ISBN 978-1-5283-7543-6
PIBN 10928217

English
Français
Deutsche
Italiano
Español
Português

www.forgottenbooks.com

Mythology Photography **Fiction**
Fishing Christianity **Art** Cooking
Essays Buddhism Freemasonry
Medicine **Biology** Music **Ancient**
Egypt Evolution Carpentry Physics
Dance Geology **Mathematics** Fitness
Shakespeare **Folklore** Yoga Marketing
Confidence Immortality Biographies
Poetry **Psychology** Witchcraft
Electronics Chemistry History **Law**
Accounting **Philosophy** Anthropology
Alchemy Drama Quantum Mechanics
Atheism Sexual Health **Ancient History**
Entrepreneurship Languages Sport
Paleontology Needlework Islam
Metaphysics Investment Archaeology
Parenting Statistics Criminology
Motivational

REPORTS

OF

CASES ARGUED AND DETERMINED

IN THE

APPELLATE COURT

OF THE

STATE OF INDIANA,

WITH TABLES OF THE CASES REPORTED AND CASES
CITED AND STATUTES CITED AND CONSTRUED
AND AN INDEX.

By SIDNEY R. MOON,

OFFICIAL REPORTER.

DANIEL W. CROCKETT, First Asst. Reporter.

LEE W. MOON, Second Asst. Reporter.

VOL. 8,

CONTAINING CASES DECIDED AT THE MAY TERM, 1893, NOT PUBLISHED IN
VOLUME 7, AND CASES DECIDED AT THE NOVEMBER
TERM, 1893.

INDIANAPOLIS:

CARLON & HOLLENBECK, CONTRACTORS FOR THE STATE.

1894.

PUBLISHED
BY
AUTHORITY OF THE STATE OF INDIANA.

Rec. Jan. 29, 1875.

TABLE OF THE CASES

REPORTED IN THIS VOLUME.

TABLE OF CASES REPORTED.

TABLE OF THE CASES

CITED IN THIS VOLUME.

(vi)

Statutes Cited and Construed.

STATUTES CITED AND CONSTRUED. xxiii

Section 5735, R. S. 1881............285
Section 6054, R. S. 1881...........680
Section 6055, R. S. 1881...........683
Elliott's Supp., section 19..........535
Elliott's Supp., section 342.......497
Elliott's Supp., section 385.......196
Ellott's Supp., section 391.......191
Elliott's Supp., section 753....... 4
Elliott's Supp., sections 812-822.234
Elliott's Supp.,sections 1077 and
1078....................................189
Elliott's Supp., section 1120.....254
Elliott's Supp., section 1122.....256
Elliott's Supp.,sections 1185 and
1186....................................878
Elliott's Supp., section 1188.....381

Elliott's Supp., section 1707.....530
Elliott's Supp., section 1710......529
Elliott's Supp., section 1758.....444
Section 336, 2 G. & H..............122
Section 784, p. 2052 R. S. 1852..672
Acts 1883, p. 140, section 3......103
Acts 1883, p. 142, section 9......529
Acts 1885, p. 66, section 3........443
Acts 1885, p. 162....................237
Acts 1885, p. 236, section 1......528
Acts 1889, p. 237....................233
Acts 1889, p. 258, section 6.....528
Acts 1891, p. 57......................444
Acts 1891, p. 323, section 2.......235
Acts 1893, p. 29, section 1, subd.
8 and 9...............................689
Acts 1893, p. 31, section 3........245

JUDGES

(xxiv)

OFFICERS

OF THE

APPELLATE COURT

CLERK,
ANDREW M. SWEENEY.

SHERIFF,
DAVID A. ROACH.

CASES

ARGUED AND DETERMINED

IN THE

APPELLATE COURT

OF THE

STATE OF INDIANA,

AT INDIANAPOLIS, MAY TERM, 1893, IN THE SEVENTY-SEVENTH YEAR OF THE STATE.

No. 942.

MORRIS ET AL. *v.* WATSON.

ESTOPPEL.—*Street Improvement.—Lien.—Damages.—Wrongful Appropriation of Land.*—In an action to enforce a lien for street improvement, an appeal having been taken from the improvement proceedings, and a judgment rendered on appeal declaring such proceedings null and void, the defendants are estopped to deny the city's right to the land appropriated for such street, and the resulting lien of the contractor, where, after such judgment annulling the improvement proceedings, the defendants accepted damages of the city for the appropriation of the land as above mentioned. And the rule is the same whether the land-owner accepts damages in proceedings under the writ of assessment or in a suit for damages.

STREETS AND ALLEYS.—*Improvement Proceedings.—Appeal from.—Effect of Appeal Judgment.—Practice.—Municipal Corporation.*—Where an appeal is taken from proceedings to improve a street, the city is not compelled to stop the work while the appeal is pending; and, in such case, if, on appeal, the city prevails, the work may be finished under the original proceedings, but if the property-owner is successful, and the court decides that there is some irregularity in the proceedings, the city may correct the same or begin anew, according to the determination of the court on appeal. If, however, the court, on appeal, adjudges the entire proceedings void, and no appeal is taken from such judgment, and the city does not proceed anew under the statute, it amounts to an abandonment of the appropriation of the land, and the title to the property reverts to the owner.

From the Clinton Circuit Court.

R. N. Lamb, R. Hill and *J. C. Green,* for appellants.
J. F. Morrison, J. E. Holman, J. O'Brien and *C. C. Shirley,* for appellee.

REINHARD, J.—This action was brought by the appellee for the enforcement of a lien claimed by him as a contractor for the improvement of a street in the city of Kokomo against the appellants, whose lands were affected by such improvement.

The action was commenced in the Howard Circuit Court, from which the venue was changed to the court below.

The complaint shows the passage of an ordinance by the city council, for the improvement of a certain street, and proceeds upon the theory that such street had an existence at the time of the passing of such ordinance.

The facts averred show the regularity of the proceedings to improve the street, the letting of the contract for the work to the appellee, the notice required by the statute, the assessments, the estimates, the particular amount assessed against the property of appellants fronting on said street, the completion of the work in accordance with the contract, and the failure of the appellants to pay the same. Upon issues joined the cause was submitted for trial to the court and there was a finding and decree for appellee over appellants' motion for a new trial.

Various errors are assigned, but the only one discussed in the brief of appellants' counsel is the overruling of the motion for a new trial, which involves the question of the sufficiency of the evidence to sustain the finding.

It appears from the evidence, that the appellant Christina L. Morris, who is a married woman and whose husband was joined as a co-defendant with her and is her co-appellant in this appeal, on the 14th day of February, 1887, was the owner of outlot No. 179 in the city of Kokomo, containing about eight acres of unplatted land used for agricultural purposes. On that day proceedings were instituted for opening Quincy and Mulberry streets through this lot, or tract of land, such proceedings resulting in the opening of Quincy street through such real estate, and condemning so much of the same as was required for the purposes of such street.

From these proceedings Mrs. Morris prosecuted an appeal to the Howard Circuit Court. In that court a demurrer was filed and sustained to the transcript treated as the complaint, and judgment was rendered thereon declaring the entire proceedings of the common council and city commissioners for the opening of said street and the condemnation of the land as absolutely null and void.

The appeal was taken under section 3180, R. S. 1881; and, while the same was pending, the city proceeded with the opening of the street, passed the ordinance referred to in the complaint for the improvement of the same, and let the contract for such improvement to the appellee.

The work was accepted by the city council, an estimate was made, and a lien declared on the land of Mrs. Morris for the amount of such assessments falling upon her land.

The appellants who were nonresidents of the State were duly notified by publication of the pendency of the proceedings, such notice inviting bids on the work before it was let.   The evidence tends to prove the other averments of the complaint.

It further appears from the evidence, that on the 4th day of April, 1889, the appellants instituted an action for trespass against the city of Kokomo, for the taking and appropriation of Mrs. Morris' land for the purposes of said street, and for the tearing down of the fences, digging up of the ground, etc.

On the 31st day of October, 1889, the city offered to confess judgment for $250 and costs, in said action, which offer was accepted by Mrs. Morris and paid by the city.   It also appears that after the bringing of this action Mrs. Morris platted the land, dividing it into city lots, and dedicating a portion thereof to the public for streets and alleys, which portion so dedicated was the same as had been appropriated by the city for street purposes.

It is earnestly insisted, by the appellants' counsel, that the judgment of the circuit court on appeal from the proceedings to open the street rendered such proceedings absolutely void, and left the parties in the position occupied by them before such proceedings were commenced; that the subsequent act of the city of improving the street was without warrant in law, and gave the contractor no lien which he can enforce in this action.

It is not denied, by the appellants, that under the act approved April 13, 1885, Elliott's Supp., section 753, the appellee would have a lien for the improvements made which he could enforce in this action, if the condemnatory proceeding of the city council had not been rendered void by the judgment of the Howard Circuit Court on appeal.   It is, therefore, proper that we should determine the effect of such judgment.

Section 3180, R. S. 1881, *supra,* under which the appeal was taken, provides what questions shall be determined by the court to which such appeal is taken, in the following language: "Upon such appeal, the regularity of the proceedings of the commissioners, and the question as to the amount of benefits or damages assessed may be tried; but such appeal shall not prevent such city from proceeding with the proposed appropriation, nor from making the proposed change or improvement."

The circuit courts are courts of general jurisdiction, and where, in such cases, appeals are authorized, they take and exercise jurisdiction under their general appellate powers. *Hamilton* v. *City of Ft. Wayne*, 73 Ind. 1.

The statute quoted from seems to confine the questions to be decided to the regularity of the proceedings of the commissioners and to the amount of damages or benefits to be assessed. There may, however, be such irregularity in the proceedings of the commissioners as to render the entire proceedings void; as, for example, where no commissioners were appointed and no proceedings were had by any commissioners whatever, or where no notice was given the property-owner of the assessments of benefits or damages, etc. If, for any such reasons, the circuit court decides that the proceedings were void, there is nothing to prevent the city council from instituting new proceedings and finishing the improvement under them. In the meantime, the city is not compelled to stop the work, while the appeal is pending. It may proceed, notwithstanding the appeal. If, in the contest in the court to which the appeal is taken, the city prevails, of course the work will be finished under the original proceedings. If the property-owner is successful, on the other hand, and the court decides that there is some irregularity in the proceedings, the municipal authorities may, doubtless, correct the same or begin anew, in accordance with the determination of the court on appeal. But if the court, upon appeal, adjudges the entire proceedings

void, and no appeal is taken from such judgment, and
the city does not proceed anew under the statute, we
think it amounts to an abandonment of the appropriation of the land, and the title to the property reverts to
the owner.

This brings us to the question as to whether the fact
that the appellants, after the judgment of the circuit
court declaring the proceedings void, proceeded against
the city in an action of trespass, in which damages were
tendered and accepted, does not estop such appellants
from questioning the right of said city to make the appropriation.   It is claimed, on the part of the appellants,
that such proceedings not only did not concede the right
of the city to take such property, but that it was an express denial of such right.

The complaint in the action for damages was in two
paragraphs, each of which contained, in substance, the
averments that the defendant (the city of Kokomo), without plaintiffs' consent or authority, wrongfully and il-
legally entered upon the land in controversy, tore down
the fences enclosing the same, and did take possession
of, use, occupy and convert to the use and benefit of said
city, a portion of said lot, 60 feet wide and 500 feet long,
and graded, graveled and macadamized the same for a
street in said city, etc.; that the land so taken, used and
converted into streets is of the value of $2,000, and no
part of which has ever been paid the plaintiff; that the
action of said defendant in entering upon said lands,
'tearing down said fences, taking possession of said land,
occupying, using, and converting the same into streets,
and thereby depriving this plaintiff of the use of her
said lands, was greatly to the damage of said plaintiff,
to wit, in the sum of $2,000, for which sum she prays
judgment, etc.

We are of opinion that the issues in such suit covered all the damages, not only for the taking away of the fences and the digging up of the ground, but also for the appropriation and use of the land. Our cases establish the doctrine that in such actions, where the injury is done under a color of right, and is of a lasting and permanent character, all damages, both present and prospective, arising from the wrongful act, must be recovered in one action, and that all injuries to the land-owner, which may naturally and proximately flow from the use of the street, may be proved upon the trial. *City of Lafayette* v. *Nagle*, 113 Ind. 425; *Indiana, etc., R. W. Co.* v. *Allen*, 113 Ind. 308; *City of North Vernon* v. *Voegler*, 103 Ind. 314; *Montmorency, etc., Co.* v. *Stockton*, 43 Ind. 328; *Lafayette, etc., Co.* v. *New Albany, etc., R. R. Co.*, 13 Ind. 90; 1 Sutherland Dam., 191.

The appellant, having elected to accept the damages for the appropriation of the land, is estopped to deny the appellee's right to the possession. Bigelow on Estoppel, 642; *Test* v. *Larsh*, 76 Ind. 452; *Sherman* v. *McKeon*, 38 N. Y. 266; *People, ex rel.,* v. *Mills*, 109 N. Y. 69; Elliott Roads and Streets, 276 and 277.

There can be no difference in the rule in cases where the land-owner accepts the money tendered him in proceedings under the writ of assessment, and those in which the money is accepted in a suit for damages, such as the one in hand.

The *gravamen* of the action here relied upon to constitute an estoppel, was the unlawful appropriation of the appellants' land for street purposes. It is clearly shown, by the averments of the complaint in that action, that it was not the mere transient injury of the removal of the fences and the digging up of the earth that appellant, Mrs. Morris, sought to have redressed in damages, but also the taking of her land for the purposes of a street or streets. This being so, she can not now be heard to say

The State v. Malone.

. that the occupancy of the street by the city is wrongful, and that the municipality was powerless to make the improvements. The tender and acceptance of the money amounted to what equity will construe to be a purchase . of the easement on the part of the city, and the appellant is precluded from asserting title afterwards. See *City of Indianapolis* v. *Kingsbury*, 101 Ind. 200; *Faust* v. *City of Huntington*, 91 Ind. 493.

There is no reversible error.

Judgment affirmed.

Filed Nov. 10, 1893.

No. 995.

THE STATE v. MALONE.

CRIMINAL LAW.—*Indictment.—Duplicity.—Obstructing Highway with Cars.*—An indictment for obstructing a highway with cars, based on section 2170, R. S. 1881, which charged that the defendant, being then and there a conductor, etc., did "unlawfully permit and suffer" the train "to remain and stand across" the street, and did "fail and neglect to leave a space of sixty feet across said street," is not bad for duplicity.

SAME.—*Indictment, Sufficiency of.—Obstructing Highway with Cars.— Name of Road not Essential.*—In an indictment founded on section 2170, R. S. 1881, it is not essential to the validity of the charge, that the railroad be named.

SAME.—*Indictment.—Joinder of Offenses in Same Count.—Offenses Mentioned Disjunctively.*—Where a statute makes it an offense to do this or that, or another thing, mentioning several things disjunctively, either one of which, when committed, would constitute one and the same offense, to which the same punishment is prescribed, all the things mentioned in the statute may be charged conjunctively as constituting but a single offense.

From the Adams Circuit Court.

A. G. Smith, Attorney-General, and *R. H. Hartford*, Prosecuting Attorney, for State.

A. P. Beatty, *L. C. De Voss* and *T. J. O. Brien*, for appellee.

Lotz, J.—This was a criminal prosecution against Thomas Malone, for obstructing a public highway, and was commenced before a justice of the peace. There was a trial and conviction before the justice, and, from the judgment rendered, an appeal was taken to the circuit court. In the circuit court, the affidavit upon which the prosecution was based, was quashed on the motion of the defendant, and the defendant discharged.

The State appealed to this court, and has assigned as error the decision of the court quashing the affidavit.

Omitting the formal parts, the affidavit is as follows: "James O. Ball swears that Thomas Malone, on the 7th day of February, 1893, at and in the county of Adams, and State of Indiana, being then and there the conductor and person having charge of and running a certain railroad train carrying, or used for carrying, freight, did then and there unlawfully permit and suffer the same to remain standing across a certain public street in the city of Decatur, Indiana, to wit, Monroe street, and did then and there fail and neglect to leave a space of sixty feet across said street."

The section of the statute on which this prosecution is based is in these words: "Whoever, being a conductor or other person having charge of or running a railroad train carrying or used for carrying freight, permits or suffers the same to remain standing across any public highway, street, or alley; or who, whenever it becomes necessary to stop such train across any highway, street, or alley, fails or neglects to leave a space of sixty feet across such public highway, street, or alley, shall be fined not more than twenty dollars nor less than three dollars." Section 2170, R. S. 1881.

The purpose of this statute is to prevent the obstruction of the public highways of the State by freight trains, at such points as the railroads cross the same.

The statute above set out defines two distinct offenses, to which the same penalty is attached; the first one consists in permitting or suffering a freight train to stand across the highway. The "standing across," as here used, does not mean for an instant merely, but it means that such standing shall continue or remain long enough to become an obstruction and prevent the free enjoyment of the highway by the citizens of the State, who may have occasion to use the same. The standing across contemplated is one of a transient character. The second offense defined consists in bringing the train to a stop, coupled with the failure or neglect to leave a space of sixty feet vacant across the highway. The statute recognizes that there may be occasions, in the management of freight trains, when it is necessary to make a stop of longer duration than a mere transient one; and whenever such an occasion arises, and the train extends across a highway, it is made the duty of the person having the management to cut the train and leave a space of sixty feet between the ends and across the highway.

The affidavit in this case charges that the defendant did "unlawfully permit and suffer" the train "to remain standing across" the street, and did "fail and neglect to leave a space of sixty feet across said street."

Is the affidavit bad for duplicity, in that it charges the defendant with having committed two distinct offenses in the same count? Repugnancy and duplicity are not good causes for quashing a criminal charge, as a general rule. But if the indictment or information charge the defendant, in a single count, with two or more distinct offenses, it is bad for duplicity, and a motion to quash should be sustained. *Knopf* v. *State*, 84 Ind. 316; *State* v. *Weil*, 89 Ind. 286; *Joslyn* v. *State*, 128 Ind. 160.

Where a statute, like the one above quoted, makes it an offense to do this or that, or another thing, mentioning several things disjunctively, either one of which, when committed, would constitute one and the same offense to which the same punishment is prescribed, all the things mentioned in the statute may be charged conjunctively as constituting but a single offense; or, in other words, where the acts charged were done by the same person, at the same time, and as a part of the same transaction, and subject the offender to the same punishment, they constitute but one offense, and may all be joined in one count. *Davis* v. *State*, 100 Ind. 154; *Fahnestock* v. v. *State*, 102 Ind. 156; *State* v. *Wells*, 112 Ind. 237.

The two offenses defined by the statute under consideration, that is, permitting the train to stand across the highway and stopping the train across the highway and failing to cut the same, each culminate in producing the same result, that is, obstructing the highway, and can both be done by the same party in the same time. The last act is but a continuation of the first. The affidavit is not bad for duplicity.

The affidavit does not state or give the name of the railroad that crossed the street obstructed. The forms given for prosecutions under similar statutes state the name of the railroad (Gillett's Crim. Law, sections 717, 718 and 719). We do not consider it essential, however, to the validity of such charge, that the railroad be named. It is true that it adds one more degree of certainty to the charge, but the charge is sufficiently specific without it. The essential element of the offense is the obstruction of the highway by a freight train. If the highway is specifically described, and the obstruction designated, the indictment or information is sufficiently specific to apprise the defendant of the charge which he is required to meet.

"It is not the law that an indictment shall be so distinct and minute in its description of the offense or the

offender as to constitute, without parol proof, a bar to a second prosecution for the same offense.   The identity of the two accusations may always be shown by parol."
State v. *Smith*, 7 Ind. App. 166, 34 N. E. Rep. 127.

The motion to quash should have been overruled.

Judgment reversed, with instructions to overrule the motion to quash.

Filed Nov. 3, 1893.

---◆---

No. 1,136.

BOLLENBACHER ET AL. *v.* THE FIRST NATIONAL BANK OF BLOOMINGTON ET AL.

PARTNERSHIP.—*Surviving Partners.—Continuing Partnership Business. —Trustee and Cestui Que Trust.—Insurance.—Receiver.—Assets.*—When a member of a partnership dies, the surviving partners hold the property and money of the partnership in trust for the partnership creditors; and where the surviving partners continue the business of the partnership in another firm-name, and insure the property in such name, and pay the premiums thereon, any money realized on the insurance policy, as well as all other funds of the partnership, belong to the *cestui que* trust, and primarily to the creditors of the firm; and, in such case, a receiver having been appointed, he is entitled to the possession and control of all the firm assets, including insurance money obtained by the surviving partners on a policy procured by them, and including profits realized in the continuance of the partnership business.

From the Monroe Circuit Court.

J. R. East, R. A. Fulk and *E. Corr,* for appellants.

J. H. Louden, W. P. Rogers and *P. K. Buskirk,* for appellees.

DAVIS, J.—The special finding of facts is substantially as follows:

1st. That on the 17th of September, 1885, there was

a firm in Bloomington, known by the name of Bollenbacher & Sons, and consisting of George Bollenbacher, Sr., George W., Martin C., and William P. Bollenbacher; that on said 17th of September, 1885, said George Bollenbacher, Sr., died testate; that, by the terms of his will, his sons, other than George W., were to have all of said decedent's interest in the said firm, consisting of real and personal property.

2d. That the firm of Bollenbacher & Sons had been in existence since 1881, engaged in the manufacture of spokes.

3d. That at the time of the death of George Bollenbacher, Sr., said firm was indebted to the First National Bank of Bloomington in the sum of $17,500; that a great part of said indebtedness still continued until the application of the sum of money described in plaintiff's complaint, and that said firm is still indebted to said bank.

4th. That upon the death of George Bollenbacher, Sr., in September, 1885, the firm of "Bollenbacher's Sons" was organized; that said firm was composed of George W., William P., Martin C., Samuel, and Jacob I. Bollenbacher, all sons of George Bollenbacher, Sr., and all members of the old firm, except Samuel and Jacob I.

5th. That all the interest that William P., Martin C., Samuel, and Jacob Bollenbacher had in the firm of Bollenbacher's Sons was the interest owned by George Bollenbacher, Sr., at the time of his death, in the firm of Bollenbacher & Sons, except what interest William P. and Martin C. had in the firm of Bollenbacher & Sons.

6th. That all the capital, property and stock and choses in action that the firm of Bollenbacher's Sons had at the time of its organization in September, 1885, was the capital, property and stock and choses in action of the firm of Bollenbacher & Sons, as it existed at the time

of the death of George Bollenbacher, Sr.; that the same
was worth the sum of $15,000.

7th. That the firm of Bollenbacher's Sons continued
the business of manufacturing spokes, from September,
1885, until 1888, since which time it has done no business with any one.

8th. That in December, 1888, said firm of Bollenbacher's Sons had deposited to its credit in the First National Bank of Bloomington the sum of $1,573.09, and
that said sum has never been paid over to said firm by
said bank.

9th. That on the 4th day of April, 1887, the factory
that belonged to the firm of Bollenbacher & Sons was
burned down and destroyed; that there was a policy of
insurance on said building and contents in the name of
Bollenbacher's Sons; that said policy was put on said
building and contents by the said firm of Bollenbacher's
Sons, and they paid the premium on said policy.

10th. That said policy amounted to the sum of $4,-
000, and that it was collected by the said firm of Bollenbacher's Sons and deposited in the First National Bank
of Bloomington to their credit, and that in September,
1888, $300 of this same insurance money still remained
in said bank.

11th. That on the 28th of September, 1885, there was
deposited in the First National Bank of Bloomington, to
the credit of the firm of Bollenbacher & Sons, the sum
of $1,493.28, and that this sum of money was on that
day transferred from the account of Bollenbacher & Sons
to the credit of Bollenbacher's Sons, and that said money
was so transferred at the instance and request of the firm
of Bollenbacher's Sons, and that from that time continuously the moneys of the firms of Bollenbacher & Sons
and Bollenbacher's Sons were commingled.

12th. That the outstanding indebtedness of the firm

of Bollenbacher & Sons was never all paid; that at the time the firm of Bollenbacher's Sons quit business in 1888, the firm of Bollenbacher & Sons still owed the First National Bank of Bloomington $10,000, with interest thereon.

13th. That a mortgage for $8,000 on the spoke factory and machinery and stock of the firm of Bollenbacher & Sons, to the said bank, was paid off by the firm of Bollenbacher's Sons, and that a large portion of the insurance money was used by said firm to pay said mortgage indebtedness.

14th. That the affairs of the firm of Bollenbacher & Sons have never been settled by any one, but that one Charles McPheeters has been duly appointed receiver of and for said firm.

15th. That before the filing of this suit, one John R. East, as attorney of the plaintiffs, during banking hours, and at the place of banking of the First National Bank of Bloomington, made a demand and presented a check duly signed "Bollenbacher's Sons," for the sum of $1,- 573.09, to the cashier of said bank, and demanded payment of the same, but that payment of said check was refused.

16th. That on the 15th day of November, 1888, Charles McPheeters, receiver of the firm of Bollenbacher & Sons, checked out of the said First National Bank of Bloomington the sum of $1,573.09 that was credited in said bank to the firm of Bollenbacher's Sons, and applied the same on the indebtedness of Bollenbacher & Sons to said bank.

As a conclusion of law the court found for appellees.

The only error discussed is that the court erred in its conclusion of law on the special finding of facts.

Counsel for appellants contend that "the firm of Bollenbacher's Sons had an insurable interest in the property formerly owned by Bollenbacher & Sons, which was insured by Bollenbacher's Sons," and, therefore, "the money derived on the policy belonged to Bollenbacher's Sons,—amounting to $4,000,—and the $1,575 in bank ought to have been paid to them."

This contention is based on the general proposition that a partner has an insurable interest to the amount of the value of the entire partnership property. It may be conceded that, ordinarily, an insurance by one partner in his own name, on partnership property, does not inure to the benefit of the partnership, but the question is whether the rule on which appellants rely is applicable to the facts in this case.

It should be borne in mind that there was a commingling of the funds of the two firms, and that only $300 of the insurance money is included in the amount in controversy.

In this connection, we quote the following from the brief of counsel for appellees:

"On the death of George Bollenbacher, Sr., in September, 1885, the law invested the surviving partners with the exclusive right of possession and management of the entire property of the partnership, for the purpose of settling up the business of the firm and paying off the debts. They were trustees primarily for the creditors of the firm. Accordingly, it has been correctly laid down that 'the surviving partners are held strictly as trustees. * * * Their trust is to wind up the concern in the best manner for all interested, and, therefore, without unnecessary delay.' *Valentine* v. *Wysor*, 123 Ind. 47; Parsons Part., p. 442; *Jones* v. *Dexter*, 130 Mass. 380; *Holland* v. *Fuller*, 13 Ind. 195.

"The surviving partners had no right to use the property of the firm for any other purpose than to convert the same into money in the best manner possible. It was a trust property, and to màke use of it was a violation of the trust. This is true, not only as to the money and choses in action, but also as to the real and personal property of the firm.

"In White and Tudor's Leading Cases in Equity, vol. 1, part 1, p. 303, the law is stated thus: 'On the other hand, the surviving partner, though he may be clothed with the whole legal title, has no right or power to divert the trust property to his own private uses, in derogation of the rights of the creditors of the firm.'

"The Supreme Court of Arkansas, in *Cline* v. *Wilson*, 26 Ark. 154, say: 'A surviving partner has a right to the possession and control of the partnership property for the purpose of settling and closing up the business, and not for the purpose of carrying it on.'

"The Supreme Court of New York, in *Skidmore* v. *Collier*, 15 N. Y. 50, says: 'A surviving partner, though he has a legal right to the partnership effects, yet, in equity, is considered merely as a trustee to pay the partnership debts, and to dispose of the effects of the concern for the benefit of himself and the estate of his deceased partner. If he continues the partnership business with the partnership funds, he is, as a general rule, liable to account for all profits made thereby, and the losses, if any, must be borne by himself.'

"Bispham, in his Principles of Equity, section 514, says: 'In taking the partnership accounts, a surviving partner will be regarded as a trustee, and will be ordinarily responsible for any profits which he may have made after the dissolution.'

* * * * - -

"The facts show that the surviving partners, on the 17th day of September, 1885, took possession of the part-. nership property of Bollenbacher & Sons, valued at $15,-

000, and $1,493.28 in money, and used the same in violation of their trust, for their own benefit. The fact that Samuel and Jacob I. Bollenbacher were in the concern with them, can make no difference. They paid nothing and had no interest in the firm, unless something was left after paying off the indebtedness of Bollenbacher & Sons. The rights of the heirs or legatees of a deceased partner are subject to the adjustment of all claims, and attach only to the surplus which remains when the partnership debts are paid. Until all the debts are paid, the rights of the heirs do not attach. *Grissom* v. *Moore*, 106 Ind. 296; *Valentine* v. *Wysor, supra; Walling* v. *Burgess*, 122 Ind. 299; *Deeter* v. *Sellers*, 102 Ind. 458.

"Under what name the surviving partners did business, can make no difference. They may call themselves Bollenbacher's Sons, or Bollenbacher's Surviving Partners, or Bollenbacher's Trustees, or whatever other name may strike their fancy, they were trustees of the property for the benefit of the creditors, and all the money they made from the use of the property belonged to the trust estate, until the indebtedness was adjusted and paid off. A trustee can not make any profit at the expense of a trust estate." See, also, *Brackenridge, Admr.*, v. *Holland*, 2 Blackf. 377 (382).

In our opinion, on the facts found and under the authorities cited, the persons composing the firm of Bollenbacher's Sons should be regarded as holding the property and money in trust for the partnership,—and primarily for the creditors,—of Bollenbacher & Sons. Lindley on Partnership (Ewell), 664, and notes; Pomeroy's Equity Jurisprudence, section 1046.

The insurance money, as well as the other funds in controversy, belonged to the *cestui que trust.* Sections 487, 553, Perry on Trusts.

On the appointment of the receiver he became at once

entitled to the possession and control of all the firm assets, including the money in controversy, to the exclusion of the members of the partnership. High on Receivers, sections 538, 541.

Whether the receiver had the right to pay the money to the bank, or whether the bank had the right to apply the money on deposit in payment of the indebtedness, under the rule enunciated in *Bedford Bank* v. *Acoam,* 125 Ind. 584, we need not determine. If appellants recover, it must be on the strength of their own right. The burden was on them. It was incumbent on appellants to show that they were entitled to the money.

If we are right in our conclusion that Bollenbacher's Sons were trustees primarily for the creditors of Bollenbacher & Sons and that the receiver, under the supervision of the proper court, was entitled to the possession and control of the money, then it necessarily follows that there is no available error of which appellants can complain in the judgment of the court below.

Judgment affirmed.

Filed Nov. 10, 1893.

No. 768.

The Second National Bank of Springfield, Ohio, *v.* Hart.

Pleading.—*Answer, Inconsistent and Repugnant.*—*Demurrer.*—Where a paragraph of answer to a complaint on a promissory note, was that the note was given in part payment of a wheat-harvesting machine which was sold upon a written warranty, alleging a breach of such warranty, and that the plaintiff did not become the owner or holder of the note in suit until after maturity, "or if it did become such owner, it was only for the purpose of collecting the same * * or with the agreement and understanding * * that * * [said

assignor] would keep * * the plaintiff whole and harmless,"—
the answer is so inconsistent and repugnant that it can not withstand
a demurrer.

From the Daviess Circuit Court.

W. H. DeWolf and *G. G. Barton*, for appellant.
J. H. O'Neall and *M. G. O'Neall*, for appellee.

REINHARD, J.—Action by the appellant against the
appellee on a note governed by the law merchant. The
note had been executed by the appellee to Amos Whitely
& Co., a corporation, and assigned to the appellant.

The appellee answered—first, the general denial, and
second, special affirmative matter.

The overruling of a demurrer to the second paragraph
of the answer is urged as error. This paragraph sets up
that the note was given in part payment of a wheat har-
vesting and binding machine purchased by the appellee
of Amos Whitely & Co.; that the machine was sold upon
a written warranty, and that there was a breach of such
warranty; that the appellant did not become the owner
or holder of the note sued on until after maturity; "or,
if it did become such owner, it was only for the purpose
of collecting the same for said Amos Whitely & Co., or
with the agreement and understanding with said Amos
Whitely & Co. that said Amos Whitely & Co. would keep
said bank, the plaintiff, whole and harmless."

The objection pointed out to the averment which we
have quoted is that it is so inconsistent, indefinite, and
illogical that it is not an averment of a fact or of facts.
We are, after careful consideration, constrained to concur in this view. True, under the code, much liberality
is indulged in the construction of pleadings. A demurrer will not be sustained for mere inconsistency, indefiniteness, or repugnancy, if some fact or facts are averred
positively, and the indefiniteness, inconsistency, or re-

pugnancy is not such as to render the averment meaningless.

But, in the paragraph under consideration, there is an utter absence of the averment of a necessary fact left standing, when the entire statement is considered. If the allegation that the "plaintiff did not become the holder or owner of the note sued on until after maturity," stood by itself, and unaffected by the other statements, it might be sufficient. And so with the statements following it. But, as it is, the one statement following the other, coupled by the disjunctive *or*, the whole averment is rendered nugatory and meaningless. It is like averring that the plaintiff either did not purchase the note in good faith before its maturity or did not purchase it at all, but that it was transferred for collection only; or, if neither of these propositions be true, that it purchased the note with an understanding that Amos Whitely & Co. would keep the bank whole and harmless. Such statements are not averments of a fact or facts. It might as well be argued that an answer to a complaint upon a promissory note is sufficient which alleges that the note had either been paid or was executed without consideration, or that the defendant had never executed it at all. All of these allegations can not be true, and we are not informed in the pleading before us which of them is true. We are told that it is either the one thing or the other which is true. But the pleader should have alleged affirmatively the facts he intended to rely upon in defense of the action. We therefore regard the pleading so inconsistent and repugnant as to be obnoxious to the demurrer. Repugnancy is ordinarily not a ground for demurrer, when the second allegation is merely superfluous and redundant, and, in that case, the latter may be stricken out or disregarded, and will not vitiate the pleading. But it is otherwise where the pleading is so inconsistent with itself as to destroy the meaning. The objection here goes to the substance, and not to the form merely. Stephen on Pleading (Heard's 9th Am. ed.), 377; Gould's Pleading, section 173.

If a pleading is so uncertain or indefinite as not to state a good cause of action or defense, it will be subject to demurrer. *Lewis, Guar.*, v. *Edwards*, 44 Ind. 333.

Besides the failure of consideration, or the breach of warranty relied upon as a defense, the appellee was bound to show by his plea that the appellant was not a *bona fide* holder of the note, for value, before maturity. Having failed to do this, his plea is bad for that reason.

Objections are urged, also, to that portion of this answer which attempts to set forth a breach of the warranty, but as the paragraph may be reformed in this respect, before another trial is had, we need not pass upon the objection.

The demurrer to the second paragraph of the answer should have been sustained.

Judgment reversed.

Filed Nov. 8, 1893.

———————•———————

No. 879.

THE QUEEN INSURANCE COMPANY OF LIVERPOOL, ENGLAND, *v.* THE HUDNUT COMPANY.

PLEADING. — *Action on Insurance Policy.* — *Answer.* — *Confession and Avoidance.* — *General Denial.* —To a complaint on an insurance policy, alleging loss of insured property by tornado, cyclone or hurricane, the defendant answered that the loss was caused by a very high wind forcing a boat of the Cincinnati and Memphis Packet Co. against the property. The answer is insufficient as a confession and avoidance, neither is it good as a denial, and no defense is stated to the action. The further allegation of an investigation by the assured and the insurer, and the bringing of an action for damages by the insured against the Cincinnati and Memphis Packet Co. did not show a release of the insurer from liability.

SAME.—*General Allegations Controlled by Special.*—Special allegations in a pleading, inconsistent with the general allegation, control the general statement.

From the Vanderburgh Circuit Court.

A. Gilchrist and *C. A. De Bruler*, for appellant.

G. V. Menzies, S. B. Davis and *G. M. Davis*, for appellee.

Ross, J.—This action was brought by the appellee to recover, on a policy of insurance, the value of a building alleged to have been destroyed by a cyclone or hurricane. The policy sued on was issued by the appellant to the Mt. Vernon Hominy Mill Company, insuring said building against loss or damage by cyclones, tornadoes and hurricanes, and, after the loss complained of, the rights under the policy were assigned by the insured to the appellee.

The appellant filed an answer to the complaint in two paragraphs, in each of which it set up matter in avoidance. No answer of general denial was pleaded. Demurrers were overruled to each paragraph of the answer, and the appellee replied specially.

The second paragraph of the reply was addressed to the first paragraph of the answer, and the fourth paragraph of the reply to the second paragraph of the answer. Demurrers were filed to each of these paragraphs of the reply, and the court, in ruling thereon, carried the demurrers back and sustained them to each of said paragraphs of answer. The appellant refusing to plead further, judgment was rendered in favor of the appellee.

The errors assigned by appellant in this court are as follows:

"1st. The court erred in overruling appellant's demurrer to the second paragraph of the reply."

"2d. The court erred in overruling appellant's demurrer to the fourth paragraph of the reply."

"3d. The court erred in holding the first paragraph of appellant's answer insufficient in law to constitute a defense to plaintiff's complaint."

"4th. The court erred in holding the second paragraph of appellant's answer insufficient in law to constitute a defense to plaintiff's complaint."

As the record comes to this court, the only ruling of the court below, to which appellant could take exception, was in carrying the demurrers back and sustaining them to each paragraph of the answer. By this ruling of the court, the replies were virtually stricken from the record. When the answers went out, the replies thereto followed. Without an answer in the record no reply was necessary, because it required none to form an issue. The first and second errors assigned present no question on the ruling of the court in carrying the demurrers back and sustaining them to the answers. Do the third and fourth?

Section 655, R. S. 1881, provides: "No pleadings shall be required in the Supreme Court upon an appeal, but a specific assignment of all errors relied upon, to be entered on the transcript in matters of law only, which shall be assigned on or before the first day of the term at which the cause stands for trial; and the appellee shall file his answer thereto."

The assignment of errors is the appellant's complaint, and each specification must be specific. If the error assigned is predicated upon a ruling on a demurrer to a pleading the assignment should so state, designating specially what ruling is complained of. See Elliott's App. Proced., section 308, and cases cited.

While these assignments may not meet the requirements of the statute and the rules of this court in this respect, we shall, nevertheless, in this instance, consider the questions which are sought to be presented thereby.

In the first paragraph of the answer it is alleged, in substance, that the warehouse described in the policy and in the complaint was not blown down by the immediate action of a cyclone, tornado or hurricane, but was destroyed as a result of a collision with a steamboat navigating the Ohio river; that after attempting to make a landing, in which it was unsuccessful, and while endeavoring to leave the wharf-boat, which was the public landing for steamboats at Mount Vernon, said boat, by reason of the force of a very high wind then prevailing, was driven against said building, causing it to fall. It was further alleged that said building was not blown down by a tornado or by any cyclone or hurricane, or by the force of the wind in any way, but was knocked down by the collision with said steamboat.

The second paragraph of the answer contains the material allegations of the first paragraph, with the following additional averments, viz.: "that after that accident the defendant and the assured—the Mount Vernon Hominy Mill Company—each investigated the facts of the loss, and were satisfied that said loss was the result of the negligence of the officers and servants of the Cincinnati and Memphis Packet Company in so negligently navigating said steamer;" that the assured and the defendant elected to treat the loss of said building and property as caused solely by the negligence of said packet company, and the assured thereupon elected to bring an action against said packet company to recover therefor, and that it did bring such action, but upon trial thereof judgment was rendered against the assured.

It is also averred that the policy sued on provides that, in all cases of loss, the assured shall assign to the insurer all his rights to recover from any other person or persons, corporations, etc., for such injury and loss, and that the assured had not done so, but had sought to recover from such corporation in his own right.

Do the facts pleaded in either of these paragraphs constitute a defense to the plaintiff's cause of action? A single paragraph of answer can not serve the double purpose of an answer of confession and avoidance of the entire cause of action, and also of a denial thereof. *Coble v. Eltzroth*, 125 Ind. 429.

But it may avoid part and deny part. *State, ex rel., White* v. *St. Paul & Morristown T. P. Co.*, 92 Ind. 42; *Colglazier, Admr.*, v. *Colglazier*, 117 Ind. 460.

Neither of these answers states facts sufficient to withstand a demurrer, as an answer in confession and avoidance, and if good at all, they are so only because they are argumentative denials.

It is alleged in the complaint that the property insured was destroyed by a cyclone or hurricane. The assurers deny that the loss was occasioned by a tornado, cyclone or hurricane, but that it was caused by a very high wind forcing the boat against it. Is this not a confession that a tornado, cyclone, or hurricane caused the injury?

The words tornado and hurricane are synonymous, and mean a violent storm, distinguished by the vehemence of the wind and its sudden changes. While the definition of a cyclone is, "A rotatory storm or whirlwind of extended circuit." Webster's Unabridged Dictionary.

It is evident, therefore, that a hurricane is a very high wind. That the hurricane itself, coming in contact with the building, did not alone cause the damage is not material, but if it caused another body to come in contact and do the damage, the hurricane would be the direct and controlling cause. The special allegations as to the cause of the injury are inconsistent with the allegations that the loss was not occasioned by a tornado, hurricane, or cyclone, hence they control such general allegation. *Evansville, etc., R. R. Co.* v. *Crist*, 116 Ind. 446; *Warbritton* v. *Demorett*, 129 Ind. 346; *Moyer* v. *Fort Wayne, etc., R. R. Co.*, 132 Ind. 88.

The allegations relative to the investigation by the assured and the insurer, and the bringing of the action by the assured against the Cincinnati and Memphis Packet Company, did not show a release of appellee from liability, and added nothing to the answer. Neither paragraph of the answer was good for any purpose, and the court did not err in sustaining the demurrers thereto.

Judgment affirmed.

Filed Nov. 9, 1893.

———————— ◆ ————————

No. 843.

MAZELIN ET AL. *v.* ROUYER ET AL.

APPELLATE COURT PRACTICE.—*Sufficiency of Evidence.*—The Appellate Court can not, on appeal, weigh conflicting evidence to ascertain the real facts, but it must take that view of the evidence most favorable to the appellee, and affirm the judgment if there be evidence which fairly supports the finding.

TRUST AND TRUSTEE.—*Power of Court to Remove Trustee.*—A court of chancery has power, even independent of any statutory provision, or of directions contained in the instrument, to remove a trustee for good cause.

From the Marion Circuit Court.

R. Denny and *N. M. Taylor*, for appellants.

A. C. Ayres, A. Q. Jones, E. Marsh and *W. W. Cook*, for appellees.

GAVIN, C. J.—The appellant, both individually and as

trustee for Victoria Mazelin, filed, in the Marion Circuit Court, his petitions for partial distribution of the assets of the estate of John B. Mazelin, deceased.

The court ordered the distribution upon the execution of a proper refunding bond by the legatees.

In requiring this bond, the court but followed the plain mandate of the statute. Section 2380, R. S. 1881.

The case of *Smith, Exec., v. Smith,* 76 Ind. 236, decides nothing to the contrary.

A cross-complaint was filed, seeking the removal of the appellant Edward Mazelin from his position as trustee of his sister Victoria. No question is made as to the propriety of the mode of procedure adopted. Upon the issues formed on the cross-complaint, in which there are no charges of want of integrity or misconduct against the appellant, there was a trial before a probate commissioner, who recommended appellant's removal. Upon a subsequent presentation to the circuit court, there was a finding and judgment against appellant, and an order for his removal as trustee.

Numerous technical objections have been urged by appellee, which we have not deemed it necessary to examine.

All the objections argued by appellant, to the action of the court, arise upon the question of the sufficiency of the evidence. There are nearly 600 pages of type-written matter presented to us as the evidence in the cause. This we have read over and examined with care. .The rule is thoroughly established that this court can not, on appeal, weigh the conflicting evidence to ascertain the real facts, but that it must take that view of the evidence most favorable to the appellee, and if there be any evidence which fairly supports the verdict or finding, then the action of the trial court must be sustained.

Counsel for appellant concede the correctness of the

rule, but strenuously contend that it is not applicable in this cause, because here there is a total want of evidence. With this view, however, we are unable to agree. ' No good purpose would be subserved by going into the details of the evidence in this case. It is an unfortunate one in many of its aspects, but keeping in mind the narrow limit allowed to us, as an appellate tribunal, for the review of the facts, we are constrained to hold that there is some evidence to sustain the action of the trial court, and its determination of the questions involved must be considered final. It is well settled that a court of chancery has power, even independent of any statutory provision, or of directions contained in the instrument, to remove a trustee for good cause. *Ex Parte Kilgore,* 120 Ind. 94; *People* v. *Norton,* 9 N. Y. 176; Pomeroy Eq. Jur., section 1086. See, also, section 2980, R. S. 1881.

The judgment is affirmed.

Filed Nov. 8, 1893.

No. 911.

The Grand Rapids and Indiana Railroad Company v. Cox.

Interrogatories to Jury.—*Refusal to Submit.*—*When Not Available Error.*—Where answers to interrogatories refused, taken in connection with the answers made to interrogatories submitted to the jury, could not have controlled the general verdict, there was no available error in refusing them.

Same.—*When General Verdict Controlled By.*—It is only when the answers to interrogatories are absolutely irreconcilable with the general verdict that the general verdict will be controlled by them.

Instructions to Jury.—*Those Given not in Record.*—*No Question as to Those Refused.*—*Presumption.*—Where instructions given are not in the record, no available question is presented as to those asked and refused, as it will be presumed that those given covered all proper points included in those refused.

CONTRIBUTORY NEGLIGENCE.—*Railroad Crossing.*—*Exception to Rule Requiring Traveler to Stop and Listen.*—A person approaching a railroad crossing is required to look and listen, because it is the part of a prudent man to do so, for the reason that a due regard for his own safety requires it. If, however, the facts and circumstances under which he approaches it are such as to mislead him, and such as would naturally create in his mind a sense of security and belief that there is no danger, to such an extent that a man of prudence would ordinarily act upon it, then the reason and rule for the precaution fails, as where one railroad train follows another, at a high rate of speed, with but twelve seconds of time between them, the view of the track being materially obstructed.

SAME.—*When a Question of Law.*—*Question of Fact.*—Where the facts are undisputed, and but one legitimate inference can be fairly drawn from them, the court may take the question of negligence from the jury; but if the undisputed facts are of such a character that different men might reasonably and fairly base upon them different conclusions, then the determination of the question is for the jury.

From the LaGrange Circuit Court.

T. J. O'Brien, J. H. Campbell and *F. D. Merritt*, for appellant.

O. L. Ballou and *J. D. Ferrall*, for appellee.

GAVIN, C. J.—The appellee recovered judgment for injuries received in a collision with one of appellant's trains at a highway crossing.

There was clearly no error in the overruling of appellant's motion for judgment on the answers to interrogatories returned by the jury with their general verdict. It is only when the answers to interrogatories are absolutely irreconcilable with the general verdict that the general verdict will be controlled by them. *Schaffner* v. *Kobert*, 2 Ind. App. 409; *City of Greenfield* v. *State, ex rel.*, 113 Ind. 597; *Lockwood* v. *Rose*, 125 Ind. 588.

The court substituted its own interrogatories for those prepared by appellant.

By those interrogatories, appellant's counsel say they

would have shown "that appellee could see and hear; that he lived within eighty rods of the crossing, and had crossed over and been acquainted with it for years, and knew the situation; that he was in a top buggy with the top lowered; that it was about ten o'clock at night; that there was a bright headlight blazing on the locomotive that struck him; that after he got within forty feet of the track, there was nothing to obstruct his view of the track for over forty rods in the direction of the approaching train, and from at least thirty-six feet from the track to the track, he drove in the glare of the blazing headlight and must have been at least ten feet from the track when he saw the light approaching fifty feet away.

There is, in the interrogatories, nothing which would have developed the fact that he drove in the glow of the blazing headlight for any distance. Even though at forty feet back the track might have been clear to the view for forty rods, at the relative speed of the train and appellant in approaching it, the train could have been only 120 feet distant. Conceding that all the facts proposed to be shown and called for by the interrogatories were true, still they would not be sufficient to overturn the general verdict, when taken in connection with the answers made to the interrogatories propounded by the court.

Appellant's own breach of duty and its own conduct may have been such as to have misled appellee and to have relieved him from a portion of that diligence which would otherwise have been required of him, and when finally apprised of the peril in which he had been placed the jury may well have found that he did all that could reasonably be required.

Where the answers to interrogatories refused could not have controlled the general verdict, there is no available error in refusing them. *Indiana Stone Co.* v. *Stewart*, 7 Ind. App. 563, 34 N. E. Rep. 1019; *Chicago, etc., R. R. Co.* v. *Hedges, Admx.*, 105 Ind. 398; *Cleveland, etc., R. W. Co.* v. *Asbury*, 120 Ind. 289.

The instructions given by the court are not properly in the record. They are not brought in by bill of exceptions, but an effort is made to save the exceptions under section 535, R. S. 1881.

To do this it has long been held that it is absolutely essential that the record should show that the instructions were filed. Section 533, R. S. 1881; *Louisville, etc., R. W. Co.* v. *Wright*, 115 Ind. 378, and cases there cited; *Supreme Lodge, etc.*, v. *Johnson*, 78 Ind. 110; *Beem* v. *Lockhart*, 1 Ind. App. 202; *Starnes* v. *Schofield*, 5 Ind. App. 4.

The record in this case nowhere shows that the instructions were filed. According to the authorities above referred to, the insertion of them in the record by the clerk is not sufficient.

The instructions given not being in the record, no available question is presented as to those asked and refused, as it will be presumed that those given covered all proper points included in those refused. *Close* v. *McIntire*, 120 Ind. 262; *Puett* v. *Beard*, 86 Ind. 104.

Counsel contend that the evidence fails to show freedom from contributory negligence upon the part of plaintiff.

There was evidence, either direct or circumstantial, tending to show the following state of facts: Appellee was familiar with the crossing, which was a country crossing over a single track approached at a down grade on the highway. About nine o'clock at night, he drove toward the crossing, riding in a buggy with the top down. Knowing a train was about due, he listened and heard it, checked up his horse to a slow walk, and when he was one hundred feet from the crossing the train passed. His horse then started up in a trot. Appellee drove on,

without looking further, until his horse's feet were almost
on the track, and his body perhaps ten feet from it, when
he saw another train within apparently about fifty or
sixty feet, coming at fifteen or twenty miles per hour.
Believing this to be his only chance for escape, he struck
his horse with the lines, and was caught by the train as
he crossed the track. The train approached without
giving the statutory signals, and without appellee's hearing it. The road was narrow, making it very difficult to
turn or back near the track. Both the road and the
railroad ran through cuts, so that the approaching train
could not be seen until the traveler was within thirty-
five feet of the crossing. The rear train was three hundred feet behind the first train, or, measured in time,
it was only twelve seconds behind.

Appellant claims that the failure to look and see when
he could have seen, is necessarily such contributory negligence upon the part of appellee as defeats his recovery.
The jury was justified in finding, that appellee was approaching the crossing with proper care and upon the
lookout when the first train passed; that when it passed,
he was thereby led to believe that no other train was
within such distance as to place him in danger in crossing. He saw the train when ten feet from the railroad.
He could have seen it first when thirty-five feet away.
His failure to look when looking would not have availed,
can not, of course, be ascribed to him as negligence.
The only negligence then possible was during the time
he passed over this twenty-five feet, which would occupy,
at the proved rate of five miles per hour, less than four
seconds of time.

Under such circumstances, can it be said that the failure to look was contributory negligence *per se?*

It is conceded by counsel that it is the law in Indiana

that, ordinarily, a traveler approaching a railroad cross-
ing is required to look and listen for approaching trains,
and that when his neglect to do so contributes to the ac-
cident, it is contributory negligence, and prevents a re-
covery. *Thornton, by Next Friend,* v. *Cleveland, etc., R.
W. Co.,* 131 Ind. 492; *Mann* v. *Belt R. R. and Stock Yard
Co.,* 128 Ind. 138; *Baltimore, etc., R. R. Co.* v. *Walborn,
Admr.,* 127 Ind. 142; *Cadwallader* v. *Louisville, etc., R.
W. Co.,* 128 Ind. 518; *Ohio, etc., R. W. Co.* v. *Hill,
Admx.,* 117 Ind. 56; *Cincinnati, etc., R. W. Co.* v.
Grames, 34 N. E. Rep. 714.

It is also true that while the failure to give the statutory signals is *per se* negligence upon the part of the
railroad company, yet such failure will not, of itself, relieve the traveler from the exercise of due care upon his
part. *Cleveland, etc., R. W. Co.* v. *Harrington,* 131
Ind. 426; *Cadwallader* v. *Louisville, etc., R. W. Co.,
supra.*

There is, however, a well recognized exception to the
rule requiring that the traveler shall look for approaching trains, and this exists when he has been, by conduct
and fault of the company, misled and thrown off his
guard, and thus prevented from taking the precaution
which he would otherwise have observed.

A man approaching a railroad crossing is required to
look and listen, for the reason that it is the part of a prudent man to do so, because a due regard for his own safety
requires it. If, however, the facts and circumstances under which he approaches it are such as to mislead him,
and such as would naturally create in his mind a sense of
security and belief that there is no danger, to such an
extent that a man of prudence would ordinarily act upon
it, then the reason for the precautions fails.

This exception to the general rule does not mean that
the traveler is relieved from the exercise of due care, but

it simply means that the *quantum* of care required from the traveler may be lessened by the acts and conduct of the railroad company, which create and justify in his mind the belief that he can safely dispense with a portion of that diligence ordinarily required.

It is said, in *Chicago, etc., R. R. Co.* v. *Hedges, Admx., supra:* "A prudent man's attention may be diverted so that he will fail to look and listen, and the evidence may be such as to make it proper to leave to the jury the question whether it was negligence for him to so fail. There may be circumstances which excuse the taking of the usually necessary precaution of looking and listening."

This language was used while considering the correctness of an instruction which gave to the jury the general rule, and then added: "If, however, in this case, you shall find from the evidence that the deceased was thrown off his guard and induced to refrain from taking this precaution by seeing the defendant's engine pass the crossing immediately before he stepped upon the railroad track, I will submit to you the question whether or not, under all the circumstances then surrounding the deceased, he was guilty of negligence."

Of this instruction it is finally said: "If there was any evidence tending to show that the plaintiff's intestate was thrown off his guard by such means as might have such effect upon an ordinarily prudent man (and we think there was some such evidence), it was not wrong to submit to the jury the question of contributory negligence."

In passing again upon this same case in 118 Ind. 5, Judge MITCHELL holds that on the facts, as found specially, the deceased was not in fact misled, because the one train did not follow the other until after several minutes, and the deceased was himself perfectly familiar with the custom. The court, however, clearly recognizes that such a case might be, saying: "His attention was not distracted by one train following so close upon another, without warning, as to mislead him or throw him off his guard."

In *Ohio, etc., R. W. Co.* v. *Hill, Admx., supra,* it is said: "There are cases where there may be a recovery, although the plaintiff may have gone upon the track without looking and listening for approaching trains, as the above stated rule requires, as, for example, where, by the negligence or misconduct of the railway company, another is suddenly put in peril, and when in such peril, and acting under the impulse of apparently well grounded fear, seeks to escape; or where the railway company acting through its servants, by its own negligent or wrongful acts or omissions, throws the plaintiff off his guard; or where it so acts as to invite him to go upon the track, or to create the impression that there is no danger when, in fact there is."

In *Cadwallader* v. *Louisville, etc., R. W. Co., supra,* where a footman entered upon the track without looking, COFFEY, Judge, uses this language: "Had the flagman done anything to induce the appellant to attempt a crossing at the time she was hurt, or anything to throw her off her guard, then the question of her negligence would have been a question for the jury. *Chicago, etc., R. R. Co.* v. *Hedges, Admx., supra.*"

In *Cleveland, etc., R. W. Co.* v. *Harrington, supra,* the same judge says: "In the absence of some evidence to the contrary, we think the appellee had the right to presume that the appellant would obey the city ordinance and would not run its trains at a greater rate of speed than four miles an hour at the point where the injury occurred, and while the wrongful conduct of the appellant in this regard would not excuse her from the exercise of reasonable care, yet in determining whether she did use such care, her conduct is to be judged in the light of such presumption." See, also, *Chicago, etc., R. R. Co.* v. *Boggs*, 101 Ind. 522, and *Pennsylvania Co.* v. *Stegemeier, Admx.*, 118 Ind. 305.

In *Evansville, etc., R. R. Co.* v. *Marohn*, 34 N. E. Rep. 27, 6 Ind. App. 646, this court approved the language quoted from *Ohio, etc., R. W. Co.* v. *Hill, Admx., supra.*

In *Eichel* v. *Senhenn*, 2 Ind. App. 208, it approved the principle of the case of *Chicago, etc., R. R. Co.* v. *Hedges, supra.*

From these authorities it is plain that our court has repeatedly recognized the existence of the exception to the general rule, and that where the traveler is deceived and thrown off his guard by the conduct and fault of the company, he may be deemed to have been in the exercise of proper care without taking all the precautions which would otherwise be required.

In *Cleveland, etc., R. W. Co.* v. *Harrington, supra,* the Supreme Court refused to adjudge it to be negligence as a matter of law, for a traveler on foot to fail to look and see an approaching train after she was within thirty-seven feet of the track.

The circumstances in the case of *French* v. *Taunton, etc., R. R.*, 116 Mass. 537, were quite similar to this case.

The company was there making a flying switch. A woman approached the track, driving in her carriage at the rate of four or five miles an hour. She saw a train pass, and drove on to the track without stopping or looking. Her carriage was struck by a flat car which had been detached from the train and was following it. At a point forty-six feet from the track, she could have seen up the track forty-six feet. At thirty feet from the crossing she could have seen up the track for a long distance. She did not look, because she did not suppose one train would follow so closely upon another. It was held that the question of her due care was properly for the jury. This case was followed in *Griffin* v. *Boston, etc., R. R. Co.*, 148 Mass. 143.

Ferguson v. *Wisconsin, etc., R. R. Co.*, 19 Am. and Eng. Ry. Cases, 285, supports the same doctrine, which is followed by *Ward* v. *Chicago, etc., R. W. Co.*, 55 N. W. Rep. 771, where it is said with reference to a similar accident: "The plaintiff did not look in the direction of this car coming. He was watching and waiting for the train to pass. His attention was diverted from that direction, and as soon as the train was over and away from the crossing * not supposing or having any reason to expect or think that this detached car was following after the train. No ordinarily reasonable man would have so expected or thought, situated as the plaintiff was. The duty of a traveler before crossing a railway to look both ways and listen depends upon the conditions that he might reasonably expect the coming of a train at any and all times, and that his attention is not reasonably arrested or diverted."

In *Breckenfelder* v. *Lake Shore, etc., R. W. Co.*, 79 Mich. 560, the deceased was struck by a detached car, which he did not look for, relying upon the train's having passed the crossing shortly before. The court held the question of care properly submitted to the jury.

Thus, we find this exception to the general rule recognized by our own cases, and those of other States as well.

No man would naturally expect that one railroad train should follow another, at a high rate of speed, with but twelve seconds of time between the two. Such a reckless disregard, both of their own safety and of the interests of their employers, no man would ordinarily expect.

"It certainly is negligence to create an appearance of

safety where there is, in fact, danger, and such a false appearance is created when one train follows another so closely as not to allow time for giving the signals prescribed by statute." *Chicago, etc., R. R. Co.* v. *Boggs, supra.*

It is only where the facts are undisputed, and where but one legitimate inference can be fairly drawn from them, that the court is authorized to take the question away from the jury. Even though the facts be undisputed, if they are of such character as that different men might reasonably and fairly base upon them different conclusions, then the determination of the question is for the jury. *Citizens' Street R. R. Co.* v. *Spahr,* 7 Ind. App. 23, 34 N. E. Rep. 446, and cases there cited; *Cincinnati, etc., R. W. Co.* v. *Grames,* 8 Ind. App. 112, 34 N. E. Rep. 613.

In accordance with this principle, and under the facts of this case, we think it was for the jury to determine whether or not appellee was in the exercise of due care, whether or not he was deceived and thrown off his guard by appellant's breach of duty, and whether or not he had a right to, and did, rely upon the false appearance of safety produced by appellant, and whether or not his failure to look and see during the four seconds of time in which he might have done so was contributory negligence.

It can not be said that, because he saw the train before he was actually on the track, he was therefore necessarily guilty of negligence in trying to cross. When a man is suddenly, without his own fault, confronted with an imminent peril by reason of another's fault, the law does not require from him the same coolness and wise determination which might otherwise be deemed necessary, and it is ordinarily for the jury to say whether he acted with due care when thus brought face to face with the unexpected danger. *Louisville, etc., R. R. Co.* v. *Kelly,* 6 Ind. App. 545, 33 N. E. Rep. 1103; *Woolery, Admr.,* v. *Louisville, etc., R. W. Co.,* 107 Ind. 381; *Indianapolis, etc., R. R. Co.* v. *Stout,· Admr.,* 53 Ind. 143.

The judgment is, therefore, affirmed, at appellant's costs.

Ross, J., concurs in the result, but not in all the rea-·soning.

Filed Nov. 10, 1898.

———————◆———————

No. 1,135.

COLTON ET AL. *v.* LEWIS ET AL.

APPELLATE COURT PRACTICE.—*Reversal of Judgment.*—*Special Verdict.* —*New Trial.*—*Question of Fact.*—The jury are the exclusive judges of all questions of fact; and where the trial court has overruled a motion for a new. trial, one reason for which was that the verdict fails to find all the facts proven by the evidence, the appellate tribunal will not disturb that ruling unless it clearly and affirmatively appears from uncontradicted evidence that the facts established thereby, if stated in the special verdict, would have authorized a different judgment.

From the Warren Circuit Court.

W. L. Rabourn, for appellants.
J. McCabe and *E. F. McCabe,* for appellees.

DAVIS, J.—This suit was brought by the appellants, who alleged in their complaint, that on the 13th day of March, 1884, appellees, Lewis and wife, conveyed to them, by a deed containing covenants of general warranty, seven hundred and fifty-four acres of land in Lawrence county, in the State of Tennessee; that the covenant of seisin was broken in this, that at the time the deed was executed one Voss was in the adverse possession of a part of the tract so conveyed, holding the same by title para-

mount to that of the grantors; that the appellants had
never obtained possession of the premises so adversely
held, and that they had thereby sustained damages, for
which they prayed judgment.

The record does not disclose that any answer was ever
filed. The cause was submitted to a jury for trial, and
a special verdict returned, on which judgment was rendered in favor of appellees.

The only error assigned is that the court erred in overruling appellants' motion for a new trial. The only
reasons discussed are that the verdict is contrary to law,
contrary to the evidence, not sustained by sufficient evidence, and that it fails to find all the facts proven by the
evidence.

The evidence is, in some respects, conflicting, and in
others it is indefinite and uncertain. For instance, as
we understand it, the description of the seven hundred
and fifty-four acres which appellees conveyed to appellants, begins: "Eight poles west from the northwest
corner of entry No. 846, in the name of Abner Pillow,
for thirty acres," and the deed to Voss, which is claimed
to constitute a paramount title to one hundred and thirty-
two acres, in the northwest corner of said first mentioned
tract, has the following beginning: "A part of entry
No. 786, in the name of Thomas M. Scott, for 612 acres,
granted to said Scott and bounded as follows, to wit:
Beginning at the southwest corner of said entry No. 786,
thence," etc.

It is earnestly insisted, by counsel for appellees, that
there is no "evidence in the record, that tends even re-
motely to establish the identity of the parcels described
in appellees' deed to the Coltons and the deeds to Voss."

There is evidence in the record tending to show that
appellees were, under claim of ownership, in the possession of seven hundred and fifty-four acres of land, which

they conveyed to appellants, also that by reason of the claim of ownership of said Voss, appellants did not acquire or hold possession of one hundred and thirty-two acres of land, but whether the description in the deed to Voss, on which this claim was based, included any part of the real estate described in the deed executed by appellants, does not clearly appear to us. The fact that there is ample evidence from which the trial court or jury might have drawn the inference that said 132 acres was a part of the real estate described in the deed to appellants, is not a sufficient reason to warrant this court in disturbing the conclusion reached by that court.

The special verdict is, it is true, indefinite and uncertain, but in this respect the verdict harmonizes with the evidence. *Shelbyville, etc., Turnpike Co.* v. *Green*, 99 Ind. 205.

The jury are the exclusive judges of all questions of fact. *Brazil etc., Coal Co.* v. *Hoodlet*, 129 Ind. 327.

The verdict also has the approval of the trial court. *Madison, etc., R. R. Co.* v. *Taffe*, 37 Ind. 361; *Winslow* v. *State*, 5 Ind. App. 306.

It is conceded, so far as this appeal is concerned, that appellants were not entitled to judgment on the verdict. The motion for a new trial presents the question as to whether appellants were entitled to recover on the evidence. Had the trial court been of the opinion that, on the evidence, appellants ought to recover, it would have been the duty of that court to sustain the motion for a new trial. The trial court having overruled the motion, this court will not disturb that ruling, unless it clearly and affirmatively appears from uncontradicted evidence, that the facts established thereby, if stated in the verdict, would have authorized a judgment in favor of appellants. In this case, the record, in the condition in which it comes before us, does not convince the court that the jury erred in failing to find and return, in their verdict, sufficient material facts, under the issues, as would have sanctioned a judgment thereon in favor of appellants.

Judgment affirmed.

Filed Nov. 8, 1893.

<hr>

No. 799.

KEESLING ET AL. *v.* DOYLE.

INSTRUCTIONS TO JURY.—*Refusal to Give.—When not Error.—Given in Substance.*—It is not error to refuse to give an instruction which is as fully and completely covered in substance, by an instruction given.

MALICIOUS PROSECUTION. — *Probable Cause.—Malice.— Instruction to Jury.*—The court, in an action for malicious prosecution, instructed the jury that in determining the question of malice and want of probable cause, they might take into consideration certain things, all being issuable facts and proper to be considered by the jury in determining whether the prosecution was malicious and without probable cause. In this there was no error.

EVIDENCE.—*Objection, When not Well Made.*—An objection to evidence that it is irrelevant and immaterial, is unavailable, unless the evidence shows on its face that it is incompetent.

SAME.—*Malicious Prosecution.—Record of a Previous Action.— When Admissible.*—In an action for malicious prosecution, the record of a previous action is admissible in evidence, when it tends to prove or disprove malice or want of probable cause.

SAME.—*Joint Objection.— When Unavailable.*—Where offered evidence is admissible against one of two or more parties, it is not error to overrule a joint objection thereto.

SAME.—*Public Records.—Notice.*—Public records are notice to the world, and it is not necessary to prove that a person has examined a record in order to bind him with notice of its contents.

SAME.—*Conversation.—Real Estate.—Rent.*—Where the right to the possession of certain land is in litigation, a conversation had during such time, by one of the parties, as to his intention to rent the land, is inadmissible.

From the Madison Circuit Court.

F. S. Ellison, for appellants.
W. A. Kittinger and *L. M. Schwinn*, for appellee.

Ross, J.—This action was brought by the appellee, against the appellants, to recover damages for alleged malicious prosecution. There was a trial by jury and a verdict returned, assessing appellee's damages in the sum of fifty dollars, upon which, after overruling a motion by the appellants for a new trial, judgment was rendered for the appellee. But one error is assigned in this court, viz: the overruling of the appellants' motion for a new trial. Many reasons were assigned in the motion for a new trial, which we will consider as they are presented by the appellants.

It is first insisted that the court erred in refusing to give to the jury the following instructions: "Unless the evidence shows clearly that the accusers had no grounds for the proceedings in the case, only a desire to injure the accused, you would not be warranted in finding for the plaintiff." The appellee insists, not only that the instruction does not state the law correctly, but that no question is presented on this appeal concerning it, for the reason that it is not properly in the record. We deem it unnecessary, at this time, to determine either of these questions, although the latter objection seems to be well taken, because we think that the court, by its own instructions, fully explained to the jury that the appellee must prove, in order to recover, not only that the criminal prosecution was begun by the appellants through malice, but also that at the time they began such prosecution there was no probable cause for commencing the same. The instruction given by the court was as full and complete as that asked by the appellants. The court was not bound to reinstruct upon the same branch of the case.

Instruction numbered three, of those given by the court of its own motion, is objected to by appellants, it being insisted that the court therein directs the jury that if they found certain facts to be true, they would be justified in finding that the appellants began the prosecution maliciously, and without probable cause. We can not give such a construction to the instruction. The court, by this instruction, simply told the jury that in determining the question of malice and the want of probable cause, they might take into consideration certain things, but the court does not say that the finding of any given state of facts as true, would constitute malice or want of probable cause. All of the issuable facts stated in the instruction were proper to be considered by the jury, in determining whether or not such prosecution was malicious and without probable cause.

Other instructions are assailed, but we find no error in them. In fact, the court, construing all of the instructions together, seems to have stated the law clearly and sufficiently.

It is next insisted that the court below erred in admitting in evidence the complaint, amended complaint, and judgment rendered in an action brought by Isabelle Doyle and the appellant James Doyle against the appellee, in ejectment. The only objection made by the appellants to the introduction of this evidence was that it was irrelevant and immaterial. Such an objection is too general, unless the evidence, on its face, shows that it is incompetent. *Heap* v. *Parrish*, 104 Ind. 36; *McCullough* v. *Davis*, 108 Ind. 292.

The evidence was clearly competent as tending to show not only the right of the appellee to the possession of the land out of which arose the prosecution for which dam-

ages are asked in this action, but also to show malice and
want of probable cause on the part of the appellant James
Doyle in the prosecution. If, as counsel insists, the
evidence was not admissible against one of the appellants, he should have objected separately to its introduction, for a joint objection by him with his codefendant
as against whom the evidence was admissible, raises no
question upon which he can predicate error. If the evidence was admissible for any purpose against either of
the appellants, the overruling of a joint objection thereto
is not error. It is true that the appellant Keesling was
not a party to the action in ejectment, yet he was bound
to take notice of it, for the reason that he acquired his
rights, if any he had, to the possession of the property
through said James and Isabelle Doyle. Public records
are notice to the world, and it is not necessary to prove
that a man has examined a record in order to bind him
with notice of its contents. If the record is one which
it was his duty to take notice of, he will be presumed to
know its contents. The judgment of a court of record is
such that every person is bound to know its contents
when dealing with those against whom such judgments
had been rendered.

It is also urged that the court erred in refusing to admit evidence of a certain conversation between the appellee and the appellant James Doyle, had in 1890, concerning the intention of the appellee to rent the farm of said
James and Isabelle Doyle for another year. This evidence was clearly incompetent, for the right to possession
of the farm was in litigation when the prosecution was
commenced, and was afterwards determined in favor of
the appellee. It is clear, therefore, that this evidence
could be introduced for no purpose other than to show a
right of possession to the property in the appellant
Keesling, which, in effect, would be to impeach that

judgment. The cases cited by appellants have no application in this case, for the reason that the right of the appellee to the possession of the property had been adjudicated under a claim of right superior to any claim of appellant Keesling; both parties claiming the right of possession through the same source. The evidence of the appellant Keesling shows that he was conversant with the claims of the appellee prior to the filing of the affidavit charging him with the supposed trespass, and that he knew that if the appellant James Doyle was defeated in his action in ejectment then pending against the appellee, he, Keesling, had no right to possession. All of counsel's argument that appellant Keesling was innocent of malice and begun the prosecution in good faith, is not sustained by the verdict of the jury. The jury, after hearing all the evidence, by which it clearly appears that the appellants were acting together, and that appellant Keesling knew of appellee's rights and claims, found that the prosecution was maliciously begun and without probable cause.

The evidence is sufficient to sustain the verdict.

Judgment affirmed.

Filed Nov. 3, 1893; petition for a rehearing overruled Nov. 24, 1893.

No. 1,146.

THE LAKE ERIE AND WESTERN RAILROAD COMPANY *v.* GRIFFIN.

PLEADING.—*Corporate Existence.—When Sufficiently Shown.*—Where an action is brought against a defendant implying a corporation, the complaint need not expressly allege that the defendant is a corporation.

SAME.—*Railroad.—Allowing Fire to Escape from Right of Way.—Negligence, General Allegation of.*—In an action for damages against a railroad company, for allowing fire to escape from its right of way, etc., the complaint is sufficient where it charges negligence in general terms, without alleging the specific acts constituting the negligence; and the same is true as to the freedom of plaintiff from contributory negligence.

RAILROAD.—*Fire Escaping from Right of Way.*—*Insurance Indemnity no Defense.*—Where, by the actionable negligence of a railroad company, fire escapes from its right of way to adjoining property, which is thereby consumed, the owner of such property can recover his entire loss from such company, without regard to the amount of insurance that may have been paid to him thereon.

From the Benton Circuit Court.

W. E. Hackedorn, T. L. Merrick and *I. H. Phares,* for appellant.

D. Fraser and *W. H. Isham,* for appellee.

DAVIS, J.—This action was brought by appellee against appellant, to recover damages occasioned by the negligent acts of appellant's agents and employes in setting fire upon its track and right of way, and negligently allowing said fire to escape to appellee's premises, destroying his meadow, hay and corn.

Appellant answered by general denial, and also by set-off on account of money paid to appellee by an insurance company. A trial by the court resulted in judgment for appellee.

The errors assigned are:

1. That the court erred in overruling appellant's demurrer to the complaint.

2. That the court erred in sustaining appellee's demurrer to the second paragraph of appellant's answer.

3. That the court erred in overruling appellant's motion for a new trial.

The first objection urged to the complaint is that it fails to charge "that appellant was a railroad corporation owning and operating its railroad at the time the fire was set out." It is alleged in the complaint "that the defendant is a railroad corporation doing business in the State of Indiana, and owning and operating a railroad through Benton county, and in and through plaintiff's lands adjacent thereto; that on the 20th day of December, 1890, the defendant company, in the operation of its trains and locomotives, carelessly and negligently set fire,'' etc.

The complaint in this respect is sufficient. The objection thereto is not tenable. The averments in relation to the corporate nature of appellant are stronger. than necessary. The rule is that where an action is brought against a defendant in a name implying a corporation, the complaint need not expressly allege that the defendant is a corporation. *Adams Express Co.* v. *Hill,* 43 Ind. 157; *Indianapolis Sun Co.* v. *Horrell,* 53 Ind. 527.

The next objection is that it does not sufficiently aver that appellant negligently suffered or caused the fire to escape from its right of way to appellee's premises. The allegation on this point is ''that said fire also, by the carelessness and negligence of defendant, was allowed to, and did, spread from defendant's right of way to the plaintiff's meadow, and burned,'' etc. A complaint is sufficient, in such case, to withstand a demurrer, where it charges negligence in general terms without alleging the specific acts constituting the negligence. *Ohio, etc., R. W. Co.* v. *Craycraft,* 5 Ind. App. 335.

The further objection is made that the complaint fails to aver that the loss resulted without the negligence of the plaintiff. The general allegation is made that the plaintiff was ''without any fault, blame or negligence.'' This was sufficient. *Chicago, etc., R. R. Co.* v. *Barnes,* 2 Ind. App. 213.

It is next insisted that the court erred in sustaining appellee's demurrer to the second paragraph of answer.

The rule is well settled that where, by the actionable negligence of a railroad company, fire escapes from its right of way to adjoining property, which is thereby consumed, the owner of such property can recover his entire loss from such company without regard to the amount of insurance he may have been paid thereon. *Cunningham v. Evansville, etc., R. R. Co.,* 102 Ind. 478.

The answer was not good, either as a set-off or defense in bar or mitigation.

The only remainining error that has been discussed by counsel is that the damages assessed are excessive "in view of the fact that appellee has already received one hundred and fifty dollars from the insurance company for the same loss."

On the authority cited *supra,* we are constrained to hold against appellant on this question.

There is no error in the record.

Judgment affirmed, at costs of appellant.

Filed Nov. 9, 1893.

———————◆———————

No. 882.

DERRY ET AL. *v.* MORRISON, ADMINISTRATOR.

PLEADING.—*Complaint, Sufficiency of.—Indemnity Bond.—Failure to Show Right of Action in Plaintiff.*—A., as attorney for B., received from the clerk of the court certain money as the distributive share of B. in her father's estate. Because of certain claims made upon him by others who asserted a right to the funds superior to B.'s, A. refused to pay the fund over to B., and in order to procure the money from A., B. and her husband executed an indemnifying bond to A., payable on demand, in case A. should be ordered to repay the money, or any part thereof, to any claimant, to the clerk of the court, or to the administrator of the estate. In a suit by C., a claimant against the estate, B. was ordered to pay over the money so received by her from A., to the administrator of the estate; and, on failure to do so, the administrator instituted suit on the bond executed to A.

Held, that the bond having been executed expressly for the protection
of A. alone, the complaint was insufficient which did not show that
it had been assigned or transferred to plaintiff, the administrator.
SAME.—*Insufficiency of Facts.—Parties.*—In such case, the fact that A.
was made a party defendant to answer to his interest, does not aid
the complaint in showing a right of action in plaintiff.

From the Hancock Circuit Court.

W. R. Hough and *Davis & Martz*, for appellants.
A. C. Ayres and *A. Q. Jones*, for appellee.

GAVIN, J.—The appellee brought suit upon a written
bond executed by the appellants to one James A. New.
The cause was tried on the answer of general denial to
the complaint.

The bond is as follows:

"This is to certify that I and my wife, Martha A.
Derry, have this day received of James A. New the sum
of six hundred and twenty-five dollars ($625), money
collected in the suit of Morrison, administrator, against
Dean, in the circuit court of Marion county, and that I am
empowered and authorized by the said Martha to receive
said sum of said New, and that, whereas, further, a suit
is instituted in the Marion Circuit Court against said New
demanding that he shall return said money to the clerk's
office of said county, and the said New is refusing to
turn said sum of money over to me on account thereof.

"Now, we each hereby agree and bind ourselves unto
said James A. New in the said sum of $625, in case he is
ordered to refund or repay said sum, or any part thereof,
to the plaintiff Noble Warrum, to the clerk of said court
or to the administrator of said estate; that we will pay
said New said sum on demand, and in default will be
liable to said New in damages to that amount.

(Signed)   "JOEL DERRY,
                                   "MARTHA DERRY."

To the complaint a demurrer for want of facts was overruled, with an exception.

The following are the facts as found specially, and the conclusions of law thereon:

"*First.* That on the 27th day of June, 1884, the defendant James A. New, as the attorney of and for the defendant Martha Derry, received from the clerk of the circuit court of Marion county, Indiana, as her, the said Martha's, distributive share of the estate of her father, John C. Atkinson, deceased, the sum of $1,389.

"*Second.* That afterwards, on the —— day of ———, 1884, the defendant New, as the attorney of the defendant Martha Derry, as and for a part of the money so received by him for her, as above found, delivered to her his check on bank for the sum of $600, and also surrendered for cancellation a certain promissory note for the sum of $25, which had been executed to him by the defendant Joel Derry, in part consideration for his services as the attorney for said Martha in the suit and matter wherein said moneys had been collected and received, and that at the time the defendants, Martha and Joel, executed to the defendant New the written instrument sued on and set out in the amended second paragraph of complaint herein, which said instrument, in substance, certifies."

After reciting the substance of the contract heretofore set out, the finding then proceeds:

"And that the only consideration for the execution of said instrument by said Martha and Joel was the delivery of said check for the sum of $600, and the surrender of said note for $25, as aforesaid.

"*Third.* That after the execution of said written instrument, on the 3d day of May, 1887, in the certain action pending in the circuit court of Marion county men-

tioned in said instrument, and wherein Noble Warrum
was plaintiff, and Frank W. Morrison, James A. New,
Martha Derry, Logan Galbreath, and Flora Fishburn
were defendants, said court did, among other things
therein, order and decree that the defendant Martha
Derry, should, within sixty days thereafter, pay over to
Frank W. Morrison, as administrator of the estate of
John C. Atkinson, deceased, the moneys so received by
her from the defendant New, as hereinbefore found by
the court.

"*Fourth.* That the defendant New was not in the action named in the last finding above, nor has he been
in any action by any court, ordered or directed to assign,
transfer or deliver the written instrument sued on and
set out in the amended complaint herein, to the plaintiff.

"*Fifth.* That the defendant New did not, at any time
before the commencement of this action, nor has he at
any time since, assigned, transferred or delivered to the
plaintiff said written instrument sued on herein, otherwise than by the institution and prosecution of this proceeding as the attorney for the plaintiff herein.

"*Sixth.* That no order has at any time been made by
the Marion Circuit Court for the repayment to Noble
Warrum, or to the clerk of said court or the administrator of the estate of said John Atkinson, deceased, by
said James A. New, or by any person other than the defendant Martha Derry, of the $625 so found to have been
paid the said defendant by said New; that said money
was so paid to the defendant Martha Derry, as a part of
her distributive share as one of the heirs of said John C.
Atkinson, deceased, and that the same is the $625 men-
tioned in said instrument of writing, and that said instrument was executed to secure the payment of the same
if required and ordered by said Marion Circuit Court to

be paid by said New; and that the same has not been re-paid by said Martha Derry to said James A. New, or to the clerk of said Marion Circuit Court, or to the adminis-trator of said estate, or to any other person, but is now retained by her.

"From the facts so found, I conclude that the plaintiff is entitled to recover of the defendants, Joel Derry and Martha Derry, said sum of $625.

"WM. H. MARTIN, Judge."

The facts found show, that there were in the hands of New, her attorney, certain moneys received by him for appellee Martha Derry, as part of her distributive share in her father's estate; that he refused to pay them over to her because of certain threatened claims upon him made by others who asserted a right to the funds superior to hers; that in order to procure the moneys from him, she executed the bond sued on, payable to him, wherein the obligors agree to pay to him said sum on demand "in case he is ordered to refund or repay said sum, or any part thereof, to the plaintiff Noble Warrum, to the clerk of said court, or to the administrator of said estate."

It is expressly found by the court that New never has been ordered to pay this money to Warrum, nor to the clerk, nor to the administrator, nor to any one else.

We are unable to construe this bond to be other than a simple bond of indemnity made for the protection of New. Its words are plain and unambiguous. There is in it not the least hint that it is for the protection of the administrator or the estate. The court find expressly as a fact that it was executed to protect New. There is no pretense that New has ever been ordered to refund or re-pay the money, or damnified in any manner. If he has not, no cause of action has accrued to him or any one else upon the bond. There is no right to maintain an

action on this bond shown to exist in favor of the appellee, under the facts as found. The bond is executed to
New. He is made a party to answer to his interest, but
there is no finding of its transfer to appellee in any manner whatever. There is a finding that he was not ordered to transfer it, and also a finding that he never did
transfer it to appellee "otherwise than by the institution
and prosecution of this proceeding as attorney for the
plaintiff herein," which is equivalent to a finding that
he did not transfer it. His bringing suit in appellee's
name could not be a transfer. It might be evidence of
a transfer, but nothing more.

The bond having been executed to New alone and there
being no averment that it had been assigned or transferred to appellee, his complaint is bad. *Holman* v. *Langtree,* 40 Ind. 349; *Green* v. *Louthain,* 49 Ind. 139; *Richardson* v. *Snider,* 72 Ind. 425.

The fact that New was made a party to answer to his
interest does not aid the complaint in this respect. His
presence or absence as a party does not affect the sufficiency of the complaint, on a demurrer for want of facts.
Whether he is made a party or not is immaterial as a
matter of pleading, unless the question is raised by demurrer for defect of parties defendant. *Strong* v. *Downing,* 34 Ind. 300; *Shane* v. *Lowry,* 48 Ind. 205; *Leedy* v.
Nash, 67 Ind. 311.

There might be facts such as the insolvency of New,
or an order of the court to transfer, and refusal by him,
which might enable the appellee to be subrogated to the
rights of New in the bond, but none such are alleged.

Counsel for appellee rely, with apparent confidence,
upon the case of *Chandler* v. *Morrison, Admr.,* 123 Ind.
254, as conclusive of this cause and identical with it.
We are unable to so hold. There is between the two
cases a marked and wide difference. In that case the

bond was, upon its face, made for the benefit and protection of Morrison as well as New.   It was therein expressly agreed that "if any suit shall be instituted by any
pretended creditor of said estate against either said New
or said Morrison, arising out of their doings in said estate, and their receipt and disbursement of said funds,
then this obligation shall protect them against said litigation or liability to said extent of $625."   In the bond
in this case there is no effort to protect Morrison.   The
question there arose on demurrer to the complaint, which
alleged that in a suit against said New and others, said
proceedings, by which the payment of said money to the
heirs had been ordered, had been set aside, and said New
had been ordered to pay to the clerk all said moneys in
his hands and all notes and collaterals, including the
bond sued on, which should be taken by the administrator for the benefit of said estate, and that under said
order he did turn said bond over to said administrator.
In this case, there was no order against New, and no
transfer by him.

There are other averments in that complaint which
evidently influenced the mind of the court, and which
do not appear in the facts as found in this cause.   It is,
however, unnecessary to go into these in detail.   We
have already called attention to essential allegations in
that complaint, which are entirely lacking in the facts as
found by the court in this case, and which supply the
very things which are wanting here.   We are, therefore,
of the opinion that the court erred in its conclusions of
law.

If it be granted, which we do not hold, that there is in
the complaint a sufficient averment of an order of the
court requiring New to repay this money, the complaint
is still bad for want of direct averment of an assignment
or transfer of the bond to appellee.

The judgment is reversed, with instructions to the court to sustain the demurrer to the amended second paragraph of complaint, with leave to amend.

Filed May 10, 1893; petition for a rehearing overruled Nov. 7, 1893.

———◆———

No. 808.

THE EVANSVILLE AND TERRE HAUTE RAILROAD COMPANY *v.* KEITH ET AL.

COMMOM CARRIER.—*Loss of Goods.*—*When Unnecessary to Aver Want of Contributory Negligence.*—In an action against a common carrier for goods destroyed while in its possession, it is unnecessary to aver that the loss was not occasioned by plaintiff's negligence, the carrier for hire being an insurer against loss or injury from whatever cause, except only the acts of God and the public enemy.

SAME.—*Delivery, What Amounts to.*—*Complaint, Sufficiency of.*—In such case, the complaint is sufficient as showing a delivery of the goods (baled hay) intended for immediate transportation, which alleges the placing of the goods, in a condition to be carried, at the usual place of loading the same.

SAME.—*Freight Charges.*—*When Prepayment Waived.*—*Liability.*—While a common carrier is not bound to receive freight for transportation until the charges therefor have been paid, the right to prepayment may be waived, and the liability of the carrier attached in the absence of such payment.

SAME.—*Freight Charges.*—*Tender, When Unnecessary to Aver.*—In such case, where the complaint shows that the goods were tendered to, and accepted by, the carrier, and were destroyed by fire before being shipped, it is not necessary to aver that the charges for transportation were tendered.

EVIDENCE.—*Railroad.*—*Sparks.*—*Damages.*—*Scope of Inquiry.*—In an action against a railroad company, for negligently permitting sparks from its engine to be communicated to plaintiff's goods, it may be shown that other engines of the defendant, passing over the road where the property was destroyed, threw sparks, and that other fires occurred along or near the right of way, about the time the loss occurred, as tending to show the negligent habit of the officers and agents of the company.

The Evansville and Terre Haute Railroad Company *v.* Keith *et al.*

SAME.—*Railroad.*—*Spark Arrester.*—*Expert Testimony.*—In such case, it is proper for an expert witness to give his observation with reference to a certain spark-arresting device, for the purpose of showing its efficiency for the purpose intended. And there was no error in refusing to permit such witness to be contradicted by showing that fires occurred along the line of such road while such device was in use.

INSTRUCTIONS TO JURY.—*Contributory Negligence.*—*When not a Bar to Recovery.*—In an action where certain paragraphs of the complaint make a case wherein the defendant is liable regardless of any contributory negligence on part of plaintiff, it is not error to refuse an instruction making contributory negligence a bar to recovery.

Dissenting opinion by ROSS, J.

From the Vigo Superior Court.

J. E. Iglehart, E. Taylor, S. B. Davis and *G. M. Davis,* for appellant.

C. McNutt and *J. G. McNutt,* for appellees.

LOTZ, J.—The appellees sued the appellant to recover for three hundred tons of hay and two warehouses, which were destroyed by fire in January and November, 1887. Their complaint was in eleven paragraphs. There was a trial by jury and a verdict and judgment for appellees in the amount of $1,965.50.

The errors assigned and discussed by counsel are the overruling of the demurrer to the amended first, the fourth and fifth paragraphs of complaint, and the motion for a new trial. All other assignments are waived by a failure to discuss them.

The amended first paragraph avers, that on and before the 17th day of January, 1887, appellees were partners, under the firm name of Keith & Bledsoe, engaged in buying, selling and shipping grain; that the appellant was a railroad corporation, operating a railroad through the town of Pimento, where appellant had a station, depot, side-track and switch, and where it received and discharged goods, farm produce, and passengers, and was a common carrier for hire; that on January 1, 1887, plaintiffs had seventy tons of baled hay which they desired to ship over said railroad, and had a chance to buy eighty tons of baled hay additional, at a profit, provided they could procure cars to ship the same at an early day; that previous to said date appellant had not furnished appellees with sufficient cars to carry hay, and the latter had been compelled to refuse hay, or, after purchasing it, to allow it to lie exposed in the open weather, on account of appellant failing to furnish sufficient cars; that at this time, under these circumstances, appellees wrote to appellant a letter, complaining about discriminations and asking for information, and notifying appellant of the offer which appellees had to buy eighty tons of hay, to which the general freight agent answered as follows:

"EVANSVILLE, IND., January 4, 1887.
"Keith and Bledsoe, Pimento, Ind.:

"DEAR SIR—I am advised this morning by our general manager that he will be able to supply all hay and other cars required at once. I think you can safely rely on a full supply of cars as needed henceforth.

"Yours truly, G. J. GRAMMER."

That relying and acting upon said undertaking, obligation and contract, appellees purchased the said eighty tons of baled hay, and one hundred and fifty tons additional, and placed the hay so purchased, as well as the seventy tons already on hand, at a point adjacent and contiguous to appellant's side-track at the town of Pimento, at the usual and customary place of loading hay into appellant's freight cars at the said town and station; that the hay was properly packed and baled; that appellees notified appellant that the hay had been placed at the usual and customary place of loading at said town and station, and demanded cars upon which to ship the same, and requested appellant to transport said hay; that appellees were ready and willing to pay appellant its reasonable charges for said transportation; that appellant wrongfully failed and refused to carry said hay, and wrongfully refused to furnish sufficient cars to transport the same within a reasonable time after said demand; that afterwards said hay was, at the said place, wholly and totally destroyed by fire, to the damage of appellees in the sum of $3,000.

The objections urged against the sufficiency of this paragraph are (1) that it does not show that the loss was not occasioned by the negligence of the plaintiffs, and (2) that it does not show the actual delivery of the property to, and placing it in the custody of, the defendant, and (3) that it does not allege that the plaintiffs had tendered the price of carriage, or were ready to pay the same under proper circumstances.

Whether the letters referred to in this paragraph constitute a contract for the transportation of hay, is a matter of some doubt. *Chicago, etc., R. R. Co.* v. *Dane*, 43 N. Y. 240; *Riggins* v. *Missouri River, etc., R. R. Co.*, 73 Mo. 598; *Tilley* v. *County of Cook*, 103 U. S. 155.

They may be treated simply as a request for cars, and an offer to comply therewith. In either event, the paragraph proceeds upon the theory that the appellant is liable as a common carrier, for the loss of the hay by fire. A common carrier of goods for hire is an insurer against loss or injury from whatever cause arising, except only acts of God and the public enemy. *Walpole* v. *Bridges*, 5 Blackf. 222; *Pittsburgh, etc., R. W. Co.* v. *Hollowell*, 65 Ind. 188.

The loss of the goods and the manner in which it occurred are sufficiently averred. In order to invoke the liability which the law imposes upon a common carrier, the goods or articles designed for transportation must be actually delivered to the carrier. When goods are designed for immediate transportation, the placing of the goods in a condition to be carried, at the usual place of loading, and in pursuance of the usage of the parties, constitutes a delivery. *Louisville, etc., R. W. Co.* v. *Flanagan*, 113 Ind. 488; *Louisville, etc., R. W. Co.* v. *Godman*, 104 Ind. 490; *Merriam* v. *Hartford, etc., R. R. Co.*, 20 Conn. 360.

Such deposit made under such circumstances constitutes a delivery, although made without notice, and although the superintendent of the railroad did not know of the usage which the local agent had permitted to grow up, contrary to the positive order of the management. *Montgomery, etc., R. W. Co.* v. *Kolb*, 18 Am. and Eng. R. R. Cases, 512.

The paragraph is sufficient in this respect.

A railroad company, like any other common carrier, has the right to demand that its charges for transporting the goods shall be paid in advance. It is not obliged to receive them unless such charges are paid. Section 3925, R. S. 1881; *Randall* v. *Richmond, etc., R. R. Co.*, 108 N. C. 612; 3 Woods Railway Law, section 428; *Bastard* v. *Bastard*, 2 Show. 82; 2 Redfield Railway Law, section 176.

As the general custom is to receive and collect the freight upon delivery to the consignee, the right to prepayment is waived, and the carrier·can rely only upon its lien or responsibility of the consignee, if it accepts the goods without prepayment. 3 Woods' Railway Law, section 428; *Pittsburgh, etc., R. W. Co.* v. *Morton*, 61 Ind. 539; *Pittsburgh, etc., R. W. Co.* v. *Hollowell, supra; Bastard* v. *Bastard, supra; Barnes* v. *Marshall*, 18 Q. B. *785; *Pickford* v. *Grand Junction R. W. Co.*, 8 M. and W. 372.

We think the paragraph sufficient.

Appellant's counsel say that the fourth and fifth paragraphs of complaint are defective because it is not

averred that the charges for transportation were tendered, and that it is not averred that the fire occurred
without the fault of the plaintiff.

Each of these paragraphs proceeds upon the theory of
a liability arising against the defendant as a common
carrier of goods.   Each shows that the goods were tendered to, and accepted by, the appellants, to be transported, and were destroyed by fire before being shipped
from the station.   No such averments as contended for
are necessary.

On the trial, the court permitted appellant Bledsoe and
many other witnesses to testify that all the engines of
the defendant passing the station where appellee's property was situated threw sparks, and that other fires had
occurred along or near the right of way of the railroad,
about the time the loss occurred.

The correctness of a ruling on the admission or exclusion of evidence depends, in a large measure, upon
the issues, and the other evidence then in hand.   Some
of the paragraphs of the complaint proceed upon the
theory of negligence, in that the appellant's engines were
improperly constructed, did not have sufficient and
proper spark arresters, and were run at a high and unnecessary rate of speed, etc.

It appears that there were two fires; one on January
17th, 1887, and one on November 5th, 1887, both of
which destroyed buildings and hay.   Appellees sought
to show that the first fire was caused by an engine attached to a passenger train going north, and that the
second fire was caused by an engine attached to a freight
train going north.   It was in this condition of the evidence, and while giving their evidence in chief, that appellees offered the evidence of which complaint is made.
Appellant contends that the engines which it was sought
to show produced the fires, were sufficiently identified;

that the proof of the defective construction and of the throwing of sparks should have been confined to such engines, and that it was error to permit the appellee to give evidence of the faulty construction of, and of the throwing sparks by, other engines. In support of this position, the following cases are cited: *Gibbons* v. *Wisconsin Valley R. R. Co.,* 58 Wis. 335; *Allard* v. *Chicago, etc., R. W. Co.,* 40 N. W. Rep. 685; *Phelps* v. *Conant,* 30 Vt. 277; *Baltimore, etc., R. R. Co.* v. *Woodruff,* 4 Md. 242; *Boyce* v. *Cheshire R. R.,* 42 N. H. 97; *Warner* v. *New York, etc., R. R. Co.,* 44 N. Y. 465 (472); *Robinson* v. *Fitchburgh, etc., R. R. Co.,* 7 Gray (Mass.), 92; *Sherman* v. *Kortright,* 52 Barb. 267; *Jacques* v. *Bridgeport, etc., R. R. Co.,* 41 Conn. 61; *Bailey* v. *Trumbull,* 31 Conn. 581.

Some of these cases seem to support appellant's contention. Their application, however, depends upon whether or not the engines had been identified when the testimony was offered. When this evidence was offered, the appellant had not yet identified the engines by their number. Nor was the objection based upon the ground that the engines had been identified. We are of the opinion that the mere fact that an engine was attached to a certain train on a certain occasion does not constitute a specific identification of the engine.

The train is sufficiently identified, but not its constituent parts. The same engine may have been used to move many different trains over the road. It is a difficult matter to identify a passing engine moving rapidly, particularly so after dark, as it appears from the conceded facts was the case here.

It was said by Valentine, J., in *Atchison, etc., R. R. Co.* v. *Stanford,* 12 Kan. 354, 15 Am. Rep. 362: "Indeed, in our opinion it would be extremely unreasonable to require a stranger to the company to do any such

thing. The engines are all alike to him. He does not
know them apart. Nor does he know when any particular engine is used, or who manages it. And when it
passes at the rate of fifteen or twenty miles an hour, he
could not see enough of it to ever afterwards identify it."

In *Koontz* v. *Oregon R. W. & Nav. Co.,* 23 Pac. Rep.
820, it was held that owing to the difficulty in identifying
a passing engine, and for the reason that the business of
operating a railroad supposes a unity of management and
a similarity in the construction of engines, it is proper
to admit evidence as to other and distinct fires. We
think the great weight of authority is against appellant's
position. *Grand Trunk R. R. Co.* v. *Richardson,* 91 U. S.
454; *Sheldon* v. *Hudson River R. R.,* 14 N. Y. 218; *Field*
v. *N. Y. Central R. R.,* 32 N. Y. 339; *Pennsylvania Co.*
v. *Stranahan,* 79 Pa. St. 405; *Huyett* v. *Philadelphia, etc.,*
R. R. Co., 23 Pa. St. 373; *Crist* v. *Erie R. W. Co.,* 58 N.
Y. 638; *Smith* v. *Old Colony, etc., R. R. Co.,* 10 R. I. 22;
Annapolis, etc., R. R. Co. v. *Gantt,* 39 Md. 115; *Cleveland* v. *Grand Trunk R. W. Co.,* 42 Vt. 449; *Longabaugh* v.
Virginia City, etc., R. R. Co., 9 Nev. 271; *Missouri Pac.
R. W. Co.* v. *Kincaid,* 11 Am. and Eng. R. R. Cases,
83; *Diamond* v. *Northern Pacific R. R. Co.,* 13 Pac. Rep.
367; *Steele* v. *Pacific Coast R. W. Co.,* 15 Pac. Rep. 851;
Butcher v. *Vaca Valley R. R. Co.,* 8 Pac. Rep. 174; *Nor-
folk, etc., R. R. Co.* v. *Bohannan,* 7 S. E. 236.

The identical question under consideration arose in
Grand Trunk R. R. Co. v. *Richardson, supra,* and the
court, by Justice Strong, said: "The question has often
been considered by the courts in this country and England; and such evidence has, we think, been generally
held admissible, as tending to prove the possibility, and a
consequent probability, that some locomotive caused the
fire, and as tending to show a negligent habit of the officers and agents of the railroad company." This de-

cision on this point has been cited with approval by the Supreme Court of this State. *City of Delphi* v. *Lowery, Admx.,* 74 Ind. 520 (524).

The court refused to permit the appellant to show by a witness, C. H. Bledsoe, the number of cars furnished by it to appellees during the months of August and September, 1887, and during the months of October, November, and December, 1886. This ruling is complained of and made one of the causes for a new trial. The court, however, did permit appellant to show the number of cars which it furnished appellees during the month of October, 1887, and up to the 5th day of November of that year; and the number of cars furnished from the fourth day of January, 1887, the day when the letter requesting cars was written, until the 17th of the month, the time of the first fire.

If the cars furnished during such time were sufficient to ship the hay of appellees then on hand, this was all that could be required of it in this respect, and what cars were furnished and what shipments made on other occasions would seem to be immaterial.

It is also insisted that the trial court erred in permitting the appellees to prove that, after their barn was full, they stacked a part of their hay on the outside. It was certainly competent to show where the hay was and its condition, under some of the paragraphs of the complaint.

One James Bargly, foreman in the boiler shops of the Vandalia Railroad, was called as an expert for appellees, and testified that a device to prevent the emission of sparks, known as the extension front, was in use on the Vandalia Railroad in 1887. He also testified, over the objection of appellant, that, with proper use and handling, he had never known of a fire resulting from an engine so equipped.

Appellant's counsel say: "The law recognizes, as a question of fact, that no device has been invented to prevent the emission of sparks, and that the court so instructed the jury." If it was error to admit this testimony, then the error by appellant's own admission was corrected by the court. But we do not think it was error. The witness was only asked to give his own observation with reference to a certain device. The only effect of such statement was to show the efficiency of the device for the purposes intended. Nor was there any error in refusing to permit the appellant to contradict the statement of such witness by showing that fires had occurred along the line of the Vandalia Railroad while such device was in use. The only purpose of the witness' testimony was to show that appellant had been negligent in not providing the best appliances for arresting sparks. It was not a question of fires or no fires along the Vandalia Railroad, but whether or not the appellant had been diligent in providing the best and most improved machinery. This could not be established by showing that certain fires had occurred when a particular device was in use. Persons of experience and knowledge in the use of such appliances might give their opinions as to the utility of the various devices and which one is best adapted for the purposes designed. It would lead to a never-ending controversy, if the particular fires along the various railroads, where different devices are in use, should be arrayed against each other and the jury compelled to consider a great mass of evidence in order to ascertain which one is the best.

The last contention of appellant is that the trial court refused to give instructions Nos. 26 and 27, asked by it. No objection is pointed out as to No. 26, and No. 27 is too broad and sweeping in its terms. It is predicated upon the theory that the appellees were guilty of contributory negligence, and directs a verdict for appellant, regardless of the other paragraphs of the complaint. Under some of the paragraphs, the appellees may have been entitled to recover regardless of the question of negligence.

We find no reversible error in the record.

Judgment affirmed, at costs of appellant.

Filed Nov. 7, 1893.

DISSENTING OPINION.

Ross, J.—I can not concur in the view of the majority of the court in holding that the first paragraph of the complaint "proceeds upon the theory that the appellant is liable as a common carrier for the loss of the hay by fire," and that it is good upon that theory. That part of this paragraph relative to a delivery to and acceptance by the defendant, is as follows: That the "plaintiffs purchased the said eighty tons of baled hay, and thereafter purchased one hundred and fifty tons of hay, and placed the hay so purchased, as well as the seventy tons, at a point adjacent and contiguous to the defendant's said side-track at the town of Pimento, and at the usual and customary place of loading hay into defendant's freight cars at the said town and station." Is the allegation that the plaintiffs "placed" their hay at a point adjacent and contiguous to a side-track, which was the usual and customary place for loading hay into the defendant's cars, equivalent to an allegation that the plaintiffs delivered the hay to, and it was accepted by, the defendant?

To support the reasoning of the majority in holding the complaint good upon the theory that the defendant is liable as a common carrier, it is said: "When goods are designated for immediate transportation, the placing of the goods in a condition to be carried, at the usual place of loading, and in pursuance of the usage of the parties, constitutes a delivery." To hold that the mere placing of goods, in a condition to be carried, at the usual loading place, is a delivery to the carrier, is much broader than I ever knew the law to be. In fact, I believe the law grants to the carrier the right to choose the kind of goods which it will undertake to carry; the kind of conveyance it will use in such transportation; the time for transit, and to require the prepayment of its charges. The carrier may refuse to receive the goods offered because they are dangerous, or because they are improperly or defectively packed; because they are consigned to a point to which he does not carry; because of a blockade, a mob or an accident which prevents their being transported within a reasonable time, as well as for a want of facilities with which to transport, or a refusal on the part of the consignor to prepay the charges. To constitute a delivery to the carrier, there must be not only a tender of the thing for which transportation is asked, but an acceptance thereof by the carrier. It is the offer on the part of the one and the acceptance on the part of the other that constitutes the contract for a violation of which liability attaches. To constitute a delivery to the carrier, he must be given exclusive possession, for so long as the consignor retains possession there is no delivery. That class of goods which the consignor is to load, the carrier simply furnishing the cars in which to load them and then to transport them, are not delivered to the carrier, so as to create a liability as a common carrier for their safety and preservation, until actually put aboard the cars.

The case of *Louisville, etc., R. W. Co.* v. *Flanagan,* 113 Ind. 488, is not in conflict with the views above expressed. That case was not to recover damages for injury to goods received for transportation, but for damages sustained by reason of the carrier's failure to receive and transport.

If, as this court says in the original opinion, that "Such deposits made under such circumstances constitutes a delivery, although made without notice," is a correct statement of the law, it would not require an acceptance by the carrier to make the delivery complete. In other words, it puts it in the power of one desiring to ship goods to make a forced delivery to a carrier without his knowledge or consent, without giving him a right to refuse to accept for any reason, thereby creating against him the liability of a common carrier.

I think the first paragraph of the complaint is insufficient upon that theory, and the demurrer thereto should have been sustained.

Again, the majority of the court hold that evidence of the condition of other engines than the one that set the fire is admissible for the purpose of showing the condition of the engine which did set the fire. I can not agree with the majority on this question. It may be conceded, for the purposes of this case, that when the origin of the fire has not been established, proof may be made of the condition of all the engines which passed the place where the fire originated, immediately preceding or about the time the fire started, and that they emitted sparks. Such evidence is admissible for the purpose of establishing the origin of the fire. But when it has been established what particular engine set the fire, it is not proper to prove that other engines set fires. The identity of the engine which set the fire, if the fire thus originated, having been established, it is proper to prove that it, both preceding and succeeding the setting of the fire complained of, set other fires or emitted an unusual number of sparks, or of an unusual size. But it can not be said, with even a semblance of justice, that evidence of the defective condition of other engines, which it is conceded did not set the fire complained of, is admissible to prove that the engine which is presumed to have set the fire, was also defective. In this case the evidence is uncontradicted that the engine attached to a particular train, which passed the point where the fire started just prior to the time the fire was discovered, is the one that set the fire, if it originated from an engine, and it is conceded that the engines concerning which plaintiff's witnesses testified did not set the fire. It matters not, therefore, what the condition of other engines might have been, so long as the engine which is presumed to have set the fire is in good condition and repair, and did not emit sparks. If evidence of the condition of other engines is admissible to prove that the engine in question is out of repair, the converse is true, and it is proper, by such evidence, to prove that it is in good condition and repair, even though the evidence may be clear and uncontradicted that it did emit sparks. *Erie R. W. Co.* v. *Decker*, 78 Pa. St. 293; *Gibbons* v. *Wisconsin Valley R. R. Co.*, 58 Wis. 335.

Railroad companies not only have the right, but they are compelled, to use fire to generate steam to operate their roads, but in that use they are required to use due care to prevent others from being injured thereby, and it has been long settled by an unbroken line of decisions that when the most approved spark arresters in general use on the best regulated railroads, are used, and they are kept in repair, and the engine is properly operated and managed, the company is not liable for the escape of fire.

The fact that the fire originated from sparks emitted from an engine raises no presumption of negligence. *Sheldon* v. *Hudson River R. R. Co.*, 14 N. Y. 218; *Rood* v. *New York, etc., R. R. Co.*, 18 Barb. (N. Y.) 80; *Terry*

v. *New York Central R. R. Co.*, 22 Barb. (N. Y.) 574;
Field v. *New York Central R. R. Co.*, 32 N. Y. 339; *Ellis*
v. *Portsmouth, etc., R. R. Co.*, 2 Neb. 138; *Hull* v. *Sac-
ramento, etc., R. R. Co.*, 14 Cal. 387; *Henry* v. *Southern
Pacific R. R. Co.*, 50 Cal. 176; *Philadelphia, etc., R. R.
Co.* v. *Yerger*, 73 Pa. St. 121; *Railroad Co.* v. *Yeiser*,
8 Pa. St. 366; *Kansas, etc., R. W. Co.* v, *Butts*,
7 Kans. 308; *Atchison, etc., R. R. Co.* v. *Stanford*, 12
Kans. 354; *Burroughs* v. *Housatonic R. R. Co.*, 15
Conn. 124; *Ruffner* v. *Cincinnati, etc., R. R. Co.*, 34
Ohio St. 96; *Gandy* v. *Chicago, etc., R. R. Co.*, 30 Iowa,
420; *Garrett* v. *Chicago, etc., R. W. Co.*, 36 Iowa, 121;
McCummins v. *Chicago, etc., R. R. Co.*, 33 Iowa, 187;
Redfield on Railways, section 125; Pierce on Railroads,
pages 436 and 437, *Indianapolis, etc., R. R. Co.* v. *Para-
more*, 31 Ind. 143; *Pittsburgh, etc., R. W. Co.* v. *Hixon*,
110 Ind. 225; *Chicago, etc., R. R. Co.* v. *Ostrander*, 116
Ind. 259.

The mere fact that fire is discovered shortly after the
passage of a train raises no presumption that sparks were
emitted and the fire originated therefrom. *Karsen* v.
Milwaukee, etc., R. W. Co., 29 Minn. 12; *Brusberg* v. *Milwaukee, etc., R. W. Co.*, 55 Wis. 106.

The evidence not only fails to establish a delivery of
the hay to the defendant, but, on the contrary, shows
that the defendant refused to accept it. The plaintiff
himself testified that the defendant refused to accept the
hay, saying that it could not get cars in which to ship
the same. Without evidence to establish a delivery to
the defendant, there could be no recovery under the first
paragraph of the complaint.

The evidence also fails to show that the plaintiff did
not contribute to his own injury, but, on the contrary,
shows that knowing the danger to which his hay would
be subjected if placed in close proximity to the defend-

ant's railroad, he did so place it, thereby contributing to his own injury.

As said by the Supreme Court of Wisconsin in the case of *Murphy* v. *Chicago, etc., R. W. Co.*, 45 Wis. 222: "We see no reason why a man who recklessly and unnecessarily exposes his property to destruction by fire in the immediate vicinity of a railroad, which from the necessity of the case must use the dangerous element in carrying on its business, should as a general rule be protected, if by the use of ordinary care he could have avoided its destruction, any more than the man who recklessly and unnecessarily places his property upon the track, and it is thereby destroyed."

For one to place property of a highly inflammable character upon the right of way of a railroad and so near the track that fire is liable to be communicated thereto from passing engines, does not take such precautions for the preservation of his property as an ordinarily prudent man would do. Such acts are not merely evidence of negligence, but constitute negligence itself.

There could be no rightful recovery under those paragraphs of the complaint wherein it is sought to recover on account of the negligence of the defendant, for the reason that the plaintiff contributed thereto.

For the above reasons, very hastily prepared, I think the judgment should be reversed.

Filed Nov. 7, 1893.

No. 832.

THE WESTFIELD GAS AND MILLING COMPANY ET AL. *v.* ABERNATHY.

VERDICT.—*Action in Tort.*—*When Verdict must be General.*—*When Damages can not be Apportioned.*—*Joint or Several Tort-Feasors.*—*Gravel Road.*—In an action against a gravel road company and several other defendants, for personal injuries sustained by reason of plaintiff's horse becoming frightened on the road and precipitating plaintiff and his horse into an open ditch close to the beaten track of the highway, charging defendants with having negligently left said ditch open and unguarded for an unreasonable length of time, and where the duties of the defendants as to the care to be exercised in relation to the ditch are *several* and *not joint*, but such neglect results in but a single injury, the verdict of the jury must be general against all of the defendants found guilty, and the verdict can not apportion the damages among the defendants found guilty.

SAME.—*When Amounts to Acquittal of Part of Defendants.*—In such case, where the verdict of the jury is against but two of the defendants, it is equivalent to a finding in favor of the other defendants.

JUDGMENT.—*Arrest of.*—*When Motion for Will Lie.*—*Verdict Against Part Only of Defendants.*—*Motion to Modify.*—*Venire de Novo.*— Where a verdict does not find against all the defendants in the action, and the court is proceeding to render judgment against all, the defendants against whom there is no finding may move in arrest of judgment as to them, there being an intrinsic cause appearing on the face of the record which shows that some of the defendants were entitled to such relief because there was no verdict against them. Other, and perhaps more appropriate, remedies would be by motion for judgment in their favor, motion to modify, or for *venire de novo.*

From the Hamilton Circuit Court.

T. J. Kane, T. P. Davis and *W. Garver,* for appellants.

J. A. Roberts, W. Fertig and *H. J. Alexander,* for appellee.

LOTZ, J.—The complaint in this case, in some respects, is a peculiar one. Its sufficiency is not questioned in this court.

We call attention to its averments for the purpose of aiding in the interpretation of the verdict rendered upon it.

Omitting the formal parts it is as follows:

"The plaintiff, for his amended complaint in said cause, says that the defendant, the Noblesville and Eagletown Gravel Road Company, was, on the second day of January, 1889, and had been continuously for the several years last past, owning, controlling, and operating a turnpike or gravel road, leading from the town of Noblesville to the town of Westfield, in said county of Hamilton, in the State of Indiana; that during the month of December, in the year 1888, the defendants negligently constructed and excavated an open ditch nearly two feet in depth and fifteen inches in width, and more than one mile in length, along and in said gravel road and near the beaten track in said road, and running said distance, nearly parallel with said beaten track; that the defendants carelessly and negligently permitted said ditch to remain open and unguarded for an unreasonable length of time next before and at the time of the happening of the injury herein complained of; that on the said second day of January, 1889, the plaintiff was traveling over and along said gravel road in a buggy; that the horse attached to the buggy, although of a gentle disposition, without any fault or negligence on the part of the plaintiff or the driver of said horse, became frightened, and shied from the beaten track in said road; that while endeavoring to keep said horse from overturning the buggy, and without any fault or negligence on the part of the plaintiff, plaintiff and said horse were precipitated into and over said ditch, whereby plaintiff's shoulder was dislocated, and he was severely and permanently injured, and has since said time suffered much pain and anguish from said injury; that said injury occurred by reason of said ditch being so constructed in said highway, and being open and unguarded.''

The defendant, the Noblesville and Eagletown Gravel Road Company, filed an answer of general denial. All the other defendants joined in an answer of general denial. The cause was submitted to a jury for trial, and a verdict returned in favor of the plaintiff, in the words and figures following, to wit:

"We, the jury, find for the plaintiff, and assess his damages at fifteen hundred dollars ($1,500); the West-field Gas and Milling Company to pay nine hundred dollars ($900), and the Noblesville and Eagletown Gravel Road Company to pay six hundred' dollars ($600).

"WILLIAM HOLLAND, Foreman."

The plaintiff moved for a judgment in his favor for $1,500 on the verdict, and against all of the defendants. Pending a ruling on this motion, the defendants, except the Gravel Road Company, filed a joint and several motion for a new trial. This motion was overruled. The Westfield Gas and Milling Company then separately moved the court in arrest of judgment. This motion was overruled. The defendants, William G. Pierce, John D. Edwards, Mahlon Perry, Aaron Harris, John L. Moore, Nathan E. Mills, Arlington L. Benford, and Orpheus E. Talbert, then jointly and severally moved the court in arrest of judgment against them. This motion was overruled. The Westfield Gas and Milling Company separately moved the court in arrest of judgment, except as to $900 and costs, and this motion was overruled. The defendant, the Gravel Road Company, then separately moved the court for a new trial, which motion was overruled. The court then sustained the plaintiff's motion for judgment on the verdict, and rendered judgment against all the defendants in the sum of $1,-500. The appellants excepted to these various adverse rulings, and have assigned each of them as error in this court. No motion for a *venire de novo* or to modify the judgment was made.

The verdict above set out is a general one. A general verdict, when perfect, covers all the issues in the case. It becomes important to ascertain what issues were joined by the pleadings, which the jury was required to determine.

There are two acts stated in the complaint, which are charged to have been negligently done by the defendants, (1) "constructed and excavated an open ditch, near two feet in depth, and fifteen inches in width, and more than one mile in length, along in said gravel road, and near the beaten track in said road," and (2) "permitted said ditch to remain open and unguarded for an unreasonable length of time."

A highway is a way open to the use of all the people of the State. The right to preclude the citizens of the State from traveling thereon, unless they comply with certain conditions, is a high privilege, and can not be exercised without assuming corresponding obligations. "The consideration for the right to exact toll, is the undertaking of the owner of the road to maintain it in a reasonably safe and convenient condition for travel." Elliott Roads and Sts., 68.

If the owner of such road create an unauthorized obstruction or excavation therein, or knowingly permit the same to be done, or fail to remove the same after notice thereof, or if any person, without authority, create or make such obstruction, he is liable to the traveler who sustains an injury resulting therefrom, when without fault. In such cases, it is not a question of negligence, but the wrong consists in creating or continuing a nuisance. And the same is true of such an excavation made so near a highway as to render it dangerous to the traveler. *Irvine* v. *Wood*, 51 N. Y. 224; Wood on Nuisances, section 266.

The liability, in such instances, does not spring from the manner in which the obstruction is made or guarded, but from its noxious character. But every excavation made in or near a street or highway is not a nuisance. They are often lawfully made. When lawfully made and properly guarded no action will lie for an injury resulting. The duty of a corporation, which owns and controls a toll road, to keep it reasonably safe for those who travel thereon, is one imposed upon it by law, and it is liable to the traveler who is injured without his fault, whether the defect or excavation was made with or without its consent, or whether such excavation is in or so near its line as to render it dangerous to the traveler. It is sufficient to charge the company with liability, if it had notice of such defect, or if the defect has existed such a length of time, as by the exercise of diligence, it could have known of it. Moak's Underhill on Torts, 230; *City of Delphi* v. *Lowery, Admx.,* 74 Ind. 520; *City of Crawfordsville* v. *Smith,* 79 Ind. 308.

It is also the law that persons who lawfully make excavations within or near the line of a highway and leave them unguarded, are liable for an injury resulting to a person who is without fault. *Noblesville Gas and Imp. Co.* v. *Teter,* 1 Ind. App. 322; *Graves* v. *Thomas,* 95 Ind. 361; Wood on Nuisances (2d ed.), section 266; *City of Indianapolis* v. *Emmelman,* 108 Ind. 530; *Stratton* v. *Staples,* 59 Me. 94; *Barnes* v. *Ward,* 9 C. B. (Manning) 392; *Bishop* v. *Trustees, etc.,* 29 L. J., Q. B. 53.

The complaint charges that the ditch was negligently constructed. Negligence is always unlawful; but, as an excavation may be lawful, the word negligence, as here used, relates to the manner in which the excavation was made, and not to the excavation itself. A lawful excavation, properly guarded, can give rise to no cause of action; but improperly or negligently guarded, and an action may arise. The evident purpose of the pleader here is to charge that the actionable negligence consisted in carelessly permitting the ditch to remain open and unguarded for an unreasonable length of time. We have alluded to these principles for the purpose of calling attention to the *gravamen* of the complaint. As the law imposed the duty upon all persons who were instrumental in making the excavation, to securely guard it and protect the traveler against injury, it is this duty that the complaint charges the defendants with having violated, and this is the gist of the action.

What is said in the complaint with reference to the construction of the ditch, is matter of inducement, merely introductory to the essential grounds of the complaint. The legal duty of guarding the excavation rested upon the defendants, either severally or jointly. The negligent act charged against the defendants, and which constitutes the cause of action, is one of omission, and not of commission. It is true that the act is a tort, but not of the aggravated kind. It is within the sphere of the law to attach the kind of liability to a given act. The law may say of the liability that it shall be joint or several, or joint and several, but the law can not make a fact. When an act is jointly done by two or more persons, volition, intention and concurrence of the minds of the actors are necessary concomitants. Persons who have jointly committed one and the same wrong, may be sued jointly or severally, and whether sued jointly or severally, their liability is always several.

"The action may be against all or any number of them. Separate actions may be prosecuted at the same time against the respective parties charged with the same wrong, and separate verdicts and judgments taken against them, whether for the same or different amounts, though the plaintiff can have but one satisfaction; but whether the judgment be joint or several, there is no right of contribution which can be enforced as between the defendants." *American Express Co.* v. *Patterson*, 73 Ind. 430; *Livingstone* v. *Bishop*, 1 Johns. *290; *Fisher* v. *Cook*, 17 N. E. Rep. 763; *Baltes* v. *Bass, etc.*, *Works*, 129 Ind. 185 (188); *Fleming* v. *McDonald*, 50 Ind. 278.

There are some exceptions to these general rules. There are cases where, although the law holds all the parties liable as wrongdoers to the injured party, yet, as between themselves, some of them may not be wrongdoers at all, and they may compel the other wrongdoers to respond for all the damages. There are many cases where the wrong is unintentional, or where the party, by reason of some relation, is made chargeable with the conduct of others; as, for instance, where a servant, at the command of the master, commits a tort, there is a liability over in favor of the servant against the master; or, if the master has been compelled to pay for the willful misconduct of his servant, he may have recourse against his servant. Cooley Torts, 166; Pollock Torts, 171.

There is a marked distinction between the tort and the liability arising from the tort. The liability as between the plaintiff and the defendants is always several, but the wrong itself may be jointly done, or severally done, by the defendants. If it be jointly done, the defendants are joint tort-feasors. If it be severally done, that is, without any concert of action between them, they are several tort-feasors. "When the suit is against several joint wrongdoers, the judgment must be for a single sum against all the parties found responsible." Cooley Torts, p. 136; *Everroad* v. *Gabbert*, 83 Ind. 489.

If a joint verdict of guilty be returned against more than one defendant, and several damages be assessed

against them, the plaintiff may, if the tort be a joint one,
cure the irregularity by entering a *nolle prosequi* against
all but the one whom he may elect to charge with the
damages assessed by the jury against such defendant.
Lyman v. *Hendrix*, 1 Ala. 212; *Beal* v. *Finch*, 11 N. Y.
128; *Halsey* v. *Woodruff*, 9 Pick. 555; *Everroad* v. *Gabbert, supra.*

But if more than one tort be charged in the same suit
against several defendants, and the defendants plead
severally, the jury may assess the damages for each tort
jointly against those defendants who jointly committed it.
Proprietors, etc., v. *Bolton*, 4 Mass. 419; *Allen* v. *Wheatley*, 3 Blackf. 332.

When a person neglects those conventional duties
which the law imposes upon him, he is liable for the injury resulting. So, if the same duty rests upon several
persons, and they all neglect it, they are all liable. The
character of the tort, whether joint or several, may exert
a controlling influence in interpreting the verdict rendered. As the plaintiff in this action has sustained but
one injury, he is entitled to but one satisfaction. Where
the separate and independent acts of negligence of two
parties are the direct causes of a single injury, and it is
not possible to determine in what proportion each contributed thereto, either is responsible for the injury.
Slater v. *Mersereau*, 64 N. Y. 138.

As between the defendants, there may be a right of
contribution depending upon their relations towards each
other. Is the tort declared on in the complaint the joint
tort of all the defendants or the separate tort of each?

In *Furguson* v. *Earl of Kinnoull*, 9 Cl. and F. 251, it
was held that if several are jointly bound to perform a
duty cast upon them by the law, they are liable jointly
and severally. In that case, however, the duty enjoined
was one that could only be performed by a majority of

the presbyters of a certain church, and as the act was one that required the coöperation of a majority of the presbyters to perform it, the refusal to perform the act also could only be brought about by the coöperation of a majority. The duty, in such case, was held to be a joint duty.

In *City of Detroit* v. *Chaffee*, 37 N. W. Rep. 882, it appeared that it was the duty of a lot-owner to repair the sidewalk in front of the lot, and in case of his default, it was the duty of the city to make such repairs. Both neglected the duty. The court said: "The parties are not joint tort-feasors. There was a duty resting upon both with respect to the same thing, but it was a separate duty imposed on each, and not joint. The neglect was likewise the separate neglect of each, and not the joint neglect of both."

Bretherton v. *Wood*, 6 Moore, 141, was an action to recover damages for personal injuries sustained. It appeared that ten persons owned a stage coach, and that while the plaintiff was being carried as a passenger thereon, the coach was overturned by the negligence of the driver and the plaintiff injured. The action was brought against all of the owners. The jury found two of the defendants not guilty, and the other defendants guilty, and assessed damages against them. The court held the action to be founded in tort, a breach of that duty imposed by law, to safely and securely carry the plaintiff so that no damage or injury happen him by default or negligence, and that from the nature of the case such duty was several and not joint, and might be maintained against one or all of those against whom it was brought, and that a judgment might be rendered against those found guilty and in favor of those found not guilty.

The breach of duty in failing to properly guard the excavation charged against the defendants, in the case in hearing, is the separate tort of each defendant, and not the joint tort of all. The verdict of the jury must be construed in the light of this fact. The plaintiff sustained but one injury. That injury resulted from a violation of a legal duty, which duty rested upon the defendants severally. He sued them jointly for their several torts, as he might lawfully do, when such torts produced but a single injury. The liability being several, may the jury apportion the damages among the several tortfeasors? We have seen that the jury may apportion the damages when there are separate torts from which separate injuries flow.

But here the damages are not divisible, and the whole must be assessed against all the defendants found guilty. If a separate injury flowed from the separate tort of each defendant, then there might have been a separate verdict and judgment against each defendant. But here a single injury was sustained. The jury, by their verdict, assessed the whole damages at $1,500. It then undertook to apportion this amount between two of the defendants. This it could not do. *Currier v. Swan*, 63 Me. 323.

But this apportionment demonstrates the intention of the jury. Damages in some amount is of the essence of a verdict or finding in favor of the plaintiff. As the whole of the damages was apportioned to only two of the defendants, it must have been the intention of the jury that the other defendants should pay no part thereof, and the verdict as to them is equivalent to a finding in their favor. When four persons are sued in trespass, a finding of guilty as to three, without naming the fourth, is equivalent to a finding of not guilty as to the fourth. *Wilderman v. Sandusky*, 15 Ill. 59.

A failure to find upon any material fact in issue is

equivalent to a finding against the party upon whom the burden rests to establish such facts. *Brazil, etc., Coal Co.* v. *Hoodlet*, 129 Ind. 327.

A verdict, no matter how informal, is good if the court can understand it. It is not to be avoided except from necessity. It should have a reasonable intendment, and should have a reasonable construction. It should not be disregarded on account of technical defects, if rendered upon substantial issues of fact, presented by the pleadings. *Clark* v. *Clark*, 132 Ind. 25; *Daniels* v. *McGinnis, Admr.*, 97 Ind. 549.

Our construction of the verdict is that it is a finding against the Westfield Gas and Milling Company and the Noblesville and Eagletown Gravel Road Company, in the sum of $1,500, and that it is a finding of not guilty or in favor of the other defendants.

The appellee contends that a motion in arrest of judgment, will not reach a defect in the verdict; that, if the appellants wished to avail themselves of any irregularity in the verdict or judgment, they should have moved for a *venire de novo* or to modify the judgment. A motion in arrest of judgment arises from intrinsic causes appearing on the face of the record. It is not confined to the pleadings, but may reach a defective verdict. 3 Bl. Com., 393; 2 Tidd Prac., 918; 3 Stephens Com., 628; Buskirk's Prac., 264; *Boor, Admr.*, v. *Lowrey*, 103 Ind. 468.

If there was no verdict against any one of the appellants, the better practice would have been for such one to move for a judgment in his favor; or, if a judgment had been entered, to move to modify it. But as neither of these motions was made the question is, can such defendant reach the defect in the verdict by a motion in arrest when the court is proceeding to render judgment, and point out the fact that there was no verdict against him? We think there is an intrinsic cause appearing on the face of the record which shows that some of the appellants were entitled to have the judgment arrested because there was no verdict against them. This may not be the best way, but it is one way of reaching the defect. By it the attention of the court is called to the fact that there is no verdict against certain defendants. When the court is apprised of such fact, no matter by what means, it is its duty to prevent a judgment from being rendered against a party in whose favor a finding has been made. So, to hold otherwise is to deny the court the power to do justice in such a case.

In an action sounding in tort, where the general issue only is pleaded, the verdict is either guilty or not guilty. In such cases a motion for a *venire de novo* will not lie.

On the trial the appellants excepted to certain instructions given by the court on its own motion, and excepted to the refusal of the court to give certain instructions asked by them. The undisputed facts of the case are, that the excavation was unguarded; that the appellee was in a buggy drawn by a gentle horse; the horse became frightened at some object, either in or near the road, and suddenly shied to the right and fell into the ditch; the appellee took hold of the bridle near the head, to assist the horse in getting out. The horse floundered, and, in a sudden wrench, appellee's shoulder was dislocated and seriously injured.

There was no evidence that the appellee acted heedlessly or recklessly. Under such circumstances, a recovery against some of the defendants was inevitable. We do not think there was any error in giving, or refusing to give, the instructions complained of. The court should have sustained the motion of the individual appellants in arrest of judgment. The other motions in arrest were properly overruled.

Judgment reversed as to William G. Pierce, John D. Edwards, Mahlon Perry, Aaron Harris, John L. Moore, Nathan E. Mills, Arlington L. Benford, and Orpheus L. Talbert, with instructions to sustain their motion in arrest of judgment.

The judgment below is affirmed as to the appellants, the Westfield Gas and Milling Company and the Noblesville and Eagletown Gravel Road Company, with costs.

Ross, J., dissents.

DAVIS, J., does not participate.

Filed Nov. 9, 1893.

--------◆--------

No. 633.

THE UNION CENTRAL LIFE INSURANCE COMPANY v. PAULY.

APPELLATE COURT PRACTICE.—*Sufficiency of Complaint on Appeal.— How Tested.*—A single paragraph of a complaint containing several paragraphs can not be questioned for the first time in the appellate tribunal. Only the entire complaint can be thus questioned.

LIFE INSURANCE. — *Warranties, What Amounts to. — Cancellation of Policy.*—Warranties in insurance policies are not favored in law, and the court will construe as a warranty that only which the parties have plainly and unequivocally declared to be such. And where the terms of the policy prescribe the penalty for misrepresentations in the application to be a right of cancellation of the policy by the company, it can not be held, by reason of the indefinite provisions of the application, to have intended a much severer penalty.

SAME.—*Warranties.—Construction of Policy.*—Where it is uncertain whether statements in an application for insurance are to be taken as warranties or representations, the construction most favorable to the policy-holder will be adopted.

SAME.—*Consummated Contract.—Failure of Payment of Premium and Delivery of Policy.*—While a consummated contract may exist without either payment of premium or delivery of policy, yet such cases are exceptional, and must be supported by very strong and satis-factory proof. And where all the evidence is consistent with the idea that there were simply negotiations looking toward an insur-ance, such a contract can not be established thereby.

SAME.—*Constructive Delivery of Policy.*—*Waiver of Payment of Premium.* —*Agent Holding Policy in Trust.*—Where there is no indication of any purpose to contract other than by a policy to be made and de-delivered upon payment of at least half of the premium, the fact that the insurance agent wrote the person seeking insurance, saying, "Your policy has come; the first time you are in town come around and get your policy," does not show a constructive delivery of the policy, a waiver of payment, and a consummation of the con-tract, neither does it show that the agent simply held the policy in trust for the insured.

SAME.—*Refusal of Agent to Consummate Contract,—Sickness and Death of Insured.*—Considering the facts that the negotiations for a policy occurred about September 28; that the insured was notified by postal card of the arrival of his policy; that two or three weeks thereafter a son of the insured called for the policy and tendered the amount of the premium, the insured being sick October 10th, and still sick November 21st and 28th, and still sick and unable to go and get his policy on the 6th of December, the date of tender of the premium, the agent was justified in refusing to consummate the contract, and, upon the death of the insured, was justified in re-turning the policy to his principal.

From the Gibson Circuit Court.

J. H. Miller, T. Duncan, W. M. Ramsey, L. Maxwell and *R. Ramsey,* for appellant.

M. W. Fields and *J. W. Ewing,* for appellee.

GAVIN, C. J.—The appellee brought suit against ap-pellant to recover the amount of a policy ($2,000) alleged to have been executed by appellant upon the life of her husband, William Pauly, who died March 1, 1890. The policy is dated October 1, 1889. The principal allega-tions of the complaint, in detail, are that appellants so-licited said William Pauly to take out insurance, and he thereupon applied for a $2,000 policy upon the en-dowment life-rate plan, payable to appellee: that appellant refused to accept this application and notified its agent of such refusal, but at the same time notified him that the insurance would be accepted on the ten-year endowment plan; that on October 25, the agent, Daily, so notified said William Pauly, who agreed to accept the same, upon the agent's promise to wait for the first premium until December, and until said William Pauly sold his hogs; that thereupon, by his direction, said agent notified the company that Pauly would accept a $2,000 policy on the ten-year endowment plan, payable to said appellee,— whereupon, said company made out such a policy and mailed it to said agent for delivery; that on November 20th said agent notified Pauly, by card, that his policy had come, and to send in for it; that on November 29, said Pauly sent his son to pay the premium and get the policy, but the agent refused to deliver it or to accept the premium, but promised to bring it out to him in a few days, but he failed and refused to deliver it, and, on April —, 1890, returned it to appellant; that said William Pauly and this plaintiff have in all things complied with the provisions of said contract of insurance.

To this complaint there was an answer of general denial, and also of breach of warranty as to certain statements in the application.

The insufficiency of the third paragraph of the complaint is assigned for error in this court. Our statute does not authorize the separate paragraphs of a complaint to be thus questioned for the first time in the Appellate Court. It is only the entire complaint which can be thus tested. *Tachau* v. *Fiedeldey,* 81 Ind. 54; *Ashton* v. *Shepherd,* 120 Ind. 69.

No question is therefore presented for our determination under this assignment.

After trial by a jury, and verdict for appellee, judgment was rendered in her favor over the appellant's motion for a new trial.

The action of the court in overruling this motion is the error urged here.

Under this motion, the sufficiency of the evidence and the correctness of the court's action as to certain instruc· tions and interrogatories are brought before us.

In the application, this question was contained: "Have you required the services of a physician during the last seven years? If so, state what for and when; also give his name and address."

To this, the answer was "No."

It is urged, by appellant, that this statement consti- tuted a warranty, for a breach of which the policy was avoided.

With this view of the law we are unable to agree.

By reason of their stringent character, warranties in insurance policies are not favored in law. The court will construe as a warranty that only which the parties have plainly and unequivocably declared to be such. *Sup. Lodge, A. O. U. W.,* v. *Hutchinson,* 6 Ind. App. 399, 33 N. E. Rep. 817; *North Western, etc., Life Ins. Co.* v. *Hazlett,* 105 Ind. 212; *Rogers* v. *Phenix Ins. Co.,* 121 Ind. 570; *Penn., etc., Life Ins. Co* v. *Wiler,* 100 Ind. 92.

We are by no means ready to decide that, even by the terms of the application, this statement is made a war- ranty; but even if it were, it could not be so construed in the light of the provisions of the policy. By the ex- press terms of the policy, it is issued on condition that "in case any statements or declarations made in the ap- plication for this policy are in any material respect un- true," * * * "the company may, at its option, can- cel this policy." Having, by this express language, provided the remedy for any false statements, and pre- scribed the character of false statements to which the penalty shall attach, it can not be held, by reason of the

indefinite provisions of the application, to have intended
a much severer penalty for any untruth in the statements
made regardless of their materiality. The policy and
application must be construed together, and if, when so
construed, it is left uncertain whether statements are to
be taken as warranties' or representations, the construction most favorable to the policy-holder is to be adopted.
This subject has been but recently fully discussed by
Judge DAVIS, in the case of *Indiana Farmers', etc., Ins.
Co.* v. *Rundell, Admr.*, 7 Ind. App. 426, 34 N. E. Rep.
588, to which we refer, and to the numerous authorities
therein cited.

We next come to the question as to whether or not the
verdict is sustained by the evidence, when applied to an
issue formed by the general denial. As to the evidence
itself, there is substantially no conflict, the differences
between counsel being with reference to the inferences
of fact which are fairly and reasonably deducible from
the evidence, and the result of the application of the law
thereto.

Dr. Paul H. Curtner testified that he made the medical
examination of deceased, September 28, 1889; that he
had a conversation with Daily, the agent, two or three
weeks afterwards, at the post-office, in which he told
Daily that Pauly was very sick, and Daily said: "I have
just received Pauly's policy, and I will take it out to him
this evening or in the morning."

D. O. Daily: I was agent of Union Central Life Insurance Co. in September and October, 1889. I received
this policy on the 10th day of October, 1889. I sent this
application of William Pauly to the Union Central Life
Insurance Co. I sent the policy back to the company
about the 10th of March, 1890. I sent a postal-card to
William Pauly on the subject of life insurance.

The policy was offered in evidence, and contains this

provision as a condition upon which it is accepted: "First. This policy shall not be valid or binding until the first premium is paid to the company, or its authorized agent, and the receipt hereto attached, countersigned by the company's agent and delivered during the lifetime of the insured."

The policy is dated October 1, 1889, for $2,000, upon the ten-year endowment plan.

The application is for $2,000 on the endowment life plan.

Nancy Pauly: "Daily was at our house talking life insurance in wheat-sowing time. Last time Daily was there was before the Vincennes fair. He asked William which he wanted, the ten or twenty-year plan. William answered: "Fix it whichever way you think is best." I did not hear all the conversation. I saw a postal-card from Daily, which is now lost. There was but one card.

Newton Pauly: Saw Daily at our house several times, once in a field with another man in wheat sowing time. Saw card. It read: "Mr. Pauly—Your policy has come. The first time you are in town come around and get your policy, and oblige, D. O. Daily." Don't remember that Daily was there any more. Remember selling the hogs. Card came about one week before Brother Willis and others took the hogs off. Don't remember date, but it was after wheat sowing. Am son of Wm. Pauly. Sold hogs three or four weeks after we sowed wheat. We sowed wheat last of September. Father was sick in bed when the card came. Last time I knew of father's being in Hazelton was on Thursday of Vincennes fair, first part of October. Father got his mail at Hazelton about once or twice a week. Got the card through Hazelton postoffice.

Willis Pauly: Knew of postal card coming. Went to see Daily afterwards at father's request. We took the

hogs to Hazelton two or three weeks after postal card
came. I told Mr. Daily that I came after the policy.
He said he couldn't send it out. I told him I had the
money for him. Daily says: I suppose you have, but
you will have to wait until your father gets better. I
will bring it out in a few days, after he gets better. I
went to see Daily one or two weeks after selling the hogs.
I had the money to pay the insurance when I went to
see Daily. We sold the hogs November 28th, 1889. I
went to see Daily a week or so after that date. Father
was not with us when we sold the hogs. Father was not
able to go along when I went to get the policy. He was
sick at both of these times.

Letter of secretary of the company says: "The company acknowledges no liability under policy No. 63,913
that had been issued by it on the life of Wm. Pauly in
October last," but sends blanks as a matter of courtesy.

E. P. Marshall: Secretary of appellant. From its
organization to the present time our company has pursued but one method of writing insurance, and that is
upon a written application of the insured.

Wm. Pauly's application for $2,000 life rate endow-
ment was received by us from Chicago department and
referred to medical department. Medical directors decided that a policy should not issue on the plan proposed,
but that a ten year endowment policy might issue, and a
policy upon this plan was then prepared and sent through
the Chicago agency to Daily in the expectation that he
could induce him to accept it instead of a policy such as
he had applied for. It was sent without any special instructions to Daily as to its return if declined, but subject to the uniform rule of the company, which appears
in the printed manual held by all agents, including
Daily. This rule is that policies not delivered to the insured and paid for shall be returned to the home office

within sixty days from date of issue. We received no notice from the time the policy was sent, in reference to it. Pauly never made any other application. We issued no other policy. No premium was ever paid. The agent was not authorized to deliver the policy without payment of the premium, and he had no authority or power to deliver it at all after sixty days from its date, under the rule of the company, under which Daily was then working. After the sixty days, it could only be delivered upon the certificate of the medical examiner that the applicant was still in good health, upon receipt of which the company authorized the delivery and not otherwise. It was also a rule of the company, which was known to Daily and constituted a part of his instructions, that no policy is to be delivered to a sick man, except where, in advance of the policy, there has been executed special printed binding contract signed by the agent, and accompanied by payment of the premium. In this case there was no authority given to the agent to vary from these rules. Policy was never delivered, and was returned to us in March, 1890.

Our register has a memorandum of the policy (setting it out) showing date, amount, etc., made when policy was sent out to Chicago agency, and a notation of the amount of first premium charged to it.

This comprised the appellee's evidence.

For the defendant.·

D. O. Daily: My only instructions were in a manual, viz.: "When you receive a policy from the home office for collection, you must not deliver if you know of any unfavorable change in the habits or health of the person on whose life it is issued. You must not, in any case, deliver a policy or renewal receipt until the premium is paid." And, again, the manual contained this instruction: "Should the health of the applicant become impaired, or anything transpire or come to the knowledge of the agent, making the risk less desirable after the application is taken and before actual delivery of the policy, the agent must notify the company of the facts and not deliver, but return the policy to the home office immediately.'' I had the above instructions, and none others, at the time I refused to deliver the policy. Pauly never saw the policy. I received it about October 10th, 1889. I went to Pauly's house to tell him that the company had declined his application on the plan proposed, but would accept the risk on another plan. The ten year endowment plan. The premium on the plan proposed first was $63 per $1,000, while on the latter plan it was $93. Pauly objected to the increase of premium. Finally he said, I guess I will take $1,000 on the plan you name. I wrote the postal card October 10th, and called at Pauly's house October 14th. I saw one of Pauly's sons and told him to come and get the policy. No one came until Willis came. Pauly never wrote me and never paid anything on the policy.

When Pauly agreed to take the $1,000 I agreed to give him six months on the half, he to pay half cash. I probably said to Dr. Gudgel in the month of March or April that I had to give Pauly time on one-half the premium. This was October 6th, and last time I saw Pauly. It was after I had received word that the company would not accept his application on first plan. There was nothing said about waiting until he sold his hogs.

Dr. Gudgel testified that in March, shortly after Pauly's death, Daily told him that in order to get Pauly to take insurance he had to give him time on one-half the premium.

There is here neither payment to the company nor actual delivery of the policy. Is the evidence such as to justify us in saying that a verdict, that there was a valid contract of insurance, is sustained by it?

It is undoubtedly true that while, as a general rule, the delivery of the policy and payment of the premium, either in money or by note, both accrue when the contract is consummated, still it is also true that there may be a valid and enforceable contract of insurance without payment or without a manual delivery of the policy. *Hamilton* v. *Lycoming, etc., Ins. Co.* 5 Barr (Pa. St.), 339; *Cronkhite* v. *Accident Ins. Co.*, 35 Fed. Rep. 26; *Carpenter* v. *Mutual, etc., Ins. Co.*, 4 Sandf. Ch. 408; *Tayloe* v. *Merchants, etc., Ins. Co.*, 9 How. (U. S.) 390; *Fried* v. *Royal Ins. Co.*, 50 N. Y. 253; *Kentucky, etc., Ins. Co.* v. *Jenks*, 5 Ind. 96.

Such contract may also exist without either payment of premium or delivery of policy. *Bragdon* v. *Appleton, etc., Ins. Co.*, 42 Me. 259; *Collins* v. *Ins. Co.*, 7 Phil. 201; *Kohne* v. *Ins. Co.*, 1 Wash. (C. C.) 93; *Sheldon* v. *Conn., etc., Ins. Co.*, 25 Conn. 207; *Hallock* v. *Commercial Ins. Co.* 2 Dutch. 268; *Commercial Ins. Co.* v. *Hallock*, 3 Dutch. 645; *Xenos* v. *Wickham*, 2 L. R. (H. of L. Cases), 296; *New England Fire, etc., Ins. Co.* v. *Robinson*, 25 Ind. 537.

Yet such cases are recognized as exceptional, and in order to sustain them the proof, whether direct or circumstantial, should be of such a character as to reasonably support the assertion.

Bliss on Life Insurance, p. 229, section 154, enunciates this rule: "In life insurance, the policy always provides that it is not to take effect until the first premium is paid. In such cases, if there is no actual delivery of the policy under such circumstances that a waiver of payment of the premium may be inferred, there must be some satisfactory proof that the premium was so paid, or that its payment was in fact waived. While neither payment nor delivery nor both combined are conclusive, it would, on the one hand, require very strong proof to show a binding contract where neither had taken place, as, on the other hand, it would require strong proof to overcome the presumption of a completed contract arising from payment and delivery combined."

In *Cronkhite* v. *Accident Ins. Co.* (Fed.), 17 Ins. Law Jour. 509, BREWER, J., says: "A party should not be called on to pay where it has in fact received nothing, unless there is some clear and positive reason upon which the demand rests."

Keeping in mind the well established rule of our court that where there is a conflict of evidence we will not undertake to weigh it, we are still unable to find in the evidence of this case any from which it may be reasonably and legitimately inferred that there was here a binding and completed contract of insurance. All of the evidence is consistent with the idea that there were simply negotiations looking toward an insurance.

There is no indication of any purpose to contract other than by a policy to be made and delivered upon payment of at least half of the premium. *Heiman* v. *Phœnix Mut. Life Ins. Co.*, 17 Minn. 153; *Markey* v. *Mut. Ben. Life Ins. Co.*, 103 Mass. 78.

There is here an entire want of proof that the agent in any manner waived payment or gave any credit, except as to one-half the premium.

Counsel for the appellee rely largely upon the postal-card, for proof that there was a constructive delivery of the policy and a consummation of the contract. It is urged that by the language, "your policy," used in this card, the idea is conveyed that the policy then actually belonged to Pauly, and that the agent simply held it as a trustee for him. When all the surrounding circumstances, as to which there is no dispute, are regarded, such a construction seems to us untenable. Such an inference can not fairly and legitimately follow simply from the language of the card, which, when considered in the light of attendant circumstances, can mean only that the policy written for Pauly had come.

Counsel for the appellee support their proposition that the "contract was executed, and that there was nothing further to be done," when the postal card was written, by the cases of *Cooper* v. *Pacific Mut. Life Ins. Co.*, 7 Nev. 116, and *Tayloe* v. *Merchants' Fire Ins. Co.*, 9 How. (U. S.) 390.

In the former of these cases, $50 was paid when the application was made, which was, according to the company's regulations, to be applied on the first year's premium, provided the company should conclude to make the insurance. The company did so conclude, entered its conclusion on its books and forwarded policy to agent, and the money paid thereby became the money of the company, and the beneficiary became entitled to a policy upon complying with the other terms of the contract, which she offered to do in strict accordance therewith, although her husband had taken sick and died after the acceptance of the application and before the delivery of the policy to her.

In the Tayloe case, Tayloe applied for insurance, the company wrote the agent it would take it at a certain rate. The agent so notified Tayloe, telling him that if he desired to effect insurance to send him a check and the "matter is concluded." On the day after receiving this letter, Tayloe sent a check by mail, with directions to leave the policy at a bank. The insurance was held to take effect from the mailing of the check, the matter being then "concluded" so far as effecting a completed contract was concerned.

These cases present very different features from the

one at bar, where there is neither payment nor waiver nor anything shown to have been accepted as a compliance with the contract.

In the cases of *Kentucky, etc., Ins. Co.* v. *Jenks, supra,* and *New England Fire, etc., Ins. Co.* v. *Robinson, supra,* there were clear and distinct contracts for insurance, the terms of which were fully complied with by the insured.

If the minds of the parties ever met, and an agreement for an insurance was made, it must have been upon the 6th of October, which was the last time that Daily saw Pauly. Whatever the arrangement then made was, whether for $1,000 or $2,000, there is not a scintilla of evidence that there was any waiver of payment of more than half the premium. Pauly then understood he was to pay half cash, at least. Word was left with his son, on the 14th, that the policy had come, yet he made no move toward payment or consummation of the contract until December 6th.

The agent certainly acted with diligence. He wrote him a card about the 10th, and went out in person on the 14th, but no response came from Pauly. We are unable to see that it was incumbent upon the agent to specifically urge payment upon Pauly as a condition to his policy's becoming effectual, nor can we hold, as urged by counsel, that his failure to do so is to be deemed a waiver of payment. Presumptively, the payment of the premium and the delivery and effectiveness of the policy would go hand in hand. May on Insurance, section 56; *Heiman* v. *Phœnix Mut. Life Ins. Co., supra.*

Pauly had no right to expect anything else, unless by special agreement.

There was, as we construe it, nothing in Daily's postal card which could have tended to raise in Pauly's mind the belief that his policy was in force, although not paid for.

Under the circumstances of this case, taking into consideration the time which elapsed between the negotiations and the tender, and the fact that Pauly was sick about the 10th of October; was sick about the 21st of November; was sick and unable to go to sell his hogs on November 28th, and was sick and unable to go to town on the 6th of December, we are of opinion that the agent was justified in declining, and in good faith to his company he was required to decline, to consummate the contract on the 6th of December, when the tender was made.

The judgment is reversed, with instructions to the trial court to sustain appellant's motion for a new trial.

Filed Nov. 1, 1893.

No. 910.

LEITER v. JACKSON.

PLEADING.—*Paragraph of Complaint.*—*Repeated in Same Form.*—*Demurrer.*—Where the facts alleged in a paragraph of complaint are provable under another paragraph, requiring neither more nor less evidence to authorize a recovery, it is not error to sustain a demurrer to such paragraph.

NEW TRIAL.—*Causes for.*—*Cause Improperly Assigned Raises no Question on Appeal.*—Rulings on motions to strike out pleadings and on demurrers are not proper causes for a new trial, and raise no question when assigned as such.

VERDICT.—*Instructing Jury to Find for Defendant.*—*When Error.*—*Recovery.*—*Sufficiency of Evidence.*—*Practice.*—When there is any evidence, although conflicting, tending to support and make out the plaintiff's case, and sufficient to sustain a verdict, the court should not instruct the jury to return a verdict for the defendant, but the question of recovery should be left to the jury.

From the Fulton Circuit Court.

M. L. Essick, O. F. Montgomery, G. W. Holman and *R. C. Stephenson*, for appellant.

E. C. Martindale and *H. Bernetha*, for appellee.

Ross, J.—The appellant sued the appellee, alleging in the first paragraph of his complaint that on the 29th day of August, 1891, the appellee, claiming to be the owner in fee of a strip of land containing forty acres in Fulton county, Indiana, proposed to trade or sell the same to appellant at and for the price of thirty dollars per acre, and the same was to apply on the sale of a stock of goods sold by appellant to appellee; that appraisers were to be appointed to appraise the goods, and also the land at *its value per acre;* that the goods were appraised and accepted by appellee at their appraised value, and the land was appraised at thirty dollars per acre; that the appellee represented to appellant that there were forty acres in said strip of land, and, relying upon such representations, he accepted the same at the rate of thirty dollars per acre, making the purchase price therefor twelve hundred dollars.

It is also alleged that the appellee, at the time he made said representations, knew them to be false, and that he made them for the purpose of misleading and deceiving the appellant, and that appellant was ignorant of the truth, but relied upon said representations of appellee; that said tract of land, in truth and fact, contained but thirty-one acres, and that as soon as he learned that said tract of land contained but thirty-one acres he demanded of appellee the repayment of the amount paid in excess of the value of the land conveyed.

The complaint is in three paragraphs, the first and second being the same in substance, except that the second contains no allegations of fraudulent representations. A demurrer was sustained to the third. The sustaining of the demurrer to the third paragraph of the complaint is the first error to be considered by this court.

This paragraph of the complaint states the same cause of action alleged in the first and second paragraphs of the complaint, except it was not as specific in stating the facts.

A party is permitted to plead his cause of action in as many different forms as he may see fit, but he must not repeat it in the same form in several different paragraphs. In this case it required neither more nor less evidence to entitle the appellant to recover under the third paragraph than would be necessary to entitle him to recover under the first, hence there was no error in sustaining the demurrer to this paragraph.

It is next urged that the court below erred in overruling the motion made by appellant to strike out the second paragraph of appellee's answer. The overruling of a motion to strike out a pleading properly filed, is not reversible error.

The second paragraph of the answer is sufficient as an answer to either paragraph of the complaint, hence there was no error in overruling the demurrer thereto.

The last error assigned is that "the court erred in overruling plaintiff's motion for a new trial."

Rulings on motions to strike out pleadings and on demurrers are not proper cause for a new trial, hence no questions are presented by the first and second reasons contained in the motion.

After the appellant closed his case in chief, the court, of its own motion, instructed the jury to return a verdict for the appellee.

This action, on the part of the court, is the sixth cause assigned in the motion for a new trial. We think the court erred in directing a verdict for the appellee. A careful reading of the evidence convinces us that there was sufficient evidence to submit the questions in issue to the jury. Counsel for appellee have failed to point out wherein there is a want of evidence upon any material question presented by the issues, and we find no such lack of evidence. When there is any evidence, although conflicting, tending to support and make out the plaintiff's case, and sufficient to sustain a verdict, the question as to whether or not the plaintiff should recover should be left to the jury.

Counsel for appellee seem to think that it is only when there is a conflict between the evidence introduced by the plaintiff and that introduced by the defendant, that the question should be submitted to the jury. Such is not the rule. There may be a conflict in the testimony of the plaintiff, and no evidence introduced by the defendant at all, and yet it should be left to the jury to determine which evidence they will believe. There was ample evidence, if believed by the jury, to have supported a verdict for the appellant.

Judgment reversed, with instructions to grant appellant's motion for a new trial.

Filed Nov. 22, 1893.

----◆----

No. 952.

DALTON ET AL. *v.* HOFFMAN ET AL.

MECHANIC'S LIEN.—*Notice.*—*Sufficiency of Description.*—*Materialman.* —A notice of intention to hold a materialman's lien, which described the property as "lot 6, 7 or 8 in Pray and Hunt's addition to the city of Indianapolis, Indiana, on the west side of Quince street, and about three-fourths of a square south of Prospect street," etc., is a sufficient description, being sufficiently certain "to enable a party familiar with the locality to identify the premises intended to be described, with reasonable certainty."

SAME.—*Complaint, Sufficiency of.—Notice.—Variance.—Description.—* In such case, where the complaint based upon the notice avers that lot 6 was the one on which the building was erected, the complaint makes a *prima facie* case, and the question as to whether the description in the complaint is at variance with that in the notice should be submitted for trial.

From the Marion Superior Court.

J. Coburn, for appellants.

C. S. Wiltsie and *J. W. Kealing,* for appellees.

REINHARD, J.—This action was instituted by the appellants, against the appellees, for the foreclosure of a materialman's lien. The only error assigned is the sustaining of the demurrer to the appellants' complaint.

It is shown by the complaint that the appellants, who are lumber dealers in the city of Indianapolis, furnished one Van Eaton, who was a defendant below, the materials for the wood work of a dwelling house, which materials were used by said Van Eaton in the construction of a dwelling house of the appellee Mary Hoffman, for the building of which he was the contractor. Henry Hoffman, the husband of Mary, was also made a party defendant, and is one of the appellees here.

The only infirmity claimed to exist in the complaint is in respect to the description of the property forming the subject of the lien, contained in the notice upon which the complaint is founded, and of which it is made a part. We are not favored with a brief by the appellees, but are informed by appellants' brief that the court below held the notice insufficient on account of a defective description of the premises. The notice is as follows:

"SEPTEMBER 28, 1891.

"To Mrs. Mary Hoffman, No. 8 Quince street, and all others concerned:

"You are hereby notified that we intend to hold a

mechanic's lien on lot 6, 7 or 8, in Pray and Hunt's addition to the city of Indianapolis, Indiana, on the west side of Quince street and about three-fourths of a square south of Prospect street, owned by you, as well as upon the dwelling house recently erected thereon by you, for the sum of two hundred and fifty dollars and thirty-three cents, for work and labor done and materials furnished by us in the erection and construction of said house; which work and labor done and materials furnished, was done and furnished by us at your special instance and request, and within the last sixty days.

"(Signed)   N. F. Dalton,

"For N. F. Dalton & Co."

It has often been decided in this State that the description of the premises in a notice of a lien of this character should be sufficiently certain to ascertain and locate the same.   *Howell* v. *Zerbee*, 26 Ind. 214; *Munger* v. *Green*, 20 Ind. 38; *Caldwell* v. *Asbury*, 29 Ind. 451; *Caldwell* v. *Asbury*, 46 Ind. 438; *City of Crawfordsville* v. *Johnson*, 51 Ind. 397; *City of Crawfordsville* v. *Boots*, 76 Ind. 32; *White* v. *Stanton*, 111 Ind. 540; *McNamee* v. *Rauck*, 128 Ind. 59.

This rule is in harmony with that laid down by Phillips as probably the best on the subject, that there should be enough in the description "to enable a party familiar with the locality to identify the premises intended to be described, with reasonable certainty."   Phillips Mech. Liens, section 379; Kneeland Mech. Liens, section 195.

Our statute only requires the description to be such as to render the property capable of being identified.   Act March 6, 1883, Acts 1883, p. 140, section 3.

It has also been held in this State that where more land is included in the notice than is necessary to discharge the lien, the notice will not be invalid.   *Scott* v. *Goldinghorst*, 123 Ind. 268.

It must follow, from this holding, that if the notice had described the premises as lots 6, 7 *and* 8, instead of 6, 7 *or* 8, the description would not be insufficient. Does the use of the disjunctive *or* in place of the conjunctive *and* vitiate the description? We think not.

An uncertain and imperfect description may be aided by extrinsic evidence, when the proper averments are laid in the complaint. *White* v. *Stanton, supra.*

From the description in the notice in the case in hand, we get the facts that the property is located on the west side of Quince street, and about three-fourths of a square south of Prospect street, in Pray and Hunt's addition to the city of Indianapolis. The complaint alleges that the actual number of the lot is 6, while the notice may be construed to declare that the lot is numbered either 6 or 7 or 8—the writer being uncertain as to which of the three was the true number. The number serves to aid in identifying the lot, and the giving of it in the description is not essential to the validity of the notice. The lot might be identified by any other designation, such as A, B and C. The notice says, in substance, that the property is situated at a point about three-fourths of a square south of Prospect street, on the west side of Quince street, in Pray and Hunt's addition to the city of Indianapolis, and is known as lot 6, or lot 7, or lot 8. The complaint says that lot 6 was the proper one. It does not appear that appellee also owned a house on lot 7 or 8. If, therefore, there was but one lot upon which she built a dwelling house, and this lot was located at or near the point designated as three-fourths of a square south of Prospect street, and on the west side of Quince street, we are not able to see how any one, especially if familiar with the locality of the premises, could possibly be misled by the description. We think, under the rule that "that is certain which may be made certain," that

the description is not void, and aided as it is by the averment that lot 6 was the one upon which the house was
erected, the complaint makes a *prima facie* case, and the
question as to whether the description in the complaint
is actually at variance with that in the notice should
have been submitted for trial. Phillips Mech. Lien,
section 384.

Judgment reversed, with instructions to overrule the
demurrer to the complaint.

Filed Nov. 7, 1893.

———————◆———————

No. 1,015.

SMITH *v.* THURSTON.

PLEADING.—*Complaint, Sufficiency of.—Promissory Note.—Delivery.—
Title.*—In an action on a promissory note, the complaint is sufficient as showing delivery to, and title in, plaintiff, where the complaint, when taken in connection with the note, shows that the note
was executed to plaintiff, for a valuable consideration; that plaintiff transferred the same, by indorsement, to V., and that V., by
like means, transferred it back to plaintiff.

JURY.—*Misconduct of.—Taking Note in Suit to Jury Room.—Plea of Non
Est Factum.—Signature.—Harmless Error.—Practice.*—When an action is brought on a promissory note, and a plea of *non est factum*
is entered, and the jury are allowed, over defendant's objection, to
take the note sued on to their room, but the record fails to show
that they also took to their room the plea mentioned, to which defendant's signature was attached, and fails to show any comparison
of the signature, there is no available error.

From the Tipton Circuit Court.

J. I. Parker, for appellant.

J. N. Waugh and *J. P. Kemp*, for appellee.

REINHARD, J.—The overruling of appellant's demurrer
to the amended first paragraph of the appellee's com-

plaint is the first error complained of.   It is insisted, in argument, that the complaint does not sufficiently aver that the note declared upon was executed and delivered by the appellant to the appellee, or that appellee has any title to the same.   The note which was filed as an exhibit shows, on its face, that it was executed by Smith to Thurston, and contains a promise to pay the latter fifty dollars.   The averments of the complaint, when taken in connection with the note itself, abundantly show, that the note was given the appellee by the appellant for a debt of fifty dollars for a plow purchased of appellee by the appellant; that the note was transferred by the appellee, by indorsement, to one William W. Vaughan, who, by like means, transferred it back to the appellee, and that it was wholly due and unpaid.   The complaint is sufficient to withstand the objections urged against it, and there was no error in overruling the demurrer.

The remaining error assigned involves the correctness of a ruling of the court upon the trial in allowing the jury to take to their room, over appellant's objection, the note sued upon, which was attached to the complaint as an exhibit.   It is conceded, by appellant's counsel, that under the decisions of our Supreme Court such ruling would not ordinarily be reversible error.   *Shulse* v. *McWilliams*, 104 Ind. 512; *Summers* v. *Greathouse*, 87 Ind. 205; *Snyder* v. *Braden*, 58 Ind. 143.

But it is contended that the case at bar differs from those in which the act of permitting the jury to take such papers to their room was declared within the discretion of the court, for the reason that in the case at bar a plea of *non est factum* had been filed, and the genuineness of the appellant's signature put in issue, which was not the case in the decisions referred to.   It is claimed, by appellant's counsel, that the appellant was prejudiced in his

The Walter A. Wood Mowing and Reaping Machine Co. *v.* Field.

rights, in that the jury were thus permitted not only to take the note and the attached signature to their room for examination, but also to institute a comparison between such signature and that appended to the plea of *non est factum.*

We have diligently searched the record but have not been able to find that the jury also took to their room the paper containing the plea just named, or that they made, or were permitted to make, in their room, any such comparison as the one complained of. Nothing is disclosed that makes it appear that the appellant was in any way injured by any such act as he complains about. We need not decide, therefore, whether the filing of a plea of *non est factum* makes the case at bar an exception to the rule by which the court may permit the jury to take to their room a note or other instrument attached to the complaint.

We find no available error.

Judgment affirmed.

Filed Nov. 21, 1893.

———◆———

No. 734.

The Walter A. Wood Mowing and Reaping Machine Company *v.* Field.

ASSIGNMENT OF ERRORS.—*Joint Assignment.—Admitting Sufficiency of One Ground of Error.—Effect.*—Where an appellant assigns as error that the answers of appellee do not state facts sufficient to constitute a defense to appellant's complaint, and, also, in another assignment, avers that the overruling of appellant's demurrer to the second, third, and fifth paragraphs of answer, and then concedes the sufficiency of the second paragraph of answer, no question is presented by such assignments.

PLEADING.—*Answer, Sufficiency of.—Demurrer.— Warranty, Breach of.— Promissory Note.*—In an action on a promissory note given as evi-

The Walter A. Wood Mowing and Reaping Machine Co. *v.* Field.

dence of the purchase price of a reaping machine, an answer setting
up a warranty that the machine was made of good material and
would do good work when properly managed, and alleging a breach
thereof, is sufficient on demurrer, although the allegations are not
full and specific.

INSTRUCTIONS TO JURY.—*Erroneous Instruction.*—*Warranty.*—*Breach of.*
—*Machine.*—Where a machine is warranted to do good work when
properly managed, an instruction to the jury that if, on fair trial,
the machine could not be made to "work profitably and successfully," it did not comply with the warranty, and the buyer might
refuse to pay for it, is erroneous.

From the Orange Circuit Court.

W. F. Townsend, J. Wilhelm and *T. B. Buskirk,* for
appellant.

DAVIS, J.—The appellee executed his note to appellant as evidence of the purchase-price for a reaping machine. An action on this note resulted in a judgment
in the court below in favor of appellee.

The errors assigned by appellant in this court are:

"*First.* The answers of the appellee do not state facts
sufficient to constitute a defense to plaintiff's (appellant's) complaint.

"*Second.* The court erred in overruling appellant's
demurrer to the second, third, and fifth paragraphs of appellee's answer and cross-complaint.

"*Third.* The court erred in overruling appellant's demurrer to amended fourth paragraph of appellee's answer to appellant's complaint.

"*Fourth.* The court erred in sustaining appellee's demurrer to the second paragraph of appellant's reply to
the fourth paragraph of appellee's answer.

"*Fifth.* The court erred in overruling appellant's motion for a new trial."

It is conceded that the second paragraph of the answer
states facts sufficient to withstand the demurrer, and,

therefore, no question is presented for our consideration by either the first or second errors assigned.

The amended fourth paragraph of the answer, which alleges, in substance and effect, that the machine in question was warranted by appellant to be well made, of good material, and that with proper management it would do good work, and which further avers that the machine was not, in certain particulars, well made, of good material and would not, with proper management, do good work, is not a model pleading and is not, in some respects, so full and specific as it ought to be, yet in our opinion it is not insufficient on demurrer.

The reply thereto was an argumentative general denial, and there was no error in sustaining the demurrer thereto.

We have not been favored with a brief in behalf of appellee, but we have carefully read the entire record. While it is true that the evidence is not on some points clear and satisfactory, this court will not attempt to review or weigh it. The instructions in the main are correct statements of the law applicable to the evidence under the issues, but in one instruction, which is not modified or withdrawn in any other instruction the court said, in substance and effect, to the jury, that if, on a fair trial, the machine could not be made to "work profitably and successfully," it did not comply with the warranty, and the buyer might refuse to pay for it. This instruction is erroneous. The machine was not warranted to work "profitably." It was, in this respect, only warranted "to do good work with proper management." If it did this, the requirements of the warranty were fulfilled.

If it did good work, in compliance with the terms of the warranty, this was certainly sufficient, although the work so done may not have been profitable to appellee.

We can not, under the circumstances of this case, say that the instruction was not misleading and harmful.

Judgment reversed, with costs.

Filed Nov. 21, 1893.

No. 847.

GREEN ET AL. *v.* BROWN, ADMINISTRATOR.

DECEDENTS' ESTATES.—*Final Settlement.*—*What Does not Amount to.*—*Administrator De Bonis Non.*—Where an administrator filed what purports to be his final report, to which exceptions were filed by claimants, but the exceptions are subsequently withdrawn, with right to enforce and collect their claims in the future, and the order concludes as follows: "And the estate is continued as to matters embraced in the exceptions only for further administration as the court may authorize and direct, and said * * [A.] now tenders his resignation as such administrator, which is accepted, and said administrator finally discharged," the provisions of the order continuing the estate for certain purposes, and accepting the resignation of the administrator, are wholly inconsistent with the idea of final settlement, and an administrator *de bonis non* may be appointed under the provisions of section 2240, R. S. 1881.

From the Hamilton Circuit Court.

S. Claypool and *J. W. Claypool,* for appellants.

W. R. Fertig and *H. J. Alexander,* for appellee.

GAVIN, J.—This was an application by appellants, to revoke letters granted to appellee as administrator *de bonis non* of the estate of Seth Green, deceased.

The former administrator of this estate filed in said court, in which the trust was pending, what purported to be his final report in said estate, on April 4th, 1888. Proper notices were given, and on September 28th, 1888, the following order was made thereon by the court:

"And the court, having seen and examined said report, and being sufficiently advised in the premises, does approve and confirm the same in all respects as to everything embraced therein, and discharges the administrator from further duty or liability as to the matters embraced in said report.

"And come now Joseph R. Gray, William A. Semans, James R. Christian and A. J. Fryberger and file exceptions herein in the words and figures following, to wit: [here insert] And' come now said exceptors and withdraw their exceptions as to matters embraced in said report, and consent to its approval, reserving their right to enforce and collect their claims in the future. And the estate is continued as to matters embraced in the exceptions only for further administration as the court may authorize and direct, and said Ezra Swain now tenders his resignation as such administrator, which is accepted, and said administrator finally discharged."

The question presented for our determination is whether or not this constitutes a final settlement of said estate.

While there is considerable confusion in this entry, we think it clear that it does not constitute a final settlement of the estate. The entire entry must be construed together, and a consistent interpretation then given to it if possible.

An order of final settlement necessarily means a determination of all matters proper to be included therein, unless they are excepted therefrom, in accordance with the express provisions of the statute, as is, for example, provided by section 2401, R. S. 1881.

In this case the court expressly continued the estate for certain purposes. The court also accepted the resignation of the administrator.

These provisions of the order wholly exclude the idea of a final settlement of the estate.

The appointment of the appellee was, therefore, within the provisions of section 2240, R. S. 1881, which authorizes the appointment of an administrator *de bonis non* in the event of the resignation of the administrator of an estate.

The authorities to which we have been referred by appellant, are applicable only to cases where there has been an order showing an actual, final, and complete settlement regularly entered by the court, or to cases where the conclusiveness of report and resignation duly approved has been questioned collaterally.

Some questions of practice have been suggested by counsel for the appellee, which we have deemed it unnecessary to consider in the view we have taken of the main question.

Judgment affirmed.

Filed April 11, 1893; petition for a rehearing overruled Nov. 24, 1893.

No. 805.

THE CINCINNATI, INDIANAPOLIS, ST. LOUIS AND CHICAGO RAILWAY COMPANY v. GRAMES.

RAILROAD.—*Contributory Negligence.—Special Verdict.—When Plaintiff is Free from Negligence.—Railroad Crossing.—Personal Injury.*—A. and B., as shown by special verdict, approached a railroad crossing with a wagon and team of horses, under the following circumstances and manner: A. driving and B. sitting in seat with A. On both sides of the street forming the crossing were buildings, which obstructed the view of persons approaching the railroad and materially interfered with their hearing approaching trains; also, box cars projecting into the street from each side, on a switch eight feet from main track, between main track and A. and B., obstructed the view of approaching trains. A. and B., who had made the crossing but a short time before, from the east, were returning. When about

Cincinnati, Indianapolis, St. Louis and Chicago Ry. Co. v. Grames.

fifty feet from the tracks, they stopped their team and looked and listened for approaching trains, and could see and hear none. Then they started to make the crossing, driving in a walk, one listening and looking south for approaching trains and the other listening and looking north for the same. In such manner they approached the crossing, neither seeing nor hearing any, nor any signal of an approaching train, and could not have seen or heard the approach of the train, the company failing to give the statutory signals. While the horses were upon the main track, a train coming from the south and running at the rate of thirty miles an hour, ran against and upon the team and the wagon, injuring B., etc.

Held, that the facts found by the special verdict are sufficient to warrant the court in inferring that B. exercised care commensurate with the danger encountered, and was not guilty of contributory negligence.

SAME.—*Railroad Crossing.—Care Required of Traveler in Crossing.*—It is incumbent upon a traveler on a highway, riding in a wagon and about to cross a railroad track, who can not see or hear an approaching train on account of obstructions which are known to him, to use greater precaution to protect himself from injury than where the view is unobstructed, and the opportunity for using the senses of sight and hearing is unimpaired. Care commensurate with the known danger is required.

SAME.—*Presumptions.—Lawful Conduct.—Statutory Signals.—Railroad Employes.—Traveler.*—While a traveler on a highway may presume that the employes of a railroad company will obey the law and give the required warning, so, also, those in charge of the train may assume that the traveler will take every precaution commensurate with the danger which he is about to encounter.

SAME.—*Presumption of Contributory Negligence.—Recovery.*—Where a traveler is injured at a railroad crossing, the law raises the presumption that the fault was his own, and he must rebut this presumption before he can recover.

SPECIAL VERDICT.—*Province of Jury, of Court.—Conclusion of Law.*—Where a special verdict is requested, it is the province of the jury to find only the ultimate facts established by the evidence, leaving the conclusions of law thereon to be stated by the court.

JUDICIAL NOTICE.—*Judges.—Terms of Office.*—The Appellate Court judicially knows who the judges of the courts of general jurisdiction of the State are, and when their terms of office expire.

BILL OF EXCEPTIONS.—*Who May Sign.—Expiration of Judge's Term of Office.*—A person who was judge and presided at the trial of a cause, has no power to sign a bill of exceptions and make the same a part

of the record in such cause, after he has ceased to be judge. Such
function should be performed by his successor.

WAIVER.—*Motion for Judgment.—Motion for New Trial Pending Above
Motion.—Right to Exception not Waived.*—Where a motion of plaintiff
for judgment is pending, the defendant does not waive the right to
call in question the action of the court in rendering judgment for
plaintiff, by filing a motion for a new trial while the motion for
judgment was pending.

From the Boone Circuit Court.

J. T. Dye, A. Baker, E. Daniels, B. K. Elliott and *W.
F. Elliott*, for appellant.

A. C. Harris, P. H. Dutch and *J. G. Adams*, for appellee.

Ross, J.—The appellee brought this action to recover
damages for personal injuries sustained by being struck
by one of appellant's trains, at a point in Thorntown
where Main street intersects appellant's railroad.

The cause was tried by a jury, and at the request of
the appellee they returned a special verdict, upon which
the court, after overruling a motion made by appellant
for a new trial, rendered judgment for the appellee.

To the ruling on the motion for a new trial, and in
rendering judgment on the verdict in favor of appellee,
the appellant at the time excepted, and these are the only
errors assigned in this court.

Several questions of practice, touching the regularity
of the record, have been urged by counsel for appellee,
in their brief, which it is necessary to consider before
taking up for consideration the errors assigned by appellant.

The record discloses, that the issues were formed, trial
had, motion for a new trial made and overruled, judgment rendered for the appellee, and time granted appellant to file bill of exceptions, by and before the Honorable T. J. Terhune, sole judge of the twentieth judicial
circuit; that within the time allowed by the court the

appellant presented to the Honorable J. A. Abbott, then sole judge of said judicial circuit, his bill of exceptions, which was duly signed by him and filed as a part of the record in this cause.

This court judicially knows who the judges of the courts of general jurisdiction of the State are, and when their terms of office expire, hence it knows that Judge Abbott was the successor of Judge Terhune.

A person who has been judge and presided as such at the trial of a cause has no power to sign a bill of exceptions and make the same a part of the record in such cause, after he has ceased to be judge. *Smith* v. *Baugh*, 32 Ind. 163; *Ketcham, Admx.*, v. *Hill*, 42 Ind. 64; *Toledo, etc., R. W. Co.* v. *Rogers*, 48 Ind. 427; *Reed* v. *Worland, Exr.*, 64 Ind. 216.

There is nothing in the contention of appellee's counsel that appellant has waived the right to call in question the action of the court in rendering judgment on the verdict in favor of appellee by filing a motion for a new trial, while the motion of appellee for a judgment was pending, and without waiting for the ruling thereon.

The sustaining of the motion of the appellee for a judgment on the verdict did not bar the right of the appellant to apply for a new trial, and by the filing of the motion for a new trial it did not waive its right to an exception to the ruling of the court in sustaining and rendering judgment in favor of the appellee, on his motion therefor. The filing of the motion for a new trial, by appellant, was not equivalent to a concession that unless a new trial was granted the appellee was entitled to a judgment on the verdict. •

The special verdict returned by the jury is very voluminous, and, besides repeating the same facts, has embodied in it both legal conclusions and part of the evidence.

The material facts found, so far as we are able to determine them, are as follows: That on and previous to the 31st day of August, 1887, the appellant was a railroad corporation owning and operating a line of railroad running from north to south through the town of Thorntown, in Boone county, Indiana, intersecting Main street in said town, which street was one of the principal thoroughfares thereof and in frequent use, and that said town contained a population of about seventeen hundred persons; that Main street was one hundred feet wide, and run east and west, and intersected appellant's railroad almost at right angles; that at such intersection appellant's railroad consisted of a main track and a side track, the side track, which was about eight feet distant from the main track and on the west side thereof, extended both north and south of Main street; that on said day there were several box cars standing on the side track, two of which, one on each side of Main street, extended out into the street, the one on the south side projecting into the street up to a plank crossing sixteen feet wide, which was placed about the center of the street; that on both sides of the street, from within a few feet of appellant's railroad and west thereof, were buildings which obstructed the view of persons approaching the railroad from the west, and very materially interfered with their hearing trains approaching from either direction; that on said day the appellee, who was nearly fourteen years of age, in good health and of ordinary intelligence, and possessed of "perfect eyesight and hearing," in company with his brother, who was twenty-two years of age, came into Thorntown from the east at ten o'clock in the forenoon, "with a load of wheat on a farm wagon drawn by two horses," driving westward along Main street, crossed over appellant's railroad tracks, and saw the situation and surrounding of the crossing and the position of the

box cars, which were then standing on the switch in said
street; that in a short time they started to return along
Main street, and to recross appellant's tracks, and that
when about fifty feet distant from the tracks they stopped
their team and looked and listened for approaching
trains, and could not see and did not hear the approach
of any; that they stopped for one minute, and while so
stopping with said team and just before and at the time
of starting their team toward the railroad crossing, fifty
feet distant from where they then were, Richard Grames,
the brother, who was and had been driving the team,
spoke to the appellee directing him to keep a watch to
the north side and listen for the locomotives, engines,
and cars, while he looked and listened for the locomotives, engines, and cars on the south side; that while the
appellee and his brother were sitting on the seat in the
wagon with the horses standing still at said point, and
before starting the team of horses, he and his brother
looked and listened for the approach to said crossing of
any locomotive, engine and cars upon appellant's railroad track; that neither the appellee nor his brother
heard or saw any locomotive, engine, or cars approaching said crossing, or signal given, or noise of an approaching train, and did not see any signal of warning
given by any flagman at the crossing or any warning
given by any one that a locomotive, engine, or cars were
approaching the crossing; that immediately after so looking and listening they drove said team of horses and
wagon easterly on said Main street to said railroad track
at said crossing; that in approaching the railroad crossing from the place of stopping to look and listen appellee's brother drove said team in a walk, and at no time
between said point of stopping and said crossing did he
drive faster than a walk; that continuously from the
time of starting, fifty feet west of the said crossing, the

appellee and his brother looked and listened for the approach of any locomotive, engine, or train of cars to said crossing on said railroad track, up to the time the horses drawing said wagon had passed upon appellant's main track at said crossing; that neither appellee nor his brother saw or heard the approaching locomotives, engine, or train of cars approaching said crossing; that neither appellee nor his brother, in so approaching said crossing, could have seen or heard the approach of appellant's locomotive, engine, or cars, by the exercise of their senses of sight or hearing; that as they were driving said team across appellant's tracks, and while the horses were upon the main track, a train coming from the south, and running at the rate of thirty miles per hour, ran against and upon said team of horses and the wagon in which appellee and his brother were sitting, injuring appellee, etc.; that if the box car which projected into the street had not been standing on said side track at said crossing the appellee and his brother could have seen and heard appellant's locomotive, engine and cars approaching the crossing, before driving their team of horses upon either the side or main track at said crossing, and in time to have stopped their team before driving upon the main track.

It is further found that no whistle was blown or bell rung on said engine before or while approaching said crossing, neither was there any signal of any kind given of the approach of said engine and cars to said crossing, and that if appellant's servants had caused the whistle to be blown or the bell to be rung, appellee and his brother could have heard it in time to have avoided the injury. It is also found that other streets in said town cross said railroad.

As already stated, the verdict contains many repetitions of the same facts intermingled, with which are extracts from the evidence, as well as many conclusions of law, and for that reason it has been a matter of much difficulty to give a clear statement of the facts. That part of the finding, after the jury find that no bell was rung or whistle blown on appellant's engine, where they find that if the bell had been rung or the whistle blown, the appellee *would have heard them and would have avoided the injury complained of*, are conclusions. The law presumes that when a person is apprised of danger, he will not voluntarily throw himself in its way.

In determining the legal effect of the facts found, we can consider only the ultimate facts, disregarding evidentiary facts as well as conclusions of law embraced in the special verdict. "A special verdict is that by which the jury find the facts only, leaving judgment thereon to the court." Section 545, R. S. 1881.

Ultimate facts only are to be found and set out in a special verdict, and not evidentiary facts, evidence, mixed questions of law and fact or legal conclusions. *Pittsburgh, etc., R. R. Co.* v. *Spencer*, 98 Ind. 186; *Indianapolis, etc., R. W. Co.* v. *Bush*, 101 Ind. 582; *Cook* v. *McNaughton*, 128 Ind. 410; *Perkins* v. *Hayward*, 124 Ind. 445.

"A special verdict is where the jury find the facts of the case, leaving the ultimate decision of the cause, *upon those facts*, to the court, concluding conditionally that if, upon the whole matter thus found, the court should be of opinion that the plaintiff had a cause of action, they then find for the plaintiff, and assess his damages; if otherwise, then for the defendant." 3 Black Proof and Pleading Accident Cas. 378; Boote Suits at Law, 158.

"It is of the very essence of a special verdict that the jury should find the facts on which the court is to pronounce judgment according to law." 1 East, 111; Lord Raymond, 1581.

In *Pittsburgh, etc., R. W. Co.* v. *Adams,* 105 Ind. 151, the court says: "The purpose of a special verdict is to avoid the mistakes that the jury may make in the application of the law to the facts. When a special verdict is demanded, the jury are to find the facts, and the court declares the law upon those facts."

It is settled, therefore, that when the jury are to return a special verdict, they shall find and set out in their verdict the facts, omitting therefrom legal inferences and evidentiary facts. It devolves upon the court very often to instruct the jury what are facts and whether it is necessary to embody in a special verdict the facts relative to a certain question, and this leads us to determine whether or not certain questions, among which are the questions of negligence and contributory negligence, are facts to be found and set out in such a verdict.

It was right and proper for the jury in this case to find and set out in their verdict whether or not the bell was wrung or the whistle blown, on appellant's engine, and whether or not, if the bell had been rung and the whistle blown, appellee could have heard them; but they had no right to conclude that he would have heard them, and having heard them, would have avoided the injury. It was for the jury to determine, from the evidence, not only what the appellant's servants did, or failed to do, in the operation of its train, but also to find what the appellee did and what he failed to do before going upon the railroad track; but it was wholly beyond their province to say what the appellee would have done under different circumstances. The question at issue was not what he might or would have done under different circumstances, but what did he do under the circumstances in this case?

When a traveler on a highway is injured at its intersection with a railroad, by being struck by a train, the

fault is *prima facie* his own.   *Indiana, etc., R. W. Co.*
v. *Hammock*, 113 Ind. 1.

And the law assumes that he actually saw what he
could have seen, had he looked and heard what he could
have heard had he listened.   *Cones, Admr.,* v. *Cincinnati, etc., R. W. Co.*, 114 Ind. 328.

And a special verdict which shows a person to have
been injured at such a point, in order to hold the railroad company answerable therefor, must show facts that
will warrant the court in concluding, as a matter of law,
not only that the injury was inflicted by reason of the
negligence of the railroad company, but that the injured
person was free from fault contributing thereto.

Some confusion apparently exists in the decisions of
the courts of last resort in this State, as to when it is
proper for a jury to determine the questions of negligence
and contributory negligence.   It is settled, however, that
the question of negligence is either purely a question of
law or a question of mingled law and fact, and that it is
never a question purely of fact.

In the case of *Toledo, etc., R. W. Co.* v. *Goddard*, 25
Ind. 185, the Supreme Court says: "The court, at the
request of the plaintiff, submitted to the jury the following special interrogatories, to which they returned the
answers annexed:

" 'Was not the defendant guilty of negligence in placing the freight car on the side-track, on the street, thereby obstructing the same?'   To which the jury answered:
'Yes.'

" 'Was not the defendant guilty of negligence in not
placing some visible signal at or near the southwest corner of the woodshed, to indicate the approach of the
backing train, to prevent collision?'   To which the jury
answered: 'Yes.' "

These interrogatories, we think, should not have been

submitted to the jury. The answers to them do not constitute a special verdict under the statute. They were probably intended to be submitted under the last clause of section 336 of the code, 2 G. & H. 205, which provides that the court, "in all cases, when requested by either party, shall instruct the jury, if they render a general verdict, to find specially upon particular questions of fact, to be stated in writing, which special finding is to be recorded with the verdict." These interrogatories do not conform to the statute. They do not ask the jury to find upon any particular questions of fact; they simply assume that certain facts existed, and ask the jury if they do not constitute negligence.

The question of negligence is ordinarily a mixed one of law and fact, but when the facts are found, then their legal consequences constitute purely a question of law for the court, and not for the jury. If the jury had been asked to find specially whether the defendant had placed a freight car on the side-track, on the street, thereby obstructing the same, and whether the company had placed a visible signal at or near the southwest corner of the woodshed, to indicate the approach of the backing train, to prevent collision, and the jury had answered the first in the affirmative, and the second in the negative, these would have been facts specially found by the jury, and then it would have devolved upon the court to determine, as a question of law, whether the facts so found by the jury constituted such negligence as to make the defendant liable for the injury complained of.

In *Bellefontaine R. W. Co. v. Hunter, Admr.*, 33 Ind. 335, it was said: "But while negligence is, in general, a mixed issue of law and fact, yet it is equally true that when the fact which it is claimed constitutes negligence is found, its legal character and consequences become a matter of law."

In *Pittsburgh, etc., R. R. Co.* v. *Spencer, supra,* Judge ELLIOTT says: "Conclusions of law in a special verdict are without force, and a general statement that an act was negligently done is but a conclusion of law. The facts showing how the act was done are essential, for without them the court can not ascertain or pronounce the law. All the authorities agree that the law is exclusively for the court in cases where special verdicts are returned, but if it be held that a general statement of negligence is good, then nothing at all is left to the court, for the jury have determined both the law and the facts. To allow this would be to permit the jury to usurp the functions of the court and decide the whole case. In that event the court would be without power and without functions, and this surely can not be the law. If the jury's decision, stated in general terms, that an act is negligent, is sufficient, then what need for a court? All that would be necessary, if that were the law, would be to take a special verdict embodying the jury's opinion. Something is to be done by the court in every case of a special verdict, and that something is to declare the law upon the facts found; but if we hold that the jury's general statement that an act was negligent is sufficient, we affirm the converse of this, because, by so holding, we declare that the verdict of the jury settles everything, the law as well as the facts, leaving the court nothing to do except make the mere formal entry of judgment.

"We understand it to be a fixed principle that the court does rule upon all questions of negligence. If it were otherwise, there would be no element of law in such a case; everything would be pure matter of fact, nothing would be matter of law. It would be strange indeed if in any case a judgment could be had without the application of rules of law, and in all civil cases the law comes from the court. It has been said, scores and scores of times that negligence is generally a mixed question of law and fact, and it has also been often said that where the facts are undisputed, and the inferences to be drawn from them unequivocal, it may be a question of law. If it be true, as undeniably it is, that the question is always either one of law, or one of mixed law and fact, then it must be true that in all cases the court must pronounce the law. In the case of a special verdict, it is only possible to do this by action upon the facts stated in the verdict.

"Where a general verdict is sought, the court instructs the jury as to the law of negligence, and thus pronounces the law of the case; but in cases where a special verdict is asked, the law is pronounced, not in instructions to the jury, but upon the facts stated by the jury. If the jury for themselves state the law, then the court is a mere passive spectator, at most a mere moderator. In general verdicts, the law enters as a factor; because the jury are required to decide the case 'according to the law and the evidence;' but in special verdicts, they simply state the facts. It is clear that unless all the material facts are stated in the special verdict, the court can not declare the law, and the result is that the law is not declared at all, or is declared by the jury.

"We have said that when the facts are found the legal character and consequences are matters of law for the court, and we now give our authority for this statement. In a recent work it is said: "And though negligence is generally a mixed question of law and of fact, yet when the fact from the existence of which it is claimed that the negligence flows, is found by the jury to be true, then its legal character and the consequences flowing therefrom become a matter of law for the court.' 2 Rorer Railroads, 1030.''

In *Purcell* v. *English,* 86 Ind. 34, ELLIOTT, Judge, says: "When the cause of action declared on is negligence, the court may direct a verdict for the defendant, in cases where the evidence wholly fails to make out a *prima facie* case. It is true that the question of negligence is generally one of mingled law and fact, but there are cases where the question is purely one of law."

In *Indianapolis, etc., R. W. Co.* v. *Watson,* 114 Ind. 20, ELLIOTT, J., says: "The question of negligence is never one exclusively of fact. The jury find the facts, but if from the facts one inference only can be drawn, and that is that there was negligence, it must be so adjudged as matter of law; or, conversely, if it can be clearly affirmed as matter of law that there was no negligence, the court must so declare. In no case where negligence is the issue does the court entirely abdicate its power, for as to the law it must always rule, although, in some instances, the jury ultimately decide whether there is, or is not, negligence; but in every case the court must declare the law."

In *Brannen* v. *Kokomo, etc., Gravel Road Co.,* 115 Ind. 115, the court says: "In the case before us the facts were found by the jury, and hence, as to whether appellant, upon those facts, was, or was not, negligent, is a question of law for the court."

In *Chicago, etc., R.R.Co.* v. *Ostrander,* 116 Ind. 259, 264, it was said: "It has practically become a legal maxim in this State that negligence is a mixed question of law and fact, and is a question of law where the facts are undisputed, and the inferences to be drawn from them unequivocal. But no question of negligence as a legal proposition arises until the facts from which negligence is supposed to have resulted are in some manner established."

In *Baltimore, etc., R. R. Co.* v. *Walborn, Admr.,* 127

Ind. 142, COFFEY, J., says: "Ordinarily, negligence is a mixed question of law and fact, but it has often been held by this and other courts, that, generally, where the facts are undisputed, the question of negligence becomes one of law."

In the case of *Korrady, Admx.,* v. *Lake Shore, etc., R. W. Co.,* 131 Ind. 261, the court says: "The appellant complains of a ruling of the trial court declining to permit an interrogatory to go to the jury. That interrogatory reads thus: 'Is it not a fact that Korrady was not negligent in crossing Wide alley where he did if he did not know said engine was approaching at a speed of more than ten miles an hour?' The complaint is not well founded. The appellant had a right to elicit the facts, but had no right to ask for a general conclusion, intermixing matters of fact with matters of law."

This leads us to inquire: When is the question of negligence one of law and fact to be determined by the jury, and when purely a question of law to be decided by the court?

Whether or not the question of contributory negligence, on the part of the plaintiff, or of negligence on the part of the defendant in a given case, is one to be determined by the court as a question of law, or by the jury, under the instruction of the court, as a question of mixed law and fact, is always an important and often a very difficult question to determine.

As Elliott, J., in *Perkins* v. *Hayward, supra,* says: "One of the most perplexing questions in the wide range of the law is whether a statement embodies a mere conclusion or contains a recital of an ultimate fact. The line between conclusions and ultimate facts is so shadowy and indistinct that it is often almost impossible to discover and follow it."

"Negligence, like ownership, is a complex conception.

Just as the latter imports the existence of certain facts, and also the consequence (protection against all the world) which the law attaches to those facts, the former imports the existence of certain facts (conduct), and also the consequences (liability) which the law attaches to those facts." Holmes' Common Law 115. And, again, on page 120, he says: "When a judge rules that there is no evidence of negligence, he does something more than is embraced in an ordinary ruling that there is no evidence of a fact. He rules that the acts or omissions proved or in question do not constitute a ground of legal liability, and in this way the law is gradually enriching itself from daily life, as it should."

"The question of legal liability is therefore one of negligence, and its consideration demands, first, a determination of what negligence is. To reach this we are not to look solely at a man's acts or his failure to act: the term is relative, and its application depends on the situation of the parties, and the degree of care and vigilance which the circumstances reasonably impose. That degree is not the same in all cases: it may vary according to the danger involved in the want of vigilance." Cooley on Torts, 751.

"Negligence is the omission to do something which a reasonable man, guided upon those considerations which ordinarily regulate the conduct of human affairs, would do, or doing something which a prudent and reasonable man would not do." Alderson B., in *Blyth* v. *Birmingham Water Works Co.*, 11 Exch. H. & G. 781.

Judge Wharton, in his work on negligence, section 3, says: "Negligence, in its civil relations, is such an inadvertent imperfection, by a responsible human agent, in the discharge of a legal duty, as produces, in an ordinary and natural sequence, a damage to another."

And Buswell, in his Law of Personal Injuries, section

91, says: "Negligence, whether on the part of the plaintiff or of the defendant, may be defined as the want of ordinary or reasonable care in respect of that which it is the duty of the party to do or to leave undone."

The word negligence, however, in its use by text writers, as well as courts, does not always stand for or include all the elements embraced in what is considered this "complex conception," and we must not consider that when it is said either in the text books or the opinions of the court, that the question of negligence is a question of mixed law and fact, or in others where it is said to be a question of law, that it is intended as announcing a legal principle applicable alike in all cases, but the sense in which the word negligence is used in the particular case may be ascertained and determined from the particular facts and circumstances with which used, and we may thus avoid apparent confusion of thought.

"But another, and perhaps the chief cause of the difficulty of determining in a given case whether the conclusion as to negligence is one of law or of fact, arises from another source, which we will now consider. The conception of negligence, as we have seen, involves the idea of a duty to act in a certain way towards others, and a violation of that duty by acts or conduct of a contrary nature. The duty is imposed by law, either directly by establishing specific or general rules of conduct binding upon all persons, or indirectly through legal agreements made by the parties concerned. It is with duties not arising out of contract that we are here concerned. There is further involved in the legal conception of negligence, the existence of a test or standard of conduct with which the given conduct is to be compared, and by which it is to be judged. The question whether the given conduct comes up to the standard is frequently called the 'question of negligence.' The result of comparing the conduct with the standard is generally spoken of as 'negligence' or the 'finding of negligence.' Negligence, in this last sense, is always a conclusion or inference, and never a fact in the ordinary sense of that word." *Farrell* v. *Waterburg Horse R. R. Co.*, 60 Conn. 239.

Where the law directs the precise conduct required under given circumstances, the standard by which such conduct is judged is found in the law. For instance, in many cases decided in this, as well as other States, the rule of law has been declared that a person's conduct shall be measured by what an ordinarily prudent man should have done under like circumstances. This general rule, however, has been prolific of many misapplications, arising not so much from a misunderstanding as to the degree of care to be exercised, as from the failure to know who defines the measure of the duty and determines whether or not the acts of the party meet the legal obligation imposed, the jury or the court.

In many well considered cases it has been held that while the law prescribes the degree of care and determines whether or not the facts proven are sufficient in law to satisfy the requirements of the law, it is always for the jury to determine, from the evidence, what facts have been proven. In fact by most of the courts of last resort in this country, as well as in England, it has been decided, and most rigidly adhered to, that it is for the court to say to the jury what facts, if proven, constitute negligence, and it is then for the jury to say whether or not such facts have been proven. And this rule seems to be the correct and proper rule, for were it otherwise, either that the court should have the right to draw the inferences of fact or the jury to determine the measure of duty, the greatest aim of justice, namely that the rule of duty by which one's conduct shall be measured as declared by the law on the one hand, and the right to have the acts of omission or commission determined by one's peers, would be entirely eradicated, and if left entirely to the jury they would not only determine the facts, but they would declare the measure of duty, or recognize or eradicate the duty as they should see fit, while if the court were to be permitted to determine the facts proven, it would authorize the court to set up its judgment as against that of twelve others equally sensible and competent to determine what facts have been proven by the evidence.

The Supreme Court of Illinois, however, has decided that an instruction to the jury that certain facts, if proven, constitute negligence, is erroneous. *Pennsylvania Co.* v. *Frana*, 112 Ill. 398; *Myers, Admx.*, v. *Indianapolis, etc., R. W. Co.*, 113 Ill. 386.

If the inference of negligence is one to be drawn by the jury, it is their province to draw it free from limitation or restriction imposed by the court, and their determination of the question is final and not subject to review, either by the court before whom the cause is tried, or the Appellate Court, on appeal, because their opinion of what a man of ordinary prudence would or would not do under the circumstances, is the rule of decision in that case. They would then conclude not only what an ordinarily prudent man should and would do under the circumstances, but they would determine whether the person in the particular case did or omitted to do what they have concluded is the measure of duty for an ordinarily prudent person under the circumstances. Relieved of all consideration of what he actually did and omitted, they would simply be required to determine whether or not he was an ordinarily prudent man. Such a perversion of the rules of law which define the duties of all persons, whether ordinarily prudent or otherwise, can not be sanctioned.

"The main object is to ascertain the facts. When they are ascertained, the question of negligence is for the court." *Doggett* v. *Richmond, etc., R. R. Co.,* 78 N. C. 305.

And the first requisite in establishing negligence is to show the existence of the duty which it is supposed has not been performed. If negligence can not be imputed, except a duty has been violated, and we assume that without the violation of a duty, either by omission or commission, negligence can not exist, then the law alone defines the duty, and it is not for the jury to say whether or not a duty exists.

HACKNEY, J., in *Louisville, etc., R. W. Co.* v. *Schmidt,* 134 Ind. 16, says: "Our embarrassment has been in determining how far the finding of the jury, by the general verdict, was an adjudication of negligence as a question of fact, and as to the privilege of the court to determine whether the facts were such that negligence, as a question of law might be inferred therefrom. It is often a difficult question to determine the line dividing the privilege of the jury from the power of the court in determining what facts constitute actionable negligence."

Bishop, in his work on Non-Contract Law, section 444, after referring to the different rules of law as established by the different courts, says: "In spite of the rule that the question of negligence is for the jury, the other rule which requires the judge to pass upon the admission of evidence, and its effect, and the sufficiency of the allegations, renders it necessarily a matter of law whether or not in a given case a particular act or omission is negligence."

In this State a party bringing an action to recover

damages occasioned by the negligence of another may be required to allege specifically the acts or omissions upon which negligence is predicated. *Pennsylvania Co. v. Dean, by Next Friend*, 92 Ind. 459.

And when the facts are pleaded, the court determines whether or not they constitute actionable negligence. *Weis* v. *City of Madison*, 75 Ind. 241; *Louisville, etc., R. W. Co.* v. *Schmidt*, 106 Ind. 73, and cases cited.

And from the same facts found by a jury in a special verdict, the court must of necessity draw the inference of negligence or want of negligence. If the court must determine, as a question of law, whether or not the facts pleaded constitute negligence, it is also the duty of the court to determine, where those same facts are found in a special verdict, whether or not negligence shall be inferred. Were it otherwise, the court, in passing upon a pleading, would determine that a given state of facts constituted negligence, and, on the trial of the cause, the jury from the same facts might conclude that the inference of negligence did not arise.

In *Faris* v. *Hoberg*, 134 Ind. 269, HACKNEY, J., says: "Numerous authorities are cited, by the appellant, to the proposition that in a case involving questions of negligence, the court is not at liberty to take such questions from the jury, but must leave them to the jury for decision. These cases all belong to that class where a question of fact is controverted, and that question is one necessary to plaintiff's recovery, or essential to the defendant's proper defense. None of them hold that the jury are the exclusve judges of the existence or nonexistence of negligence as an ultimate fact. A moment's reflection will show the error of a rule which would deprive the court of the right to determine whether a given state of facts, uncontroverted, does or does not constitute actionable negligence. When the facts are submitted to the court upon demurrer to a complaint, the court exercises the power of determining whether such facts, if proven, will constitute actionable negligence. When, under the practice prevailing, the jury does not return a general verdict, but returns findings of fact by special verdict, the court must determine whether the facts so found are sufficient to warrant the conclusion of the existence of negligence.''

If any apparent inconsistency exists in the law as announced in this State, it is not that it is improperly stated, but rather because principles are announced as general which have but a limited application.

In a number of recent cases, in which general verdicts were returned, the following general legal proposition has been announced, viz.: That in cases where negligence is the issue, and the facts are undisputed, and but one inference can be drawn therefrom, the court may draw that inference; *but where the facts are controverted, or where more than one inference may be reasonably drawn from the facts, the question is generally one for the jury, under proper instructions from the court. Rogers v. Leyden,* 127 Ind. 50; *Baltimore, etc., R. R. Co. v. Walborn, Admr., supra; City of Franklin v. Harter,* 127 Ind. 446; *Shoner v. Pennsylvania Co.,* 130 Ind. 170; *Eichel v. Senhenn,* 2 Ind. App. 208.

ELLIOTT, Judge, in *City of Franklin v. Harter, supra,* uses this forcible language: ''As the question in cases where a municipal corporation is sought to be held liable for injuries caused by a defect in a street is one of negligence, it is seldom that the court can determine the question as one of law, for in by far the greater number of cases the question is a complex one, in which matters of law blend with matters of fact. In all such cases the duty of the court is to instruct the jury as to the law, and that of the jury is to determine whether, under the law as declared by the court, there is actually negligence.

Nor does this general rule fail in all cases where the facts are undisputed, since the rule has long been settled in this State that where an inference of negligence may or may not be reasonably drawn from admitted facts, the case is ordinarily for the jury, under proper instructions, but where only one inference can be reasonably drawn from the facts the question of negligence or no negligence may be determined by the court, as one of pure law. The rule, as we have outlined it, is the law of this State and must be so accepted, notwithstanding expressions occasionally found in some of the cases which seem to indicate a different doctrine. It would overthrow a long line of cases to deny the rule, and it would also lead to the subversion of sound and salutary principles. In the old, as well as in the recent cases, the doctrine we here declare has been strongly and explicitly asserted, and to that doctrine we give an unwavering and unhesitating adherence, disapproving all statements which seem to deny its soundness.''

The principle declared in these cases is applicable in the cases in which announced, which were cases where general verdicts were returned, and the same principle of law applies in all cases of that nature; but it has no application in cases where special verdicts are returned by the jury.

When a special verdict is required, no instructions are given to the jury as to the law of the case. *Louisville, etc., R. W. Co.* v. *Buck, Admr.*, 116 Ind. 566, and cases cited.

And this is so for the reason that when the facts have been found, the court will apply the law to such facts in determining the rights of the parties. The statute provides for special verdicts for the express purpose of taking from the jury the duty of applying the law to the facts. This is to avoid a misapplication of the law to the facts, and to prevent, as far as possible, any purpose on the part of the jury, either through sympathy or prejudice, from bending the facts to the law in order that a favored litigant may succeed. We think the correct principle, applicable alike in cases where either a general or a special verdict is returned by the jury, is announced by OLDS, Judge, in the case of *Rush* v. *Coal Bluff Mining Co.*, 131 Ind. 135, where he says: ''It is the province of the jury to weigh evidence where there is evidence from which two conclusions may reasonably be drawn, but it is the province of the court to determine whether or not there is or is not evidence supporting any particular fact or theory of a case, and if there is no evidence authorizing a reasonable inference of such fact or theory essential to a recovery or sufficient to create a reasonable difference of opinion in the minds of impartial men sitting in judgment on the case, then it is the duty of the court to instruct the jury to return a verdict against the party having the burden of establishing such material facts essential to a recovery. If, however, the evidence is such as that impartial men may differ as to the conclusions to be drawn from the evidence, then the court must submit the question to the jury. Such we believe to be the well-established rule of the law. Jurors can not, without evidence reasonably authorizing an inference of negligence, arbitrarily declare there was negligence. Neither can they, in the face of undisputed facts showing conclusively that a party was guilty of negligence contributing to an injury, declare that he was free from contributory negligence.''

In cases where the jury are to return a general verdict, it is settled that if the facts are undisputed, or where but one inference of fact can be drawn from the evidence, the court may instruct the jury, as a matter of law, whether or not such facts constitute negligence, but if the evidence is conflicting, or the inferences of fact to be drawn from the evidence are such that two minds, equally sensible and impartial, may differ as to the inferences of fact to be drawn from the evidence, the question of negligence should be left to the jury under proper instructions from the court.   In such cases it devolves upon the court to say, as matter of law, what amounts to negligence or contributory negligence, and upon the jury to say as matter of fact, in the light of the instructions of the court, whether or not the evidentiary facts proven establish the ultimate facts which the court has instructed constitute negligence or contributory negligence.   In many cases has this question been decided, so that it seems settled beyond all question.   Beach on Contributory Negligence, section 161; *Ohio, etc., R. W. Co. v. Collarn,* 73 Ind. 261; *Indiana Car Co. v. Parker,* 100 Ind. 181; *Woolery, Admr., v. Louisville, etc., R. W. Co.,* 107 Ind. 381; *Evans v. Adams Express Co.,* 122 Ind. 362; *Board, etc., v. Chipps, Admr.,* 131 Ind. 56; *Eichel v. Senhenn, supra.*

When a jury is to return a special verdict, they should find and return facts only.   They have no right to embody in a special verdict, either the evidence, legal conclusions, opinions or mixed questions of law and fact. And when they have found the facts they have no right to conclude whether or not the defendant was guilty of negligence or the plaintiff guilty of contributory negligence.   Were it otherwise, the jury would be the exclusive judges of what constitutes negligence, and the court could only render judgment upon the verdict, for the party in whose favor the jury have concluded.   If they have a right in a special verdict to draw the conclusion of negligence or want of negligence, that inference must be a fact, to be found and embodied in the verdict, while the facts upon which the inference is based would be merely evidentiary facts, and should not be embodied in the verdict. But, as we have decided, negligence is never a question purely of fact, it can not be found as a fact in a special verdict.

Whether a party has been negligent under certain circumstances includes two questions, namely: 1st. Whether a particular thing has been done or omitted; this is a pure question of fact. And, 2d. Whether the doing or the failure to do this thing was a legal duty; this is a pure question of law. *Metropolitan R. W. Co.* v. *Jackson*, L. R. 3 App. C. 193.

As the court said in *Pittsburgh, etc., R. R. Co.* v. *Spencer, supra:* "Conclusions of law in a special verdict are without force, and a general statement that an act was negligently done is but a conclusion of law. The facts showing how the act was done are essential, for without them the court can not ascertain or pronounce the law."

In *Indianapolis, etc., R. W. Co.* v. *Bush, supra*, which was an action to recover damages for personal injury received by being struck by a train at a highway crossing, the jury returned a special verdict, and on appeal ZOL- LARS, Chief Justice, speaking for the court, says: "At the close of the verdict are conclusions by the jury that appellee was not guilty of contributory negligence, and that the injury was the result of carelessness and negligence on the part of appellant. These conclusions are conclusions of *law* that the jury could not make, and hence must be disregarded in deciding as to the sufficiency of the verdict."

In *Western Union Telegraph Co.* v. *McDaniel*, 103 Ind. 294, ELLIOTT, J., says: "We put our decision upon the ground laid down by the Supreme Court of Pennsylvania in a case not unlike the present. It was said by that court: 'The cases are numerous that upon an undisputed state of facts it is the province of the court to pass upon the question of defendant's negligence.' *Koons* v. *Western Union Telegraph Co.*, 102 Pa. St. 164. The rule stated in the case cited is the rule of this court. *Pittsburgh, etc., R. R. Co.* v. *Spencer*, 98 Ind. 186. These cases, it is true, speak of the negligence of the defendant, but negligence is negligence whether on the part of the plaintiff or of the defendant, and the rule as to how it is to be determined and by whom, is the same in the one case as in the other.''

In the case of *Conner* v. *Citizens' Street R. W. Co.*, 105 Ind. 62, the jury returned a special verdict, and after setting out the facts proven, concludes as follows: "12th. That the conduct of plaintiff on the occasion of the injury was ordinarily prudent and cautious under the circumstances, and that he did not wholly contribute to said injury by any fault or negligence on his part, but that said injury was caused mostly by the agent of the defendant driver of said car.''

Judge Mitchell, in passing upon the sufficiency of the facts found, says: ''In determining the legal value and quality of the facts found, the paragraph above set out is not to be regarded as a finding of facts. It contains nothing more than inferences or conclusions, drawn by the jury upon the precedent facts, and upon these it was not the province of the jury, in their special verdict, either to express opinions or draw conclusions. In framing and returning a special verdict, the whole duty of the jury is discharged when they have found and set forth, in an orderly and intelligent manner, all the principal facts which were proven within the issues submitted to them. * * * * * * * *

''When, upon an issue involving negligence, the principal or ultimate facts are determined by the jury, it then becomes the function of the court to decide, as a question of law upon the facts found, whether or not the party to whom negligence is imputed was negligent.

"A civil case can not be conceived of in which it is the province of the jury by special verdict to determine the facts, and also to draw inferences in the nature of legal conclusions upon the facts found. When the jury find and return a special verdict, it must then be considered that the facts in that case are no longer in dispute. They are ascertained and settled by the special verdict. Unless it can be maintained that the inference or conclusion which may be drawn from all the ascertained and undisputed facts is also a fact, it must follow that it is not the province of the jury to draw inferences or state conclusions. It is settled by decisions so numerous that we need not cite the cases, that where the facts are undisputed it is the province of the court to settle the question of negligence as a question of law. This must be so in the nature of things. If it is otherwise, there is a class of cases in which, upon the undisputed facts, the court is incapable of reaching a conclusion, or of determining whether such facts constitute negligence or not. As in cases where the question is whether, upon an ascertained state of facts, the conclusion of fraud, conversion of goods, payment or probable cause for the institution of a suit may be drawn. So, where the question is whether negligence has intervened when the facts are ascertained by the instrumentality selected for that purpose, the court must determine whether, in law, negligence can be predicated upon the facts ascertained.

"Concede that in some sense negligence is, as it is sometimes said to be, a mixed question of law and fact, it can not be so after the facts are ascertained. In cases involving negligence, as in all other civil cases, a point must be reached at some time when the facts and the law are to be considered as separate and distinct, when the litigants have the right to invoke the judgment of the court, and require it to determine whether, upon the facts as they are agreed to be, the law declares that negligence intervened. Such a point, we think, is arrived at when the jury have agreed upon and returned to the court in a special verdict the principal, contested facts in issue.''

In *Louisville, etc., R. W. Co.* v. *Balch,* 105 Ind. 93, it was said: ''A special verdict is a finding of the facts only. In this, the jury have nothing to do with the law. The court does not instruct them as to the law, but in the rendition of the judgment, applies the law to the facts found by the jury.''

In *Woolery, Admr.,* v. *Louisville, etc., R. W. Co., supra,* MITCHELL, Judge, again says: ''It was the exclusive province of the jury to ascertain the facts, and apply them, when ascertained, to the law, and return their general verdict accordingly. In doing this, however, they were to be guided by proper instructions from the court as to the law of the case. In that connection it was the duty of the court to instruct the jury what facts within the issues in the case, if established by the proof, would or might, under the circumstances, constitute contributory negligence, leaving to the jury the duty of discovering whether such facts and circumstances were proved or not. Simply to have told the jury that the plaintiff must have been free from contributory negligence, without stating what facts might constitute contributory negligence, would have been to leave the jury without any direction whatever in respect to the legal effect of the facts in the case. The practical result of the doctrine contended for would be to submit both the law and the facts to the determination of the jury.

''It can not be maintained that a civil case can arise in which the court is incompetent to declare the law upon the facts, when the facts are either admitted or satisfactorily proved. Where the essential facts are ascertained in any case, the litigants have a right to call upon the court to declare the law. *Wanamaker* v. *Burke*, 111 Pa. St. 423.

"If the court can do nothing more than deal in abstract generalities in its charge, then in every case involving negligence the jury are left at sea, a law unto themselves. It is the duty of the court, in every case in which a general verdict is to be returned, to instruct the jury as to the force and legal effect of the facts which may have been proved within the issues."

In *Perkins* v. *Hayward, supra*, ELLIOTT, Judge, says: "It is well settled that a special verdict must find the facts and state neither conclusions of law nor mere matters of evidence, and, as we have seen, what is true of a special verdict is true of a special finding."

In *Chicago, etc., R. W. Co.* v. *Burger*, 124 Ind. 275, COFFEY, J., says: "A finding that one of the parties has been guilty of negligence has often been held by this court to be a mere statement of a conclusion."

When the facts are found or undisputed, it is for the court to determine, as a question of law, whether or not they constitute negligence. *Louisville, etc., R. R. Co.* v. *Eves*, 1 Ind. App. 224; *Toledo, etc., R. W. Co.* v. *Goddard, supra; Pittsburgh, etc., R. R. Co.* v. *Spencer, supra; Louisville, etc., R. W. Co.* v. *Balch, supra; Woolery, Admr.*, v. *Louisville, etc., R. W. Co., supra.*

The principle, and oftentimes the only, questions of law, in an action brought to recover damages for personal injuries, are the questions of negligence on the part of the defendant, and of contributory negligence on the part of the plaintiff, and if they were to be left to the determination of the jury, there would be nothing for the court to do. Where the jury is to return a special verdict, the court should not instruct them as to what does or does not constitute negligence or contributory negligence, because they have no right to apply the law to the facts to determine whether or not negligence exists; neither have they a right to know that if they find a given state of facts, the court, in applying the law, will infer negligence. *Toler* v. *Keiher*, 81 Ind. 383; *Louisville, etc., R. W. Co.* v. *Frawley*, 110 Ind. 18; *Louisville, etc., R. W. Co.* v. *Hart*, 119 Ind. 273; *Stayner* v. *Joyce*, 120 Ind. 99; *Sprinkle* v. *Taylor*, 1 Ind. App. 74.

It is simply their province to find the ultimate facts, not knowing what legal inference the court may draw therefrom when the law is applied. From ultimate facts, but one legal conclusion can be drawn. In the trial of a cause, the evidentiary facts may all be admitted, from which more than one inference of an ultimate fact may be drawn, in which case it is always the province of the jury to draw the inference of the existence of the ultimate fact, and when the ultimate facts are found, the court concludes the law. The questions of negligence and contributory negligence are not ultimate facts, but are legal conclusions drawn from the ultimate facts. *Louisville, etc., R. R. Co.* v. *Eves, supra; Hankey* v. *Downey*, 3 Ind. App. 325; *Indianapolis, etc., R. W. Co.* v. *Bush, supra; Pennsylvania Co.* v. *Marion*, 104 Ind. 239; *Conner* v. *Citizens' Street R. W. Co., supra; Woolery, Admr.*, v. *Louisville, etc., R. W. Co., supra; Chicago, etc., R. R. Co.* v. *Ostrander, supra.*

In approaching the crossing, as found by the jury, without blowing the whistle or ringing the bell on the engine, as required by the statute, the appellant was guilty of negligence, and if the appellee was injured by reason thereof, and without fault on his part contributing thereto, he would be entitled to recover. *Baltimore, etc., R. R. Co.* v. *Walborn, Admr., supra.*

But the failure of the railroad company to do what the statute directs does not excuse one who approaches a railroad crossing from exercising the care and taking the precaution which the law enjoins upon him. *Mann* v. *Belt R. R.*, *etc.*, *Co.*, 128 Ind. 138; *Cadwallader* v. *Louisville*, *etc.*, *R. W. Co.*, 128 Ind. 518; *Thornton* v. *Cleveland*, *etc.*, *R. W. Co.*, 131 Ind. 492, 31 N. E. Rep. 185.

The only question left to be determined is whether or not the appellee was guilty of contributory negligence. Do the facts found show a failure to perform a duty imposed by law? The burden rests upon the appellee to show affirmatively that he has performed every duty imposed upon him by law, before the court can say that he did not contribute to his injury. *Hathaway* v. *Toledo*, *etc.*, *R. W. Co.*, 46 Ind. 25; *Toledo*, *etc.*, *R. R. Co.* v. *Brannagan*, *Admx.*, 75 Ind. 490; *Lyons* v. *Terre Haute*, *etc.*, *R. R. Co.*, 101 Ind. 419; *Indiana*, *etc.*, *R. W. Co.* v. *Greene*, *Admx.*, 106 Ind. 279; *Belt R. R.*, *etc.*, *Co.* v. *Mann*, 107 Ind. 89; *Chicago*, *etc.*, *R. W. Co.* v. *Hedges*, *Admx.*, 118 Ind. 5; *Cincinnati*, *etc.*, *R. W. Co.* v. *Howard*, 124 Ind. 280, and cases cited; *Miller*, *Admr.*, v. *Louisville*, *etc.*, *R. W. Co.*, 128 Ind. 97.

For, as MITCHELL, C. J., in the case of *Cincinnati*, *etc.*, *R. R. Co.* v. *Butler*, 103 Ind. 31, says: "In such an occurrence, he is one of the independent actors, charged with duties correlative with the duties of the railroad company. He is able and he must show whether his duty was performed. Thousands of persons pass safely over a given crossing over which thousands of trains are run, under every variety of circumstances, before one is injured, and, therefore, it may be said a presumption arises that the crossing may be safely passed by all those who observe such care as prudent persons ordinarily observe. Out of the thousands who crossed, the one who sustained injury is the exception. Because the thousauds who crossed in safety are supposed to represent the ordinary course of conduct better than the one, a presumption of fact is indulged that he, too, would have passed in safety had he observed the caution which prudent men ordinarily observe under like circumstances. This presumption is at least sufficient to require from him an explanation of his relation to the occurrence, and an affirmative showing that the circumstances were such, and his conduct such, that he was not in fault, and as his own conduct and his relation to the occurrence are peculiarly known to himself, and may be unknown to the railroad company, the requirement is a reasonable one.''

It is incumbent upon a traveler on a highway, riding in a wagon and about to cross a railroad track, who can not see or hear an approaching train on account of obstructions which are known to him, to use greater precaution to protect himself from injury than where the view is unobstructed, and the opportunity for using the senses of sight and hearing is unimpaired. The greater the danger, the greater the precaution required of him. He must not only do what an ordinarily prudent man would do under like circumstances, but he must exercise such care and diligence as are commensurate with the danger which confronts him. *Toledo, etc., R. W. Co.* v. *Shuckman, Admr.*, 50 Ind. 42; *Nave* v. *Flack*, 90 Ind. 205; *Board, etc.*, v. *Dombke*, 94 Ind. 72; *City of Indianapolis* v. *Cook*, 99 Ind. 10; *Cincinnati, etc., R. R. Co.* v. *Butler*, 103 Ind. 31; *Town of Gosport* v. *Evans*, 112 Ind. 133; *Griffin* v. *Ohio, etc., R. W. Co.*, 124 Ind. 326.

And a person going along a highway who drives upon a railroad track at a place known to him to be peculiarly dangerous because of the obstructions which impair and hinder the free use of his senses of sight and hearing, simply relying upon the servants of the railroad company performing their duty in blowing the whistle and ringing the bell, does not show himself, in the eyes of the law, to have been diligent and prudent. For, as the distinguished Judge SHARSWOOD, in *Pennsylvania R. R. Co.* v. *Beale*, 73 Pa. St. 504, says: "If the traveler can not see the track by looking out, whether from fog or other cause, he should get out, and if necessary lead his horse and wagon. A prudent and careful man would always do this at such a place. * * There never was a more important principle settled than that the fact of the failure to stop immediately before crossing a railroad track, is not merely evidence of negligence for the jury, but negligence *per se*, and a question for the court."

In the case of *Seefeld* v. *Chicago, etc., R. W. Co.*, 70 Wis. 216, the court, after reviewing many cases cited, says: "The rule to be deduced from these cases is this: If the view of a traveler on the highway approaching a railroad crossing is so obstructed that he can not see an approaching train in time to stop his team before colliding with it, if he knows that a train is due at such crossing at or about such time, and if he is unable to hear the approaching train when his team is in motion, whether by reason of the force and direction of the wind or of noises in the vicinity, made by his own wagon, or other causes, ordinary care requires him to stop his team while he may do so and listen for the train."

In *Brady* v. *Toledo, etc., R. R. Co.*, 81 Mich. 616, it appeared, that the plaintiff was driving a team attached to a lumber wagon, on a highway, toward the defendant's railroad; that intervening objects obscured a view of the track so that he could not see a train approaching, until within twenty or twenty-five feet of the crossing, and then only when the train was but a short distance from the crossing. He was familiar with the crossing, and in addition to the view being obscured, a mill in the vicinity made considerable noise. He drove his team upon the crossing without stopping just before going upon the track, to look and listen, and was injured, and the court held that it was not sufficient that plaintiff looked and listened for the train as he drove along, but he should have stopped his team and listened; and the court, concluding its opinion, says: "A greater duty was imposed upon the plaintiff in the present case by the fact that he knew the crossing to be a dangerous one. He knew its condition and that he would be unable to see the train until arriving at the crossing. He had no right to close his ears and drive along without stopping when he must have known that the noise of his wagon and of the mill would shut off the sound from the approaching train."

In the case of *Haas, Admr.*, v. *Grand Rapids, etc., R. R. Co.*, 47 Mich. 401, the facts were that the deceased, while driving along a highway approaching where it crossed the appellee's railroad, and when about three rods from the crossing he stopped his team and looked and listened and then proceeded on his way to the crossing, where he was struck and killed by a passing train. Judge Cooley, speaking for the court in passing upon the facts, says: "The peculiar risks of the crossing imposed upon the decedent the duty of special caution also; and as he knew that a regular train was due at the crossing at about that time, he was under the highest possible obligation to observe such precaution as would be needful to avoid a collision. We may concede that the railroad company failed to sound the bell; but this did not relieve the decedent from the duty of taking ordinary precautions for his own safety. And what ordinary prudence would demand must be determined on a view of all the circumstances. It is vain to urge or to pretend that ordinary precautions were made use of in this case. To move forward briskly as the decedent did, from a point whence an approaching train would not be seen, at a time when it was known by him that a train was due, and not to pause until the train was encountered, was so far from being ordinary prudence that it approached more nearly to absolute recklessness." See, also, *Pennsylvania R. R. Co.* v. *Righter*, 42 N. J. L. 180; *Wilds* v. *Hudson, etc., R. R. Co.*, 29 N. Y. 315; *Gorton* v. *Erie R. W. Co.*, 45 N. Y. 660; *Pennsylvania Canal Co.* v. *Bentley*, 66 Pa. St. 30; *Henze* v. *St. Louis, etc., R. W. Co.*, 71 Mo. 636; *Turner* v. *Hannibal, etc., R. R. Co.*, 74 Mo. 602; *Marty* v. *Chicago, etc., R. W. Co.*, 38 Minn. 108, and *Fletcher* v. *Fitchburg R. R. Co.*, 149 Mass. 127.

While a traveler on a highway may presume that the employes of a railroad company will obey the law and give the required warning, yet those in charge of the train may assume that the traveler will take every precaution commensurate with the danger which he is about to encounter, and will avoid going upon the track in front of the train.

The court, in *Hathaway* v. *Toledo, etc., R. W. Co.*, *supra*, says: "Although the negligence of the defendant was a cause, and even the primary cause of the occurrence, yet the occurrence would not have happened without a certain degree of blamable negligence on the part of the plaintiff."

A railroad crossing is a place of danger, and one who does not exercise every sense or faculty to protect himself from possible injury, before attempting to cross, can not be said to have exercised due care. Self-preservation is the first and greatest law of nature, and ordinarily it will lead to the employment of all the precautions which the situation naturally suggests to an individual in danger of harm. It implies not only the doing of those things which an ordinarily prudent man would do under like circumstances, but the doing of every practicable and available thing within his power, which the law says he should do. And it is no excuse that he did all that an ordinarily prudent man would have done under like circumstances, unless the things done were all the law declares an ordinarily prudent man should have done. It is the law that measures the duty, for a prudent man may do that which the law forbids, or he may omit to do that which the law enjoins, nevertheless the doing of the one or the omission of the other is negligence. The most prudent men are not always exempt from carelessness, and when actually negligent the law attaches the same consequences to their conduct as to similar conduct in others. *Bellefontaine R. W. Co. v. Hunter, Admr., supra; Pennsylvania Co. v. Marion, supra.*

In this case the appellee and his brother, when fifty feet distant from the track, stopped, looked, and listened, and from that point the horses approached and went upon the railroad track in a walk, the appellee looking and listening for approaching trains. That when and where they stopped they could neither hear nor see an approaching train on account of obstructions. It is also found that the appellee saw the situation and surroundings of the crossing. And while the appellant was guilty of negligence in placing the cars in the street, it was appellee's duty to approach the crossing under the apprehension that a train was liable to come at any moment; and while he had a right to presume that those in charge of the engine would obey the law by giving warning of its approach, the law nevertheless required that he obey the instincts of self-preservation, and not thrust himself into a situation of danger, knowing that he could not see or hear a train approaching, except those in charge of the train gave the statutory signals.

Cincinnati, Indianapolis, St. Louis and Chicago Ry. Co. *v.* Grumes.

When a crossing is so dangerous that for one to attempt to cross is equivalent almost to courting injury, he can not recover if, knowing the danger, he assumes the responsibility and attempts to cross and gets injured.

"Where there is danger, and the peril is known whoever encounters it voluntarily and unnecessarily can not be regarded as exercising ordinary prudence, and therefore does so at his own risk." Ray's Negligence of Imposed Duties, p. 129.

In *Town of Gosport* v. *Evans, supra*, the court says: "One who knows of a dangerous obstruction in a street or sidewalk, and yet attempts to pass it when, on account of darkness or other hindering causes, he can not see so as to avoid it, takes the risk upon himself. For a much greater reason does he take the risk upon himself, if, seeing an obstruction, and knowing its dangerous character, he deliberately goes into or upon it, when he was under no compulsion to go, or might have avoided it by going around."

As heretofore stated, the fact that he was injured raises the presumption that the fault was his own, and it was for him to rebut that presumption. The facts found show that this was a street in a populous part of the town, and that where it crossed appellant's railroad the obstructions were such that to cross it one took great risk. Whether or not he was justified in taking the risk must depend upon the circumstances. He can not shut his eyes to dangers which are apparent, and, if injured, recover therefor.

"A person is bound to use the senses, and exercise the reasoning faculties with which nature has endowed him. If he fails to do so, and is injured in consequence, neither he, in life, nor his representatives after his death, can recover for resulting injuries." *Stewart, Admx.*, v. *Pennsylvania Co.*, 130 Ind. 242.

In *Shoner* v. *Pennsylvania Co.*, *supra*, McBRIDE, J., says: "When a traveler approaches a railroad with the intention of crossing it, he is bound to know that to attempt to cross near and in front of a moving train involves more or less of danger. If he is so heedless of his personal safety that he braves the danger, or so careless that he does not use the senses nature has given him to look and listen, that he may learn if there is danger, only one inference, that of negligence, can be drawn from his conduct."

The facts do not show that at any point nearer than fifty feet from appellant's track the appellee stopped and looked and listened.

In the case of *Thornton* v. *Cleveland, etc., R. W. Co.*, *supra*, the court says: "While the plaintiff was not required to enter into a calculation of the comparative speed of a traveler walking towards a railroad track, and a train of cars passing along that track at ordinary speed, he must, as a matter of common observation, have known that while he would walk one hundred and fifty-five feet, the train would cover a considerable distance, sufficient, at least, to require him to look for its approach at some point during his journey. He had no right to look from a given point, and then close his eyes and pass upon the track."

It is a matter of common knowledge, hence is judicially known, that a train of cars moving along a railroad track necessarily makes a noise. That noise of itself is a warning to those about to go upon the track to look out and guard against danger. It is, therefore, the duty of one, before going upon the track, to listen for the sound which necessarily follows a moving train, and if there are any obstructions which interfere with his hearing readily, he must stop and listen. *Louisville, etc., R. W. Co.* v. *Stommel*, 126 Ind. 35.

And it is not always sufficient that he do so when one hundred or fifty feet away from the track, but he must do so at the last opportunity before going upon the track, when by so doing he could have heard.

In the case of *Louisville, etc., R. W. Co.* v. *Stommel, supra,* the court says: "We are at a loss to understand what difference it could make as to the caution to be used by the appellee's servant, whether there was or was not a statute requiring the giving of signals. It was his duty to stop and look for an approaching train, if there was any point within a reasonable distance from the crossing from which he could observe a train approaching; and if no train was to be seen it was his duty, when nearing the crossing, to stop and listen for the sound which ordinarily follows a moving train; and a statute requiring signals to be given, though violated, does not excuse this vigilance."

And COFFEY, J., in *Mann* v. *Belt R. R., etc., Co., supra* (144), says: "When it is said that a person approaching a railroad crossing must look and listen attentively for approaching trains, it is not to be understood that he may look from a given point, and then close his eyes; but it is to be understood that he must exercise such care as a reasonably prudent person, in the presence of such a danger, would exercise to avoid injury. The courts can not close their eyes to matters of general notoriety, and to matters of every-day observation. We must know that a train of cars passing over iron or steel rails at a speed of thirty miles an hour does not do so without noise. * * * As a rule, it is not necessary to stop and listen or look where approaching danger can be otherwise ascertained, but one approaching such crossing must exercise such care as will enable him, under the circumstances, to inform himself of the extent of the danger attending the crossing of the track if he can reasonably do so."

A majority of the court (the writer of this opinion not included) are of the opinion that the facts found by the jury, disregarding conclusions as well as evidentiary facts set out in the verdict, are sufficient to warrant the court in inferring that the appellee exercised care commensurate with the danger encountered, and, therefore, was not guilty of contributory negligence, and that the appellee was entitled to judgment thereon.

Appellant insists that the court below erred in permitting a witness, called by appellee, to testify concerning a conversation had with one Wheatley concerning the removal of the appellant's cars which were standing in Main street.

We are unable to see wherein this evidence, even if material, could have been prejudicial to the appellant. The appellant had no right to block the street with its cars, and it required no notice to remove them to make it guilty of negligence in having them there.

We find no error in the record, for which the judgment should be reversed.

Judgment affirmed.

Filed June 21, 1893.

PER CURIAM.—The majority of the court concurred in the result reached in the original opinion in affirming the judgment of the trial court, but not in all the reasoning therein contained. The cause having since been compromised, the parties, by agreement, ask leave to withdraw the petition for a rehearing heretofore filed.

With these observations such leave is accordingly granted.

Filed May 9, 1894.

Miles, Trustee, etc., *v.* De Wolf *et al.*

No. 878.

MILES, TRUSTEE, ETC., *v.* DE WOLF ET AL.

ATTORNEY AND CLIENT.—*When Such Relation Exists.*—*Contract.*—*Professional Services.*—*Attorney's Fees.*—*Decedents' Estates.*—A. died testate, devising almost his entire estate to B. and C., in trust for D., E. and F., three nieces. C. did not qualify, but B. qualified to look after the interest of his wife, a *cestui que trust.* G. was appointed administrator with the will annexed. A suit was instituted to set aside the will. G., as administrator, employed, among other attorneys, H. and I. to defend and sustain the will, for which services they were paid in full, the first ·trial resulting in a disagreement of the jury. Before the second trial of the case, G. resigned his trust, and H. was appointed administrator *de bonis non*, with the will annexed, and I. was appointed guardian of a minor child of D., deceased. In the second trial, B., H. and I., among others, were defendants in their respective trust capacities. H. and I. prepared the case for trial, interviewed witnesses brought to their office by B., and assisted at the trial, as attorneys, in the presence of B. H. and I. bring suit against B. for professional services rendered for him in the second trial of the cause.

Held, that the fact that H. and I. interviewed witnesses brought to their office by B., in preparation for trial, and assisted, as attorneys at the trial, in the presence of B., raises no presumption of employment by B.

Held, also, that the evidence is insufficient to sustain the verdict rendered in favor of plaintiffs.

From the Knox Circuit Court.

H. S. Cauthorn, W. F. Townsend and *J. Wilhelm*, for appellant.

W. A. Cullop and *C. B. Kessinger*, for appellees.

DAVIS, J.—The complaint filed in this case in the court below was in the words and figures following, to wit:
"STATE OF INDIANA, KNOX COUNTY, ss:

"WILLIAM H. DE WOLF,

SMILEY N. CHAMBERS,

EDGAR H. DE WOLF,

vs.

WILLIAM R. MILES, Trustee under the last will and testament of William J. Wise, deceased.

"Knox Circuit Court, March Term, 1890.

"The plaintiffs, late copartners, doing business under the firm name of De Wolf, Chambers & De Wolf, complain of the defendant, and say that said defendant is indebted to them in the sum of six thousand dollars, for services, as attorneys, rendered said defendant at his special instance and request in the defense of the suit of Jacob Shugart *et al.* against said defendant and others, and for special services rendered said defendant in the management of said trust, a bill of particulars being filed herewith and made a part hereof. And plaintiffs say that said account is due and remains wholly unpaid. Wherefore they demand judgment for six thousand dollars.   CULLOP & KESSINGER,

Attorneys for Plaintiffs."

In the bill of particulars, the alleged services in the Shugart case were estimated at $5,000, and the services rendered in the management of the trust at $1,000.

The answer was a general denial, payment, and set-off, but the alleged payment and set-off were founded on items of nominal amount only, and, therefore, these answers are not material so far as the questions presented for our consideration are concerned.

There is no averment in the complaint that said Miles was trustee under any will or for any person. Neither is there any averment as to the extent, character, value or condition of the estate, if any, in his hands. In fact, it is not alleged that he had any trust estate in his hands or under his control, or that he was, in such trust capacity, a party to any suit, or that, as trustee, he required the services of an attorney, or that, as trustee, he employed appellees to perform any services for him, or that any such services were necessary.

On whatever theory the parties to the action may have proceeded in the court below, the case, as it comes to us on the record, appears, under the authorities, to have been merely a personal action against said Miles, to recover from him the alleged value of the services rendered by appellees. *Turner* v. *Flagg, Guar.*, 6 Ind. App. 563, and authorities there cited.

What we have said on this subject has been for the purpose of getting an accurate statement of the pleadings, and the theory of the case before us, in order to determine whether there is available error in the record.

The cause was submitted to a jury for trial, and resulted in a general verdict for appellees in the sum of two thousand four hundred and eighty dollars, on which verdict a personal judgment was rendered against William R. Miles.

The history of the case, with a general statement of the facts, may be summarized as follows:

"William J. Wise, of Vincennes, died testate January 4, 1884, leaving a large estate. He left no issue, as he was never married. By his will, he devised almost his entire estate to William R. Miles and John M. Boyle, in trust for the use and benefit of Elizabeth'S. Miles, Catharine A. Fay, and Mary B. Ryder, his three nieces, one equal third to each.

"The said nieces were all married, and their husbands living, at the date of the death of testator. By the provisions of the will, if either of the husbands of the *cestui que trust* should die, then the one-third interest of his estate should absolutely vest in the surviving widow, freed from the trust. And if either of said nieces should die before their husbands, and leave issue surviving, then the one-third interest in his estate should absolutely vest in her surviving issue, also freed from the trust. Catharine A. Fay and Mary B. Ryder, two of the nieces, died before their husbands, and before the estate was settled, and while it was in litigation. They both left minor children, and, by the terms of the will, one-third of the estate of the testator vested in their children. F. M. Fay, the surviving husband of one, was appointed guardian of her children, and Smiley N. Chambers was appointed guardian of Emma W. Ryder, the minor child of Mary B. Ryder. This left under the charge and control of the trustees under the will only one-third of the estate, the interest of Elizabeth S. Miles.

"John M. Boyle, one of the trustees named in the will, did not qualify, but William R. Miles, the husband of Elizabeth S. Miles, qualified to look after the interest of his wife.

"After the death of William J. Wise, the testator, Richard J. McKenney was appointed administrator, with the will annexed, of his estate, and made an inventory, collected many thousands of dollars of notes and other choses in action, settled and adjusted a partnership of over thirty years' duration, of which testator had been a member, involving assets of over $200,000, and, in fact, administered the estate and had the assets ready for distribution, and filed a final account showing the complete settlement of the estate and the character of the assets in hand ready for distribution. Distribution was alone prevented and postponed by pending suits to contest the will, in order to ascertain whether distribution was to be ordered according to the will, if sustained, or according to the law, if it was annulled. The estate was in this condition when McKenney resigned the trust, and when William H. De Wolf was appointed administrator *de bonis non*.

"McKenney was allowed, for his services in settling the estate, in all, $4,750.

"After the death of testator, and the probate of his will, Henry K. Wise, a brother of testator, commenced an action in the Knox Circuit Court to set it aside. This action was tried in said court before a jury, and resulted in a verdict sustaining the will. On this trial, which lasted some four weeks, substantially all the evidence tending to sustain and uphold the will was hunted up, as well as most of the evidence relied on to defeat it, and the same was taken down in shorthand and embodied in a bill of exceptions. The appellees in this case had no connection with that litigation or the estate of testator in any way.

"Henry K. Wise, the contestant, died, and the appeal was never prosecuted from the judgment of the Knox Circuit Court.

"Afterwards Jacob Shugart and other heirs of testator commenced an action in the Knox Circuit Court to contest his will. This action was, on the application of contestants for a change of venue, sent to the Sullivan Circuit Court for trial. At the time this second action was commenced, the interests of Catharine A. Fay and Mary B. Ryder had vested in their minor children, by their death, and Frank M. Fay and Smiley N. Chambers, the guardian of Emma W. Ryder, the sole heir of Mary B. Ryder, were both made defendants in that suit, as also Richard J. McKenney, the administrator with the will annexed of the testator, his estate being unsettled, and William R. Miles, the trustee who had charge, under the will, of the one-third interst of Elizabeth S. Miles, his wife.

"The first trial of the said second suit brought by Shugart and others, in the Sullivan Circuit Court, before a jury, resulted in the jury failing to agree. On that trial Richard J. McKenney, the administrator, employed William H. De Wolf and Smiley N. Chambers, among other attorneys, to defend and sustain the will, and paid them in full for the services rendered on said trial under said employment. The testimony on the trial of that cause to sustain the will was practically the same as the testimony on the first trial of the case of Henry K. Wise.

"After the said first trial, it was deemed advisable to get rid of McKenney as administrator, as he was thought unsafe on account of his wife being interested in defeating the will, as one of the general heirs of testator, and taking an active part in the pending suit to accomplish it. To prevent measures being taken to remove him, McKenney resigned as administrator, and settled the estate ready to deliver all the assets to a successor, which assets were in fact turned over to his successor before the second trial of the cause.

"The second trial of the case of Shugart, had in the Sullivan Circuit Court, before a jury, resulted in a verdict sustaining the will. This second trial was not as long continued as the preceding one, and the evidence to sustain and support the will, was practically the same as the evidence on the two former trials, and the evidence on the preceding trial of Shugart, resulting in the jury failing to agree, was also taken down in full by a stenographer appointed by the court.

"On the last trial of the Shugart case, which resulted in a verdict sustaining the will, a question of law arising on the ruling of the court admitting certain testimony was reserved for the decision of the Supreme Court, on appeal. A bill of exceptions embodying the question reserved was filed and the appeal prosecuted, resulting in the affirmance of the judgment of the Sullivan Circuit Court.

"After the first trial of the Shugart case and after the resignation of McKenney as administrator, William H. DeWolf, one of the appellees, was appointed administrator de bonis non, with the will of testator annexed, and was properly substituted as a defendant in lieu of Mc-

Kenney in the Shugart contest, before the trial of the cause.

"In the last trial of the case of Shugart in the Sullivan Circuit Court, the following attorneys were especially employed to defend the will in said court, and also to defend or prosecute any appeal in the Supreme Court, that might be taken from the judgment of the Sullivan Circuit Court, and their receipts were drawn so as to evidence this special contract and agreement: Hays & Hays, of Sullivan; Gardiner & Taylor, of Washington; Harrison, Miller & Elam, of Indianapolis, and McDonald, Butler & Snow, of Indianapolis.

"Messrs. Gardiner & Taylor of Washington, Frederick W. Viehe and Mason J. Niblack of Vincennes, were retained and took part in all the three trials had to contest the will of the testator.

"The attorneys for the defense participating in the trial of the Shugart case paid all their own expenses. The expenses of William H. DeWolf, who was defendant as well as administrator, were paid out of the estate of testator before it was settled and distribution made. The expenses of Smiley N. Chambers, who was guardian of Emma W. Ryder and also a defendant, were also paid out of the estate before distribution.

"The same assets that McKenney had on hand when he resigned the trust, passed to DeWolf as his successor, and DeWolf procured an order of court to authorize him to suffer the assets so received by him to remain in bank in the same manner that they had been kept by McKenney. After the judgment of the Sullivan Circuit Court was rendered sustaining the will, and before the appeal was taken to the Supreme Court therefrom, DeWolf filed his final account as administrator, showing that the assets of the estate were in the same condition and consisted of same items as turned over to him by McKenney, only increased in amount by interest that had accrued and been received on United States bonds. He claimed for his services $10,000, which was resisted by appellant as being excessive. Pending adjudication of the amount of his allowance, the court ordered him to distribute all the estate in his hands among the parties entitled thereto, under the will, except the $10,000 claimed by him for his services as administrator, and he accordingly dis- tributed the same, one-third to Smiley N. Chambers, one of appellees, who was guardian of Emma W. Ryder; one-third to F. M. Fay, guardian of the minor heirs of Catharine A. Fay, and one-third to William R. Miles, as trustee for his wife, Elizabeth S. Miles. The $10,000 claimed for services were to be held for further order on proof of the value of his services. On hearing proof of the value of his services, the court allowed him $6,820, and ordered the $3,180 remaining to be distributed to the parties entitled thereto under the will, which was accordingly done by DeWolf, and the estate was declared settled and he was discharged. William H. DeWolf was only practically administrator about seven months, and the assets he distributed were the same he had received from McKenney, with the exception of interest received on the United States bonds.

"The court, in hearing proof on the claim of DeWolf for services as administrator, admitted and received testimony as to the appointment of DeWolf as administrator *de bonis non*, the amount of bond he gave as such, the amount of the assets, his services as an attorney in defending the suit of Shugart to contest the will in both the Sullivan Circuit Court and in Supreme Court on appeal, and all matters and things done and performed by him in connection therewith, as to loss of time and attendance at court in a foreign county, and every matter connected with or growing out of said suit, excepting his expenses, which were paid out of the estate without question, and which payment of his expenses was admitted by DeWolf, but it does not appear that the court allowed him anything for his services as attorney.

"After the final settlement of the estate and distribution of the assets, the appellees, as partners at law, filed in the Knox Circuit Court, on the 28th day of February, 1890, the complaint in this case to recover from appellant for professional services rendered by them in the Sullivan Circuit Court and in Supreme Court on appeal, and for advice given him as trustee at his special instance and request, and making an account current for him. The appellant denied the indebtedness *in toto*, except as to an account current, and that he ever employed appellees to render any service whatever for him, either in the Sullivan Circuit Court or in Supreme Court in the Shugart case, and denied seeking or obtaining any advice from them in the management of the trust, and that the only service rendered by appellees for him as trustee or otherwise was simply copying the items of receipts and disbursements from his account book, in the form of a report, to submit to court, of his trust, and that appellees had in their hands twenty dollars of money for his use, which was sufficient to cancel and offset the services rendered by them in making his account as trustee. The twenty dollars claimed was not denied."

There are in some other particulars material facts, which will, further on in the course of this opinion, be more fully stated.

The first error discussed is that the court below erred in overruling appellant's motion for judgment in his favor on the answers of the jury to the interrogatories.

The facts found by the jury in answers to the interrogatories are, in substance, as follows:

First. That William H. DeWolf was administrator *de bonis non, cum testamento annexo,* of the estate of William J. Wise, at the time of the last trial in the Sullivan Circuit Court.

Second. That Smiley N. Chambers was guardian at law of Emma Ryder during the last trial in the Sullivan Circuit Court.

Third. William H. DeWolf was appointed such administrator in October, 1887.

Fourth. That he was discharged as such in February, 1889.

Fifth. That said William H. DeWolf, administrator, was party defendant upon said last trial.

Sixth. That William H. DeWolf had received for his services, as such administrator, six thousand, eight hundred and twenty dollars.

Seventh. That the appellees were partners in the practice of the law in May and June, 1888.

Eighth. That Smiley N. Chambers was guardian at law of Emma Ryder, and party defendant in the suit tried in the Sullivan Circuit Court.

"Int. 9th. Did the defendant William R. Miles, trustee, etc., employ the plaintiffs as attorneys to defend the action of *Shugart* v. *Miles,* on the last trial thereof, in May and June, 1888, in the Sullivan Circuit Court?

"Ans. We decide that the plaintiffs were in his employ.   J. R. HADDEN, Foreman."

"Int. 10th. If you find any such employment was made as inquired about in the ninth interrogatory, state when the contract was made, where made, and with which one of the plaintiffs was it made.

"Ans. We decide that they were employed in the first trial at Sullivan, and were not discharged.

"J. R. HADDEN, Foreman."

Eleventh. That said firm of attorneys made out a report for William R. Miles as trustee, and filed the same in court.

Twelfth. That William R. Miles employed said firm of attorneys in the appeal to the Supreme Court.

Thirteenth. That said firm of attorneys assisted in preparing the brief, and were present when the case was argued.

It is earnestly insisted that this motion should have been sustained, because one of the appellees, William H. DeWolf, was, as administrator, a party defendant, and another of the appellees, Smiley N. Chambers, was also a party defendant as guardian of the person and property of Emma Ryder, in the identical cause for which they seek compensation in this action as attorneys.

The contention is that the law forbade appellees, William H. DeWolf and Smiley N. Chambers, occupying the position they did—one as administrator of the estate of William J. Wise, deceased, and the other as guardian of the ward whose property interests were involved,—from accepting employment and receiving compensation as attorneys for the discharge of duties which the law imposed upon them from the first moment after they qualified and became responsible for the legal protection of the interests involved in the trusts committed to their hands.

It is well settled that an administrator can not recover for services rendered by him as an attorney in the settlement of an estate, and neither is a law firm of which he is a member entitled to such compensation. Sections 2396 and 2398, R. S. 1881; *Taylor* v. *Wright, Admr.*, 93 Ind. 121; *Pollard* v. *Barkley*, 117 Ind. 40.

The appellees in argument do not controvert the law as enunciated above and supported by the authorities cited, but they urge "That one defendant may employ his co-defendant to represent and defend his interest, although they may be co-trustees representing the same fiduciary interest. In the case at bar, they were not co-trustees in any sense whatever, but represented entirely different and distinct interests with entirely different and distinct relations, duties, and responsibilities.''

Many authorities are cited by counsel in support of the proposition that the offices of trustee and administrator are distinct, and involve different duties. Schuyler's Execs. and Admrs., sections 46, 472; Williams' Execs. and Admrs., section 472; Lewin on Trusts, section 205; *Valentine* v. *Valentine*, 2 Barb. Ch. 430; *Lansing* v. *Lansing*, 31 Howard's Pr. Rep. N. Y. 55; *Wheatly* v. *Badger*, 7 Pa. St. 459; *Simpson* v. *Cook*, 24 Minn. 180; 7 Am. and Eng. Encyc. of Law, p. 179, and notes; *Drury* v. *Natick*, 10 Allen (Mass.) 169, 174.

And, further, when one trustee acts as solicitor or attorney for another trustee, in a litigation in which both, by reason of their trust relation, are involved, that such solicitor or attorney is entitled to compensation from his co-trustee for the services so rendered. *Cradock* v. *Piper*, 47 Eng. Ch. Rep. 663; *Lyon* v. *Baker*, 5 DeGex and Smale's Reps. 622.

The Cradock case, on which appellees rely in support of their position on this question, was one in which there were four trustees and where three of them had employed the fourth, who was a solicitor, to represent them as such trustees in several important litigations in which the trust estate was involved, and, so far as appears, the trustee who so acted was the sole and only solicitor who appeared for the trust in the litigation, and it was held, under the facts in that case, that he was entitled to have his costs taxed as such solicitor, in order that the same might be paid out of the trust estate. But whatever view may be taken of the application to this case, of the authorities cited, and without at this time entering upon an analysis of the interrogatories and answers thereto, it will suffice to say that it is doubtful whether, on any theory, the answers of the jury to the interrogatories are so effectually and irreconcilably antagonistic to the general verdict as to overthrow it and control the result, and we will, therefore, for the present, pass on to the consideration of other questions which are pressed upon our consideration. *Gaar, Scott & Co.* v. *Rose,* 3 Ind. App. 269; *Baldwin* v. *Shill,* 3 Ind. App. 291.

The next assignment of error is overruling appellant's motion for a new trial. It should be borne in mind that for services in the Shugart case, Mr. De Wolf, as administrator, paid attorney fees as follows:

Harrison, Miller & Elam $5,000
McDonald, Butler & Snow............ 5,000
Gardiner & Taylor.................. 2,000
John T. Hays..................... 2,000

Pursuant to the written request of Chambers, Miles and all the parties in interest, he was directed "to pay the fees of counsel in the contest of the will." In addition thereto, De Wolf and Chambers were paid by the administrator for services rendered by them on the first trial in the Sullivan Circuit Court, and Viehe and Niblack were also paid by the administrator, out of the trust estate in his hands, for services rendered on each trial. It is not claimed that De Wolf and Chambers were employed by appellant in the first trial. The uncontradicted evidence also shows that when the proposed appointment of De Wolf was under consideration, Mr. De Wolf said to Mr. Miles: "If he was appointed administrator it would cut him off of any claim or right to compensation as an attorney."

In this connection we quote, at length, extracts from brief of counsel for appellant, as follows:

"1. The verdict of the jury is not sustained by the evidence, but is contrary to both the law and the evidence.

"The complaint in this case is to recover for professional services alleged to have been rendered under a contract of employment. The general denial which was pleaded imposed upon appellees the burden of proving, by a fair preponderance of the evidence, every material fact necessary for a recovery. This is clear, and will not be questioned. Therefore, the jury, before they could find any verdict in favor of appellees, must first find from the evidence, that the services sued for were rendered under a contract with appellant. The evidence of appellees is all in the record. The only evidence in the case that has any bearing whatever upon this material question, is the evidence of Mr. De Wolf and of Mr. Chambers. We invite the careful attention of the court to their evidence. It will be found that Mr. Chambers, in his evidence, says nothing whatever about the services being rendered under any contract with appellant, or at his special instance and request. Nothing whatever, in his evidence, appears to throw any light whatever upon this question of employment by appellant, which is absolutely necessary for a recovery. Nothing appears to show that the services he rendered were not rendered in discharge of his duties as guardian of Emma W. Ryder. And, in the absence of all proof on the subject, the legal presumption is that he performed the services in discharge of the duties devolved upon him by law as guardian of Emma W. Ryder. And there is nothing whatever in the evidence of Mr. De Wolf that has any tendency whatever to show that the services sued for were rendered under a contract with appellant or at his special instance and request. The only statement in his entire evidence in the least concerning appellee is a naked assertion, where he says: 'I rendered the services for the defendant.' Leaving out this naked and unsupported assertion, there is absolutely nothing in his evidence that has any tendency to show that the services were not rendered in the discharge of his duties as administrator. And this statement is not of a fact and does not even assert that appellant employed or requested him to perform said services. From all that appears, he may have done so voluntarily and without solicitation. The bare statement that he performed them for the appellant is not sufficient of itself to raise any presumption of an employment by appellant, or even to negative the legal presumption that he was not doing his duty as administrator. We confidently rely upon this total failure of proof of an employment, or that the services were rendered at the special instance and request of appellant, for a reversal of the case. This case is not one where the rule applies that a case will not be reversed upon a bare preponderance of the evidence. It is a case where there is a total want of evidence upon a point material to any recovery. The evidence of appellees is in the record, and our positive assertion of the want of any evidence to sustain the verdict on this material question is fully sustained by the record. The most that can be claimed for it on behalf of appellees, is that they rendered certain professional services in a case, in which there were several parties defendant, among them two of the appellees, F. M. Fay and appellant. But who employed them, nowhere appears in the evidence, and no attempt was made to show it. The only thing the evidence discloses affecting in any way appellant, is that he was present in court when the services were rendered. But this presence of appellant at the time the services were rendered furnishes no ground to presume that he employed them to perform the services, more than any of the other defendants to the suit who were also present.

"The appellees, in the court below, relied upon this presence and knowledge of appellant as being sufficient of itself to warrant a presumption of employment, and the court below gave color to this claim in one of the instructions to the jury. The verdict of the jury can not be sustained in the absence of proof of an employment of appellees by appellant. His mere presence at the trial when the services were rendered in a case in which he was not a sole party, and in which the appellees, who actively rendered the services, were themselves parties with him and upon whom the law imposed the duty to render and perform them, can not raise any presumption against him to aid appellees or sustain the verdict.

"In the case in which the services were rendered, Mr. De Wolf, one of the appellees, was a defendant as administrator, and Mr. Chambers, another appellee, was also a defendant as guardian of Emma W. Ryder. The law specially imposed upon them, as such defendants, the imperative obligation of rendering the services in person, or to employ some attorney to do so. The trust character in which they were clothed required this of them, and to have failed to do so would have been a gross violation of their trust duties. In the absence of all proof on the subject, the reasonable and legal presumption is that they performed the services in fulfillment of their duties as such trustees. Besides, F. M. Fay, as guardian of the children of his deceased wife, was a party defendant, and was also present when the services were rendered. He represented the same interest as Chambers, and they both represented an equal interest in the litigation as appellant. Why should the mere fact of presence at the trial raise any presumption against appellant of an employment of appellees, more than against Fay?

"Besides, the action of appellees show clearly, we think, that at the time these services were rendered they were in fact rendered on their own behalf and in discharge of their duties as trustees, and not otherwise. It was the duty of Mr. De Wolf, as administrator, to defend the suit and sustain the will, if he believed it a valid instrument. And in so doing, all his reasonable expenses incurred in good faith, including attorneys who were employed to defend, would be allowed him, and paid out of the estate, whether the result of the litigation was favorable or unfavorable to the validity of the will involved in the litigation. *Bratney, Admr.,* v. *Curry, Exec.,* 33 Ind. 399.

"And this is what was actually done in this case before any distribution of the assets. All the expenses of Mr. De Wolf and Mr. Chambers, as defendant, and the fees of the attorneys employed to sustain the will, were thus paid. The written order Mr. De Wolf took from the beneficiaries of the estate to pay attorney fees show this. It was demanded by Mr. De Wolf, and given by the beneficiaries for his satisfaction, although the law would have protected him in making the payment of reasonable attorney fees without it. It may have been feared by Mr. De Wolf that some trouble might arise on account of the fees paid by him to attorneys being unreasonable, owing to the number employed and paid by him. That order to pay attorney fees was signed by Mr. Chambers and Mr. Fay, as well as by appellant, and they represented all the interest involved. If there were any attorney fees due appellees, or claimed by them, why were they not paid out of the estate before distribution of the assets? Or is it equitable and just, after the estate has been settled and the assets distributed, to assert such a claim against appellant alone, representing, as he does, but a one-third interest in the estate, the same as represented by Mr. Chambers and Mr. Fay?

"So far as any presumption of employment from the fact the services were rendered with the knowledge and in the presence of appellant is concerned, we hold no such presumption can be indulged in this case. Even if Mr. De Wolf, under any possible circumstances, could claim attorney fees, occupying the relation he did to the Shugart case (which right to claim attorney fees by him from any one, we expressly deny), still, in this case, the claim of appellees can not be aided by any presumption. If an attorney in no way connected with a suit as a party renders professional services for a sole party in his presence and with his knowledge, a presumption of employment reasonably and properly arises. But where such services are rendered in a case where there are several parties on the same side, in aid of which rendered and in the presence of all, no presumption of an employment arises hostile to any one in particular to the exclusion of the others. And where the attorney who performs the services is himself a party to the suit, in a case where the law required him to perform such services as a part of his sworn duty, the presumption, in the absence of proof on the subject, certainly is, they were rendered in the line and discharge of his duty, and not otherwise. And such, we insist, is the case we are considering."

This is a part only of the argument of counsel for appellant on the question under consideration, and we quote in full all that counsel for appellees have said with reference to the alleged employment, in which is embodied the substance of the testimony of appellees as to the character and value of the alleged services:

"The legal right upon the part of Miles to employ the firm of appellees being thus established, the question that remains for this court to investigate is: Was there evidence before the jury tending to support their verdict? If there was such evidence, under the frequent rulings of this court the verdict will not be disturbed.

"William H. DeWolf testified that during the years 1887, 1888, 1889, the firm was composed of William H. DeWolf, Smiley N. Chambers and E. H. DeWolf. 'I was connected with said suit as one of the attorneys for the defense; after the first trial of the case in the Sullivan Circuit Court, we began to prepare for the next trial of the case; from that time we were almost constantly employed, except Sundays, perhaps. I made two trips to McConnelsville, Ohio, one to Peabody, Kansas, the pleadings were reformed and new issues added; I personally attended to same, made two trips to Indianapolis for consultation with General Harrison, one of the attorneys, and interviewed Dr. Fletcher, and also Dr. Thomas. * * *

" 'Mr. Miles brought the witnesses for the defense to our office to ascertain to what they would testify. *

" 'Chambers and DeWolf attended to all the legal work required in relation to the witnesses. * * *

" 'I interviewed the witnesses for the defense in my office. I was employed this way day and night. Mr. Miles was there very often. Mr. Miles was in my office almost every day, and sometimes several times a day. * * *

" 'I myself prepared a memorandum of legal questions. On the second trial of the case there were about seventy-five witnesses on each side. There were also a vast number of depositions taken and used in the case on both sides. . There were also new witnesses, quite a number, and new evidence adduced. I was present every hour in the court-room during the progress of the trial. Every witness for the defense was privately examined at our rooms, sometimes it was myself and sometimes Harrison and Gardiner who interrogated. * * *

" 'Edgar H. DeWolf, one of the plaintiffs, had personally no connection with the trial of the case, except that during the time it was on trial in the Sullivan Circuit Court he remained at the plaintiffs' office in Vincennes to be prepared to send witnesses to Sullivan as they were needed, and attended to that duty, and had witnesses go to Sullivan as required. * * *

" 'I went to Spencer, before Judge Franklin, concerning the case arising on questions involved upon the bill of exceptions. Chambers was also before the judge at a subsequent day, and the bill of exceptions was finally signed by the judge. * * *

" 'I can not give the language used by Mr. Miles when he employed us; he said once that he had spoken to Viehe to represent him in the trusteeship, and that Mr. Viehe did not want to take the case.' * * *

"Smiley N. Chambers testified as follows: 'After the disagreement of the jury on the first trial, another trial of the case was a matter of course. The attorneys for the defense agreed among themselves that the first thing to be done to insure a successful issue for the defense was to get rid of McKenney; I was finally deputized to call on McKenney and notify him that unless he voluntarily resigned the trust that charges would be made against him, and that he would be legally forced to give up the trust. Finally, Mr. McKenney made his final settlement of the estate and resigned the trust, and Mr. DeWolf was appointed in his place. We then commenced preparations for the second trial of the cause in earnest. Mr. Miles was in our office nearly every day, and sometimes several times a day. He brought many witnesses to our office who were to give evidence for the defense, in order to have them examined, and they were examined by Mr.

DeWolf or myself. This took up about all our time. We were the only local attorneys that took charge of the case for the defense, and the work of preparing for the coming trial devolved upon us. The second trial of the case commenced in May, 1888, and lasted about six weeks. I suggested to General Harrison that the issues in the case should be amended by a plea of former adjudication, and the issues in the case were accordingly amended. On the second trial of the case, there were a number of new witnesses and much new matter was brought out in evidence. I took notes of the testimony as it was given by the witnesses, with the expectation of making an argument in the case, but different arrangements were made and I did not make an argument. * * *

" 'I went to Spencer on business connected with the bill of exceptions. The brief in the case on appeal to the Supreme Court was originally prepared by John T. Hays. After he had prepared the same, he brought the brief to our office and it was read over and corrected. I went to Washington to consult with Gardiner concerning the brief, read it over to him and with him made corrections and additions. I superintended the printing of the brief. * * *

" 'Our firm also did work for Mr. Miles as trustee; we gave him legal advice concerning his duties as trustee; we commenced to advise him concerning his duties in 1887 sometime, I do not remember the date. He was continually consulting us and getting our advice. Mr. DeWolf also made out a report for him as trustee, which was filed in this court. It took considerable time and labor to prepare this report; it was quite lengthy and Mr. DeWolf was in all two weeks in preparing it. It was a difficult report to make; it was his first report as trustee; there were many collections to make. Mr. De Wolf worked several nights until a late hour. The great difficulty in preparing the report was in making the calculations of the premiums of the bonds which he had in his hands. A reasonable fee for the services rendered him as trustee in this respect by our firm was $1,000.' "

The fourth reason assigned in the motion for new trial is "The damages assessed by the jury are excessive in amount," and the fifth reason is "The assessment by the jury of the amount of recovery is erroneous, being too large."

We have carefully read the evidence, and in view of all the facts and circumstances surrounding the case, we fail to find any evidence in the record fairly tending to support the theory that appellant, either individually or as trustee, employed appellees as attorneys to appear for and represent him or any one else in the Shugart case, on the second trial, in the Sullivan Circuit Court, to contest the will of William J. Wise.

Neither of appellees has testified to any fact or circumstance, conversation with, or statement made by said William R. Miles indicating any such employment. The evidence and the answers of the jury to interrogatories indicate that any such agreement was an implied one predicated upon the previous employment of Messrs. De Wolf and Chambers by the former administrator on the first trial of the Shugart case. Any such employment made by said McKenney prior to or on the former trial could not be a continuous one, as his powers to employ and retain counsel ceased before the second trial, and Mr. DeWolf succeeded him as administrator.

The law firm of appellees seems to have been afterwards formed. When Mr. De Wolf accepted the appointment as administrator, he entirely changed his relation to the case, and conceding, without deciding, that he, or the firm of which he was a member, might thereafter have accepted retainer and employment therein as at-

torneys for the trust estate represented by appellant, yet
nothing is shown to have been said or done by Mr. Miles,
after the first trial, which can be construed as an intent
on his part to so retain and employ appellees. The fact
that he may have had frequent conversations with them
in regard to the case, or that he took witnesses to their
office, or that he knew they were devoting their time to
preparation for the trial, or that he was present at the
trial and saw and knew they were assisting as attorneys
therein, when considered separately or together, are not
(under the other conceded facts in this case) circumstances indicating or tending to establish such employment by him.

Nothing appears in the record, on this branch of the
case, which can be construed as tending to create an obligation, either personally or as trustee, on the part of
William R. Miles.

The late esteemed Chief Justice MITCHELL said: "A
relation, which the law recognizes as contractual, may
arise between the parties in three ways: (1) The terms
of the agreement may have been uttered, avowed, or expressed at the time it was made; in which case an express contract results. (2) Circumstances may have
arisen, or acts may have been done which, according to
the dictates of reason and justice, and the ordinary course
of dealing, or the common understanding of men, show
a mutual intention to contract; in which case an implied
contract arises. (3) There may have been no intention
to contract at all, and yet one may have come under a
legal duty to another of such a character that the law
precludes him from asserting that he did not agree to
perform it, and thus, by a fiction of law, a contract results by construction, or implication." Ramsey v. Ramsey, 121 Ind. 215 (220).

We do not find anything in the evidence tending to

support the proposition that there was an express contract, or that there was a mutual intention to contract, or from which a · contract results from construction. Nothing is shown to have been done or said by appel-. lant which could be fairly construed by appellees as an employment of their firm as attorneys by him on the second trial.   There is an entire absence of evidence to sustain the theory that the minds of the parties ever met on the vital question now in dispute.

The evidence was taken at the trial in longhand, in narrative form, and some material parts thereof, may have been inadvertently omitted.

Ordinarily, it is true that where an attorney appears in court for and in behalf of one of the parties involved in a litigation, and performs services in the action, as such attorney, in the presence of the party, the law implies a contract between the attorney and the person who receives the benefit of the services, and in the absence of an agreement as to terms and amount, the client is under obligations to pay the reasonable value of the services so rendered, but under the circumstances of this case that rule is not applicable.   It does not appear in this case that appellant knew, or that the circumstances were such that he ought to have known, that appellees were claiming that they specially represented him, or that they were expecting compensation from him.

In fact, the evidence, together with the acts of the parties, and all the facts and circumstances in the case, tend strongly, without contradiction, to support the theory that all of the attorneys who represented the defense in the contest of the will, appeared generally for all of the defendants in interest, and no attorney or firm of attorneys is shown to have been employed by, or to have appeared for or represented the interest of any one person or defendant especially.   Further, as we read and understand the record, the agreement implied, if not expressed, seems to have been that all of the fees of the different attorneys, who appeared in the interest of the defendants, were to be paid in full by said De Wolf as administrator of the estate of William J. Wise, deceased, out of the trust funds in his hands, before distribution.

The isolated and independent expressions, "when he employed us," or "I rendered the services for the defendant," standing alone and without explanation, can not be construed as the statement of any conversation, fact, or circumstance on which to base a contract of employment in the case to contest the will. The qualified expression or assertion, "when he employed us," is not preceded or followed by any statement or explanation tending to show there ever had been any employment of appellees by appellant, so far as the litigation is concerned, and so far as anything to the contrary appears, the expression, for whatever it may be worth, may refer to the services mentioned in the second item of the claim in question.

In his fiduciary capacity, the administrator represented all of the parties in interest in that litigation, and as between themselves, Mr. Chambers, Mr. Fay and appellant each represented a one-third interest, which he was to receive on final settlement of the administrator and distribution of the estate, and no circumstance has been mentioned, either in the evidence or argument, which, in justice and fair dealing, should impose the liability on appellant, either personally or as trustee, to pay the entire fee of appellees, for services rendered by them on the second trial.

The rule has been thoroughly established, in a long line of unbroken decisions, that where there is evidence in the record, fairly tending to sustain the verdict of the jury on every material point in the case, this court will not, on the weight of the evidence, disturb the judgment of the trial court rendered thereon, but when the evidence is wholly insufficient in any essential particular, as it is in the respect hereinbefore set out in this case, to support such verdict, the judgment will be reversed. *Louisville, etc., R. R. Co.* v. *Eves,* 1 Ind. App. 224; *Nichols* v. *Pressler,* 3 Ind. App. 324.

Several other questions are presented and discussed, which, in some instances at least, do not constitute substantial error, and if others were construed as reversible error, the decisions thereof are unnecessary in view of the conclusion we have reached in the case.

Since this case was submitted, William R. Miles has departed this life, and Mary W. Miles, as administratrix, has been substituted as appellant.

Our conclusion is that while there is some evidence tending to sustain the second item of $1,000 mentioned in the complaint and bill of particulars, there is no evidence in the record, for the reasons stated, to support the first item, and, therefore, the judgment of the court below is reversed, as of the term when submitted, at costs of appellees, with instructions to sustain appellant's motion for a new trial.

Filed May 11, 1893; petition for a rehearing overruled Nov. 23, 1893.

No. 674.

SMITH *v.* DOWNEY ET AL.

GARNISHMENT.—*Certificate of Stock of Foreign Corporation.—Nonresident Defendant.—Not Subject to.—Replevin.—Answer of Res Adjudicata, Sufficiency of.*—Suit was brought in this State against a nonresident, notice being given such defendant by publication. Proceedings in attachment and garnishment were instituted, which resulted in the garnishment of a certificate of stock of a foreign corporation, belonging to defendant, and held in trust for him, the only appearance, answer, or defense to such garnishment proceeding being an answer by the garnishee defendant, admitting that he held the certificate of stock as the property of the defendant. The defendant in the principal action was defaulted, and judgment being rendered against him, the certificate of stock was ordered to be sold. The defendant instituted an action in replevin against above plaintiff for recovery of possession of the certificate of stock. The defendant answered, setting up the above facts as a plea of *res adjudicata* in defense to the action.

Held, that the answer was insufficient on demurrer, it appearing that the principal defendant (plaintiff here) in the garnishment proceedings was a nonresident, and that the certificate of stock was issued by a foreign corporation, and, hence, not subject to garnishment in this State.

From the Marion Circuit Court.

A. C. Harris and *L. A. Cox,* for appellant.

S. M. Shepard, A. C. Ayres and *A. Q. Jones,* for appellees.

DAVIS, J.—In the court below, in an action of replevin, appellees recovered judgment against appellant for the possession of "a certain certificate of stock issued by the Snow-Storm Mining and Milling Co., of Durango, Colo., an incorporated company existing in and created under the laws of the State of Colorado, and doing business therein, the said certificate consisting of 110,000 shares of said stock."

The principal question presented for our consideration

on this appeal arises on the ruling of the court below in sustaining a demurrer to appellant's answer.

The material facts alleged in the answer are, that appellant, in 1887, instituted an action in the Marion Superior Court, against James E. Downey, to recover damages for breach of covenants in a deed of warranty for conveyance of real estate; that said Downey was a non-resident of the State, and due notice was given him of the pendency of the action by publication as required by statute; that an affidavit in attachment against Downey, and an affidavit in garnishment against Theodore P. Haughey, a citizen of Marion county, Indiana, were duly filed, alleging that Haughey had in his possession, and under his agency and control, property credits and effects of said James E. Downey which could not be reached by a writ of execution, and that proper writs of attachment and garnishment were issued, and said Haughey was duly served as such garnishee defendant, and that said corporation was also duly served with a writ of garnishment issued on proper affidavit, charging that said company held property rights and credits of said James E. Downey which could not be reached by execution; that said Haughey afterwards appeared and filed his answer in said cause, admitting that he had in his possession, at the time of said service, the said property of said Downey, hereinbefore described.

It is also alleged in said answer, that said corporation had its office and place of business, and its books and papers, in Indianapolis, in said county, and that its officers and directors were citizens of, and resided in, said county of Marion; that on failure of said James E. Downey and said company to answer, they were each duly called in open court, and made default, and that the cause, being at issue as to Haughey, was submitted to the court for trial, on the 5th day of June, 1888, on said answer of Haughey, and the default of the other defendants, and resulted in judgment in favor of appellant against James E. Downey for $5,950, also sustaining the attachment proceedings and ordering the sale of the shares of stock evidenced by said certificate.

It is also averred in said answer, in general terms, that said James E. Downey "at one time, by counsel, appeared in said suit," but when, how, or for what purpose he so appeared is not stated, and, also, it is in like manner alleged that appellees were represented in said suit by counsel, who defended said suit as to the attachment and garnishment proceedings for the purpose of protecting said certificates and stock from being held by said attachment proceedings as the property of James E. Downey, but when, how or through what issue such defense was made or attempted, is not stated.

The answer of Haughey was an admission that he held the certificates of stock now in controversy as the property of James E. Downey, and the other defendants made default.

It is earnestly insisted, by counsel for appellant, that this answer is good as a plea of *res adjudicata*.

In the first place, notwithstanding the unsatisfactory character of the averments in relation to the connection of appellees with the former suit, and the apparent inconsistencies between such averments, and the other facts which appear in the answer, it might be conceded, if it appeared that any answer had been filed or defense made by or in the name of James E. Downey, that appellees would be bound by the result as fully as said Downey might be. *Roby* v. *Eggers*, 130 Ind. 415.

Yet the difficulty remains, so far as shown in the answer, that no defense was made or attempted by or in the name of Downey or any other defendant to the action.

The doctrine of *res judicata*, as to persons who are not parties to the record, can only arise by virtue of some issue joined or contest made in the name of another, and it logically follows that when there is no such issue joined there can be no former adjudication. For the same reason the answer can not be sustained on the theory that it shows there is a prior action pending between the same parties. The appellees can not be regarded, under the facts stated therein, as attachment defendants under section 1266, R. S. 1881.

If appellees had been joined as defendants in the former action, or if they had appeared therein by counsel to sustain or contest any issue joined between the parties, a different question would be presented. The facts disclosed in the answer, however, clearly show there was no such issue tendered or contest made.

The statement that James E. Downing "also, at one time, by counsel appeared in said suit," should not be construed as an averment that he appeared to the attachment and garnishment proceedings, but if such construction was given, it could not, in any event, be so extended as to hold that an answer had been filed or issue joined by him as to the attachment proceedings. For aught that is shown, he may have appeared on the occasion referred to for the purpose of ascertaining the amount of the claim or in order to be heard, notwithstanding the default, on the question of the measure of damages.

The general allegations that appellees "in said suit were represented by counsel," and that such counsel "defended said suit as to the attachment and garnishment proceedings for and on behalf of the plaintiffs (appellees) in this action, and with their knowledge and by their authority, for the purpose of protecting the said certificate and stock from being held by said attachment

proceedings, as the property of said James E. Downey,''
and ''because their interests were represented, and the
litigation controlled, by them for the purpose aforesaid,''
can not overcome the affirmative showing that no issue
was joined as to the attachment proceedings, and that no
answer was filed therein (except the admission of
Haughey, as garnishee defendant, that he held the certificate of stock for, and as the property of, James E.
Downey), and that there was no defense or contest in the
case, and that there was no appearance to attachment
and garnishment proceedings, except by Haughey, and
that judgment was rendered, as to other defendants, by
default. ,

If issue had been joined or defense made, either by or
in the name of Downey, the question would arise whether
such appearance, defense, and judgment would constitute
a former adjudication, in the event it should be determined that the court had no jurisdiction over the thing
in controversy. Brown on Jurisdiction, section 10.

The vital question is, can the stock of a nonresident,
in a foreign corporation created and existing by virtue
of the laws of another State, be garnisheed in an action
in a court in this State, when the certificate of stock is
held here in trust?

On investigation we find that the great weight of authority is against the proposition.

Mr. Cook, in his excellent work, says: ''Shares of
stock in a corporation are personal property, whose location is in the State where the corporation is created. It
is true that, for the purpose of taxation and some other
similar purposes, stock follows the domicile of its owner;
but considered as property separated from its owner,
stock is in existence only in the State of the corporation.
All attachment statutes provide for the attachment of a
nonresident debtor's property in the State, and gener-

ally, under such statutes, the stock owned by a nonresident in a corporation created by the State wherein the suit is brought may be attached and jurisdiction be thereby acquired to the extent of the value of the stock attached. But under no circumstances can an attachment be levied on a defendant's shares of stock in an action commenced outside of the State wherein the corporation is incorporated. For purposes of attachment, stock is located where the corporation is incorporated and nowhere else. The shares owned by a nonresident defendant in the stock of a foreign corporation can not be reached and levied upon by virtue of an attachment, although officers of the corporation are within the State engaged in carrying on the corporate business. Nor can such an attachment be levied, although the foreign corporation has a branch registry office in the State where the attachment is levied, and although the certificates of stock are also in such State. Certificates of stock are not the stock itself—they are but evidence of the stock; and the stock itself can not be attached by a levy of the attachment on the certificate. As was well said by the Supreme Court of Pennsylvania, stock can not be attached by attaching the certificate, any more than lands situated in another State can be attached by an attachment in Pennsylvania levied on title deeds to such land.'' Section 485, 2d ed., Cook's Stock, Stockholders and Corporation Law. See, also, *Plimpton* v. *Bigelow*, 93 N. Y. 592; *Christmas* v. *Biddle*, 13 Pa. St. 223, *Winslow* v. *Fletcher*, 13 Am. and Eng. Corp. Cas. 39; *Armour Bros. Banking Co.* v. *Smith*, 20 S. W. Rep. 690; section 607a, Freeman on Judgments; section 474, Drake on Attachment; section 245, Waples on Attachment.

It is not necessary in this case to enter upon the discussion of the question as to the power of the Legislature to authorize the seizure and sale under judicial process of certificates of stock in foreign corporations that maintain agents and officers, keep the books, aud conduct business in this State.

Sections 913, 1285, 3022, 3023, and 5501, R. S. 1881, do not, in any respect, authorize such proceeding. Section 3023, *supra*, which provides that agents of foreign corporations, before entering upon the duties of their agency in the State, shall deposit in the clerk's office of the county the power of attorney or authority under or by virtue of which they act as agents, authorizes actions against such corporations in the courts of this State on claims or demands "arising out of any transaction in this State with such agents."

This controversy did not arise out of any transaction with any agent of the corporation.

In Missouri the statute provides that shares of stock in any corporation may be attached in the same manner as the same may be levied upon under execution, but it was held that such provisions applied to domestic corporations alone. *Armour, etc.*, v. *Smith, supra.*

Section 723, R. S. 1881, authorizes the levy of an execution on shares of stock, and section 931, provides the manner in which shares of stock in a corporation may be reached through process against the corporation as a garnishee defendant. Such authority, however, under the authorities cited, does not extend to shares of stock in a foreign corporation, although such corporation may have a branch of its principal office in this State where its books and records are kept, the meetings of its directors held, and its principal business transacted. *Plimpton* v. *Bigelow, supra.*

In the case of *Young* v. *South, etc.*, 85 Tenn. 189, the principles enunciated in the authorities cited are recognized as correct statements of the law, but it was held that under the policy and legislation in that State, and

---

Smith *v.* Downey *et al.*

---

the acts of the corporation in question, the situs and status of said corporation was that of a domestic corporation.

In conclusion, we repeat that James E. Downey was a nonresident of the State. The only process against him was by publication. No answer was filed or defense made by him or in his name. The shares of stock which it was sought to attach were issued by a foreign corporation. In the language of Judge ANDREWS: "It seems impossible to regard the stock of a corporation as being present for the purpose of judicial proceedings, except at one of two places, viz.: the place of residence of the owner, or the place of residence of the corporation." *Plimpton* v. *Bigelow, supra.*

Therefore, in view of our opinion that appellees, under the facts disclosed in the answer, stand in the position of strangers to the proceedings in the former action and that the stock in a foreign corporation, under the authorities, is not subject to attachment in this State, it is not necessary to further consider the other questions of minor importance presented by the record.

Judgment affirmed.

Filed Sept. 19, 1893.

ON PETITION FOR A REHEARING.

DAVIS, J.—The learned counsel for appellant have filed an able and earnest petition for a rehearing in this case. We concur in much that has been urged upon our consideration by counsel, but the great difficulty in this case is that on the facts shown in the answer, and to which we have called special attention in the original opinion, there was no issue joined or defense made to the attachment proceedings either by or in the name of James E. Downey.

The averments, "And defendant further shows that

although the plaintiffs herein, Mrs. Downey and Mrs. Brouse, were not parties of record to said suit and proceeding, yet they, in said suit, were represented by counsel, which counsel in said action in said superior court, defended said suit as to the attachment and garnishment proceedings for and on behalf of the plaintiffs in this action, and with their knowledge and by their authority, for the purpose of protecting the said certificate of stock from being held by said attachment proceeding as the property of said James E. Downey. And, by such action, sought to defeat the garnishment and suit in order to prevent the same (said stock) being taken under said attachment, and to keep and hold the said certificate and stock from under said garnishment proceedings."

And further, "Their interests were represented and the litigation was controlled by them for the purpose aforesaid, and to, and did, contest said claim of plaintiff in said case," must be considered and construed in the light of the facts disclosed in said answer in substance and to the effect that no answer was filed or defense made by or in behalf of said James E. Downey, defendant of record therein, but that judgment was rendered as to said attachment proceedings, on default.

Notwithstanding the fact that appellees herein were not parties to said attachment proceedings, yet if they had defended that suit in the name of another to protect their rights, they would have been as much bound by the result of that suit as they would be if they were parties of record. *Roby* v. *Eggers, supra.*

But the trouble is, as before stated, that no such issue was joined or defense made by or in the name of any person who was a defendant therein.

The rule, as we understand it, as to persons who are not parties of record, is correctly stated by Judge VAN-FLEET, as follows: "On the contrary the doctrine of *res judicata* can not arise except by virtue of some issue joined and actually contested on the trial." Vanfleet's Collateral Attack, section 17.

It is clear, from the allegations contained in the answer, that no such issue was joined and actually contested on the trial of the attachment proceedings.

The infirmity in the answer is not the result of any oversight or lack of skill on the part of the pleader. It is apparent, from the facts stated, that no amendment or revision of the answer could have brought it within the rule enunciated in *Roby* v. *Eggers, supra*.

Whether, if they had been parties to the attachment proceedings, the rule stated in *Markel* v. *Evans*, 47 Ind. 326 (330), would have applied, it is not necessary to decide; but no reason occurs to the writer, at this time, why it could not have been invoked against appellees in this case, under such circumstances.

The petition for rehearing is accordingly overruled.

Filed Nov. 24, 1893.

No. 975.

CHICAGO AND SOUTHEASTERN RAILWAY COMPANY *v.* ROSS.

PLEADING.—*Complaint, Sufficiency of.—Railroad.—Action for Constructing Fence Along Right of Way.—Notice.—Exhibit.*—When an action is brought against a railroad company for labor performed and material furnished in constructing a fence along the company's right of way, by the adjacent land-owner, a copy of the written notice to the company need not be set out in the complaint, it not being the foundation of the action.

From the Boone Circuit Court.

W. R. Crawford and *J. A. Abbott*, for appellant.

C. M. Zion, for appellee.

LOTZ, J.—The appellee commenced this action against the appellant, to recover for the value of work and materials furnished in the construction of a fence along the line of appellant's right of way and appellee's improved lands.

The work was done and the materials furnished under the provisions of sections 1077 and 1078, Elliott's Supp. The court below overruled a demurrer to the complaint. This ruling is the only error assigned in this court.

It is insisted that the complaint is defective because it does not set out a copy of the thirty days' notice which section 1078, *supra*, requires the land-owner to serve upon railway company's agent. The complaint avers that such notice was given.

Section 362, R. S. 1881, provides that when any pleading is founded on any written instrument or an account the original or copy thereof must be filed with the pleading. A bill of particulars of the costs of the fence was filed with the complaint. We do not regard the thirty days notice which the land-owner is required to serve upon the company, as the foundation of the cause of action. The purpose of the notice is to apprise the company of the land-owner's intention and to give him the right to enter upon the right of way and construct the fence if the same be not done by the company. The work and labor done and materials furnished, which have enured to the benefit of the company, is the foundation of the cause of action. When a written instrument is not the basis of the cause of action or defense, but is only referred to as one among other facts material to the pleading, a copy or exhibit need not be filed with, or made a part of, the pleading. *Hight* v. *Taylor*, 97 Ind. 392; *Black* v. *Richards*, 95 Ind. 184.

Judgment affirmed, at costs of appellant.

Filed Nov. 22, 1893.

No. 970.

McCLOSKEY, ADMINISTRATOR, *v.* DAVIS, ADMINISTRATRIX.

ADMISSIONS.—*When Sufficient to Shift Burden of Proof.*—*Open and Close.*—*Promissory Note.*—*Attorney's Fees.*—*Chattel Mortgage.*—*Decedent's Estate.*—Where an administrator, in an action on a contested claim, for the purpose of obtaining the opening and close of the evidence and argument in the case, after the jury had been impanneled and before the claimant had introduced any evidence, admitmitted the execution of the notes (they being secured by chattel mortgage) forming the basis of the claim, and also admitted the reasonableness of attorney's fees as set forth in the claim, such admissions are not sufficient to entitle the estate to the open and close in the case, for the reason that the admissions do not shift the burden of proof so that the claimant might have complete recovery and relief on his claim, without the necessity of introducing evidence, the claimant being entitled to make proof of attorney's fees, above the amount stated in the claim, and, also, to make proof of the chattel mortgage, the admissions not being broad enough to satisfy the issues in these respects.

EVIDENCE.—*Objections, How Made.*—All objections to the introduction of evidence, to be available on appeal, must be specific.

Concurring opinions by DAVIS, J., and GAVIN, J.

From the Montgomery Circuit Court.

G. D. Hurley and *M. E. Clodfelter,* for appellant.

W. T. Brush and *E. C. Snyder,* for appellee.

Ross, J.—The appellee, Amanda Davis, as administratrix of the estate of James Davis, deceased, filed two notes, secured by chattel mortgage, as claims against the estate of Albert Allen, deceased, of which estate the appellant was acting as the administrator. The claims were not allowed by the administrator, and, at the proper time, were transferred to the issue docket for trial. The appellee recovered judgment in the court below in the sum of twelve hundred and fifteen dollars.

The appellant has assigned, on this appeal, the following reasons for the reversal of said judgment, viz.:

"1st. The court erred in overruling appellant's motion for a new trial.

"2d. The court erred in overruling appellant's motion for leave to assume the burden of the issue and open and close the evidence and argument in the cause."

The second error is not well assigned in this court. If the court below committed an error in its ruling on appellant's application for the open and close, that was cause for a new trial.

The first cause assigned in the motion for a new trial is that the court erred in overruling the appellant's motion for leave to assume the burden of the issues and open and close the evidence and argument in the case. The record discloses that after the jury had been impanneled, and before the appellee had introduced any evidence, the appellant made the following admission, viz.: "The defendant, for the purpose of obtaining the opening and close of the evidence and argument in this case, admits the execution of the notes sued on, and also admits that $52.20 is a reasonable attorney fee on the first note; $34.35, the amount claimed, is a reasonable attorney fee on the second note, as set forth in the claim. Upon these admissions, we ask the opening and close of the evidence and argument."

The court overruled the request for the open and close, and the appellant excepted.

The appellant insists, that upon making the above admission, he was entitled to the open and close of the evidence and argument; that by the admission the appellee's case in chief was made out and the burden shifted to appellant. On the other hand, the appellee insists that the right to the open and close is determined from the pleadings alone; that while the appellant had the right under the statute (Elliott's Supp., section 391) to make any defense, except set-off or counterclaim, without a plea, yet he had the right to file an answer if he so desired. We think it can not be controverted, that under the above section of the statute, it is not necessary for the administrator of an estate to plead specially any defense except a set-off or counterclaim. *Castetter, Admr.,* v. *State, ex rel.,* 112 Ind. 445.

When a general denial is pleaded, all defenses may be proven under the issues thus formed, except a set-off or counterclaim. *Griffin, Admr.,* v. *Hodshire,* 119 Ind. 235.

It remains, therefore, to be determined, first, whether or not it is necessary for an administrator to file an answer of general denial; and, second, whether, having filed no answer at all, he can, on the trial, waive proof of the claim and thus shift the burden of the issue.

Section 391, *supra,* provides that it shall not be necessary for the administrator to plead any matter by way of defense. The fair interpretation of this language is that the law puts in a general denial for him, under which he may make all defenses except set-off and counterclaim.

It further provides that "If the executor or administrator plead any other matter by way of defense, the claimant shall reply thereto."

The effect of this part of the section is to permit the executor or administrator to admit, if they should see fit, the execution of the instrument which is the basis of the claim, and yet plead specially in avoidance. If an administrator undertakes to answer the defenses which are admissible under the general denial, pleading matter in avoidance only, he thereby affirmatively waives the right to make the defenses under the general denial which the law otherwise puts in for him; and he is confined to the defenses so pleaded.

The law does not contemplate that the same issue shall

be formed by more than one answer, hence it would be folly to say that the sustaining of a demurrer to a pleading setting up a defense of which the party has the benefit under the general denial, would be error. In fact, it has been repeatedly held that it is not error to sustain a demurrer to a paragraph of answer setting up a defense which is available under the general denial, also pleaded. *Wabash R. R. Co.* v. *Williamson*, 3 Ind. App. 190; *Sluyter* v. *Union Central Life Ins. Co.*, 3 Ind. App. 312; *Wickwire* v. *Town of Angola*, 4 Ind. App. 253; *Kidwell* v. *Kidwell*, 84 Ind. 224; *Epperson* v. *Hostetter, Admr.*, 95 Ind. 583; *Mason* v. *Mason*, 102 Ind. 38; *Ralston* v. *Moore*, 105 Ind. 243; *Landwerlen* v. *Wheeler, Trustee*, 106 Ind. 523; *Rush* v. *Thompson*, 112 Ind. 158; *Cincinnati, etc., R. W. Co.* v. *Smith*, 127 Ind. 461; *Messick* v. *Midland R. W. Co.*, 128 Ind. 81; *Baltes* v. *Bass Foundry, etc.*, 129 Ind. 185; *Pattison* v. *Babcock*, 130 Ind. 474; *Butler* v. *Thornburg*, 131 Ind. 237; *Palmerton* v. *Hoop*, 131 Ind. 23.

True, in a certain class of cases, namely, in actions to quiet title and in ejectment, all defenses are admissible under the general denial. *Brown* v. *Fodder*, 81 Ind. 491; *West* v. *West*, 89 Ind. 529; *Eve* v. *Louis*, 91 Ind. 457; *East* v. *Peden*, 108 Ind. 92; section 1055, R. S. 1881.

The defendant, in addition to an answer of general denial, may plead his defenses specially. *Over* v. *Shannon*, 75 Ind. 352; *Eve* v. *Louis, supra*.

But it is not error to sustain a demurrer to such special answers, even if they state a good defense, because they are useless, the party having advantage of the same defenses under the general denial. *West* v. *West, supra; Ratliff* v. *Stretch*, 117 Ind. 526.

The rule is different, however, when no general denial

is filed, in which event the sustaining of a demurrer to an answer stating a good defense would be error.

The law puts in the general denial for an estate when a claim is transferred to the issue docket for trial, under which the administrator or executor may prove all defenses except set-off and counterclaim. But they are not precluded from waiving the benefit of the denial so put in by the law and filing special answers in confession and avoidance only. By setting up affirmatively the defenses which are admissible under the general denial, without pleading the general denial, they waive the benefit of the answer which otherwise the law assumes to put in for them.

The right to the open and close is usually determined from the issues formed by the pleadings. When the answers filed all allege affirmative matter, and admit so much of the complaint as relieves the plaintiff from making any proof to entitle him to recover, the burden shifts to the defendant, and he has the open and close, unless the plaintiff, by reply, admits the defense pleaded and avoids it by affirmative matter, when the burden would again shift to the plaintiff to prove the matter in avoidance set up in the reply. *French* v. *Howard*, 10 Ind. 339.

The party upon whom rests the burden of the issue, is entitled to the open and close. R. S. 1881, section 533; *Donahoe* v. *Rich*, 2 Ind. App. 540; *Starnes* v. *Schofield*, 5 Ind. App. 4; *Kimble, Assignee,* v. *Adair*, 2 Blackf. 320; *Downey* v. *Day*, 4 Ind. 531; *Moore* v. *Allen*, 5 Ind. 521; *Shank* v. *Fleming*, 9 Ind. 189; *McLees* v. *Felt*, 11 Ind. 218; *Judah* v. *Trustees of Vincennes University*, 23 Ind. 272; *Goodrich* v. *Friedersdorff*, 27 Ind. 308; *Fetters* v. *Muncie Nat'l Bank,* 34 Ind. 251; *Hamlyn* v. *Nesbit, Admr.*, 37 Ind. 284; *Camp* v. *Brown*, 48 Ind. 575; *Indiana State Board of Agriculture* v. *Gray*, 54 Ind. 91; *Heilman* v.

Shanklin, 60 Ind. 424; *Hyatt* v. *Clements*, 65 Ind. 12; *Bannister* v. *Jett*, 83 Ind. 129; *Reynolds* v. *Baldwin*, 93 Ind. 57;. *Rahm* v. *Deig*, 121 Ind. 283.

If the appellant had filed an answer in avoidance only, the appellee would not have been required to adduce any evidence to entitle him to recover, and the issue would have shifted, and the burden rested upon the appellant. Not having filed any answer, but resting upon the issues formed by the answer of general denial which the law put in for him, could he afterwards waive the issues thus formed and admit the truth of appellee's complaint and take upon himself the burden of the issue? We can see no reason why he may not do so. When he admits either by his pleadings, or admissions, made before the introduction of evidence by the appellee, that the material allegations of the complaint are true, thus obviating the making of any proof to sustain the complaint, he takes upon himself the burden of the issue, and is entitled to the open and close. *City of Aurora* v. *Cobb*, 21 Ind. 492.

The admission, however, must be sufficient to obviate the introduction of any evidence whatever by the plaintiff. *Starnes* v. *Schofield*, *supra*.

Was the admission by the appellant sufficient? The appellant admitted the execution of the notes sued on, which was sufficient to entitle the appellee to recover the principal and interest due thereon. The notes, however, provided for reasonable attorney's fees, which the claim or complaint stated as $52.20 on the one note and $34.35 on the other, which amounts were admitted to be reasonable.

In the late case of *Lindley* v. *Sullivan*, 133 Ind 588, 32 N. E. Rep. 738, which was an action brought by the appellants against the appellees upon a promissory note, providing for attorney's fees, there was an allegation in the complaint that the appellees were indebted to the appellants in a certain sum for principal, interest and attorney's fees, the amount demanded exceeding the principal and interest by $53.

To the complaint an answer in two paragraphs was filed, each of which set up special matter in defense. The issues were closed by a reply of general denial. When the case was called for trial the appellants demanded the open and close, but this demand was overruled.

The Supreme Court says: "While good pleading requires that, in an action upon a note providing for attorney's fees, the value of the services should be stated, evidence may be admitted without such averment, and a recovery had for such fee, provided the whole recovery does not exceed the amount for which judgment is demanded in the complaint, the evidence being admissible under the general claim for damages."

The attorney fees to be allowed in the collection of a note in which they are provided for, but not defined, depends upon the services rendered, hence the demand for attorney's fees which would be reasonable, made on filing a claim of a note against an estate, would not be sufficient in the event the claim was not allowed and its collection litigated. The attorney's fees demanded, in a claim of that character, filed against an estate, must be simply for the amount due for services for collecting without litigation.

The statute (section 385, Elliott's Supp.) requires the claim to be verified as to its correctness, and that it is due and wholly unpaid. The statement of the amount due on a note at the time it is filed as a claim against an estate, does not necessarily preclude the party on the trial from proving and recovering the amount actually due, although it exceeds the amount specified in the statement as due. It follows, therefore, that on the trial of the cause, an admission of the correctness of the amount of attorney's fees at the time the claim was filed is not sufficient to preclude the claimant from making proof of attorney's fees. *Camp* v. *Brown, supra.*

The appellee was entitled to make proof of the amount of attorney's fees which he should recover in the case, and until the appellant made an admission sufficiently broad to cover such attorney's fees the appellee had a right to make proof thereof.

If the appellant was satisfied with the admission as to the amount of attorney's fees, no additional proof was necessary. That he was not satisfied with the admission, but sought a larger amount, is shown by the fact that he made proof of the value thereof. In another particular was the admission insufficient, in this that the admission was not broad enough to relieve the appellee from introducing in evidence the chattel mortgages given to secure said notes. Section 385, *supra*, specially provides that if a claim filed against an estate is secured by a lien on real or personal property, such lien shall be particularly set forth in such statement and a reference given to where the lien, if of record, will be found. It was also necessary to make proof thereof.

The appellant was not entitled to the open and close under the issues formed by the pleadings, and we think the admissions made were not sufficient to give him that right.

Objections are urged to the ruling of the court in the admission of evidence offered by the appellee in rebuttal.

In this we find no error. The evidence complained of, which consists of a single question and answer, was not prejudicial to the appellant. Again, the objections, made at the time, were not sufficiently definite and specific. To object to the introduction of evidence because irrelevant, incompetent, and immaterial presents no question for review on appeal, unless the evidence on its face appears to be incompetent. *Ohio, etc., R. W. Co.* v. *Wrape,* 4 Ind. App. 108; *Noftsger* v. *Smith,* 6 Ind. App. 54, 32 N. E. Rep. 1024; *Forbing* v. *Weber,* 99 Ind. 588; *Heap* v. *Parrish,* 104 Ind. 36; *Chapman* v. *Moore,* 107 Ind. 223; *McCullough* v. *Davis,* 108 Ind. 292; *McKinsey* v. *McKee,* 109 Ind. 209; *Ohio, etc., R. W. Co.* v. *Walker,* 113 Ind. 196; *Metzger* v. *Franklin Bank,* 119 Ind. 359; *Litten, Admr.,* v. *Wright School Tp.,* 127 Ind. 81; *Swaim* v. *Swaim,* 134 Ind. 596, 33 N. E. Rep. 792.

All objections to the introduction of evidence, to be available on appeal, must be specific. The objections made to the introduction of the evidence complained of were too general.

For the same reason, there was no error in overruling the motion to strike out the evidence of the same party. When a general objection is made to evidence, any part of which is proper, it is not error to overrule the objection. *Pape* v. *Wright,* 116 Ind. 502; *Jones* v. *State,* 118 Ind. 39; *McGuffey* v. *McClain,* 130 Ind. 327.

The reason assigned for a new trial, relative to the admission of the evidence of the witness Paul, is too general under the authority of *Harvey* v. *Huston,* 94 Ind. 527.

The instructions, taken altogether, stated the law correctly. With the instructions, given at the request of the appellant, before them, the jury could not be misled as to the law of the case.

The cause seems to have been tried upon its merits, and that being the case, the judgment will not be reversed, except the appellant show material error which was prejudicial to his rights.

The judgment of the court below is in all things affirmed.

Filed Nov. 1, 1893.

CONCURRING OPINION.

DAVIS, J.—I am not able to agree with all the reasoning in the opinion of the majority of the court. The burden of the proof, as determined by the issues, should, in my opinion, govern the right to the open and close, and the burden can not be shifted by an admission made after the trial has begun. So far, however, as the offer is concerned, if it was otherwise sufficient, I am of the opinion that when the amount of the attorneys' fees claimed is specifically stated in the complaint, an admission that the same is correct is all that is required.

GAVIN, C. J., concurs in the result in this case and in the statement of law in the opinion of DAVIS, J.

Filed Nov. 1, 1893.

◆

No. 1,026.

THE LAKE ERIE AND WESTERN RAILROAD COMPANY *v.* YARD.

APPEAL.—*Appellate Court.—Jurisdiction.—Money Demand.—Originating Before a Mayor.*—An appeal can not be taken from a judgment of a circuit court on a money demand not exceeding $50, exclusive of interest and costs, where the action originated before a mayor of a city.

From the Miami Circuit Court.

R. P. Effinger, W. E. Hackedorn, L. Walker and *W. B. McClintic,* for appellant.

C. A. Parsons, W. E. Antrim and *J. N. Tillett,* for appellee.

REINHARD, J.—The question of jurisdiction confronts us at the threshold of this case. The action originated before the mayor of the city of Peru, and was one in which damages were claimed for the killing of the appellee's cow of the value of $50. The appellee recovered $50 before the mayor. An appeal was taken by the railroad company to the circuit court, where the appellee again recovered the amount of $50.

From this judgment the present appeal is attempted to be prosecuted.

Section 632, R. S. 1881, authorizes an appeal from such judgment as the one under consideration only in cases where the amount in controversy, exclusive of interest and costs, exceeds fifty dollars. *State, for Use,* v. *Wills,* 4 Ind. App. 38; *Cincinnati, etc., R. W. Co.* v. *McDade,* 111 Ind. 23.

The amount in controversy in the present case, exclusive of interest and costs, does not exceed fifty dollars, and as the case was commenced before the mayor of a city, no appeal will lie from the judgment of the circuit court. The appellee's motion to dismiss the appeal must, therefore, be sustained.

Appeal dismissed, at appellant's cost.

Filed Nov. 23, 1893.

———————◆———————

No. 861.

REHMAN *v.* THE NEW ALBANY BELT AND TERMINAL RAILROAD COMPANY ET AL.

PLEA IN ABATEMENT.—*Assessment of Damages.*—*Instituting Another Suit Pending Writ of Assessment.*—*Making Additional Defendants.*—*Railroad.*—During the pendency of a proceeding under a writ of assessment of damages for land appropriated by a railroad company, and for consequential damages, the plaintiff can not, over a plea in abatement, setting forth the pendency of the writ for assessment of damages, prosecute another action involving the same subject matter, and affecting the same party defendant; and the fact that in

Rehman *v.* The New Albany Belt and Terminal Railroad Co. *et al.*

the subsequent action plaintiff makes another party a co-defendant, can avail nothing as against the plea in abatement of the common defendant to both actions, setting up the pendency of the former suit; and the plea in abatement of the co-defendant joined in the subsequent action, setting up the same facts, can not prevail against a demurrer.

ASSESSMENT OF DAMAGES.—*Presumption.*—*Plea in Abatement.*—Whatever damages, present and prospective, that might properly have been assessed in a proceeding under a writ of assessment of damages, will be presumed to have been assessed, and such assessment, unless appealed from, is a final adjudication for such injuries, and the land-owner can not seek any other remedy against the same party or parties defendant, while such proceeding is pending.

From the Floyd Circuit Court.

C. L. Jewett and *H. E. Jewett,* for appellant.

A. Dowling, for appellees.

Ross, J.—The appellant, by her complaint, seeks to recover damages from the appellees, for injury to her property and business, alleged to have resulted from the building, maintaining, and operating of an elevated railroad along and upon Upper Water street in the city of New Albany. To the complaint, the appellees filed separate pleas in abatement, in which it was alleged that another action against the appellee The New Albany Belt and Terminal Railroad Co. was begun by the appellant prior to the bringing of this action, alleging the same cause of action here declared on, which action was still pending, and for which reason they asked that this action abate. Demurrers to these pleas were filed and overruled, and the appellant replied by a general denial. Upon the issue formed on the pleas in abatement, the cause was submitted to the court for trial, and after hearing the evidence, the court, at the request of the parties, made a special finding of the facts, with conclusions of law thereon. Judgment was rendered on the facts found, in favor of the appellees, abating the action, and the appellant, from that judgment, prosecutes this appeal.

The appellant has assigned, in this court, three errors, the first and second of which call in question the ruling of the court on the demurrers to the pleas in abatement.

A plea in abatement, based upon the pendency of another action, in order to be sufficient as such, must show not only that such other action is for the same cause of action, but also that it is between the same parties. *De Armond* v. *Bohn*, 12 Ind. 607; *Loyd* v. *Reynolds*, 29 Ind. 299; *Dawson* v. *Vaughan*, 42 Ind. 395; *Merritt* v. *Richey*, 100 Ind. 416; *Bryan* v. *Scholl*, 109 Ind. 367.

By the statement, "between the same parties," is not meant that both actions shall be brought by the same plaintiffs against the same defendants only. If the same plaintiffs bring two actions, at different times, upon the same cause of action, the first one instituted being against a single defendant, and the second being against the defendant in the prior action, and also against another joined as a defendant, the action will, so far as the defendant who is a party defendant to both actions, be between the same parties, and the second action as to him, by reason of the pendency of the prior action, may be abated. *Atkinson* v. *State Bank, Assignee, etc.*, 5 Blackf. 84.

We think the answer in abatement of the appellee The New Albany Belt and Terminal Railroad Co. is good, and there was no error in overruling the demurrer thereto. The answer in abatement of the Kentucky and Indiana Bridge Co. is not good, and the court erred in overruling the demurrer to it.

This answer, while it is exactly the same as the one filed by the New Albany Belt and Terminal Railroad Co., and as to that company stated facts sufficient, does not state facts sufficient to abate this action as to said Kentucky and Indiana Bridge Co., for the reason that the facts alleged that no prior action is pending against it for the same cause of action. There is nothing in its plea to show that any such relation exists between it and its codefendant that an adjudication in the former action, either for or against said New Albany Belt and Terminal Railroad Co., would be an adjudication of its liability in this action. The appellant may have a cause of action, and recover against the appellee The New Albany Belt and Terminal Railroad Co. in the previous action, and yet, while such recovery would be a bar to a recovery against it, in this action, that judgment does not necessarily bar a recovery against said Kentucky and Indiana Bridge Co. in this action.

The facts found by the court are as follows:

First. That on the 17th day of November, 1890, the plaintiff, Margaret Rehman, filed her complaint and application for writ of assessment of damages, in the Floyd Circuit Court, in and for the county of Floyd and State of Indiana, claiming and alleging in such complaint and application that she was the owner in fee-simple of real estate in the city of New Albany, Floyd county, Indiana, described as follows: Beginning at the southeast corner of lot number sixteen (16), on Upper Water street, running thence westwardly along the front line of lots sixteen (16) and fifteen (15), one hundred and twenty (120) feet, and extending southwardly between parallel lines of the same width of one hundred and twenty (120) feet, to the bank of the Ohio river at low water mark.

Alleging that the defendant was a railroad corporation engaged in the construction of a steam railroad through a part of the city of New Albany, the line of which is surveyed, laid out and projected, passed over and along the plaintiff's real estate aforesaid.

Alleging that on the first day of August, 1890, and on divers other days between that day and the time of filing such application, the said railroad company entered upon, fixed, located, and established its line of steam railroad over and upon the real estate of the plaintiff above described, and appropriated to its own use a strip of said real estate fifty (50) feet wide, extending from the east line thereof to the west line thereof, thereby rendering the remainder of said real estate useless and of no value to said plaintiff.

Alleging that the defendant ever since maintained its line of railroad on said real estate, and that it appropriated the same, and wholly excluded the plaintiff from all benefit and use thereof, and that the said strip of land was appropriated by the defendant by virtue of the provisions of section 3907, of the Revised Statutes of the State of Indiana.

Alleging, that the real estate so taken by the defendant is, and was, at the time it was appropriated, of the value of four thousand dollars ($4,000), and that by reason of its appropriation the real estate of the plaintiff had been damaged in the sum of four thousand dollars ($4,000), and that such damages were due and unpaid, and that no damages had ever been assessed, tendered or paid to the plaintiff by the defendant; that in and by said complaint and application the plaintiff prayed the court that a writ of assessment of damages might issue to the sheriff of Floyd county, pursuant to the statute in such cases, and that her damages might be assessed, and that she have judgment therefor.

Second. That on the same day a writ of assessment of damages, in due form, was issued out of the said court, sealed with the seal and signed and attested by the clerk of said Floyd Circuit Court, addressed to the sheriff of Floyd county, reciting the facts of the application of the said Margaret Rehman for such writ, and commanding the sheriff to impanel a jury of six disinterested freeholders of the county of Floyd to meet upon the land and real estate described in the application, and belonging to the said Margaret Rehman, on a day to be fixed by said sheriff, and there to proceed to cause the damages of the said Margarat Rehman to be assessed as provided by law; and further requiring the said sheriff to give ten days' notice to the said New Albany Belt and Terminal Railroad Co., and to the said Margaret Rehman, of the time and place where said jury were to meet to assess the damages above mentioned.

Third. That the said sheriff, in pursuance of the command of the said writ, did fix the 29th day of November, 1890, at ten o'clock, A. M., as the time when the jury named in said writ should meet upon the real estate therein described, to assess the damages of the plaintiff; and that the said sheriff gave notice to the said plaintiff and the said defendant of the time and place when and where such assessment would be made, more than ten days before the time fixed for the meeting of said jury; that the said sheriff did, on the day fixed for such assessment, summon a jury of six persons, who were disinterested freeholders of the county of Floyd, and not owning land within one mile of the railroad described in the said application; that the said jury did, on the said 29th day of November, 1890, after being duly sworn and charged by the sheriff, proceed to make an assessment of the damages alleged to have been sustained by the plaintiff, and that they then and there assessed her charges for the real estate taken by the defendant, at the sum of six hundred dollars ($600), and they then and there assessed the damages sustained by the plaintiff by reason of the construction of the defendant's railroad over and along her real estate, at twenty-four hundred and forty dollars ($2440); that the said writ was returned into the circuit court by said sheriff on the first day of December, 1890; that on the 9th day of December, 1890, the de-

fendant company filed its exceptions and objections to
the said proceedings, assessment, and return; that on
the 26th day of December, 1890, the plaintiff filed her
reply thereto, and that the said proceeding is yet pending in the said Floyd Circuit Court.

Fourth. That on the 4th day of September, 1891, the
said plaintiff, Margaret Rehman, filed her complaint in
the Floyd Circuit Court, against the defendants, the New
Albany Belt and Terminal Railroad Company, and the
Kentucky and Indiana Bridge Company, wherein and
whereby she alleges that she, the said plaintiff, owned
and occupied as a residence and boarding-house a large
dwelling situated on said lot No. 16, on the corner of
Upper Fourth and Water streets, in the city of New Albany.

Alleging that said Water street was a public street in
the city of New Albany, and had been so for many years,
and that there had been no obstruction thereon prevent-
ing the free use of the same by the plaintiff, or prevent-
ing her, her servants, lodgers, or others from having
free view of, and access to, the Ohio river, which is south
of the plaintiff's premises.

Alleging that on the 1st of September, 1890, and divers
other days between that day and the time of bringing
the action, the defendants, against the wishes, and over
the opposition of the plaintiff, constructed upon and
along East Water street, and near the middle line thereof,
a trestle or elevated railroad, built of heavy, rough timbers, laid upon piles driven in the said street, and extending ten feet above the surface of said street, forming
an obstruction along the length of said street, and shut-
ting off the view of, and access to, the Ohio river, of the
plaintiff, her servants, lodgers, etc.

Alleging that the said trestle and railroad had been
maintained by the defendants as a permanent obstruc-

tion to the use of the said street, and that the defendants had been engaged during the hours of the day and night in running thereon locomotives drawing freight cars and trains of cars, which locomotives emitted large quantities of smoke, soot, and sparks, and caused great and unusual noise in passing over said railroad, to the injury and annoyance of the plaintiff.

Alleging that such soot, smoke, and noise penetrated into the house and building of the plaintiff, and interfered with the sleep and rest of the inmates thereof.

Alleging that the defendants threatened to continue and permanently maintain the said railroad and to use the same in the manner and for the purposes herein set forth, to the damage of the plaintiff, praying judgment for one thousand dollars ($1,000) damages, and that the defendants be perpetually enjoined; that on the said 4th day of September, 1891, a writ of summons was issued upon the said complaint by the clerk of the Floyd Circuit Court, for the defendants, the New Albany Belt and Terminal Railroad Company, and the Kentucky and Indiana Bridge Company, requiring them to appear in said Floyd Circuit Court on the second Monday of September, 1891, to answer the said complaint, and that said writ was duly served upon the said defendants at said county on the said 4th day of September, 1891, by the said sheriff.

Fifth. That afterwards, on the —— day of September, 1891, the said plaintiff, Margaret Rehman, filed in said Floyd Circuit Court her amended complaint, alleging, in substance, that she was the owner of lot number sixteen (16) on the corner of Upper Fourth and Water streets, in the city of New Albany, Floyd county, Indiana, and that she had been such owner for more than ten years last past; that during all of said time the plaintiff had owned, occupied, and enjoyed, as a residence and boarding-house, a large dwelling situated upon said lot, near the corner of said Upper Fourth and Water streets; that said Water street was, and for more than fifty years had been, a public street and highway, one hundred feet wide, in the city of New Albany, and that for more than fifty years prior to the filing of said complaint said street had been used by the plaintiff, her grantors, and by the other owners and occupants of said lot sixteen (16), and by her servants, boarders and lodgers, and inhabitants of said city, and the public generally as a public highway and street; that during said time there was no obstruction in said street which prevented the free use thereof, and the passage over and along the entire length and width thereof by the plaintiff and other persons, in going to and from plaintiff's premises and the Ohio river, which lies south of said premises; that there had been, previous to the construction of said railroad, no obstruction in said street, which prevented the plaintiff, her servants, lodgers, etc., from having a free view of the Ohio river, nor was there maintained in said street any trestle, bridge, or other obstruction, over which cars, emitting smoke and cinders, and making great and unusual noises, passed, and that the plaintiff's residence and premises were free from smoke, soot, and bad odors, and the health and comfort of the plaintiff, and other occupants of said house were not interfered with or injured by reason of smoke, cinders, bad odors, and loud and unusual noises during the day or night time, and that, by reason thereof, the plaintiff's lot was of the value of five thousand dollars ($5,000); that on the 1st day of September, 1890, and on divers other days between that day and the beginning of said action, the defendants, against the wishes and over the opposition of the plaintiff, constructed on said East Water street, and near the middle line thereof, a wooden structure called a trestle or elevated railroad, extending above the surface of the street more than ten feet, forming an immovable obstruction along the entire length of said street, and entirely shutting off the view of, and access to, the Ohio river, of the plaintiff, her servants and lodgers; that the said trestle and railroad were constructed, and had been maintained as a permanent obstruction to the use of said street, and that the defendants had been engaged, and were, at the time of the commencement of the said action, engaged in running thereon locomotives drawing freight cars, and trains of cars, which locomotives emitted large quantities of smoke, soot, and sparks, and caused great and unusual noise in passing over said railroad, to the injury and annoyance of the plaintiff, and to the interruption of the free use of her property; that the said smoke, soot, and noise penetrated her house and building, and interfered with the sleep and rest of the inmates thereof, to the injury of her and their health, and to their discomfort and annoyance; that the defendants threaten and intend to permanently maintain said railroad, and to continue the nuisance and wrongs in which they were engaged, and alleging that such maintenance, and use of said railroad would cause lasting and irreparable damage to the plaintiff and her property to the amount of one thousand dollars ($1,000); that the city authorities of the city of New Albany, although requested, refused to remove such obstruction or abate such nuisance, and praying for judgment against the defendants for one thousand dollars ($1,000) damages, and for a perpetual injunction against the maintenance of said railroad, and the obstruction of said street.''

Upon the foregoing facts, the court concluded, first, that at the time of the commencement of the present action, another action between the same parties for the same cause was pending, and, second, that the action ought to abate.

To the conclusions of law the appellant at the time excepted.

The real controversy to be determined is whether or not, under the writ of assessment of damages, appellant must recover all damages for the property actually taken and for the injury, present and prospective, which the remainder sustains. It is not controverted that the damages sought to be recovered are for injuries to one and the same piece of property.

The statute, sections 881–912, R. S. 1881, provides who may apply for the writ, and the manner in which the proceedings shall be had, and what shall be taken into consideration in assessing the damages. It shall be the duty of the jury summoned, first, to view and assess the value of the land taken; second, to examine the adjacent lands, mansion-house, gardens, or any improvements or appurtenances thereto belonging, and if they are damaged by the construction and operating of the railroad, to assess damages therefor, and, third, to assess any other damages that may be sustained by the property owner.

The statute contemplates the assessment of all damages, not only for the land taken, but for all injury to the remainder of the land which resulted, or might reasonably result, from the appropriation of the part of the land and the proper construction, maintenance, and operation of the railroad thereon. It would be absurd to hold that the uses to which the land taken is to be put, in the running of railway trains and the interference with egress, the inconvenience and annoyance from dirt and smoke, the risk from fire, and exposure of personal property, as well as depreciation in value and income of the rental, and interruption of facilities of business and communication attached to the property, were not injuries contemplated by the legislature, and which should be considered in assessing damages. The true purpose of the act is to grant, in one suit, a right to recover all damages, both present and prospective.

"Damages assessed upon the taking of property in the exercise of the power of eminent domain, include prospective as well as present damages, they are an entirety; and all such as will proceed from that cause and be suffered in the future, are presumed to have been anticipated." I Sutherland on Damages, 191.

Judge Redfield, in his work on Railways, section 71, says: "But the appraisers are to assess all the damages, present and prospective, to which the party will ever be entitled, by the prudent construction and operation of the road." And again, in section 74: "So it is settled that the appraisal of land damages is a bar to claims for injuries by fire, from the engines obstructing access to buildings, exposing persons or cattle to injury, and many such risks. And it will make no difference, that the damages were not known to the appraisers, or capable of anticipation at the time of assessing land damages."

"In this class of cases the damages are assessed once for all, and the owner of the land is entitled to compensation for every injury resulting from the appropriation." Eggleston on Damages, section 308.

In Pierce on Railroads, p. 177, it is said: "The final award is a bar to an action for an injury which the appraisers could have legally estimated, irrespective of their action, upon the claim for injury, or even knowledge or ignorance of its existence. They are conclusively presumed to have performed their duty, except in a direct proceeding to set aside the award, or on appeal."

"The presumption is that every injury which, in judgment of law, would result to the other adjacent property of the owner from taking a part of his land for the construction of the road, and from the use of it in a proper manner when constructed, was foreseen by the apprais-ers, and included in their first estimate. The award made by the statutory tribunal is exhaustive; and the land-owner can not maintain an action for damages which should have been but were not assessed and al-lowed in that proceeding; even though he claimed them there, and they were erroneously disallowed." 2 Wood's Railway Law, section 256.

The question is not a new one in the courts of last re-sort in this State, for the Supreme Court has, in many cases, decided that the appraisers are required to consider and to award compensation for all damages of every character which is, or may be, sustained by reason of the appropriation of the land to the uses contemplated.

In the case of *Chicago, etc., R. W. Co.* v. *Hunter*, 128 Ind. 213, the court says: "The rule in condemnation proceedings is that all damages, present or prospective, that are the natural or reasonable incident of the im-provement to be made, or work to be constructed, not including such as may arise from negligence, or unskill-fulness, or from the wrongful act of those engaged in the work, must be assessed. Damages are assessed once for all, and the measure should be the entire loss sustained by the owner, including in one assessment all injuries resulting from the appropriation."

That this has been the opinion of the Supreme Court, by an unbroken line of cases from its earliest decisions to the present time, is unquestioned. *Lafayette Plank Road Co.* v. *New Albany, etc., R. R. Co.*, 13 Ind. 90; *White Water Valley R. R. Co.* v. *McClure*, 29 Ind. 536; *Grand Rapids, etc., R. R. Co.* v. *Horn*, 41 Ind. 479; *Baltimore, etc., R. R. Co.* v. *Lansing*, 52 Ind. 229; *Pitts-burgh, etc., R. W. Co.* v. *Swinney*, 59 Ind. 100; *Swinney* v. *Ft. Wayne, etc., R. R. Co.*, 59 Ind. 205; *Lafayette, etc., R. R. Co.* v. *Murdock*, 68 Ind. 137; *Indiana, etc., R. W. Co.* v. *Allen*, 100 Ind. 409; *Indiana, etc., R. W. Co.* v. *Allen*, 113 Ind. 308; *White* v. *Chicago, etc., R. R. Co.*, 122 Ind. 317; *American Cannel Coal Co.* v. *Huntington, etc., R. R. Co.*, 130 Ind. 98.

If the damages sought to be recovered in this action are such as can or could have been assessed in the proceedings for the assessment of damages for the appropriation, this action can not be maintained. Whatever damages might properly have been assessed in those proceedings will be presumed to have been assessed, and such assessment, unless appealed from, is a final adjudication for such injuries. And it is settled in this State that where a railroad company had appropriated the lands of another, and had instituted proceedings to have the damages assessed, such owner could not seek any other remedy while the appropriation proceedings were pending. *Ney* v. *Swinney*, 36 Ind. 454; *Pittsburgh, etc., R. W. Co.* v. *Swinney, Exx.*, 97 Ind. 586; *City of Ft. Wayne* v. *Hamilton*, 132 Ind. 487, 32 N. E. Rep. 324.

If this is true where the proceedings have been instituted by the railroad company, how much more reasonable must it seem when both actions have been instituted by the land-owner himself.

That the injury for which damages are sought in this action necessarily arise from the construction and operation of the railroad of said New Albany Belt and Terminal Railroad Co., and are embraced in the proceedings for a writ of assessment of damages, is clear, and no action therefor could be maintained pending those proceedings.

The judgment is therefore affirmed as to the New Albany Belt and Terminal Railroad Company, and reversed as to the Kentucky and Indiana Bridge Co., with instructions to sustain the demurrer to its plea in abatement, and for further proceedings not inconsistent with this opinion. Costs to be taxed one-half to appellant and one-half to appellee The Kentucky and Indiana Bridge Co.

GAVIN, C. J., absent.

Filed Nov. 7, 1893.

No. 834.

THE CITY OF LAFAYETTE v. ASHBY.

MUNICIPAL CORPORATION.—*Personal Injury.*—*Defective Sidewalk.*—*Notice.*—*Liability for Act of Licensee.*—*Sufficiency of Complaint.*—*Theory of.*—In an action against a municipal corporation, for personal injuries sustained by tripping upon a guy wire which had been erected by an electric light company, licensed to use the street, extending from the top of a pole, across the street, and attached to a tree, the complaint is sufficient, on demurrer, which proceeds upon the theory that the defendant had notice, when the wire was stretched across the street, that it was fastened to a decayed and unsafe tree outside and beyond the street (such tree having been blown down, and such wire suspended but a few inches above the sidewalk about an hour before the accident complained of), and that, by the exercise of reasonable diligence, appellant might have known of the continuance (about nine months) of such unsafe attachment up to the time of the accident, and alleging want of contributory negligence.

VERDICT.—*Sustained by the Evidence.*—That the evidence is sufficient to sustain the verdict, see opinion.

INSTRUCTIONS TO JURY.—*Error in Giving and Refusal to Give.*—*Presumption of Harm.*—*Unsatisfactory Evidence.*—Where the evidence is so unsatisfactory on the vital points in the case as to render it extremely doubtful, in the mind of the court, whether the verdict was right, error in giving and refusal to give instructions will be presumed to have been harmful, and will work a reversal.

Concurring opinion by REINHARD, J.

Opinion on petition for rehearing, PER CURIAM.

From the Clinton Circuit Court.

J. F. McHugh, for appellant.

J. R. Coffroth and *W. R. Coffroth*, for appellee.

DAVIS, J.—This was an action to recover damages on account of personal injuries. The complaint was in two paragraphs, and separate demurrers to each paragraph were overruled. The answer was a general denial. As the result of a trial before a jury, judgment was rendered against appellant for two thousand dollars.

The errors assigned bring in review the rulings on the demurrer to each paragraph of the complaint, and also the overruling of appellant's motion for a new trial.

We will consider them in the order in which they are presented.

It is alleged, in substance, in the first paragraph of the complaint, that the Brush Electric Lighting Co., in January, 1888, erected, at the corner of certain streets in the city of Lafayette, as a part of its plant for lighting the streets of said city with electricity, a pole about ten inches in diameter and twenty feet in height, at the top of which it caused to be attached its electric lighting wires, and that, for the purpose of keeping said pole in position, said Brush company, "with the knowledge of said defendant," caused a guy wire to be attached to the top of said pole and stretched the same a distance of three hundred feet over, above, and beyond the street, and there "carelessly and negligently caused said guy wire, with the knowledge of said defendant, to be fastened and attached to an insecure and dead tree," and that said company carelessly and negligently continued to suffer and permit said wire to be stretched over said street and to remain fastened to said insecure, decayed and dead tree, and that said appellant might have known said facts by the exercise of reasonable diligence.

It is alleged that afterwards, on Friday, October 19, 1888, said decayed and dead tree, from its own weight and the strain of said guy wire, fell over and upon the ground, and thereby greatly loosened said guy wire, "which was suffered to remain stretched across said street during said day, attached to said pole and fallen tree, at a distance of about eight inches above the sidewalk, and "that on the evening of said 19th day of October, 1888, at about the hour of six o'clock, the plaintiff, while passing over and along the sidewalk of said Fourteenth street, without knowledge of said fallen wire, and in the exercise of care, and without any fault or negligence on his part, was caught by said wire and thrown violently forward upon the sidewalk and into the gutter," and was injured "through the fault and negligence of the defendant aforesaid," etc.

The second paragraph is substantially the same as the first paragraph, except it charges that the Brush company did the acts complained of, without objection upon the part of the city, and that appellant, with full knowledge of all the facts, "suffered and permitted said wire to remain suspended over and across said Fourteenth street, well knowing that the wire was attached to said insecure tree, and was liable to fall and unlawfully obstruct said street;" and further, "That early in the day of Friday, October 19, 1888, said insecure, decayed and dead tree, from its own weight and the strain of said guy wire, fell over and upon the ground in the direction of said pole, and thereby greatly loosening said guy wire, and said guy wire, during said day, was, by the defendant, carelessly and negligently suffered to remain stretched upon and across said Fourteenth street," and that appellant had negligently permitted said street at said point to become and remain out of repair, and in a dangerous and unsafe condition, in this, that there was a hole in the gutter, etc.

It will be noticed that it is charged, in the first paragraph, that the guy wire was carelessly and negligently, with the knowledge of appellant, so fastened and attached

to said insecure, decayed, and dead tree, in January, and
that said company carelessly and negligently continued
to suffer and permit said wire to be stretched over and
across said street and to remain fastened and attached to
said insecure, decayed and dead tree until the ensuing
October, when the accident occurred, and that the appellant might have known of such continuation of said wire
by said company, by the exercise of reasonable diligence.
And that, in the second paragraph, it is charged that the
wire was so negligently attached to the insecure tree,
with the knowledge of appellant, and that the alleged
negligent continuation thereof was with such knowledge
on part of appellant.

We have examined the authorities cited by counsel for
the respective parties, and we call attention thereto.

"It is the duty of municipal corporations to keep all
of their streets in a reasonably safe condition for travel,
so as not to endanger the persons and property of those
lawfully using them, and they are liable for negligently
suffering them to become unsafe." *City of Aurora* v.
Bitner, 100 Ind. 396.

This duty extends upwards indefinitely for the purpose
of the preservation, safe use, and enjoyment of the street.
Grove v. *City of Ft. Wayne*, 45 Ind. 429.

"Where a defective and unsafe condition of a street or
sidewalk in a city is caused by the act or omission of a
third person, and the city, *after due notice of the defect*,
fails to have it remedied within a reasonable time, it is
as much responsible for the injury caused thereby as if
the defect had had its origin in the acts of the city itself,
through its officers in charge of the streets, or otherwise."
City of Huntington v. *Breen*, 77 Ind. 29.

(The italics in the quotations throughout this opinion
are our own.)

It has been held that "the indirect and inferential

averments, that the highway, within the corporate limits of the city and where the wagon ran into the ditch, was carelessly and negligently permitted to be out of repair, and that the city had knowledge that it was so out of repair, fairly and plainly imply that the city had notice of the bad condition of the street when the plaintiff and his daughter were injured," but in that case the sufficiency of the complaint was not challenged by demurrer in the court below, and in conclusion of the above sentence the court said: "After verdict we will infer that the notice was in time to have enabled the city to repair the street if it had desired to do so." *City of Madison* v. *Baker,* 103 Ind. 41. See, also, *City of Michigan City* v. *Ballance,* 123 Ind. 334; *City of Logansport* v. *Justice,* 74 Ind. 378; *City of Indianapolis* v. *Murphy,* 91 Ind. 382.

In another case Judge ELLIOTT says: "Where the obstruction which causes the injury is not placed in the street by the city itself, *there must be actual notice,* or the obstruction must have remained in the street such a length of time as to make it the duty of the corporate authorities to take notice of its existence." *City of Warsaw* v. *Dunlap,* 112 Ind. 576; *Dooley* v. *Town of Sullivan,* 112 Ind. 451.

It is also settled that a general averment of negligence is sufficient to withstand a demurrer. *City of Anderson* v. *East,* 117 Ind. 126.

It will be noticed that it is not alleged in either paragraph that the obstruction was placed or remained in the street under such circumstances and for such length of time as to make it the duty of the corporate authorities to take notice of its existence, but the charge is that *appellant had notice when the wire* was stretched across the street that it was fastened to a decayed and unsafe tree outside of and beyond the street, and that by the exercise of reasonable diligence appellant might have known of the continuance of such unsafe attachment thereafter up to the time of the accident.

It should be borne in mind that in this instance the work was not undertaken by the city, nor was it apparently dangerous in itself. It was proper to permit the streets to be used by the Brush company for the purpose of lighting the city with electricity. Aside from the alleged actual notice on part of appellant, that the wire when erected was attached to said unsafe tree, nothing is shown which would indicate that the wire was, or would likely become, an obstruction. The distinction which exists between a work undertaken by a municipal corporation itself and work undertaken by another should be kept in view.

Whatever our views of the question under consideration might have been as an original proposition, we are constrained under the decision of the Supreme Court to hold each paragraph of the complaint sufficient. The demurrer concedes the truth of the averments relative to notice, on the part of appellant, of the alleged negligence of the company in the erection of the wire, across the street, in the unsafe condition described in the complaint, and as the result of which negligence the injury occurred. With actual notice or knowledge of such negligence and carelessness of the company in fastening the wire to an secure and decayed tree, in the unsafe manner deribed, it was the duty of appellant, under the authoris cited, to have given the subject proper attention, and have exercised at least reasonable diligence in having wire removed or safely secured, and suffering the tinuation thereof for nine months, in the negligent unsafe manner described, renders the appellant le under the circumstances stated in the complaint. here is evidence tending to show that on the after- of Friday, October 19th, 1888, there was a wind and rain storm, during which the tree in question was blown down, and that as appellee was returning to his home, perhaps an hour thereafter, he fell over the wire and was injured. The testimony as to whether appellee fell or was injured, is, it is true, conflicting. In fact all the witnesses who saw the appellee on that occasion, except himself, say that he did not trip or fall, but that when he reached the wire he discovered it was there, and that the appellee, with the assistance of his neighbors, then and there cut and removed it. That the heavy wind blew the tree down does not seem to have been controverted, and that the wire was removed on the evening of the 19th appears to be conceded. In this connection we pause to remark that appellee concedes he said nothing to either his family or any one else on that evening concerning his fall or injury. The evidence is, however, in several respects contradictory, and where there is any evidence in the record favorable to appellee he is entitled to the benefit thereof, on this appeal, without reference to any conflict, and regardless of the weight of such evidence.

There is no allegation in the complaint that appellant suffered or permitted the wire to remain down or across the sidewalk an unreasonable length of time. In fact, there is no claim either in the complaint or evidence that appellant had any knowledge, prior to its removal, that the wire was down. Neither is it alleged that the defect in the street, mentioned in the second paragraph, was a proximate or contributing cause of appellee's injury. The theory of the appellee, on which the cause was tried in the court below, seems to have been, except as indicated in instructions, that said Brush company, *with knowledge of appellant*, negligently and carelessly attached the guy wire to a dead and insecure tree, and that therefore appellant was responsible for such negligence of said com-

The City of Lafayette *v.* Ashby.

pany, and should respond in damages for the injuries sustained by appellee in falling over the wire when down across the sidewalk on that evening.

Doctor Washburne, who was the family physician of appellee, and who treated him professionally, both before and after the alleged injury, testified, as a witness on the trial, in behalf of appellee, that he was, and for ten years had been, a member of the city council of Lafayette, and that the guy wire was fastened to a hickory tree in the commons. He states that he saw the tree while it was lying on the ground a day or two after the accident. He also testified that the tree was ten inches in diameter, and that it was green in both branches and body, "down to within just above the ground a piece," and that the tree bore hickory nuts the year before.

We quote the greater part of his testimony as follows:

"Were you present when the Brush Electric Lighting Company fastened its guy wire to this tree, running it from the pole to the tree?

"I was not.

"Do you know how long had this guy wire been run from this pole to this tree in question?

"I don't know.

"You may state, so far as you have any knowledge of its existence there, how long it had been before this 20th of October, 1888.

"I have no knowledge of the length of time; I don't know anything at all about it.

"You practice medicine a good deal all over that part of the city, don't you?

"I am over that part of the city quite often; yes, sir.

"And in passing along you had noticed the wire running from the pole to this tree, had you?

"I had observed the wire; yes, sir.

"How long, now, before the time this accident is alleged to have occurred had it been since you observed it?

"I couldn't say.

"State whether or not it was for a considerable time or only a short time?

"I couldn't say the period of time, but it was before this accident or the tree blew down.

"Well, was it several years or several months, or what was it?

"I remember seeing this wire attached to the tree, and that is all I can say. As regards the period of time prior to the time the tree blew down, I don't know.

"It was sometime before, was it?

"Sometime before that; how long I wouldn't undertake to say.

"Can you state whether it was two or three months before?

"Yes, it was two months before; how much longer I don't know."

He also testified that a fire had been built on one side of the tree several years before by his son, and that one-half of it had been burnt off, but whether he noticed this fact prior to accident is not clear, and that the inside of the tree was dead and decayed and the outside was apparently green, at the time of the accident.

Other witnesses testified that fires had been built at and around said tree several times after the wire was fastened thereto, and prior to the time it blew down.

As to when and under what circumstances Doctor Washburne observed the condition of the tree prior to the alleged accident does not appear, except as indicated in his testimony, to which reference has been made. It appears, however, that he had seen the tree and knew a fire had been built there several years before, and that one side of the tree was burned; that the tree bore hickory nuts the year before, and that "the body of the tree was green (and the branches were green), with the exception of down close to the ground," and that he knew the guy wire was fastened thereto, but it is not shown, except inferentially, that he knew at any time prior to the accident that the tree was insecure or decayed, except the burn near the ground.

In fact we have referred to the sole and only evidence, to which our attention has been called, or which we have observed, tending to show any knowledge on the part of appellant, in relation to the fastening of the guy wire to the tree, or of its continuance prior to the 19th of October, 1888, and there is no evidence whatever in the record, tending to prove that the city had any knowledge, at any time, of the condition of the tree, except the testimony of Doctor Washburne.

It is insisted "that appellee has wholly failed to show that there is a particle of evidence to sustain the very essential fact that the city knew, *at the time the guy wire was attached to the tree,* that the tree was dead, decayed and rotten. This is the basis of both paragraphs of the complaint."

It is conceded that there is a variance between the allegations and the proof, in this, that the evidence fails to show that appellant had such knowledge "at the *very time* it was so fastened."

It is insisted, however, by counsel for appellee, that under all the surrounding circumstances disclosed by the evidence, appellant had constructive knowledge of the alleged negligence of the company and unsafe condition of the wire, a sufficient length of time to have remedied the defect as to the street, before the happening of appellee's injuries. In this view we can not concur. The tree was on the commons, which belonged to private parties, and was some distance from the street. There was nothing in the appearance of the wire to indicate that it was in any manner unsafe. In the absence of actual knowledge or notice as to the condition of the tree, it does not appear that anything could be observed from the street, indicating that it was rotten or unsafe.

The variance referred to, however, will not justify a reversal of the judgment of the trial court, if, as insisted by counsel for appellee, the evidence fairly tends to prove *such actual knowledge* on the part of appellant; as to the alleged negligence of the company and the unsafe condition of the wire for such period prior to the accident as would have given appellant a reasonable time in which to have taken the necessary steps to remove or safely secure the wire. *Steinke* v. *Bentley*, 6 Ind. App. 663.

The evidence relative to such notice or knowledge on the part of appellant, and, also, in reference to other material points in the case, is not satisfactory, but there was evidence tending to show that Dr. Washburne knew the tree had been burned, at least partly away, several years prior to the time in question, and that one end of the guy wire was fastened to the tree at least two months prior to the accident. In view of all the facts and circumstances which appear in the record, we can not say there was an entire failure of proof on this proposition, or as to the alleged injury. There was no evidence in support of the allegation in relation to the hole in the gutter, or that the tree fell from its own weight and the strain of said guy wire.

Complaint is made of the third instruction given by the court at request of appellee, in substance and to the effect that if the city knew the sidewalk was obstructed a reasonable time before the happening of the injury, the city was liable for the injury occasioned by such obstruction. There was no evidence whatever tending to show that appellant, prior to the alleged injury, had any knowledge of the fact that the wire was down or across the sidewalk. The instruction was not applicable to either the issues or the evidence.

The same objection is urged to the fourth instruction, but it is insisted, by counsel for appellee, that "if they were not relevant, as counsel contend, the giving of them is no cause for reversal, for the reason that it clearly appears that no harm could have resulted to appellant therefrom."

When the evidence clearly justifies the verdict, and it appears to the Appellate Court that the merits of the cause have been fairly tried and determined in the court below, the giving of irrelevant and erroneous instructions, where it is clear that such instructions have done no injury, constitutes harmless error, for which the judgment of the trial court will not be reversed. Section 658, R. S. 1881. *Felkner* v. *Scarlet*, 29 Ind. 154; *Garrigan* v. *Dickey*, 1 Ind. App. 421.

Absolute accuracy and perfection can not be obtained, ordinarily, in all the stages of an important trial. It is, therefore, not enough to reverse a judgment, that the court below committed some error in the course of a cause. Errors which have no effect on the verdict occur in the proceedings and trial of almost every cause before a jury. Appellate courts are not created to either reverse or affirm judgments, but are organized and maintained as a part of the judicial system, the administration of which is intended and calculated to secure to parties involved in litigation their substantial rights, freely and without purchase, completely and without denial, speedily and without delay, but where error is shown to have occurred in the trial court which it appears was probably prejudicial to appellant, it is the duty of the Appellate Court to reverse the judgment. Practically, more or less delay in judicial proceedings is unavoidable, and, moreover, correct results can not always be secured. Notwithstanding painstaking investigation and careful consideration, unimportant errors will occasionally be deemed prejudicial, and now and then hurtful rulings may be considered harmless. There is not so much uncertainty in the general principles of the law or the rules of practice, but the difficulty in the practical enforcement of these principles and rules in and by an Appellate Court oftentimes is in determining what errors in the trial court were probably influential on the result. So it is in this case. For instance, in the fourth instruction referred to, without any reference to whether the obstruction had remained in the street under such circumstances and for such length of time as to make it the duty of the city to take notice of the existence thereof, the jury were told that appellant was liable if the city, "by the use of ordinary and reasonable diligence, might have known of such obstruction a reasonable time before the occurrence of said alleged injury." Whatever may be said concerning the instruction, it certainly was not pertinent to any issue in the case. Whether the instruction had any effect on the result, prejudicial to appellant, the court can not say. We can only theorize, speculate and indulge in presumptions and probabilities in relation thereto. The rule is that instructions of the court must be applicable to the issues. *Myers* v. *Moore*, 3 Ind. App. 226 (227).

Counsel for appellant insist that the court erred in refusing to give to the jury instructions numbered six, seven, and ten, asked by defendant.

The substance of the tenth instruction was that the jury, in determining the weight and credibility of the appellee's testimony in relation to whether he tripped and fell over the wire, as claimed by him, had the right to take into consideration his conduct immediately following the alleged accident, together with the other evidence in the case.

It is contended by counsel for appellee that the use of the word "duty" in the instruction, in this connection, namely, "it is your duty to look into his conduct," etc., renders the instruction improper. *Unruh* v. *State, ex rel.,* 105 Ind. 117.

Under the facts and circumstances disclosed by the evidence in this case, the reasoning in the case last above cited is not applicable, and does not sustain the objection urged to the instruction in question. *Robertson* v. *Monroe,* 7 Ind. App. 470, and authorities there cited.

In our opinion, the instruction was a proper one to have been given to the jury. It correctly states the law applicable to the evidence on that branch of the case. It does not necessarily follow, however, that the refusal to give such correct and pertinent instruction constitutes reversible error.

The fifth, sixth, and seventh instructions asked by appellant are as follows:

"5. If you find from the evidence, that the tree to which said guy wire was attached was rendered insecure by reason of its having been set fire to sometime after the guy wire had been attached to it, then I instruct you that the plaintiff can not recover unless the defendant had knowledge or notice of such insecurity of said tree, or unless such insecurity had existed for such a length of time before the alleged accident that the city authorities, under the circumstances disclosed in the evidence, by the exercise of reasonable care, should have known of its existence.

"6. If you find from the evidence that the tree to which the guy wire is alleged to have been attached was rendered insecure by reason of fires having been made

against it after the time said tree was observed by the
witness Washburne, and that prior thereto said tree was
a reasonably secure tree to which to attach a guy wire
for the purposes alleged in the complaint, then I instruct
you that knowledge on the part of the witness Washburne of the prior condition of said tree would not, alone,
amóunt to a knowledge or a notice on the part of the defendant of the insecurity of said tree at the time of the
alleged accident.

"7. In determining the question whether the defendant should have had notice of the insecurity of said tree to
which said guy wire was attached, prior to the alleged
accident, you should take into consideration, with the
other evidence in the cause, the distance of said tree from
a public street, the character, location and visibility of
the defect or burn, if any, which rendered said tree insecure, and the likelihood of its having been observed
by any of the city authorities prior to the alleged accident."

In the language of NIBLACK, C. J.: "As applicable
to the facts of this case," we see no objection to the sixth
instruction. *Wiseman* v. *Wiseman*, 89 Ind. 479 (483).

The fifth instruction, which was given, does not em-
brace all of the material and pertinent parts of the sixth
instruction, which was refused. In view of the fact that
there were no circumstances, aside from the knowledge
of Dr. Washburne, in regard to the condition of the tree,
tending to show that appellant might have known of the
insecure condition of the wire, prior to the accident, the
fifth instruction, to say the least of it, stated the law,
under the issues and the evidence, on the proposition
contained in the conclusion thereof, fully as favorable
as appellee was entitled to. If, in fact, the tree was
rendered unsafe by reason of the burning thereof after the time Dr. Washburne observed it, the sixth in-

struction should have been given in connection with the other instructions.

The seventh instruction was also refused.

The general statement of an abstract legal rule, although accurately stated, can not, in all cases, be properly embodied in an instruction. A party, however, has a right to have specific instructions applying to the facts of the particular case as developed by the evidence. *Unruh* v. *State, ex rel.*, *supra; Hipes* v. *State*, 73 Ind. 39; Elliott's App. Proced., section 706.

The theory of each paragraph of the complaint was that the wire was originally negligently attached, by said Brush company, to the decayed and insecure tree, *with the knowledge* of appellant, but the instructions given by the court at the request of appellee were in substance and to the effect that (without any knowledge on the part of appellant either in relation to the original insecure attachment or to the continuation thereof in an unsafe condition), the appellant was liable, "if, by the exercise of ordinary or reasonable diligence," the city might have known of such negligence, on the part of the company, several months before the happening of the accident in question.

It is true, as contended by counsel for appellant, that a complaint must proceed on a single definite and distinct theory. *First Nat'l Bank, etc.*, v. *Root*, 107 Ind. 224. And that the instructions must be applicable thereto. *Myers* v. *Moore, supra.*

These rules should be construed and applied in the spirit which underlies the code. Sections 391, 392, 393, R. S. 1881.

But conceding, without deciding, that the instructions so given by the court, at request of appellee, to the jury, relative to constructive notice on the part of the appellant of the alleged negligence of said company, correctly

state the law applicable to the case, then the seventh instruction asked by appellant under the circumstances of
this case should have been given.

It is not necessary to decide whether, if appellee's instructions, of which complaint is made, had not been
given, or if appellant's instructions which were refused
had been given along with them, or whether if all of the
instructions in question had been refused, there would
have been, in any such event, reversible error in the
record.   It is sufficient to say that in the view we have
taken of the case, any one of the errors which we have
hereinbefore mentioned, standing alone, may have been
harmless, but when the entire case, as presented by the
record, is examined and considered as a whole, we can
not say it appears "to the court that the merits have
been fairly tried and determined in the court below," or
that the errors referred to do "not affect the substantial
rights" of appellant.   Sections 398, 658, R. S. 1881;
Elliott's App. Proced., sections 594, 632.

This case does not come within the rule that where the
record affirmatively shows that the verdict is right upon
the evidence the judgment will not be reversed because
the court erred in the instructions given to the jury, or
for error in refusing to give instructions.   *Woods* v.
Board, etc., 128 Ind. 289 (292).

An appellate court, in the light of the observation and
experience of *nisi prius* courts and of the members of the
profession who have had an extensive and long continued practice in the trial of causes before juries, may,
and ordinarily will, assume that the giving of merely
irrelevant or slightly inaccurate instructions do not have
any controlling influence on the result, and therefore the
presumption in such cases is that a just conclusion was
reached in the trial court (and this rule may apply in
some case where the instructions are more radically er-

The City of Lafayette *v.* Ashby.

roneous, and also where correct and, pertinent instructions are refused), but where the evidence is so unsatisfactory on the vital points in the case as to render it extremely doubtful, in the mind of the court, whether the verdict was right, while it is true the court will not weigh the evidence, it will, where there is such error in the record as is shown to exist in this case, proceed on the theory that the errors were hurtful.

In this case the record discloses, in the opinion of the court, under the facts and circumstances to which we have called attention, such prejudicial error in the giving and refusing of instructions, on account of which, for the reasons indicated, the judgment of the court below is reversed, with instructions to grant a new trial.

Filed May 23, 1893.

CONCURRING OPINION.

REINHARD, J.—I concur in the result, but think the judgment ought to be reversed on the evidence also. In my judgment, there is no evidence tending to show any knowledge of the unsafe condition of the tree. It is not shown at what particular time Dr. Washburne discovered that the tree had been scorched, nor does it appear that he knew the extent to which it had been injured. It was the duty of the appellee to prove knowledge of the defective condition, in the city.

Filed May 23, 1893.

ON PETITION FOR A REHEARING.

PER CURIAM.—Counsel for appellant has filed a petition for a rehearing, in which he urges that the justice of the cause requires that it should be remanded with instructions to the court below to render judgment for appellant. Section 660, R. S. 1881; 2 Works' Practice, p. 138.

The majority of the court is of the opinion that there was some evidence at least in support of the verdict on every material point in issue. The jury were the exclusive judges of the credibility and weight of the evidence, and, therefore, the court would not reverse the judgment of the court below because of the insufficiency of the evidence to sustain the verdict, with instructions to render judgment for appellant.

Counsel for appellee earnestly insist that a rehearing should be granted on the ground that the errors in giving and the refusal to give the instructions, as stated in the original opinion, were harmless.

In this contention, the majority of the court do not agree with counsel. The court is not able to say, in this case, that the record so clearly and affirmatively shows that the verdict is right upon the evidence as to render the errors referred to in the original opinion harmless.

Each of the petitions for a rehearing is therefore overruled.

Filed Nov. 24, 1893.

———————◆———————

No. 699.

KOONS v. CLUGGISH ET AL.

STREETS AND ALLEYS.—*Improvement Lien.*—*Complaint, Sufficiency of.*— *Statute Repealed.*—*Act of 1869.*—*Act of 1889.*—Where the theory of a complaint for the foreclosure of a lien alleged to have accrued by reason of certain street improvements, was that the contract was made and work performed under the act of 1869, relating thereto, the complaint was insufficient on demurrer, the contract having been made and work performed under the act of 1889, relating to the same subject and repealing the former act.

From the Henry Circuit Court.

J. Brown and *W. A. Brown*, for appellant.

M. E. Forkner and *W. E. Jeffrey*, for appellees.

DAVIS, J.—In and prior to April, 1891, the appellant was the owner of a parcel of land containing one acre situate in the town of Mooreland, Henry county, Indiana. The street on which said real estate fronts, was improved during that year by appellees as contractors, under order of the board of trustees of said town. The assessment against appellant's real estate, on account of said improvement, amounted to $61.56. The description indicates that the real estate was unplatted and extended back more than one hundred and fifty feet.

We have not deemed it necessary to set out the substance of the averments in the complaint. Suffice it to say the theory of the complaint is that, by reason of the improvement of the street, under the provisions of the act of 1869, appellees acquired a lien on all of said real estate, and that they were entitled to a foreclosure of the lien against the real estate, and to personal judgment against appellant.

It is not necessary to consider or discuss, at this time, the question whether appellees, under the act of 1869, were entitled to personal judgment. The record discloses that there was no foreclosure of the lien, and that personal judgment was rendered against appellant for the amount of the assessment. This appears to have been done without objection or exception.

The first error discussed by counsel, is that the court below erred in overruling appellant's demurrer to the complaint.

The main and controlling question which is presented by this assignment, for our consideration, is whether the act in force April 27th, 1869, in relation to the improvement of streets in towns, was repealed by implication by the act providing for the improvement of streets in cities and towns approved March 8th, 1889, p. 237.

It is conceded, by counsel for appellees, that the street

improvement, which forms the basis of this action, was made under the act of 1869. Sections 3364, 3365 and 3366, R. S. 1881.

If that act was repealed by implication, by the act of 1889, the complaint is insufficient. Elliott's Supp., sections 812 to 822, inclusive.

The act of 1889 covers the whole subject-matter of the former law, as will be seen by a comparison of the two acts. The act of 1869 required a petition by "a majority of all the resident owners," etc. Section 3364, supra.

The act of 1889 requires a petition by the resident "owners of two-thirds," etc. Section 812, supra.

Under the act of 1869 the lien of the assessment attached to the entire lot or tract fronting on the street, whether platted or not. Section 3365, supra.

On the failure to pay such assessment it was provided, in the language of the act, that the contractor "may immediately, by suit in any court of competent jurisdiction, recover against such owners of lots or parcels of land the amount of such estimate," and further provides for the sale of such lot or tract on the judgment. Section 3366, supra.

Under the act of 1889, the lien attaches to the lots or land fronting on the street, but as to the improvement "along or through any unplatted land" the lien extends "back to the distance of one hundred and fifty feet from such front line" only. Section 814, supra.

Under the act of 1869 there was no lien in favor of the town. The lien was in favor of the contractor alone. Section 3366, supra.

Under the act of 1889 the lien is in favor of the "incorporated town and contractor." Section 814, supra.

The owner may pay the whole or any part of the assessment when the improvement is completed, or, on failure so to do, the amount so assessed is placed on the tax duplicate. Section 818, *supra.*

The town may pay for the improvement, or any part of it, out of the general revenue of the town. Section 816, *supra.*

Or, the town may issue certificates to the contractor, who may foreclose the lien and collect the assessment. Sections 814 and 820, *supra.*

It will be observed that the act of 1889 is more comprehensive than the act of 1869. The act of 1869 does not provide for any notice in relation to either the petition, improvements or assessment, except "advertising to receive proposals" for the performance of the work. Section 3364, *supra.*

The act of 1889 provides for notice to the property-owners, in certain contingencies at least, before the improvement is made, and also for another notice, in all cases, after the completion of the work and before the assessment is made. Sections 813, 818, Elliott's Supp.; Acts 1891, p. 323, section 2. See *McEneney* v. *Town of Sullivan*, 125 Ind. 407; *De Puy* v. *City of Wabash*, 133 Ind. 336, 32 N. E. Rep. 1016.

The title of the act of 1889 contains, among other things, the following: "And repealing all conflicting laws."

The only act prior thereto on the subject of improvement of streets in towns was the act of 1869. This is the only law which could have been in conflict, in any respect, as to improvement of streets in towns, with the act of 1889. The Legislature evidently intended the act of 1889 as a substitute for the act of 1869. The provisions of the two acts are, in some respects, as indicated in the foregoing partial review, inconsistent and repugnant. While the new statute, as before stated, covers the same subject-matter as the older statute, and is more specific and comprehensive, the provisions in the later act which are inconsistent with or different from the provisions of the former act, can not, in our opinion, be so reconciled as to permit both to stand.

In this connection, the statement of Judge COFFEY is applicable: "Underlying all the rules for the construction of statutes is the cardinal and general one, that in construing a statute the court will seek to discover and carry out the intention of the Legislature in its enactment. In the search for that intention, the court will look to each and every part of the statute; to the circumstances under which it was enacted; to the old law upon the subject, if any; to the other statutes upon the same subject or relative subjects, whether in force or repealed; to contemporaneous legislative history, and to the evils and mischiefs to be remedied." *Barber, etc.*, v. *Edgerton*, 125 Ind. 455.

Also, we quote the pertinent language of Judge NIBLACK, in another case: "It is true, as insisted, that repeals by implication are not favored in the construction of statutes. * * * It is, nevertheless, a well-recognized rule of statutory construction, that where a new statute covers the subject-matter of an older statute, and contains some provision or provisions inconsistent with, or different from it, the new statute operates as an implied repeal of the older one." *Crowell* v. *Jaqua*, 114 Ind. 246.

The rule is thus stated in *Water Works Co.* v. *Burkhart*, 41 Ind. 364 (383): "It must appear that the subsequent statute revised the whole subject-matter of the former one, and was evidently intended as a substitute for it, or that it was repugnant to the old law. In other words, it must appear that it was the intention of the law makers to repeal the former law. When that appears, the will of the law makers is just as manifest as if it had been shown by express words."

We think it is clear that the purpose of the act of 1889 was to prescribe a comprehensive and uniform system of procedure for the improvement of streets in cities and towns, and that the Legislature intended that the provisions thereof should be a substitute for the former act, and that all laws in conflict therewith should be repealed. Therefore, when the principles enunciated in the cases cited are applied, we are of the opinion, after careful consideration and mature reflection, that the act of 1869 was repealed, by implication, by the act of 1889.

This conclusion is, as we construe it, in harmony with the reasoning of Judge ELLIOTT in the case of *Robinson* v. *Rippey,* 111 Ind. 112, relied on by counsel for appellee.

In that case it was insisted that the gravel road law of March 3, 1877, was repealed by the act of April 8, 1885, p. 162, but in the latter act there was the following proviso: "This act is not intended to repeal any law now in force for the construction of gravel or macadamized roads."

It was there held "that the enactment of the new statute covering the whole subject is an expression of an intention to repeal the old law," but that the rule did not apply where it was unequivocably asserted in the act that there was no intention to repeal the old law. In this case the act of 1889 not only covers the whole subject, but there is in addition the intention expressed in the title, for whatever it may be worth, whether much or little, that all conflicting laws were repealed.

We can not declare that the law of 1869 was not repealed by the act of 1889, without ignoring the familiar rule, above stated, "that the enactment of a new statute covering the whole subject is an expression of an intention to repeal the old law," and also disregarding the words in the title supporting this view.

The repeal of the law of 1869 by the act of 1889, by implication, in our opinion, which we state in the language used by the court of appeals of New York, "will not operate as a repeal, so as to affect a duty accrued under the prior law, although as to all new transactions the later law will be referred to as the ground of obligation." *In re Prime's Estate*, 32 N. E. Rep. 1091 (1093). See, also, *People* v. *Wilmerding*, 32 N. E. Rep. 1099.

The statutes conferring power to make assessments for street improvements are strictly construed. *Niklaus* v. *Conkling*, 118 Ind. 289.

While it is perhaps true, on the facts stated in the complaint, that appellant, having received the benefits, should, in equity and good conscience, pay for the improvement, yet the court can not make contracts for parties, nor create a legal or equitable liability. The courts can only afford the remedy where the right exists by reason of the contract or conduct of the parties, or growing out of some statutory enactment, or created in some other recognized manner. The interest of appellees should have admonished them to ascertain that the proceedings were such as would create a binding obligation on some one to pay for the work, before entering into the contract. *Kiphart* v. *Pittsburgh, etc., R. W. Co.*, 7 Ind. App. 122.

The appellees have not, and, in view of the conclusions reached, perhaps can not bring the case within the rule stated in *Prezinger* v. *Harness*, 114 Ind. 491, and other similar cases.

All we now decide, however, is that the complaint does not state facts sufficient to constitute a cause of action.

Judgment reversed, with instructions to sustain demurrer to complaint.

GAVIN, C. J., did not participate in the decision of this case.

Filed June 23, 1893; petition for a rehearing overruled Nov. 23, 1893.

No. 855.

THE BANK OF WESTFIELD *v.* INMAN ET AL.

HARMLESS ERROR.—*Error Cured by Instruction.—Recovery.—Pleading, Bill of Particulars.*—In an action on account, the party is restricted, on recovery, to the items designated in the bill of particulars, and where evidence of items not so included is given, which might have been embraced in the verdict, any error which otherwise might have occurred will be deemed cured by an instruction that "the defendant would not be entitled to a verdict against the plaintiff on any item not included in such bill of particulars."

EVIDENCE.—*Subsidiary or Corroborative Fact.*—When the principal fact is given in evidence without objection, it is not reversible error to give in evidence a subsidiary or corroborative fact.

INSTRUCTIONS TO JURY.—*Items of Account.—Restricting Consideration of Jury.—Exclusiveness.—Erroneous.*—Where many matters are given in evidence, among which are several hundred items of account, conversations, notes, and bank checks, without objection, an instruction which singles out three items of account and says, "these are all the matters proper for you to consider in arriving at a conclusion as to whether the defendant * * was indebted to plaintiff at the date of the execution of the note in suit, and as to whether the plaintiff is now, in fact, indebted to the defendant," is erroneous, the phrase, "these are all the matters," etc., conveying the idea of exclusiveness, *i. e.*, the only matters.

Opinion on petition for rehearing *per curiam.*

From the Hamilton Circuit Court.

T. J. Kane, T. P. Davis and *A. K. Kane,* for appellant.

W. R. Fertig, H. J. Alexander and *W. S. Christian,* for appellees.

Lotz, J.—The appellant sued the appellees upon a promissory note. The appellees answered jointly that the note was executed without any consideration. The appellee Robert C. Inman filed a separate answer of two paragraphs. The first paragraph of his separate answer alleged, that he was the principal, and the other appellees were his sureties; that the appellant was, at the time of the execution of the note, and at the time of filing his answer, indebted to him in the sum of fifteen hundred dollars for money had and received for his use, and which had been converted to the use of appellant.

The second paragraph of the separate answer averred that he executed the note as principal, for an alleged overdraft; that in fact there was no overdraft, but that by reason of divers errors, overcharges, and omissions in his account as a customer and depositor in said bank, there was fifteen hundred dollars due him, for which he prayed judgment. A bill of particulars was filed with each of these paragraphs, in which certain errors were specifically pointed out, and it was also stated that there were other errors in the account, which appellee was then unable to specify. No question is raised as to the sufficiency of the answer. There was a trial by jury, and a general verdict for all the appellees on the complaint, and a verdict for $1,076.92 in favor of the appellee Robert C. Inman, on his separate answers. There were no interrogatories submitted to the jury. A motion for a new trial was filed and overruled. After this ruling, and at the same term of the court, appellant filed another motion for a new trial on the ground of newly discovered evidence. The ruling upon each of these motions is assigned as error. Appellant earnestly insists that the verdict is not supported by the evidence, and that there is error in the assessment of the amount of recovery in favor of appellee Robert C. Inman.

It appears from the evidence that the appellee Robert C. Inman was engaged in buying and selling live stock, and that he did business through appellant's bank, borrowed money, discounted notes, made deposits there, and gave checks upon it. The business extended over a period of more than two years, and in the aggregate a large sum of money was deposited and checked out of said bank. The whole account of the dealings between them was given in evidence. We have looked into the evidence, and while we may have doubts as to the correctness of the verdict, yet under the familiar rule where there is any evidence tending to support the verdict the appellate courts will not disturb the judgment on such grounds. Appellant insists, that it is apparent that the jury included one item of $750 in the verdict which was not contained in the bill of particulars; that this was erroneous, and renders the amount of recovery too large. Whether or not under the pleadings the appellee was confined to the items specifically designated in the bill of particulars, we need not decide. The whole account of debit and credit, including several hundred items, was given in evidence without any objection except as to a few items. In this condition of the evidence, it is difficult to determine what items were or were not considered by the jury in reaching the verdict. The court expressly instructed the jury that "the defendant would not be entitled to a verdict against the plaintiff on any item not included in such bill of particulars." In the condition of the evidence, this court will presume that the jury followed the instruction given, and that the verdict contained only such items as were set out in the bill of particulars.

Another cause assigned for a new trial is that the court erred upon the trial in allowing the appellee Robert C.

Inman to testify relative to the execution of a note for $750 about the time of the purchase of a lot of hogs from one Roberts, and the payment of said note, for which he claimed he did not receive credit or money. This item was not embraced in the bill of particulars, and for that reason it is contended that the evidence was erroneously admitted. At no time on the trial was the objection raised that this item was not in the bill of particulars. The record shows that the appellee testified that he had made a note to the bank for $750, which should have been, but was not, credited to his account, and that he drew a check to Roberts on the same day for the amount, and paid the note off within a day or two afterwards, but received neither credit for the note nor for the money paid in its discharge. He then offered the check in evidence. To this the appellant objected, on the ground that the check was not in controversy. The principal fact to which the appellee's testimony related upon this point, was that he had made his note and paid it off, and had not received credit, although the note was charged against him in the account.

Where the principal fact is given in evidence without objection, it is not reversible error to give in evidence a subsidiary or corroborative fact.

Another cause for which a new trial was asked is that the court erred in giving to the jury a certain instruction prepared and asked by the appellee Robert C. Inman. The instruction is in these words: "If the defendant R. C. Inman executed his note to the plaintiff's bank for $950, and received credit on his deposit account for such note, in the sum of $949, being the amount of said note less the discount, and afterwards paid off said note in full by the payment of cash into the bank, for which he received no credit on said deposit account, and the amount of note, $950, was afterwards charged against him along with checks drawn on said account, or if the defendant executed a note to said bank for $750, and did not receive any money thereon, and did not receive credit therefor on his deposit account nor otherwise, and afterwards paid the said note in cash to the bank, and received no credit for the money so paid, and in like manner if the defendant made a note to said bank, $123.52, for which he received no credit for the money so paid, these are all the matters proper for you to consider in arriving at a conclusion as to whether the defendant Robert C. Inman was indebted to plaintiff at the date of the execution of the note in suit, and as to whether the plaintiff is now in fact indebted to the defendant Robert C. Inman.''

Appellees' learned counsel have not favored us with a discussion of this alleged error, and we are left in the dark as to their theory of its correctness.

These three items, the $950 note, the $750 note and the note for $123.52, are singled out by the instruction, and the jury are told that ''these are all the matters proper * * to consider'' in determining whether Robert C. Inman was indebted to the plaintiff, or whether the plaintiff was indebted to Robert C. Inman. The use of the phrase, ''these are all the matters,'' conveys the idea of exclusiveness; that is to say, the only matters. If this is the proper construction to be put upon the instruction, standing alone, we do not see upon what theory it can be upheld.

There were many matters given in evidence, there were several hundred items of account, various conversations, notes and bank checks introduced by both parties without objection, and yet the jury are told that it is proper to consider only three matters.

If the article ''the'' before the word ''matters'' was omitted, we see no objection to it, for it would then say to the jury "these are all matters proper for you to consider." But the definite article "the" before the word "matters" conveys the idea that the jury must consider only these three matters or things, and no other. To determine whether or not this instruction was misleading, it must be considered in connection with all the other instructions given in the case. There were a number of other instructions that directed the jury's attention to many other matters, and, under such circumstances, the jury could hardly be given to understand that these three notes were the only matters to be considered by them. The idea intended to be conveyed by the instruction, when considered in connection with the other instructions, no doubt was that there were only three items in the set-off that were in controversy, and that it would be unnecessary for the jury to consider any other.

When a fact or facts are admitted, or are undisputed, the court has the right, in instructing the jury, to treat them as proved, without invading the jury's province. But, as we understand the evidence, there were many other disputed items.

Appellees' counsel, in their brief, assert that it was another and different item than the $750 note, to wit, the $700 received from the express company, that went to make up the verdict. Again they say, in their brief, that "the whole account was involved in the controversy. The ultimate question was not as to any particular items of debits or credits, but as to the final balance."

We do not think the instruction can be justified upon any theory. If it was intended to convey the idea to the jury that there were only three items of evidence proper for them to consider, or only three matters in controversy, then it is clearly bad in the light of the record of this case, for it usurps the functions of the jury. Nor will it do to say that the instruction limited the jury's consideration to three items in the answer of set-off, for one of these items, the $750 note, is not found in the bill of particulars. And further, if this was the intention, it is squarely contradictory of the other instruction from which we have above quoted.

This conclusion renders it unnecessary to pass upon the other questions discussed by counsel for appellant.

Judgment reversed, with instructions to grant a new trial.

DAVIS, J., having been of counsel, did not participate in this decision.

Filed May 13, 1893.

ON PETITION FOR A REHEARING.

PER CURIAM.—It is settled by a long line of decisions that a rehearing will not be granted to enable the parties to procure a correction of the record. *Warner* v. *Campbell*, 39 Ind. 409; *Pittsburgh, etc., R. R. Co.* v. *Van Houten*, 48 Ind. 90; *Cole* v. *Allen*, 51 Ind. 122; *State, ex rel.*, v. *Terre Haute, etc., R. R. Co.*, 64 Ind. 297 (303); *Board, etc.*, v. *Hall*, 70 Ind. 469 (476); *Mansur* v. *Churchman*, 84 Ind. 573; *Robbins* v. *Magee*, 96 Ind. 174 (179); *State* v. *Dixon*, 97 Ind. 125 (126); *Board, etc.*, v. *Center Tp.*, 105 Ind. 422 (444); Elliott's App. Proced., section 556.

By section 3 of the act of February 16, 1893, Acts of 1893, p. 31, it is expressly provided that this court shall be governed in all things by the law as declared by the Supreme Court, and shall not, directly or by implication, reverse or modify any decision of that court.

Petition for rehearing overruled.

Filed June 28, 1893.

No. 643.

BIERHAUS ET AL. *v.* THE WESTERN UNION TELEGRAPH COMPANY.

TELEGRAPH COMPANY.—*Message.*—*Legal Transaction.*—*Negligence in Transmission and Delivery.*—*Special Damages.*—If a telegraphic message show that it relates to a commercial or legal transaction of value, it is sufficient to apprise the company of its character, and, for failure to use due diligence, it must respond in all special proximate damages.

SAME.—*Message.*—*Legal Transaction.*—*Damages.*—Where a telegram has been negligently and unnecessarily delayed, either in transmission or delivery, and thereby the collection of a debt has been defeated or rendered improbable, a substantial injury has been sustained for which special damages may be recovered.

SAME.—*Knowledge by Company of its Inability to Promptly Send Message.*—*Duty of.*—*Liability.*—Where a telegraph company receives a message for transmission, knowing at the time of its inability to transmit the message promptly, and does not so inform the sender, the company will be held responsible for any damages flowing from a delay in the transmission of the message.

SAME.—*Telegram.*—*Free Delivery.*—*Limitation to Certain Hours.*—*Knowledge of by Sender.*—*Liability for Delay.*—Where a telegram is received for transmission and delivery, and the sender is informed of a rule at the office of destination that free delivery of telegrams will not be made beyond a certain hour in the day, until the succeeding day, the company will not be responsible for any damages resulting from a delay in delivery, in compliance with such rule and custom.

EVIDENCE.—*Law of Foreign State Not Pleaded.*—*When May be Shown by Parol.*—Where a plaintiff seeks to establish his cause of action by showing the loss of a remedy in a foreign State, by defendant's negligence, the existence of the remedy under the laws of such foreign State may be shown, without pleading the law of such State.

From the Knox Circuit Court.

W. A. Cullop and *C. B. Kessinger*, for appellants.

J. S. Pritchett, J. T. Beasley and *A. B. Williams*, for appellee.

LOTZ, J.—The appellants sued the appellee to recover

damages alleged to have been sustained on account of the negligence of the appellee in transmitting and delivering two telegraphic messages. Issue was joined; there was a trial by jury, and a verdict for appellants in the sum of fifty cents. The court rendered judgment in favor of appellants for fifty cents damages and fifty cents costs.

The errors assigned in this court are:

1. The overruling of the demurrer to the second paragraph of amended answer.

2. The motion for a new trial.

If the appellants, in the court below, secured a judgment for all the damages recoverable under the allegations of their complaint, then they can have no valid grievance to present to this court; for where the ultimate judgment is right, no intervening error will avail in securing a reversal. *Morrison* v. *Kendall*, 6 Ind. App. 212, 33 N. E. Rep. 370; *Hamilton* v. *City of Shelbyville*, 6 Ind. App. 538, 33 N. E. Rep. 1007.

The first question presented for our consideration is whether or not special damages can be recovered under the allegations of the complaint. If only nominal damages and the sum paid for the transmission of the messages can be recovered, then appellants have no cause for complaint, for the court below meted out to them all they were entitled to recover.

The substantial allegations in that paragraph of the complaint upon which the judgment is founded are as follows:

''That the appellants were wholesale grocers and jobbers, doing business in Vincennes, Indiana, by the name of E. Bierhaus & Sons, and did business throughout that part of the State of Indiana and the adjoining State of Illinois; that they employed traveling salesmen and clerks, who solicited business for them, and they had many customers at various places in both of said States; that on the 22d day of July, 1890, and long prior thereto, they did business at Mt. Carmel, Illinois; that among their customers at said place was one P. L. Davis, who was indebted to them in the sum of $161.15; that the appellee had a line of wire extending directly from Mt. Carmel to Vincennes, a distance of twenty miles, and was engaged in telegraphing for the public generally; that on said day appellants had in their employ one M. F. Hoskinson, a competent and practicing attorney at said Mt. Carmel, who was authorized by them to make collections for them; that on said day said Davis was the owner of a stock of goods and merchandise situate in said Mt. Carmel; that on said day, at about the hour of three o'clock P. M., said Hoskinson learned and ascertained that said Davis was disposing of his stock of merchandise and converting his property into money, and preparing to leave the State of Illinois without paying his debts, and especially appellants' debt, and said Hoskinson thereupon prepared and delivered to the appellee, at its office in Mt. Carmel, directed to appellants, in their firm name, at 3:30 o'clock P. M. on said day, for transmission, the following message: 'Have you claim against P. L. Davis? Answer how much.' That the defendant then and there accepted said message and agreed to transmit the same; that said message was for the use and benefit of appellants; that said telegram was not delivered to appellants until the hour of 8:05 o'clock P. M. of said 22d day of July, four hours and thirty-five minutes after the same was delivered to appellee for transmission; that as soon as appellants received said message, they at once prepared an answer thereto and delivered the same to appellee at its office in the city of Vincennes, addressed to said Hoskinson, and requested appellee to transmit the same to Mt. Carmel, which said answer was as follows: "Yes. One hundred and sixty-one dollars and fifteen cents." That appellee then and there accepted and agreed to transmit the same for and in consideration of the sum of twenty-five cents, which appellants then and there paid to appellee; that said telegram arrived at Mt. Carmel at 8:40 o'clock P. M. of said day, but was not delivered to said Hoskinson until 9 o'clock A. M. of the 23d day of July, 1890; that before said telegram was delivered, the said Davis had disposed of all his property and converted the same into money and left the State of Illinois, and appellants' debt could not then be collected from him; that said Hoskinson was a resident of the city of Mt. Carmel; that he was then the judge of the County Court of Wabash county, and his residence and place of business was well known, and he lived near appellee's office, and could have been easily found; that appellee well knew that Hoskinson was looking for an answer to his said message, as he went to appellee's office at 8 o'clock P. M. of said 22d day of July and inquired for an answer to his telegram; that immediately after said Davis sold his property, he departed from the State of Illinois for parts unknown to appellants, and has ever since kept his whereabouts unknown to them; that if said message from said Hoskinson to appellants had been promptly transmitted and delivered, appellants would have responded at once, and if the telegram to said Hoskinson had been promptly delivered, appellants could have made and collected their debt due them from said Davis; that on account of appellee's negligence in transmitting and delivering said messages, appellants have lost the debt due them from Davis, and they were prevented from collecting the same, and have lost said debt, together with a fee of $20 which they became liable to pay to said Hoskinson."

Appellee contends, that there is nothing in the first message to apprise it of the importance of speedy transmission; that there is nothing in either of them that acquaints it of the fact that appellants desired to institute legal proceedings; that the first message may have been no more than an idle inquiry, or that Hoskinson may have wanted the information for various purposes other than legal proceedings; that it was not notified of the importance of either message, and that, therefore, no special damages can be recovered.

The transmission of information from one point to another, by means of electrical wires, is of comparatively recent origin. When persons and corporations first began to transmit such messages for hire, the courts applied to them the same rules that governed common carriers. There is little analogy between the two methods of doing business. The carrier transports the thing itself, while in telegraphy the information is not actually transported at all, but is conveyed by means of a continuous wire and electrical appliances. A language is spoken at one end which an educated and skillful operator understands and interprets at the other. The tendency has been to apply old rules to new inventions and methods.

In the celebrated case of *Hadley* v. *Baxendale*, 9 Exch. 341, it appeared that the plaintiff, owner of a steam mill, broke a shaft, and desiring to have another made, left the broken shaft with the defendant, a *carrier*, to take to an engineer to serve as a model for a new one. At the time of making the contract, the defendant's clerk was informed that the mill was stopped and that the plaintiff desired the broken shaft sent immediately. Its delivery was delayed and the new shaft kept back, as a consequence. The plaintiff brought an action for a breach of the contract with the carrier, and claimed, as special damages, the loss of profits while the mill was kept idle. But because it was not made to appear that the defendant was informed that the want of the shaft was the only thing that was keeping the mill from operating, it was held that he could not be made responsible to the extent claimed.

The reason for this rule is that the defendant not having any knowledge of one element of the damages sought, at the time he made the contract to carry the shaft, he could not be held to have contracted with reference to such possible resultant consequences.

Until recently, American judicial authority has been generally agreed that the rule for the measure of damages here laid down governs in all cases for the failure to transmit and deliver telegraphic messages correctly and promptly. That is to say, the company which undertakes to transmit the message must be apprised by the sender, or by the terms of the message itself, of the probable resultant consequences flowing from the failure to transmit and deliver promptly; that unless it has knowledge of such probable consequences it can not be said to contract in reference thereto. *W. U. Tel. Co.* v. *Hall,* 124 U. S. 444; *W. U. Tel. Co.* v. *Cooper,* 71 Tex. 507, 10 Am. St. Rep. 772, note. Many cases might be cited in support of this rule. In some of the more recent decisions, the tendency is to relax this rule, and some courts have gone so far as to entirely overthrow it.

In *Daugherty* v. *Am. Union Tel. Co.,* 75 Ala. 168, 51 Am. Rep. 435, it was held that the company was liable for special damages for the nondelivery of a cipher message, the meaning of which was not known or explained to the company's agent. So it has also often been held that the company is liable for all proximate damages where the message is couched in language the meaning of which is obscure, or unknown to the company's agent. The courts are inclined to adopt the principle that it is sufficient to render the company liable for actual damages if the message show upon its face that it relates to a business transaction, and that loss will probably result unless it is promptly and correctly transmitted and delivered, and that it is not necessary that the company be apprised of the loss that may result from its default. If the message show that it relates to a commercial or legal transaction of value, it is sufficient to apprise the company of its character, and for failure to use due diligence it must respond in all special proximate damages.

The following are some of the cases where the principle has been applied, messages as follows: "Cover two hundred September, one hundred August." *W. U. Tel. Co.* v. *Blanchard*, 68 Ga. 299, 45 Am. Rep. 480. "Ten cars new two whites Aug. shipment fifty six half." *W. U. Tel. Co.* v. *Harris*, 19 Ill. App. 347. "Sell one hundred Western Union. Answer price." *Tyler* v. *W. U. Tel. Co.*, 60 Ill. 421. "Ship hogs at once." *Manville* v. *W. U. Tel. Co.*, 37 Iowa 214. "Ship cargo at 90 if you can secure freight at 10." *True* v. *International Tel. Co.*, 60 Me. 9. "If we have any Old Southern on hand sell same before board. Buy five Hudson at board." *Rittenhouse* v. *Independent Line, etc.*, 44 N. Y. 263. "Will take two cars sixteen; ship soon as convenient, via West Shore." This was in response to the following: "Pickled hams sixteens nine and a half." *Mowry* v. *W. U. Tel. Co.*, 51 Hun, 126. "Buy fifty Northwestern—Fifty Prairie du Chien, limit forty-five." *U. S. Tel. Co.* v. *Wenger*, 55 Pa. St. 262, 93 Am. Dec. 751. "Car cribs six sixty c. a. f. prompt," sent in reply to the following: "Quote cribs loose and strips packed." *Pepper* v. *Telegraph Co.*, 87 Tenn. 554. "Send bay horse to-day; Mack loads to-night." *Thompson* v. *W. U. Tel. Co.*, 64 Wis. 531.

In the well considered case of *Postal Tel., etc., Co.* v. *Lathrop*, 131 Ill. 575, after reviewing many authorities bearing on this question, the court concludes as follows: "We think the reasonable rule, and the one sustained by authority, is, that where a message, as written, read in the light of well known usage in commercial correspondence, reasonably informs the operator that the message is one of business importance, and discloses the transaction so far as it is necessary to accomplish the purpose for which it is sent, the company should be held liable for all the direct damages resulting from the negligent failure to transmit it as written, within a reasonable time, unless such negligence is in some way excused."

No court has gone farther in this direction than the Supreme Court of Indiana. In the case of *Hadley* v. *Western Union Tel. Co.*, 115 Ind. 191, the telegram read as follows: "Want your cattle in the morning; meet me at pasture." The message was sent on the 14th day of October, but was not delivered until the morning of the 15th, at about the hour of seven o'clock. It seems that the cattle had been sold for future delivery, at the option of the purchaser, and the purpose of the message was to notify the seller to deliver the cattle at a certain time. It was the custom among stock dealers to take and weigh cattle at early daylight. On account of the failure to deliver the message promptly, the cattle were detained in a public highway for the space of thirty or forty minutes before they could be weighed; and on account of such detention and delay, they decreased in weight. It was held that the company was liable for the decrease in weight, although there was no showing that the company's agent was notified of the importance of the message, or that he had any knowledge of the sale of the cattle, or of the custom among stock dealers, or that the cattle were liable to decrease in weight by not being weighed immediately after rising in the morning. It is hard to reconcile some of the holdings with the general rules that prevail in measuring the damages in the cases of a breach of contract. A person in making a contract has the right to protect himself against liability by proper stipulation, and it is manifestly unjust to compel him to respond in damages for consequences which were unknown, and not even contemplated by him.

Telegraph companies when they are incorporated have certain extraordinary privileges granted to them by the State, and the State has the right to impose duties upon them. Accordingly they are required to receive and transmit dispatches with impartiality and in good faith, under a penalty for failure so to do. Elliott's Supp., section 1120. They are also made liable for special damages for failure or negligence in receiving, transmitting and delivering messages. Section 4177, R. S. 1881. Most all the States have similar enactments. It seems to us that it is more logical to say that there are duties imposed upon the company by law, and that for the breach of these duties it is liable for all the damages that naturally and proximately result from the breach of the duty, and not from the breach of a contract.

The appellee further contends that the complaint does not show that the appellants have lost any legal remedy; that they may still pursue the said Davis by legal process or otherwise, and collect their debt. If, however, the collection of their debt has been defeated or rendered improbable by the neglect of the appellee, we think the appellants have sustained a substantial injury. In *Parks* v. *Alta California Tel. Co.*, 13 Cal. 73, Am. Dec. 589, the plaintiffs, in reply to a message from their agent, informing them of the failure of a certain firm, and inquiring the amount due, sent the following: "Due 1,800; attach if you can find property. Will send note by to-morrow's stage." The message was delayed through the negligence of the defendant's agent, and, when it reached its destination, all the property of the firm had been attached by other creditors, and the plaintiff's claim was wholly lost. The loss of the debt was held to be the natural and proximate damages resulting from the defendant's negligence.

In *W. U. Tel. Co. v. Sheffield,* 71 Tex. 570, 10 Am. St. Rep. 790, the message read as follows: "You had better come and attend to your claim at once." The delivery of the message was delayed by the negligence of the company, so that other creditors attached and obtained first liens upon the property of the debtor. It was held that the measure of damages was the value of the debt with interest to the date of trial, and the costs of the message. The same principle was applied to similar circumstances in *Bryant v. Am. Tel. Co.,* 1 Daly 575. The complaint states a case which entitles the appellants to recover special damages.

The first part of the amended second paragraph of the answer is addressed to the first message, and is designed to excuse the appellee from promptly transmitting the same. The facts upon this point, alleged in brief, are, that said message was delivered to appellee's agent at Mt. Carmel at the hour of 5:10 o'clock in the afternoon of July 22, 1890, and at that said time, and for several hours just previous thereto, a severe storm was raging at Mt. Carmel, Ill., and along the route over which the wires extended between Mt. Carmel and Vincennes, and such storm continued with great violence for the period of three hours after said message had been delivered for transmission; that during all of said time the air was so charged with electricity, and the wires so affected thereby, that it was impossible to transmit such message over such wires, and said wires were thrown down and broken by trees falling upon them; that as soon as said storm abated the message was, at the earliest possible moment, transmitted and delivered.

Appellants assert, that these facts do not show a sufficient justification for the delay; that no one but a skilled electrician or telegrapher can determine what storms affect the wires so that a message can not be sent over them, and that none but the agents of the company could know that the wires were broken at remote points; that when the company received the message it knew of these facts, and appellants' agent did not; that when it accepted the message and money for transmission, if it failed to inform appellants of its inability to transmit, at once, that its liability became fixed from that moment; that had appellants known of the inability, they might have availed themselves of other means of communication, and thus have secured their debt.

The statute, section 1122, Elliott's Supp., requires telegraph companies to receive messages. They have no option to refuse them, except upon payment of a penalty. The law does not require of them impossible or unreasonable things. If a message can not be transmitted by reason of storms or other atmospheric influences, the company will be excused. *Western Union Tel. Co. v. Cohen,* 73 Ga. 522.

If the delay in transmitting a message is caused by conditions beyond the control of the company, it can not be compelled to respond in damages. *Beasley v. Western Union Tel. Co.,* 39 Fed. Rep. 181.

If, at the time the message is received, the company's agents have no knowledge that the wires are in such a condition that the message can not be transmitted, or if, after it is received, conditions arise which render it impossible to transmit it promptly, it will be excused. *Fowler v. Western Union Tel. Co.,* 15 Atl. Rep. 29.

But the case made by the answer does not fall within these rules. It is shown that at the time the message was received, the company's agent knew of its inability to transmit the message promptly, by reason of the electrical storm and its broken wires. There is no showing that the appellants had knowledge of these conditions, or that the company's agent gave them any such information. It is true that appellants knew that a storm was raging, but it surely will not be contended that every storm so affects the wires that messages can not be transmitted, nor that every storm causes trees to fall over and break the wires. The law requires, that the company shall deal with the public in good faith; that each party should be placed on an equal footing. It is manifestly unfair for the company to receive the message knowing that its wires are broken, and that an electrical storm is raging which renders it impossible to transmit promptly, and keep such knowledge locked up from the sender. Persons resort to telegraphy because of its rapid communication, and pay exorbitant prices for the service because it is rapid. If the company knows that it can not give quick communication, when the message is accepted, it can not excuse itself except by notifying the person presenting the message of its inability. Suppose there were several lines between the same points, operated by different companies, and that one of the lines is broken and can not be repaired for several hours, and these facts are known to the company only. A message is presented and accepted and no notice of inability is given. A delay of several hours ensue, and great damages are incurred. Would it be contended that the company would not be liable when, if it had communicated its inability, the message might have been sent by another line, and the loss avoided?

So, in this case, if appellants had been informed of appellee's inability, they might have made the communication by other means. They were only half an hour away by rail or two hours by courier. We think this part of the answer insufficient.

The second part of the answer relates to the failure to deliver the second message promptly. It is averred, that this message was delivered to appellee's agent, at Vincennes, Ind., at 8:30 o'clock P. M., of July 22d; that it was promptly transmitted to its office in Mt. Carmel, where it was received at 8:40 o'clock of the same day; that on said day, and for a long time prior thereto, there was a general rule and regulation in force at said office to the effect that if any message was received after 8 o'clock P. M. of any day, such message would not be delivered by messenger of appellee away from said office, and that such message would only be delivered on the day of reception, unless the person to whom such message was addressed employed a special messenger to make such delivery; that such custom was general and uniform at said office and place, and was well known and understood by the citizens and inhabitants of said Mt. Carmel and vicinity; that when the said M. F. Hoskinson, mentioned in the complaint, delivered the first message, referred to in the complaint, he was fully informed as to said rule and regulation, and was then notified by appellee's agent that if an answer should be received to said message after the hour of 8 o'clock P. M. of said day, the same would not be delivered away from the receiving office until the following day, unless a special messenger was employed to make such delivery; that no such messenger was employed, and that appellee delivered the same promptly on the next day. Appellants contend that these facts do not excuse the appellee for the negligence imputed to it for a failure to deliver the second message, because it is not shown that when they sent the message from Vincennes they had knowledge of, or were informed of the regulation ·at Mt. Carmel. It is well settled that a telegraph company may reasonably regulate its office hours, and its free delivery limits, according to the requirements of the business at the various points where it holds itself out for public service. It is not the regulation that is complained of here, but the failure of the company to notify appellants of the existence of such regulation.

In *Western Union Tel. Co.* v. *Harding,* 103 Ind. 505, which was an action to recover a statutory penalty, it was held that a telegraph company is not required to keep its agents informed concerning the office hours at all other points, so that when a message is presented for transmission the sender may be apprised of any probable delay which may intervene at the other end of the line. This decision, however, was not unanimous, and it was expressly limited to cases for the recovery of a penalty. The intimation, however, is that in a case to recover special damages such regulation, without being communicated to the sender, would not exculpate the company from liability. MITCHELL, J., said: "It might well be that in a case where a message was delivered, which showed upon its face the importance of speedy transmission, and other means of making the communication were available to the sender, which might be resorted to if he was informed that the one chosen was ineffectual, or his conduct might otherwise be materially controlled thereby, the company would be bound, at its peril, to ascertain and disclose its inability to serve him, or render itself liable to respond in damages."

In *W. U. Tel. Co.* v. *Broesche,* 72 Tex. 654, it was decided that a telegraph company could not relieve itself from liability for failing to deliver a message paid for and sent by it, by showing that its office at the point of delivery was closed when the message was received for transmission: A telegraph company had an office regulation at Hannibal, Mo., which confined the free delivery of messages in that city to within a radius of ten blocks. "It would, in our opinion, be quite unreasonable to expect the plaintiff to be advised of such a regulation. It would be much more reasonable to require the defendant's agent to notify the sender of a message of the free delivery limits applicable only to the place of destination." *Brashears* v. *W. U. Tel. Co.*, 45 Mo. App. 433. There are authorities which take a contrary view of this question. *W. U. Tel. Co.* v. *Henderson*, 89 Ala. 510; *Stevenson* v. *Montreal Tel. Co.*, 16 U. C. Q. B. 530; *Given* v. *W. U. Tel. Co.*, 24 Fed. Rep. 119.

In the case last cited, Mr. Justice MILLER said: "Nor do we see that it is the duty of the Western Union Telegraph Company to keep the employes of every one of its offices in the United States informed of the time when every other office closes for the night. The immense number of these offices all over the United States, the frequent changes among them as to the time of closing, and the prodigious volume of a written book on this subject, seem to make this onerous and inconvenient to a degree which forbids it to be treated as a duty to its customers, for neglect of which it must be held liable for damages." We do not concur in the statement that onerous and burdensome conditions would be imposed upon the company if it were required to inform its customers of the office hours and delivery limits at the delivery office. It is a well known fact that such companies have rate books, with the names of the stations alphabetically arranged, which its employes frequently resort to before they accept a message. By a proper designation, the office hours and delivery limits of each station could be readily indicated. Such methods are applied in the postal service.

Mr. Thompson, in his work on Electricity, section 300 says: "But it is a mere judicial assumption to say, as was said in one case (*Givens* v. *Western Union Tel. Co.*, *supra*) that the employes in a telegraph office are *not* required to know the hour at which an office of the company in another city closes. On the contrary, it is an obvious suggestion that, in any properly regulated elegraph system, the offices would be classified, and ere would be a uniform time established for the closing those of each class, of which time every agent receiv-'g dispatches would be apprised. It is probable that here is not a receiving agent in the postal telegraph service of France or Germany that does not know the hour of closing of every office in the republic or empire."

The averment here, however, is that the appellee informed appellants' agent at Mt. Carmel, before the second message was sent, of the existence of such regulation. As he was specially entrusted with the management of the business at that end of the line, his knowledge must be deemed the knowledge of his principals. *Brannon* v. *May*, 42 Ind. 92; *Phœnix Mut. Life Ins. Co.* v. *Hinesley*, 75 Ind. 1.

That part of the answer that is addressed to the failure to promptly transmit and deliver the first telegram is insufficient, and that part that is addressed to the failure to promptly deliver the second telegram is sufficient; but as the pleading attempts to answer the whole complaint, the demurrer should have been sustained.

On the trial of the cause, the appellants produced a witness, M. F. Hoskinson, who testified that he was a resident of Mt. Carmel, Ill., and had been practicing law for fourteen years and was then the county judge. Appellants then offered to show by him, that he could have sued out, under the laws of Illinois, a writ of attachment and attached sufficient property of the said Davis to have made the whole of appellants' debt had said message been promptly delivered; that he, as the attorney for appellants, could have given bond and made the affidavits for a writ of attachment and garnishment. The appellee objected to this testimony, assigning as a reason for its inadmissibility that no statute of Illinois had been pleaded.

The court excluded this testimony, and, among other things, said, in the presence of the jury, that no statute of Illinois had been pleaded. To these remarks of the court in the presence of the jury, the appellants, at the time, excepted. The court seems to have based its ruling upon the theory that it was necessary to plead the statute of a foreign State, before it could be given in evidence.

The general rule is that where a party relies upon the statute of a foreign State to give him a right of action or ground of defense, he must specially plead and prove the statute. The right of action declared upon in plaintiffs' complaint is not given by a foreign statute. The right to recover damages for failure to promptly transmit and deliver a telegraphic message exists independently of any statutory enactment, but such right is specially given by section 4177, *supra*.

The statutes of Illinois, if they were proper for any purpose in this case, were only evidence tending to establish appellants' right of recovery. It is a familiar rule that a party is not required to plead his evidence. The laws of a State to whose courts a party appeals for redress, furnish, in all cases, *prima facie*, the rule of decision, and if either party claims the benefit of a different rule, as applicable to his case, he must aver and prove it. *Buchanan* v. *Hubbard*, 119 Ind. 187.

In *Crake* v. *Crake*, 18 Ind. 156, it was said: "Where a right is sought to be enforced in one State in relation to a subject-matter existing in a foreign State, and no foreign law is proved, and no common law rule ever prescribed, and no contract exists, * * * the court will apply the law of the State in which it is sitting."

The law of the sister State of Illinois, both statutory and common, in the absence of any showing to the contrary, is presumed to be the same as that of our own State. *Hynes* v. *McDermott*, 82 N. Y. 41; *Desnoyer* v. *McDonald*, 4 Minn. 515; *Cooper* v. *Reaney*, 4 Minn. 528; *Lewis* v. *Bush*, 30 Minn. 244; *Draggoo* v. *Graham*, 9 Ind. 212.

It would seem, under these rules, that the appellants were under no compulsion to prove the statute laws of Illinois, but that they might rely upon the laws of Indiana without proof. Lawson's Expert and Opinion Evidence, p. 59.

If the appellee desired to invoke a foreign rule, the burden rested upon it to overthrow the presumption.

We may say, *en passant*, that the unwritten or common law of any other of the United States or of England may be proven by parol by persons learned in such laws. Section 476, R. S. 1881.

In England, this rule extends to the written as well as the unwritten laws.

In Baron De Brode's Case, 8 Q. B. 208, a French advocate practicing at Strasburg was permitted to depose that the feudal law had been put an end to in Alsace by the "torrent of the French Revolution" and by a decree of the national convention. This rule has been followed in that country ever since, but the American rule is less liberal. It requires the production of the written law, but will hear parol evidence of experts as to its interpretation and effect.

Section 477, R. S. 1881, provides that "The existence and tenor or effect of the laws of any foreign country may be proved as facts by parol evidence; but if it shall appear that the law in question is contained in a written statute or code, the court may, in its discretion, reject any evidence of such law which is not accompanied by a copy thereof."

The appellants were surely entitled to show that they could have given bond and procured writs of attachment and garnishment and secured their debt, under the statutes of Indiana, without pleading the statutes of Illinois. It is not necessary to prove the law of the forum. Lawson's Expert and Opinion Evidence, p. 59.

Judgment reversed, with instructions to sustain the motion for a new trial and the demurrer to the amended second paragraph of answer, and for further proceedings in accordance with this opinion.

Filed June 20, 1893; petition for a rehearing overruled Nov. 23, 1893.

No. 762.

YOUNG v. MASON.

PHYSICIAN AND PATIENT.—*Malpractice.*—*When Patient May Recover, When Not.*—*Mixed Negligence.*—In an action against a surgeon for malpractice, no recovery can be had by the patient against the surgeon, in any case, where both the surgeon and patient are free from negligence, or where the surgeon and patient are both guilty of negligence, or where the surgeon is free from fault and the patient is guilty of negligence. It is only where the surgeon is guilty of negligence, and the patient is without negligence on his part, contributing in any degree to such injuries, that the patient can recover damages of the surgeon.

SAME.—*Contributory Negligence.*—*Judgment on Answers to Interrogatories, non Obstante.*—In such an action, when the answers to interrogatories show that the patient, by his negligent conduct in disregard of his surgeon's instructions, and in interfering with the surgeon in the discharge of his duties, contributed to the injuries complained of, the defendant is entitled to judgment on such answers, notwithstanding a general verdict for the plaintiff.

From the Grant Circuit Court.

W. H. Carroll, G. D. Dean and *A. J. Remy*, for appellant.

H. Brownlee, H. J. Paulus, E. Pierce and *J. A. Hindman*, for appellee.

DAVIS, J.—In her complaint the appellant alleges that on the 9th day of July, 1891, she suffered the following injuries, to wit:

1. Broke and fractured the radius of her left forearm, near the wrist joint.

2. Dislocated laterally both bones of her left forearm, at the elbow joint.

3. Fractured the inner condyle of the humerus of the left elbow.

It is further alleged that she employed the appellee, a practicing physician and surgeon, of Hartford City, Ind., to attend and treat her said injuries. This action is to recover damages alleged to have been sustained by appellant, as the result of alleged unskillfulness and negligence on the part of appellee, in the treatment of her said injuries in the following respects, namely:

1. That he did not exercise due care and skill in setting and reducing said fractures and dislocations, and in the treatment of said injuries.

2. That he negligently, carelessly, unskillfully, and unprofessionally pretended to set and reduce said fractures and dislocations.

3. That he failed to properly reduce said dislocation of said elbow joint, and to properly bandage the same so as to hold said bones to their proper places.

4. That he too frequently changed the bandages and splints on said wounds, and prevented the union of the ' fragments of said broken bones by frequently manipulating and moving the same.

5. That he prevented the proper relocation and adjustment of said dislocated elbow by too frequently manipulating and moving it.

Whereby it is charged:

1. That said bones of said joints, by adhesion to the surrounding parts, became stiff at said joints.

2. That said left arm became permanently stiff and crooked at said joints.

3. And because of the negligence, and carelessness, and unskillfulness of appellee in improperly reducing the dislocation of the elbow joint, and in bandaging and treating said arm and hand, the appellant's hand and fingers have become stiff and permanently crooked.

The venue of the cause was changed from the Blackford to the Grant Circuit Court, where it was tried by a jury. The jury returned a general verdict in favor of appellant for $1,000, and they also returned answers to forty interrogatories submitted by appellee. Upon motion of appellee, the court rendered judgment in his favor on the answers to the interrogatories. This ruling is the basis of the only error assigned. The question presented is, whether the facts disclosed by the answers to the interrogatories can, in any way, be reconciled with the general verdict. The general verdict necessarily decided all material questions in favor of appellant. As was well said by Judge NEW, in *Gaar, Scott & Co.* v. *Rose*, 3 Ind. App. 269, "The answers to interrogatories override the general verdict only when both can not stand together, the antagonism being such, upon the face of the record, as is beyond the possibility of removal by any evidence admissible under the issues in the cause.''

In the language of Judge ELLIOTT, in another case, ''If there is no irreconcilable conflict between the general verdict and the special answers, the former must prevail, and it is likewise true that intendment will not be made in favor of the special answers. It is also true that the answers to the interrogatories can not control the general verdict if they are contradictory, although the verdict may be in irreconcilable conflict with some of these answers.'' *Matchett* v. *Cincinnati, etc., R. W. Co.*, 132 Ind. 334.

In the light of these authorities, the first proposition to be determined is whether the answers to the interrogatories conclusively show that appellee was not guilty of negligence resulting in any of the injuries for which recovery is sought in this action.

It is clearly shown, by the answers, that the appellee did possess the fair and ordinary knowledge and skill. *Jones* v. *Angell*, 95 Ind. 376; *Gramm* v. *Boener*, 56 Ind. 497.

Also that the manner in which he dressed and treated appellant's injuries was, with one exception, such as is approved and followed by the most skillful surgeons in that vicinity, and which is approved by the standard authors and text-writers upon the subject of surgery. The exception is that the answers do not conclusively show that appellee exercised due skill and care in reducing the fracture near the wrist joint. The most that can be said in behalf of appellee, in this respect, is that the answers are contradictory.

Counsel for appellee, however, contend that ''Granting, for the time being, that this fracture was not reduced, there is nothing in the entire record indicating that the appellant was injured or even inconvenienced by this omission.''

All we deem it necessary to say on this subject is that when we refer to the allegations in the complaint, to which we have heretofore called attention, which, in view of the general verdict, so far as the question now under consideration is concerned, we must regard as having been proven on the trial, the court can not say, as a matter of law, in the absence of an express finding to the contrary, that the appellant was not injured or inconvenienced by reason of the alleged negligence of the appellee in failing to reduce the fracture near the wrist-joint.

Conceding that the answers to the interrogatories fail to show that appellee was not guilty of the unskillfulness or negligence charged in the complaint, in the respect last mentioned, does it appear from these answers that the alleged injuries which are made the basis of the action, were in any degree caused by the want of proper care on the part of appellant? In other words, is appellant shown to have been guilty of any act of negligence which was the proximate cause of the injuries of which complaint is made?

The interrogatories and answers thereto bearing on this branch of the case are as follows:

''Did not the defendant, at his first visit, after having properly examined, reduced, adjusted, bandaged, and dressed the arm, and at divers other times, order and direct plaintiff not to remove her arm from the sling, but to keep it in the sling at rest? A. Yes.

''If you answer question 18 (the preceding question) in the affirmative, state if such orders and directions given the plaintiff by the defendant were proper, and whether a strict observance of the same was necessary to the proper treatment of the injuries of the arm. A. In the main it was.

"If you answer question 18 in the affirmative, state if it is not true that the plaintiff failed, refused and neglected to obey the orders and directions of the defendant by taking and removing the arm from the sling in the defendant's absence. A. She did in part.

"Is it not true that the plaintiff at divers times within the first, second, and third weeks following her injuries, remove the injured arm from the sling in violation and disregard of defendant's directions and instructions? A. Yes.

"Did not the plaintiff on divers occasions within the first, second, and third weeks following the injury, and after the said third morning, remove the arm from the sling, and leave it out for short times, placing it in different positions while out of the sling, and if this was not in violation of the defendant's instructions to her? Answer fully. A. Yes.

"Did the plaintiff obey the directions and instructions of the defendant in the matter of caring for and treating her arm in his absence? A. Not entirely.

"If you answer question 28 (last question) in the negative, state fully how and in what manner the plaintiff failed to follow defendant's directions and instructions. A. By taking her injured arm out of the sling and placing it on her lap, window-sill, and table.

"Is it not a fact that the injured arm was highly inflamed and very much swollen for a time? A. Yes.

"If you answer question 31 in the affirmative, state if the inflammation and swelling was not produced in part as the natural result of the injuries sustained? A. Yes.

"If you find that the plaintiff, at divers times within the week following the injury, removed her arm from the sling, state if it is true that the natural tendency of such conduct was not to aggravate and increase inflammation and swelling. A. It was to some extent.

"If you answer question 33 in the affirmative, state if it is not true that the inflammation and swelling of plaintiff's arm was not aggravated and increased by the removal of her arm from the sling. A. It would partially.

"Is it not a fact that the natural effect and tendency of such inflammation and swelling over and about the injured parts, and over and about the ligaments, tendons, muscles, and soft parts of the arm was to produce and cause a stiffened condition of the elbow, wrist, and finger-joints? A. Yes.

"If you find that the arm at and about the points of the injuries was greatly inflamed and swollen, and that the natural tendency of such inflamed and swollen condition was to cause stiffness at the elbow, wrist, and finger-joints, what do you find from the evidence was the proper treatment of the arm in that condition to prevent or overcome such tendency to stiffness in said joints? A. Passive motion and the application of lotions.

"Do you not find that the arm was highly inflamed and swollen for a time, and that the natural tendency of such condition was to produce stiffness in the joints if not properly treated, and that the proper treatment to prevent such results was to use passive motion. A. Yes.

"Is it not a fact that the defendant, at the proper times, used such passive motion at these joints, when allowed to do so by the plaintiff, as fully and freely as she would permit? A. Yes.

"Is it not a fact that the plaintiff, on account of the pain (caused) by the defendant's effort to produce passive motion at the elbow, wrist, and finger joints, refused to allow him to employ such means for her recovery, and that he was prevented, by such refusal, from using such passive motion at the times and to the extent proper? A. Yes.

"If you find from the evidence that there is a partial stiffness at the elbow, wrist, and finger joints, do you not find that this condition of these joints resulted, in whole or in part, from the refusal of the plaintiff to permit the defendant to subject these joints, at the proper times, to passive motion? A. In part."

Before considering the effect of these answers, we will briefly refer to the authorities which relate to the duties of the patient in such cases, and also the question of contributory negligence on his part.

In *Potter* v. *Warner*, 91 Pa. St. 362, 36 Am. Rep. 668, the court says: "It is, however, the duty of the patient to submit to the treatment prescribed, and to follow the directions given, provided they be such as a physician of ordinary skill would adopt or sanction. * * * If the injuries were the result of mutual and concurring negligence of the parties, no action to recover damages therefor will lie. A person can not recover from another for consequences attributable in part to his own wrong. Nor is it necessary that the negligence of each party be equal, to defeat a recovery. *Cattawissa R. R. Co.* v. *Armstrong*, 13 Wright, 186."

It was well said, in *Railroad* v. *Norton*, 12 Harris, 465: "The law has no scales to determine in such cases whose wrong-doing weighed most in the compound that occasioned the mischief." *Jones* v. *Angell, supra.*

Indulging every reasonable presumption and intendment in favor of the general verdict, and granting that the appellant established, to the satisfaction of the jury, every fact put in issue by the allegations in her complaint, except when the answers to the interrogatories affirmatively and conclusively show to the contrary, and giving a fair and reasonable construction to the facts, which are clearly, specifically, and without conflict or contradiction, found in said answers, we conclude that the negligence of the appellee in failing to reduce the fracture near the wrist, and the refusal of appellant to allow appellee to subject the injured joints at the proper times to passive motion concurred in producing the injuries for which recovery is sought.

It is urged by counsel for appellant that one of the injuries complained of is the failure to reduce the fracture, and that it is not shown that any negligence of appellant contributed to this injury.

We do not so understand the allegation in the complaint. The failure to reduce the fracture near the wrist is one of the alleged negligent acts of appellee. This act, with other acts of negligence, it is charged, as we have seen, caused the injuries specifically complained of, as hereinbefore stated, for which damages are sought. The bone was fractured near the wrist, and the elbow was dislocated. Appellee, in all respects, fully discharged his duty, except he failed to reduce the fracture. The appellant did not obey his directions, and refused to allow appellee to subject the injured parts at the proper times to passive treatment, and this contributory negligence on the part of appellant united with the said negligence on the part of appellee in causing the adhesion of the bones to the surrounding parts, the stiffness of the joints and the loss of the use of the arm. In other words, it is not charged that the failure to reduce the fracture is one of the injuries which resulted from his negligence, but this act is charged as the negligence which caused the stiffness of the joints. If the failure of appellee to reduce the fracture had caused the stiffness of the joints, without any negligence of appellant contributing thereto, appellee would undoubtedly be liable in damages therefor. The injuries complained of were certainly aggravated by the misconduct of appellant, and therefore appellee, under the authorities, is not liable in damages therefor. *Jones* v. *Angell, supra.*

The condition of the arm, the loss of its use, the stiffness of the joints, are the injuries of which it is alleged the negligent acts of the appellee were the proximate cause, and these injuries are shown by the answers to the interrogatories to have been the result, in some degree at least, of contributory negligence on the part of appellant. *Jones* v. *Angell, supra.*

For instance, suppose a man fractures the bones in his leg below the knee, and calls a surgeon to treat the injuries, and the surgeon negligently fails to properly reduce one of the fractures, but in all other respects gives proper treatment, and the patient, in disobedience of the directions of the surgeon, negligently removes the bandages used as a part of the proper treatment by the surgeon, or is otherwise guilty of contributory negligence, and such combined negligence of the surgeon and patient unite in producing a shortness and stiffness of the leg, for which injuries an action is brought against the surgeon, can the patient recover? The patient is certainly not responsible in such case for the original negligence of the surgeon in failing to properly reduce the fracture, but this negligence of the surgeon unites with the subsequent contributory negligence of the patient in causing the shortness and stiffness of the leg. Now, it seems clear to us under such circumstances, and the authorities cited, that the patient can not recover for the consequent shortness and stiffness of the leg. When both the surgeon and patient are free from negligence, or where the surgeon and patient are both guilty of negligence, or where the surgeon is free from fault and the patient is guilty of negligence, no recovery can be had by the patient against the surgeon in any case. It is only where the surgeon is guilty of negligence and the patient is without negligence on his part, contributing in any degree to such injuries, that the patient can recover damages of the surgeon.

In this case it appears, as we have seen, that both parties were, in some degree, at least, in fault in producing the injuries in question, and therefore the court below did not err in rendering judgment for appellee.

Judgment affirmed.

Filed Nov. 22, 1893.

END OF MAY TERM.

CASES

ARGUED AND DETERMINED

IN THE

APPELLATE COURT

OF THE

STATE OF INDIANA,

AT INDIANAPOLIS, NOVEMBER TERM, 1893, IN THE SEVENTY-EIGHTH YEAR OF THE STATE.

———◆———

No. 946.

THE CITIZENS' INSURANCE COMPANY, OF EVANSVILLE, INDIANA, v. SPRAGUE.

INSURANCE.—*Policy on Merchandise.—Provision for Inventory Each Year.—When Failure to make not Matter of Defense.*—Where an insurance policy issued upon a stock of merchandise provided, as a condition of insurance, that the insured would make an itemized inventory of merchandise * * each year, and correct records of all purchases and freight paid, and all sales made from the time one inventory is made until another shall have been taken, etc., and about two months after the issuance of the policy the property was destroyed by fire, no inventory having been made, the failure of the assured to make an inventory of the merchandise is no matter of defense by the company, the assured having yet ten months in which to make such inventory, under the terms of the policy.

From the Gibson Circuit Court.

J. E. Iglehart, E. Taylor and *J. H. Miller*, for appellant.

A. Gilchrist, C. A. De Bruler and *L. C. Embree*, for appellee.

(275)

Ross, J.—The appellee sued the appellant upon a pol-. icy of insurance, issued by it April 18, 1891, insuring his stock of merchandise for one year from that date against loss by fire. On the 18th day of June, 1891, the property insured was destroyed by fire, and appellant refusing to adjust the loss, this action was brought. The cause was tried by the court, without the intervention of a jury, a finding made, and judgment rendered in favor of the appellee.

The only questions urged on this appeal relate to the rulings of the court in sustaining the demurrers to the third, fourth, fifth, and sixth paragraphs of the answer. Each of these paragraphs of the answer is based upon the following clause in the policy, viz:

"Warranted by assured that an itemized inventory of merchandise and store furniture and fixtures shall be made once each year, and correct records of all purchases and freight paid, and all sales made from the time one inventory is made until another shall have been taken; and that such inventories and records, or duplicates thereof, shall either be kept in an iron safe or in another building located sufficiently remote from the property insured under this policy as not to be burned therewith by the same fire."

There is considerable discussion *pro* and *con*, as to whether or not the above clause is a part of the policy sued on, and, also, whether or not it amounts to a warranty. The first of these questions must be considered in the affirmative, and the second, for the purposes of this case, will be considered, in effect, as a warranty. What, then, did the appellee, under the terms of this contract, agree to do? He agreed to make out, once each year, an itemized inventory of his merchandise and store furniture and fixtures, and correct records of all purchases and freight paid, and all sales made from the time one inventory was made until another should be taken.

It is averred in each paragraph of the answer that the appellee failed to make out and deposit the inventory as provided in said policy.

Under this clause of the policy, the appellee had one year from April 18, 1891, in which to make out the inventory as therein provided. Until the expiration of one year, there was no breach of the contract on his part in not making out such inventory.

The fire which destroyed appellee's property occurred just two months after the issuing of the policy sued on. Ten months remained in which the appellee was permitted to make out the inventory of the stock of merchandise, furniture, and fixtures, and until the expiration of the year allowed, there was no breach. This is the plain meaning of the language used in the policy, and to give it any other construction would simply be to do violence to the English language.

There was no error committed in sustaining the demurrers to these paragraphs of the answer.

Judgment affirmed.

REINHARD, J., absent.

Filed Dec. 12, 1893.

Fruits *et al. v.* Elmore.

No. 901.

FRUITS ET AL. *v.* ELMORE. ·

REPLEVIN.—*Answer of Property in Third Person.—Sustaining Demurrer to.—Harmless Error.—General Denial.*—In an action of replevin, it is not available error to sustain a demurrer to a paragraph of answer which only amounts to an answer of property in a third person, such fact being provable under the general denial.

SAME.—*Possession Must be Shown.*—Replevin can not be maintained unless the evidence shows the actual or constructive possession of the property in the defendant at the time when the suit was instituted.

SAME.—*Evidence.—Judgment.—Execution.—Constable.*—In such case, the suit being against a constable, among others, who had levied an execution on the property in question, the judgment and writ of execution are admissible in evidence as tending to show the right of possession.

JUDGMENT.—*Voidable.—Collateral Attack.*—In an action for work and labor performed, on a demand for $3, the jury returned a verdict as follows: "We, the jury, find for the plaintiff," upon which the court rendered judgment for plaintiff for $3 and for costs of suit, taxed at $14.75.

Held, that the judgment was merely voidable and not void, and could not be collaterally attacked.

From the Montgomery Circuit Court.

G. D. Hurley and *M. E. Clodfelter*, for appellants.

G. W. Paul and *M. W. Bruner*, for appellee.

LOTZ, J.—The appellee was the plaintiff and the appellants the defendants in the court below. The action was to recover the possession of a certain horse. There was a trial by jury, and the appellee had judgment in her favor against all the appellants. The appellants have severally assigned errors in this court. The first error discussed by counsel is that the court erred in sustaining a demurrer to the second paragraph of the separate answer of Noah Fruits. In this paragraph, said appellant pleaded, that he was the duly qualified and acting constable of Ripley township, in Montgomery county, and that a writ of execution was duly issued and delivered to him by John L. Hankins, a justice of the peace of said township, on a judgment duly made and given in favor of one Jacob Elmore, and against one James Elmore; that as such constable he levied said writ upon the property described in the complaint as the property of said James Elmore, and that the same was the property of said James Elmore. There was no error in sustaining a demurrer to this answer. It is only equivalent to an answer of property in a third person. It is well settled that where the real defense in replevin is property in a third person, such defense may be given under the general denial. *Branch* v. *Wiseman,* 51 Ind. 1; *Lane* v. *Sparks,* 75 Ind. 278.

The next assignment of error discussed by counsel is the overruling of the motion for a new trial. On the trial the appellants, after sufficiently identifying the same, offered in evidence a judgment rendered by the appellant, John L. Hankins, as a justice of peace of Ripley township, in the case of Jacob Elmore against James Elmore, and a writ of execution issued thereon by the appellant, John L. Hankins, as such justice of the peace, which was levied upon the property in controversy by the appellant, Noah Fruits, as constable of said township. This evidence was excluded over the objection of the appellants. Replevin is a mere possessory action. Title to the property is usually but an incident in determining the right to possession. It may, or may not, be a controlling circumstance. One person may have the title and another have the right to the possession. Usually title is a strong circumstance tending to show the right of possession. In the case in hearing, it was proper, under the issues for the appellants, to show that the horse was the property of James Elmore, and that the possession under the writ and judgment was lawful and right. The general issue admits any evidence relevant to the right of possession, asserted by the plaintiff, including evidence of a right of possession in the defendant, or even in a stranger. *Smith* v. *Harris*, 76 Ind. 104. Appellee, however, contends that the judgment on its face is a nullity, and that it conferred no rights upon appellant Hankins, to issue an execution, and that the writ affords no protection to the other appellants in making the levy. The judgment offered in evidence shows that it was an action on account for work and labor done, in which a judgment in the sum of $3 was demanded. There was a trial by jury, and a verdict as follows: "We, the jury, find for the plaintiff." Upon this verdict the justice rendered judgment in favor of the plaintiff in the sum of $3 and costs of suit, costs taxed at $14.75. The writ was issued for $3 with interest, and for $14.75 costs. This writ was levied upon the property in controversy.

It has often been decided that where there is a mere finding for the plaintiff, without any assessment of damages, no judgment can properly follow. *Cincinnati, etc., R. R. Co.* v. *Washburn*, 25 Ind. 259; *Trout* v. *West*, 29 Ind. 51; *Mitchell* v. *Geisendorff*, 44 Ind. 358; *Nicholson* v. *Caress*, 76 Ind. 24; *Bunnell* v. *Bunnell*, 93 Ind. 595.

If a judgment is a nullity, the party against whom it is rendered may assail it whenever and wherever it confronts him. But is the judgment offered in this case a nullity? In the cases above cited, there was a direct attack upon the judgments, here the attack is a collateral one. We do not consider the judgment offered in evidence as being absolutely void. The justice had jurisdiction of the subject-matter, and of the person of the judgment defendant. The judgment rendered by him was erroneous but not void. It was sufficient to support an execution until set aside. A constable or sheriff, as a general proposition, is not bound to look beyond the face of the writ delivered to him to execute. If it is legal on its face, he is bound to execute it, and he can plead it as a justification, though the proceedings before the magistrate, which led to the issue of the writ, are illegal. But the rule is different where the suit is against the person who procures, or the justice who issues the writ on such void proceedings. *Ewing* v. *Robeson*, 15 Ind. 26; *Rutherford* v. *Davis*, 95 Ind. 245; *Davis* v. *Bush*, 4 Blackf. 330.

The judgment here being merely voidable, the constable had the right to levy the same on the property of the judgment defendant. Of course if the constable levied it upon the property of appellee, neither the judgment nor the writ afforded him any protection. The right to the possession was the issue to be determined. There was some evidence which tended to show that James Elmore was the owner of the horse. This being true, the judgment and writ were proper evidence to go to the jury to show the right of possession under said levy.

Again, there is no evidence in the case which tends to show that the appellant, John L. Hankins, ever had the actual or constructive possession of the property. The only connection he had with the case was to issue an execution against the property of James Elmore. He gave no command to levy it upon the particular property in controversy. Replevin can not be maintained unless the evidence shows the actual or constructive possession of the property in the defendant at the time when the suit was instituted. *Standard Oil Co.* v. *Bretz*, 98 Ind. 231; *Louthain* v. *Fitzer*, 78 Ind. 449; *Krug* v. *Herod*, 69 Ind. 78.

Judgment reversed at the costs of appellee, with instructions to sustain the motion for a new trial as to all the appellants.

Filed Sept. 21, 1893; petition for rehearing overruled Nov. 28, 1893.

———————

No. 1,010.

THE STATE, EX REL. COURTER, *v.* BUCKLES ET AL.

EXECUTION.—*When May Issue and be Levied Against a County.—Judgment.*—An execution may issue on a judgment against a county, and may be levied upon any property owned by the county and not needed for governmental or public purposes.

SAME.—*Against a County.—Failure to Make Return Within 180 Days. —Liability of Sheriff.*—If a sheriff fails to make return of an execution issued against a county within 180 days, he is liable in nominal damages, without reference to the question whether or not there was any property out of which he could have made the same.

From the Knox Circuit Court.

H. S. Cauthorn, for appellant.

O. H. Cobb, for appellees.

REINHARD, J.—This is an action by the appellant's relator, against the appellee Buckles, on his official bond, as sheriff of the county of Knox, the other appellees being sureties on such bond.

The complaint is in two paragraphs, and the breach alleged in each paragraph is that the appellee Buckles, as such sheriff, for more than 180 days failed to levy an execution, in his hands, on a judgment in favor of the relator and against the board of commissioners of the county of Knox, which judgment was rendered by, and execution issued out of, the Knox Circuit Court.

For the purposes of the questions here involved, the

averments in each paragraph are substantially the same.

The court sustained a demurrer to each paragraph of the complaint, and this ruling presents the only ground upon which a reversal is asked.

The appellee has not favored us with a brief in the case, but we are informed, by appellant's brief, that the court based its ruling upon the theory that a judgment against a county could, under no condition, be enforced by means of an execution to be levied upon and satisfied by the sale of the county's property.

The statute makes it the duty of the sheriff, when an execution comes into his hands, to serve it upon the defendant or defendants in his county, and levy the execution, if not paid, upon any property of such defendant or defendants, and make at least one effort to sell such property, within sixty days after the execution comes into his hands. R. S. 1881, section 719.

The execution is returnable within 180 days from its date. R. S. 1881, section 683.

If he neglect or refuse to levy upon property, or return such execution, as required by law, the sheriff shall be amerced to the extent of the value of the property, not exceeding the amount necessary to satisfy the execution. R. S. 1881, section 783.

It is averred, in each paragraph of the complaint, in substance, that the execution defendant had, during the time the sheriff had the said execution in his hands, and during the life of said execution, personal property subject to execution, and on which he might have levied said execution and made the whole amount of money due thereon.

The effect of the judgment upon the demurrer, therefore, if the same is to stand, is to declare the law to be that an execution is in no case proper to enforce a judgment against the board of commissioners of a county. Is this sound law?

Counties being but subdivisions of the govermental power of the State, the property held by them and used for such governmental or public purposes, such as a court house, or jail, or a public square, can not be sold upon legal process. *Lowe* v. *Board, etc.,* 94 Ind. 553; 2 Dill. Mun. Corp. (3d ed.), section 576.

"The rule rests upon the principle that the public good requires that property needed for the proper administration of local governmental affairs shall not be taken from the local authorities, lest the due administration of such affairs be so much disturbed as to cause the public to suffer." *Lowe* v. *Board, etc., supra.*

We do not think it can be said, however, that a county may never be the owner of property which is not needed for governmental or public purposes. We are not aware of any reason why a county, which, like other corporations, is an artificial person, subject to the power and authority of the courts within whose jurisdiction it is situated, may not, in a proper case, be bound and controlled by such process as an execution, as other persons within such jurisdiction are bound. We are aware that in some jurisdictions it is held that a judgment against a county or municipal corporation amounts to no more than the establishment of a valid claim, which the officers of such corporation may be compelled to pay out of the proper funds by mandate. *Emerie* v. *Gilman,* 10 Cal. 404, 70 Am. Dec. 742; *Kinmundy* v. *Mahan,* 72 Ill. 462; *Wilson* v. *Commissioners,* 7 Watts & Serg. 197; *Board, etc.,* v. *Edmonds,* 76 Ill. 544.

But this rule is not followed in all the States. *Savage* v. *Supervisors of Crawford Co.,* 10 Wis. 44.

We think the better rule is that execution may issue against a county upon a judgment rendered against it,

The State, *ex rel.* Courter, *v.* Buckles *et al.*

and may be levied upon any property owned by such county not needed for governmental or public purposes. 1 Freeman on Executions, section 126.

Our statute makes counties' bodies corporate and politic, and clothes them with power to prosecute and defend suits, and confers upon them such rights, duties, and powers generally as are incident to corporations. R. S. 1881, section 5735.

There is nothing in the law which creates these corporations, that in any manner conflicts with the view that judgments against them may be enforced by execution, if the same can be levied and made out of property other than that needed for governmental purposes. We have not been able to find any case decided by the Supreme Court, which holds that this may not be done. If there was in fact no such property, the question can be fully met by pleading the general denial. At all events, we think it was the duty of the sheriff to make return of the execution within 180 days, and, for failure to do so, he would be liable for nominal damages, without reference to the question of whether or not there was any property out of which he could have made the same.

Judgment reversed, with directions to overrule the demurrer.

Filed Nov. 28, 1893.

No. 604.

LACY *v.* ELLER ET AL.

VENDOR'S LIEN.—*Series of Installments.*—*Good Only as to the Whole.*—*Former Adjudication.*—The right to have a vendor's lien declared applies not to any single installment of a series of payments to be made, but to the entire amount of the installments, and if there was no such lien for the first installment due, neither is there one for any subsequent installment which might become due; and an adjudication as to the first installment may be answered in bar of an action on any subsequent installment demanding such lien.

ESTOPPEL.—*Real Estate.*— *Vendor and Vendee.*—*Lien.*—*Representations of Third Party.*—*Purchase on Faith of.*—Where a party, previous to a conveyance, has informed the grantor or grantee of lands conveyed, that he has no lien on such lands, and the grantee purchased the lands, relying upon such representations, the party making such representations is estopped from asserting a lien thereon, which he may have had at the time of making such representations; and it is not necessary to show that he intended, by his statements, to defraud, for the fraud consists, not in making the statements, but in attempting to enforce his lien, to the injury of the party whom he induced to purchase the land upon his representations.

From the Hamilton Circuit Court.

G. Shirts and *I. A. Kilbourne,* for appellant.

J. A. Roberts, for appellees.

Ross, J.—The appellant sued the appellee to recover a debt due him from the appellee Joseph W. Eller, seeking to have a vendor's lien declared in his favor on certain real estate owned by the appellee Gerard, and asking a foreclosure of such lien.

This cause was certified to this court, as being within its jurisdiction, by the Supreme Court.

It is alleged, in the complaint, that on the 25th day of September, 1874, the appellant was the owner of 406 acres of land in Hamilton county, Indiana, which, on that day, he conveyed to the appellee Joseph W. Eller, his son-in-law, and Albert H. Lacy, Jackson Lacy and

William Lacy, his sons, at the agreed price of twenty-five hundred dollars; that in the year 1877, the appellant commenced an action in the Hamilton Circuit Court, against said grantees, to recover the balance of the purchase-money, and that he recovered a personal judgment against them in the sum of $6,750; that afterwards, to wit, on the 15th day of December, 1877, the judgment defendants instituted an action in said court to set aside said judgment and proceedings, and that while said action was pending, namely, on the 8th day of May, 1878, the parties thereto entered into agreement compromising the differences existing between them, and that in lieu of said judgment agreed that they would each pay the appellant fifty dollars per year so long as he should live, which agreement of compromise was entered of record by the court in said cause.

It further appears, that afterwards said grantees, by diverse mesne conveyances, sold and conveyed the land to the appellee Tunis Gerard, who is now the owner thereof, and that he had personal notice of all the facts as above charged; that the appellee Joseph W. Eller is insolvent, and that he failed and refused to pay the said sum of fifty dollars, as agreed, for the year preceding the commencement of this action, and that the same was due and unpaid.

Separate demurrers were filed to the complaint, and overruled, and they thereupon filed an answer in four paragraphs, as follows: The first paragraph, a joint answer of general denial; the second paragraph, a joint answer of former recovery; third paragraph, the separate answer of Tunis Gerard, that he purchased said property in good faith for a valuable consideration, and without any notice or knowledge of appellant's claim; and the fourth paragraph, the separate answer of Tunis Gerard, wherein he alleges, by way of estoppel, that his grantor, prior to his purchase of said land, asked the appellant whether or not he had any interest in, lien or claim against, said land, and was informed by appellant that he had no interest in, lien or claim against the same, and that upon said representations, his grantor purchased the same and conveyed it to appellee by warranty deed.

Demurrers were filed and overruled to the second and fourth paragraphs of the answer, and these rulings of the court have been assigned as errors in this court.

It is urged that the second paragraph of the answer is insufficient for the reason that the proceedings and judgment pleaded as former adjudication show that the causes of action are not the same.   That action was against these appellees to recover an annuity due under said agreement of compromise, and asking that a vendor's lien therefor be declared in appellant's favor against said land, and for a foreclosure thereof.

As shown by the facts alleged in this paragraph of the answer, one of the issues in such former action was as to appellant's right to have a vendor's lien declared in his favor, against the property in controversy, for one of the installments due under the agreement of compromise. That issue was determined against the appellant, and as long as that judgment stands, is an adjudication of his right to have a vendor's lien declared for any installment due under the agreement.   The right to have a vendor's lien declared applies not to any single installment, but to the entire amount to be paid appellant, and if he did not have such lien for the first installment due, he had none for any subsequent installment which might become due.

The Supreme Court, in *Kilander* v. *Hoover*, 111 Ind. 10, says: "If it appears that the first judgment involved the whole claim, or extended to the whole subject-matter, and settled the entire defense to the whole of a series of notes or claims, and adjudicated the whole subject-matter of a defense, equally relevant to and conclusive of the controversy between the parties, as well in respect to the claim or defense in judgment, as in respect to other claims and defenses thereto, pertaining to the same transaction or subject-matter, then the first judgment operates as an estoppel as to the whole. Unless, however, it is made to appear that the defenses pleaded to the first claim, or demand, involved the whole title, or extended to the whole subject-matter, of the controversy between the parties, so as to litigate and determine the defendant's liability in respect to the whole transaction, then the judgment is a finality only as to so much of the claim and defenses as was actually litigated in the first suit."

If to a suit upon one of a series of notes executed for the same consideration, a recovery thereon is refused for want of consideration, such judgment would be good pleaded as former adjudication in an action brought on the remaining notes of the series.

In Wells on Res Adjudicata, section 233, it is said: "As to installments, the rule has already been stated to be that where there are two or more promissory notes (or bonds) executed as a part of the same transaction, so that what affects one must affect the other in like manner, an adjudication upon one will determine that upon the other, and this applies to defenses, as where a suit has been brought on the first of two notes given for installments of purchase money of real estate, and judgment is rendered for the plaintiff on a particular defense, that defense is not thereafter available in a suit on the other note." See, also, *French* v. *Howard*, 14 Ind. 455; *Turner* v. *Allen*, 66 Ind. 252; *Felton* v. *Smith*, 88 Ind. 149; *Cleveland* v. *Creviston*, 93 Ind. 31; *Farrar* v. *Clark,* 97 Ind. 447.

There was no error in overruling the demurrer to the second paragraph of the answer.

It is insisted that the fourth paragraph is insufficient because it is not alleged that appellee Gerard's grantor, at the time he purchased the land, had no knowledge that the purchase-money due appellant was unpaid, and hence it must be assumed that he had such knowledge; that if the facts (i. e., the records of the former action and the judgment of compromise) were open to him, he can not be heard to say that he was injured by appellant's representations.

Even if the record of the former proceedings had shown, which they do not, that the appellant had a lien on the land, if he represented to appellee Gerard's grantor that he had no such lien or claim, he would be bound thereby.

In the case of *Maxon* v. *Lane*, 124 Ind. 592, the court said: "If a party induces another to change his position and expend a large sum of money, equity will not permit such a party to reap any advantages from the change to the prejudice of the other; nor will it permit him to do what he has expressly or impliedly promised not to do. If a party who holds a mortgage declares it to be invalid, or agrees not to enforce it, and thus induces another to buy the property, the courts will not aid him by awarding him a decree of foreclosure."

If the appellant, as alleged in this answer, informed Gerard or his grantor that he had no lien or interest in said lands, thus inducing them to purchase it, the court will not aid him in denying such representations and thus perpetrate a fraud on appellee. It matters not what knowledge the party had of the record and proceedings in the other actions, such records were public records, of the contents of which all persons were bound to take notice; but if appellant stated that he had no lien, and the appellee purchased the property relying upon such representations, as alleged in this answer, he is now estopped from asserting such lien, and it is not necessary to show that he intended, by his statements, to defraud, for the fraud would consist not in the making of such statements, but in his attempt to enforce his lien to the injury of the party whom he induced to purchase the land upon his representations. *Wisehart* v. *Hedrick,* 118 Ind. 341; *Maxon* v. *Lane, supra,* and cases cited.

There was no error in overruling the demurrer to this paragraph.

The argument of counsel in support of the error assigned, that the court erred in overruling the motion for a new trial, is simply a review of the questions presented in arguing the insufficiency of the answers, and need not be further considered.

The evidence is sufficient to sustain the finding of the court.

Judgment affirmed.

DAVIS, C. J., did not participate in this decision.

Filed Nov. 28, 1893.

————◆————

No. 743.

CONSTANTINE *v.* EAST ET AL.

REAL ESTATE.—*Contract of Sale.*—*Construction of.*—*Title.*—*Abstract.*— *Earnest Money.*—*Forfeiture.*—Where a contract for the sale of real estate provides, among other things, that "said conveyance is to be made by warranty deed, with all liens and taxes discharged, but subject to all existing leases," and that "a full abstract is to be furnished by us, and said abstract and deed to be subject to reasonable examination and approval by," * * * the vendee, acknowledging the payment of $500, as earnest money, which the vendee should forfeit, if he failed to carry out the terms of the agreement, provided the title proved good; under such contract the vendee was not bound to consummate the purchase on failure of the vendor to furnish an abstract showing title in him, and hence the earnest money was not forfeited on failure of the vendee to carry out the terms of the contract.

SAME.—*Evidence.*—*Proof of Title by Adverse Possession.*—*Erroneous.*— In such case, in an action to recover the earnest money, it was error to admit proof of title by adverse possession.

From the Henry Circuit Court.

M. S. Robinson and *J. W. Lovett*, for appellant.

H. C. Ryan, for appellees.

Ross, J.—The appellant brought this action in the Madison Circuit Court, to recover back five hundred dollars paid by him to the appellees, as earnest money, upon a contract for the purchase of a farm situated in Madison county, Ind., and which the appellees claim to own. The venue of the cause was changed, on the application of the appellant, to the Henry Circuit Court, and a trial had, resulting in a verdict and judgment for the appellees.

The contract of purchase, the construction of which presents the real question at issue on this appeal, reads as follows:

"We hereby agree to sell and convey to Charles Constantine, or his assigns, at any time within thirty days after the completion of the gas wells now being put down on the lands of J. H. Stanley and N. C. McCullough, the following described property lying in the County of Madison, State of Indiana, namely: Part of the northeast quarter of section 18, township 19, range 8 east, bounded as follows: Beginning at the half mile post on the line dividing sections 17 and 18, thence west 4 minutes and 15 seconds south, 160 poles to a stake; thence north 42——— east, 80 perches to White river; thence with the meanderings of said river to the line dividing said sections 17 and 18, and thence south to the place of beginning, except 2⅜ acres or thereabout on the north-west corner of said tract, as marked north and south by the east line of a tract owned by R. N. Williams, form-erly the said tract supposed to contain 55 acres, more or less, and also the following described tract of land: Com-mencing at the northwest corner of the southeast quar-ter of section 18, township 19 north, range 8 east, run-ning thence south forty rods, thence east across said quarter section, thence with the east line thereof to the northeast corner of said quarter section, thence west to the place of beginning, containing 40 acres, more or less, also 5 acres, more or less, off the northeast corner of the northeast quarter of the southwest quarter of section 18, township 19, range 8 east, containing in all 100 acres, more or less, the last tract set off by the Anderson and New Columbus East Line Turnpike Road; also all that part of the northeast quarter of section No.18, in town-ship 19 north, range 8 east, that lies east of White river, and east of a line beginning at the center of said section 18, and running north 20 east to White river; said line is evidenced by a stone placed on the south or east bank of White river and marked X, and evidenced by a wit-ness stone marked W, south 20 west, and distance from said stone 25 links, except the half acre fenced in and occupied by Charles W. East, for the price and sum of fifteen thousand dollars, payable as follows: One-third in one year and one-third in two years, after date of deed, with interest at six per cent. per annum, and the sum of four thousand, five hundred dollars cash on de-livery of deed, deferred payments to be secured by mort-gage on said premises.   It is understood that there are 110 acres in said tract; if upon survey there should be more, said Constantine is to pay for the excess at same rate per acre as herein; if less, a like deduction shall be made. Said conveyance is to be made by warranty deed, with all liens and taxes discharged, but subject to all existing leases. A full abstract is to be furnished by us, and said abstract and deed to be subject to reasonable examination and approval by said Constautine. And it is agreed that, if said title shall not be good and perfect in all respects, to any or all of said land, the said Constantine shall not be required to forfeit the five hundred dollars, as hereinafter provided, but in such event it shall be returned to him. We acknowledge payment of five hundred dollars by said Constantine, which, should the title prove good, the said Constantine shall forfeit if he fail to carry out the terms of this agreement.

"Dated at Anderson, Ind., April 30, 1887.
        "Signed, D. C. ,EAST,
                MARY L. EAST,
                CHAS. W. CONSTANTINE."

The contract provides that "said conveyance is to be by warranty deed, with all liens and taxes discharged, but subject to all existing leases. A full abstract and deed to be subject to reasonable examination and approval by said Constantine."

A construction of this part of the contract is decisive of the case.

It is contended, on behalf of the appellant, that the true meaning of the above provision is that the appellant was to have a good *record* title conveyed to him, and that he was not bound, under the contract, to consummate the purchase, unless the appellees had such a title.

On the other hand, it is contended, by counsel for the appellees, that the contract does not stipulate for a good record title, and that they had a right to prove, on the trial of the cause, that they acquired title by adverse possession.

It must be conceded that it is not the province of

courts to make contracts for parties, but simply to enforce them when called upon, and in their enforcement courts must construe them according to their sense and meaning and according to the real intention of the parties thereto as expressed therein. *Gillum* v. *Dennis*, 4 Ind. 417; *Conwell* v. *Pumphrey*, 9 Ind. 135; *Durland* v. *Pitcairn*, 51 Ind. 426.

"The rule of law is not that the court will always construe a contract to mean that which the parties to it meant; but rather that the court will give to the contract the construction which will bring it as near to the actual meaning of the parties as the words they saw fit to employ when properly construed, and the rules of law will permit." Parsons on Cont., *494.

Courts will not place such a construction upon a contract as to do violence to the rules of language, nor will it adopt such a construction as will violate the contract itself, unless the words employed are susceptible of no other reasonable construction.

When the language used in the contract is plain and unambiguous, there need be little trouble to construe its meaning, but in placing a construction upon it, sentences should not be detached and construed, but the entire contract should be interpreted as a whole, and its meaning ascertained from a consideration of all its stipulations. For that reason such a construction should be adopted, if possible, as will give meaning to all its stipulations.

With a statement of these few general principles, as applied to the contract under consideration, what could have been intended by the parties by the stipulation that the conveyance is to be by warranty deed, with all liens and taxes discharged, but subject to all existing leases, and that "A full abstract is to be furnished by us, and said abstract and deed to be subject to reasonable examination and approval by said Constantine?" Was it the intention of the parties that the appellee should convey to the appellant a good and perfect title, which must be shown by an abstract? The only construction which can be placed upon the language used, without doing violence to the rules of language, is that appellees were to convey the property, by a good and perfect title, to the appellant. It can hardly be urged that the appellees agreed to give a warranty deed for property which they did not own, or to which they had no title. Can it be said, therefore, that they were to give a warranty deed for property to which they had but an imperfect title? Under the terms of this contract it was agreed that, if appellees could not convey to appellant a good and perfect title to said lands, the appellant should not forfeit his earnest money. This meant more than merely to convey the land to him by a warranty deed, it meant to vest in him a good and perfect title. If it was not necessary that the appellees possess a title in order to convey to the appellant, there would be no necessity for an abstract. If there was to be an abstract at all, it was for the purpose of disclosing the title of appellees. If it did not disclose a record title, it would show nothing, for an abstract is simply a compilation in abridged form of the record of the title. When the appellees failed to furnish appellant with an abstract showing title in them, appellant was not bound to consummate the purchase, unless we adopt such a construction of the contract as will make that part of it, which provides for an abstract meaningless. That we can not do.

But it is contended that the appellees, although they could not show a title of record, did have a title by adverse possession, which they were permitted to prove on the trial of this cause. The appellees might be able to establish in this action a title by adverse possession, but such a showing would not be binding against the person or persons holding the legal title to the property. Until the rights of the party holding the legal title had been adjudicated in some manner, the appellees' claim, by reason of adverse possession, is not settled. As to just what is necessary to be shown to establish a title by adverse possession, need not be decided, but for the purposes of this case it is sufficient to say that the appellant, under the terms of the contract, was not bound to consummate the purchase, unless the appellees could give him a good and perfect title subject to the leases as provided in such contract. Such a construction should have been given the contract by the trial court, and it was error to admit proof of title by adverse possession.

Judgment reversed, with instructions to grant a new trial.

Filed Nov. 28, 1893.

No. 904.

THE LAKE ERIE AND WESTERN RAILROAD COMPANY
v. ARNOLD.

RAILROAD.—*Passenger.*—*Demanding Extra Fare for Part of Passage Covered by Surrendered Ticket.*—*Rights of Passenger.*—*Expulsion.*— Where A. purchased a railroad ticket entitling him to passage from X. to Z., and boarded a train carrying passengers between such points, and surrendered his ticket to the conductor, which was accepted, and upon the arrival of the train at Y., an intermediate station between X. and Z., the conductor demanded fare of A. from Y. to Z., claiming that A.'s ticket entitled him to passage only from X. to Y., it was not the duty of A. to pay the extra fare demanded of him and afterwards settle the question in dispute, with the company or its agents. The passenger was as much entitled to stand on his rights (having paid his fare) as the company was to

The Lake Erie and Western Railroad Company *v.* Arnold.

stand on theirs (believing the fare not to have been paid), and whether he should pay the extra fare and stay on the train, or refuse pay and suffer expulsion, was a matter solely in the discretion of A.

INSTRUCTIONS TO JURY.—*Correct Statement of Law, Irrelevant.—Refusal to Give.—Modification by Court.*—Where an instruction, as asked, correctly states an abstract proposition of law, but is not relevant to the issue, it is not prejudicial error to refuse the instruction asked, or to give the instruction as modified by the court.

RECORD.—*Affidavits in Support of Motion for New Trial.—How Made Part of Record.—Bill of Exceptions.—Order of Court.*—Affidavits in support of a motion for a new trial can only be made a part of the record by bill of exceptions or order of the court; simply attaching the affidavits to the motion, and marking them as exhibits, is not sufficient.

From the Tipton Circuit Court.

W. E. Hackedorn, J. B. Cockrum, R. B. Beauchamp and *W. W. Mount,* for appellant.

J. C. Blacklidge, C. C. Shirley and *B. C. Moon,* for appellee.

LOTZ, J.—The appellee was the plaintiff, and the appellant the defendant, in the court below. In his complaint, appellant charged, in brief, that he purchased a ticket of the defendant's agent in the city of Kokomo, which ticket entitled him to ride upon the defendant's passenger train from the city of Kokomo to the city of Indianapolis; that he took passage upon defendant's train at said city of Kokomo and presented his said ticket to defendant's agent, the conductor of said train, and that said ticket was received and accepted by said conductor; that he was carried upon said train to a point beyond the city of Noblesville, when said conductor came to him, and, in the presence of other passengers, demanded of the plaintiff that he pay his fare from Noblesville to Indianapolis, stating that the ticket taken by him from plaintiff only entitled plaintiff to ride upon said train to Noblesville; that plaintiff refused to pay said additional fare wrongfully demanded of him, and that said conductor then demanded of plaintiff, in the presence and hearing of other passengers, that he leave said train, which plaintiff refused to do; that said conductor used towards plaintiff opprobrious epithets, and accused him of attempting to defraud, by riding without paying his fare; that when the train reached a station called New Britain the said conductor again demanded of plaintiff that he pay his fare, and plaintiff again refused, and said conductor then wrongfully and by force ejected plaintiff therefrom; that plaintiff was greatly angered, mortified, and disgraced thereby, and endured great mental suffering and physical pain.

The defendant answered this complaint by general denial.

There was a trial by jury and a verdict for the plaintiff in the sum of $500.

The assignment of error discussed by appellant's counsel is that the court erred in overruling the motion for a new trial. It is strenuously insisted that the verdict is not sustained by sufficient evidence.

We have examined the evidence with some care, and while it is in some respects conflicting, yet we think it fairly supports the verdict. The elaborate and forcible argument made by the appellant's counsel, on this point, we presume was presented to the trial court. If it was unavailing there, under the fixed rules governing appellate courts, it must surely prove futile here.

Another cause assigned for a new trial is that the damages assessed by the jury are excessive.

The action made by the complaint sounds in tort. It seeks to recover damages for the humiliation and shame laid upon appellee, and for an injury done to his person.

In this class of cases it is the peculiar province of the jury to assess the damages.

In the case of *Coleman* v. *Southwick*, 9 John. 45, KENT, C. J., said: "The question of damages was within the proper and peculiar province of the jury; it rested in their sound discretion under all the circumstances of the case, and unless the damages are so outrageous as to strike every one with the enormity and injustice of them, so as to induce the court to believe that the jury must have acted from prejudice, partiality or corruption, we can not consistently, with the precedents, interfere with the verdict. It is not enough to say that, in the opinion of the court, the damages are too high, and that we would have given much less. It is the judgment of the jury, and not the judgment of the court, which is to assess the damages in actions for personal torts and injuries."

This language has been quoted with approval by the Supreme Court of this State. *Ohio, etc., R. W. Co.* v. *Collarn*, 73 Ind. 261 (274).

Under the allegations of the complaint, and under the instructions of the court, in order to entitle the appellee to a verdict, the jury must necessarily have found that the appellee purchased a ticket from Kokomo to Indianapolis, and that the conductor was in the wrong in expelling appellee from the train. It may be, and we think the evidence shows, that the conductor was acting in good faith; and that he honestly believed that the ticket taken up by him only entitled appellee to ride to Noblesville.

But the jury must have found that the conductor either made a mistake or purposely tried to extort an additional fare from appellee. In either event the appellant would be liable for his tortious conduct.

Counsel for appellant insist, that the conductor treated the appellee in the most courteous and gentlemanly manner possible under the circumstances; that he advised appellee to pay his fare and then settle the matter with the agent at Kokomo; and that even after the expulsion from the car he advised him to purchase a ticket or pay his fare and continue his journey to Indianapolis; that appellee refused to do this, although he had the money with which to pay his fare; that his expulsion was largely due to his own conduct, and was invited by him for the purpose of laying the foundation for an action; that under such circumstances the damages are excessive, and show that the jury were improperly influenced by prejudice or partiality.

It is true that the appellee was offered an opportunity to pay his fare and continue his journey unmolested, and that he had the money with which to pay, and was advised to settle the matter with the agent at Kokomo; and that he refused to do so; and that he refused to leave the car until the conductor took hold of him, and that no great violence or injury was done his person.

The attitude and manner of the conductor was firm and attended with some asperity, and the attention of the other passengers was attracted by the controversy between them. The conductor testified that the appellee got off under protest and against his will, and that he was prepared to use force if necessary to put him off.

We do not concur in the doctrine that it was the duty of the appellee to pay the extra fare demanded of him and afterwards settle the question in dispute with the company or its agents. It is true that the amount demanded was trifling, but the principle involved is the same as if the sum demanded had been a large one.

However much we may commend the conduct of that person who yields his rights to avoid a difficulty, it is nevertheless the privilege of every person to stand upon his strict legal rights, and the law does not require him to yield them, or make concessions to avoid trouble.

The argument that the damages are excessive, impliedly admits that some damages are recoverable. The jury found that the appellant's agent was in the wrong. Its attitude before the court then is this: "It is true that the appellee purchased a ticket from Kokomo to Indianapolis, and that the conductor inadvertently made a mistake, but gave appellee good advice and opportunity to pay his fare and save himself from expulsion and mortification, therefore only nominal or a small amount of damages ought to be assessed." .

Such circumstances might tend to rebut malice, but the damages were not assessed upon the theory of malice. There is no such charge in the complaint. Again it may be urged that there was a doubt, at the time, as to whether appellee's ticket was from Kokomo to Indianapolis or from Kokomo to Noblesville, and that such circumstances ought to go in mitigation of damages. If there was a doubt, it was as much the duty of appellant's agent to forego ejecting appellee as it was appellee's duty to pay the fare and continue his journey when the opportunity was offered. Appellant chose to stand upon what it conceived to be its strict legal rights. It can not now be heard to complain if the appellee chose to do the same. It comes with an ill grace for the appellant, after it has pushed what it believed to be its rights to the last extremity, to say that because it offered to carry appellee if he would pay his fare, the damages ought to be mitigated. Appellee was under no legal obligation to accept any offer, no matter how considerately made. In fact, the offer itself was only what the appellant would have been compelled to give to any person who would pay the fare demanded. The time to be magnanimous was before the expulsion occurred. Appellant can not excuse or palliate the wrong or mitigate the damages flowing therefrom by its subsequent acts. Nor will it be permitted to palliate its own sordid conduct by the want of magnanimity in the person it has aggrieved. The appellee, by the acts of appellant's agent, was placed in a very unpleasant position before the passengers on the train. By conduct, if not by words, he stood charged with an attempt to defraud the railroad company, and of endeavoring to ride from Noblesville to Indianapolis without paying the fare therefor. His attitude, as thus made to appear, was that of a dishonest man, and brought shame and discredit upon him. If he had paid the extra fare demanded after such accusations, legitimate inference might be drawn therefrom that he was guilty of the dishonesty attributed to him. Whether he should pay and stay on the train, or refuse pay and suffer expulsion, was a matter which the law left to the sole discretion of ppellee. It was his rights that were being infringed, nd he was the sole arbiter of the course he should pursue.

Under the circumstances of this case, the verdict does not strike us as so excessive and enormous as to ad us to believe that the jury acted from prejudice or artiality. *Lake Erie, etc., R. W. Co. v. Fix*, 88 Ind. 81; *Lake Erie, etc., R. R. Co. v. Close*, 5 Ind. App. 444, 2 N. E. Rep. 588; *Pittsburgh, etc., R. W. Co. v. Annigh*, 39 Ind. 509; *Chicago, etc., R. R. Co. v. Conly*, 6 Ind. App. 9, 32 N. E. Rep. 96; *Louisville, etc., R. R. Co. v. Conrad*, 4 Ind. App. 83; *Chicago, etc., R. R. Co. v. Graham*, 3 Ind. App. 28; *Louisville, etc., R. W. Co. v. Wolfe*, 128 Ind. 347; *Indianapolis, etc., R. W. Co. v. Howerton*, 127 Ind. 236; *Lake Erie, etc., R. W. Co. v. Acres*, 108 Ind. 548; *Toledo, etc., R. W. Co. v. McDonough*, 53 Ind. 289; *St. Louis, etc., R. W. Co. v. Myrtle*, 57 Ind. 566; *Indianapolis, etc., R. R. Co. v.*

Milligan, 50 Ind. 392; *Pittsburgh, etc., R. W. Co.* v. *Hennigh*, 39 Ind. 509.

It is also contended that the court erred in modifying instruction No. 9, requested by appellant, and in giving the same to the jury as modified.

This instruction, as asked, read as follows: "The conductor of a railroad is not required to accept the statement of a passenger as to his right to be carried on said train; the ticket, as presented by the passenger, is conclusive as to whether or not he is entitled to passage on said train, and if such ticket shows on its face that the passenger is not entitled to passage on said train, the conductor may lawfully eject him therefrom, unless he pays his fare."

This instruction was not relevant to the evidence. The controversy did not arise until after the ticket was taken up, and the disputed point was whether or not it was from Kokomo to Indianapolis or from Kokomo to Noblesville. The ticket itself was not produced on the trial. It was a conceded fact that the appellee was entitled to passage on the train, but the point to which he was entitled to go was the controverted question. The modification did not harm the appellant. The instruction asked and refused, as an abstract proposition, correctly states the law, but it was not applicable to the evidence or the issue tendered by the complaint. Appellee could only succeed on the theory stated in the complaint. Under the issues and facts disclosed, there was no error in refusing the instruction asked.

The sixth and last cause for a new trial, discussed by counsel, is that for newly discovered evidence. The affidavits in support of this cause are attached to the motion, marked exhibits, and are copied into the record, but they are not made a part of the record by a bill of exceptions or by order of the court. Such affidavits must be brought into the record by a bill of exceptions, or made a part thereof by order of the court. *Elbert* v. *Hoby*, 73 Ind. 111; Elliott's App. Proced, section 817.

In this condition of the record, we can not consider them.

We find no reversible error in the record.

Judgment affirmed, at the costs of appellant.

Filed Sept. 20, 1893; petition for a rehearing overruled Nov. 28, 1893.

———————— ♦ ————————

No. 482.

HALLETT *v.* HALLETT ET AL.

HUSBAND AND WIFE.—*Right of Wife of Insane Man to Support Out of His Estate.*—*Remedy.*—*Can not Bring Action Against.*—*Guardian and Ward.*—The wife and minor children of an insane man, whose estate is in the hands of a guardian, should be provided, out of the estate, with such things as are reasonably necessary for their comfort and welfare, and if the guardian fail to make suitable provisions for them, application therefor may be made to the court under whose authority the guardian is acting, and the court should direct the guardian to make proper provisions; but the wife has no right of action, under such circumstances, against her husband's estate, for such support.

SAME.—*Right of Wife and Children of Insane Man to Crops Raised by Them on His Lands.*—*Seizure by Guardian.*—*Remedy.*—The wife and minor children of an insane man have a right to the use, for their support, of grain (wheat) raised by them on the lands of the husband and father, previous to the appointment of a guardian for him. The guardian has no right to the custody of such grain, and, on a seizure of the same by him, no right of action lies against him therefor, as guardian; but if any exists, it would be against him as an individual.

From the Montgomery Circuit Court.

G. D. Hurley and *M. E. Clodfelter*, for appellant.

W. T. Wittington, H. D. Van Cleave and *H. A. Wilkinson*, for appellees.

VOL. 8—20

Ross, J.—The appellant, in May, 1891, filed her complaint in three paragraphs, alleging, that she and the appellee Elijah P. Hallett were husband and wife, having been married fifteen years prior to the filing of her complaint; that they lived and cohabited together from the time of their marriage until in the year 1888, at which time her said husband became of unsound mind, and was sent to the Hospital for the Insane at Indianapolis, where he is now confined; that as a result of such marriage there were born to them five children, all of whom are now living, and range in age from four to fourteen years; that at the time her husband became insane he was the owner of an undivided one-third interest in two hundred acres of land, said interest therein being of the value of twenty-two hundred dollars; also the owner of personal property of the value of three hundred dollars; that there were situated on said land a dwelling house and other necessary out-buildings, which were occupied and used by appellant, her husband, and their children, and after her husband became an inmate of the hospital she and their children continued to reside on said land, and occupy said dwelling house as a home, and continued to use the real estate and personal property of her said husband in supporting herself and children; that by the use of all of her husband's property, and by the most persevering industry and strictest economy, she was hardly able to support herself and children from the use of said property; that about two years after said Elijah P. Hallett became insane the appellee Henry D. Vancleave was appointed his guardian, who, as such guardian, immediately took possession of all the property and effects of his ward, together with eighty-five bushels of wheat which she had raised on said land, of the value of seventy dollars; and that he afterwards returned to the appellant about three hundred dollars

worth of the personal property, consisting of live stock
and household goods; that in October, 1890, in a suit
brought by the owners of the other two-thirds of said
land, against said Vancleave, as guardian, for partition,
there was set off to said Elijah P. Hallett sixty-six acres
and seventy-two hundredths of an acre, the greater part
of which was in timber, there being no dwelling house
thereon; that said guardian, under an order of the court,
sold timber from the land, receiving therefor the sum
of four hundred and ten dollars; that she has been deprived of her only means of support for herself and
children, by reason of the taking from her of the husband's
said property, and that she and her infant children are
dependent upon charity; that in the care and support of
their children during the year preceding the filing of her
complaint, she incurred liabilities in the sum of two hundred and fifty dollars, which she requested said guardian
to pay, and that he refused to pay the same, or in any
manner provide for her or her children; that soon after
⸱⸱   ᵼardian procured the order for the sale of said
she demanded that he turn over one-third of the
₂ds of such sale to her, which he promised to do,
ᴊas failed and refused to do.

ᴐ each paragraph of the complaint the defendants
d demurrers, which were sustained by the court, and
the plaintiff refusing to amend, judgment was rendered
in favor of the defendants.

In support of the sufficiency of the facts alleged to
constitute a cause of action, it is insisted, first, that appellant and her children are entitled to support out of
the husband's estate, and for a failure to furnish the
same a cause of action accrued in her favor against the
guardian; second, that appellant, having an inchoate interest in her husband's real estate, the timber being a
part of the real estate, a sale thereof by the guardian

gave her a vested right in one-third of the proceeds of such sale, and third, that she was entitled to recover the value of the eighty-five bushels of wheat which she raised on her husband's lands, and which was taken from her by said guardian.

This action is virtually against the husband for support. Under the common law no such right of action existed in favor of the wife, hence we must look to the statute for a remedy if any exists.

A husband is liable for necessaries furnished his wife, although not furnished at his request, nor under an express promise to pay therefor. *Eiler* v. *Crull*, 99 Ind. 375. It is the duty of a husband to support his wife, and this legal obligation creates a liability in favor of one furnishing her the necessaries for such support, and while the common law afforded the wife no personal remedy for which she could bring an action and enforce such remedy, yet through the rules of agency she was enabled to bind his credit, thus procuring the desired result.

Numerous statutes have been enacted by the legislature of this State, enlarging the rights and remedies of the wife. For instance, section 5132, R. S. 1881, provides that "A married woman may obtain provision for the support of herself and the infant children of herself and husband, in her custody, in any of the following cases:

"First. Where the husband shall have deserted his wife, or his wife and children, without cause, not leaving her or them sufficient provision for her or their support.

"Second. When the husband shall have been convicted of a felony and imprisoned in the State prison, not leaving his wife or his wife and children sufficient provision for her or their support.

"Third. When the husband is an habitual drunkard,

and by reason thereof becomes incapacitated or neglects to provide for his family.

"Fourth. When a married man renounces the marriage covenant, or refuses to live with his wife in the conjugal relation, by joining himself to a sect or denomination, the rules and doctrines of which require a renunciation of the marriage covenant or forbid a man and woman to dwell and cohabit together in the conjugal relation according to the true intent and meaning of the institution of marriage."

Again, section 2966, R. S. 1881, provides that, "In all cases where the guardian of any person of unsound mind, under the direction of any court of competent jurisdiction, has made or may hereafter make sale of any lands of such person of unsound mind, the wife of such person of unsound mind may, by her separate deed, release and convey all her interest in and title to such land; and her deed, so made, shall thereafter debar her from all claim to such land, and shall have the same effect on her rights as if her husband had been of sound mind and she had joined with such husband in the execution of such conveyance."

The law of descent, section 2492, R. S. 1881, reserves to the widow and children the use of the family dwelling house and the messuages thereunto pertaining, and fields adjacent, not exceeding forty acres, free of rent for one year from the death of the husband; and section 2262, R. S. 1881, reserves, in case of the husband's death, for the use of the widow and minor children, all the provisions on hand, provided for consumption by the family.

Admitting, as we must, that for a husband to become hopelessly insane is a greater misfortune to his family than his removal by death, yet none of the above sections of the statute provides a remedy in case of his in-

sanity, whereby the wife may either sell or encumber her
husband's estate, or have any interest therein set off to
her in her own right. Whether the husband is sane or
insane, the wife is entitled to support, and while she can
neither dispose of his estate, nor sue and recover means
from his estate with which to support herself, except in
the cases provided by section 5132, *supra*, she may procure the necessaries for the support of herself and children, and the husband's estate will be answerable therefor.

In the case of *Booth* v. *Cottingham, Guar.*, 126 Ind.
431, which was an action brought by the appellant to
recover for medical services rendered the wife of appellee's ward, the court says: "It would be a reproach to
the law if the wife of an insane man, whose estate is in
the hands of a guardian, were denied the necessaries of life
(and, surely, medical attention in illness is necessary),
but no such reproach rests upon the law. For many
years it has been settled that the wife of an insane man
shall be provided with such things as are reasonably necessary to her comfort and welfare."

As long as no guardian had been appointed to take
charge of and manage her husband's estate, the appellant
had a right to manage and use it for the support of the
family, but upon the appointment of the appellee Vancleave, as guardian, he became the proper custodian of
all his ward's estate. If such guardian failed or refused
to make suitable provision for appellant and her children, she might have applied to the court under whose
authority the guardian was acting, and the court would
direct the guardian to make proper provision. This
seems to have been the course pursued in the case of
State, ex rel., v. *Wheeler*, 127 Ind. 451, which meets our
approval as to the proper course to pursue.

It is true that the timber while standing upon the land,

was a part of the realty itself, but when it was severed, it at once became personal property.

Among other facts alleged in the first paragraph of the complaint, it is averred that appellant raised eighty-five bushels of wheat on her husband's land the year preceding the appointment of the appellee Vancleave, as guardian, which he, as such guardian, took possession of and sold. The appellant and her children had such an interest in the wheat raised by them previous to the appointment of appellee Vancleave, as entitled them to use the same for their maintenance and support, and to the possession of which he had no right as such guardian.

While we find no direct provision authorizing the wife, in case of the involuntary absence of the husband, to cultivate his lands and thus provide for the support of herself and children, an unwritten law grants to the wife the right, by her own exertions, to provide sustenance and clothing for herself and those left helplessly in her charge, and to that end may use the property of her husband.

In *Loy* v. *Loy*, 128 Ind. 150, which was an action brought by the appellant to enjoin the use and removal of personal property claimed by appellant under a chattel mortgage, given by the husband after he had deserted his wife and children, the mortgagee being cognizant of the facts; the wife set up in defense the fact of such desertion and failure to provide by the husband, and that her children, after such desertion, had planted the crops mortgaged, which had been cultivated for the support of herself and children, the same constituting their sole dependence for subsistence. This answer was sustained by the lower court, and on appeal the Supreme Court says: "A husband who wrongfully abandons, and refuses to support his wife and family, not only subjects himself to the various civil and criminal penalties pro-

vided by legislative enactment, but he impliedly clothes
her with authority to feed and clothe herself and children by the ordinary use and consumption of the property left in her possession, and, to a limited extent, to
exercise such authority and control over his property
and ,business as may be necessary for its preservation,
and the support of herself and children.'' Such seizure
and conversion by the appellee Vancleave, vests no right
of action in appellant against him as such guardian, but
if any exists, it would be against him as an individual.
Rose v. *Cash*, 58 Ind. 278.

Counsel for appellant, while pointing out with great
clearness the justness of a wife's claim to support out of
the estate of her insane husband, have failed to cite
either statute or adjudicated case wherein the wife is
given a right of action against her husband's estate, for
such support, and we are unable to find any such authority.

There was no error in sustaining the demurrers to each
paragraph of the complaint.

Judgment affirmed.

Filed Sept. 20, 1893; petition for a rehearing overruled Nov. 28, 1893.

———————◆———————

No. 830.

Baldwin v. Threlkeld.

PLEADING.—*Complaint, Sufficiency of.—Theory of.—Damages.—Sale of
Forged and Worthless Note.*—Where a paragraph of complaint alleges, substantially, that the defendant sold and assigned to the
plaintiff, by separate instrument, a certain promissory note, alleging date of note, date of assignment, amount of consideration, names
of makers and payee; that the note so sold and assigned was a
forgery; that by reason thereof the note is absolutely worthless, and
that plaintiff has been damaged in the sum of $800, etc., such plead-

Baldwin *v.* Threlkeld.

ing is sufficient on the theory of injury and damage by reason of the sale to plaintiff of the forged and worthless note.

SPECIAL FINDING.—*When Sufficient.*—A special finding will be sufficient which contains the ultimate facts necessary to support the conclusions of law, disregarding evidentiary facts and conclusions of law stated therein.

SAME.—*When Delivery Need Not Be Shown.*—*Presumption.*—It is not necessary that a special finding, in an action for balance of purchase price of a personal chattel, should show a delivery. The sale being complete, it will be presumed that the vendee obtained possession.

VENDOR AND VENDEE.—*Sale.*—*Assignment of Forged and Worthless Note.*—*Action for Value of Articles Sold.*—*Personalty.*—Where a vendor sold a horse of the value of $500, and accepted therefor the vendee's note for $50 and the assignment of another note which proved to be forged and worthless, the vendor had a right to disregard the assignment and sue for the value of the horse.

APPELLATE COURT PRACTICE.—*Discussion, What Amounts to.*—Simply referring to a ground of objection stated in the trial court, and insisting that the objection there made should have been sustained, does not amount to a discussion, and presents no question for the consideration of the court.

SAME.—*When Ruling of Trial Court Will be Upheld.*—If the ruling of the trial court can be supported upon any theory, whether the same was advanced at the time of the ruling or not, it must be upheld.

EVIDENCE.—*Transcript of Record of an Action.*—*When Admissible in Subsequent Action.*—*Assignment.*—Where a written assignment of a note shows that an action on the note was pending at the time the assignment was executed, it is proper to admit in evidence, in a subsequent action thereon by the assignee, a certified transcript of the record of such action showing the result thereof.

SAME.—*Proof of Contents of Destroyed Letters.*—*Discretion.*—The court may, in its discretion, reject evidence offered by plaintiff to prove the contents of letters destroyed by him after he had instituted his action; the court having the right to deduce from such act, the inference of fraudulent design.

SAME.—*Original Evidence, When May be Given.*—*Discretion.*—It is within the discretion of the court to admit original evidence at any stage of the proceeding, and unless abuse of discretion is shown, there can be no cause for reversal.

Opinion on petition for rehearing by REINHARD, J.

From the Clinton Circuit Court.

G. W. Paul and *M. W. Bruner,* for appellant.

P. S. Kennedy and *H. H. Ristine,* for appellee.

REINHARD, J.—The appellee sued the appellant in the court below, the complaint being in two paragraphs. There was no demurrer filed to either paragraph of the complaint, but there is an assignment of error that the first paragraph fails to state facts sufficient to constitute a cause of action.

The substance of the averments of this paragraph is, that on the 8th day of October, 1888, the appellant sold and assigned to the appellee, by separate instrument, a certain promissory note, dated November 8, 1887, and purporting to be signed by John L. Bryan and William Bryan, payable to the order of the appellant, for the sum of $582.05, and due one day after date; that the consideration paid for said note and the assignment thereof was a stallion of the value of $700; that copies of the written assignment and the note are filed with' this paragraph of complaint; that the promissory note so sold and assigned to the appellee was a forgery, and was not executed by said William Bryan; that, by reason of such forgery, the said note is absolutely worthless, and that appellee has been damaged in the sum of $800, for which he demands judgment.

The appellant's counsel have not pointed out any objection to this complaint, which would render it bad on assignment of error, and we have discovered none. Its theory is that the appellee has been damaged by reason of the sale to him of the forged and worthless note.

Counsel argue that there is a wide difference between an assignment and an indorsement of a note, and we fully agree with them in their position. But there is no need for drawing any such distinction here, for the reason that this is not an action against an indorser, and is not claimed to be such. Some question is also at-tempted to be made as to the correct measure of damages in such a suit, but no such question is involved in the objection to the complaint. The appellee, by this paragraph, shows himself entitled to recover some damages. He would be entitled, on the facts averred, to recover the amount he paid for the note. Whether the amount he should recover would be the actual value of the horse or the price agreed upon, without regard to the value, is not raised by this pleading.

The second paragraph of the complaint was in the nature of an action on an account for the value of a horse sold and delivered by appellee to appellant, for the price of $650, of which sum $50 had been paid by the appellant. To this paragraph an answer was filed in two paragraphs, viz:

1. The general denial.

2. Payment for the horse before the action was commenced.

The appellee filed a general denial in reply to the second paragraph of answer, and the cause was submitted to the court for trial.

At the request of the parties, the court made a special finding of facts and legal conclusions.

The second specification of error is that the court erred in its conclusions of law from the facts found. It is insisted, in the first place, that the special finding contains only items of evidence and not ultimate facts. The special finding is, in substance, that on the 8th day of October, 1888, the appellant commenced an action in the Chancery Court of Kenton county, Kentucky, against John L. Bryan and William Bryan, upon a promissory note of the tenor set out in the finding; that afterwards, on the same day, appellee sold to appellant a saddle horse, of the value of $500, and received from appellant his note for $50, which was afterwards paid, and a certain written assignment of the note sued on in the Kentucky court and the proceeds thereof. The assignment

is also set out in the finding. It is further found that
this note was executed by John L. Bryan, but that William Bryan did not sign it; that John L. Bryan signed
William's name to the note without legal authority to do
so, and without the knowledge or consent of said William; that at the time said suit was commenced in the
Kenton Chancery Court of Kentucky, said John L. Bryan
was wholly insolvent, and was a nonresident of the State
of Kentucky; that William Bryan was then solvent; that
in said suit the said William Bryan filed a separate answer of *non est factum*, duly verified; that upon the filing
of such answer, John L. Bryan dismissed said action;
that the note so sued upon was given in renewal of another note before executed by John L. and William
Bryan to the appellant for a valuable consideration, the
said John L. signing the name of said William Bryan to
said original note, with full authority to do so from said
William; that no part of said assigned note has been
paid; that, at the time appellee accepted said assignment,
he knew that said John L. Bryan was insolvent, and
that he relied upon the genuineness of said note so assigned and upon the solvency of said William Bryan for
its payment.

From these facts the court concludes:

1. That the assignment of the note in question was
not a payment of any part of the value of said horse so
sold by appellee to appellant.

2. That appellee is entitled to recover the unpaid balance of such value, viz., $450.

We think, while these findings contain some evidentiary facts, they also contain sufficient ultimate facts to
warrant the conclusions drawn by the court.

It is objected that the findings fail to show that there
was any delivery of the horse. It is found that the appellee sold the horse to the appellant. The execution of

the $50 note, even without the assignment of the Bryan note, made the sale a complete and not an executory one, and the title in the horse passed to the appellant. Possibly the appellee might have had the right to have the sale annulled for the fraud of the forged note transaction, but certainly the appellant could not treat the sale as void for that reason. The sale was not void under the statute of frauds, because the $50 note was a part payment of the price of the horse, and entitled the appellant, to possession so long as the sale was not disavowed by the appellee. The title in the horse having passed to the appellant, he could have brought replevin for him in case the appellee had refused to deliver him, and we must presume that he obtained such possession. Having thus purchased the horse, he was legally bound to pay for him. This he could not do with a forged note, and hence the finding that this note was no payment is correct. It was not essential that the finding should show a delivery.

It is further complained that the finding fails to show the ultimate fact that the horse was not paid for, the appellant insisting that there can be no recovery without the finding of such fact. If it be conceded that there is no such finding, it by no means follows that the failure to so find defeats the appellee's right to recover. The answer of payment raised an affirmative issue which the appellant was bound to prove. If the facts found do not determine this issue in his favor, the appellant fails in his plea. *Vannoy* v. *Duprez*, 72 Ind. 26; *Dodge* v. *Pope*, 93 Ind. 480; *Gray* v. *Taylor*, 2 Ind. App. 155.

It is further urged that the ultimate fact as to how much was due the appellee was not found by the court. But the facts found, when taken together, show that there was due the appellee the sum of $450. The appellant had purchased the horse, and it was of the value of

$500; $50 of this amount had been paid. These facts warranted the inference drawn by the court in its second conclusion, that the appellee was entitled to recover the unpaid balance of that value, to wit, $450, without a specific statement that the amount of $450 was still due.

Some question is made, also, that the facts found show no diligence in the collection of the note. We have already seen that the facts found amply support the second paragraph of the complaint, and the question of the assignment of the note may, therefore, be entirely disregarded. But if the first paragraph of the complaint were essential to a recovery upon the special finding, still the appellant's contention can not prevail on this point. The assumption underlying this contention is that the suit is upon an indorsement. Even if this were true, it would not be necessary to show diligence when diligence was unavailing. That it would have been unavailing, was shown by the fact that as to William Bryan the note was a forgery, and that John L. was insolvent and a nonresident of the State of Kentucky, where the appellee resided. But the first paragraph does not count upon an indorsement of the note, as we have already seen. It is an action for damages for the assignment of a forged and worthless note. The measure of damages in such case is the amount paid for the note, which, in the case at bar, was the value of the horse, less the amount paid.

The indorser of a note warrants the genuineness and ability of the maker to pay. *Alleman* v. *Wheeler*, 101 Ind. 141; *Herald* v. *Scott*, 2 Ind. 55.

If the maker is a nonresident of the State at the time of the maturity of the note, suit need not be brought against the maker before suing the indorser. *Sayre* v. *McEwen*, 41 Ind. 109; *Titus* v. *Seward*, 68 Ind. 456.

We are of the opinion, therefore, that the appellant's liability is established by the finding, even if he was sued as an indorser of the note. But we think the appellee had a right to disregard the assignment and sue for the value of the horse, as he did in the second paragraph of his complaint. The exceptions to the conclusions of law are not sustained.

The last assignment of error is the overruling of the appellant's motion for a new trial. It is urged that the evidence is insufficient to support the finding. The appellant insists that there is no evidence of the fact that the note was not genuine as to William Bryan, other than the plea of *non est factum* filed in the Kentucky court, and that this plea furnishes no proof whatever of the forgery alleged. In the last conclusion we quite agree with counsel, but they are in error in their assumption that no other evidence was adduced upon the point of the non-genuineness of the note. The record discloses that "plaintiff, by his counsel, with the permission of the court, and consent of counsel on the other side, introduced and read in evidence the depositions of James W. Bryan and E. D. Seeley, * * * in words and figures following, to wit:" After stating that he was a lawyer, and resided in Covington, Ky., the witness, Bryan, testified that the note in question was written by him, at his law office in Covington, Ky., and that it was given in renewal of another note signed by John L. and William Bryan, which he held for collection; that John L. Bryan signed his own name and that of William Bryan in the presence of the witness, and also in the presence of the appellant, and that John L. Bryan then stated, in the presence of the two, that he had no written authority to sign William's name, while Baldwin stated that 'it made no difference, as it would be settled through Lucky Baldwin, for whom John L. Bryan was to work in California. D. A. Coulter, a banker, testified as an expert that in his opinion both names were written by the same hand. The appellant testified that William Bryan had signed his own name to the note, but the court was not compelled to accept this testimony as against that of the other two witnesses. The appellant did not proceed upon the theory that John L. Bryan had signed William's name by the latter's authority and consent, but that William himself wrote his name to the note. In view of these facts the court had a right to accept the theory of the appellee, that the name of William Bryan was signed by John L. Bryan without the consent and authority of the former. We regard the evidence as sufficient to warrant the court in its conclusion.

The next ground assigned in the motion for a new trial is, that the finding of the court is contrary to law.

The only discussion of this point made by appellant's counsel is a reference to their argument upon the first reason for a new trial, and, as we have already disposed of that, no further notice of the same will be necessary.

The appellant next complains of error of law occurring at the trial. This alleged error consists of the admission in evidence of the written assignment of the note described in the complaint. The only discussion of this question made by counsel, in their brief, is a reference to the grounds of objection stated in the trial court, and insisting that the objection there made should have been sustained. We do not think the question is "discussed," and it is therefore not presented for our determination. Elliott's App. Proced., section 445.

Complaint is also made of the ruling of the court in admitting in evidence a certified transcript of the Kentucky Chancery Court showing the suit upon the note in question, the plea of *non est factum* filed in the cause, and the dismissal of the action. We agree with appellant's counsel that this transcript furnishes no sort of evidence tending to establish the forgery of the note. It does not appear that it was admitted for this purpose. We think the transcript was competent as a part of the history of the transaction. The written assignment shows that an action on this note was pending in the Chancery Court of Kenton county, Kentucky, at the time such assignment was executed. It was proper to show what had become of this action, whether it had been prosecuted to final judgment in the appellant's name, or, if not, how it was taken out of court. The steps taken in the suit were taken by the appellant himself, who was the plaintiff.. If he dismissed his action after the plea of *non est factum* was filed, it was a circumstance- tending to show the appellant's want of faith in the genuineness of the note. This was, of course, subject to any explanation he might desire to make concerning the dismissal, and was in no wise conclusive upon him. But we can not say that the court had no right to consider it. Of course the plea of *non est factum* could not be considered as evidence of the forgery, and there is nothing to show that it was admitted for any such purpose. There was no error in admitting the transcript in evidence.

The court sustained an objection of the appellee to proving the contents of certain letters testified to by the appellant after he had practically admitted that he voluntarily destroyed the letters after he had commenced the suit on the note against the Bryants. The court had a right to deduce, from the act of destruction after the commencement of such suit, the inference of a fraudulent design to do away with the letters themselves, and upon this theory the exclusion of the evidence was proper. *Anderson Bridge Co.* v. *Applegate,* 13 Ind. 339; *Rudolph* v. *Lane,* 57 Ind. 115.

A reversal is finally asked because the court permitted

the appellee to examine an expert witness as to the hand-writing in the signatures to the note. Appellant had testified that the signature of William Bryan had been placed there by William himself. To rebut this the appellee sought to show that John L. Bryan had signed both names to the note. The expert witness was permitted to testify that in his opinion both names were written by the same hand. There was no error in this ruling. Even if the testimony was original, it was within the discretion of the court to admit it at any stage of the proceeding, and unless a clear abuse of such discretion were shown there would be no cause for reversal because of the introduction of the testimony out of its order. *Stewart* v. *Smith*, 111 Ind. 526.

This disposes of all the questions presented, and we find no available error.

Judgment affirmed.

Filed Sept. 26, 1893.

ON PETITION FOR A REHEARING.

REINHARD, J.—The appellant's learned counsel have presented a petition for a rehearing upon the ground that this court erred in holding that the court below committed no error in excluding the proposed testimony of the contents of certain letters claimed to be material to the defense.

We held the ruling of the lower court proper for the reason, as stated in the former opinion, that the trial court had a right to deduce, from the act of destruction of the original letters by the appellant, the inference of a fraudulent design to do away with them. We are now met with the proposition that the ruling of the circuit court was not grounded upon this theory. In support of this proposition, we are directed to the statement in the record forming the basis of the objection as urged by appellee's counsel at the time it was proposed to introduce the evidence of the contents of the letters.

We do not think the position is tenable. The appellant here asserts that an error was committed. It is his duty to show such error affirmatively. If the ruling of the trial court can be supported upon any theory, whether the same was advanced at the time of the ruling or not, it must be upheld. If the appellee had interposed no objection whatever, and the court had excluded the testimony of its own motion, the ruling must stand in this court, unless the appellant succeeds in showing that it was wrong upon any theory. It is different where the court admits the proposed testimony and the appellant asserts error in such ruling. It then devolves upon the appellant to show that he made timely objection, and stated the reasons for the incompetency of the testimony. He will then be confined to the reasons urged below, because here, again, he must make it appear affirmatively that there was error, and he is confined to the grounds presented to the trial court. See Elliott's App. Proced., section 721

We did not undertake to adjudge what was the force and effect of the evidence of the destruction of the letters. We only held, and now hold, that the court had the right to infer from it a fraudulent design to do away with such proof as militated against his case. Of the competency of the evidence, we have no doubt. Upon its weight or effect, we do not undertake to decide.

Petition overruled.

Filed Nov. 28, 1893.

No. 804.

DOAN ET AL., EXECUTORS, *v.* DOW.

GUARDIAN AND WARD.—*Contract.*—*When the Terms of May be Partly Enforced and Partly Disregarded.*—Where a ward, within three years from the final settlement of his guardian, employed counsel to institute suit to set aside certain allowances and to recover certain sums from the guardian, and the guardian promised that if he would not bring suit against him, he would hold all of such sums for him, and manage them for him until he, the ward, should marry and settle down, and then he would pay him all of such sums with their accretions, and would make him his, the guardian's, heir, the contract to make the ward the guardian's heir and to pay the sums of money are distinct and separate matters, and the promise to pay the sums of money may be separated from the promise to make the ward an heir, and be enforced against the guardian or his estate, without working any injustice, the forbearance to sue being sufficient consideration for such promise.

SAME.—*Family Relation.*—Where the family relation exists, whether natural or assumed, there is, in the absence of an express agreement, or circumstances from which an agreement may be fairly inferred, no implied obligation to pay for board on the one hand or for work on the other.

SAME.—*Evidence.*—*Statements of Guardian to Judge.*—*To a Former Attorney.*—In an action by a ward against his guardian to set aside certain allowances made the guardian, the presiding judge was competent to testify concerning the statements made by the guardian to procure the allowance of his claims; and, to the same effect, the statements of a person who had formerly, but was not at the time of the transaction testified to, been the attorney of the guardian, are admissible in evidence.

SAME.—*Evidence.*—*Declarations of Guardian.*—*Amount of Estate.*—In such case, declarations of the guardian as to the amount of the ward's estate, or what he expected it to be, were admissible in evidence to show its amount, and also to show that heavy charges made just before the close of the trust, were an afterthought, and were not contemplated nor intended by him when the ward was living with him as a member of his family.

EVIDENCE.—*Admission Without Objection.*—*Appellate Court Practice.*—The admission of evidence, without objection, can not be complained of on appeal.

From the Hendricks Circuit Court.

L. A. Barnett, W. J. Beckett and *W. S. Doan*, for appellants.

T. S. Adams, J. G. Miles and *E. A. Miles*, for appellee.

GAVIN, J.—The appellee's complaint or claim against the estate of Mordecai Hadley, represented by the appellants, was in three paragraphs. Since the special findings of the court show that the judgment rests upon the third paragraph, it is unnecessary for us to consider the sufficiency of the others. *Hill* v. *Pollard*, 132 Ind. 588, 32 N. E. Rep. 564.

In presenting claims against decedents' estates, no formal complaint is necessary. It is sufficient if the statement sets forth the nature and amount of the claim with sufficient precision to bar another action, and shows a *prima facie* right to recover. *Lockwood, Admr.*, v. *Robbins*, 125 Ind. 398; *Hileman, Admr.*, v. *Hileman*, 85 Ind. 1; *Taggart* v. *Tevanny*, 1 Ind. App 339; *Knight, Admr.*, v. *Knight*, 6 Ind. App. 268, 33 N. E. Rep. 456.

The third paragraph of the complaint alleged that Mordecai Hadley became the guardian of appellee in 1868, and received, from pension and bounty, $2,000 for said ward, whom he took to live with him as a member of his family; that appellee thus lived with him and worked for him; that said Hadley, in his various reports to the court, obtained credits for board, clothing, etc., for his said ward, without disclosing to the court that he was all the time living with the guardian as a member of his family and working for him; that the guardian loaned the money at 10 per cent. interest and only accounted for 6 per cent.; that he failed to charge himself with several installments of pension received and with considerable amounts of interest received; that in 1883 he filed his final report, which was approved, and paid appellee the amount he then claimed to be due him; that within three years from the time of such settlement, appellee employed counsel to institute suit to set aside such allowances, and recover said sums from the guardian; that said guardian then promised that if he would not bring suit against him he would hold all of said sums for appellee, and manage them for him until plaintiff should marry and settle down, and then he would pay him all of said sums with their accretions, and would make him his heir; that in reliance upon this agreement appellee did not bring such suit, and in 1886 married and settled down, and became steady, and decedent expressed his entire satisfaction, and renewed his said promises, but has wholly failed and neglected to pay said sums or any part thereof. To this paragraph a demurrer was overruled.

Under the facts set forth there was abundant cause shown for setting aside the final settlement of this guardianship, and requiring the guardian to account for the sums wrongfully withheld. *Marquess* v. *La Baw*, 82 Ind. 550; *Wainwright* v. *Smith*, 117 Ind. 414.

Where the family relation exists, whether natural or assumed, there is, in the absence of an express agreement, or circumstances from which an agreement may be fairly inferred, no implied obligation to pay for board on the one hand, or for work on the other. *Lockwood, Admr.,* v. *Robbins,* 125 Ind. 398; *James, Admr.,* v. *Gillen,* 3 Ind. App. 472.

"The general rule is that a guardian can not exact money for the board of a ward whom he makes one of his family." *Marquess* v. *La Baw, supra.*

The concealment from the court of this fact, that the ward was living with him as a member of his family, was a wrong. So also was his failure to account for the interest and pension money actually received. The court could have no knowledge of these facts except as reported by him.

Appellee was required to bring his action to set aside the settlement within three years, else all matters embraced within his reports would be deemed finally adjudicated. *Briscoe* v. *Johnson, Exec.*, 73 Ind. 573; *Wainwright* v. *Smith*, 106 Ind. 239; *Horton* v. *Hastings*, 128 Ind. 103.

Having a clear right of action against the decedent, appellant's surrender of this right was a sufficient consideration for the promise by the decedent. *Ditmar, Guar.*, v. *West*, 7 Ind. App. 637, 34 N. E.; 1 Parsons on Cont. *441.

Appellants' counsel contend that decedent's promise "to make him an heir" is within the statute of frauds, and therefore void; also, that the contract is inseparable, and as part must fall, that therefore all must fall. Even if it be conceded that this part of the decedent's promise is within the statute and unenforceable, or if it be deemed so uncertain as to be unenforceable, still the conclusion reached by counsel by no means follows.

No claim is made nor recovery had for breach of the contract to make appellee an heir. The claim simply is that he has not repaid him his money, as promised.

The agreement to make him an heir, and the agreement to repay the money are separate, distinct, and severable matters. There is no connection between the two, nor any interdependence of the one upon the other.

Where the promisee has rendered the entire consideration, it would be inequitable and even iniquitous to say that because the law would not enforce all of the agreements made by the promisor, therefore he could not enforce even that in which there was no infirmity whatever.

The rule is well expressed in *Rand* v. *Mather*, 11 Cush. 1: "On principle, and according to numerous modern adjudications, the true doctrine is this: If any part of an agreement is valid, it will avail *pro tanto*, though another part of it may be prohibited by statute; provided the statute does not, either expressly or by necessary implication, render the whole void; and provided, further-more, that the sound part can be separated from the un-sound, and be enforced without injustice to the defend-ant.''

The case of *Hynds* v. *Hays*, 25 Ind. 31, decides that where the consideration of a note is in part legal and in part illegal, but they are clearly divisible, the contract, a bill of exchange, will be supported so far as it depends upon the valid consideration.

Here the agreements of the decedent are divisible, and the enforcement of the one part only, and the omission of the other, works no injustice to the decedent's estate.

The complaint is not liable to any of the objections offered to it.

There was a special finding by the judge, which em-braces abundantly sufficient of the material allegations of the complaint to justify the conclusions of law thereon.

There is no provision in the statute requiring notice of final report of a guardian, but the ward must take notice thereof. *Castetter, Admr.*, v. *State, ex rel.*, 112 Ind. 445.

It does not follow, however, that because he is thus required to take notice thereof for some purposes that his only remedy against wrong in the proceedings is by ap-peal, as asserted by counsel. On the contrary, numer-ous cases, some of which have already been cited, hold that he may maintain his action, in proper time, to set aside the final settlement.

The evidence of the presiding judge concerning the statements made by the guardian to procure the allow-ance of his claim for board, etc., was clearly admissible. It was part of appellant's case to prove the fraud or mis-take in the report. The testimony of Cofer, so far as material, was, for like reasons, admissible; so far as im-material it was harmless. Miles, also, was a competent witness to testify as to what transpired between the judge and the guardian. The guardian's statements to the court could not be deemed confidential communications to the attorney, and such only are privileged. *Borum* v. *Fouts*, 15 Ind. 50; *Hanlon* v. *Doherty*, 109 Ind. 37.

Neither was Miles, by reason of having formerly been the attorney of the guardian, disqualified from giving evidence as to statements made to him by the guardian when he was no longer a practicing attorney, and was employed in the auditor's office. The evidence shows that the conversation did not occur between them as attorney and client.

The declarations of the deceased guardian were not admissible in behalf of his estate. *Bristor* v. *Bristor, Admx.*, 82 Ind. 276.

The statements of various witnesses, who testified to what the guardian told them concerning the amount of the ward's estate, or what he expected it would be, were admissible to show its amount, and also to show that the heavy charges made just before the close of the trust were an afterthought, and were not contemplated nor intended by him when the ward was living with him as a member of his family.

Objection is made to the certified statement of the pension agent, because it was not shown to be genuine, and was not properly identified. No objection was made to its genuineness in the court below, and for this reason it can not be heard now.

Counsel have not referred us to any statute requiring the certificates of a pension agent to be under seal. No claim is made that the amount of pension received, as shown by this statement, varies materially from the showing made by decedent's own reports, which were in evidence.

No objection was made on the trial to the introduction

of the report in the estate of the deceased guardian. The deposition of Haynes does not appear to have been in evidence. No errors can therefore be predicated upon the court's action regarding it.

There are some other objections to evidence which have not been set out, but we are unable to find any material error in the rulings of the trial court. We are strongly of the opinion that the cause was fairly tried and correctly determined.

Judgment affirmed.

Filed Nov. 28, 1893.

———————◆———————

No. 1,167.

JACKSON SCHOOL TOWNSHIP v. SHERA.

CONTRACT.—*Common Schools.*—*Employment of Teacher.*—*Verbal Contract Valid.*—*Township Trustee.*—A verbal contract of employment as a teacher in the public schools, entered into by a township trustee and the teacher, is valid and binding, there being no statute requiring it to be reduced to writing.

INSTRUCTIONS TO JURY.—*Instruction Stating Ground of Recovery.*—*Omission of Essential Element.*—*Reversible Error.*—Where an instruction purports to set out all the material averments necessary to be proven in order to entitle the plaintiff to recover, it is fatal error to omit any such material averment.

From the Decatur Circuit Court.

W. A. Moore and *F. E. Gavin*, for appellant.

S. A. Bonner, *M. D. Tackett* and *B. F. Bennett*, for appellee.

DAVIS, C. J.—This was an action by the appellee to recover damages for breach of contract entered into between appellee and appellant, for services as a teacher in the public schools of said township.

The material allegations in the complaint are the same as in *School Town of Milford* v. *Zeigler*, 1 Ind. App. 138, with the exception that in the case cited the contract was in writing, and the action was against the school town, while this is against the school township.

The learned counsel for appellant, in a cogent brief, earnestly contend that the complaint is bad because the school township can not be held to respond in damages for the breach of an executory contract of this kind, when the corporation has received no benefit whatever, and cite, in support of this proposition, *Bloomington School Township, etc.,* v. *National School Furnishing Co.,* 107 Ind. 43; *Boyd* v. *Mill Creek School Township,* 114 Ind. 210; *Honey Creek School Township* v. *Barnes,* 119 Ind. 213; *Litten* v. *Wright, etc.,* 1 Ind. App. 92.

We heartily concur in the principles enunciated in those cases, but whatever our conclusion might be relative thereto, as applied to this case, it will suffice for the present to say that under the decisions of the Supreme Court, although the exact question here presented does not seem to have been considered, the liability of the school township for damages on account of the breach of such executory contract on the part of the trustee has been recognized. *School Town of Milford* v. *Powner,* 126 Ind. 528; *Reubelt* v. *School Town of Noblesville,* 106 Ind. 478.

It is also insisted that the contract was invalid because it was merely verbal, and should have been reduced to writing. No authority, however, has been cited which supports this proposition. The statute, so far as our attention has been called thereto, does not so provide. Sections 4444 and 5993, R. S. 1881.

In *Fairplay School Township* v. *O'Neal,* 127 Ind. 95, Judge ELLIOTT, in speaking for the Supreme Court, says: "It is, we may say in passing, not altogether clear that the statute does not require that all contracts shall be in writing and be recorded, but we do not deem it necessary to decide that question."

The learned judge does not cite any section of the statute or decision in support of the above dictum, and we are not prepared to say there is any statute in force that would bear such construction. The writer not only agrees with Judge ELLIOTT that "There is much reason for scrutinizing with care contracts made so far in advance of the opening of the school year as was that here sued on, and sound policy requires that the terms should be so definitely fixed and made known that all interested may have full and reliable information," but is also of the opinion that sound policy requires that the law making power should prescribe that when the minds of the parties meet as to the terms of such contract, the same should be reduced to writing and signed before the school corporation shall be held liable in damages for the subsequent violation thereof by the officer. In the absence, however, of such statutory provision, we are of the opinion that the complaint states facts sufficient to withstand the demurrer.

One of the material allegations contained in the complaint is in substance and to the effect that said appellee "held himself in readiness at all times during said school year to perform his said contract," etc.

The court undertook to instruct the jury as to the material averments of the complaint, and, after setting them out, said to the jury that if such facts were proven they should return a verdict in his favor. It omits entirely any reference to the allegation that the plaintiff was ready and willing to perform his contract of teaching the school. This is a fatal defect in the instruction.

It was incumbent on appellee to prove the contract,

the repudiation thereof by appellant, and the performance or readiness to perform the same·on his part.

An instruction which purports to set out all the material averments necessary to be proven, in order to entitle the plaintiff to recover, must be corréct and complete. *Kentucky and Indiana Bridge Co.* v. *Eastman*, 7 Ind. App. 514, 34 N. E. Rep. 835.

There are other errors in the record to which it is not necessary to call attention, as they may not arise on another trial.

For error in giving the instruction referred to, the judgment of the court below is reversed, with instructions to grant a new trial.

GAVIN, J., did not participate in this decision.

Filed Nov. 28, 1893.

No. 767.

THE TOLEDO, ST. LOUIS AND KANSAS CITY RAILROAD COMPANY *v.* TRIMBLE.

MASTER AND SERVANT.—*Employing a Minor.*—*Rules Governing Master's Liability.*—*Coemploye, Incompetency of.*—*Injury by.*—*Railroad.*—If one knowingly hire a minor and require him to perform dangerous service, in opposition to the parent's will, he will be liable to the parent, if injury befall such minor while engaged in such service. In such case it is not a question of negligence that gives rise to the liability, but the wrong consists in opposing the will òf the parent. But where such employment is simply without the consent of the parent, not against his express will, the question of liability is governed by the general rules applicable to such relation, viz.: Instructing servant if unexperienced, providing usually safe machinery, tools, and place to work, and competent and skillful fellow-servants; and in case of an injury resulting from the incompetency of a fellow-servant, damages can not be recovered where it is not affirmatively shown that the injured party had no knowledge of such incompetency.

From the Clinton Circuit Court.

S. O. Bayless and *C. G. Guenther*, for appellant.
M. Bristow and *J. T. Hockman*, for appellee.

LOTZ, J.—The appellee's minor son was killed while in the employ of the appellant as a night switchman. This action was brought to recover damages for the loss of his services during his minority. The complaint proceeded upon the theory that the son had been employed by the appellant in a dangerous and hazardous service, without the consent of the appellee; that he was inexperienced, and appellant failed to give him proper instructions, and that the son's death resulted from the unskillful and negligent conduct of the engineer in charge of the engine. There was a trial by jury and a special verdict returned.

Several errors are assigned, but the only ones discussed by appellant are that the court erred in overruling the motion for judgment in favor of the appellant on the special verdict and in overruling the motion for a new trial. The special verdict is as follows:

"First. We find that the defendant is a corporation duly organized under the laws of the State of Indiana, and as such corporation is now, and has been, for more than two years last past, conducting and managing a general railroad business between the cities of Toledo, Ohio, and St. Louis, Missouri, and controlling and operating locomotive engines, cars, and other property upon the defendant's said railroad.

"Second. That the railroad track of defendant passes through the county of Clinton and State of Indiana.

"Third. That as a part of said railway of defendant and its appurtenances thereunto belonging, the defendant has maintained for more than two years last past, in and adjacent to the city of Frankfort, in said Clinton county, a large yard covered with switches (side tracks), which are used by the defendant for standing cars and general switching purposes, upon which tracks trains are made up by the defendant preparatory to their being transported over the defendant's said railroad, both east and west, from said yard.

"Fourth. That at and in said yard, and for the purpose of conducting the business thereof, the defendant employed locomotive engines propelled by steam, and crews of employes, one of which crews, for more than two years last past, has attended to such duties of switching from the hour of six o'clock in the evening until six o'clock the next morning, at which time another crew takes charge of such switching work.

"Fifth. That the said city of Frankfort is, and has been for more than two years last past, a division point in the defendant's said railway system, and at the aforesaid yards all freight trains are rearranged before being transported over the defendant's said railway, both east and west from said Frankfort and from said yards.

"Sixth. That to do said service of said night switching in said yard, it required the services of the said night crew the entire night, and until six o'clock of the following morning, to get the said freight trains ready to move.

"Seventh. That the work of switching during the night time, and the making up of trains during that time, was, from April 2d to May 7th, 1891, dangerous to the persons of the said night crew, and required skilled and experienced persons to operate the locomotives, and shift and switch the cars in said yard.

"Eighth. That from April 2d to May 7th, 1891, in said yard of the defendant, and at the switches and side tracks in said yard adjacent to said defendant's railroad track, no lights were kept to aid said night crew in their said work of switching, except the small lanterns carried

... es engaged in said work and the headlight
. .g engine.

.. That said work of night switching during
_ ast aforesaid was also hazardous and danger-
. ...s—that by reason of the short runs made each
.. . .nanging the situation of the cars, the sudden
.... . _ and stopping of the locomotive and cars attached,
_ a.s caused by the coming together, the constant
..g.ng and uncoupling of the cars, requiring a switch-
... each time to go between the cars, the necessity of
sw.tchmen having to ride upon the tops of the cars much
, the time during switching, all of which rendered the
employment and duties of night switchmen particularly
hazardous and dangerous, and especially so to employes
of immature years and inexperience in this class of labor.

"Tenth. That on April 2d, 1891, the defendant, without the consent of the plaintiff, employed one Charles C.
Trimble, a son of the plaintiff, to serve in said yard of
defendant, in the capacity of night switchman; that at
the time of said employment of plaintiff's son by defendant, said Charles entered the service of said defendant and continued in said service until the day of his
death, to wit: May 7th, 1891.

"Eleventh. That said Charles, pursuant to the terms
of said employment, went on duty as such night switchman, with said night crew, at six o'clock in the evening
of each day, served during the entire night at such work
until six o'clock the next morning, except the morning
of May 7th, 1891. That under said employment, and as
a part of the duty of said Charles, he did, during said
employment in the night time, couple and uncouple cars,
open and close switches, and was compelled, in the
proper discharge of his duties at such times, to ride upon
the tops of the cars; that during the time of such employment, and while said Charles was on duty at said

The Toledo, St. Louis and Kansas City Railroad Company *v.* Trimble.

work, said cars were shifted and changed from place to place by means of a locomotive engine propelled by steam.

"Twelfth. That said Charles, at the time of said employment by defendant, was nineteen years of age, had never served in the capacity of switchman, and was wholly inexperienced to do such duties incumbent upon him in such service, with safety to his person. That at the time said Charles entered the service of the defendant as aforesaid, the defendant had knowledge of his · youth and inexperience to perform the duties attending the service of night switchman, but at the time of said employment the defendant failed to instruct said Charles of the dangers attending such service, and failed to give him the necessary instructions as to how to avoid the dangers attending the same.

"Thirteenth. That on the evening of May 6th, 1891, said Charles went on duty in said service as switchman, to serve until six o'clock of the morning of the 7th day of May. That the night switching crew on duty on said night consisted of George Beech, engineer; Alfred Allison, fireman; George V. Keefer and said Charles C. Trimble, switchmen. That the switching locomotive engine used by said crew on said night, and until the following morning at five o'clock, was known as engine No. 94. This engine was at said time owned and operated by the defendant. It was formerly a narrow gauge engine, and had been widened to standard gauge prior to said night. That said engine was of low build, the cylinder cock being about three to five inches above the tops of the rails.

"Fourteenth. That about five o'clock of the morning of said May 7th, it became necessary in the line of duty for said crew to move five freight cars from said yard of defendant to the "house switch" of defendant in said

city; that said switching engine, with said engineer
Beech in charge, was fronting to the east, and pushed
said cars from the yard east, toward the said house
switch.

"Fifteenth. That when said engine and cars were
moving toward said house switch, said Charles and the
associate switchman were riding upon the top of the east
end of the fifth freight car. When the front car was within
about (200) two hundred yards of the house switch, the
engineer, Beech, was signaled to slacken up for the
switch; at or about the time said signal was given to the
engineer, said Charles, who was standing about the center of the last or fifth car, started to go to the east end of
the car, where the ladder was, for the purpose of going
down to throw the house switch; that when he was near
the end of said car, the engineer unnecessarily reversed
said engine and caused said engine and cars to stop with
such suddenness that said Charles, by reason thereof,
was thrown forward over the end of the car upon the
track below, with his head and upper part of the body
resting on the south side of the south rail of said track,
and, with his legs over and upon said south rail of said
track; that at the time said Charles fell as aforesaid, said
engine and cars were moving toward where said Charles
was lying; that said Charles was caught under the
wheels of said car and one leg crushed below the knee,
while the other foot was also crushed; that all of said
cars, including the engine, passed over said Charles.

"Sixteenth. That when said Charles fell, and was
lying with his head and upper part of his body at nearly
right angles with said track, he was on the engineer's or
right side of the track, and could have been seen by said
engineer; that said engineer carelessly permitted said
engine and cylinder cock to pass over and crush his

body, which could have been avoided had the said Beech been attending to his duty.

"Seventeenth. That said Charles died from the effects of the injuries received as aforesaid, on the 7th day of May, 1891, at 12:30 o'clock P. M.

"Eighteenth. We further find that said Charles was in the employment of the defendant at the time he received said injuries, was in the line of his duty as assigned him by the defendant, and that in assisting to transfer said freight cars he was doing the same under the direction of the defendant.

"Nineteenth. That the plaintiff was never present about the defendant's track or yard when the said Charles was on duty as night switchman.

"Twentieth. We further find that the death of said Charles was caused by the cars and cylinder cock of the engine of defendant passing over his body, mangling and bruising the same.

"Twenty-first. We further find that said Beech was not regularly employed by the defendant as an engineer; neither was he sufficiently skilled or competent to act in the capacity of engineer, or to have the management of said locomotive engine, all of which facts of incompetency and unskillfulness were known to the defendant at the time of the accident, and prior thereto; that said Beech was, from April 2 to May 7, 1891, upon the payroll of the defendant as "day hostler," and not as an engineer, and at the time of said accident, and when and before said Beech was assigned to duty upon said switching engine No. 94, the defendant had notice that the said Beech was an incompetent and unskilled engineer.

"Twenty-second. We further find that engineer Beech was well acquainted and familiar with the switches and said tracks of the defendant in and adjacent to the city of Frankfort, in said county, on the 17th day of May,

1891. We also find that it was unnecessary, in the switching of said five cars and placing the same in the house switch, that said engineer Beech should check said engine and cars so suddenly at the time said Charles was thrown from the car as aforesaid; that when said engineer Beech received said signal to stop said engine and cars, the front freight car was 230 yards west of said house switch, and said engine and cars could have been stopped before reaching said switch without any sudden checking of said engine and cars. We further find that at the time said Beech checked said engine and cars for entering said house switch, said Beech did not sound the whistle of said engine nor give any warning to said Charles.

"Twenty-third. We further find that the death of said Charles, as aforesaid, was caused through the incompetency and unskillfulness of said engineer Beech, and that the defendant showed a want of care and diligence in putting said Beech in charge of said engine No. 94 on the night of May the 6th, and on the morning of May 7, 1891, for the purpose of doing the switching as aforesaid.

"Twenty-fourth. We further find that said Charles C. Trimble was nineteen years old on the first day of January, 1891, and that at the time of his death as aforesaid, was nineteen years, four months and six days old.

"Twenty-fifth. That said Charles, at the time of said employment and at the time of his death, was living in plaintiff's family as a member thereof, and had never been emancipated by plaintiff.

"Twenty-sixth. That said Charles, at the time of said employment, and of the accident aforesaid, and for seven years prior thereto, was able-bodied and capable of earning and did earn wages, and was, at the time of said accident, earning two dollars ($2.00) per day.

The Toledo, St. Louis and Kansas City Railroad Company *v*. Trimble.

"Twenty-seventh. We further find that the value of the services of said Charles, from the time of his death to the time when the said Charles would have attained the age of twenty-one years, less the cost of his maintenance during said term, is the sum of eleven hundred dollars.

"If, upon the foregoing fact, the law be with the plaintiff, we find for the plaintiff and assess his damages at eight hundred dollars. If, upon the foregoing facts, the law be with the defendant, we find for the defendant."

Several causes of action are alleged in the complaint:

First. That the minor son was employed and set to work in a dangerous service, without appellee's consent.

Second. That the son was inexperienced, and that the appellant failed to give him proper instructions so that he might avoid injury.

Third. That the appellant knowingly employed an unskillful and incompetent engineer, which fact was unknown to the deceased.

If either one of these causes be found by the special verdict, the appellee is entitled to a recovery. The father is entitled to the services and society of his child until he reaches his majority. Whoever deprives the father of the child's services against his will must respond in damages. *Rogers* v. *Smith*, 17 Ind. 323.

If one knowingly hire a minor and require him to perform dangerous service in opposition to the parent's will, he will be liable to the parent if injury befall such minor while engaged in such service. In such a case it is not a question of negligence that gives rise to the liability, but the wrong consists in opposing the will of the parent. *Grand Rapids, etc., R. R. Co.* v. *Showers*, 71 Ind. 451 (454); *Ft. Wayne, etc., R. W. Co.* v. *Beyerle*, 110 Ind. 100.

The mere fact that a minor is employed without the

consent of the parent will not make the employer liable
in case injury befall him.   There is a difference between
the want of consent and active opposition to the parent's
will.   In the last instance, the injury proximately results from opposing the parent's will, while in the other
instance the employment itself may not be wrongful,
and if injury befall the minor, it can not be said that the
injury proximately results from the employment.   In a
special finding or verdict, every fact necessary to the
plaintiff's recovery must be found, or the judgment must
be for the defendant.   The want of consent may give
rise to the presumption that the employment was against
the will of the parent, but such presumption is not conclusive, nor is it an ultimate fact upon which the right
of recovery rests.   Something more must concur to make
the employer liable.   He must have failed to instruct
him if he was inexperienced, or failed in the discharge
of some of the master's duties, such as providing him
with reasonably safe machinery, tools, places to work and
competent, and skillful fellow-servants.   *Pennsylvania
Co.* v. *Long*, 94 Ind. 250 (254).

The special verdict here finds that the deceased was
employed without the consent of the appellee, but does
not show that the employment was in opposition to his
expressed will.   In this respect it is insufficient to support a recovery.

As to the second cause, the finding is that the deceased
was inexperienced, and that the appellant failed to instruct him, but there is the further finding that the deceased was more than nineteen years of age, and had
worked as night switchman for more than a month at
the time he met his death.

The services which he was required to perform were
specially hazardous, and their dangers were as well
known to him as any one.   Minors are ordinarily held

The Toledo, St. Louis and Kansas City Railroad Company *v.* Trimble.

to assume the risks of the employment in which they are engaged and which are open and obvious to them. Buswell Personal Injuries, section 204; *Levey* v. *Bigelow*, 6 Ind. App. 677, 34 N. E. Rep. 128, and cases there cited.

As to the third cause, the finding is that the appellant directed Beech to perform the duties of engineer, knowing that he was incompetent; but there is no finding that the deceased did not know of his incompetency. If he knew of his incompetency and entered or continued in the service with such knowledge, he assumed the risk attending such incompetency. In order to sustain an action for an injury resulting from the negligence or incompetency of a coemploye, the plaintiff must prove that at the time the injury occurred he had, or that his decedent had, no knowledge of the incompetency or negligence of the fellow-servant, or facts from which the want of such knowledge may be inferred. *Lake Shore, etc., R. W. Co.* v. *Stupak*, 108 Ind. 1 (4).

The want of such knowledge must be affirmatively shown. There are no facts found by the special verdict from which such want of knowledge affirmatively appears. There is a marked difference with reference to the duties of the court in dealing with a special and a general verdict in actions for negligence. Negligence being usually a mixed question of law and fact, a general verdict may cover questions of both law and fact. Not so with a special verdict. It is the duty of the court to declare the law on a special verdict, and in such cases the jury have no concern with the law. The special verdict above set out fails to find sufficient facts upon which the judgment can find support.

Judgment reversed, at cost of appellee, with instructions to sustain the motion for a new trial.

Filed Nov. 28, 1893.

No. 955.

BALDWIN v. RUNYAN.

EVIDENCE.—*Objection to, When Properly Made.*—An objection to evidence on the ground that it is incompetent, immaterial and irrelevant, is insufficient. The reason why it is incompetent, etc., should be stated.

JUSTICE OF THE PEACE.—*When Acting as Collecting Agent Does not Deprive Justice of Jurisdiction.—Collateral Attack.—Presumption.—Waiver.*—Where a justice of the peace sits in judgment on the trial of a case based on account, the accounts having been, previous to bringing suit, placed in the hands of the justice for collection, the previous action of the justice as a collection agent of the subject-matter of the suit did not disqualify the justice to the extent of depriving him of jurisdiction, and a judgment rendered by the justice under such circumstances is not void and subject to collateral attack, except the disqualification is made to appear on the face of the record, or unless it was not known when it occurred; and it will be presumed that the parties had knowledge of any such disqualification until the contrary is made to appear affirmatively. Such disqualification may be waived, and would be waived unless disclosed at the earliest opportunity.

SAME.—*Appeal from, How Tried.—Jurisdiction on Appeal.—How Determined.*—Where a case is appealed to the circuit court, from a justice of the peace, the cause is tried *de novo*, and the circuit court only inquires into the jurisdiction of the justice for the purpose of deciding whether it has itself jurisdiction, and when it has so found, it tries and disposes of the case as an original action.

Dissenting opinion by Ross, J.

From the Montgomery Circuit Court.

G. W. Paul and *M. W. Bruner*, for appellant.

B. Crane and *A. B. Anderson*, for appellee.

REINHARD, J.—This action was on an account by the appellee against the appellant, and was commenced before a justice of the peace, after which it was appealed to the circuit court, where there was a recovery by the appellee.

But two questions arise in the case. The first of these

is an alleged error of the trial court in admitting in evidence, over appellant's objection, what purports to be an account or settlement sheet, showing the amount due from appellant to the appellee. The grounds of objection stated in the trial court, when the paper was offered, are as follows: "The defendant objected to the introduction of plaintiff's account now offered in evidence, on the ground that it is immaterial, incompetent, and irrelevant; that the plaintiff has no right to introduce, to prove an account or any issue in the case, not competent for any purpose."

We do not think any valid objection is pointed out to the introduction of the paper. The mere fact that it was "an account" certainly falls short of rendering it improper evidence, for it may have been made by both parties in a settlement had between them, and this is the contention of appellee's counsel. Nor is it sufficient to base the objection upon the ground that the evidence is "incompetent, immaterial, and irrelevant." The objection should state why it is incompetent, irrelevant, or immaterial. Nor is it apparent that the account was not in issue. On the contrary, it was directly in issue. If the appellant desired to object to the introduction of the account, because the same was prepared or written by the appellee himself, and the appellant is not bound by it, he should have made this the basis of his objection. Elliott's App. Proced., section 770, and cases cited.

We proceed to consider the second alleged error. During the progress of the trial in the circuit court, and after witnesses for both sides had been examined, one of the appellant's counsel interposed the following oral motion: "I now, based upon the evidence of George Runyan and Matthew R. Scott, move the court to strike this case from the record, on the ground that the justice of the peace before whom it was tried was an agent and at-

torney of the plaintiff in the case, and had the account
itself for collection at ten per cent.; brought the suit before himself, issued the summons to bring it before himself, and had the trial before himself and entered up the
judgment—on the grounds it was an absolute nullity."

The court overruled the motion, and the appellant
saved an exception to the ruling.

Was this error?

The evidence disclosed the fact that the account sued
on, or a portion thereof, had been, by the appellee, with
some other accounts, turned over to the justice of the
peace before whom this cause originated, for collection,
with the understanding that such justice was to receive
a commission of ten per cent. for all collections placed
in his hands by said appellee, if made without suit; that
the said justice attempted to collect the same without
suit, but being unable to do so, issued process thereon
the same as if the account had been left with him for
suit, and subsequently tried the cause.

Just at what point of time this supposed disqualification was discovered by the appellant, is not made to appear. We are of the opinion that the disqualification of
the justice was not such as necessarily deprived him of
jurisdiction, either of the person or of the subject-matter.
The utmost that can be made of the fact that he had
previously attempted to collect the claim is that it might,
if a proper showing were made, disqualify him as an
impartial trier of the case. It is, however, such a disqualification as might be waived, and we think it would
be waived, unless made known at the earliest opportunity. That this was the first opportunity the appellant
had for making the objection should also be made to appear by the appellant. That an objection to a trial judge,
on account of such a disqualification as is here relied
upon, may be waived, if not seasonably made, we think

is in conformity to the spirit of our decisions. As stated by Judge ELLIOTT, in his excellent work on Appellate Procedure: "The authority of the person who assumes to discharge the functions of a judge is presumed to be lawful. This presumption applies to a special judge unless the record shows a well founded objection to his capacity to act as judge. The later cases declare the doctrine we have stated and they rest on sound principle, since it would be unreasonable to assume that parties quietly sat by and permitted their cause· to be tried by an intruder or usurper. * * * The appellate tribunal will presume that the courts were held at the proper time and place, and that all was done that the law requires, to make the holding of the court regular and legal." Elliott's App. Proced., section 714, and cases cited.

This doctrine fully meets our approbation. It would, in our judgment, be a dangerous rule that would permit a party to a judgment to assail it upon any and all occasions, as void, when the record thereof utterly fails to disclose anything to impeach it. Such a practice would render many judgments, regular upon the face thereof, subject to collateral attacks for reasons that might, for aught that appears, have been known and disclosed prior to the rendition. If the appellant in the present case was aware of the alleged disqualification of the justice at the time he tried the cause, it was his imperative duty to make it known, and object to his acting as judge in such trial. He could not be permitted to sit quietly by and await the result of the trial, and then, in the event of an adverse decision, raise an objection to the judge after the rendition of the judgment.

We are bound, in the present case, to presume that the appellant had knowledge of the alleged disqualification, for everything must be presumed in favor of the rulings of the court below, until the error relied upon is made to appear affirmatively, and this includes every step necessary to establish such error.

We do not think the cases relied upon by appellant's counsel support their contention.

The case of *Chicago, etc., R. W. Co.* v. *Summers,* 113 Ind. 10, was a proceeding by a judgment plaintiff to enforce the payment of a judgment rendered by a justice of the peace for the killing of animals by the locomotive of a railroad company, under the provisions of section 4030, R. S. 1881. The answer in that proceeding showed not only the disqualification of the justice who rendered the original judgment, by reason of his having been regularly employed and acting as attorney in said cause pending before himself, but also that such disqualification was made to appear upon the trial of the original action by plea to the jurisdiction duly verified and filed, and that, therefore, the record of the judgment sought to be enforced showed upon its face the disqualification and incompetency of the justice who rendered the same.

There is a wide difference between the character of the judgment in the present case and the one disclosed by the record in the case cited. In the case in hand, no such plea or other motion was interposed showing that the justice was incompetent for any reason to try the cause, while in the case cited, as we have seen, the objection was made as soon as an opportunity was presented.

In the case of *Waterman* v. *Morgan,* 114 Ind. 237, one of the attorneys in the case, who assisted at the trial, was subsequently elected as judge of the circuit court to succeed the judge who presided at the trial, and after becoming judge he signed the bill of exceptions. These facts were all disclosed by the record. It was held, in that case, that there was no proper bill of exceptions in the record.

Again, in the case of *Fechheimer* v. *Washington*, 77 Ind. 366, it was held that a judgment was void, which was rendered by one of the attorneys of record, in such judgment, acting as judge, when the statute required that in case of such disqualification the cause should be transferred from the common pleas court, in which it was pending, to the docket of the circuit court.

It must be borne in mind that in the case at bar the justice had not been, properly speaking, acting attorney in the case for one of the parties, prior to his assuming jurisdiction of the same as such justice. The justice, upon the theory of the motion, had, at the most, been acting only as a collection agent, and there is no claim or pretense that he was ever employed as counsel in the trial of the cause. While we do not desire to be understood as deciding that the assumption of the duties of a collecting agent may not disqualify one from sitting as judge or justice in the trial of a cause in which it is shown that the chose in action forming the subject of the litigation had been in his hands for collection as such agent, we are decidedly of the opinion that this fact will not make void a judgment rendered by such judge or justice upon a collateral attack, unless the disqualification is raised and made to appear on the face of the record, or unless it appears that it was not known when it occurred. It is true that this is not, strictly speaking, a collateral attack upon the judgment rendered by the justice, yet the principle upon which we must treat the motion is the same. If the judgment of the justice was not void upon collateral attack, it can not be said that there was such a want of jurisdiction in him as rendered all the proceedings taken by him nugatory to such an extent that even the circuit court, where the cause is tried *de novo*, would have no jurisdiction on appeal. The circuit court is not a court of error, and does not undertake to review the proceedings before the justice. It can only inquire into the jurisdiction of the justice for the purpose of deciding whether it has itself jurisdiction, and when it has so found, it proceeds to try and dispose of the case as an original action.

We find no error for which the judgment should be reversed.

Judgment affirmed.

Filed Nov. 28, 1893.

DISSENTING OPINION.

Ross, J.—It developed, on the trial of this cause in the Montgomery Circuit Court, that the account sued on was placed by appellee in the hands of Mathew R. Scott, who was then an acting justice of the peace for Wayne township, in said Montgomery county, as the agent of the appellee, for collection, for which services he was to receive a sum equal to ten per cent. of the account; that said Scott instituted this action before himself as such justice, and tried the cause and entered judgment against the appellant. As soon as these facts were disclosed on the trial in the circuit court, the appellant, by his counsel, at once moved the court to dismiss the cause for want of jurisdiction, which motion was overruled by the court, and appellant excepted.

It has been suggested by my worthy associate who wrote the opinion of the majority, that the appellant should have pleaded to the jurisdiction, or if not acquainted with the facts in time to have pleaded them, should have shown by his motion to dismiss that that was the first opportunity he had for interposing his objection to the court's jurisdiction. It is new to the writer that a party can, by statements in a motion, either make

or contradict a record, and while it must be conceded
that a party must interpose his objection to the court's
jurisdiction over his person at the first opportunity, the
question of jurisdiction of the subject-matter may be
raised at any time. The record in this case, until the
making of the motion to dismiss, does not disclose in
any way that said Scott was acting for the appellee in
procuring said judgment. When the witness Scott was
on the stand, it then developed, for the first time, that
while he was acting as a court, he was at the same time
acting for the appellee as his attorney. Thereupon the
appellant interposed his objection, and moved to dismiss
the cause.

It is against the policy of the law that any man shall
sit in judgment upon his own case. That which the law
forbids the principal to do it will not tolerate on the part
of his agent. Section 1457, R. S. 1881, provides that no
constable or justice of the peace shall act as the agent or
attorney of a party to an action pending in such justice's
court.

While a justice of the peace ordinarily has jurisdiction
of the class of cases similar to the one in controversy, he
can not acquire jurisdiction either of the subject-matter
or of the person, even of a case falling within that class,
if the law forbids it.. His right to jurisdiction both of
the subject-matter and the person of the defendant is
limited, and if he assumes to do that which the statute
forbids in acquiring jurisdiction, his acts are void. As
the Supreme Court, in the case of *Chicago, etc., R. W.
Co.* v. *Summers*, 113 Ind. 10, says: "If at the time
his action against appellant was pending before the first
justice, appellee in person had been a qualified and acting justice of the peace, of Starke county, and if, when
the change of venue was granted, the action had been

sent to appellee, as such justice, and he had tried and decided the case, and had rendered and entered judgment therein in his own favor and against appellant, no one could doubt that such judgment was wholly void and could not be enforced; for such a judgment would be in direct violation of the old and well known legal maxim, namely, *Nemo debet esse Judex in propria sua causa.*"

It is affirmatively shown by the record that as soon as it developed, on the trial of the cause in the circuit court, that the justice rendering the judgment was at that time acting in the dual position of attorney and court, the appellant denied the jurisdiction of the court. It has often been asserted that a judgment is void only when the thing lacking or making it void is apparent on the face of the record, and again it has been decided that the enforcement of a judgment can not be enjoined except it is void, but such statements are not absolutely correct, for a judgment may be enjoined which does not on its face show that it is void. I need cite no authorities upon these propositions, because our reports are full of such decisions.

The judgment in this case could have been enjoined, because upon a showing of the facts it would have appeared that the court had neither jurisdiction of the subject-matter of the action nor of the person of the defendant. In fact, on the trial of this cause in the circuit court, it was the duty of the court to have dismissed the cause, when the facts became known, without any formal motion. "Without even a suggestion, *ex mero motu*, a court will set aside a judgment rendered without jurisdiction." *Doctor* v. *Hartman*, 74 Ind. 221.

If the justice of the peace had no jurisdiction, the circuit court acquired none on appeal. *Snell* v. *Mohan*, 38 Ind. 494; *Mays* v. *Dooley*, 59 Ind. 287; *Horton*

v. *Sawyer*, 59 Ind. 587; *Brown* v. *Goble*, 97 Ind. 86. I think it was error to overrule the motion to dismiss, and that the judgment of the court below should be reversed.

. Filed Nov. 28, 1893.

———————◆———————

No. 794.

RICHARDS, ADMINISTRATOR, v. HOLLIS.

DECEDENT'S ESTATE.—*Right of Widow to Take Both Under the Will and the Law.*—If a widow accept a bequest, she does not thereby forfeit her statutory allowance ($500), where there is nothing in the will inconsistent with the widow's right to take both the bequest and the statutory allowance.

From the Grant Circuit Court.

J. A. Kersey, for appellant.

J. T. Strange and *E. A. Huffman*, for appellee.

DAVIS, C. J.—William Hollis departed this life testate on the 15th of April, 1891, leaving appellee, who was his second wife, without children, surviving him as widow. By the terms of his will said William Hollis devised to appellee five hundred dollars out of his personal property, and also one-third of his real estate during her natural life. After making bequests of specific amounts to several of his children and grandchildren, he devised the residue of his estate, personal and real, to his children and grandchildren. Aside from the real estate, the personal estate, which came into the hands of appellant as administrator, amounted to $2,446.11. After the payment of debts and expenses, the amount remaining for distribution was $2,196.60. On the 13th of May, 1891, appellee filed her written election to take the lands devised to her, as provided in section 2505, R. S. 1881, and

VOL. 8—23

also stated therein that she would accept the "property bequeathed, but in no case shall the acceptance thereof preclude my rights to the five hundred dollars provided for under section 2269 of the Revised Statutes of 1881."

The section last cited provides that "the widow of the decedent, whether he die testate or intestate," shall have five hundred dollars, either in personal property or "in cash out of the first moneys received," etc.

The court below held that the appellee was entitled to the five hundred dollars bequeathed to her in the will, and also to the five hundred dollars allowed a widow under the statute. Counsel for the administrator insist that this decision was wrong, and that having accepted the five hundred dollars devised to her under the will, she has forfeited the statutory allowance. *Shafer* v. *Shafer, Exec.*, 129 Ind. 394. In this case, it should be borne in mind, that under the law appellee would have taken one-third of the real estate for life, also the five hundred dollars statutory allowance, and also one-third of the residue of the personal estate after the payment of such allowance, debts, and expenses. Section 2487, R. S. 1881.

The general rule is that when it clearly appears from the will, either by express statement or otherwise, that the provisions therein made for the wife are intended to be in lieu of that made by the law, she must elect between the will and the law, and can not have the provision made by both, but this rule should not have an unreasonable, arbitrary, and technical construction against the widow.

The cases in which the general rule has been applied are not in all respects harmonious. The difficulty lies in determining whether a given state of facts and circumstances bring each particular case within the rule.

As to the personal estate, there was then no statute in force requiring a widow to elect whether she would accept the provision made for her in the will, or claim her rights under the law, and if the acceptance of the five hundred dollars given appellee under the will is held to bar her right to receive the statutory allowance, such result must be deduced from the principles of equity, and because of such manifest repugnancy between that right and the will that they could not possibly stand together.

In this case the husband, by the will, did make provisions for his widow, but he did not in terms declare that such provisions should be in lieu of her rights under the law. The testator then made specific provision for his children and grandchildren, in the way of particular bequests for them for different amounts, and concluded by making a general disposition of all the residue of his property to his children and grandchildren.

The circumstances under which this will was made, and the principles which should control the rights of the parties, are, it seems to us, correctly enunciated in *Shipman* v. *Keys, Admr.*, 127 Ind. 353, and we quote, as applicable to the question under consideration, the language of Judge McBRIDE, as follows:

"A general disposition of all the residue of his property by residuary devise or bequest, not purporting to be in lieu of such absolute claim, is not enough, however, to compel an election. Such devise or bequest will be construed as made in view of her absolute statutory rights, and subject thereto, and only operates on the residue after the payment of debts and expenses of administration, and the satisfaction of specific devises, legacies and rights. There is nothing in the will in this case inconsistent with the widow's claim to take both the statutory allowance of five hundred dollars and the provision made for her by the will."

Judgment affirmed, at costs of appellant.

Filed Nov. 28, 1893.

No. 1,005.

PARRETT, ADMINISTRATOR, v. PALMER, ADMINISTRATOR.

HUSBAND AND WIFE.—*Wife's Separate Estate.*—*What Consists of.*—Not only is the property actually acquired by gift, devise, or descent, preserved to the married woman, but also the proceeds of such property, whether the natural increase or the money procured by its sale or other property purchased with that money.

SAME.—*Wife's Separate Estate.*—*Use of by Husband with Wife's Consent.*—*Trustee.*—*Gift.*—Where the husband, with the wife's consent, used money belonging to the wife, as part of her separate estate, in building a family residence, and there was nothing to indicate that the wife intended the money as a gift, it will be presumed that, as to such money, the husband is the trustee of the wife, and the husband or his estate is liable to the wife for such money.

SAME.—*Personal Property.*—*Rights in, How Affected by Marriage.*—*Governed by Law of Husband's Domicil.*—The respective rights of the husband and wife in their personal property, acquired by them by their marriage, are determined by the law of the place of their marital domicil, and that, in the absence of any contrary intention, is the domicil of the husband at the time of the marriage.

From the Fountain Circuit Court.

W. A. Tipton, C. S. Wesner, H. H. Stilwell and *W. F. Stilwell,* for appellant.

J. A. Lindley and *O. P. Lewis,* for appellee.

GAVIN, J.—The appellee, as administrator of the estate of Caroline Parrett, deceased, filed a claim against the estate of her deceased husband, William Parrett, for her $500, and also for additional sums received by him from her in 1857.

There was a trial and special finding of facts, with a motion for new trial and exceptions to the conclusions of law overruled.

From the facts found, it appears that at the time of his marriage to Caroline, in 1856, William Parrett was a resident of Fountain county, Indiana, while she was a resident of the State of Ohio, where they were married; that Caroline received, as the proceeds of the real and personal property owned by her in the State of Ohio, the sum of $2,900, which money was received by her after her marriage with said William, and while they were both temporarily in the State of Ohio. Afterwards, and prior to 1860, $1,200 of this money was used by her husband, with her consent, in the erection of a dwelling house upon his lands, to be used as a family residence, in which both lived until their death, in 1892, the husband dying intestate three days before the wife. No express agreement was made to repay the money so used by William.

Upon these facts the court concluded that appellee was entitled to recover the $500, and also the further sum of $1,272.

The appellant insists that the conclusion as to the $1,272 is erroneous.

The laws of Ohio are not before us, and appellant contends that the common law is presumed to be in force there, and that the law of Ohio determines the right to the money received by Mrs. Parrett, because she was married in Ohio and received it there.

We do not so understand the rule. The respective rights in their personal property, acquired by husband and wife, by their marriage, are determined by the law of the place of their matrimonial domicil, and this, in the absence of any contrary intention, is the domicil of the husband at the time of the marriage, which was in Indiana. Story on Conflict of Laws, sections 191–199; Wharton on Conflict of Laws, section 190; 5 Am. and Eng. Encyc. of Law, 868.

By her marriage, the wife acquired the domicil of the husband. *McCollem* v. *White*, 23 Ind. 43; *Jenness* v.

Jenness, 24 Ind. 355; *Cooper* v. *Beers*, 33 N. E. Rep. 61;
5 Am. and Eng. Encyc. of Law, 868.

Appellant further contends that even under the law of
Indiana in force from 1856 to 1860, when the wife sold
her separate property and received money for it, the
money became the property of the husband, because it
was not acquired by gift, devise, or descent, but by purchase, and was not the money of the wife at the time of
her marriage.

Section 5116, R. S. 1881, which was then in force,
provides that "No lands of any married woman shall be
liable for the debts of her husband; but such lands, and
the profits therefrom, shall be her separate property, as
fully as if she were unmarried: *Provided*, That such
wife shall have no power to incumber or convey such
lands, except by deed in which her husband shall join."

By section 2488, R. S. 1881, in force since 1853, "The
personal property of the wife held by her at the time of
her marriage, or acquired, during coverture, by descent,
devise, or gift, shall remain her own property to the
same extent and under the same rules as her real estate
so remains."

We can not concur in giving to these provisions the
narrow construction claimed by counsel. On the contrary, we are strongly of the opinion that not only the property actually acquired by gift, devise, or descent, is preserved to the married woman, but also the proceeds of
such property, whether the natural increase or the money
produced by its sale, or other property purchased with
that money. It would be a barren ideality, indeed, to
hold that a woman should have the rent, corn that grew
on her land, or could own a drove of hogs given her by
her father, but if she sold them the money would be her
husband's. Such a holding would not accord with the
spirit of later times.

The case of *Mahoney* v. *Bland, Admr.*, 14 Ind. 176, is relied upon by appellant in support of his proposition, and it does sustain it, but it has been repudiated by later cases.

In *Ireland* v. *Webber*, 27 Ind. 256, it is said: "We can not see why property purchased with the proceeds of the sale of the wife's lands is not as much hers as that purchased with the proceeds of the rents, issues and profits therefrom." "It is claimed that, inasmuch as the property in controversy (having been bought with the proceeds from the sale of her lands) was not held by the wife at the time of her marriage, and was not acquired by her during coverture by descent, devise or gift, it is liable to attachment as the property of the husband, for the payment of his debts. We think otherwise.

"The appellant relies on *Mahoney* v. *Bland, Admr.*, 14 Ind. 176, for a reversal of the judgment in the case at bar. But we do not think that the case can be reconciled with the ruling in *Johnson* v. *Runyon*, 21 Ind. 115."

In *Bellows* v. *Rosenthal*, 31 Ind. 116, it is decided that goods purchased with money which was her separate estate, or the proceeds thereof, were the separate property of the wife.

In *Derry* v. *Derry*, 98 Ind. 319, it is said that a trust results to the wife where the husband takes in his own name title to land purchased with the "proceeds or accumulations" from his wife's separate estate in his hands.

In *Garner* v. *Graves, Admr.*, 54 Ind. 188, our Supreme Court held that notes taken by the husband in his own name, in payment for his wife's real estate, belonged in equity to her, and not to his estate.

Whatever language there may be in *Abshire* v. *State, ex rel.*, 53 Ind. 64, which would seem in its literal interpretation to be inconsistent with these holdings, must be considered with reference to and limited to the circumstances of that particular case.

The principle asserted is no new one. We find it supported by Story's Eq. Jur., section 1375, where he is speaking of the separate allowances to a wife at common law: "And if such allowances are invested in jewels or other ornaments, or property, the latter will be entitled to the same protection against the husband and his creditors." See also *Liebes* v. *Steffey* (Ar.), 32 Pac. Rep. 261; *Knapp* v. *Smith*, 27 N. Y. 277; *Schurman* v. *Marley*, 29 Ind. 458.

We think the rule is well expressed by the language of the court in *Spooner* v. *Reynolds*, 50 Vt. 437: "If a married woman purchases personal property with money of her own, the property thus purchased is as much hers as was the money with which she purchased it."

It being established that this money was, in the hands of Mrs. Parrett, her separate property, and governed by our statute, the question then arises as to whether or not under the facts stated there is any liability upon the part of the husband's estate to account to her.

The facts found are quite meager, but we are compelled to determine the correctness of the legal conclusions from the facts stated alone, without their being aided by inferences which might have been fairly and with propriety drawn from the evidence.

We have here a case where the wife's money passes directly and voluntarily from her hands to that of her husband, with no finding as to whether a gift was intended, or whether he received the money simply as an agent or trustee for her. Under such circumstances what is the presumption of the law?

It has long been conceded to be the law that a woman could bestow her separate property upon her husband by way of gift, unless prevented by some special limitation of her powers over it, but courts of equity view such transactions with care and caution, and in dread of undue influence. Story Eq. Jur., section 1395.

"There is no doubt that courts should narrowly scrutinize cases of alleged gifts from the wife to the husband." *Hardy* v. *Van Harlingen*, 7 O. St. 208.

"As regards the corpus of the separate estate, no presumption arises in favor of a husband who has received it. He is *prima facie* a trustee for his wife, and a gift from her to him will not be inferred without clear evidence." 2 Lewin on Trusts, *778.

"A simple payment by the wife to the husband of the income of her separate estate may be treated as a gift to him. * * The receipt by him of separate capital moneys of the wife stands on a different footing. A transfer of her separate property into his name is *prima facie* no gift." Crawley's Law of Husband and Wife, 268.

So also in Eversley on Dom. Rel. 409. "She may make a gift of her separate property to her husband for his own use, or that of the family, but the onus lies upon the husband of proving that a gift was intended, and that he has not influenced her act and conduct." *Rich* v. *Cockell*, 9 Ves. 369; *Hughes* v. *Wells*, 9 Hare, 749; *Wales* v. *Newbould*, 9 Mich. 45; *Boyd* v. *De La Montagnie*, 73 N. Y. 498; Reeves Dom. Rel. (4th Ed.), 216, note; *McNally* v. *Weld*, 30 Minn. 209; *Green* v. *Carlill*, 4 Ch. Div. 882; *Jones* v. *Davenport*, 44 N. J. Eq. 33; *Bergey's Appeal*, 60 Pa. St. 408.

In our own State the holdings of the Supreme Court strongly support the doctrine announced above.

In *Hileman, Admr.*, v. *Hileman*, 85 Ind. 1, the ruling was to the effect that the presumption of law, under the statute of this State, is that the separate property or money of a wife, which is taken into the possession of the husband, is to be considered as taken by him for her use and benefit, until such presumption is overcome by evidence that a gift was intended.

Judge MITCHELL says in *Armacost, Admr.*, v. *Lindley, Admr.*, 116 Ind. 295: "Transactions between husband and wife are presumably influenced by the peculiar relation which exists between them, and where a husband obtains possession of the separate money or property of his wife, it must appear from all the circumstances that the wife intended to make a gift of it to him."

In the case from which we have last quoted, it was decided that where the notes for the purchase-money of her land were taken, payable to the husband, with the wife's consent, but at his suggestion, the law would presume, nevertheless, that he thus took her separate estate as her trustee, and not for his own benefit.

In *Denny* v. *Denny*, 123 Ind. 240, the holding in *Hileman, Admr.*, v. *Hileman, supra*, is reaffirmed, and the distinction between the income and the principal of the fund is clearly drawn. It is there decided that where the husband, with the consent of the wife, receives and uses her separate income for the benefit of the family, a gift will be presumed, but it is said, "A well established distinction exists, however, when the husband receives and appropriates the corpus or principal of his wife's separate property."

The trust and confidence ordinarily reposed by the wife in the husband, her natural reliance and dependence upon him for the management of her business; the fact that as a rule the husband is possessed of general business experience, while the experience of the wife is usually limited; all these considerations sustain us in the conclusion that where the wife voluntarily delivers her money to the husband, the law presumes that he takes it as trustee for her, and not as a gift, even though there be no express promise to repay.

Parrett, Administrator, v. Palmer, Administrator.

There are some cases maintaining a different doctrine, but we do not believe them to be in harmony with the legislation or the judicial interpretation of our State. Nor is the mere fact that the huband in this case, with her consent, used the money in building a family residence on his land, in itself sufficient, as the case comes to us on a special finding, to rebut and overthrow this presumption. This, taken in connection with other circumstances, such as the respective values of their estates, failure to assert any claim for a long period of time, and any others which might throw light on the intentions of the parties, might justify a trial court in drawing the inference of fact that a gift was in truth intended, but no such intention is found by the facts in this case, and such intention is an essential element of appellant's case, and must be specifically found before the opposite presumption can be deemed overcome.

There is, in our judgment, sufficient evidence to sustain the findings. The claim was not barred by the statute of limitations, which does not run as to dealings between husband and wife. *Barnett* v. *Harshbarger, Admr.*, 105 Ind. 410.

The claim was stated with sufficient accuracy to enable the appellee to recover on the proof made. *Hileman, Admr.*, v. *Hileman, supra.*

In presenting claims against estates, it is sufficient if the statement shows the nature and amount of the claim with sufficient precision to bar another action, and show a *prima facie* right to recover. *Lockwood, Admr.*, v. *Robbins*, 125 Ind. 398; *Doan* v. *Dow*, 35 N. E. Rep. 709.

We find no error in the record.

Judgment affirmed.

Filed Nov. 28, 1893.

No. 993.

THE WESTERN UNION TELEGRAPH COMPANY *v.* CLINE.

TELEGRAPH COMPANY.—*Telegram.*—*Liability of Company for Mental Suffering Caused by Its Negligence.*—A recovery may be had for the mental anguish and suffering caused by negligence in transmission and delivery of a telegram, although no pecuniary loss other than the cost of the message be shown.

SAME.—*Gist of Action.*—*Secondary Evidence.*—*Telegram.*—*Duty of Jury.*—In an action against a telegraph company for failure to transmit and deliver a telegram with due diligence, the negligence in transmission and delivery, and not the message, is the foundation of the action; and when some evidence of the terms of the original message is given without objection, the original not being in evidence, it is the duty of the jury to weigh the evidence, such as it was, and the court can not remove this duty by instructing them to return a verdict for the defendant.

From the Monroe Circuit Court.

J. H. Louden and *T. J. Louden,* for appellant.
J. R. East and *R. G. Miller,* for appellee.

LOTZ, J.—This action was commenced by the appellee to recover damages for the alleged failure of the appellant to transmit and deliver to appellee, within a reasonable time, a telegraph message sent by one John Evans, of Spencer, Ind., directed to the appellee, at Bloomington, Ind.

The message was in these words: "Joe Cline. Come at once. Mother is dying." A demurrer was overruled to the complaint. This is the first error assigned.. An examination of the complaint shows it to be sufficient to withstand the demurrer. Issues of fact were joined and tried by a jury, which returned a verdict for appellee in the sum of $125. A motion for a new trial was made by appellant, which was overruled. This is the only other error assigned.

Appellant insists that there is a total failure in the evidence to show that the appellee sustained any damages. It was averred, and conceded on the trial, that the person referred to in the message as dying was the mother-in-law of the appellee, and there was evidence tending to show that if the message had been transmitted and delivered promptly, the appellee and the members of his family might have been present at the time of her death, and that by reason of the delay they were prevented from being present. It is settled by the decisions in this State that there may be a recovery for mental anguish and suffering, although no pecuniary loss other than the cost of the message be shown. *Western Union Tel. Co.* v. *Newhouse*, 6 Ind. App. 422, 33 N. E. Rep. 800; *Western Union Tel. Co.* v. *Eskridge*, 7 Ind. App. 208, 33, N. E. Rep. 238; *Western Union Tel. Co.* v. *Stratemeier*, 6 Ind. App. 125, 32 N. E. Rep. 871; *Reese* v. *Western Union Tel. Co.*, 123 Ind. 294; *Renihan* v. *Wright*, 125 Ind. 536.

Counsel for appellant strenuously insist that the evidence shows that the message was delivered to its agent at Spencer at 7:35 P. M., and that the agent informed the sender that it would have to be sent by way of Indianapolis and Louisville, and that the office would close at Bloomington at 8 P. M., and that it could not, in the usual course of business, transmit the message before the closing hour of its office at Bloomington. If this were the undisputed evidence in the case, the position would be well taken, but we have examined the evidence on this point and find it conflicting. We must decline to weigh it.

It is next insisted that the original message delivered to appellant's agent at Spencer was not given in evidence, nor was its absence properly accounted for. The agent at Spencer to whom the message was delivered was a witness for appellant on the trial, and on his cross-examination he gave the contents of the message delivered to him, without objection. There was also parol evidence of the contents of the message received at Bloomington. The appellant asked the trial court to instruct the jury that, as the original message had not been introduced in evidence, nor accounted for in any way, it should return a verdict for the defendant. The court refused to give this instruction, and this refusal is one of the causes assigned for a new trial. The instruction asked proceeds upon the theory that in the absence of the original, or properly accounting for it, there is a total failure of proof on a material question, and a recovery can not be had. There was some evidence of the terms of the original message given to the jury without objection. This being true, the court would have no right to direct a verdict for the defendant.

It was the duty of the jury to weigh the evidence, such as it was, and the court had no right to take from them this duty. The best evidence should always be produced if possible, before secondary evidence is allowed, but if secondary evidence is given without objection, it is to be considered and weighed by the jury as any other evidence.

The message is not the foundation of this action. The failure to transmit and deliver within a reasonable time is the gist of the controversy. That a certain message was delivered for transmission was a substantive fact necessary to be proved, and the rule is, that when parol evidence is as near the fact testified to as the written, then each is primary. *Hewitt* v. *State*, 121 Ind. 245. There is no reversible error in the record.

Judgment affirmed, at costs of appellant.

Filed Nov. 28, 1893.

NOVEMBER TERM, 1893. 367

The Toledo, St. Louis and Kansas City Railroad Company *v.* Hauck.

No. 948.

THE TOLEDO, ST. LOUIS AND KANSAS CITY RAILROAD COMPANY *v.* HAUCK.

RAILROAD.—*Duty to Keep Premises Safe for All Persons Transacting Business With It.—Delivering and Receiving Freight.*—A railroad company, which is a common carrier of goods, and by its conduct invites or induces the public to use its premises, such as depots and other places set apart for receiving and discharging freight, is under special obligation to keep such premises safe for such use' for all persons coming upon the premises to transact business with such company, and among those who are entitled to this protection are such persons as come there for the purpose of delivering or receiving freight.

SAME.—*Freight, Delivering and Receiving.—Safe Premises, Duty of Company as to.—Notice.*—Where a box car had been left on a side track, to be loaded with freight, and the consignee of the car was storing her goods therein at the precise point where she was directed to use it for that purpose, there was an implied agreement that the company would protect her from all approaching trains, and that she should not be molested or endangered in her person or property by any act of the company or its servants; and, in such case, the mere fact that a freight train had arrived and passed the box car, on the main track, was no notice to her that such train would enter the side track and endanger her safety by being pushed violently against the car in which she was lawfully engaged in her work of putting away her goods; nor was it her duty, under such circumstances, to leave the car and watch the movements of the freight train.

APPELLATE COURT PRACTICE.—*Searching the Record.—Error Should be Specifically Designated.*—The appellate tribunal will not search the record, for appellant, to find error which is asserted to have been committed. It is his duty to direct the court to the place or places in the record where it is made to appear that the error was committed.

From the Grant Circuit Court.

S. O. Bayless and *C. G. Guenther,* for appellant.

W. Stephenson, H. Brownlee and *H. J. Paulus,* for appellee.

REINHARD, J.—The appellant has assigned numerous

errors, but we shall notice such only as are discussed in the supersedeas brief of counsel, which is the only one filed by them.

The action was brought to recover damages for a personal injury sustained by the appellee through the alleged negligence of the appellant while appellee was loading some household goods to be carried upon a freight car set apart to the appellee for that purpose by the agents of the appellant. It is claimed, in argument, on behalf of appellant, that the special verdict of the jury, when purged of mere evidentiary facts and legal conclusions, is insufficient to show culpable negligence on the part of appellant and freedom from contributory fault on the part of appellee, and that the court consequently erred in overruling the appellant's motion for judgment in its favor upon the special verdict.

From the facts found, it appears, in substance, that the appellant was, at the time of the alleged grievances, a common carrier of goods and freight, for hire, over a line of railroad operated by it, the main track of which ran through the town of Swayzee, in Grant county, Indiana, where the appellant maintained a station, switch and side track for the use and convenience of persons receiving and transporting freight, which station and the business connected therewith were under the management and direction of a station agent of the appellant; that the side track at the point mentioned branched off from the main track, running east and west on the north side thereof, running for a distance of 1,000 feet or more, where it again joined the main track, and was so constructed and arranged that the cars and engines could pass from the main track over and upon the side track from either the east or west end thereof; that the appellee, who resided in the town of Swayzee, desired to have transferred and carried by the appellant, over the line of its railroad, from the said town to a point east thereof on said line, certain household goods and furniture belonging to her, and for that purpose, on the 13th day of May, 1890, called upon the appellant's said station agent at said place, and informed him of her desire to ship said goods, and requested him to have a car placed upon said side track, in which to load such goods, which said agent then agreed to do, and, on the 16th day of May, 1890, he caused to be placed upon said side track, at said town, at a point a short distance east of the station building, a box car completely and tightly closed at the sides, ends, bottom and top, with an open doorway on the north; and, on the evening of the day last named, informed appellee of the arrival of the car and directed her to place her goods therein for shipment without any unnecessary delay, whereupon, on the same evening, the appellee placed a portion of such goods in said car, placing the remainder therein the next day; that with the assistance of others and with her own hands, and with the knowledge and consent of such agent, she placed the goods in said car through the open door on the north side thereof; that in order to protect the goods from injury and damage while in transit, it was necessary that many articles be wrapped with cloth, carpet, and other material, and that the same be stored in proper position in the car, and for this purpose, and with the knowledge and consent of the station agent, she went into the car and began the work of wrapping and arranging such goods; that while appellee was in said car and so engaged, one of appellant's east-bound freight trains was drawn along and upon the main track, to or near said station, and, after a short stop, the agent and employes of the appellant in charge of such train caused the same to be run at a rapid speed on its way east and along and upon said main track, passing the

car in which appellee was so engaged, until the rear car
passed the east end of the side track, when its movement
was reversed, and it was backed into and upon the side
track westwardly to such a distance and with such speed
and force as that it struck said car with such violence as
to move it suddenly a distance of four feet or more; that
when said train so left the station, going eastwardly, and
when it was so backed in upon the side track, the said
station agent knew that all the goods of the appellee were
not in said car ready for shipment, and so believing and
knowing, said agent failed and neglected to so inform the
agents and employes of the appellant in charge of the
train; that such train, after passing such car, and before
it reached the east end of the side track, was so far away
that its movements could not be and were not heard by
the appellee in said inclosed box car, and that the appellee had no knowledge that her goods and car were to be
taken from the side track by said train, or that the train
would be backed in upon the side track, and there was
no other car or cars than the one already mentioned, on
such side track before and at the time the said train was
so backed upon the same; that when the train passed the
car going east the appellee was in the closed box car engaged as aforesaid, and was not able to see said train,
and was unable to know its movements after it passed
the car going east and beyond her hearing, and that she,
having no knowledge that her goods were to be taken by
said train, or that the same would be run upon the side
track, and knowing as she did that the station agent
knew of her being in and about said car, and that the
same was not ready for removal, she had reason to believe, and in good faith did believe, and so believing did
rely thereon, that said train, after its movement beyond
her hearing, had continued on its way eastward, and so
believing, and being wholly ignorant that said train

would be backed upon the side track and against said car, thereby endangering her life and limb, she remained, in said car placing and arranging her goods as aforesaid, and was so engaged when said car was struck as aforesaid; that being in said car without any warning of the approach of said train, or of the danger threatening her, she was, by the said movement of the car, caused by the same being violently struck by the train, thrown violently out of and from said car, through said doorway, to and upon the ground or such obstruction as may have been there, and by such fall she sustained the injuries complained of, which are more minutely described in the verdict.

It is further found, that in order to get into the car the appellee had placed a board about ten feet long and eight inches wide, with one end upon the ground and the other in the iron stirrup under the open door of the car, and then placed a chair upon the ground at the side of such board in such position that she could and did climb upon it, thence to the board and into the car; that in taking the train upon the side track, the appellant or its agents and employes in charge of the same gave no warning of the approach of said train, and did not sound the whistle or ring the hell of the locomotive; that they did not place or have a brakeman or other person at the rear end of said backing train or at the said car for the purpose of watching and controlling the approach of the train, and to make the coupling with the car; that at the time the train so struck said car in which appellee was engaged, the board and chair referred to were in the position as above described, and had been in such position for more than fifteen minutes prior thereto, and that a large quantity of appellee's carpets, parcels of her said household goods, was then, and for more than an hour had been, lying on the ground in front of said open door,

and could have been seen by a brakeman or other employe, had he been in the position required; that appellant's station agent knew that the appellee was, on the
evening of the day of the injury, so loading her goods in
said car; that he knew, when said train stopped as aforesaid at said station, that appellee was still loading her
goods in said car, but that he failed and neglected to
make any inquiry or effort to ascertain whether or not
appellee had completed the loading of said car, as did
also the agents and employes in charge of said train, and
said station agent failed and neglected to notify said employes as to the condition of appellee and her said car,
or the completion or otherwise of the loading of the car;
that appellee had no knowledge or notice of the approaching train so backed in upon the said track, and
that no means were afforded her to learn or know of its
approach, and that the injuries she sustained were received without any fault or negligence on her part contributing to the same.

Negligence may be defined to be a violation of some
legal duty which one person owes to another. If the appellant, therefore, owed the appellee such duty, and failed
to perform the same, and by reason of such failure the
appellee received the injury complained of, there is a
legal liability, unless the appellee, by her own negligence, was instrumental in bringing about the result.

A person engaged at some certain place in some particular business, trade, or occupation to which he either
expressly or by implication invites others for the purpose
of transacting the ordinary business there, is in duty
bound to keep such place in a reasonably safe condition
for those so invited, and, failing to do so, any such vis-
itor sustaining an injury solely by reason of such failure
has his right of action against the proprietor for the

damages sustained. *Howe .v. Ohmart,* 7 Ind. App. 32, 33 N. E. Rep. 466.

A railroad company, which is a common carrier of goods, and by its conduct invites or induces the public to use its premises, such as depots and other places set apart for receiving and discharging freight, is under special obligation to keep such premises safe for such use for all persons coming upon the premises to transact business with such company, and among those who are entitled to this protection are such persons as come there for the purpose of delivering or receiving freight. *Shelbyville, etc., R. R. Co.* v. *Lewark,* 4 Ind. 471; *Newson* v. *New York Central R. R. Co.,* 29 N. Y. 383; *Stinson* v. *New York Central R. R. Co.,* 32 N. Y. 333; *Barton* v. *New York Central, etc., R. R. Co.,* 1 Thompson & C. 297; *Chicago, etc., R. W. Co.* v. *Fillmore,* 57 Ill. 265; *Toledo, etc., R. W. Co.* v. *Grush,* 67 Ill. 262; *Illinois Central R. R. Co.* v. *Hoffman,* 67 Ill. 287; *Campbell* v. *Portland Sugar Co.,* 62 Me. 552; *Railroad Co.* v. *Hanning,* 15 Wall. 649; *New Orleans, etc., R. R. Co.* v. *Bailey,* 40 Miss. 395; 1 Thompson Neg., 313.

This duty includes the further one of furnishing to persons lawfully upon the railroad track of such company, engaged in loading or unloading freight, protection from injury by approaching trains or locomotives. In such cases, a person having business with the company of the character indicated, has a right to occupy a position designated by the agent of the company, even if such position be hazardous, and to rely upon the diligence of the company to protect him from danger. *Newson* v. *New York Central R. R. Co., supra;* 3 Lawson's Rights and Rem., section 1193, and authorities cited; *Wabash, etc., R. W. Co.* v. *Locke, Admr.,* 112 Ind. 404.

In the present case, the servants of the company knew, or had good reason to know, that the appellee was in the

box car engaged in storing her goods. She had no information that it was the intention of the appellant to remove the car before she had finished loading it, nor was
she informed by the station agent, who had set apart the
car for her use at the designated point on the side track,
that the freight train in question was to back in on such
track for the purpose of coupling the car on to it. Not
even common diligence was used by the employes in
charge of the train, such as sounding the whistle or ringing the bell of the locomotive, but without any warning
to the appellee, who was excusably ignorant of the approach of the train, the latter was run against the car at
a rate of speed causing it to move at least four feet, and
that, too, without any brakeman or other person being
upon the rear end of the train or in the vicinity of the
car to give the signals or make the coupling.

Had the station agent notified the appellee that the car
was to be taken by the freight train, or had he informed
the trainmen of the presence of the appellee in or about
the box car, as we think he was in duty bound to do, it
is probable that the accident would not have occurred,
and, if it had, there might be some ground for the claim
now made that negligence on the part of the appellant
was not shown, unless, after such notice to them, the
trainmen in charge had persisted in making the coupling
in the manner in which the jury found it was made, notwithstanding the notice given them of the presence of
the appellee at the car.

It is our opinion that the facts found by the jury show
culpable negligence on the part of appellant's servants,
for which it should respond in damages, unless the appellee was herself in some fault.

Nor do we think the finding warrants the conclusion
that there was contributory negligence. Certainly it can
not be maintained that the appellee was in a place where

The Toledo, St. Louis and Kansas City Railroad Company *v.* Hauck.

she had no right to be, or that she was negligent in remaining in ignorance of the movements of the train. She had a right to assume, without notice to the contrary, that she would be permitted to complete the loading of the car without molestation. The car had been placed at her disposal, and she was storing her goods in it at the precise point where she was directed to use it for that purpose by the appellant's agent. There was an implied agreement that the appellant would protect her from all approaching trains, and that she should not be molested or endangered in her person or property by any act of the appellant or its servants. The mere knowledge of the fact that a freight train had arrived and passed the box car on the main track was no notice to her that such train would enter the side track and endanger her safety by being pushed violently against the car in which she was lawfully engaged in her work of putting away the goods. She was not bound, under such circumstances, to leave the car and watch the movements of the freight train.

The rule of looking and listening has no application to a case where the injured person has been lulled into a feeling of safety by the conduct of the company, through the negligence of which the injury was inflicted. The case is somewhat analogous to one in which a person employed to do work on the railroad track is run over or injured while engaged in such work. It is no want of diligence for such person to become so engrossed in his labor as to be oblivious to the approach of a train, relying, as he may, upon the performance of the duty imposed by law upon the railroad company with reference to him. 2 Thomp. Neg., p. 461, and cases cited.

The appellant's counsel, in their supersedeas brief, also make some complaint of a ruling of the trial court in the admission of alleged incompetent testimony. The point is stated thus in the brief referred to:

"The appellee was permitted to introduce testimony, over the objections of the defendant, which we contend was incompetent; and without calling attention to all the testimony of this class, we shall only refer to one or two of the errors of the court:

"Error D.—'Q. What would she say about sleeping when she came down stairs?' 'A. She complained of her arm hurting; she said it pained her so she could not sleep.'"

Counsel then proceed to argue the inadmissibility of the testimany quoted, without designating the witness who gave it or referring in any manner to the place in the record where the same may be found.

We do not think this is a compliance with the well known rules of both this court and the Supreme Court, requiring the counsel to point out in their brief the particular page and line of the transcript where the alleged erroneous ruling was made. The court will not search the record in any case, for the appellant, to find the error which counsel assert has been committed. It is the duty of the appellant to establish error affirmatively, and in connection with such obligation, he must direct the court to the place or places in the record where it is made to appear that the error was committed. Elliott's App. Proced., section 440, and cases cited.

We have considered all the alleged errors discussed by counsel, and found none for which the case should be reversed.

Judgment affirmed.

Filed Nov. 28, 1893.

Louisville, New Albany and Chicago Ry. Co. *v.* State, *ex rel.* Ward.

No. 1,112.

THE LOUISVILLE, NEW ALBANY AND CHICAGO RAILWAY COMPANY *v.* THE STATE, EX REL. WARD, COMMISSIONER.

JUDGMENT.—*Railroad.*— *Drainage Lien.*— *Foreclosure of.*— *When Personal Judgment May be Rendered Against Railroad Company.*—A personal judgment may be rendered against a railroad company, in an action to foreclose a drainage lien against the railroad of the company, a sale of the road under the lien- being forbidden upon the ground of public policy, and the court having the power to furnish a remedy for an existing right.

Dissenting opinion by Ross, J.

From the Lake Circuit Court.

E. C. Field, C. C. Matson and *W. S. Kinnan,* for appellant.

J. W. Youche, for appellee.

GAVIN, J.—The appellee brought suit to foreclose a drainage lien against appellant's railroad, alleging appellant's continued ownership of the road, and refusal to pay the lien. Appellant answered by a general denial. There was a trial and finding in favor of appellee, and judgment for a foreclosure of the lien. There was no order for the sale of appellant's road, but a personal judgment was rendered against the appellant for the amount of the assessment, the attorneys' fees and costs of suit.

Appellant objected and excepted to the personal judgment rendered against it, and its motion to modify the judgment by striking out this portion was overruled. Appeal was taken to the Supreme Court, and the cause transferred by order of that court to this.

It is urged that this action of the court was erroneous, because the court was not authorized to render a personal judgment against it.

It is questionable whether appellant's motion was well taken, even if counsel were correct in their general proposition, for the reason that the motion seeks to strike out the judgment for costs as well as for the amount of the general lien.   If a motion applies to several matters as an entirety, and is not well taken as to all it asks, the court may oftentimes overrule the entire motion without error, not being required to analyze and dissect the motion and sort out the good from the bad.   *Waymire* v. *Lank*, 121 Ind. 1; *Jones* v. *State*, 118 Ind. 39; *Pape* v. *Wright*, 116 Ind. 502; *DeVay* v. *Dunlap*, 7 Ind. App. 690.

We do not, however, stop to determine this question, but pass to the merits of the cause.

Appellant contested the ditch proceedings by appeal, and was defeated.   It then refused and failed to pay its assessments, and resisted in the circuit court the validity of the proceedings and its liability to pay.   It was again defeated, and now comes to this court, not controverting the justness of the assessment, nor the validity of the lien, but still endeavoring to evade its payment.   Its position is not one which entitles it to ask any favor at the hands of the court, yet it is entitled to whatever rights the law gives it.

The ordinary mode of collecting such assessments, and the mode evidently contemplated by the legislature, has been by a sale of the property benefited, when the owner refuses to pay.   The legislature plainly contemplated that railroad companies should pay their assessments. Express provision is made in the statute for giving such companies notice, and for the mode of describing their right of way.   Elliott's Sup., sections 1185–1186.

The law, by reason of considerations of public policy, takes away, in cases of railroad companies, the ordinary process of collection by sale of the property benefited. *Louisville, etc., R. W. Co.* v. *Boney*, 117 Ind. 501; *Louis-*

ville, etc., R. W. Co. v. *State, for Use,* 122 Ind. 443. Unless the law provides some other remedy, the company would be relieved from bearing its proper share of the burden imposed by reason of the benefit received. It is a general rule that where the law gives a right it will also furnish a remedy for its enforcement. *VanSickle* v. *Belknap,* 129 Ind. 558; *Eisenhauer* v. *Dill,* 6 Ind. App. 188, 33 N. E. Rep. 220.

To relieve the railroad company entirely from paying, would be unconscionable and manifestly unjust.

In *Louisville, etc., R. W. Co.* v. *Boney, supra,* it is expressly decided that no such result will follow from the holding that a railroad may not be sold for the enforcement of a mechanic's lien. It is said: "As it appears in the present case that the debt remains unpaid, the lien affords the basis for the exercise by a court of chancery of its flexible jurisdiction to coerce payment of the debt."

This power the trial court seems to have exercised by making an order against the appellant to pay the amount due in the form of a personal judgment. In so doing they followed the course directly approved by the Supreme Court in the case of *Louisville, etc., R. W. Co.* v. *State, for Use, supra,* wherein the railroad company appealed from a judgment to enforce a drainage lien. Judge MITCHELL, speaking for the court, says: "The court rendered judgment against the company for a certain sum, and made a decree of foreclosure and order for the sale of the right of way of the railroad through certain described sections of land in Lake county, for the satisfaction of the judgment. So far as respects the order directing the sale of the railroad, it is enough to say that it is not maintainable. The statute creates a lien upon the road, but does not authorize the body of the railroad to be sold. *Louisville, etc., R. W. Co.* v. *Boney,*

117 Ind. 501. To the extent that the judgment fixes the amount due, and awards the right of process for its collection, it is affirmed."

In this case the court below acted in strict conformity with the course approved by the Supreme Court in the above case, and in so doing committed no error.

Judgment affirmed.

Filed Nov. 28, 1893.

DISSENTING OPINION.

Ross, J.—As stated in the opinion of the majority of the court, this is an action to enforce a drainage lien, and the only question presented on this appeal is whether or not, in such a proceeding, a personal judgment could rightfully be rendered against the appellant instead of a foreclosure of such lien. It seems to be the opinion of the majority that a personal judgment can be rendered for the collection of a ditch assessment. Whether this supposed equitable remedy is to be invoked only as against railroads, or whether it is to apply to individual persons as well, the opinion does not disclose.

The judgment of a court must be responsive to the facts proven or admitted. And it is elementary law that no court can go outside the issues presented, and render a judgment determining other rights and privileges not involved in the controversy before it. In courts of law, judgments are rendered which are enforcible by execution, which may be levied upon any property of the judgment defendant. In courts of equity decrees are rendered which are enforced either by direct order of the court compelling their obedience, or by the sale of specific property decreed to be sold in case the order of the court is not complied with. No court has authority to assume legislative powers and provide a remedy where one exists. And it has been held that if a court, acting

NOVEMBER TERM, 1893.   381

Louisville, New Albany and Chicago Ry. Co. *v.* State, *ex rel.* Ward.

solely under the authority conferred by the law, either common or statutory, and renders a judgment requiring satisfaction to be made in any other way, or by any other means, than those provided by law, the same would be stricken out, on appeal, by the Appellate Court. *Reed* v. *Eldredge*, 27 Cal. 348; *Whetstone* v. *Colley*, 36 Ill. 328; *Burling* v. *Goodman*, 1 Nev. 314; *Buchegger* v. *Shultz*, 13 Mich. 420.

There is a legal maxim which has almost become a rule of law, that for every wrong there is a remedy. But with due deference to the learned courts that have used the maxim, I beg to say that while for most wrongs there is a remedy, there are exceptions to the rule. The majority of the court say that, "Where the law gives a right it will also furnish a remedy for its enforcement." Admitting it to be true, for the purposes of this opinion, that where the law gives a right it will furnish the means by which that right may be enforced, it can hardly be said that when the legislature has created a liability, and has prescribed the means for its enforcement, that courts can furnish another and different remedy.

The appellant, as shown by the record, has enforced upon it a legal liability, not created by its own contracting or with its consent, but by operation of law. The law creating the liability provides that it shall be in the nature of a lien only, and against specific property, and that if it becomes necessary to collect the assessment, it shall be by enforcing the lien upon the tract or tracts of land assessed, and "*such judgment shall not be a lien on any other real estate belonging to the owner of such tract; nor shall any other property than the lands so assessed be sold to satisfy such judgment.*" Elliott's Sup., section 1188.

It is a fundamental rule that taxes imposed upon individuals as the owners of property, either real or personal, for the maintenance of the government—State, county, or municipality, is a personal tax, but when a tax is levied for the purpose of making public improvements in the way of roads, streets, sidewalks, alleys, drains, sewers, etc., contiguous to or of special benefit to particular lands, the tax is not a personal one, but special to the specific property benefited by the improvement.

In the case of *Craw* v. *Village of Tolono*, 96 Ill. 255, the court says: "Taxation for revenue is imposed on the citizens of the State or resident of the municipal corporation, or person doing business within the jurisdiction thereof, to compel him to contribute to the maintenance of the government, State or municipal, by which his life, liberty and property or business are protected, in common with that of all other citizens and residents. This, under our system, is a personal tax, imposed upon the owners of property in proportion to the value of the property of each, and to secure its collection such tax is made a lien upon the property of the person thus taxed. It is entirely competent to declare such a tax a *personal* liability of the person so taxed. To pay it is a duty he owes to the government.

"*Not so with special taxation, for local improvements on property contiguous to the improvement.* The owner of such property is not supposed to derive any special benefit from the improvement, except so far as his contiguous property is to be benefited by the improvement. * * * Special taxation of contiguous property can no more be made a *personal* liability of the owners of the contiguous property so taxed than can a special assessment be made a personal liability of the owners of property against which an assessment is. made on account of supposed benefits."

"If there can be a personal assessment, or the owner

can be made *personally* liable for the tax thus imposed, then we have the remarkable result that for a tax which is imposed on a lot of land, upon the theory that its pe-cuniary value is increased by the improvement, the lot may be sold, and if there is a deficiency, the owner may be required to pay it; or, in other words, for the benefit conferred on the property, the property may be confis-cated, and the owner, for the privilege of having it con-fiscated, may be required to pay a tax into the treasury of the city." Burroughs on Taxation, 475.

And Judge Cooley, in his work on Taxation, p. 675, says: "The levy is made on the supposition that that estate, having received the benefit of a public improve-ment, ought to relieve the public from the expense of making it. In such a case, if the owner can have his land taken from him for a supposed benefit to the land, which, if the land is sold for the tax, it is thus conclus-ively shown he has not received, and he then be held liable for a deficiency in the assessment, the injustice—not to say the tyranny—is manifest." And again, on page 676, he says: "But where and what are the bene-fits to the individual for which he can be called upon to pay any deficiency after a sale of the estate? Unless the whole legal basis of these assessments has been misun-derstood by the courts, it would seem that there are none whatever."

In the case of *Neenan* v. *Smith*, 50 Mo. 525, the court says: "The sole object, then of a local tax being to benefit local property, it should be a charge upon that property only, and not a general one upon the owner. The latter, indeed, is not what is understood by a local or special assessment, but the very term would confine it to the property in the locality; for, if the owner be person-ally liable, it is not only a local assessment, but also a general one as against the owner. The reasonableness of this restriction will appear when we reflect that there is no call for a general execution until the property charged is exhausted. If that is all sold to pay the assessment, leaving a balance to be collected otherwise, we should have the legal anomaly—the monstrous injustice —of not only wholly absorbing the property supposed to be benefited and rendered more valuable by the improvement, but also of entailing upon the owner the loss of his other property.''

The right to assess property for public improvements is statutory, and in making such assessments the statute must be followed. If the statute does not provide the mode for making and collecting an assessment the courts can not. The creation of liens and their incidents is a legislative matter, and courts can not create such liens. The statute creating the lien must determine its character and the extent thereof. *State, ex rel.,* v. *Ætna Life Ins. Co.,* 117 Ind. 251.

And if the statute creating the lien provides an insufficient remedy, or provides no remedy whatever for its enforcement, the courts can not provide a remedy. It must come from the law-making power. The remedy which courts are permitted to provide for the enforcement of a right applies only to common law rights, and not such as are conferred specially by statute.

In *Niklaus* v. *Conkling,* 118 Ind. 289, ELLIOTT, C. J., speaking for the court, says: ''The authority to levy the assessment is purely statutory, and no other assessment than such as the statute prescribes can be made. As it is solely by virtue of the naked statutory power that cities have a right to levy an assessment, they can not levy it upon other property, or upon more property than the statute authorizes.''

The statute here creates a lien and provides that it may be enforced by a sale of the particular property against which it is created, for the payment of the benefits assessed; the courts have held that as to railroads the lien can not be enforced if the property against which the assessment is made is a part of its right of way.

Because such lien can not be enforced by a sale of the property, the majority of this court say: "Where the law gives a right, it will also furnish a remedy for its enforcement," and this, notwithstanding the fact that the statute creating the lien provides that in its enforcement *"the judgment shall not be a lien on any other real estate belonging to the owner of such tract; nor shall any other property than the lands so assessed be sold to satisfy such judgment."*

Under the common law there is no remedy by which to enforce a special assessment for an improvement, and courts can not create a statutory remedy. Courts can only enforce rights where either the statute or the common law afford a remedy. A careful research on the part of the writer of this opinion fails to bring to light a single case decided by *any* court, where it is announced that the court may create the right, and then create and apply a remedy.

"The assessment made for improvements is strictly *in rem*, and gives no right of action against the land owners, assessed as individuals." *Killian* v. *Andrews*, 130 Ind. 579.

It is settled that a judgment *in rem* can not be the basis for a personal judgment. A review of a few of the cases of our own courts on this question is appropriate at this time.

In *Henrie* v. *Sweasey, Admr.*, 5 Blackf. 335, it is said: "When in a suit, the defendant has been served with process, and has appeared, or might have appeared to defend it, the judgment of the court is, in general, con-

clusive between the parties as to the indebtedness of the
defendant to the amount of the judgment.   On such a
judgment an action will lie, and the defendant can not
deny the debt.   This principle is familiar.   But in the
process by attachment, the proceedings are against the
property only of the defendant, and where execution is
awarded, it issues against the property attached, and
nothing else.   If it pays the debt, it is well; if not, the
original debt, so far as it remains unpaid, continues.
Judge STORY, in his Conf. of Laws, page 461, speaking
of the proceedings by attachment against the property of
non-residents, says: 'In such cases, for all the purposes of the suit, the existence of such property, within
the territory, constitutes a just ground of proceeding to
enforce the rights of the plaintiff, to the extent of subject-
ing such property to execution upon the decree or judgment.   But it is to be treated to all intents and purposes, if the defendant has never appeared and contested
the suit, as a mere proceeding *in rem*, and not personally binding upon the party as a decree or judgment *in
personam.*' ''

In *Roose* v. *McDonald*, 23 Ind. 157, the court says:
''A judgment in attachment, when the defendant does not
appear, can not be made the foundation of an action.''
''A mere judgment of foreclosure, without any personal
judgment for the debt or the residue of the debt secured
by the mortgage, after applying the proceeds of the sale,
is exhausted by a sale of the mortgaged premises, and
can not become the foundation of another action, for the
purpose of making the balance of the debt secured by
the mortgage.   It is merely a judgment *in rem*, and
when the property has been sold, the judgment has no
more vitality.''   *Lipperd* v. *Edwards*, 39 Ind. 165.

''And it has been repeatedly decided that a judgment
in rem can not become the foundation of another action.''

Louisville, New Albany and Chicago Ry. Co. *v.* State, *ex rel.* Ward.

says this court in the case of *Moyer, Guard.*, v. *Bucks*, 2 Ind. App. 571. See also *Marshall* v. *Stewart*, 65 Ind. 243.

That a personal judgment can not be rendered against the owner of property, on account of special assessments for benefits or improvements to such property, without a statute authorizing the same, seems to be well settled. Elliott on Roads and Streets, page 399. The drainage act does not create a personal liability against the land owner. *State, ex rel.*, v. *Ætna Life Ins. Co.*, *supra*. It has also been held that a statute authorizing such judgments is unconstitutional. *City of St. Louis* v. *Allen*, 53 Mo. 44; *City of St. Louis* v. *Bressler*, 56 Mo. 350; *Higgins* v. *Ausmuss*, 77 Mo. 351; *Town of Macon* v. *Patty*, 57 Miss. 378; *Taylor* v. *Palmer*, 31 Cal. 240; *City of Virginia* v. *Hall*, 96 Ill. 278; *Wolf* v. *City of Philadelphia*, 105 Pa. St. 25.

If, then, an "Assessment made for improvements is strictly *in rem*, and gives no right of action against the land owners assessed as individuals," and "a judgment *in rem* can not become the foundation of another action," the judgment of the court below is without a foundation, and can not be upheld.

The case of *Louisville, etc., R. W. Co.* v. *State, for Use*, 122 Ind. 443, cited as authority in the opinion of the majority, is not decisive of this case, for the reason that no question was presented by the record in that case, or decided by the court, relative to the right of a court to render a personal judgment against a railroad company for the collection of a ditch assessment.

Not a single authority has been cited in support of such a proposition, and I think none can be cited.

I think the judgment should be reversed.

Filed Nov. 28, 1893.

No. 1,057.

THE TOLEDO, ST. LOUIS AND KANSAS CITY RAILROAD COMPANY *v.* CUPP.

RECORD.—*Plat, When May be Inserted After Bill is Signed by Judge.— Certiorari.—Presumption.—Appellate Court Practice.*—It is not necessary to incorporate a plat into a bill of exceptions before the judge has signed the same, but it is sufficient to refer to such evidence (the plat) by the words "here insert," and afterwards insert the plat in its proper place in the record, and such action will not be ground for *certiorari*. In the absence of any showing or statement to the contrary, the court will presume that the transcript of the record, on appeal, duly authenticated by the certificate of the clerk, is correct.

From the Adams Circuit Court.

S. O. Bayless and *C. G. Guenther*, for appellant.
E. R. Wilson and *J. J. Todd*, for appellee.

DAVIS, C. J.—The appellee has filed a petition and motion herein, asking for a writ of certiorari for the correction of the transcript of the record, in this, that the bill of exceptions contains what purports to be a plat of Barwell and Hall's addition to the city of Bluffton, when, in truth and in fact, it is alleged that "said plat never was incorporated in said bill of exceptions signed by Judge Heller."

The plat, as shown by the record, was introduced in evidence by agreement, and was marked exhibit A. The bill of exceptions recites that "thereupon said map was introduced in evidence, and is as follows," and then follows the plat.

It is not contended that the plat set out in the bill of exceptions was not in fact introduced in evidence. Neither is it claimed that the plat has been inserted in the bill of exceptions since the record was made by the

The Toledo, St. Louis and Kansas City Railroad Company *v.* Cupp.

clerk. The sole and only contention in behalf of appellee is that the plat was not incorporated in the bill of exceptions when signed by the judge. The definition of the word incorporated is, "united in one body." It was not necessary to incorporate—bodily insert—the plat into the original bill of exceptions, prior to the signing thereof by the judge. Section 626, R. S. 1881.

It was sufficient to refer to such plat, where the appropriate place therefor was designated by the words "here insert."

For aught that appears in the showing made in this case, the plat was, when the bill was signed, referred to at the appropriate place by such words, and when the same was copied by the clerk the plat so introduced in evidence was inserted by him at the appropriate place in the record. If there was any claim that such was not the fact, a different question might be presented, but the mere fact that the plat was not bodily incorporated into the bill of exceptions when it was signed by the judge, is not sufficient, for the reasons stated, to authorize the court to grant the writ directing the clerk to place "nothing therein that was not contained in the bill of exceptions as signed by the judge."

All we now decide is that it was not necessary to incorporate said plat into the bill of exceptions before the judge signed the same, but it was sufficient to refer to such evidence if its appropriate place was designated by the words "here insert," and, in the absence of any showing or statement to the contrary, we will presume that the transcript of the record on this appeal, duly authenticated by the certificate of the clerk, is correct.

The motion is therefore overruled.

Filed Dec. 15, 1893.

No. 864.

JUDSON v. ROMAINE ET AL.

CONTRACT.—*Made for Benefit of Third Person.*—*May Accept and Enforce, or Rescind.*—A person in whose favor a contract has been made, may accept the same and enforce it; as, where A. assumes the payment of a debt owing by B. to C., C. may accept and enforce the contract against A., or C. may rescind it before it is accepted.

ATTORNEY'S FEES.—*When Recoverable.—Contract.—Attorney and Client.*—A contract to pay attorney's fees is a contract of indemnity to secure the holder of the note against any liability which he may incur in the event he should be compelled to employ an attorney to enforce the collection of the debt, and the plaintiff is not entitled to judgment for attorney's fees, unless an attorney, of necessity, was employed to collect the debt.

PRACTICE.—*Question, How Saved for Appellate Court.—Appeal.—Appellate Court Practice.*—In order to present a question for decision to the Appellate Court, as to irregularities or abuse of discretion in the proceedings of the trial court, the foundation must be laid in an exception to the ruling of the trial court.

From the Elkhart Circuit Court.

F. E. Baker and *C. W. Miller*, for appellant.

H. C. Dodge, for appellees.

LOTZ, J.—On the 14th day of October, 1884, the appellee Levi W. Deitch was the owner of a stock of goods and merchandise of the value of $2,000. He was indebted to divers creditors in the sum of $2,468, for which he had given his several promissory notes, on some of which, aggregating $1,423, one Henry Deitch had become the surety of said Levi, and on the others, aggregating the sum of $775, the appellant had become surety of said Levi. At that time the said Levi Deitch proposed to said Henry Deitch and the appellant, Judson, that he would transfer and turn over to them the whole of said stock of goods if they would pay the debts on which they were severally liable, and save him, the said

Levi, entirely harmless and free from said debts. This proposition was accepted, reduced to writing, and signed by the parties, and the stock of goods was turned over and placed in the possession of said Henry Deitch and John L. Judson. The notes on which the said Henry Deitch and said Judson had become surety were described in the written agreement. Thereafter, on November 20th, 1884, the creditors of Levi Deitch having reduced some of the notes on which Henry Deitch was surety to judgment, the said Henry Deitch and John L. Judson thereupon entered into a new agreement, whereby the said Judson became replevin bail for stay of execution on the judgments rendered against said Levi and Henry Deitch, and the said Henry Deitch transferred his interest in said goods to said Judson. Levi W. Deitch was not a party to this contract. At the time said Judson became replevin bail, he did not understand that, by the terms of the original agreement, he was liable for, or had agreed to pay, all the notes described therein, but believed that he was liable only for the notes which he had signed as surety. Thereafter, on November 25th, 1884, the said Henry Deitch and the said Judson made another agreement with each other, whereby the said Henry Deitch became the purchaser of all of said goods, and in consideration thereof executed his notes payable to said Judson for the sum of $800, and secured the same by mortgage on real estate. The purpose of the mortgage was to indemnify the said Judson from the liability he had incurred as replevin bail for Henry Deitch, as aforesaid. Said notes and mortgage having been duly executed, the goods were accordingly delivered to said Henry Deitch, and said Henry Deitch placed the said Levi Deitch in possession, to make sale of the same for him, the said Henry Deitch. All of the notes described in the original agreement were not paid. Several of the notes were made payable to Edward R. Kerstetter, who was then the guardian of the appellee, Romaine. One of such notes was reduced to judgment by said Kerstetter, but said judgment has never been paid. Romaine having attained his majority, the notes and judgment were transferred to him. This action was brought on the agreement for the payment of the notes. The notes which it was sought to make the appellant liable for were three, one of $250 and one of $500, and the one reduced to judgment. Issue was joined, and certain questions of fact were submitted to the jury. The court, at the request of the parties, made a special finding of the facts, and stated the conclusions of law. The special findings show that one note for $250 was included in the agreement by the mutual mistake of the parties, and as to this note there was a finding in favor of the appellant on his counterclaim. The court found for the appellee on the $500 note, and on the note which had been reduced to judgment. It also found that $200 was a reasonable attorney's fee, and rendered judgment in favor of Romaine in the sum of $1,400.50. Appellant excepted to the conclusions of law, and this is one of the errors assigned. He then moved to modify the judgment, and made a motion for a new trial. These motions were overruled, and each of these rulings is assigned as error. It is well settled by the decisions in this State that a contract made for the benefit of a third person may be accepted and enforced by him. *Carnahan* v. *Tousey*, 93 Ind. 561. It is equally well settled that such contract may be rescinded before it is accepted. *Berkshire Life Ins. Co.* v. *Hutchings*, 100 Ind. 496.

Appellant's contention is that the facts show that the contract for the payment of the notes was rescinded before acceptance. In this we can not agree. Levi W. Deitch parted with the title to the stock of goods in consideration that the notes described in the agreement should be paid. He never received the title back, nor do the findings show that he ever received anything in lieu thereof, except the promise to pay the notes described in the agreement. He has never been placed *in statu quo.*

The motion to modify the judgment was based upon the amount of attorney's fees allowed by the court. A contract to pay attorney's fees is a contract of indemnity. Its purpose is to make the holder of the note secure against any liability which he may incur in the event he should be compelled to employ an attorney to enforce collection of his debt. The $500 note is not the basis of this action, nor is there any finding that the note was ever placed in the hands of an attorney for collection, or that any liability was incurred for that purpose. We think the appellee was not entitled to recover attorney's fees, and that the motion to modify should have been sustained.

Appellant has discussed several questions arising under the last assignment of error, the overruling of the motion for a new trial. It is first insisted that the findings are not sustained by the evidence. We find the evidence conflicting, and must decline to weigh it.

The next causes discussed are the alleged irregularities in the proceedings of the trial court and the abuse of discretion by the court in having required the jury to try certain questions of fact, and then without intimating that it was not satisfied with the jury's answer, setting them aside and making a finding of its own contrary thereto.

It is not necessary for us to determine the merits of this contention, for the record shows that at the time such action was taken by the court, the appellant made no objection thereto and took no exception to such proceedings. The general rule is that in order to present a question for decision to an appellate court, the foundation must be laid in an exception to the ruling of the trial court. *Taylor* v. *Trustees, etc.*, 7 Ind. App. 388, 34 N. E. Rep. 655.

We have carefully examined the other causes discussed by counsel, and find no error authorizing the granting of a new trial. Appellee's counsel has expressed his willingness to enter a remittitur of the attorney's fees if this court should hold the amount assessed improper. The cause is therefore affirmed on condition that the appellee enter a remittitur of $200 of the principal of the judgment, as of the day of rendition, within thirty days, in the court below, otherwise the cause will be reversed. Appellee to pay costs of this appeal.

REINHARD, J., absent.

Filed Dec. 12' 1893.

No. 1,009.

O'HALLORAN v. MARSHALL.

PRACTICE.—*Pleading, Sustaining Demurrer to.—Exception.—Leave to Amend.*—Where a demurrer is sustained to a pleading, and exception is taken to such ruling, and leave is granted to amend, the excepting party may stand on his pleading and exception, or he may abandon his exception, and amend his pleading.

PLEADING.—*Counterclaim, Sufficiency of.—Action for Attorney's Fees.—Misconduct of Attorney.—Damages.*—In an action for attorney's fees, a counterclaim is sufficient, on demurrer, which alleged, in substance, that the plaintiff, as defendant's attorney in cases forming the basis of the fees, acted in disregard and contrary to defendant's instructions, in continuing the cases until the next term of court, thereby causing defendant, by such wrongful conduct, to pay —— dollars additional costs, to his damage.

From the Jasper Circuit Court.

F. Foltz, for appellant.

J. T. Brown, E. G. Hall and *R. W. Marshall,* for appellee.

GAVIN, J.—The appellee filed his complaint against appellant for services rendered him as his attorney in various cases. Appellant filed a counterclaim, to which a demurrer was sustained. This ruling is assigned for error.

The counterclaim alleges, that appellee was employed by appellant as his attorney in two cases pending in the circuit court, and that he, as such attorney, for a valuable consideration, undertook the management of them; that they were set down for trial upon a certain day; that appellant was present with his witnesses ready and anxious for trial, as appellee well knew; that appellant instructed appellee to use all proper means to bring said causes to trial on the day set for their hearing, but appellee, in disregard of such instructions, and of his duty to appellant, secretly, and without the knowledge of this appellant, agreed and consented to a continuance of said causes, whereby they were continued until another term; that without such agreement the trials of said causes would not have been postponed; that by reason of such consent and agreement, and the appellee's said wrongful conduct, appellant was compelled to pay the sum of two hundred dollars additional costs occasioned by such continuance. Whereby he was damaged in such sum; that the cases thus referred to are two of the cases for which appellee seeks to recover fees in his complaint.

No argument is offered by appellee to sustain this ruling of the court, but it is insisted, with apparent confidence, that because, after appellant properly saved his exception to the ruling, leave to amend was given, and the error, if any, thereby waived.

The record is: "Defendant excepts, and has leave to file amended counterclaim on tomorrow morning."

Whether this leave was granted by the court of its own motion or at the request of appellant, does not appear.

Upon the following morning, the record shows the rule closed against appellant by reason of his having failed to file his amended pleading.

Appellee's proposition is supported by counsel by reference to *Patrick* v. *Jones,* 21 Ind. 249, and *De Armond* v. *Stoneman,* 63 Ind. 386, which hold, as do many other cases, that where a party files an amended pleading, he thereby waives the sustaining of a demurrer to the original pleading. This result, however, follows the filing of the amended pleading, and not the granting of leave to so do.

The rule is thus stated by CRUMPACKER, Judge, in *Evans* v. *Queen Ins. Co.,* 5 Ind. App. 198: "A party can not have the benefit of exceptions to an adverse ruling upon a demurrer to a plea, and exercise the privilege of amending the plea at the same time. He is compelled to abide by his exceptions or waive them by amendment."

The language of numerous cases is that the amended pleading supersedes the old one.

Here the exception was regularly saved. The appellant did no act inconsistent with this exception. We find no case sustaining counsel's contention, nor are we able to see any good reason why it should be the law. On the contrary, the rule adopted by us is sustained by the holdings of our Supreme Court.

In *Washburn* v. *Roberts,* 72 Ind. 213, a demurrer was sustained to several paragraphs of answer, with exceptions and leave taken to amend. One paragraph was amended, but not the other. The court held that the exception to the ruling on the paragraph not amended was not lost. It says: "Court and counsel were advised by the exception to the ruling and the failure to amend the third paragraph, that appellant elected to let that paragraph stand upon the exception entered."

This ruling is followed in *Daggett* v. *Flanagan,* 78 Ind. 253. The language there used is applicable here. "The exception was not withdrawn. No amendment was made, and the exception previously entered remained in full force. Nothing was done to impair its efficacy. No act was done by appellant which can be construed into an abandonment of his exception."

Until the amended pleading has been filed, there is clearly no waiver.

We are unable to discover any serious defect in the counterclaim. It seems to show plainly a disregard of appellee's duty to appellant with reference to the cases, and damage resultant therefrom.

If this be true, and the demurrer so admits, then appellee should respond. *Nave* v. *Baird,* 12 Ind. 318; *Reilly* v. *Cavanaugh,* 29 Ind. 435.

The judgment is reversed, with instructions to overrule the demurrer to the counterclaim.

Filed Dec. 15, 1893.

No. 997.

THE AMERICAN WIRE NAIL COMPANY *v.* CONNELLY.

DEMURRER.—*Uncertainty as a Ground.*—Uncertainty is not ground for
demurrer, unless the pleading is so vague as not to state a cause of
action or a defense.

PLEADING.—*Complaint.*—*Sufficiency of, How Determined.*—*Theory of.*—
The theory and sufficiency of a complaint must be determined from
the facts alleged, and not simply from the statements or admissions
of the parties.

JUDGMENT.—*On Answers to Interrogatories.*—*Employer and Employe.*—
Co-Employe.—*Personal Injury.*—In an action for personal injuries
received by the negligence of a co-employe, the defendant was entitled to judgment on answers to interrogatories, which established
the fact that such co-employe was competent to do the work in
which he was engaged at the time of the injuries.

From the Madison Circuit Court.

W. A. Kittinger and *L. M. Schwinn*, for appellant.

E. D. Reardon, E. B. Goodykoontz and *G. M. Ballard*,
for appellee.

Ross, J.—The appellee sued the appellant to recover
damages for personal injuries received while in its employ, the same alleged to have been caused by appellant's negligence.

The appellant assigns three errors in this court for a
reversal of the judgment rendered by the court below.
The first and second errors call in question the ruling of
the court in overruling appellant's demurrers to the first
and second paragraphs of the complaint.

The material allegations of the first paragraph of the
complaint are admitted to be as follows:

"That on the —— day of January, 1890, the appellant
employed appellee to work for her in her nail mills in
the city of Anderson, at an employment known as
"scrapping," which consists of taking the refuse wire

away from the rolls and out of the mill; that on the 31st
day of January, 1890, while appellee was engaged in said
work of scrapping, the appellant's foreman, one Richard
Harris, who had full charge of the workmen in that department of appellant's business, and authorized to employ and discharge the workmen in said department,
ordered appellee to leave his occupation of scrapping and
go to work at a much more dangerous occupation in said
mill, known as "sticking in on the reels;" that appellee
at first refused to accept said new occupation, for the
reason that he was entirely inexperienced in said occupation and considered the same dangerous; that he had no
means of knowing the danger, and that the actual danger
was not apparent to him; that said foreman assured
him that said occupation was not dangerous, and would
not harm him, and that he, in reliance upon the statement of said foreman, left his former occupation of
scrapping and went to work at sticking in on the reels;
that a part of his duty in said occupation of sticking in
on the reels was to remove the kinks in the wire rods
which lay upon the floor after passing through the rolls
and before being wound upon the reel; that said rods were
heated to a great heat, and were very difficult and dangerous to handle; that it was necessary and customary
to stop the reels while appellee should remove the kinks
in the wire, and after he had removed the kinks in the
wire and returned to a place of safety the reels were
again started by the man whose duty it was to start them;
that on the 31st day of January, 1890, the reeler, who
was operating the reel on which the appellee was working, was one Walter Ramsey, an employe of said appellant; that it was part of the duties of said reeler to stop
said reel while appellee was taking out and removing the
kinks from said wire rods aforesaid, and to start the reels
when appellee had retired to a place of safety; that, on

said day, one of the rods which was being run on the
reel became kinked, and the reeler stopped the reel for
the appellee to go and remove the kink; that he started
to do so, and was just in the act of removing the kink
when the said Ramsey negligently and carelessly started
the reel again, well knowing the danger in which the
appellee was placed, and without giving him any opportunity to retire to a place of safety, by reason of which
negligent and careless starting of the reel by said Walter
Ramsey, appellee was greatly injured, by having his
foot and leg caught by the heated rod, which circled.
around appellee's foot and leg, burning the flesh and
bone of appellee's foot and leg, and dragging him by
said heated iron rod into said reel; that the reeler, Ramsey, who was operating the reel for the appellant at the
time, was incompetent and wholly unfit for the position
that he occupied, and for which appellant had employed
him, all of which was known to the appellant and unknown to the appellee, and that the appellant retained
said Walter Ramsey as her servant and employe after
having knowlege of his incompetency and unskillfulness
a sufficient length of time to have discharged him; that
by reason of said negligence and carelessness the appellee was injured as aforesaid, and without any fault on his
part.''

This paragraph is assailed upon the ground that its
averments are ''too vague and uncertain,'' and because
''the act complained of, being a simple act of carelessness,'' does not necessarily show the servant complained
of to be incompetent.

That the allegations of a complaint are vague, indefinite,
and uncertain, is not cause for demurrer. If the appellant desired a more definite and explicit statement of the
facts alleged to constitute the negligent acts complained
of, the remedy was by a motion to make the complaint

more specific. *Sluyter* v. *Union Cent. Life Ins. Co.*, 3 Ind. App. 312; *Cleveland, etc., R. W. Co.* v. *Wynant*, 100 Ind. 160; *Cincinnati, etc., R. W. Co.* v. *Gaines*, 104 Ind. 526; *Town of Rushville* v. *Adams*, 107 Ind. 475; *Louisville, etc., R. W. Co.* v. *Jones*, 108 Ind. 551; *Pittsburgh, etc., R. W. Co.* v. *Hixon*, 110 Ind. 225; *Mississinewa Mining Co.* v. *Patton*, 129 Ind. 472; *Sheeks* v. *Erwin*, 130 Ind. 31; *Garard* v. *Garard*, 135 Ind. 15, 34 N. E. Rep. 442; *Evansville, etc., R. R. Co.* v. *Maddux, by Next Friend*, 134 Ind. 571, 34 N. E. Rep. 511.

In *Adamson* v. *Shaner*, 3 Ind. App. 448, this court says: "Uncertainty is not generally a cause for demurrer, unless the pleading is so vague as not to state a cause of action or ground of defense, in which case only a demurrer will lie."

The second paragraph of the complaint, in addition to the facts alleged in the first paragraph, contains the following additional allegations, viz: That the appellee was injured by reason of the appellant's failing to inform and notify the appellee of the dangerous character of the work, and the means to avoid said danger.

It is urged, against both paragraphs of the complaint, that notwithstanding the allegations that appellee had no "knowledge of the actual danger of said occupation," and that such dangers were not apparent to appellee, and that the facts specially pleaded which are alleged to constitute the dangers to which he would be exposed, show that the danger was apparent to any person who would exercise the sense of sight; that the appellee was conversant with the dangers incident to the work, from the allegation "that when first ordered by the said foreman to go to work at said occupation of sticking in on the reels, plaintiff refused to do so, for the reason that he was entirely inexperienced in the duties of said occupation, and considered the said occupation as dangerous.''

It is also alleged, in the complaint, that the appellee was induced to undertake the performance of the new duties upon the representation made by appellant that the work was not dangerous.

When a servant undertakes to engage in a master's service, and to perform certain duties, the master has a right to assume that he is qualified to perform the duties of the position he seeks to occupy, and competent to apprehend and avoid all the apparent and obvious hazards of such service. *Louisville, etc., R. W. Co.* v. *Frawley,* 110 Ind. 18.

But if an experienced servant, such want of knowledge being known to the master, is induced to engage in the performance of certain duties, the dangers of which are not apparent, upon the assurance that no danger attends the performance of such duties, and the servant is injured without fault on his part, the master must answer in damages therefor.

It is averred, in both paragraphs of the complaint, that a part of his duties in ''sticking in on the reels'' ''was to remove the kinks from the wire rods which came from the rolls and lay upon the floor preparatory to being wound upon the reels.'' ''That said wire rods were heated to a great heat and very difficult and dangerous to handle.''

So far as we are able to determine from the allegations of the complaint, the appellee was a person of mature years and possessed of the faculties and understanding of ordinary persons; hence, was able to see apparent dangers and to anticipate and realize the results liable to flow therefrom.

The jury rested their verdict upon the first paragraph of the complaint, hence it is necessary only to consider the sufficiency of that paragraph. While counsel for appellee insists that the complaint is drafted upon the theory that the appellant removed the appellee from the work he was engaged to perform, and set him to work at a more dangerous and hazardous occupation, we can not accept that as its theory. This court can not determine the theory and sufficiency of a complaint simply from the statements or admissions of the parties, but from the facts alleged. The theory of the first paragraph of the complaint is that the appellee was injured by reason of the careless and negligent acts of his fellow-servant, Walter Ramsey, in starting the reel, causing the heated rod to encircle appellee's foot and leg, burning the flesh and bone thereof, and dragging him into the reel, it being alleged that said Ramsey was incompetent and wholly unfit for the position he occupied, which fact was known to the appellant and unknown to the appellee. Upon this theory the complaint is sufficient, so far as any defects therein have been pointed out.

The jury, at the request of the appellant, answered and returned with their general verdict numerous interrogatories, among which were the following:

"4th. Was not Walter Ramsey, the reeler testified about, a fellow-employe with the plaintiff at the time the plaintiff was injured? Ans. Yes.

"5th. Was the injuries to the plaintiff caused by the negligence or carelessness of Walter Ramsey, the reeler? Ans. Yes.

"6th. If you answer the last preceding question in the affirmative, then state whether the said Walter Ramsey was competent to do the work in the position in which he was working at the time of the injuries. Ans. He was competent."

These interrogatories and answers show that the ap-

The Louisville, New Albany and Chicago Railway Co. *v.* Renicker.

pellant was not entitled to recover on the theory of this paragraph of the complaint.

The court erred in overruling appellant's motion for judgment on the answers to the interrogatories.

Judgment reversed, with instructions to render judgment in favor of appellant on the answers to the interrogatories, notwithstanding the general verdict.

REINHARD, J., absent.

Filed Dec. 15, 1893.

───────────◆───────────

No. 1,002.

THE LOUISVILLE, NEW ALBANY AND CHICAGO RAILWAY COMPANY *v.* RENICKER.

ASSIGNMENT OF ERRORS.—*Questioning Admissibility of Evidence.—Errors Jointly Assigned.—When Unavailable.*—When an assignment of error is that the court erred in the admission of certain testimony given by several witnesses upon divers subjects, the assignment is unavailable if any part of such evidence was properly admitted.

RECOVERY.—*When Contrary to Law.—Theory.*—A party must recover *secundum allegata et probata*, or not at all. If the evidence fails to establish the material allegations of the complaint, a recovery by the plaintiff would be contrary to law. The plaintiff must recover, if at all, upon the theory of the complaint.

From the Jasper Circuit Court.

G. W. Kretzinger, E. C. Field, W. B. Austin and *W. S. Kinnan,* for appellant.

S. P. Thompson, for appellee.

Ross, J.—The appellee filed her complaint in one paragraph against the appellant, as follows:

"The plaintiff, Anna Renicker, complains of the defendant, The Louisville, New Albany and Chicago Railway Co., and says that the defendant is a corporation

duly organized under the laws of the State of Indiana,
and, on the 26th day of June, 1891, owned and operated
a certain railroad, known as the Louisville, New Albany
and Chicago Railway Co., with the track, cars, locomotives and other appurtenances thereto belonging, and
was a common carrier of passengers for hire between
Delphi, in Carroll county, Indiana, and the towns of
Rensselaer and Fair Oaks, in Jasper county, Indiana,
from which and to which the said railroad was built, operated and run for a long time before, at, and since said
date; that on the said 26th day of June, 1891, the plaintiff, who was then aged nineteen years, purchased of
the defendant a first-class ticket from the city of Delphi
to the town of Rensselaer, aforesaid, and took passage on
defendant's regular passenger train; that defendant, by
its agents, to wit, its engineer, conductor, and brakeman,
so negligently ran and operated said train of cars that
the same did not stop at the platform and depot of the
defendant at Rensselaer, Indiana, but ran by said platform a distance of six hundred feet before stopping. The
plaintiff proposed to the defendant's servants, who were
then and there acting in the line of their duty, to try to
get off such train, but was assured that the train would
back down to the platform, and plaintiff was, by said
servants, while in the line of their duty, ordered and
commanded to keep her seat until the train backed down
to the platform, and, in obedience to said directions, the
plaintiff made no effort to then get off the train. The
defendant's servants, however, unlawfully neglected and
refused to back said train to the depot at said station, and
started towards Chicago, and, after going some distance,
informed plaintiff that the train would stop at Surrey, a
distance of five miles from Rensselaer, and the plaintiff
consented thereto; whereupon said conductor, brakeman
and engineer of the defendant, while acting in the line

of their duty, unlawfully and negligently stopped the train on a grade one mile from Surrey, and with great force and violence commanded and compelled the plaintiff to alight from the said train some six miles from the town of Rensselaer, and one mile from Surrey, and not at any platform or station, and in attempting to alight the plaintiff, by the negligence of defendant, was cast suddenly to the ground on an incline, and by reason thereof she sprained, bruised, and injured her ankle, knee, leg, and back to such an extent that she has been helpless and unable to perform labor, and has suffered, and still suffers, bodily pain, to her damage ten thousand dollars, and is also, by reason thereof, crippled and maimed and prevented from actively pursuing business for life, and without any fault or negligence of the plaintiff; and that her said injuries were all caused by the negligence, carelessness, willfulness, and improper acts of the defendant and its servants. Wherefore, the plaintiff says she ought to recover ten thousand dollars.

"The plaintiff alleges that although she is under the age of twenty-one years, yet her father, being a poor man, had, before the time of this accident, allowed and permitted the plaintiff to work for herself, and now consents that plaintiff prosecute this action in her own name, and plaintiff files herewith her father's relinquishment of his right of action, and his consent to act as her next friend, marked exhibit A, and made a part of this complaint. Wherefore plaintiff demands judgment for ten thousand dollars, and for all other relief."

To the complaint, appellant filed a demurrer for want of facts, which was overruled by the court and exception saved. There was a trial before a jury and a verdict for the appellee, assessing her damages at $700.

The appellant moved for a new trial. The motion was

overruled and judgment rendered on the verdict in favor of the appellee.

The appellant assigns, in this court, three errors, but inasmuch as counsel have not argued the first and second errors assigned, they are waived.

The third error assigned is "The court erred in overruling appellant's motion for a new trial."

The motion embraces the following reasons for which a new trial was asked, viz:

"First. That the evidence wholly fails to prove or establish the averments as alleged in the complaint as amended.

"Second. That the evidence further changes the theory of the complainant's case as made and laid in the complaint as amended, and then, even though the evidence gives a right of action, it proceeds upon a different theory than that stated in the complaint.

"Third. That the plaintiff is not permitted, by evidence, to change the theory of the case as made in the complaint.

"Fourth. That the plaintiff having stated specific. acts of negligence, she is required to rely thereon, and, failing thereon, leaves the case, as alleged and made in the complaint, without sufficient proof to entitle the complainant to a verdict or judgment, motion overruled, defendant excepts, and thereupon the court overruled said motion, which was error.

"Fifth. The court erred in refusing instructions requested to be given the jury by the defendant.

"Sixth. The court erred in giving instructions asked by the plaintiff.

"Seventh. The verdict of the jury is contrary to the evidence.

"Eighth. The verdict of the jury is contrary to the law.

"Ninth. The verdict of the jury is contrary to, and in disregard of, the instructions given by the court.

"Tenth. The damages awarded by the jury are excessive."

To all and each of which matters and things and rulings of the court above stated, the defendant then and now objects, and takes exceptions thereto, and to each of them severally.

"Eleventh. During the course of said trial, the following questions were propounded plaintiff, to which questions the defendant, by its attorneys, then and there objected and moved to strike out the answers thereto, which questions, objections, and reasons therefor, exceptions and answers to such questions and motions to strike the same and exceptions, thereto, were in the words following, to wit:

"Dr. M. B. Alter.

"Doctor, you may state if you know what the usual results are in restoring the system, after it is wounded or sprained, to a perfect condition, under the ordinary practice among the physicians?

"The defendant objects to this question upon the ground that a perfect state of restoration is not necessary; that it is immaterial; that a proper foundation has not been laid, for the plaintiff has not shown that this witness knows the difference between the highest state of restoration possible within his knowledge, and to prove the prior condition of the individual upon which he based his judgment. And the facts upon which opinion is to proceed are not stated, and question does not limit witness to facts proved or stated to jury, and under both of these conditions, his evidence is not admissible.

"Objection overruled.

'A. In a country practice, as the physicians are in this town, there are but few cases of fractures or bad dislocations, and, under those existing, there are but very small per cent. of them become perfect.

"Mrs. Eliza Renicker.

"Q. State what has been her condition as to being able to do work, say, since the 26th day of June, 1891.

"The defendant, objects on the ground it calls for a conclusion.

"Objection overruled. Defendant excepts.

"A. She complained of her knee and her back.

"Answer stricken out.

"Q. What I want to know is, how much work she could do.

"A. She could not do much work; she would complain it would hurt her back if she stood much on her feet.

"Defendant moves to strike out the part of the answer 'she would complain,' also the part of the answer 'that it would hurt her back,' because conclusions.

"Motion overruled. Defendant excepts.

"John Renicker.

"Q. I will ask you to state to this jury whether or not you visited the place on the railroad where your sister claims that she got off the train.

"A. Yes, sir.

"Q. Now, where was that place?

"Defendant objects. Objection overruled. Defendant excepts.

"Samuel B. Thornton.

"Q. Now, how was the railroad track at this time?

"Defendant objects to the question because it relates to track and its condition at a time after alleged accident, and, therefore, not admissible or relevant.

"Objection overruled. Defendant excepts.

"Edgar Thornton.

"Q. Now, were you informed where she alighted from the cars?

"Defendant objects.   Objection overruled.   Defendant excepts.

"A. On the grade.

"Q. How far was that from the station?

"A. In my judgment, between 95 and 100 rods.

"Grant Renicker.

"Q. Where did you see her?

"A. At my brother John's home.

"Q. Now, you may state whether your brother John was married at that time.

"A. Yes, sir.

"Q. You may state if it was the only place she had relatives near Surrey.

"Defendant objects.   Objection overruled.   Defendant excepts.

"A. Yes, sir.

"Q. Now, Mr. Renicker, you may state to the jury what your sister has been able to do in the way of work since that time, so far as you have observed.

"Defendant objects to the word 'able'.

"Q. What has she been doing about the house?

"A. She has not done so very much.

"Q. State just what you know.

"A. She was not able to wash, or to walk around hurt her.

Q. (By the court) Are you testifying now from what she told you?

"A. Yes, sir.

"Annie Renicker.

"Q. What is the fact, Annie, about how many times you have traveled on the cars?

"Defendant objects to the question upon the ground that

it is wholly immaterial whether she was ever on the cars previous to this day, alone or with anybody.

"Objection overruled.   Defendant excepts.

"Dr. Longhridge.

"Q. You have not had a pass on their road lately?

"A. Not for a year or so.   I always charged the company for whatever I did for them.

"The defendant moves to strike out the question and answer of witness touching the evidence as to a pass or free transportation over company's road, upon the ground that the evidence does not tend to show witness in employ of defendant, does not tend to prove issues, and upon these two grounds, and upon general rules, it is certainly inadmissible, irrelevant, and immaterial.

"Motion overruled.

"By the court: The jury are not to consider the question as to whether the doctor had a pass over the road, only so far as his credibility is concerned, as it was last year he had a pass.   The jury are only to consider it for the purpose of credibility, and for no other purpose.

"Q. Suppose, doctor, a young person is excited and scared, and jumped from a train and injured her leg, and tried to walk some distance on the railroad ties, walking eighty rods, and then walked upon smooth ground, and stopping, left her satchel and rested, it is not impossible for her to walk that distance; there is nothing unusual in that?

"Defendant objects. Objection overruled.   Defendant excepts.

"A. No.

"Q. Now, suppose a person should receive a sprain in the leg and should go lame and would apply liniments, such as arnica and other medicines of that kind, and rub the parts that were injured, and take what rest they could, would that be proper treatment, so far as it went?

"A. Yes, sir.

"Q. Suppose they continued that treatment for a short time and then consulted a physician, and then, substantially following the physician's directions, what would you say to that?

"Defendant objects to the question upon the ground that the plaintiff failed to follow the directions of the physician.

"Objection overruled. Defendant excepts.

"A. I think they should have been followed directly.

"Annie Renicker.

"Q. Where was Mr. Kenton when you went to the house that morning?

"A. When I first came to the house I did not see him. When I came in Mrs. Kenton had the breakfast just nearly ready, when he came in, and we were talking about what times we had, and we went back into the room, and I told them how it came I did not get off at Rensselaer.

"Defendant objects. Objection overruled. Defendant excepts. And, for reasons appearing upon the face of said record, defendant prays for a new trial."

The first, second, third and fourth reasons are not well assigned.

The fifth, sixth, ninth and tenth reasons are waived because not argued.

The eleventh cause assigns as error the admission of the testimony of several witnesses upon divers subjects. Under this reason for a new trial, if any part of the evidence objected to was proper, the assignment is not well taken. A considerable portion of the testimony objected to was proper, and there was no error in overruling the objections thereto.

It also appears that the objections to the evidence offered were too general. Objections to evidence must be reasonably specific.

The seventh reason is no longer a statutory reason for a new trial. Section 559, R. S. 1881.

The eighth reason is the only one which can be considered by this court.

It is insisted, on behalf of the appellant, that the case established by the evidence is not the cause of action alleged in the complaint.

"A motion for a new trial, upon the ground that the verdict or decision is contrary to law is somewhat in the nature of a demurrer to the evidence. It admits all the evidence given upon the trial, but says that as the verdict or decision based upon such evidence is contrary to the general principles of the law applicable to the issues involved, judgment should not be rendered thereon. Such a motion presents to the *nisi prius* and appellate courts a question of law merely. Each court is required to make an application of the law to the evidence, and determine whether the verdict or decision is contrary to the principles of law which should govern the cause." Buskirk's Prac., 239; *Bosseker* v. *Cramer*, 18 Ind. 44; *McGuire* v. *State*, 50 Ind. 284.

It is the settled law that the plaintiff must recover, if at all, upon the theory of her complaint. *Boesker* v. *Pickett*, 81 Ind. 554; *Hewitt* v. *Powers*, 84 Ind. 295; *Western Union Tel. Co.* v. *Reed*, 96 Ind. 195; *Ivens* v. *Cincinnati, etc., R. W. Co.*, 103 Ind. 27; *Chicago, etc., R. R. Co.* v. *Bills*, 104 Ind. 13; *Pennsylvania Co.* v. *Marion*, 104 Ind. 239; *Louisville, etc., R. W. Co.* v. *Godman*, 104 Ind. 490; *Spencer* v. *McGonagle*, 107 Ind. 410.

What, then, is the theory of the cause of action alleged in the complaint? Is it to recover damages for being carried past her destination or for injuries received while alighting from appellant's train? . The complaint is wholly insufficient as stating a cause of action upon the former theory. *Pittsburgh, etc., R. W. Co.* v. *Lightcap*, 7 Ind. App. 249, and cases cited; *Chicago, etc., R. R. Co.* v. *Bills, supra*, and cases cited.

We think, however, that the gist of the action is that the "defendant unlawfully and negligently stopped the train on a grade one mile from Surrey, and with great force and violence commanded and compelled the plaintiff to alight from the said train some six miles from the town of Rensselaer and one mile from Surrey, and not at any platform or station, and, in attempting to alight, the plaintiff, by the negligence of the defendant, was cast suddenly to the ground on an incline, and by reason thereof she sprained, bruised, and injured her ankle, knee, leg, and back," etc.

Upon this theory must the evidence sustain the verdict, or it will be contrary to the law of the case.

There is no evidence to make a case under the issues. While the evidence may be sufficient to entitle the appellee to recover for being carried past her destination, she was not entitled to a verdict and judgment upon that theory, because that is not the cause of action alleged in her complaint. In fact the evidence wholly fails to establish the fact that the appellee was injured at the time or under the circumstances alleged in the complaint.

Counsel for appellee, in his contention, says: "The appellee wanted to go to her mother's house, near Rensselaer. Rensselaer was her first choice, Surrey second choice, and Fair Oaks third choice. This choice was compulsory and caused by the wrongful and negligent acts of the appellant in not permitting appellee to alight where her ticket entitled her to a discharge. Appellee bought a ticket at Delphi for Rensselaer; at Rensselaer appellant's train passed the platform, promised to go back, but went on. The brakeman hallooed Surrey three times, took appellee's valise out of the car and set it on the ground, reached his hand out as if to support appellee, and she jumped. The support was not given, and appellee was deceived. She had a right to rely on the professed support of appellant's servant in the line of his duty. The command or call was repeated three times, and no doubt with great force and violence, Surrey, *Surrey, Surrey.* * * * The evidence thus clearly makes out a plain case of negligence against appellant, and there was no perceptible change of theory."

If we are correct in our conclusions as to the theory of the complaint, and we think our conclusions as to its theory is correct, the evidence fails to establish the material allegations of the complaint; hence it follows that the verdict can not stand, because it is contrary to the law applicable to the case. It is not sufficient to say that the evidence is sufficient to entitle the appellee to recover upon some theory, but the question is, does it entitle her to recover upon the theory of the issues. The evidence must establish the case made by the complaint, and if there is no evidence to sustain the cause of action upon the theory of the complaint, the verdict is contrary to law.

As said by the court in *Bosseker* v. *Cramer, supra:* "We think that a verdict which is contrary to law, is one which is contrary to the principles of law as applied to the facts which the jury were called upon to try; contrary to the principles of law which should govern the cause." *Robinson Machine Works* v. *Chandler*, 56 Ind. 575.

In the case of *Boardman* v. *Griffin*, 52 Ind. 101, the court said: "When the trial of a cause is by the court, instead of a jury, whether the court is required to find

the facts specially or not, it can not, any more than a
jury can, go outside of the case made by the pleadings.
In such cases, as well as in others, the parties must recover
upon the allegations of the pleadings. They must recover *secundum allegata et probata*, or not at all. It must
be so, in the nature of things, so long as our mode of
administering justice prevails. It would be folly to require the plaintiff to state his cause of action, and the
defendant to disclose his grounds of defense, if, on the
trial, either or both might abandon such grounds and
recover upon others, which are substantially different
from those alleged.'' *Paris* v. *Strong,* 51· Ind. 339;
Terry v. *Shively,* 64 Ind. 106; *Judy* v. *Gilbert,* 77 Ind.
96; *Hays* v. *Carr, Admr.,* 83 Ind. 275; *Thomas* v. *Dale,*
86 Ind. 435; *Cleveland, etc., R. W. Co.* v. *Wynant,* 134
Ind. 681; *Hasselman* v. *Carroll,* 102 Ind. 153; *Brown* v.
Will, 103 Ind. 71; *Louisville, etc., R. W. Co.* v. *Godman,*
104 Ind. 490.

A new trial ought to have been granted the appellant,
for the reason that the verdict of the jury is contrary to
the law applicable to this cause.

Judgment reversed, at the cost of appellee, with instructions to sustain appellant's motion for a new trial.

Filed Dec. 20, 1893.

---◆---

No. 909.

Hindman *v.* Timme.

PLEADING.—*Complaint.*—*Negligence.*—*General Allegations Sufficient.*—
In an action based on tort, negligence may be alleged in general
terms without setting forth the specific acts constituting the same.

SAME.—*Indefiniteness.*—*Remedy for.*—The usual remedy for indefiniteness in pleading is by motion to make more specific.

VARIANCE.—*Immaterial.*—*Pleading and Proof.*—Where an allegation in the complaint was that plaintiff was injured while "attempting to drive them [his horses] and pass" the object, and the proof was that plaintiff was injured while attempting to "lead" his horses past the object after failing to drive them by, there was at most an immaterial variance which would be deemed cured by sections 391 and 392, R. S. 1881.

INSTRUCTIONS TO JURY.—*Joint Assignment.—When Unavailable.*—An assignment of error, which questions the sufficiency of instructions jointly and not severally, can avail nothing, unless all the instructions thus assigned are erroneous.

SAME.—*Incomplete Instruction.—Remedy.*—If an instruction is correct as far as it goes, the party who desires a more complete and fuller statement of the law must ask for it, and thus only can error be ordinarily predicated upon the action of the court.

SAME.—*Not Signed by Party or Attorneys.—Refusal not Error.*—It is not error to refuse instructions which are not signed by a party or his attorneys.

SAME.—*Assuming Fact to be True.*—It is not error to assume an issuable fact as true in an instruction, if the fact be uncontroverted.

CONTRIBUTORY NEGLIGENCE.—*Mixed Question of Law and Fact.—Province of Jury.*—As to whether a party is guilty of contributory negligence in attempting to lead his horses past an object in the highway, at which they had taken fright, and so attempting was injured, is a mixed question of law and fact, the determination of which properly rests with the jury.

NEGLIGENCE.—*Leaving Sick and Disabled Cow in Highway.—Injury from Fright of Horses.*—In an action for damages for personal injury by reason of plaintiff's horses taking fright at defendant's dead cow in the highway, defendant's negligence was sufficiently established when shown that he left the sick and disabled cow in the highway, having good reason to believe that she would die and was liable to frighten the horses of passers-by, whether he knew, previous to the accident, that the cow had died.

From the Greene Circuit Court.

A. G. Cavins, E. H. C. Cavins and *W. L. Cavins,* for appellant.

W. L. Slinkard and *D. W. Crockett,* for appellee.

GAVIN, J.—As appellee was traveling along a public highway his horses became frightened at a dead cow lying in the highway. Being unable to drive them by, he undertook to lead them past, but, by reason of their fright, they ran away, and he was injured by being thrown against a wire fence.

He brought suit against appellant for negligently leaving the cow in the road, and recovered damages.

The complaint was tested by demurrer, which was overruled to the first and third paragraphs, with proper exceptions.

When fairly construed, the allegations of the first paragraph show that the body of his dead cow was, by appellant, carelessly and negligently left lying in a public highway, whereby appellee's horses became frightened and ran away and caused the injuries complained of, while appellee was traveling on said highway, and, in the exercise of proper care and diligence, was "attempting to drive them and pass the said object."

While the allegations as to appellant's negligence are made in general terms, the complaint is not thereby rendered insufficient on demurrer. On the contrary, it has long been recognized as the rule in Indiana that the general allegation that an act was negligently done is sufficient without setting forth in detail the specific acts constituting the negligence. *Louisville, etc., R. W. Co. v. Berkey*, 35 N. E. Rep. 3.

We do not find, in their essential features, any material difference between the two paragraphs. Upon the ground that it is indefinite, objection is made to one of the allegations of the third paragraph. The usual remedy for such a defect is by motion to make more specific. *American Wire Nail Co. v. Connelly*, 8 Ind. App. 398, 35 N. E. Rep. 721, and cases cited therein.

Furthermore, the allegation itself was a needless one, the matter covered by it being included in the general allegation.

There was no error in overruling the demurrer.

Hindman *v.* Timme.

An examination of the evidence convinces us that there was sufficient evidence to sustain the verdict.

While it does not show that appellant knew that the cow was dead before the accident, there was sufficient to authorize the jury to find that he left the sick and disabled cow in the highway, where he had good reason to believe that it would die and was liable to frighten the horses of passers-by, as did actually occur. While he did not know that the results which occurred would happen, he had good reason to expect them.

That appellee was injured while attempting to lead his horses past the body, after failing to drive them by, instead of while "attempting to drive them and pass" it, as alleged in the complaint, would be at the most an immaterial variance and not a failure of proof, and would be deemed cured by the provisions of sections 391 and 392, R. S. 1881. *Steinke* v. *Bentley*, 6 Ind. App. 663, 34 N. E. Rep. 97; *Bristol Hydraulic Co.* v. *Boyer*, 67 Ind. 236.

Under the facts of this case, the question of the negligence of the appellee, in attempting to lead his horses past the body, was essentially one for the determination of the jury, and with their determination we do not feel justified in interfering.

One cause assigned for new trial is that the court erred in giving "instructions 6 and 7 of its own motion." As contended by counsel for appellee, this assignment questions the sufficiency of these instructions jointly and not severally. To sustain the motion upon this ground both must be bad. *Devay* v. *Dunlap*, 7 Ind. App. 690, 35 N. E. Rep. 195; *Ohio, etc., R. W. Co.* v. *McCartney*, 121 Ind. 385; *Wallace* v. *Exchange Bank*, 126 Ind. 265; *Rees* v. *Blackwell*, 6 Ind. App. 506, 33 N. E. Rep. 988.

The only objection presented to the 6th instruction is that it authorizes a recovery upon proof that appellee was injured while attempting to "lead" instead of drive his horses. What we have heretofore said shows this objection to be untenable.

The only criticism offered to the seventh is that it assumes that appellant had a dead cow in the highway. If this be granted, the fact was uncontroverted. No harm could possibly result from the courts assuming such a fact to be true. *Louisville, etc., R. R. Co.* v. *Utz, Admr.,* 133 Ind. 265.

That the court erred in giving "instructions 1, 2, 3, 4 and 5 asked by plaintiff," is another cause for new trial. Like the preceding cause, this also questions the sufficiency of all these instructions jointly, and not of each one separately. All the instructions must be overthrown to sustain the assignment.

Instruction No. 1 states that "where negligence is one of the issues in a case, in order for the plaintiff to recover, he must use ordinary care," and then proceeds to give a definition of ordinary care. This instruction counsel assert to be erroneous "because it does not take into consideration any of the elements of negligence and the recovery therefor, except that the plaintiff must use ordinary care."

Did the instruction undertake to tell the jury all that was necessary to enable the plaintiff to recover, then the contention of counsel would be correct. *Kentucky, etc., Co.* v. *Eastman,* 7 Ind. App. 514, 34 N. E. Rep. 835; *Jackson School Township* v. *Shera,* 35 N. E. Rep. 842.

But the instruction does not do this. It simply informs the jury as to one element of his right to recover, and that this is an essential one. That it is indeed an essential element is not and can not be gainsaid. It is settled that when an instruction is correct as far as it goes, the party who desires a more complete and fuller statement of the law must ask for it, and thus only can any error be ordinarily predicated upon the action of the court. Elliott's App. Proced., sections 647 and 736; *Western Union Tel. Co.* v. *Buskirk*, 107 Ind. 549.

The objection to the third instruction is not well taken.

No objection whatever is made to the fifth instruction. Thus there are three instructions out of the five to which no well founded objection is presented. The cause for new trial is, therefore, not sustained.

The last reason for a new trial argued in this court is that the court erred in refusing certain instructions asked by the appellant. These instructions do not appear, from the record, to have been signed by the appellant or his attorneys. This being true, appellee must be sustained in his contention that there was no error in refusing them. *Darnell* v. *Sallee*, 7 Ind. App. 581, 34 N. E. Rep. 1020; *State, ex rel.,* v. *Sutton*, 99 Ind. 300; *Board, etc.,* v. *Legg, Admr.*, 110 Ind. 479; Thornton on Juries, section 159.

We have considered all the questions presented to us by counsel, and find no available error.

Judgment affirmed.

Filed Dec. 20 1893.

No. 940.

WELSH, EXECUTOR, *v.* BROWN.

PRINCIPAL AND AGENT.—*Agent Acting in Disregard of His Principal's Instruction.—Liability of Agent.—Damages.—Measure of.*—Where A. left money in the hands of B., as his agent, with instructions to loan the same to C., when C. and his wife should execute a mortgage upon a certain eighty acres of land unincumbered, and B., in disregard of such instructions, loaned the money to C. with a preëxisting mortgage on the land, he is liable to A. therefor, if loss resulted therefrom, in a sum not exceeding the amount of the preëxisting mortgage.

SAME.—*Evidence.—When a Witness May Testify to a Conversation with*

Decedent.—Decedent's Estate.—In an action by a decedent's representative, against decedent's agent, for damages resulting from a disregard, by the agent, of instructions concerning the loaning of money, the party with whom the agent contracted is competent to testify to a conversation which he had with the decedent before the agent turned over the money left with him by the decedent to loan and accepted a mortgage, wherein the decedent directed witness to tell said agent to turn over the money and accept a second mortgage.

DEMURRER.—*Overruling to Insufficient Answer.— When Reversible Error. — When Harmless.*—The overruling of a demurrer to a paragraph of answer not stating a defense to the action is reversible error, unless it affirmatively appears that the verdict rests wholly upon one or more paragraphs of the answer which are good.

ASSIGNMENT OF ERRORS.—*Assignment Must be Based Upon Proper Exception.—Misconduct of Counsel.*—Where error is predicated upon the misconduct of counsel, no question is presented, on appeal, unless the trial court was given an opportunity to correct the error. No valid exception can be saved unless based upon a ruling of the court.

From the Wayne Circuit Court.

J. M. Morris, L. P. Mitchell and *R. A. Jackson,* for appellant.

Brown and *Brown,* for appellee.

Ross, J.—The appellant, Josiah A. Welsh, as executor of the estate of Joseph Welsh, deceased, brought this action against the appellee in the Henry Circuit Court, and the cause was sent, on change of venue, to the Wayne Circuit Court, where there was a trial, and verdict and judgment in favor of the appellee.

The complaint is in two paragraphs, the first being, in substance, as follows: That in January, 1887, the deceased, desiring to make a loan to one Albert Brown, placed in appellee's hands, as his attorney and agent, the sum of $2,500, and requested and instructed him to loan and pay the said sum to the said Albert Brown, upon the execution by Brown and his wife of a mortgage upon eighty acres of land which he owned in Henry county,

Indiana, but not to pay over said money until said land
was clear of all incumbrances; that the appellee undertook the performance of the said matters and the making of said loan, for and on behalf of decedent; that, instead of obeying his instructions, he carelessly and negligently paid over said money to said Albert Brown, while
there was a senior mortgage for $1,600 still upon said
real estate, the existence of which mortgage was known
to the appellee; that both said mortgages were foreclosed,
the property sold and bid in by the decedent for $2,900,
of which sum after the payment of the first mortgage,
the balance was paid upon decedent's mortgage, leaving
a balance due thereon of $1,800, which is due and un-
paid; that Albert Brown, at the time of making the loan,
was, and still is, insolvent; that when the decedent accepted the mortgage he was ignorant of the fact that
there was an older mortgage on the property.

The second paragraph contains substantially all the
facts alleged in the first, and in addition charges that
the appellee purposely defrauded the decedent, in this,
that he was the brother of said Albert Brown, and at the
time of the making of the loan was surety for him on
certain notes to the amount of $2,000, which were then
overdue, and that the loan was made in order to save
himself from liability as such surety, for the payment of
which debts the money borrowed was used. It is also
averred in this paragraph that the property mortgaged
was worth but $2,900 and was incumbered for $1,600,
which appellee well knew at the time he turned over the
$2,500.

To the complaint the appellee filed an answer in four
paragraphs:

1st. A general denial.

2d. Payment.

3d. That the loan was made under the direction of the

decedent, he having full knowledge of the existence of the prior mortgage.

4th. That, upon the foreclosure of the mortgage, the mortgaged property was sold and bid in by the decedent for $2,900; that it was worth $4,500, which was ample to pay both mortgage debts.

A demurrer was filed and overruled to the fourth paragraph of the answer, and the ruling of the court thereon is the first error assigned in this court.

Under the allegations of the complaint, the decedent directed the appellee, as his agent, to loan the money, when said Albert Brown secured him with a mortgage upon eighty acres of ground, which he owned, said land to be unincumbered. If the appellee disregarded his instructions and loaned the money with a preëxisting mortgage still on the land, he was liable to decedent therefor, if loss resulted therefrom, to the extent of a sum not exceeding the amount of the preëxisting mortgage. An answer in confession and avoidance, in order to withstand a demurrer, must overcome, by affirmative allegations, the *prima facie* case which it confesses and seeks to avoid. *Racer* v. *State, for Use*, 131 Ind. 393.

It is prejudicial to the rights of a plaintiff, and hence error, to hold an answer to be sufficient as a bar to his action, which does not contain facts constituting a defense. *Abdil* v. *Abdil*, 33 Ind. 460; *Over* v. *Shannon*, 75 Ind. 352; *Sims* v. *City of Frankfort*, 79 Ind. 446; *Thompson* v. *Lowe*, 111 Ind. 272; *Messick* v. *Midland R. W. Co.*, 128 Ind. 81; *Scott* v. *Stetler*, 128 Ind. 385.

If the fourth paragraph of the answer is insufficient, the overruling of the demurrer to it would be error, and the judgment would have to be reversed unless it affirmatively appears that the verdict rests wholly upon one or more of the other paragraphs of the answer, which are good. *Taylor* v. *Wootan, by Next Friend*, 1 Ind. App. 188; *Glass* v. *Murphy*, 4 Ind. App. 530.

The appellant, in support of his complaint, in addition to establishing what the property sold for on foreclosure sale, introduced a number of witnesses, who testified as to its value, some of whom placed its value at more than $2,900, and one, at least, said it was worth four thousand dollars. The appellee made proof of its value, but none of his witnesses placed it higher than four thousand dollars, and inasmuch as the original mortgages amounted to $4,100 it is clear the verdict does not rest upon this answer to sustain which it was necessary to establish the fact that the mortgaged property was worth more than the mortgage debts. Even if the jury had accepted as its value the value placed upon it by appellee's witnesses, they must still find that it did not equal the amount of the two mortgages. The jury returned a general verdict for the appellee, hence it must have been either upon the theory that the appellant failed to establish his complaint, or that the appellee established one or more of the defenses pleaded in the good paragraphs of his answer.

There was no error in admitting and afterwards in overruling the motion of the appellant to strike out that part of the testimony of Albert Brown relative to a conversation which he had with the decedent before the appellee turned over the money and accepted the mortgage from him, wherein the decedent directed the witness to tell appellee to turn over the money and accept a second mortgage.

Counsel for appellant calls attention to section 500, R. S. 1881, wherein it is provided that "no person who shall have acted as an agent in the making or continuing of a contract with any person who may have died, shall be a competent witness, in any suit upon or involv-

ing such contract, as to matters occurring prior to the
death of such decedent, on behalf of the principal to
such contract, against the legal representatives or heirs
of the decedent, unless he shall be called by such heirs
or legal representatives," and insist that said Albert
Brown was acting as an agent in the making or continuing of a contract; that if the decedent, after placing the
money in appellee's hands with special instructions as
to how and to whom he was to loan it, should change
his mind as to the terms of the loan and should inform
the borrower of new terms therefor; that such borrower,
in conveying the information to the appellee, was the
agent of appellee, and therefore an incompetent witness.

We think this objection untenable. Albert Brown is
not a party to this action and can not in any way be
considered to have been the agent either of appellee or
of the decedent. The appellant sought to recover from
the appellee for damages sustained by reason of appellee's neglect of duty, and this evidence went to prove
another state of facts which, if established, would show
no breach of such duty. It was to establish the contract
made between the decedent and said Albert Brown, and
if appellee turned over the money to Brown pursuant to
the terms of such contract last entered into, without any
knowledge even that the decedent had changed the terms
of the loan, there would be no breach of duty for which
a recovery could be had, although such delivery was
contrary to the instructions originally given appellee by
the decedent.

The only question to be determined was whether or
not the decedent got the security he was to have to insure the repayment of his money. If he agreed to accept a second mortgage, and in fact got it, he could not
afterwards complain and recover from appellee because
it was not a first mortgage.

The objections to instructions given are not well taken. While in several of the instructions there are expressions which, considered by themselves, would seem to be improper, but when we consider the instructions altogether, we can not see wherein they are erroneous or could in any manner have misled the jury or prejudiced appellant's rights.

It is next insisted that a new trial should have been granted on account of the misconduct of counsel for the appellee in argument to the jury. The record discloses that when counsel for appellee made the objectionable statement, counsel for appellant objected and the court at once stated to the jury that the remarks made by appellee's counsel, to which objection had been made, should not be considered by them. Counsel for appellee then continued his argument, and repeated the remarks to which exception had been taken.

The record then recites as follows: "To which latter statement of the said John F. Robbins the plaintiff at the time objected and excepted." This is not a showing of any ruling of the court upon which error can be predicated. Unless the court below was given an opportunity to correct the error, no valid exception can be saved. If the court was asked to compel counsel to withdraw his statement, to instruct the jury to disregard it, or to discharge the jury on account of such statement, and refused to do so to appellant's injury, and the proper exception was saved, this court would have some question to review, but no question is presented by the record as it comes to us.

We pass again to the consideration of the error in overruling the demurrer to the fourth paragraph of the answer. Courts of appeal will reverse a cause for errors of the court below in making up the issues when injury has resulted. And, as heretofore stated, when the court has held an answer good on demurrer, which does not state a defense, the presumption arises that the plaintiff was injured by such ruling. However, this court will search the record, and if it finds that the verdict does not rest upon such bad answer, and that the cause has been fairly tried and determined in the court below, the judgment will not be reversed for the error in overruling the demurrer to such answer, the error in such a case being harmless.

It is the object of this court, in reviewing the judgment and proceedings of the court below, to see that justice has been done the parties, and when the record discloses that there has been a fair trial and neither party deprived of a legal right, intermediate errors will not avail. *Board, etc.*, v. *Lomax*, 5 Ind. App. 567, and cases cited.

We think this case was fairly tried and the right result reached, the court having given the appellant greater latitude in making his case than is usual or to which he was entitled in a case of this character.

There is no error in the record for which the judgment should be reversed.

Judgment affirmed.

REINHARD, J., absent.

Filed Dec. 14, 1893

No. 1,039.

CITY OF VALPARAISO v. CARTWRIGHT.

MUNICIPAL CORPORATION.—*Open Drain or Sewer.*—*Failure to Keep in Repair.*—*Damages.*—*Complaint, Sufficiency of.*—Where the gist of an action stated in the complaint is negligence of the municipality in failing to keep a drain or open ditch in repair, by carelessly and negligently allowing the same to fill up with sand and other obstructions, and by building across the drain approaches to adjoining alleys without placing drains under the approaches, by reason of which obstructions the water overflowed the drain, and flowed into plaintiff's cellar, keeping it damp and unhealthful, injuring the foundation of the house, and destroying large quantities of personal property mentioned, the complaint states a cause of action.

SAME.—*Special Verdict.*—*Sufficiency of.*—In such case, where the facts found by the special verdict were, substantially, those alleged in the complaint, and, in addition, that the ditch was so defectively constructed as not to be adequate to carry off the water, the special verdict is sufficient to support the theory of the complaint, and plaintiff is entitled to recover.

From the Porter Circuit Court.

N. L. Agnew and *D. E. Kelly*, for appellant.

J. E. Cass, for appellee.

REINHARD, J.—The overruling of the appellant's demurrer to the complaint, and of its motion for a judgment in its favor upon the special verdict of the jury, are the only errors assigned and discussed.

The action was brought by the appellee, against the appellant, for damages for injury to the former's real estate by water alleged to have been caused by the appellant to flow upon it, by reason of a defective sewer or drain alongside of the street next to appellee's said real estate.

The gist of the action stated in the complaint is negligence in failing to keep the said drain or open ditch in repair, and carelessly and negligently allowing the same to fill up with sand and other obstructions, and building across the said drain approaches to the adjoining alleys, and failing and neglecting to place any drain under such approaches to carry off the water.

It is averred in the complaint that by reason of these things the flow of the water in the drain became greatly impeded, and, by reason of the obstructions aforesaid, was turned back and flowed into appellee's cellar and kept it damp and unhealthful at all times, and injured the foundation of the house by weakening the same, and destroyed large quantities of personal property described in the complaint.

We think the complaint states a cause of action. A municipal corporation is liable in damages to one injured, not only for negligently constructing a sewer, but for negligently suffering the same to get out of repair. Elliott on Roads and Streets, pages 364, 365.

The appellant's counsel misconceive the theory of the complaint. The *gravamen* of the negligence charged is not in collecting the surface water and running it onto the appellee's lot, but it is, as has been shown, the negligent failure to keep in proper order and repair the sewer or drain which was designed to carry off the water. The cases cited by appellant's counsel are, therefore, not in point.

We are likewise unable to agree with counsel in the statement that the complaint discloses that the appellee's property is situated on a hillside and in a ravine on the lower side of the street, "so that the natural course of the water is across the street, which runs at right angles with the ravine and along the hillside." The complaint discloses no such facts as these, and we are unable to see how, even by the closest scrutiny of the pleading, any such inference could be drawn.

It is charged that the appellee is the owner of a certain described lot in the city of Valparaiso, which is adjacent to a certain street "upon which the city has a sewer which is an open drain along said street; that the same is adjacent to said premises, through which large quantities of surface and waste water escape and find their way into the general outlet."

Then follows a description of the defective drain, the substance of which we have already set out in the introductory portion of this opinion, and this description is followed by the averment and specification of the damages claimed.

We are unable to discover any such complaint as the appellant's counsel criticise, and we know of no valid reason why the same is not sufficient as against the demurrer.

Appellant's counsel further contend that the special verdict is wholly insufficient to authorize the court to render a judgment upon it. We have examined the special verdict with some care, and are unable to reach the same conclusion as that at which counsel have arrived.

It is quite true, as contended, that a sewer is not usually an open drain, but a subterranean channel for the passage of drainage water and filth. We know of no reason, however, why municipalities should not be required to keep in repair an open drain constructed by the city, for the purpose of carrying off surface water directed into it by the municipal authorities. It would be strange law, indeed, that would permit a city, by its negligence, to injure the property of the citizen by overflow of water from an open drain, where the same might, perhaps at inconsiderable expense, be kept in such a condition as to carry off such water without material injury to the property owner.

We quite agree with counsel that no damages can be

recovered from a city for injury done by surface water collecting on land "in consequence of its being lower than the grade of the street, which the city has a right to establish." Elliott on Roads and Streets, page 364. *Weis* v. *City of Madison*, 75 Ind. 241.

But we have here no such case as that. Here the water backed over the drain, as the special verdict finds, and flowed upon the premises of the appellee by reason of the fact that the city negligently allowed the drain and the tiling connecting with the same to become obstructed and filled with sand and other refuse matter. It is true the verdict also finds, as an additional cause of the overflow, that the ditch was so defectively constructed as to be inadequate to carry off the water.

Just what proportion of the damage was occasioned by defective construction, and what by the accumulation of obstructions, is not shown, but to the extent, at least, that the injury was occasioned by such obstruction of the drain from sand and other accumulations, the verdict supports the theory of the complaint and the appellee was entitled to recover.

There was no motion for a new trial or for a modification of the judgment, and we are, therefore, not able to determine whether the damages were in excess of the amount the appellee was entitled to recover under the facts found.

Our conclusion is that the record contains no reversible error.

Judgment affirmed.

Filed Dec. 20, 1893.

No. 964.

SHIVELY *v.* KNOBLOCK ET AL.

TENDER.—*Purpose of.*—When a tender has been made for one purpose, it can not be diverted to another.

ARBITRATION.—*Nature of.*—*Estoppel.*—*Notice.*—*Waiver.*—An arbitration partakes of the nature of judicial proceedings, and is regarded with great respect by the courts; and when an award is valid, it is, so far as the question of estoppel is concerned, equivalent to a valid judgment. The award, to be valid, must be rendered after notice has been given to the parties submitting their rights to arbitration, unless notice is waived. The parties, by agreement, may fix the time and place of hearing and the manner in which notice may be given.

SAME.—*Notice.*—*Waiver.*—*Evidence.*—Where an arbitration and award is set up in answer by way of cross-complaint, which is answered, averring want of notice, the question of notice or waiver of notice is for the determination of the trial court, where the evidence relating thereto is uncertain and conflicting.

From the St. Joseph Circuit Court.

A. L. Brick, for appellant.

A. Anderson and *L. Hubbard,* for appellees.

LOTZ, J.—On the 30th day of January, 1888, the appellant, being the owner of the Grand Central Hotel, situated in the city of South Bend, by indenture leased the same to the appellees for the term of three years from that date, with the privilege of renewing the same for three years longer, the said lessees agreeing to pay the sum of $1,400 per annum as the rent therefor, payable monthly at the end of each current month on the last day thereof, in equal monthly installments of $116.67 each. It was stipulated in the lease that the premises were in good order when received by the lessees, and that the lessees should, at the expiration of the lease, surrender the premises in as good condition as when received, damages by fire and ordinary wear excepted.

The appellees availed themselves of the privilege in the lease, and renewed the same for a further period of three years.

The appellant brought this action on the lease to recover rent alleged to be due for the months of January, February, March, and April, 1892.

The appellees answered:

1. The general denial.

2. That, before the commencement of the action, they tendered to the appellant the full amount of the rent due, to wit, the sum of $466.68, in legal tender money, and continued and made said tender good by bringing the same into court for the appellant.

The appellees also filed a cross-complaint, which states, in brief, the execution of the lease, and the renewal thereof by them; that subsequently differences arose between them and the appellant with reference to injuries and damages done to the premises while occupied by appellees; that, in order to adjust and settle these differences, they and the appellant entered into a written agreement for the arbitration of such differences. By the terms of the agreement it was stipulated "That in order to settle the amount of damages and repairs that John C. Knoblock and Otto M. Knoblock shall pay to D. M. Shively, by reason of their occupancy of D. M. Shively's building, * * * and also by reason of any negligence or other damages accruing to said Shively from said Knoblocks in reference to said premises, that they will allow the same to be adjusted and settled by three men (naming them). They (the arbitrators) to take the said lease, and estimate the damages and repairs according to the terms of the lease, and all other damages accruing to the said Shively from the said Knoblocks, by reason of their occupancy of said building, which may be legally due in favor of said Shively and against Knoblocks, in reference to and flowing from said premises.''

It is further averred that it was the intention of the parties that said contract should contain a stipulation that the lease should be canceled and the appellees should deliver up said premises to the appellant; that by the mistake of the scrivener who wrote said article, and by the mutual mistake of the parties, said stipulation was omitted from said contract; that said arbitrators, in pursuance with said agreement, did make an estimate and finding of the damages in the sum of $91.15, which sum, together with the amount of the rents due and the keys to said premises, the appellees tendered to the appellant, and continued and made good said tender by bringing the money into court.

The prayer is that said contract be reformed so that said omitted stipulation be inserted therein; that said lease be cancelled; that the plaintiff take nothing by his complaint, and that the appellees have all relief to which they may be entitled.

The plaintiff answered the cross-complaint by a general denial, and by a special answer, in which he averred that he had no notice of the meeting of the arbitrators; that he revoked said arbitration agreement, and that said award was void.

There was no reply to the second paragraph of answer to the complaint, nor any reply to the second paragraph of the answer to the cross-complaint. None of these pleadings were tested by demurrer, nor is their sufficiency assailed in this court. The issues were tried by the court. The court made a general finding for the defendants (appellees). The judgment rendered was that "the plaintiff take nothing by his action herein, and that the defendants recover of the plaintiff their costs."

A motion for a new trial was overruled. This ruling is the only error assigned in this court.

It appears, from the uncontroverted evidence, that the Knoblocks tendered to Shively $694.48. The date of the tender was April 5th, after all the rent sued for had accrued. The tender was for more than the amount due, and was kept good and the money brought into court. The tender included the rent due for a period of five months, the damages assessed, and $20 attorney's fees, as provided for by the arbitration contract.

Appellees insist that their second paragraph of answer has been fully proven by the evidence, and that the judgment of the court is correct, and that it is unnecessary to consider any other question. The tender, however, was not made in discharge of the lease, but in discharge of the arbitration contract. When a tender has been made for one purpose, it can not be diverted to another. The finding and judgment of the court are very brief and somewhat uncertain when considered in connection with the issues. Whether it is a finding for the defendants on their answers, or on their cross-complaint, is left in doubt. The reformation of the contract sought by the cross-complaint was an equitable proceeding, and would require a specific decree and judgment in order to effect a cancellation of the lease. No motion was made to modify the judgment, and we do not determine its sufficiency in this respect.

It is conceded that the award is one at common law, and not statutory. Appellant insists that it is void because he had no notice of the time when the arbitrators met. Appellees insist that the award is like a judgment, and can not be attacked collaterally; that the appellant.

if he wished to avoid its force, must have impeached it by a direct assault.

When an award is valid, it is, so far as the question of estoppel is concerned, equivalent to a valid judgment. 1 Freeman Judg., section 320.

An arbitration partakes of judicial proceedings. An award by arbitrators is regarded with great respect by the courts, for it is the decision of persons chosen by the parties to settle their differences. But it can hardly be considered of equal dignity to a judgment rendered by a court having jurisdiction of the persons and subject-matter. A court speaks by the force and power of the law, while an award speaks by consent and contract of the parties. A judgment that is a nullity may be assailed by the party against whom it purports to be rendered, whenever and wherever it confronts him, but he can not assail it for mere errors or irregularities, except by a direct attack. An award is no better than a judgment. An award, to be valid, must be rendered after notice has been given to the parties who have submitted their rights to the arbitration. The agreement of the parties may fix the time and place of hearing, and the manner in which the notice may be given to the parties, but when it is silent on the question of notice, as in this case, notice is implied from the agreement to submit, unless it is waived. Without notice, the award is a nullity. This has often been decided. *Vessel Owners' Towing Co.* v. *Taylor*, 126 Ill. 250, 18 N. E. Rep. 664; *Lutz* v. *Linthicum*, 8 Pet. 163; *Curtis* v. *City of Sacramento*, 64 Cal. 102.

It is true that an award can not be impeached collaterally for irregularities, or for misconduct of the arbitrators of the opposing party. Story Eq., Juris., section 1452; Morse Arbitration and Award, 595.

Notice goes to the foundation of the award; without it, it must fall.

Elmendorf v. *Harris*, 23 Wend. 628, was a suit on an arbitration bond. It was there held that an award made without notice of the hearing to the losing party was void, and that such defense might be set up to the action on the bond, without first asking a court of equity to set the award aside.

The case of *Curtis* v. *City of Sacramento, supra*, was an action to enforce the award itself. It was held that the invalidity of the award for want of notice of the hearing might be shown as a defense, and without first appealing to a court of equity to amend it.

In judicial tribunals, the law fixes the method of procedure by which jurisdiction is acquired, by the service of notice. If the parties undertake to create a private tribunal for the determination of their differences, they may fix the method of giving notice of the hearing. The law only interferes to the extent of saying to them: You must give some notice.

If the manner in which the notice is to be given is not determined by the parties, then the general rule is that the arbitrators shall give notice of the hearing. Morse Arbitration and Award, 118.

The same author, on page 120, says: "What will be regarded as such reasonable notice is a matter regulated by no arbitrary rule of law. It is necessarily left, in each case, very much in the discretion of the arbitrator. It has been said that if he acts in good faith, it will be sufficient, since his action is within the authority conferred upon him by the submission; and his award will be valid at law, though he actually mistakes the true rule as to what is reasonable notice. But another case takes a different view, and declares that the question, whether or not reasonable notice was given, is one prop-

erly to be determined by a jury in view of the circumstances in each case."

And, on page 121, it is said: "The right to, or necessity for, notice may be waived or dispensed with by a
party."

The evidence in this case shows that the appellant was
very solicitous that the arbitrators should perform their
duty. He spoke to two of them and urged them to proceed with the arbitration. He said nothing about wanting to be present or wanting any notice of a hearing.
The terms of the contract are somewhat uncertain as to
whether or not the arbitrators should consider the statements of witnesses or of the parties. None of the parties
to the controversy, nor their attorneys, were present at
the time the arbitrators made an examination of the
premises, nor was the statement of any person or witnesses taken. The arbitrators obtained the lease from
appellant's attorney on the day before they proceeded
with the examination, and left a copy of the award at his
office for him when it was completed.

There was evidence tending to show that both the appellant and the appellees had knowledge of the fact that
the arbitrators were engaged in making the award at the
time it was done. The evidence makes the impression
that it was the intention and purpose of the parties that
the arbitrators should take the lease and make an examination of the premises and estimate the damages, without hearing any evidence or that the parties should be
present. Two of the arbitrators seem to have been d
selected by the appellant, because of their knowledge c
the property.   ... and

We think it was a question for the trial cou a result.
termine whether or not the appellant h' be interpreted
whether or not he waived notice. The ev ith proof before

questions being uncertain and conflicting, we must refuse to disturb the judgment on the evidence.

Judgment affirmed, at costs of appellant.

Filed Dec. 20, 1893.

No. 1,126.

THE STATE v. GARDNER.

APPEAL.—*Trial, What Amounts to.—Mayor.—Misdemeanor.— Plea of
not Guilty.—Finding of Guilty by Agreement.*—Where a person was
arrested upon an affidavit filed before a mayor, and, upon arraignment, pleaded not guilty, but consented, by his attorney, that the
court, without the hearing of testimony, might find the defendant
guilty as charged, and the court, in accordance with the agreement,
found the defendant guilty, the defendant is entitled to an appeal,
there having been a trial in legal contemplation, whether the court
actually heard any evidence or not.

From the Putnam Circuit Court.

A. G. Smith, Attorney-General, *F. A. Horner*, Prosecuting Attorney, and *J. H. James*, for State.

GAVIN, J.—Appellee was arrested upon an affidavit
filed before the mayor of Greencastle, charging him with
a misdemeanor.

The transcript of the proceedings before the mayor
shows the filing of the affidavit, and the arrest, and "the
defendant being arraigned for plea says that he is not
guilty as charged, but the defendant, by his counsel,
James J. Smiley, consents and agrees that the court,
sithout the introduction of any evidence or hearing of
ferretstimony, shall find the defendant guilty as charged,
be valid uirt, as per said agreement, finds the defend-
rule as to whcharged and assesses a fine against him in
takes a differe dollar." An ordinary judgment then
whether or not r

The appellee appealed to the circuit court, where he was tried and acquitted.

In the circuit court the appellant moved to dismiss the appeal upon the ground that the transcript showed the appellee had entered a plea of guilty before the mayor and because he was adjudged guilty without trial, by agreement.

This motion was overruled with an exception, and this is assigned for error.

Section 3062, R. S. 1881, gives to the mayor of a city the same power over cases of this character as is possessed by a justice of the peace. By this statute the right of appeal is given in cases tried by the mayor, "under the same restrictions and in the same manner as in a justice's court."

Section 1643, R. S. 1881, gives to any prisoner, against whom any punishment is adjudged in a justice's court, a right of appeal "within ten days after the trial."

Counsel for appellant argue, with great ingenuity, that the record shows a plea of guilty and a judgment without trial, by agreement. Since there was no trial, he argues, there is no right of appeal, because an appeal can be taken only within ten days after the trial.

We are unable to conclude that this record shows a plea of guilty. It shows an arraignment and a clear plea of not guilty. This plea can not reasonably be deemed withdrawn by the agreement that the court should find him guilty without evidence. Had it been intended to withdraw the plea of not guilty, it would have been easy to say so.

Such a statement would have been the simplest and most natural expression to accomplish such a result. Neither do we think the agreement is to be interpreted as anything more than a dispensing with proof before the mayor.

It is not an agreement for a judgment, but an' agreement for a finding. The judgment then follows the finding.

It is true that in *Holsclaw* v. *State*, 114 Ind. 506, it is held that where there has been a plea of guilty and the judgment rendered thereon has been stayed by replevin bail no appeal lies, and this holding is based upon the argument that where there is a plea of guilty there is no trial. Here, however, was an unequivocal plea of not guilty.

The word trial, in its general sense, means the investigation and decision of a matter in issue between parties, before a competent tribunal. *Jenks* v. *State*, 39 Ind. 1.

Where issue has been joined by the parties and the cause submitted to and determined by the court, there has been a trial in legal contemplation, whether the court actually hears any evidence or not.

There was no error in the action of the trial court.

Judgment affirmed.

Filed Dec. 21, 1893.

———————◆———————

No. 1,012.

HOCHSTETTLER v. MOSIER COAL AND MINING COMPANY.

MINES AND MINING.—*Falling In of Mine.*—*Right of Action.*—*Failure to Furnish Timbers for Props, etc.*—*Statutory Requirement.*—*Negligence.* —*Personal Injury.*—*Damages.*—Where, during the operation of the statute of March 6, 1885, requiring the owners or operators of coal mines to supply the workmen therein with suitable timber for props and supports to secure the workings from falling in, an employe therein, by reason of a failure to furnish such timbers, was injured by the falling in of the mine, but an action for such injuries was not commenced until after the taking effect of the act of March 9, 1891, relating to the same subject, there was a right of action against the operator of the mine, whether conferred by the act of 1885 or not, such right of action for negligence being given by common law; and the question whether or not the act of 1885 was repealed by that of 1891 can make no difference, as the statute of 1885 only defined what should be regarded as negligence *per se* in that particular.

SAME.—*Contributory Negligence.*—*When Sufficiently Negatived.*—*Complaint.*—In such case, the complaint alleged that "without any fault or negligence on his part the slate which composed the roof in said mine at the point where he was at work fell upon him, greatly injuring him," etc., also averring that at the time the roof fell in upon him, he "was using all due care," and "had no knowledge of the unsafe and dangerous condition of the roof." These several averments, when construed together, are equivalent to one that the injury was incurred without any fault or negligence on appellant's part.

SAME.—*Complaint, Sufficiency of.*—*Assumption of Risk of Employment.*—*Failure of Operator to Discharge Statutory Duty.*—Nor does the fact that the complaint, in such case, avers that plaintiff requested defendant, three days before the injury occurred, to furnish the caps and props "so that he [plaintiff] might make said neck or room secure and safe," disclose such a state of facts as would cast upon plaintiff the assumption of the risk of the employment, after defendant's refusal to furnish the supports.

From the Clay Circuit Court.

S. W. Curtis, C. McNutt, J. G. McNutt and *G. A. Knight*, for appellant.

E. S. Holliday and *G. A. Byrd*, for appellee.

REINHARD, J.—The appellant sued the appellee for damages, alleged to have been sustained by him as the result of a personal injury received from the caving in of the roof of a coal mine or shaft in which he was at work while in the employ of the appellant as a coal miner. The sustaining of the appellee's demurrer to the complaint is the only error assigned and discussed. The complaint proceeds upon the theory of negligence on the part of the appellee in failing to comply with the provisions of section 3, p. 66, of the act approved March 6, 1885, requiring the owners or operators of coal mines to sup-

ply the workmen therein with suitable timber for props
and supports to secure the workings from falling in.
Elliott's Supp., section 1758.   It is contended by appellee's counsel that this section was repealed by implication by the act approved March 9, 1891 (Acts 1891, page
57), and that for this reason no liability existed at the
time this action was instituted.

No special right of action was conferred, in terms, by
this statute, but it made the failure to supply the appliances described in the section quoted, an act of negligence *per se*, on the part of the mine owner, agent, or
operator.

The act approved March 9, 1891, reënacted the substantial provisions of the section hereinbefore quoted,
provided penalties for the violation thereof, and conferred a special right of action in damages to any person
injured by reason of failure on the part of the mine
owner, agent, or lessee.

It is agreed by the parties that the right of action in
this case, if any, accrued while the act of 1885 was in
full force.   It is also agreed that when the present action was commenced the law of 1891 was in force, and if
it had the effect of repealing the act of 1885, the latter
had ceased to operate when this action was instituted.

It is the contention of appellee's counsel, and this
seems to have been the conclusion reached by the court
below, that inasmuch as the act of 1885 was repealed
when this action was commenced, the reënactment of
the section by the law of 1891 did not save the appellant any rights he might have had under the former
law, and that hence no recovery can be had in this action.   Appellant's counsel, on the other hand, contend
that by virtue of another statutory provision all his
rights under the repealed act are saved to him.

The section of the statute just alluded to is as follows:

"Whenever an act is repealed which repealed a former act, such act shall not thereby be revived, unless it shall be so expressly provided. And the repeal of any statute shall not have the effect to release or extinguish any penalty, forfeiture or liability incurred under such statute, unless the repealing act shall so expressly provide; and such statute shall be treated as still remaining in force for the purpose of sustaining any proper action or prosecution for the enforcement of such penalty, forfeiture, or liability." R. S. 1881, section 248.

It will be observed that the only feature calculated to save any rights in this section is in respect to the right of recovering a penalty or forfeiture, or upon a liability incurred under the act repealed. The contention of appellant's counsel is met by appellee's counsel by the argument that the act of 1885 does not create any liability or confer any right of action, and that hence nothing could have been saved to the appellant by virtue of section 248, *supra*. In this view of the law we can not concur. We incline to the opinion that the failure to comply with the statutory requirements constituted negligence *per se*, and, if injury resulted, there was a right of action in the appellant, and a liability on the part of the appellee, at the time the injury was incurred. If such right was created, and such liability existed, solely by virtue of the act of 1885, then it was saved by reason of section 248, *supra*.

But if the law of 1885 conferred no such right and created no such liability, then the same existed by virtue of the common law and independently of the statute, otherwise there would have been no such right or liability even while the statute was in force,—a position not sought to be maintained by the appellee.

If we take the view that the right and liability existed independently of the act of 1885, it must have been because negligence was actionable at common law, and the statute in question only defined what should be regarded as negligence in this particular.

In either case there was a liability and a right of action at the time the injury was sustained, and the question whether or not the act of 1885 was repealed by that of 1891 can make no difference. We think that if the appellee violated the statutory duty as set forth in the complaint, and an injury resulted to the appellant without his fault, the appellee is liable to the appellant, and the present action must be upheld.

It is further insisted, however, on behalf of appellee, that, even if the complaint is sufficient in this respect, it is radically defective for the further reason that it fails to aver the appellant's freedom from contributory fault.

The complaint contains a statement that "without any fault or negligence on his (appellant's) part, the slate which composed the roof in said mine at the point where he was at work fell upon him, greatly injuring him," etc.

This averment is not equivalent to one that the injury occurred without appellant's fault. The appellant may not have been guilty of any negligence in connection with the falling in of the roof, and he may yet have contributed in some way to the injury; as, for example, by going into the mine shortly before the collapse, when he was aware of the impending danger.

In another portion of the complaint it is averred that at the time the roof fell upon him, the appellant "was using all due care, and had said defendant furnished him said props and caps, as the law provides, and as he demanded, as aforesaid, he would not have received the injuries herein complained of."

We do not think this averment supplies the place of one that appellant was free from fault in sustaining the injury. He may have been at fault in venturing into the mine when the roof was in apparent danger of collapsing, or when he had otherwise received knowledge of the danger, and yet without fault in causing the roof to fall. Nor does the statement that the injury would not have occurred but for the negligence of the appellee, cure the vice in the complaint. All these averments may be literally true, and yet the appellant may have been guilty of the grossest negligence.

There is still another averment in the complaint, however, which, we think, supplies the defect in this respect. It is averred that appellant had no knowledge of the unsafe **and dangerous** condition of the roof, he having been at work in said mine for only ten days before the injury occurred.

We are of opinion that if appellant was ignorant of the dangerous condition of the roof he could not have been at fault in entering the mine prior to, and remaining in the same up to, the time of the accident; and that if, when the roof caved in, he was in the exercise of due care, he must have been without fault when the injury was sustained. The several averments, when construed together, are equivalent to one that the injury was incurred without any fault or negligence on appellant's part.

Nor do we think the complaint discloses such a state of facts as would cast upon the appellant the assumption of the risk of the employment, after the appellee's refusal to furnish the supports. The mere fact that appellant demanded of appellee the compliance with the statutory requirement three days before the injury occurred, does not necessarily imply that appellant had any knowledge that the roof was in danger of falling in. It is true that the complaint states that appellant requested appellee to furnish him such props and caps, ''so that he might make said neck or room secure and safe"; but this can not be taken as an admission that appellant knew the roof to be unsafe, in the face of the direct averment that he was ignorant of the unsafe and dangerous condition of the mine.

It is easy to see, we think, how there might have been some danger anticipated against which the appellant desired to protect himself, although such danger was not at the time apparent or known to him. The statute under consideration, as well as the later one upon the subject, was designed to protect the employes in mines from dangers not only apparent and imminent, but also from those remote and not apparent. If the rule contended for should be adopted, the statute would furnish such employe but little protection.

The mere refusal of the owner to furnish the safeguards provided for by the statute would then be sufficient to exonerate him from liability if the employe continued in the work and sustained an injury in the manner set out in the complaint, for it could be argued with equal plausibility, in every other such case, that the mere demand for the safeguards, coupled with an expression that they were required to guard against danger, was indicative of a knowledge of the hazardous condition of the mine.

We think the complaint sufficiently shows the appellant's freedom from contributory fault, and is otherwise sufficient to withstand the demurrer.

Judgment reversed.

Filed Dec. 19, 1893.

No. 949.

THE WABASH VALLEY PROTECTIVE UNION *v.* JAMES.

PLEADING.—*Complaint, Sufficiency of.*—*Exhibit.*—*Insurance.*—*Damages.*
—*Fraudulent Representations.*—Where a controversy arose between
an insurance company and the beneficiary of a policy issued by it, and
the controversy was settled by a compromise agreement, in which the
company paid the beneficiary $600, the policy being for $3,000, and
subsequently the beneficiary brought suit to recover damages alleged to have been sustained through false representations in procuring the settlement and compromise; the *gravamen* of the complaint is the fraud alleged to have been perpetrated upon plaintiff,
and a copy of the policy need not be filed with the complaint.

SAME.—*Answer.*—*Sustaining Demurrer to.*—*By-Law.*—*Contract.*—*Tort.*
—In such case, it was not error to sustain a demurrer to an answer
in bar setting up a by-law of the company, for the reason that the
action is not on the policy nor on contract, but in tort.

SAME.—*Counterclaim.*—*Essential Averments.*—*Can not be Aided by Other
Pleadings.*—A counterclaim, to be sufficient, must contain all the
essential averments of a complaint, and must state a cause of action
in favor of the defendant and against the plaintiff, growing out of
the subject-matter alleged in the complaint, without aid by reference to other pleadings.

SAME.—*Counterclaim, When Insufficient.*—*Release.*—*Warranty, Breach
of.*—In an action for damages for fraudulent representations in the
settlement of a disputed insurance policy, wherein it appears that
the plaintiff is standing upon and retaining the consideration of the
settlement, it was not error to sustain a demurrer to a counterclaim
for damages, founded upon a breach of warranty, in the release executed to defendant by plaintiff, to defend the payment, in settlement, against all claimants whomsoever.

PRACTICE.—*Order for Production of Books for Inspection.*—*When
Proper.*—The propriety of making an order, by the court, requiring
one party to produce and give another party inspection of certain of
its books, depends upon the averments of the pleadings and issues
joined.

EVIDENCE.—*General Objections, When not Sufficient.*—Unless from the
offered evidence itself, a sufficient reason for excluding it appears,
it is not error to admit it over general objections.

From the Tippecanoe Superior Court.

VOL. 8—29

G. D. Hurley, *M. E. Clodfelter* and *W. E. Humphreys*, for appellant.

LOTZ, J.—The appellant is a mutual life insurance corporation organized under the laws of this State. It issued a joint policy of insurance upon the lives of Hugh B. and Annie M. James, in the sum of $3,000. By its terms, the insurance money was payable to the survivor in the event of the death of either of the assured.

Annie M. James died, and the appellee made due proof of her death, and demanded payment of the policy. The appellant made an assessment upon its policy-holders and collected money with which to pay said policy. A controversy arose between the appellant and appellee as to the amount which should be paid in the discharge of the policy. This controversy was settled in a compromise agreement, in which the appellant paid the appellee the sum of $600, and appellee executed a written release and assignment of the policy to the appellant. The appellee brought this action to recover damages alleged to have been sustained through fraudulent representations in procuring the settlement and compromise.

The issues joined were tried by the court. The court made a special finding of the facts, and stated the conclusions of law thereon. A judgment was rendered in favor of the appellee in the sum of $2,662.40. Many errors are assigned. We consider those only which counsel have discussed.

The first is the overruling of the demurrer to the complaint.

Appellant insists that the cause of action is based upon the policy of insurance, and that a copy thereof should have been filed with the complaint. In this contention counsel are in error. The *gravamen* of the complaint is the fraud alleged to have been perpetrated upon the appellee. A party may retain the property received through a fraudulent transaction and sue for the damages sustained by the fraud perpetrated upon him. He may affirm the contract and recover or recoup the damages sustained by him. But he can not repudiate the contract and retain its benefits at the same time. *English* v. *Arbuckle*, 125 Ind. 77; *Nysewander* v. *Lowman*, 124 Ind. 584; *Johnson, Admr.*, v. *Culver, Admx.*, 116 Ind. 278.

The fraud is sufficiently averred in the complaint, and there was no error in overruling the demurrer to it.

It is next insisted that the court erred in sustaining appellee's demurrer to the third paragraph of answer. This answer pleaded, as a bar to the action, a by-law of the appellant, which was as follows: "No suit or action shall be sustainable in any court of law or chancery upon any death claim unless the same shall be commenced within twelve months after the death of any member."

It is alleged that, when this action was commenced, one year had elapsed since the death of Annie M. James. It is not necessary for us to determine whether or not such stipulation is valid, for this is not an action on the policy, nor is it an action on a contract. It is an action in tort which arose when the fraud was perpetrated.

The demurrer was correctly sustained to this answer.

The fourth paragraph of answer was in the nature of a counterclaim. It alleges, in substance, that the policy was procured by the false representations of the appellee and of the said Annie M. James, as to the condition of her health; that this fraud was kept concealed from the appellant until after the assessment had been made and appellee had obtained the $600. The conclusion is that the appellant sustained damages in the sum of $1,-500, for which it asked judgment.

It is a familiar rule of pleading that a counterclaim

must contain all the essential averments of a complaint.
It must state a good cause of action in favor of the defendant and against the plaintiff, growing out of the subject matter alleged in the complaint.   It can not be aided
by reference to other pleadings, but must be complete
within itself.   The pleading under consideration refers
to the policy and assessment as described in the complaint.   If it be considered independently of such aid or
reference, it is hardly intelligible.   The inducement upon
which its important averments depend are wanting.
There is nothing to show that any policy was ever issued,
or that an assessment was ever made except as a matter of
inference.   Nor is there anything to show the character
of the appellant or its right to do an insurance business,
or that it had incurred any liability on account of a policy issued by it, except inferentially.

There was no error in sustaining the demurrer to this
paragraph.

The fifth paragraph of answer is also pleaded by way
of counterclaim.   It is based upon the breach of this
written instrument:

"Received of Wabash Valley Protective Union of
Crawfordsville, Indiana, the sum of six hundred dollars,
in full of all claims under and to the written certificate
of membership numbered 940, on the life of Annie M.
James, late of Hedrick, Indiana, and hereby surrender
all my rights, titles and interest under and to the same,
and releasing said association from all liability in the
premises, also warranting and defending said payment
against any and all claimants whomsoever.

"HUGH M. JAMES."

It is averred, that by the terms of the agreement the
plaintiff agreed to warrant and defend said payment
against all claimants whomsoever, and that there has
been a breach of said warranty on the part of the plain-

tiff in the prosecution of this action; that defendant has been put to large expense in defense of the action, in the employment of counsel and loss of time, in the sum of $500. It is not averred that the payment of the $600 is questioned by the appellee's action. It appears, from the complaint, that he is standing upon and retaining the payment. He is not seeking to have the contract of settlement annulled. He affirms the contract and sues for the fraud. There was no error in sustaining the demurrer to this counterclaim.

It is next insisted that the court erred in the order made upon the affidavit and motion of the appellee, requiring the appellant to produce and give appellee an inspection of certain of its books.

The propriety of making such orders depends upon the averments of the pleadings and the issues joined. Considering the issues and the showing made by the affidavit, we think the order of the court was right. The same is true of the next assignment, that the court erred in requiring the appellant to answer certain interrogatories. The order was proper in view of the issues to be determined. The interrogatories to which objection is made called for information which was proper to be given in evidence on the trial.

The last assignment discussed is the overruling of the motion for a new trial. A good many of the causes for the motion are based upon the admission of certain evidence over the objection of the appellant. The objections to the admission of the evidence are very general. They are nearly all based upon the grounds that the evidence was "irrelevant, incompetent, and immaterial." The incompetency, irrelevancy and immateriality should be specifically pointed out. Unless, from the offered evidence itself, a sufficient reason for excluding it appears, it is not error to admit it under such general objections.

Baldwin *v.* Hutchison.

The appellant gave no evidence in the trial, and the cause was submitted on the evidence given by the appellee alone. It is earnestly insisted, that the findings and judgment are not supported by the evidence; that there is no evidence whatever to show that more than $600 was realized from the assessment made to pay the appellee's policy, and that there is no evidence whatever to show that there was any reserve funds on hand out of which the policy or any part of it could be paid. It is true that the appellant's secretary so testified; but he was a hostile witness. There was other evidence given of statements contained in the circulars and advertisements of the appellant, and statements of its secretary tending to show that the company was prosperous and had a large membership and reserve fund at or about the time the appellee's claim matured.

Under the circumstances, we can not disturb the judgment on the weight of the evidence.

Judgment affirmed, at costs of appellant.

Filed Dec. 13, 1893.

No. 797.

BALDWIN *v.* HUTCHISON.

HARMLESS ERROR.—*Overruling Demurrer to Paragraph of Complaint.*—Any error in overruling a demurrer to a paragraph of complaint will be deemed harmless, where it clearly appears that the judgment is founded upon another paragraph of the complaint.

PLEADING.—*Complaint, Sufficiency of.*—*To Recover Money Obtained by Duress.*—*Threatened Prosecution for Statements as Witness.*—*Privileged Communication.*—In an action to recover money obtained through duress and without consideration, the complaint was sufficient which alleged, in substance, that plaintiff, having been duly subpoenaed, testified as a witness in the trial of a cause to which defendant was a party, and, in response to questions asked him, testified that the character of defendant's son, a witness, was bad for truth and veracity, and that plaintiff testified on cross-examination that he had heard one A. and wife say that said son had stolen a sheep, all of which answers were made in good faith, and without malice, believing them to be true; that the defendant, the next day, threatened to prosecute plaintiff for such testimony, unless plaintiff paid him a certain sum of money; that plaintiff was a person of weak mind, of little education and experience in business affairs, ignorant of the law and of his rights and liabilities as a witness, easily influenced and overcome by a person of strong mind, all of which was known to defendant, and that defendant was a shrewd business man of wide experience, and of force and determination; that plaintiff, believing that defendant would carry out his threats, and by being put in fear of defendant, and against plaintiff's will, and upon defendant's promise not to prosecute him on account of said testimony, plaintiff paid defendant the sum of $900, which he seeks to recover.

DEMAND.— *Money Wrongfully Obtained.*—Where money has been wrongfully obtained by means of a voidable contract, for which there was received no valuable consideration, a demand before suit is not necessary.

From the Montgomery Circuit Court.

G. W. Paul and *M. W. Bruner*, for appellant.

B. Crane and *A. B. Anderson*, for appellee.

GAVIN, J.—The appellee's complaint was in two paragraphs, each of which was attacked by demurrer. The special verdict of the jury clearly shows that the judgment is founded upon the second paragraph of complaint. It is therefore unnecessary for us to consider the sufficiency of the first paragraph, since, if the second is good, any error in overruling a demurrer to the first will be deemed harmless. Elliott's App. Proced., section 637; *Doan* v. *Dow*, 8 Ind. App. 324.

By the second paragraph of complaint the following state of facts is shown:

Appellee was regularly subpoenaed and testified as a witness in the trial of a cause to which appellant was a party. In response to the questions asked him, appellee

stated that the character of appellant's witness, his
son, was bad for truth and veracity. In response to
questions asked by appellant's counsel, he also testified,
on cross-examination, that he had heard that he had
stolen a sheep, and that he had heard one Elstun Sayers
and his wife say so. All of these answers were made in
good faith, without any malice, and in the belief that
they were true. Appellee had, in fact, heard it said that
said Baldwin had stolen a sheep, and it was his recollection that he had heard it from Sayers and wife. On
the next day, after dark, appellant came to appellee's
house in a buggy and waited outside while one McComas
came into the house and told appellee that the Baldwins
were very mad over his testimony, and had been to see
the Sayers, who denied having made the statement, and
that appellant would send appellee to the penitentiary,
and put him behind the bars, and cause him to lose his
farm unless he fixed the matter up satisfactorily; that it
would take from $3,000 to $5,000 to fix it up. McComas
advised appellee to go out and talk to appellant, and fix
it up. Appellee went out and talked with appellant, who
told him if he didn't fix the matter up and pay him a
large sum of money, appellant would send him to the
penitentiary, put him behind the bars, and cause him to
lose his farm, and informed appellee that he could have
nutil seven o'clock next morning to decide. Next morning
the appellant came at seven and renewed his threats, and
demanded $1,000. Appellee was a farmer, who had al-
ways lived on his farm, and a person of weak mind, of
little education and experience in business affairs, ignorant of the law and of his rights and liabilities as a witness, easily influenced and overcome by a person of
strong mind; all of which was known to appellant, who
was a shrewd and keen business man of more than ordinary skill and ability, of wide experience in business

and ways of the world, and known to appellee to be a man of force and determination. Appellee believed that appellant could and would carry out his said threats, and was thereby put in fear of appellant, and by reason thereof, and against his will, and upon the appellant's promise not to prosecute nor molest him on account of said testimony, he paid him the sum of $900, which he seeks to recover.

Upon these facts, there was clearly no consideration for the payment of this money. Neither the appellant nor his son had against appellee even a colorable claim of any kind whatsoever, arising from the testimony which he had given in good faith, without malice, believing it to be true, and which was responsive to questions by appellant's attorneys; nor had any crime been committed by appellee.

His statements, as a witness, under the circumstances, were absolutely privileged. *Hutchinson* v. *Lewis*, 75 Ind. 55; Townshend on Libel and Slander, section 223; *Nelson* v. *Robe*, 6 Blackf. 204; *Grove* v. *Brandenburg*, 7 Blackf. 234; 1 Hilliard on Torts, 86; Cooley on Torts, 210; *Calkins* v. *Sumner*, 13 Wis. 193.

In *Stevens* v. *Rowe*, 59 N. H. 578, it is said: "Public policy, and the safe administration of justice, require that witnesses, who are a necessary part of the judical machinery, be privileged against any restraint, excepting that imposed by the penalty for perjury."

In *United States, etc., Co.* v. *Henderson*, 111 Ind. 24, the court approves this language, used in *Warey* v. *Forst*, 102 Ind. 205: "A threatened litigation founded merely on the defendant's belief, without any fact to support the belief, amounts to nothing, and the purpose to avoid such a litigation was no consideration for the plaintiff's promises." *Jarvis* v. *Sutton*, 3 Ind. 289;

Smith v. *Boruff*, 75 Ind. 412; *Harris* v. *Cassady*, 107 Ind. 158.

Counsel for appellant vigorously contend that the payment was a voluntary one, and the money not recoverable, for that reason. With this proposition we can not agree.

Under the allegations of the pleading, the payment was not made by appellee of his own volition, but against his will, and because he was controlled by and overpowered with fear.

In *Bush* v. *Brown*, 49 Ind. 573, the law is thus expressed: "To give validity to a contract, the law requires the free assent of the party who is to become chargeable thereon; and it therefore avoids any promise extorted from him by terror or violence."

It is decided, by this case, that threats of prosecution and imprisonment upon an unfounded charge are such duress as avoids the contract.

"So, if a person executed an instrument from a well-grounded fear of illegal imprisonment, he may avoid it on the ground of duress." *Walker* v. *Larkin*, 127 Ind. 100.

Counsel for appellant argue that the threats were not sufficient to constitute duress, because not of such character as should have reasonably excited the fears actually caused, and cite *Hines* v. *Board, etc.*, 93 Ind. 266, and *Darling* v. *Hines*, 5 Ind. App. 319.

The case in hand is easily distinguished from those, by the fact that appellee was a man of weak mind, ignorant of the law and his rights, as was actually known to appellant. The threats made unquestionably did excite the fear and belief that appellant could and would carry them out.

It comes with an ill grace from appellant to say that appellee ought not to have been so badly scared.

We deem the law to have been well stated by MORSE, Judge, in the case of *Cribbs* v. *Sowle*, 87 Mich. 340, where it is said: "It has been held by some of the courts that mere threats of criminal prosecution, when neither warrant has been issued nor proceedings commenced, do not constitute duress. *Buchanan* v. *Sahlein*, 9 Mo. App. 552; *Higgins* v. *Brown*, 78 Me. 473; *Town Council* v. *Burnett*, 34 Ala. 400. And, by others, that a threat of arrest for which there is no ground does not constitute duress, as the party could not be put in fear thereby. *Knapp* v. *Hyde*, 60 Barb. 80; *Preston* v. *Boston*, 12 Pick. 12. But these rules do not seem to have any regard to the condition of the mind of the person acted upon by the threat, or to take into consideration the age, disposition or intellect of the person so threatened; and leave the old, the ignorant, the weak and the timid at the mercy of the bully or the scoundrel who operates upon their fears to extort money from them. Truly, to such an action as this, the defendant who, without semblance of any legal or moral right or claim, has scared money out of an old man, can not well set up any defense of the policy of the law that it was the duty of the injured party to have resorted to the courts in the first place, or withstood the threat of being taken there until proceedings were actually begun, to defend himself from the extortion. Nor, in my opinion, is it the true policy of the law to make an arbitrary and unyielding rule in such cases, to apply to all alike, without regard to age, sex or condition of mind. Weak and cowardly people, and old and ignorant persons, are the ones that need the protection of the courts, and they are the ones usually operated upon and influenced by threats and menaces."

In cases of fraud, it is recognized that representations may be effectual in dealing with a weak-minded, ignorant man, which ought not to be relied upon by a man of ordinary knowledge and intellect. *Ingalls* v. *Miller*, 121 Ind. 188.

Our conclusion, therefore, is that the complaint shows the payment of the money was procured without any consideration and by duress through such threats as, considering all the circumstances and comparative abilities of the parties, were reasonably calculated to and did overcome the will of appellee. It was therefore good. *Line, Admx.*, v. *Blizzard*, 70 Ind. 23; *Adams* v. *Stringer*, 78 Ind. 175.

The special verdict contains some facts evidentiary merely, and some mere conclusions, yet when stripped of all unnecessary matter, it contains sufficient facts, well founded, to sustain the material allegations of the complaint. What we have already said in considering the sufficiency of the complaint, meets most of the objections urged to the verdict.

The verdict shows that appellant and his son executed to appellee an agreement not to prosecute or molest him on account of his testimony.

There was no necessity for a return of this agreement by appellee; it was wholly valueless, and conferred nothing upon appellee, and no rights were by it surrendered by appellant or his son.

"Where a contract is void, or, if being merely voidable, no rights have been actually surrendered, and no benefits acquired under it, since in either case the contract has conferred nothing, there is nothing to restore." *Higham* v. *Harris*, 108 Ind. 246.

Neither was any demand for the return of the money required before suit, because the possession of the money was wrongfully obtained by means of a voidable contract, and the appellee received nothing of value for it. *Thompson* v. *Peck*, 115 Ind. 512.

The able counsel for appellant have urged with great

ingenuity and plausibility many objections in this case which we have not deemed it necessary to set out in detail. Those which appeared to us the most important, we have discussed in this opinion. Others have been considered, but we are unable to find any cause for reversal. On the other hand, we are convinced that a just and proper conclusion has been reached, so far as disclosed by the record before us.

The judgment is affirmed.

REINHARD, J., absent.

Filed Dec. 12, 1893.

* * *

No. 980.

HARMON *v.* DORMAN ET AL.

DECEDENT'S ESTATE.—*Liability of Devisees for Breach of Decedent's Covenant.—Final Settlement.*—The devisees of a decedent are liable in damages to the covenantee for a breach of the decedent's covenant, occurring after the decedent's death and after the final settlement of the decedent's estate.

PLEADING.—*Complaint.—Allegation of Damages.—Due and Unpaid.*—In an action for damages for breach of covenant, it is not necessary to allege, in the complaint, that the damages sought are due and unpaid.

From the Dearborn Circuit Court.

G. M. Roberts and *C. W. Stapp*, for appellant.

N. S. Givan, for appellees.

Ross, J.—The appellant sued the appellees, as the devisees under the will of Nancy Hayes, deceased, to recover damages for a breach of covenant of warranty contained in a deed of conveyance made by said Nancy Hayes to the appellant. The only question on this appeal is as to the sufficiency of the complaint, the court below having sustained a demurrer thereto.

The complaint reads as follows:

"For cause of action against the defendant, plaintiff says that heretofore, to wit, on the 4th day of August, 1886, the plaintiff purchased of and from one Nancy Hayes, for the sum of two thousand dollars, the following described real estate, situated in the county of Madison and State of Indiana, to wit: Fifty-five acres off the west side of the northeast quarter of section twenty-seven (27), township twenty-one (21) north, range six (6) east; and, on said day, viz: August 4, 1886, the said Nancy Hayes, an unmarried woman, who was then in possession of the whole of said real estate, made, executed and delivered to said plaintiff her deed of general warranty, whereby she covenanted and agreed that she was the owner, in fee, of said real estate, and would warrant and defend the title thus conveyed by said deed of warranty to this plaintiff, a copy of said deed is filed herewith, made a part of this complaint and marked exhibit 'A.' "

Plaintiff avers that upon the execution of said deed the grantor therein put plaintiff in possession of the whole of said real estate, including the one-sixth interest afterwards recovered by Stephen B. Spahr, and plaintiff thereafter remained in possession of the whole of said real estate until the time of the eviction hereinafter mentioned, and until then had no knowledge of the title or claim of said Spahr in said real estate. And the plaintiff avers that the covenants of said warranty deed have been broken, in this, that the said Nancy Hayes was not, at the time of the execution of said deed, nor did she afterwards become, the owner in fee of said real estate, but that one Stephen B. Spahr was the owner, in fee, at said time, of one undivided one-sixth ($\frac{1}{6}$) part of said real estate, then and now of the value of $500, and that afterward, and after the death of said Nancy Hayes, to wit, at the October term, 1890, of the Madison Circuit Court, for Madison county, in the State of Indiana, the said Stephen B. Spahr brought his action against the plaintiff, alleging, in his complaint, that he was the owner in fee, and was entitled to the possession of the undivided one-sixth of said real estate, and this plaintiff, being brought into said court by due process of law, to answer said complaint, employed counsel and made all the defense he could, or that could be made to such action, but the court, upon trial of said cause, gave judgment to and in favor of said Stephen B. Spahr, and against this plaintiff, for the undivided one-sixth part of said real estate, and then and there found and adjudged that he, the said Stephen B. Spahr, was the owner thereof, and that his title thereto was paramount and superior to any right or title of the plaintiff or the said Nancy Hayes; that the title conveyed by said •Nancy Hayes to ,this plaintiff by said warranty deed, as aforesaid, has failed as to the said one-sixth part thereof, and that the same has been lost to this plaintiff by a paramount and permanent title, and by due course of law, and to the damage of this plaintiff in the sum of six hundred dollars.

Plaintiff further avers that after the execution of said deed, and on the 16th day of August, 1886, the said grantor, Nancy Hayes, died testate, leaving her last will and testament, by which she disposed of all her property, real, personal and mixed, which will was duly proven and admitted to probate, and recorded in the will records of Dearborn county on the 20th day of August, 1886; that by said will she devised and bequeathed to the following defendants the devises and bequests, viz: To Stephen B. Spahr, John Spahr and James Spahr, one hundred dollars each; to George Finch, five hundred dollars; to Samuel Finch and William Finch, ————;

to Carrie Guard, one thousand dollars; to Bertha Swift
and Eva Swift, two hundred dollars each; to Isaac Swift,
one note against Isaac Hayes for two hundred and seventeen dollars; to Columbus Guard, one note held
against him; to Linaeus Swift, one note held against
him and his wife; to John S. Dorman, two notes held
against him; to James Finch, Samuel Finch, Flora
Finch and Charles Finch, share and share alike, the
following real estate, situated in Union county and State
of Indiana, to wit: Beginning at the northwest corner
of section 30, township 14, range 14, thence east $27\frac{25}{100}$
chains, thence south $5\frac{25}{100}$ chains, thence west $13\frac{50}{100}$
chains, thence south 17.05 chains, thence west $13\frac{75}{100}$
chains, thence north $22\frac{50}{100}$, to place of beginning, of the
value of $1,000; to Nancy Dorman, the following real
estate, situate in Posey county, Indiana, to wit: Lots
Nos. 5 and 8 in block No. 3, and lots Nos. 5, 6, 7 and
8 in block No. 2, in the Company's Enlargement of the
city of Mt. Vernon, of the value of $1,000; to Flora
Finch and Hanna Finch, the rest and residue of all
property owned by said Nancy Hayes at her death, a
part of which residue is real estate situated in Dearborn county, Indiana, and afterwards sold in partition
proceedings, and the money arising from such sale, to
wit, $2,540, was paid unto said Flora and Hannah Finch,
by George C. Columbia, commissioner; that all said
above devisees of real estate and bequests of personalty
by said will made, were taken and accepted by said devisees and legatees respectively, and were appropriated
to their own use, and, in the aggregate, were and are of
the value of ten thousand dollars, and are held subject
to the debts of said Nancy Hayes, deceased; that said
will contains no provision whatever whereby the devise
or bequest to any one of said devisees or legatees should
be made to pay the debts of said deceased in exoneration

of any other, but, by the provisions of said will, all are liable proportionately; that the devises and bequests hereinbefore set out are all the dispositions of property contained in said will, and said will disposed of all the property owned or possessed by said Nancy Hayes at the time of her death; that the value of the property which, upon final settlement of said Nancy Hayes' estate, was distributed under said will to the defendants Nancy Dorman, John S. Dorman and Carrie Guard, was, and yet is, more than three thousand dollars; that at the commencement of this action, the defendants James Spahr, James Finch, Samuel Finch and Charles Finch were, and yet are, nonresidents of the State of Indiana, and did not then have, nor have they since, had any property in the State of Indiana, or within the jurisdiction of this court; that letters testamentary and of administration were taken out on said Nancy Hayes' estate, and said estate, and all the property thereof was fully administered upon, and final settlement thereof was made on the 9th day of March, 1889, and still remains in full force and effect; that plaintiff was not disturbed in his possession of the real estate so conveyed to him by said deed of said Nancy Hayes, nor was he evicted from said one-sixth thereof, by reason of said superior and paramount title, until in the month of February, 1891, at which time, by reason of such paramount title, he was evicted from, and lost possession of, said one-sixth, which was after the said final settlement of said estate; that at no time prior to the final settlement of said Nancy Hayes' estate, or prior to said eviction, did plaintiff know of the existence of the cause of action herein sued on, and it was impossible for plaintiff to have filed this cause of action as a claim against said estate; that at no time since the execution of said deed has this plaintiff been insane, an infant, or out of the State of Indiana.

Wherefore, he asks judgment against all of said defendants for the sum of one thousand dollars damages sustained in such just proportions as each may by law be liable for, and that he recover judgment against such defendants herein as may be within the process of this court, in the sum of one thousand dollars, and to the extent of the property so devised and bequeathed to them respectively, and that the court decree such judgment to constitute a lien upon all property now in the hands of defendants received through said will, in such proportions as may by law be right, and that the same be ordered sold to pay the plaintiff's claim, and for all proper relief.

The material question to be passed upon in considering the sufficiency of this complaint is, what, if any, liability exists on the part of the appellees as the devisees of Nancy Hayes for a breach of the covenant of warranty contained in her deed to the appellant?

It is urged, on behalf of the appellees, that no such liability exists; that there is no common law right, the same having been abolished by section 2925, R. S. 1881, and that the only liability which could exist against them as such devisees is that created by section 2442, R. S. 1881, which is as follows: "The heirs, devisees, and distributees of a decedent shall be liable, to the extent of the property received by them from such decedent's estate, to any creditor whose claim remains unpaid, who, six months prior to such final settlement, was insane, an infant, or out of the State; but such suit must be brought within one year after the disability is removed: *Provided*, That suit upon the claim of any creditor out of the State must be brought within two years after such final settlement."

That inasmuch as the complaint does not show the appellant to have been insane, an infant, or out of the State, no cause of action is stated, and the demurrer was properly sustained. It is also urged that the cause of action did not accrue until after the death of the warrantor, and for that reason was not a claim against her estate.

This is not a new question in this State, and we will call attention to the cases which we think decisive of the objection urged to the liability of the appellees.

In *Blair* v. *Allen*, 55 Ind. 409, which was an action similar to the one being considered, the court says: "In the case we are considering, the obligation could not arise until after the death of Nancy Allen,—an uncertain event, over which the vendee had no control,—nor until after the title warranted had been lost by reason of a superior title, and by due course of law, which were also events over which the vendees had no control, and which did not take place until after the estate of James Allen had been finally settled.

"It is very certain, then, that the appellee could not have complied with section 62, *supra*, by filing his claim in the clerk's office, nor brought himself within section 178, *supra*, by commencing his suit within one year after certain disabilities were removed. His claim did not accrue in time to file it under said section 62, and he labored under none of the disabilities mentioned in said section 178.

"The question, therefore, is forced upon us, whether, after lineal and collateral warranties have been abolished by section 10, *supra*, and no obligation especially prescribed by law to take their place, the appellee has any remedy at all.

"Upon full and careful consideration, we have come to the conclusion that the Legislature could not have meant to leave a meritorious class of rights without remedies for their breach. The opposite conclusion, in cases like the present, would very much impair the faith and weaken the force in warranties of land titles, and become a frightful source of uneasiness to otherwise peaceable possession.

"We must conclude, therefore, that when, from the nature of the claim, the creditor can not comply with said section 62 or 178, the heir, devisee or distributee shall be liable, on the covenant or agreement of the decedent, to the extent of the property received by him from the decedent's estate. The law does not require that to be done which can not be done; and no one shall lose his remedy for not doing what can not be done."

In the case of *Stevens* v. *Tucker*, 87 Ind. 109, which was an action brought by one of two sureties on a guardian's bond, against the heirs of his co-surety for contribution, on account of a liability on such bond after the decease of said surety and the settlement of his estate, it was urged that the heirs of the deceased surety could not be held liable for a default on the bond after the death of the decedent and after the settlement of his estate.

The court, after reviewing a number of cases, and citing the sections of the statute, *supra*, quote with approval from *Blair* v. *Allen*, *supra*, and then say: "But are they, though their claim is thus meritorious, without remedy? It would have been practically impossible for them to have filed a claim against said decedent's estate. Whether they would ever have a claim for contribution, and if so, the amount thereof, were contingencies at the time of said final settlement, and were not made certainties until the successor of said defaulting guardian had recovered a judgment on said additional bond, and they had been compelled, by reason of the insolvency of the principal, to pay the judgment.

They could not have filed 'a succinct statement of the nature and amount' of the claim, as required by statute. While the settlement of said estate was pending, the present cause of action was not simply a claim which was not then due within the meaning of the statute, the interest upon which might be rebated. It then depended upon future circumstances which they could not control or hasten, and which were not bound to happen, if ever, within a certain time. No allowance could have been made by the court in such settlement to the appellees as claimants, and the facts which they could have stated involved such contingencies that they could not have furnished a proper pretext for delaying the settlement of the estate.''

Many cases have been cited by counsel for the appellees in support of their contention, but we are unable to find that any of them have any bearing on this case, or in any manner criticise, modify, or overrule the cases of *Blair* v. *Allen, supra,* and *Stevens* v. *Tucker, supra.*

The case of *Leonard* v. *Blair,* 59 Ind. 510, was an action brought against heirs to recover on an account for goods sold and delivered to the deceased during his lifetime, his estate never having been administered upon. The court held that the action would not lie.

In *Stevens* v. *Tucker,* 73 Ind. 73, is the same case reported in 87 Ind. 109, the court, on the first appeal, holding the complaint insufficient because the facts alleged did not show that the decedent's estate had been administrated and settled.

The case of *McCurdy* v. *Bowes,* 88 Ind. 583, was an action brought by the appellants against the appellee as the heir and legatee of William R. Bowes, to recover a sum of money due them from the deceased, whose estate had been administered and finally settled, the appellee having received the entire estate amounting to $5,000.

It was alleged, by the appellants in their complaint, that for six months next preceding the settlement of said estate and at the time the action was brought they were absent from the State. The complaint was held to be sufficient.

In *Rinard* v. *West*, 92 Ind. 359, which was an action to recover money had and received, the complaint was held insufficient under section 2442, *supra*, because it was not alleged therein either that the plaintiff had a valid demand against the decedent at the time of his death, or that the claim was unpaid, or that the plaintiff was out of the State for six months prior to the settlement of the estate.

In the case of *Busenbark* v. *Healey*, 93 Ind. 450, the court held that a creditor, although a nonresident of the State, who, about eight months before the final settlement of a decedent's estate, filed his claim and continued to prosecute it until within a month of the final settlement and then dismissed his claim, could not afterwards recover his claim from the heirs, devisees, and distributees of the decedent.

The case of *Fisher* v. *Tuller*, 122 Ind. 31, counsel for appellee insists, is decisive of this case, but in this contention we can not concur.

The facts in that case were that "the appellant and Owen Tuller were partners, and as partners carried the United States mails in Missouri, under a contract with the government. During the war of the Rebellion, confederate soldiers captured and destroyed property of the partnership to the value of twenty-five thousand dollars. In the year 1866, the firm filed a claim for the value of the property, and the prosecution of the claim was entrusted to Tuller. He received from the government, in payment of the claim, in the year 1867, twenty thousand dollars, which he appropriated to his own use. He concealed from Fisher the fact that he had received the money. After the dissolution of the partnership, which occurred in 1866, Tuller informed Fisher that the claim had not been paid and that it had been disallowed, and finally disposed of by the Government. Fisher relied upon the statement of Tuller and was wholly ignorant of the fact that Tuller had received and appropriated the money due the partnership, nor did he obtain knowledge of the fact until September, 1884. Fisher has been a resident of another State since the year 1860. Tuller died in 1873, leaving as his only heirs his widow, Janet C. Tuller, George M. Tuller, Owen Tuller and Emma J. Tuller. Tuller died the owner of real and personal property of the value of one hundred and fifty thousand dollars; his estate was administered upon, and in 1879 was fully settled. The property remaining after settlement was distributed to the heirs, and ten thousand dollars was received by the appellee, George M. Tuller, from the personal estate of his father, and he also received land to the value of fifty thousand dollars, which was set off to him by an order of partition.''

This action was brought under the provisions of section 2442, *supra*, the claim having existed prior to the death of decedent, and the action not having been brought within the time designated, the court held that there was no right of action.

The further objection, that the complaint is defective, in that there is no allegation that plaintiff's claim is unpaid, is untenable. This was not an action to recover an amount due upon a contract, but to recover damages for a covenant broken. In such a case, it is not necessary to allege in the complaint that the damages sought are due and unpaid.

We think the complaint stated a cause of action, and that the court erred in sustaining the demurrer thereto.

Judgment reversed, with instructions to overrule the demurrer to the complaint.

REINHARD, J., absent.

Filed Dec. 13, 1893.

———————◆———————

.

No. 795.

POTTLITZER ET AL. *v.* WESSON ET AL.

HARMLESS ERROR.—*Sustaining Demurrer to Good Paragraph of Answer.*
—It is harmless error to sustain a demurrer to a good paragraph of answer if there is a paragraph remaining under which the same facts may be proven.

PLEADING.—*Reply, Sufficiency of.—Accord and Satisfaction.—Part Payment.*—In an action for balance due on a car load of bananas, to which the defendant answered that plaintiff received $550.70 in settlement of the car of bananas in suit, a reply that such sum was not accepted in full satisfaction of the amount due, but that it was received in part payment only, of which fact plaintiff had due notice, is sufficient on demurrer.

SALE.—*Executory Contract.—Order for Goods.—What Amounts to Acceptance of Goods.—Vendor and Vendee.*—The following order was made of Hoadley & Co., New Orleans, May 13, 1891: "Ship Pottlitzer Bros., Fort Wayne, and Pottlitzer Bros., Lafayette, car each of straight run bananas out of steamer 'Hewes,' at $1.50 per bunch," and May 14, Hoadley & Co. shipped a car of bananas to Pottlitzer Bros., at Lafayette, which arrived May 17, and vendees, on inspecting the bananas, wired vendors, May 18 and 19, that they would not accept the bananas as "straight run," to which the vendors replied at once, by telegram and by letter, that the bananas were "straight run," and that they must accept them as such, after which vendees took the bananas into their possession and sold them.
Held, that the conduct of the vendees constituted an acceptance of the bananas as per order.

ACCORD AND SATISFACTION.—*What Amounts to.—Delivery of Check for Less than Amount Due.—Debtor and Creditor.*—Where a debtor sends a creditor a check in settlement of an account, the check being less

than the amount due, an acceptance of the check by the creditor
will not amount to an accord and satisfaction of the amount due,
unless the creditor must have understood, from the words used by
the debtor, in connection with the delivery of the check, that they
were to accept it in full of their claim.

From the Allen Superior Court.

W. P. Breen, for appellants.

C. H. Worden and *J. Morris, Jr.,* for appellees.

DAVIS, C. J.—The evidence tends to establish the following state of facts:

Appellants are partners, doing business in Fort Wayne
and Lafayette, Indiana, under the name of Pottlitzer
Brothers; and appellees are partners, doing business in
New Orleans, Louisiana, under the name of Hoadley &
Co.

On the 13th of May, 1891, Leo Pottlitzer, one of appellants, gave appellees a written order for bananas, as follows: "Ship Pottlitzer Bros., Fort Wayne, and Pottlitzer
Bros., Lafayette, car each of straight run bananas out of
steamer 'Hewes,' at $1.50 per bunch."

May 14, 1891, appellees shipped a car of bananas to
appellants at Fort Wayne, which arrived the 17th or
18th of May. Appellants, on inspecting the bananas,
wired appellees May 18 and 19, that they would not accept the bananas as straight run, to which appellees at
once replied by telegrams and by letter that the bananas
were straight run and that they must accept them as
such. Appellants, after this, took the bananas into their
possession and sold them.

On the 8th of June, 1892, appellants sent appellees
their check for $550.70, and refused to pay the balance
of the $825, claimed by appellees as due for the bananas,
and this suit was brought.

On trial by jury verdict was returned for appellees in
sum of $274.30.

In answer to interrogatories, the jury found that the bananas were straight run.

Judgment was rendered on the verdict against appellants.

The errors assigned are:

1. That the court erred in sustaining the demurrer to sixth paragraph of answer.

2. That the court erred in overruling the demurrer to the second paragraph of reply.

3. That the court erred in overruling appellant's motion for judgment on the answers of the jury to the interrogatories, notwithstanding the general verdict.

4. That the court erred in overruling appellant's motion for a new trial.

It is first urged, by counsel for appellants, that the court erred in sustaining the demurrer to the sixth paragraph of the answer. Conceding, without deciding, that this paragraph contained facts sufficient to constitute a defense to the cause of action, the error, if any, was harmless, for the reason that all the evidence which would have been admissible thereunder was admissible under the fifth paragraph of the answer.

The rule is that it is harmless error to sustain a demurrer to a good paragraph of answer, if there is a paragraph remaining under which the same facts may be proven. *Wickwire* v. *Town of Angola*, 4 Ind. App. 253; *Landwerlen* v. *Wheeler*, 106 Ind. 523.

The next question presented arises on the ruling of the court below on the demurrer to the second paragraph of the reply.

In the fourth paragraph of answer it was alleged that appellees received the $550.70 in settlement for the car of bananas in suit. In reply appellees alleged that said sum was not accepted by them in full satisfaction of the amount due, but that it was received in part payment only, of which fact appellants had due notice.

In our opinion the facts therein stated constituted a good reply to the answer. The same evidence would, so far as we can see, have been admissible under the general denial, but in any event there was no error in pleading the facts specially.

Counsel for appellants next contend that the court erred in refusing to sustain their motion for judgment on the special interrogatories answered by the jury, for the reason that these interrogatories disclosed the tender to, and receipt by, appellees of the check of appellants for the bananas sued for. The jury answered that the bananas were "straight run"; that there were 550 bunches; that appellants paid appellees by check $550.70; that appellants were claiming that 340 bunches were inferior to straight run and were disputing their liability for the residue of the $825, and that the check so sent by appellants was not accepted by appellees in full payment.

The answers to the interrogatories are not so irreconcilably inconsistent with the general verdict as to entitle appellants to judgment thereon. It is well settled that special findings of fact override a general verdict only when so inconsistent that both can not stand. *Evansville, etc., R. R. Co.* v. *Weikle*, 6 Ind. App. 340, 33 N. E. Rep. 639.

On the last error assigned, two propositions of law are presented in different forms growing out of the rulings of the court below at the trial.

1. Conceding that the bananas were represented as "straight run," and that some of them were of an inferior quality or grade, upon the other undisputed facts presented by the record, was there such a warranty of the goods sold and delivered as survives acceptance?

This we regard as the vital question in the case.

It clearly appears in this case that appellants did inspect and know just what the bananas were before accepting them.   It is not pretended that there were any latent defects in the bananas, but simply that they were not "straight run," and that part of them were "thin, unmatured, green fruit, and not free from culls."

The general rule established by the authorities is that in an executory contract for the sale of personal property, words descriptive of the kind, quality, or nature of the property, do not import a warranty that survives acceptance.   The purchaser, in such case, has the right, upon inspection, to reject the goods if not of the particular description ordered, but if he accepts the property after such examination, he can not complain of the defects disclosed by the examination. *McConnell* v. *Jones*, 19 Ind. 328; *Brown* v. *Foster*, 15 N. E. Rep. 608; *Studer* v. *Bleistein*, 22 N. E. Rep. 243; *Pierson* v. *Crooks*, 22 N. E. Rep. 349; *Coplay Iron Co.* v. *Pope*, 15 N. E. Rep. 335.

In *McConnell* v. *Jones*, *supra*, there was an agreement to sell wool "to be washed on the sheep, to be put up in good merchantable order, free from tags."   The court, in holding that there was no warranty in this case, say: "According to the case of *Ricketts* v. *Hoyt*, 13 Ind. 181, the contract for the sale of the wool did not contain a warranty, proper, but an agreement to deliver washed wool.   *   *   *   But, as it (the agreement) was given for wool, to be prepared and delivered at a future time, it amounted to but an agreement to deliver, at such future time, wool of a given character; was but an executory agreement; and a failure to deliver such wool worked, not a breach of warranty of a thing sold, but a simple breach of contract for the delivery of a given kind of article; and it seems that, in the subsequent execution of such executory contract, if the party purchasing accepts the article delivered, in execution, after examining it, or with full opportunity to examine, though the opportunity is voluntary, and without any understanding with the other party, unimproved, he estops himself to deny that the article filled the requirements of the contract."

The case of *Day* v. *Pool*, 52 N. Y. 416, is not in favor of appellants. In that case the defects of the article sold were not discernible upon inspection, and there was a warranty of the quality of the syrup sold, which was obviously intended to survive the receipt and use of the syrup. It was, however, held in that case that the vendee in an executory contract can not rely upon a warranty as to defects open and visible.

In the case of *Fairbank Canning Co.* v. *Metzger*, 23 N. E. Rep. 372, there was a latent defect in the beef sold.

On the question of acceptance, it clearly appears that appellants knew that appellees sent the fruit in fulfillment of their order, and while it is true that appellants, on inspection, insisted that the fruit was not straight run, yet appellees notified them that it was straight run, and that they should so accept it. With this knowledge, appellants took the fruit into their possession and sold it.

In *Pierson* v. *Crooks, supra*, the court said: "The general rule is stated in Benjamin on Sales. In section 701, the author says: 'The buyer is entitled, before acceptance, to a fair opportunity of inspecting the goods'; * * and, in section 703 (Bennett's 6th ed.): 'When goods are sent to a buyer in performance of the vendor's contract, the buyer is not precluded from objecting to them by merely receiving them; for receipt is one thing and acceptance another. But receipt will become acceptance if the right of rejection is not exercised within a reasonable time, or if any act be done by the buyer which he would have no right to do unless he were the owner of the goods.' "

In *Brown* v. *Foster, supra*, the court said: "The evidence in this case, however, permits an inference that the plaintiff exercised a dominion over the machinery inconsistent with ownership in the defendants and consistent only with title as well as possession in himself. He used the machinery in the prosecution of his business, and, although complaining, did not intermit its use. Knowing its defects, he continued to run it. * * * The continued use of the machinery in the promotion of his own business interest, with knowledge of its imperfections, was an unequivocal act of acceptance which no words of his could qualify."

The conduct of appellants must be held to constitute an acceptance of the property.

The second question of law to consider is whether or not, upon the facts involved in the case, there was an accord and satisfaction.

On May 18th and 19th, 1891, appellees duly notified appellants that the fruit was straight run, and that they would hold appellants for the full amount of the invoice. There was no farther communication between the parties until June 8, when appellants sent the check, hereinbefore referred to, accompanied by the following letter and invoice:

(Letter): "Gentlemen—Enclosed you will find our check on Hamilton National Bank in settlement for car of bananas shipped here and held here subject to your order, which we have sold for your account."

(Invoice, omitting figures): "Sirs—We herewith hand you account sales of 550 bunches bananas received May 19, 1891, and enclose you check for $550.70 net proceeds of same. We trust the same will prove satisfactory and to hear from you again. We remain," etc.

On the same day that appellees received the check, they wrote appellants that they had received it and would place the amount to their credit; that they had placed the claim for the bananas in the hands of a collection agency, whose attorney would see appellants about paying the balance of the claim. To this letter appellants never replied.

In the first place, do the words used by appellants in connection with the delivery of their check to appellees, under the circumstances shown, necessarily imply that if appellees accepted the check they must have understood that they were accepting it in full of their claim?

In the case of *Preston* v. *Grant*, 34 Vt. 201, relied on by opposing counsel, the court say: "To constitute an accord and satisfaction it is necessary that the money shall be offered in satisfaction of the claim, and the offer accompanied with such acts and declarations as amount to a condition that, if the money is accepted, it is accepted in satisfaction, and such that the party to whom it is offered, is bound to understand therefrom that if he takes it, he takes it subject to such condition."

Counsel for appellees, among other things, say, in discussing this question:

"Were appellees bound to understand, from these words, that if they accepted the check, they accepted it subject to the condition that it was in satisfaction of their whole demand? Certainly this is not the necessary nor the obvious meaning of the words when considered in connection with the previous transaction between the parties. The words seem to mean that the sum stated is the amount that appellants consider as due appellees for the fruit; that they pay this without dispute, trusting that it will be satisfactory and to "hear again" from appellees on the subject. There is not a word used to indicate that they mean that the check is to satisfy the larger amount due. They simply mean that this is the sum in which they consider themselves to be indebted. They do not say that if appellees will not accept the check in full payment it shall be returned, nor do they in any way indicate that this is their meaning. * * *

"If words are used by one party, which can bear two constructions, and the party to whom they are addressed gives them a possible, but different construction from that intended, and informs such party of the sense in which he understands them, certainly the party using the words should make plain his meaning at once or be estopped to say that he used the words in a sense different from that in which he knew the other party understood them.

"In the case of *Curran* v. *Rummell*, 118 Mass. 482, a check for a sum less than the debt was sent by the debtor's attorney to the creditor in a letter stating that the check was "in settlement of your account." The check was received and collected in the ordinary course of business, but the court held that the creditor was not bound to treat it other than as a part payment by the debtor, to be applied in reduction of the debt only. * * *

"The case of *Hutton* v. *Stoddart*, 83 Ind. 539, cited by appellants' counsel, is entirely unlike this case. In that case the letter containing the check expressly stated that the check was to be returned if not accepted in full satisfaction of the debt." See, also, *Fuller* v. *Kemp*, 33 N. E. Rep. 1034.

In the last case cited the court says: "To make out the defense, the proof must be clear and unequivocal that the observance of the condition was insisted upon, and must not admit of the inference that the debtor intended that his creditor might keep the money tendered in case he did not assent to the condition upon which it was offered."

The case of *Hills* v. *Sommer*, 6 N. Y. Sup. 469, as stated by counsel for appellants in his brief, is more nearly in point in favor of appellants. In that case it appears that when the dispute arose the plaintiffs drew on defendants for the invoice price which draft was returned with the indorsement: "Amount incorrect. Will remit." Then to a letter from plaintiffs asking what they intended to do, defendants enclosed draft for the amount which they stated they would pay for the goods.

As applicable to the facts in this case, however, we prefer to follow the principles enunciated in *Curran* v. *Rummell*, *supra*, and *Fuller* v. *Kemp*, *supra*.

The appellants here have not brought their case clearly within the rule stated in the last case cited, and are not entitled to a reversal of the judgment of the trial court on this ground.

In this case it should also, in this connection, be borne in mind that the car contained 550 bunches of bananas, for which the original contract price was \$1.50 per bunch, or in the aggregate \$825, and if, under the uncontroverted facts to which we have hereinbefore called attention, the appellants, on acceptance, after inspection, became bound to pay the full contract price therefor, as liquidated damages an agreement, whether express or implied, if such agreement can be said to have been created, under the circumstances, by the acceptance of the check for \$550.70, to take that amount in satisfaction of the \$825 debt, is without consideration. *Stone* v. *Lewman*, 28 Ind. 97.

All, however, that we decide on this question is that under the facts and circumstances of this case the alleged accord and satisfaction has not been shown, and no error appears in the proceedings which resulted in the judgment in favor of appellees, for the excess of the debt over the sum paid, that would justify a reversal.

Judgment affirmed, at costs of appellants.

Filed Dec. 21, 1893.

No. 1,086.

THE ARCANA GAS COMPANY *v.* MOORE.

PLEADING.—*Variance Between Allegations of Complaint and Exhibit.*— *Effect of.*—Where there is a conflict between the allegations of a complaint and a written instrument which is the basis thereof, and filed as an exhibit therewith, the latter controls.

STENOGRAPHER.—*Duties of.*—*Transcript.*—*Time for.*—It is not the duty of an official reporter to know that time, or what time, has been granted in which to file a bill of exceptions. It is simply her duty to furnish the transcript within the time given her by the party ordering the same, if such time is reasonable and sufficient.

From the Grant Circuit Court.

G. W. Harvey and *A. De Wolf,* for appellant.

O. A. Baker, A. E. Steele, R. T. St. John and *W. H. Charles,* for appellee.

Ross, J.—The appellee, who was the official stenographer of the Grant Circuit Court, sued the appellant upon an account for services rendered at its instance and request, in making out a transcript of the evidence in a cause tried in said court, to which appellant was a party defendant.

A demurrer was filed to the complaint and overruled, thereupon appellant filed its answer in two paragraphs, to the second paragraph of which appellee filed a reply. There was a trial by the court, and special finding of the facts made, with conclusions of law thereon, to which conclusions exceptions were taken by the appellant. Af-

The Arcana Gas Company *v.* Moore.

ter overruling a motion for a new trial, interposed by appellant, the court rendered judgment for the appellee.

The complaint is in the ordinary form upon an account.

Counsel for appellant insist that the court erred in overruling the demurrer to the complaint, for the reason that the allegations of the complaint are that appellant is indebted to her for stenographic and transcribing services done and performed by her for it, while the account, which is filed as an exhibit to the complaint, is for "twenty-six pages, of three hundred words each, of transcript of record, * * at ten cents per one hundred words," and "six hundred and three pages, of three hundred words each, of transcript of record and testimony * * , at ten cents per one hundred words."

In support of their contention, counsel say: "The contention of the appellant is that the exhibit contradicts the complaint, and for that reason the complaint is subject to demurrer."

Where there is a conflict between the allegations of a complaint and a written instrument which is the basis thereof, and filed as an exhibit therewith, the latter controls. *Goodbub* v. *Scheller*, 3 Ind. App. 318; *Parker* v. *Teas*, 79 Ind. 235; *hines* v. *Driver*, 100 Ind. 315; *Avery* v. *Dougherty*, 102 Ind. 443; *Blount* v. *Rick*, 107 Ind. 238.

We fail to observe the distinction, contended for by counsel, that there is a variance between the allegations of the complaint and the account filed therewith. The account is not for goods sold and delivered, but for services rendered in making the transcript of the evidence. The law fixes the rate which shall be the basis of the charge for such services. Section 1409, R. S. 1881.

There was no error in overruling the demurrer to the complaint.

The court, at appellant's request, made a special finding of facts, with conclusions of law thereon. Proper exceptions were saved to the conclusions of law, and an assignment predicated thereon is made in this court.

Under this assignment, it is urged, on behalf of appellant, that the averments of the complaint are not supported by the findings, and that hence the court erred in its conclusions of law.

The court finds that the appellee, at the instance and request of the appellant, transcribed 629 pages of evidence, each page containing 300 words, for which she was entitled to recover ten cents per hundred words. We think this is sufficient as a finding that the appellee rendered services for the appellant in transcribing the evidence. The facts found are clearly within the issues.

The court found, that the case in which the appellee rendered services in making a transcript of the evidence was tried at the April term, 1892, of said court, and eighty days from May 27th, 1892, were allowed appellant in which to file its bill of exceptions; that appellant's attorney directed appellee to transcribe the evidence, and informed her that she would have ninety days in which to complete said transcript, and that she did complete and deliver it to appellant's attorney on the 18th day of August, 1892.

The appellant insists that the facts disclose that the appellee was the official court reporter, and that she was bound to know that the record disclosed that appellant had been granted but eighty days in which to file its bill of exceptions, hence, she must rely upon the record, and not upon the time granted her by appellant's attorney for making the transcript. We can not agree with counsel in this contention. Parties desiring to file a bill of exceptions containing the evidence should ask, and it is the duty of the court to allow, sufficient time in which to prepare such bill. But it is not the duty of the 'official reporter either to have the time granted or even to know that time has been granted. It is simply the duty of a reporter to furnish the transcript within the time designated by the party ordering it, if the time in which it is to be furnished is reasonable and sufficient.

There is no error in the record.

Judgment affirmed.

Filed Jan. 5, 1894.

◆

No. 826.

The Board of Commissioners of Harrison County *v.* Cole.

Pleading.—*Reply.*—*General Averment.*—*Statute of Limitations.*—To an answer setting up the six years' statute of limitations, a reply, in general terms, that defendant has made payments on the claim within six years, is sufficient without pleading the particulars.

Appellate Court.—*Decision of.*—*Law of Case.*—A decision of the Appellate Court in a case remains the law of the case throughout all its subsequent stages.

From the Harrison Circuit Court.

M. W. Funk, for appellant.

H. C. Hays and *J. H. Weathers*, for appellee.

Davis, C. J.—This case is here for the second time. *Cole* v. *Board of Commissioners of Harrison County*, 3 Ind. App. 13.

On return of the case to the lower court, appellant filed answer in four paragraphs: First. General denial. Second. Payment. Third. The statute of limitations:

that the cause of action did not accrue within six years before the filing of the claim. Fourth. That Cole accepted the individual obligation of Douglass in discharge of the debt, and that appellant, with full knowledge and consent of appellee, fully paid said Douglass.

Appellee replied in two paragraphs: First. A general denial. Second. That appellant, within six years prior to filing thereof, made payments thereon.

On the trial, after deducting credits and allowing interest at six per cent., the court rendered judgment in favor of appellee for sixty-one dollars and ninety-three cents.

The errors assigned are:

1. That the court erred in overruling the demurrer to second paragraph of reply to third paragraph of the answer.

2. That the court erred in overruling appellant's motion for a new trial.

It is urged that the reply was insufficient because it was not stated therein that the payments had been made pursuant to allowances made under the statute. It was not necessary to plead the particulars as to how or when the payments were made. The general averment that appellant had made such payment on the claim within six years, was sufficient to constitute a good reply, as against the demurrer, to the answer pleading the six years' statute of limitations.

The motion for a new trial should have been sustained. On the former appeal this court held that the instrument executed by Douglass amounted to nothing more than the written acknowledgment of the superintendent that there was a balance due appellee, and that such acknowledgment was not binding on the county. That decision, under the familiar rule so often stated that its repetition

is hardly necessary, remains the law of this case throughout all subsequent stages.

The evidence on the trial was in some respects conflicting, but it is perfectly clear that the county had not
paid anything on the claim within six years, or at any
other time, but it does appear that Douglass, who was
paid the full amount by the county, thereafter, from time
to time, made payments on the debt to appellee, a part
of which payments so made by him consisted of professional services rendered by Douglass, as a lawyer, for
appellee.

If, as held on the former appeal, the writing is to be
treated simply as the statement of the amount of an account, the right of action thereon was barred in six
years, unless it was taken out of the operation of the
statute of limitations by the alleged payment made
thereon by appellant. The payment by Douglass, in the
way of the rendition of professional services by him for
Cole, can not, under the circumstances, be construed as
such payment by appellant as would take the case out of
the statute.

In other words, there is no evidence in the record
tending to show that appellant, within six years prior to
the filing of the claim, paid anything thereon.

Conceding that as to all other questions in the case,
appellee is entitled to the benefit and advantages of all
presumptions which tend to support the conclusion
reached by the trial court, and yet, for the reasons stated,
there is nothing in the record, as we view the case,
which tends to sustain the issue tendered by the second
paragraph of the reply.

The judgment of the court below is reversed, at costs
of appellee.

Filed Jan. 5, 1894.

Haase v. The State.

No. 658.

HAASE v. THE STATE.

CRIMINAL LAW.—*Indictment.*— *Venue, When Sufficiently Laid.*—An indictment in the following words, omitting the caption: "The grand jurors for the county of Marion and State of Indiana, upon their oaths, present that Lewis Haase, on the 3d day of January, 1891, at and in the county of Marion, and State aforesaid, did," etc., sufficiently lays the venue, the "State aforesaid" being a sufficient reference to the State (Indiana) mentioned in the introductory portion.

SAME.—*Interruption of Trial.*—*Filing New Charge for Same Cause.*— *Arrest, Arraignment, etc.—Jeopardy.— Variance.*—During the progress of a trial on a criminal charge of assault and battery, the prosecuting attorney conceived the notion that there was a variance between the indictment and the proof upon the name of the injured party, and, so believing, asked the court for time to prepare and file an affidavit and information containing the true name of the injured party, to which the defendant objected, and moved the court for a finding and judgment in his favor, which motion was overruled and exception reserved; and after having prepared and filed an affidavit and information, and issued a warrant thereon, which was served upon the defendant, and due return made, appellant being duly arraigned, refused to plead thereto, and the trial under the indictment was then proceeded with before the court to whom it had been submitted, and the defendant found guilty.

Held, that such interruption in the trial on the indictment did not amount to reversible error, no substantial injury affecting the defendant's legal rights having been shown, jeopardy not having attached under the new charge.

SAME.—*Matter in Abatement.—Jeopardy.*—That another prosecution is pending against the defendant for the same offense, can not constitute matter in abatement until the defendant has been placed in jeopardy in the other action.

SAME.—*Jeopardy.*—Jeopardy attaches only after the jury has been sworn, or, if the trial is by the court, after the trial has been entered upon.

JUDGMENT.—*Sufficiency of Evidence to Support.*—The judgment of the trial court will not be disturbed where the evidence is conflicting, or where there is some evidence which supports the finding upon which the judgment is founded.

From the Marion Criminal Court.

J. W. Kern, Davis & Martz, for appellant.

A. G. Smith, Attorney-General, *F. W. Cody* and *D. L. Cody*, for State.

REINHARD, J.—The appellant was indicted, tried, and convicted, in the court below, for an assault and battery. The indictment is as follows:

"THE STATE OF INDIANA *v.* LEWIS HAASE. } Criminal Court of Marion County.

"ASSAULT AND BATTERY.

"The grand jurors, for the county of Marion and State of Indiana, upon their oaths, present that Lewis Haase, on the 3d day of January, 1891, at and in the county of Marion, and State aforesaid, did then and there unlawfully, in a rude, insolent and angry manner, touch, beat and strike one Helen J. Patrick, contrary," etc.

The appellant, at the proper time, moved to quash the indictment, but the court overruled the motion, and it is contended that this ruling was error. The particular defect is claimed to consist in the failure to lay the venue of the offense properly, by omitting to name the State in which such offense was committed.

Every indictment must name, in some certain manner, the county and State in which the offense is alleged to have been committed. It is sufficient if the State be named in the caption and afterwards referred to in some appropriate way, in connection with the venue of the offense. Gillett Crim. Law, section 130, and cases cited.

In the indictment under examination, the State was mentioned in the introductory portion, and then referred to as "the State aforesaid." This was sufficient, and there was no error in overruling the motion to quash.

The next error assigned is the overruling of the motion for a new trial.

It appears that after the trial had been in progress for some time, the prosecuting attorney conceived the notion that there was a variance between the indictment and proof upon the subject of the name of the injured party, the indictment charging the name to be Helen J. Patrick, while the evidence disclosed that it was Helen L. Patrick. While apparently laboring under this impression, the prosecting attorney asked the court for time to prepare and file an affidavit and information in which the true name of the injured party might be set forth. To this the defendant objected, and then and there moved the court for a finding and judgment in favor of the defendant, which motion was overruled and an exception reserved.

The prosecuting attorney having prepared an affidavit and information, the same was then filed, a warrant was issued upon the same and delivered to the sheriff, who arrested the appellant and made due return of the warrant. Appellant was thereupon duly arraigned upon the affidavit and information, but refused to plead thereto. The trial under the indictment was then proceeded with before the court to which it had been submitted, and the appellant was found guilty as charged in the indictment.

One of the causes assigned in the motion for a new trial is that the finding is contrary to the law.

Conceding, without deciding, that the question here sought to be presented is properly raised, it is difficult to conceive in what respect any prejudicial error has been shown. The most that can be said in support of appellant's position is that there was some interruption of the proceedings of the trial by the inopportune arrest and arraignment upon another charge, or upon the same charge presented in another form.

It is not claimed that the arrest and arraignment during the trial operated as an acquittal upon the charge for which he was being tried, nor do we think it had that effect. The mere irregularity of an interruption of the proceedings, by an arrest and placing him in custody, could not have harmed the appellant in his rights in the case, for which he was on trial. He was not taken away from court while the trial was proceeding. He was deprived of no opportunity to meet his accusers face to face or to make a full defense to the charge against him.

Had he incurred a jeopardy under the new charge, as by being required to proceed with both trials at once, a different question might arise. But there was no trial upon the information, and the jeopardy attached only in the case of the indictment.

We can not see, therefore, how the appellant was prejudiced in his rights in the trial, by the interruption. Appellant's counsel practically concede that if the arrest and arraignment had been upon some other case, entirely foreign to this, the mere interruption for the purpose of arresting and arraigning the appellant would not have been error; but they contend that as the new charge was a part of the same case and gotten up by the prosecutor upon the supposition that it would cure a supposed defect in the case pending, it in some way worked a prejudicial error.

We confess our inability to see any distinction in principle between the supposed and the real case.

The attorney-general suggests that the statute made it proper to re-arrest the appellant while under bond, and cites section 1679, R. S. 1881. But we need not, and do not, place our conclusion upon this ground.

Whether the arrest was authorized or not is of little consequence for the purposes of this case. The question is, was the appellant prejudiced in his rights in the case on trial? Whether his personal rights were otherwise invaded is a matter not now before us.

We do not understand that the appellant insists that the court erred in refusing to adjudge an acquittal as soon as the prosecuting attorney expressed his belief that there was a variance. The court evidently did not think there was such a variance, nor is it now insisted that there was.

We think the court did right in proceeding with the trial, and in refusing to make a finding before all the evidence was heard. The statement of the prosecutor did not amount to an admission that the appellant was entitled to be discharged from the case on trial, and even if it did, we question whether the court was bound to adopt that view and acquit him. Courts exist for the purpose of doing substantial justice, and a party who is really guilty can not legally escape because the prosecuting officer has made an inadvertent admission. Before we are authorized to reverse the judgment, it must be shown affirmatively that some prejudicial error was committed, affecting the legal rights of the appellant in the conduct of the proceeding in which he was tried and convicted, which we do not think has been done.

After the appellant had been arraigned upon the information, he filed a plea in abatement in this case, setting up the pendency of another prosecution for the same offense. To this plea the court sustained a demurrer, and the ruling is assigned as error. But little, if any, argument is made upon this question by appellant's counsel. The point, however, must, in any event, be decided against the appellant. That another prosecution is pending against him for the same offense can not constitute valid matter in abatement, until the defendant has been placed in jeopardy in the other action.

Many cases might be cited in support of this rule, but it can not be necessary. See, however, Gillette's Crim. Law, section 764, and cases cited.

Haase v. The State.

It will not be claimed that the appellant incurred any jeopardy here in the case upon the information. Jeopardy attaches only after the jury has been sworn, or if the trial is by the court, after the trial has been entered upon. So far as the record shows, the trial upon the information was never entered upon.

It is likewise assigned as a cause for a new trial that the evidence was insufficient to sustain the verdict. There is a sharp conflict in the evidence, and where this is the case it is not the province of this court to weigh the same.

If the testimony of the injured party was true, the appellant was guilty of an aggravated assault and battery, for which the punishment assessed, which was a fine of $500, was in no wise excessive. If the appellant's version of the affair was the true one, he was, in legal contemplation, not guilty.

It must be confessed that there were many circumstances surrounding the affair that might be construed to corroborate the appellant in his account of the occurrence. On the other hand, these circumstances are not necessarily inconsistent with the appellant's guilt.

The trial court was the more competent tribunal to judge of the act and conduct of these parties. It had both them and other witnesses before it, and was in a much better position to ascertain the exact truth than we are.

We must, therefore, adhere to the long established rule of declining to disturb the judgment when the evidence is conflicting, or when there is some evidence in support of the finding upon which the judgment is founded.

Judgment affirmed.

Filed Jan. 5, 1894.

No. 1,095.

KILLION v. HULEN.

EVIDENCE.—*Sufficiency of.*—*Judgment.*—Where the evidence is conflicting, it is for the jury to determine the facts proven, and their determination will not be reviewed on appeal.

INSTRUCTIONS TO JURY.—*Exceptions to.*—*How Saved.*—*Filing.*—Where written instructions have been given to the jury, or refused, and the proper exceptions taken, which are dated and signed by the judge, the record must show that the instructions were filed as a part of the record of the cause, or there will be no question saved, relating thereto, on appeal.

From the Daviess Circuit Court.

A. J. Padgett and *J. W. Ogdon,* for appellant.
W. R. Gardiner, C. G. Gardiner, J. H. O'Neal and *M. G. O'Neal,* for appellee.

Ross, J.—The appellee sued the appellant to recover damages for the breach of a marriage contract.

The complaint is in two paragraphs, alike in general allegations, but differing only as to when the contract was to be performed.

In the first paragraph it is alleged that the appellant promised and agreed to marry appellee "on request," while in the second paragraph the allegation is that he promised to marry her, "but no particular day for the onsummation of such marriage was fixed between them."

The appellant answered in two paragraphs, the first being a general denial, and the second that the contract had been mutually rescinded and appellant released. There was a trial by jury and a verdict for the appellee, upon which the court rendered judgment.

The appellant assigns but one error in this court, namely: "That the court erred in overruling appellant's motion for a new trial."

The evidence, although conflicting, is sufficient to sustain the verdict. Where the evidence is conflicting, it is for the jury to determine the facts proven, and their decision will not be reviewed by this court.

We do not concur in counsel's contention that the evidence fails to show a contract of marriage. The appellee testified that the appellant asked her to be his wife and that she consented thereto. The time and manner of his courtship do not rest upon appellee's testimony alone, but are corroborated by many witnesses. The appellant himself was a witness, and corroborated the appellee's testimony in most particulars, denying, however, that he ever asked her to be his wife.

There was a breach of the contract when the appellant married another. *Hunter* v. *Hatfield*, 68 Ind. 416.

The damages assessed are not excessive.

It is next urged that the court erred in giving to the jury, of its own motion, instructions number five, seven and nine, and in giving each of them.

The instructions are not made a part of the record by a bill of exceptions, but are simply copied into the record by the clerk, following a recital made by him, but which is not a copy of any order-book entry in the cause, "that the court's instructions to the jury in the above entitled cause were in writing, and are in the words and figures as follows, to wit:

Section 535, R. S. 1881, provides that a party excepting to the giving of instructions, or the refusal thereof, shall not be required to file a formal bill of exceptions; but it shall be sufficient to write on the margin, or at the close of each instruction, 'refused, and excepted to,' or 'given, and excepted to'; which memorandum shall be signed by the judge, and dated.

Under this section, it is necessary in order to save an exception to the giving of instructions, or the refusal thereof, that the exception be written on the margin of the instruction, dated and signed by the judge. The instructions complained of in this case, had the exceptions properly indorsed on the margin and were dated and signed. This alone, however, does not make them a part of the record in the cause.

Section 533, R. S. 1881, provides that the instructions given, if in writing, shall be filed as a part of the record.

It has been held repeatedly by this court and the Supreme Court that under this provision of the statute, in order to save any question on appeal, the record must show, in some manner, that the instructions were filed as a part of the record of the cause. *Beem v. Lockhart,* 1 Ind. App. 202; *Conduitt v. Ryan,* 3 Ind. App. 1; *Steeg v. Walis,* 4 Ind. App. 18; *Harlan v. Brown,* 4 Ind. App. 319; *Lockwood v. Beard,* 4 Ind. App. 505; *Starnes v. Schofield,* 5 Ind. App. 4; *Supreme Lodge Knights of Honor v. Johnson,* 78 Ind. 110; *O'Donald v. Constant,* 82 Ind. 212; *Hadley v. Atkinson,* 84 Ind. 64; *Heaton v. White,* 85 Ind. 376; *McIlvain v. Emery,* 88 Ind. 298; *Elliott v. Russell,* 92 Ind. 526; *Olds v. Deckman,* 98 Ind. 162; *Eslinger v. East,* 100 Ind. 434; *Landwerlen v. Wheeler, Trustee,* 106 Ind. 523; *Blount v. Rick,* 107 Ind. 238; *Childress, Admx., v. Callender,* 108 Ind. 394; *Fort Wayne, etc., R. W. Co. v. Beyerle,* 110 Ind. 100; *Silver v. Parr,* 115 Ind. 113; *Louisville, etc., R. W. Co. v. Wright,* 115 Ind. 378; *Butler v. Roberts,* 118 Ind. 481; *VanSickle v. Belknap,* 129 Ind. 558.

The recital of the clerk "that the court's instructions to the jury, in the above entitled cause, were in writing and are in the words and figures as follows, to wit:" does not show that these instructions were filed as a part of the record. They were not a part of the record unless filed. There is nothing in the record before us to show that the instructions were filed, hence they are not a part of the record, and we can not consider them.

This disposes of every question presented, and we find no error warranting a reversal of the judgment of the court below.

Judgment affirmed.

Filed Jan. 3, 1894.

No. 1,062.

GRAHAM *v.* THE STATE.

CRIMINAL LAW.—*Pointing Firearm.*—*Indictment, Sufficiency of.*—*Statute Construed.*—An indictment which charges the willful pointing of a firearm at another, by a person over ten years of age, is sufficient without alleging whether such act was with or without malice, or whether the firearm was loaded or empty, the *gravamen* of the indictment being the willful pointing of the firearm at another.

From the Noble Circuit Court.

P. V. Hoffman, for appellant.

A. G. Smith, Attorney-General, and *L. D. Fleming,* Prosecuting Attorney, for State.

LOTZ, J.—The appellant was indicted, tried, and convicted for the violation of section 342, Elliott's Supp.

He appealed from the judgment, and assigns as error:

1. That the facts stated in the indictment do not constitute a public offense.

2. That the court erred in overruling the motion for a new trial.

The indictment is assailed for the first time in this court.

The substantial parts of the indictment are "That

Charles Graham, on the 26th day of February, in the year 1893, at the county of Noble, in the State of Indiana, did then and there unlawfully and purposely point and aim a certain firearm, to wit, a revolver, at and toward Lizzie Kinney, May Kern, Rush Cunningham, said Charles Graham being then and there over the age of ten years.''

By section 342, *supra*, it is enacted ''That it shall be unlawful for any person over the age of ten years, with or without malice, purposely to point or aim any pistol, gun, revolver, or other firearm, either loaded or empty, at or toward any other person, and any person so offending shall be guilty of an unlawful act, and upon conviction shall be fined in any sum not less than one nor more than five hundred dollars.''

Appellant asserts that the indictment fails to charge a public offense, because there is no allegation to show whether the pointing was done with or without malice, and that there is no allegation to show whether the revolver was loaded or empty.

This contention can not prevail.

To constitute an offense, the pointing must be purposely done. The statute recognizes two classes of persons who may commit the offense, those who are actuated by malice and those who are actuated by foolish and mischievous motives. It also recognizes two kinds of firearms that may be pointed, those that are loaded and those that are empty. The evident purpose of the statute is to bring under the ban of the law the willful pointing of a firearm at another. The motive that actuates the person, or the kind of firearm, whether loaded or empty, are but incidental matters. The indictment charges a willful pointing of a firearm at another. These facts constitute a public offense.

The only cause for a new trial discussed by appellant

is that the verdict is not supported by sufficient evidence. There was some evidence, although very meager, which tended to support the verdict. Where the jury and trial court, who were in the living presence of the witnesses, have weighed the evidence and reached a certain conclusion, we are not warranted in disturbing the judgment, on the weight of the evidence.

Judgment affirmed, at costs of appellant.

Filed Jan. 3, 1894.

No. 1,034.

CLELAND *v.* APPLEGATE.

EVIDENCE.—*Account Books.*—*When Admissible.*—Where the transactions of a partnership with another firm became relevant to the issues of an action, the books of the firm with which such dealings were had, containing an account of the transactions, are admissible in evidence, the accurateness of the entries not being questioned, the entries having been made by a disinterested person.

ASSIGNMENT OF ERRORS.—*Assignment, Insufficiency of.*—*Evidence.*—Where an assignment of error is that "the court erred in refusing to allow the plaintiff * * to testify as to matters that occurred prior to the death of Nathan Gray," the assignment is not well made, and is insufficient, where the record shows that plaintiff was permitted to testify to many such matters.

From the Noble Circuit Court.

T. M. Eells, for appellant.

L. H. Wrigley, for appellee.

REINHARD, J.—This is an action on a promissory note executed to the appellant by one Nathan Gray, as principal, and by the appellee as surety.

There was a trial by jury, and a verdict and judgment for the appellee.

The overruling of a motion for a new trial is the only error assigned by the appellant.

It is insisted that the evidence does not sustain the verdict. One of the answers was that the note was executed without any consideration. The evidence tends to show that the note was given in partial settlement of a partnership transaction between Gray and the appellant. It also tends to establish the fact that the partnership continued to run after the execution of the note, and that no final settlement of the same has ever been effected.

It is admitted inferentially, by appellant's counsel, that if the evidence tends to prove these facts the plea of no consideration is established.

The only contention of appellant's counsel, upon this point, is upon the sufficiency of the evidence, and no issue is made upon the law touching the same. As indicated, we think the evidence is sufficient to support the theory that the note was given in a partnership transaction, and that no final settlement appears to have been made between the partners, and we need not prolong this opinion by attempting to quote such portions of the evidence as in our view strongly tend to make out this defense.

Upon the trial of the cause, it became material to show whether or not the appellant and Gray had been doing business in partnership about the time the note in suit was given. It was claimed that Gray and Cleland, as such partners, had been transacting business with another firm during the existence of such partnership, and over appellant's objection and exception, the books of the firm with which such dealings were had, and containing the accounts of Gray and Cleland, were admitted in evidence. It is insisted that this was error. It is claimed, in argument, that the testimony of the person who made the entries was the best evidence of the facts

contained therein, and that such entries are but secondary evidence.

The bookkeeper who made the entries testified to the
occurrences generally, as disclosed therein, but stated
that the particulars and dates of the transactions had es-
caped his recollection. Gray, one of the alleged partners, was dead, and the only remaining witness familiar
with the entire circumstances was the appellant. The
entries were made by a disinterested person, and in the
usual course of business. There was nothing to show
that they were in any degree inaccurate, and their truthfulness was vouched for by the testimony of the bookkeeper who made them.

We think the entries were competent, and that the
court did not err in admitting them. *Culver, Admx.*,
v. *Marks*, 122 Ind. 554.

One of the causes assigned in the motion for a new
trial is that "the court erred in refusing to allow the
plaintiff, Jonathan W. Cleland, to testify as to matters
that occurred prior to the death of Nathan Gray."

Appellee's counsel insist that this cause is not well assigned, and in this contention we are disposed to concur.
The record discloses that Cleland was permitted to give
testimony as to transactions occurring before the death
of Gray, but the court refused to allow him to testify in
relation to some transactions with Gray himself. Had
the court refused to let the appellant testify as to any
matters that occurred prior to Gray's death, the assignment would have been sufficient; and in that case it
would not have been incumbent upon the appellant to
show the materiality or relevancy of the proposed testimony. *Sutherland* v. *Hankins*, 56 Ind. 343.

But when, as in the present case, only a portion of
the testimony of the witness is excluded, it devolves
upon the appellant, in his motion for a new trial, to

point out what particular portion of the testimony was ruled out. *McClain* v. *Jessup*, 76 Ind. 120.

In other words, the motion for a new trial specifies, in effect, that the appellant was prohibited from testifying upon any matters that occurred prior to Gray's death, while the record shows that he was permitted to testify to many such matters.

The cause assigned is, therefore, not made out by the record, and we need not decide whether the ruling was right or wrong.

There is no available error.

Judgment affirmed.

Filed Jan. 3, 1894.

No. 798.

THE WALTER A. WOOD MOWING AND REAPING MACHINE COMPANY *v.* NIEHAUSE.

PLEADING.—*Answer.*— *When too Narrow.*—*Demurrer.*—An answer must fully cover the entire complaint, or so much thereof as it purports to answer, or it will be insufficient on demurrer.

From the Posey Circuit Court.

D. O. Barker and *F. P. Leonard*, for appellant.

L. M. Wade and *W. P. Edson*, for appellee.

DAVIS, C. J.—The foundation of this action is a written order, executed by appellee to appellant, for one "new single apron Wood binder (1891) carrier, six foot cut, including usual extras," at $128, and "one tarpaulin, $4."

The order, on the back of which a warranty is printed, is filed with, and made part of, appellant's complaint, as exhibit A.

The allegation in the complaint is that appellee agreed to pay $128 for the binder and $4 for the tarpaulin.

Appellee filed an answer in one paragraph, in the nature of a counterclaim, in which he "admits the execution of the contract or order sued on, but says that the same was executed in consideration of the sale by plaintiff to the defendant, of the mowing and reaping machine mentioned therein, and in consideration of the warranty of the plaintiff indorsed on the said order or contract sued on, and that as a breach of said warranty," etc.

There is no averment in the answer that the tarpaulin was a part of the machine or that the tarpaulin and machine constituted a joint purchase.

The only error assigned is the overruling of the demurrer to this answer.

Appellant contends that the answer is insufficient for two reasons:

"First. Because it purports to answer all of the complaint, whereas, in fact, it answers but a part therof, *i. e.*, that part seeking to recover for the price of the machine. Nowhere does the answer refer to the tarpaulin, or set up any facts in bar of a recovery of the purchase-price thereof.

"Second. Said answer is bad for the reason that the foundation thereof is the written and printed warranty upon the back of the order executed by appellant to appellee, and such warranty is not made a part of the pleading."

There is, in the answer, as we have seen, a plain reference to the contract "sued on," which the complaint alleges "is herewith filed and made a part hereof, marked exhibit A," but it should be borne in mind that the order is signed by appellee alone, and that the warranty only is signed by appellant. If the warranty was the instrument sued on, then the reference thereto in the an-

504   APPELLATE COURT OF INDIANA,

The Walter A. Wood Mowing and Reaping Machine Co. v. Niehause.

swer would be a sufficient showing that it was also the foundation of the counterclaim. *Sidener* v. *Davis*, 69 Ind. 336 (341).

The two writings should be construed together in determining the rights of the parties, but it is doubtful whether making the order signed by appellee a part of the complaint by reference thereto as exhibit A, is sufficient to make the warranty indorsed on the back thereof, signed by appellant, a part of the answer. The warranty is not incorporated or included in the order. As, in the view we take of the case, the answer is bad for another reason, it is not necessary to further consider this question.

It is conceded, by appellee, "that it is a general rule of pleading that an answer must fully answer the entire complaint, or so much thereof as it purports to answer," but it is insisted that the rule has no application in this case, for the reason that the tarpaulin was a part of the machine; that it was made for and fitted to the machine; that it was for the preservation of the machine; that the only difference between the tarpaulin and the paint is that the paint is permanently attached to the machine and that the tarpaulin, like the shifting top of a buggy, can be attached to or removed from it at the pleasure of the owner.

There is much force in the reasoning of counsel, and if the facts on which this argument is predicated were shown in the answer, the answer would perhaps be sufficient to withstand the demurrer.

We have noticed that the order mentions the machine and tarpaulin separately. They are treated as separate purchases in the complaint. There is nothing disclosing, except inferentially, that the tarpaulin was a covering for the machine. The answer ignores the tarpaulin entirely, and seeks to defeat a recovery in any amount by reason of the alleged failure of the warranty on the binder.

Judgment reversed, with instructions to sustain the demurrer to the answer, with leave on part of appellee to amend, at costs of appellee.

Filed Jan. 3, 1894.

No. 1,070.

SHIPPS v. ATKINSON.

SPECIAL VERDICT.—*Failure to Find Essential Fact.*—*Not Aided by Intendment.*—*Recovery.*—Where a special verdict fails to find any fact essential to support the complaint, the plaintiff must fail. The special verdict can not be aided by intendment.

SAME.—*Recovery.*—*Omission of Essential Fact.*—*Money Paid Out and Expended.*—In an action for money paid out and expended, on failure of the vendee to accept a phaeton ordered of plaintiff, the plaintiff can not recover, where the special verdict returned contains no finding as to the amount expended.

SAME.—*Recovery.*—*Omission of Essential Fact.*—*Damages.*—*Vendor and Vendee.*—In such case, where the plaintiff retains the property and sues for damages (the difference between the contract and the market value at date fixed for delivery), the plaintiff can not recover, where the special verdict contains no finding as to such damages.

From the Benton Circuit Court.

D. Fraser and *W. Isham*, for appellant.

J. T. Brown and *E. G. Hall*, for appellee.

GAVIN, J.—Appellant sued appellee to recover the price of a certain phaeton, which she had procured him to have constructed for her. The construction of the phaeton according to the order and its tender to appellee, together with her refusal to accept and her repudiation of the contract, are alleged in the complaint.

There was a special verdict, upon which the court rendered judgment in appellee's favor. The correctness of this action of the trial court is the only error argued in this court.

A special verdict must contain a finding of the facts, and if any fact essential to support the appellant's complaint is not found, then he must fail. Nothing can be supplied by intendment. A failure to find a fact in favor of a party upon whom the burden rests, is equivalent to finding such fact against him. *Noblesville Gas, etc., Co.* v. *Loehr*, 124 Ind. 79; *Cook* v. *McNaughton*, 128 Ind. 410; *Sult* v. *Warren School Township*, 36 N. E. Rep. 291.

Keeping this rule in mind, we are unable to say that the special verdict was sufficient to authorize a judgment for appellant for more than nominal damages at most.

The verdict, giving it the construction most favorable to appellant as to the making and terms of the contract, shows the contract as alleged in the complaint, the construction of the buggy as ordered, notice from appellant to appellee that it was ready for her, and her wrongful repudiation of the contract and refusal to carry it out. The verdict wholly fails to show that any tender or offer to deliver was made by appellant at the place where, by the contract, it was to be delivered, nor does any excuse for such failure appear, except appellee's repudiation of the contract.

Under such circumstances, the case comes squarely within the rule laid down in *Pittsburgh, etc., R. W. Co.* v. *Heck*, 50 Ind. 303' which was, in *Dwiggins* v. *Clark*, 94 Ind. 49, approved and applied to facts in principle, not distinguishable from those found in this case: "It is conceived that in all cases of contracts for the sale of personal property, where it has any market value, the vendor, before he can recover of the vendee, * * must have delivered the property to the vendee, or have done such acts as vested the title in the vendee, or would have vested the title in him, if he had consented to accept it; for the law will not tolerate the palpable injustice of permitting the vendor to hold the property, and also to recover the price of it." *Indianapolis, etc., R. W. Co. v. Maguire*, 62 Ind. 140; *Fell v. Muller*, 78 Ind. 507; *Ganson v. Madigan*, 13 Wis. 67; *Neal v. Shewalter*, 5 Ind. App. 147, 31 N. E. Rep. 851.

In *Dwiggins v. Clark, supra,* there was a contract for the manufacture of a monument with certain letters and mottoes upon it, to be delivered at Waynetown, Ind. The monument was completed according to contract, and ready for delivery, and the purchaser notified thereof, but she refused to receive it. The court holds that under such circumstances no action can be maintained for the contract price.

A repudiation of the contract by the purchaser relieves the seller from further compliance with the contract on his part so far as to enable him to maintain an action for damages for the breach of the contract, but in order to sustain an action for the contract price as upon an executed contract, he must, upon his part, comply entirely with the contract.

The appellant seeks to give to his complaint a triune character. First, he insists upon his right to recover the contract price as upon an executed contract. If that fails, he next urges that he should recover the damages suffered by reason of appellee's failure to accept the phaeton; and, lastly, he counts upon it as a complaint to recover money laid out and expended at appellee's instance and request.

We will not stop to consider whether or not the rules of pleading permit us to view the complaint as such a multiform creation,—*Chicago, etc., R. W. Co. v. Burger,* 124 Ind. 275; *Thomas v. Dale,* 86 Ind. 435,—but will briefly consider whether or not the latter positions taken by counsel are supported by the special verdict.

By the case of *Dwiggins* v. *Clark, supra*, it is established that the measure of damages, upon a breach of the contract, where the vendor retains the property as his own, is the difference between the contract price of the article and its market value at the time and place fixed for its delivery.

In *Pittsburgh, etc., R. W. Co.* v. *Heck, supra*, the rule laid down in Chitty on Cont., 11 Am. Ed. 1331, is quoted and approved: "In an action for not accepting goods, the measure of damages is the difference between the contract price and the market price, on the day when the vendee ought to have accepted the goods." Numerous cases are there cited to sustain the position taken.

To the same effect also is Benjamin on Sales, sections 1117, 1118.

In Tiedeman on Sales, section 333, it is stated that in such actions as we are now considering the measure of damages is the "difference between the contract price and the market value of the goods at the time of delivery."

This being the law, it is essential that the special verdict should show the value of the property at the time and place of delivery, else it will be impossible for the amount to be ascertained. In this verdict, such value is not shown. There is, therefore, no basis furnished by the verdict upon which the damages may be calculated. The value of the property at some time subsequent to the time of delivery will not supply the defect.

We can not say, as a matter of law, that the value remained unchanged.

In *Fell* v. *Muller*, 78 Ind. 507, the complaint was held bad because it did not show the difference between the contract price and the market price at the time and place of delivery, there being no general allegation of damages suffered.

Neither is the verdict sufficient to sustain the claim for money paid out and expended, because there is no finding as to the amount expended by appellant.

It is clear that the verdict was insufficient to authorize a judgment for appellant for either the $120 or the $20, as asked by him.

If it be conceded that he was entitled to nominal damages, the refusal to award them is not reversible error. *Wimberg* v. *Schwegeman*, 97 Ind. 528.

Judgment affirmed.

Filed Jan. 31, 1894.

———————— ♦ ————————

No. 999.

JAAP *v.* DIGMAN ET AL.

PLEADING.—*Complaint, Sufficiency of.*—*To Set Aside Final Settlement.*—*Decedent's Estate.*—*Fraud.*—The final settlement of an estate may be set aside for mistake, fraud or illegality, as provided by section 2403, R. S. 1881. And a complaint comes within the provisions of the above section which states, in substance, that the defendants, seeking to cheat and defraud plaintiff out of his right in the property left him by his father and mother, both deceased, by falsely representing to the court that this plaintiff was dead, his whereabouts not being known since 1872, it now being 1887, by reason of which representations they caused plaintiff's estate to be administered upon, etc., in which a final settlement was made, etc., all of which proceedings were unknown to plaintiff, and whereas, in truth and in fact, the whereabouts of plaintiff was known to defendants all of such time. Wherefore, etc.

From the Allen Circuit Court.

H. Colerick and *J. E. K. France*, for appellant.

T. E. Ellison, for appellees.

Ross, J.—The appellee James Digman brought this action in the court below, against the appellant, to set aside the approval of the report of appellant as administrator of the estate of the appellee James Digman, an absent person, and to require an accounting to him for his property.

There is but one question presented by the record, which is argued by counsel, which will be considered on this appeal, and that question is as to the sufficiency of the facts stated in the complaint to constitute a cause of action.

The complaint, which is in two paragraphs, is as follows:

"James Digman complains of George Jaap, Mary Jaap, James D. White and J. E. K. France, and says that said Mary Jaap is his sister and said George Jaap is her husband; that this plaintiff's father, Phillip Digman, died in 1865, leaving a small estate in this county; that Elizabeth Digman, this plaintiff's mother, said Mary, and this plaintiff were his only heirs; that said Elizabeth, shortly after the death of her said husband, became insane, and so continued until her death, in 1889, and was confined in either the State asylum or the county asylum during that period; that because of the death of their father and the insanity of their mother, this plaintiff was taken to the Catholic Orphan Asylum at Rensselaer, Indiana, when but a small child, and, having no home, he worked for such people and at such places as he could find employment, mostly in this State, from that time until now; that said Jaap wrongfully and wickedly conceived the idea of cheating and defrauding this plaintiff out of the little property left him by his father and the interest he might have in his mother's estate; that to more speedily accomplish that purpose they did, on the 10th day of January, 1887, file a petition in this court, in which they falsely and fraudulently represented to this court that the estate belonging to this plaintiff was going to waste, and that they had had no knowledge of his whereabouts since November, 1872, when in truth and in fact they knew that he was alive, and were informed where he could be found; that by reason of such fraudulent and false representations, they did procure an order from this court finding that this plaintiff was dead, and letters of administration were granted on his estate, to said George Jaap, and his said codefendants, James B. White and J. E. K. France, became and were his bondsmen as such administrator; that said bond has been lost, so that a copy of said bond can not be filed herewith; that this plaintiff does not know what property came into the hands of said Jaap, but is informed and believes that he received over twelve hundred dollars ($1,200), in property and money, belonging to this plaintiff, which he wrongfully and unlawfully converted to his own use and to the use of himself and said Mary Jaap; that to carry out said scheme, he caused the publication to be made in the Indianapolis Sentinel and in the Fort Wayne Dispatch, well knowing that this plaintiff would never hear or know of the same, when in truth and in fact he knew, or could have found out, from information he then had, just where this plaintiff was; that on the 16th day of April, 1888, said Jaap filed a pretended final report, in which he set forth that this plaintiff was deceased, and that said Mary Jaap was entitled, as the sister of this plaintiff, to one-half of his estate, and that said George Jaap, as the guardian of the said Elizabeth Digman, was entitled to the other half; that he took and kept for his own use, for his pretended services in so defrauding this plaintiff, the sum of thirty dollars ($30), and that he paid out fifty dollars ($50) of other costs and expenses wholly unnecessary and wrongfully; that in December, 1888, said Jaap made such representations to this court as to the death and decease of this plaintiff, and to his having given notice thereof, that this court did approve of said final report, and discharged said Jaap from further acting as such administrator; and the plaintiff avers that all the acts done by said Jaap were fraudulent and void as to this plaintiff, and that the representations made by him to procure the same were false, and known by him to be so at the time when made, and that they should all be set aside; that said James B. White and J. E. K. France, in the execution of said bond, wrongfully combined and conspired and made it possible for said George Jaap and Mary Jaap to commit said fraud on this plaintiff, well knowing that such proceedings were not authorized by law, and that the same were wrongful, fraudulent and void as to this plaintiff; that this plaintiff knew nothing of any of said proceedings until within the last six weeks, and never surmised that said defendants were doing or had done any of said acts.

"Wherefore this plaintiff asks that the approval of all reports and acts done by said George Jaap be set aside and declared fraudulent and void, and that he have judgment for two thousand dollars ($2,000) against all of said defendants, and that said judgment be declared to be without relief from valuation and appraisement laws, and all homestead and exemption laws, and for all other proper and equitable relief."

For a second cause of action, the plaintiff says:

"That his father, Phillip Digman, died in 1865, the owner of certain real estate in this county; that Elizabeth Digman, the wife of the said Phillip and mother of this plaintiff and the defendant Mary Jaap, shortly after the death of his said father, became insane, and so continued until her death in 1889; that John Nail became and was for several years the guardian of this plaintiff; that said George Jaap is the husband of Mary Jaap, and that they two conceived the purpose of cheating and defrauding this plaintiff out of his interest in his father's and mother's estate; that they brought an action for the partition of said real estate, and procured an order of this court that the same was indivisible, and an order appointing the defendant herein, J. E. K. France, a commissioner to sell the same, when said property could easily have been divided between said parties; that said France, as such commissioner, sold said property to said George Jaap for much less than its real value; that failing in said action to get possession of this plaintiff's interest in said real estate, they did, on the 10th day of January, 1887, file a petition in this court to declare this plaintiff dead, and made such representations to this court that said George Jaap was appointed administrator of the plaintiff's estate, and authorized to take possession of all property and assets belonging to him, and in order to enable him so to do, he filed a bond; that said bond has been lost, so that a copy thereof can not be filed herewith, executed by said James B. White and J. E. K. France as his sureties; that the plaintiff does not know what property or assets he received, but is informed and believes that the sum amounted to about twelve hundred dollars ($1,200); that in April, 1888, said George Jaap, as administrator, filed a report in this court, setting forth the decease of this plaintiff, and that said Mary Jaap and himself, as guardian for Elizabeth Digman, were entitled to all the assets in said estate, and made such false and fraudulent representations to this court that his acts as such administrator were approved, and said money was paid over to said Mary Jaap and himself, when in truth and in fact this plaintiff was known to be alive, and his

whereabouts could have been ascertained if they had so
desired; that this plaintiff did not know that any of said
facts nor that any of said acts had been done or occurred
till within three months last past.

"Wherefore plaintiff says that by reason of said wrongful acts the said defendants came into and have possession of said sum of twelve hundred dollars ($1,200), in
property and assets, belonging to this plaintiff, and plaintiff demands judgment that all of said proceedings of this
court be declared fraudulent and void, and that said defendants be required to account to him for the value of
all the property which came into their hands by any and
all of said proceedings, and that he have judgment for
two thousand dollars ($2,000), and that the same be de-
clared a trust; that said defendants be required to pay
the same to him out of any property or money they may
have, or be deemed in contempt of this court, and pun-
ishable as for contempt in failing so to do."

The appellant insists that "By this complaint, the appellee, James, in this action seeks to have the court open
up the matter of the partition judgment; wipe out collaterally the judgment finding him dead; call upon appellant again to report his stewardship as his guardian;
likewise to report as his mother's guardian, and to again
report and settle with the court as his administrator;"
and, further, that this is a collateral attack upon the
judgments pleaded, and that they are unassailable and
unimpeachable in such a proceeding.

On the other hand, it is insisted, by counsel for appellees, that this is a proceeding to set aside the final report made by the appellant as administrator, and to compel him to account for the money in his hands belonging
to appellee James Digman.

The approval of an administrator's or guardian's final
report and settlement is a final adjudication of all mat-

ters appertaining thereto, and precludes all collateral inquiry into the correctness thereof, by the parties interested therein, who have been duly notified, so long as such judgment of approval remains in force. *Pate, Exr.*, v. *Moore, Admr.*, 79 Ind. 20; *Carver* v. *Lewis, Admr.*, 105 Ind. 44; *Castetter, Admr.*, v. *State, ex rel.*, 112 Ind. 445.

The judgment of approval of the final report and settlement may be set aside at any time within three years from the date of such settlement, at the instance of any person interested in the estate, who neither appeared at the final settlement nor was personally served with a summons to attend the same, and if a minor, or under legal disability at the time of such final settlement, at any time within three years after the removal or cessation of such disability. Section 2403, R. S. 1881.

The judgment of approval is an adjudication only so far as it rests upon matters properly embraced within such report, relative to the proper management and settlement of the ward's estate. *Wainwright* v. *Smith*, 106 Ind. 239.

Under section 2403, *supra*, the approval of a final report and settlement of an estate may be set aside for mistake, fraud, or illegality. *Pollard* v. *Barkley*, 117 Ind. 40.

The complaint or petition in this case is apparently intended to come within the requirements of that section, and we think it sufficient for that purpose.

There is no error in the record.

Judgment affirmed.

Filed Jan. 4, 1894.

No. 971.

Lynch *v*. The Chicago, St. Louis and Pittsburgh Railroad Company.

EMPLOYER AND EMPLOYE.—*Personal Injury.*—*Knowledge of Defects and Danger by Employe.*—*Assumption of Risks.*—*Judgment on Answers to Interrogatories, Non Obstante.*—In an action for damages for personal injuries received while in the employment of rolling car wheels, in which a general verdict was rendered for plaintiff, it was not error for the court, on motion, to render judgment for defendant on the answers to interrogatories, which established the fact that plaintiff had knowledge of the defective condition of the track on which the wheels were rolled, and of the danger attendant thereon, the want of such knowledge by plaintiff being essential to the sufficiency of the complaint.

SAME.—*Knowledge of Condition of Appliance.*—In such case, a finding that the employe knew the condition of the track, fastens upon him not only knowledge of some, but of all the defects existing in the track.

From the Marion Superior Court.

J. E. McCullough and *L. P. Harlan*, for appellant.

S. O. Pickens, for appellee.

GAVIN, J.—The appellant sued appellee for damages occasioned by injuries suffered by him while rolling car wheels in the line of his employment and under the direction and command of appellant.

It was alleged, in the complaint, that the wheels weighed six hundred pounds and were rolled along a plank track consisting of planks laid lengthwise loosely nailed at the ends, with rotten edges and with cracks between the planks, which were filled in with dirt or other soft material and covered over with dust, so that the flanges of the wheels would run into the cracks, and fall. While engaged in rolling a wheel, it rolled into a crack between the planks, spread them apart, and thereby caught appellant's foot, and fell over on it, all without any fault on his part and solely by reason of appellee's negligence. Knowledge of the defect and danger by the appellee, and want of such knowledge upon the part of the appellant, are expressly alleged.

Upon the trial there was a general verdict for appellant, with answers to interrogatories. Upon these answers judgment was rendered in favor of the appellee over appellant's exception. The correctness of this action of the court is presented for our consideration.

From the interrogatories and answers thereto, it appears that appellant was injured, as alleged in the complaint, while engaged in the line of duty, rolling car wheels over a track formed by three rows of boards laid lengthwise, with a crack between the boards one inch or more wide, filled in with cinders; that for a month before the accident the crack had been in the same condition as at the time of its occurrence; that appellee had been employed as a roustabout forty or forty-five days before he was hurt, but had, on one occasion, rolled eight or ten wheels over this track before that day, and upon the day of the accident, had rolled four or five before he was hurt. He had been instructed how to roll the wheels and of the danger connected with rolling them, and how to avoid such danger, before the time of the injury, but not by the foreman. The danger connected with the rolling of wheels and the way to avoid it was apparent to a person of ordinary intelligence and judgment.

Appellant was forty years old, and in full possession of his sense of sight. The crack into which the wheel rolled was in such condition that it could be seen that a crack was at that place, by a person walking over the boards at that place, if he gave ordinary attention to the place where he was walking; appellant could have known of the condition of the boards and of the existence of the

crack before that day, if he had exercised ordinary care
and diligence in his work about the yards and in his
surroundings, and did know such facts prior to such
day.   He also knew, or by the exercise of ordinary care
and attention could have known, that in rolling the
wheel over the boards where he was injured it was liable
to run into a crack, and fall.   He knew also of the condition of the track where he was hurt and of the existence of the crack in question, before the wheel ran into
the crack, and that the wheel was liable to run into it.

It is undisputed that the answers to interrogatories will
not control the general verdict, unless irreconcilable with
it.   Nor will the answers be aided by intendment.   The
answers must, of themselves, establish some fact or facts
which are absolutely incompatible with the appellant's
right to recover upon any evidence admissible under the
pleadings, else the general verdict must stand.   *Ohio,
etc., R. W. Co.* v. *Trowbridge,* 126 Ind. 391; *Town of
Poseyville* v. *Lewis,* 126 Ind. 80; *Chicago, etc., R. W. Co.*
v. *Spilker,* 134 Ind. 380, 33 N. E. Rep. 280; *Evansville,
etc., R. W. Co.* v. *Weikle,* 6 Ind. App. 340, 33 N. E. Rep.
639.

The only question presented by these answers is as to
the assumption of the risk of the defective track by appellant.

Applying to the facts specially found a strict and not
a liberal rule of construction, we still think it clearly appears that since appellant knew the condition of the
track and the existence of the crack in question, and
that the wheel was liable to run into it, and also knew,
or by the exercise of reasonable care might have known,
that the wheel was liable to run into a crack, and fall, he
is chargeable with knowledge, both of the defect and of
the danger.

The finding that he knew the condition of the track

fastens upon him not only knowledge of some but of all the defects existing in the track.

The law requires the master to exercise reasonable care to provide his employes with safe working places and appliances. *Kentucky, etc., Bridge Co. v. Eastman,* 7 Ind. App. 514, 34 N. E. Rep. 835; *Evansville, etc., R. W. Co. v. Holcomb,* 36 N. E. Rep. 39, and cases there cited.

It is also settled as a general rule in Indiana that the employe can not recover from the master for injuries suffered by reason of defects in the place where he works, or the machinery or appliances with which he works where the danger is known to him at the time of his employment or where he voluntarily remains in the service after he has acquired such knowledge, or, by the exercise of due care, should have acquired it. Under such circumstances he is deemed to have assumed the risk. *Ames, Admr., v. Lake Shore, etc., R. W. Co.,* 135 Ind. 363, 35 N. E. Rep. 117; *Evansville, etc., R. R. Co. v. Duel,* 134 Ind. 156, 33 N. E. Rep. 355; *Swanson v. City of Lafayette,* 134 Ind. 625, 33 N. E. Rep. 1033; *Kentucky, etc., Bridge Co. v. Eastman, supra; W. C. DePauw Co. v. Stubblefield,* 132 Ind. 182; *Brazil Block Coal Co. v. Hoodlet,* 129 Ind. 327; *Rogers v. Leyden,* 127 Ind. 50; *Louisville, etc., R. W. Co. v. Corps,* 124 Ind. 427; *Louisville, etc., R. W. Co. v. Sandford, Admx.,* 117 Ind. 265; *Rietman v. Stolte,* 120 Ind. 314; *Indianapolis, etc., R. W. Co. v. Watson,* 114 Ind. 20.

Where the employe's continuance in the service is induced by the master's promise to remedy the defect, either express or implied, there is an exception to this general rule. *Becker v. Baumgartner,* 5 Ind. App. 576, 32 N. E. Rep. 786; *Indianapolis, etc., R. W. Co. v. Watson, supra; Joliet, etc., R. W. Co. v. Velie,* 26 N. E. Rep.

1086; *Roux* v. *Lumber Co.*, 85 Mich. 519; *Greene* v. *Min-neapolis, etc., R. W. Co.*, 31 Minn. 248.

So, also, there is an exception where by the direction of the employer he undertakes some work outside of the line of or away from the place of his regular employment. *Brazil Block Coal Co.* v. *Hoodlet, supra;* *Louis-ville, etc., R. W. Co.* v. *Hanning, Admr.*, 131 Ind. 528; *Cincinnati, etc., R. R. Co.* v. *Madden*, 134 Ind. 462, 34 N. E. Rep. 227.

There may also be other exceptions, but we are not concerned with them here.

While there is a conflict between the adjudicated cases and the text writers as to whether working with such knowledge of a dangerous defect constitutes an assumption of the risk occasioned thereby, or is simply one factor going to establish contributory negligence—Buswell on Pers. Inj., sections 207, 208, 209—the question can not be regarded as an open one in Indiana. The cases to which we have referred establish this knowledge as an independent element separate and distinct from contributory negligence.

The rule has been thus stated: "That an employe who knows, or by the exercise of ordinary diligence could know, of any defects or imperfections in the things about which he is employed, and continues in the service without objection, and without promise of change, is presumed to have assumed all the consequences resultant from such defects, and to have waived all right to recover for injuries caused thereby." *Jenney, etc., Co.* v. *Murphy*, 115 Ind. 566.

In order that he shall be deemed to have assumed the risk, he must be chargeable with knowledge not only of the defect, but of the danger therefrom. *Rogers* v. *Leyden*, 127 Ind. 50.

In *Louisville, etc., R. W. Co.* v. *Sandford, Admx.*, 117

Ind. 265, speaking concerning the master's duty to furnish a safe place to work, the court says: "But if he fails to do his full duty, and the employe has seasonable and adequate knowledge of the failure and continues in the service, he assumes the risk resulting from this failure."

Counsel for the appellant endeavor to take this case out of the general rule upon the ground that under the general verdict it may have been found that the servant did the act in doing which he was injured by the express command and direction of the master, and did not, therefore, assume the risk, even though known. This question we do not feel called upon to determine, for the reason that we are fully satisfied that this is not the case made out by the complaint, and such proof would not sustain the complaint.

Under the authorities which we have referred to, the complaint would be bad on demurrer, did it not contain the allegation of want of knowledge of the defect and danger.

The allegations of the complaint are that on the said "11th day of April, 1890, and at the time of receiving the injury hereinafter complained of, the plaintiff, acting under the command and direction of said defendant and within the scope of his said employment, was engaged in rolling car wheels," etc. * * * And, that "while so engaged, with others, in rolling car wheels over the defendant's said line of roadway, under the command and direction of said defendant, and within the scope of his said employment and without any negligence or carelessness upon his part, and while balancing and rolling said car wheels on the flanges thereof, as was the usual and customary way of rolling said wheels, and as it was his duty, and as he was required to do, the wheel which plaintiff was rolling rolled into a crack," etc. This is the only reference to command or direction by the master, and when coupled with the allegations of absolute ignorance by appellant of the defect and danger, these allegations could not be deemed supported by proof of actual knowledge and reliance upon a direct command to relieve him from the results attaching to that knowledge.   Such proof would present a case radically and essentially different from that set forth in the pleading, and where this is the case the pleading is not sustained thereby.   *Cleveland, etc., R. W. Co.* v. *Wynant,* 100 Ind. 160; *Armacost, Admr.,* v. *Lindley, Admr.,* 116 Ind. 295.

In *Becker* v. *Baumgartner, supra,* it is said: "The complaint is predicated, though imperfectly, upon the theory that appellee was ignorant of the danger, and this will not be supported by proof that he did know all about it, but remained in the service upon appellant's promise to provide a remedy."

If want of knowledge by appellant was essential to the sufficiency of his complaint, as we have held, then it necessarily follows that when that essential fact was found against him, he must fail.

We are, therefore, forced to the conclusion that there was no error in rendering judgment against him.

Judgment affirmed.

Filed Jan. 4, 1894

No. 929.

FERGUSON ET AL. *v.* DESPO ET AL.

ASSIGNMENT OF ERRORS.—*Omission of Name from Title.*—*Supplied in Body of Assignment.*—*Sufficiency.*—An omission to give the name of a party appellant in the title of an assignment of error may be supplied in the body of the assignment, and the assignment in that respect will be sufficient.

PLEADING.—*Complaint, Sufficiency of Facts.*—*No Cause of Action Against Part of Defendants.*—*Subcontractor.*—*Mechanic's Lien.*—*Personal Liability.*—A railroad company contracted with A. to construct certain piers and abutments for a bridge, and A. in turn sublet the work to B., and B. contracted with C. for labor and materials. Under such contract, C. performed labor and furnished certain materials, and in due time filed his notice of intention to hold a lien for the same. C. brought suit against A. and B. and the railroad company for the amount due, praying judgment against the several defendants, and for a foreclosure of his lien, etc. Under such circumstances has C. a cause of action against A.?

Held, that, as the facts do not disclose any state of facts which would make A. personally liable to C., there being no privity between them, nor any principle of subrogation whereby C. could succeed to the rights of A., the benefits of the labor performed and the materials furnished by C. having enured, alone, to B. and the railroad company, no cause of action existed against A.

MECHANIC'S LIEN.—*What Constitutes.*—*Labor.*—*Board, Groceries, Money Furnished, etc.*—*Railroad.*—In an action on a mechanic's, etc., lien for labor performed as a foreman in the construction of the masonry for a bridge for a railroad company, the account contained items, besides that for the labor performed, for board, groceries, tobacco, and money furnished the other employes of the contractors.

Held, that the item for labor properly constitutes a lien, but that the other items for board, groceries, etc., not being materials entering into the construction of the work, constituted no lien.

SAME.—*Railroad Laborer.*—*Lien, How Obtained.*—*Notice.*—*Statute Repealed.*—Where labor was performed for a railway company in 1889 and 1890, in constructing masonry for a bridge, the employe, whether of a contractor or subcontractor, may have a lien for such work upon filing notice of intention to hold a lien, and no other notice (as provided by the act of March 6, 1883, section 9) is necessary, such section, as to notice, having been expressly repealed by the act of March 9, 1889, section 6.

SAME.—*Demand.*—In such case, where notice of intention to hold a lien was duly filed, a demand for the money due is not necessary before an action will lie.

From the Lawrence Circuit Court.

M. F. Dunn, for appellants.

W. W. Herod and *W. P. Herod,* for appellees.

REINHARD, J.—We are asked to dismiss this appeal or affirm the judgment on the ground of an alleged defect in the assignment of errors.

The amended assignment in the title of the cause leaves out the name of one of the appellants. In the body of the assignment, however, the names of all the parties are given thus: "The above named appellants (naming each of them) file this their amended assignment of errors, making their co-defendants below in the Lawrence Circuit Court (naming them) co-appellees with said other appellee, Alfred O. Despo, for the reason that said (naming the co-appellees) have not joined in this appeal, and assign additional errors." Then follow the separate assignments of errors.

We regard the assignment as sufficient. The assignment of errors is the appellant's complaint in this court. It must contain the names of all the parties to the appeal, and a failure makes the assignment fatally defective. Elliott's App. Proced., section 322.

This is likewise required of a complaint under the code. R. S. 1881, section 338.

But it has been held that the omission to give the names of the parties in the title may be supplied by naming them in the body of the complaint. *Ammerman* v. *Crosby,* 26 Ind. 451; 1 Works Pr. and Pl., sections 344, 345.

Despo brought this action against the appellees, Cummings and Conner, partners, and the appellants, Francis

M., Emma, and Mary Ferguson, partners, and the Cincinnati and Bedford Railway Company.

The substance of the complaint is that in November, 1889, the Fergusons, as partners, entered into a contract with the said railway company for the construction of the railroad, track, and bridges of said company, or certain parts thereof; that by the contract the Fergusons were to erect and construct the abutments, piers and masonry work for a certain bridge over the east fork of White river, near Bedford, in Lawrence county, Indiana, as a part of said railway; that the Fergusons contracted with Cummings and Conner for the construction of the stone work and masonry for such bridge; that Cummings and Conner entered upon the work and completed it according to the agreement; that Despo furnished Cummings and Conner goods and merchandise on account of, and necessary to, the building and construction of said stone work and masonry to the amount of $918.44, at the special instance and request of said Cummings and Conner; that such work and labor and materials were performed, furnished, and used in the erection and construction of said stone work and masonry of said bridge; that at the time Cummings and Conner commenced said work on said bridge, they contracted with said Despo to act as foreman and manager for them in the erection and construction of said stone work and masonry of said bridge at the agreed price of $100 per month, during the time said Cummings and Conner were engaged in said work; that Despo performed all his duties as such foreman or manager from November 25, 1889, until June 20, 1890, but that he only received $116 in all for his labor, and that there yet remains due him $504, which is wholly due and unpaid, although payment has been demanded of each and all the defendants for all of said sums.

Plaintiff files herewith an itemized statement of account marked "Exhibit A." That on the 19th day of August, 1890, and within sixty days of the time of furnishing said materials and performing said work, plaintiff filed in the office of the recorder of Lawrence county, Indiana, notice of his intention to hold a lien on the property of said railway company, which notice was duly recorded on the 19th day of August, 1890, and a copy of which is filed herewith, marked "Exhibit B."

Wherefore, plaintiff prays judgment against the several defendants above named, in the sum of $2,500, for the foreclosure of said mechanic's lien and for a sale of the railway property, together with all the appurtenances thereunto belonging within said county of Lawrence, and all proper relief.

The itemized account and copy of lien notice are filed as exhibits A and B.

Among the specifications of errors following the title of the cause, and the statement hereinbefore set out containing the names of appellants and appellees, is the following: "4th. Francis M. Ferguson, Mary Ferguson, and Emma Ferguson, and each of them, say that the court erred in overruling their separate and joint demurrer to the complaint of the appellee."

The next assignment is as follows: "5th. Francis M. Ferguson, Mary Ferguson, and Emma Ferguson, for themselves, and each for himself and herself, say that the complaint does not contain facts sufficient to constitute a cause of action against them or either of them."

The record shows the filing of the following demurrer, omitting the caption and title:

"4th. Francis M. Ferguson, Mary Ferguson, and Emma Ferguson, each for themselves, separately and severally, as well as for himself and herself jointly, demur to the complaint herein, for the reason that said complaint does not contain facts sufficient to constitute a good cause of action against them, or either of them, separately or severally or jointly.''

The demurrer is signed by the attorney for defendants.

The record further shows that ''the demurrers heretofore filed are, by the court, overruled, and to this ruling the defendants each except.''

Counsel for appellee Despo insist that these assignments, and the demurrer and rulings thereon, do not present any question which this court can consider as a separate error against the Fergusons.

After a careful consideration of the question, we have come to the conclusion that the same is properly presented. The point we are to decide, therefore, is whether the complaint states a cause of action against the appellants Francis M., Mary, and Emma Ferguson.

It will be noticed, by reading the complaint, that it is nowhere alleged that the appellants above named ever, at any time, employed Despo to do any work for them. Nor does it appear that they were the owners of the property upon which the work was done. It is shown that the railway company contracted with them to construct the work, and they in turn contracted with Cummings and Conner, and that the latter, as partners, employed and contracted with Despo for the work and materials. Whatever benefit was received from the work and materials furnished by Despo enured to Cumming and Conner and the railway company, the latter as the owners of the property, and the former as the contractors who did the work. The action is not merely for the enforcement of a mechanic's and material man's lien, but it is to obtain a personal judgment against each of the defendants. In our opinion, the complaint does not disclose any state of facts which would make the Fergusons personally liable. It does not appear that they owed Cummings

and Conner anything upon the contract, or that there is
any privity between Despo and the Fergusons, and no
principle of subrogation enters in by which Despo could
succeed to any rights of said Fergusons. The demurrer
as to them should have been sustained.

The further question is made that there is no cause of
action against the railway company. Upon an investigation of the record, we entertain grave doubts as to
whether any such question as affecting said company is
properly presented, but, in view of our conclusion upon
this subject, we have thought it best to decide the question. The bill of particulars contains all the items for
which the appellee Despo seeks to recover. Besides the
item of work and labor done in superintending the stone
and masonry work, we do not think there are any for
which the railway company could be held liable, either
personally or by a charge upon its property in the way
of a lien. These items are such as board, groceries,
tobacco and money furnished the hands and workmen of
Cummings and Conner, none of them being materials
that went into the construction of the work. We think,
however, that the work and labor in superintending the
job of the stone-work and masonry on the piers and
abutments of the bridge is an item that properly enters
into Despo's lien, and for which he has a right to hold
the company if he is otherwise entitled to recover,
against it.

The work sued for was commenced in November, 1889,
and finished in 1890, and it is admitted by counsel on
both sides that the rights of the appellee Despo under
his lien must be determined by the law of 1889 in relation to mechanic's and material men's liens, unless there
are prior laws unrepealed that are applicable to it.

The act approved March 9, 1889, p. 258, in section 6
amending section 1 of the act of April 13, 1885, p. 236,

provides that all persons who shall perform work or labor, or furnish materials in the way of grading, building embankments, making excavations for the track, building bridges, trestle work, work of masonry, fencing or any other structure, etc., whether the work or labor performed or materials furnished be in pursuance of the contract with the railroad company as owner or lessee, or with a subcontractor or agent of such railroad corporation in the work of constructing or repairing any such railroad or part thereof, in this State, may have a lien to the extent of the labor performed or materials furnished, or both, upon the right of way and franchises of the corporation within the limits of the county in which such labor is performed or materials furnished, and upon all works and structures in this section mentioned. It is expressly provided that if the work is done or material furnished in pursuance of a contract with any person, corporation or company engaged as lessee, subcontractor, or agent of any railroad corporation in the construction or repairing of any railroad, as before mentioned, the person performing such labor or furnishing such material shall not be required to give notice to such corporation, as provided by section 9, p. 142, of the act approved March 6, 1883, in order to entitle him to hold a lien for such labor or material, but the performing of the labor and furnishing of the material shall be sufficient notice to such corporation.

It is further provided that all the provisions of the act of March 6, 1883, when applicable, shall remain in force, in aid of the amended section, except that part of section 9 in reference to notice. Elliott's Supp., section 1710.

A bare statement of the provisions of this section, we think, is sufficient to show that no notice is necessary to the railroad company further than the filing of the notice of intention to hold a lien, as required by section 1707, Elliott's Supp.

The contention of the appellant, therefore, that notice is still required in order to hold the company for the lien, can not prevail.

We are, therefore, of the opinion that the court committed no error against the railway company in overruling its demurrer to the complaint, and that the complaint is sufficient for a foreclosure of the lien against said company.

Error is further predicated upon the conclusions of law which the court made upon its special finding of facts. The assignment of error in this particular is joint, and there might be some question as to whether the point is properly presented. We may say, however, that we have carefully examined the special findings and legal conclusions, and so far as they affect the railway company the conclusions are fully justified by the findings. It appears that none of the improper items contained in the bill of particulars were allowed by the court, and that all proper credits to which the company was entitled were given.

It is further insisted that there is no finding that a proper demand was made of the defendants before suit. In this we think counsel are mistaken, but we do not regard it necessary that a demand should have been made of the company. If the work was done and the materials were furnished, as found, and a notice of intention to hold a lien was filed within the time and in the manner required by the statute, which the court finds was done, we know of no rule, statutory or otherwise, that requires a specific demand for the money due before an action will lie.

Other errors are assigned but not specifically discussed

in the brief of appellant's counsel, and we need not, therefore, consider them.

The judgment and decree of the court against the Cincinnati and Bedford Railway Company is affirmed, and the judgment against Francis M. Ferguson, Mary Ferguson and Emma Ferguson is reversed, with instructions to the court below to sustain the demurrer of said appellants to the appellee's complaint, and for further proceedings as between said appellee and said appellants, Francis M. Ferguson, Mary Ferguson, and Emma Ferguson, not inconsistent with this opinion.

Filed June 24, 1893.

No. 1,063.

THORNBURG, ADMINISTRATOR, v. ALLMAN.

DECEDENT'S ESTATE.—*Claim.*—*Witness.*—*Competency.*—*Adverse Interest.*—*Principal and Surety.*—In an action on a claim against a decedent's estate, wherein the claimant alleged that he, as surety for the decedent, was compelled to pay the amount due on a certain note, the note, which was introduced in evidence, purporting to have been executed as the joint and several obligation of all the makers, *i. e.*, the decedent, the claimant and one A., A. is incompetent as a witness to testify as to the question of principal and suretyship in such transaction, A.'s interest in the controversy being adverse to that of the estate, and the mere fact that A., at the time of the trial, was insolvent, does not strip him of such interest.

From the Marshall Circuit Court.

J. D. McLaren and *E. C. Martindale*, for appellant.

L. M. Lauer, for appellee.

LOTZ, J.—The appellee filed a claim against the estate of appellant's decedent. The claim was rejected and transferred to the issue docket for trial. There was a trial by jury, a verdict and an allowance in favor of the appellee.

The amended complaint avers, in substance, that on the 9th day of June, 1891, the appellee signed a certain note for one hundred dollars, due in six months from its date, payable to the order of the First National Bank of Marshall County, with eight per cent. interest after maturity and ten per cent. attorney's fees, as the surety of appellant's decedent, Harvey Thornburg; that said note was the last of a number of renewal notes that had been given to said bank, the original of which was executed by one Bernard E. Ryder as principal, and the said Thornburg and plaintiff as the sureties of the said Ryder, the date of said original note being October 23, 1879; that said note was renewed from time to time until the year of 1884 or 1885, when, by the contract of all the makers of said note, the plaintiff became the surety of said decedent only, and continued in that relation on all the subsequent renewals; that suit was instituted on said note against the plaintiff, and he was compelled to and did pay the same, with interest, costs, and attorney's fees.

A copy of the last note is filed with the complaint and made an exhibit. This note was signed by Ryder, Thornburg, and the appellee, Allman, as makers, and was the joint and several note of each.

On the trial of the cause, the appellee gave the note in evidence, and he also called as a witness in his own behalf, the said Ryder. The appellant objected to the competency of the said Ryder as a witness, assigning, among other causes, that he was a party in interest, being one of the makers of the note. This objection was overruled, to which ruling the appellant saved an exception, and properly assigned the same as a cause for a new trial.

The competency of Ryder as a witness for the appellee is the controlling question in this case.

Ryder testified, in brief, that when the first note was made, in 1879, he received the whole of the money; that he was the principal and Thornburg and Allman sureties for him; that this relation continued until the year of 1886. Prior to this time he had placed in the hands of Thornburg collaterals to secure said Thornburg against liability on such indorsement. Thornburg had derived money enough from the collaterals to pay the note, and Ryder wanted it applied in payment. Thornburg, desiring to use the money, made an arrangement with Allman, by which Allman was to become the surety of Thornburg, and it was agreed that the note should be renewed at the bank, by all the parties signing the renewals in the same order as before.

This action is not a suit on the note, but is a suit to recover money paid by a surety for the use and benefit of his principal. It was not necessary to make the note or a copy thereof an exhibit to the complaint. It was necessary, however, for the plaintiff to aver that he had paid money for the benefit and use of the decedent, or of his estate, in discharge of a duty or obligation resting upon him. It was also necessary to aver what that obligation was. The complaint contains several unnecessary averments, but it sufficiently appears that the plaintiff. paid the money as the surety of the decedent. To prove merely that the appellee paid the money would not establish his right to recover. He must prove that he paid the money for the benefit of the decedent or the estate. Suretyship became an important element in establishing his right to recover. A contract of suretyship is collateral to, and predicated upon, a primary obligation. In order to establish suretyship, it is first essential to prove the existence of the primary contract. The note

or written instrument was the best evidence of this contract.

The appellee, in support of his claim, gave in evidence
the original note. This note, upon its face, purported to
be the joint and several obligation of all the makers.
The relation of the makers toward each other must be
shown in order to establish suretyship. This may be
done by parol if the witnesses are competent. The witness Ryder was interested in the question of suretyship.
If the decedent was the principal in the note, then his
estate was liable for the whole debt. If the decedent was
a cosurety with the appellee, then his estate was liable
to the appellee for only one-half of the debt. The principal subject of controversy in this action was the question of suretyship, and upon its solution depended the
respective rights of Ryder, Allman, and the estate of the
decedent. Ryder's interest in this controversy was adverse to that of the estate.

By section 498, R. S. 1881, it is enacted that "In suits
or proceedings in which an executor or administrator is a
party, involving matters which occurred during the lifetime of the decedent, where a judgment or allowance may
be made or rendered for or against the estate represented
by such executor or administrator, any person who is a
necessary party to the issue or record, whose interest is
adverse to such estate, shall not be a competent witness
as to such matters against such estate."

The purpose of this statute is to prevent undue advantage from being taken of the estates of deceased persons. The policy of the law is to place the estate and
the person asserting a claim against it upon the same
footing. Death having sealed the lips of one party to a
transaction, the law closes the lips of the other.

This statute has received a liberal construction in order to effectuate the legislative purpose.

Thornburg, Administrator, v. Allman.

"In determining the competency of a witness, the accepted rule is not to regard the mere letter of the statute, but to look to its spirit and purpose." *Durham* v. *Shannon*, 116 Ind. 403; *Clift, Admr.*, v. *Shockley*, 77 Ind. 297; *Wiseman* v. *Wiseman*, 73 Ind. 112; *Ketcham, Admx.*, v. *Hill*, 42 Ind. 64; *Peacock* v. *Albin*, 39 Ind. 25.

This policy of liberal construction has received the sanction of legislation. By section 19, Elliott's Supp. it is enacted that "In all cases in which executors, administrators, heirs, or devisees are parties, and one of the parties to the suit shall be incompetent, as hereinbefore provided, to testify against them, then the assignor or grantor of a party making such assignment or grant voluntarily shall be deemed a party adverse to the executor or administrator, heir, or devisee, as the case may be."

Ryder's competency did not depend upon his being a party to the issue or record, but upon his interest in the controversy. We think he came within the spirit if not the letter of the statutes. By such interest is meant such an interest as may affect him pecuniarily. The mere fact that he may have been insolvent at the time of the trial, does not strip him of his interest. An insolvent may become solvent.

We think it was manifestly unfair to the estate to permit Ryder to give his version of a transaction which relieved him of any responsibility and placed it upon the estate of the deceased. If this practice can be upheld, it is readily conceivable how great frauds might be perpetrated upon the estates of deceased persons. One of the makers of a note might pay it, and, by collusion with his surviving comaker, charge the decedent with being the principal, and use the other survivor to prove the relationship.

To hold that Ryder was a competent witness would be

to make plain a way for avoiding the statutes and defrauding estates.

Judgment reversed, at costs of appellee, with instructions to sustain the motion for a new trial.

Filed Jan. 2, 1894.

No. 1,094.

TYLER v. JOHNSON ET AL.

ESTOPPEL.— *Mortgage Deed.* — *Conveyance by Mortgagee.*— *Action by Mortgagor for Improvements Made at Request.*—Where A. conveyed land to B. as indemnity for a debt of security, by a deed absolute upon its face, though in fact only a mortgage, and B. conveys the land without the consent of A., by such conveyance B. will be held to have treated the deed as an absolute conveyance, and in an action by A. for improvements made on such land at the instance and request of B., B. will be estopped from asserting that the deed from A. to him was only a mortgage.

From the Tippecanoe Superior Court.

W. P. Rhodes and *W. L. Rabourne,* for appellant.

E. F. McCabe, for appellees.

REINHARD, J.—George C. Tyler, a brother of the appellant, claims to have made certain improvements on the farm of the latter, and at his instance and request. For this alleged indebtedness he made out an itemized account, which he assigned to the appellees Miles Starry and William L. Hamilton, and to one George Johnson, now deceased. The assignees instituted this action on the account, in the Warren Circuit Court, making both the appellant and George B. Tyler defendants thereto. Issues were joined and a trial was had, resulting in a judgment in favor of the appellant, the defendant below. On appeal to this court, the judgment was reversed.

Johnson v. *Tyler*, 1 Ind. App. 387. When the cause came back to the docket of the Warren Circuit Court the pleadings were amended so as to conform to the ruling of the Appellate Court, the death of one of the plaintiffs. was suggested, and his executors were substituted in his stead. Thereupon the venue of the cause was changed to the court below, where there was a trial by the court and a finding and judgment in favor of the appellees, the plaintiffs below. The case comes here upon a single question, viz, the sufficiency of the evidence to sustain the finding.

There was evidence tending to show that George C. Tyler made the improvements in suit at the instance and request of the appellant. It is contended, however, on the part of the appellant, that these improvements were made upon a farm which, in reality, belonged to George C. Tyler, although at the time they were made, he (appellant) held the legal title to the same. The theory of the appellant is that the farm was conveyed to him by his brother simply as an indemnity for a debt of security, and that though the deed was absolute in form upon its face, it was in fact only a mortgage.

He further claims that he and his brother George made a rough estimate of the amount paid by him for George, and found that it was about $500 more than he had realized out of the rents and profits of the farm, and that thereupon, in pursuance of an agreement between the two brothers, appellant conveyed the farm to Robert A. Chandler and De Witt C. Andrews, the sons-in-law of George, and that they paid him said amount of $500 in discharge of all indebtedness to him of said George.

The evidence strongly tends to sustain this contention. On the other hand, there is some testimony tending to prove that although the deed from George to appellant was only a mortgage, yet the appellant made the conveyance of the farm to Chandler and Andrews without any agreement or consent on the part of George C. Tyler. This is the testimony of George.

We must therefore assume that the court was fully warranted in its conclusion that the evidence sufficiently proved the alienation of the farm by the appellant, without the permission or consent of George C. Tyler. By conveying the land without such consent, under the circumstances of this case, the appellant treated the deed from George C. Tyler to himself as an absolute conveyance, and he was, therefore, precluded from asserting, afterwards, that it was only a mortgage. *Shubert* v. *Stanley*, 52 Ind. 46.

Furthermore, there was evidence tending to show that the appellant had claimed and treated the land as his own property.

If the farm was the property of the appellant, and the improvements were made at his instance and request, as there is evidence tending to prove, the appellant should, in equity and good conscience, be required to pay for such improvements.

There is no available error.

Judgment affirmed.

Filed Jan. 24, 1894.

No. 1,073.

MINNICH *v.* DARLING ET AL.

PRINCIPAL AND AGENT.—*Contract.*—*Ratification, How Pleaded.*—*Estoppel.*—*Law and Fact.*—Ratification, as the term is applied to principal and agent, is a fact, and not a legal conclusion, and, as such, may be pleaded in general terms; but when used in a sense akin to estoppel, it is not proper to plead it in general terms, but the acts constituting the ratification must be specially pleaded.

SAME.—*Contract.*—*Ratification, Definition of.*—The contract ratified must be one that the parties might have lawfully made in the first instance, and the person who acts as agent must purport to be the agent of the principal, and the contract must be made upon the faith and credit of the principal, ratification being an adoption of that which was done for and in the name of another.

LAW AND FACT.—*Commingling of.*—*Effect.*—*Special Findings.*—*Conclusions of Law.*—*Appellate Court Practice.*—Where a conclusion of law is cast among the finding of facts, it must be disregarded, and can not be used to help out the conclusions of law as stated by the court; and the same rule applies where a fact is stated among the conclusions of law. The appellate tribunal will not transpose a fact improperly cast among the conclusions of law, and *vice versa.*

GAVIN, J., and DAVIS, J., dissent.

From the Elkhart Circuit Court.

H. C. Dodge, for appellant.

W. L. Stonex and *E. A. Dausman*, for appellees.

LOTZ, J.—It affirmatively appears that the judgment rendered by the trial court was based upon the first paragraph of the appellee's complaint. It is the ordinary action to recover judgment and to foreclose a materialman's lien for materials furnished to the owner of real estate for the construction of a dwelling house thereon.

The appellant filed an answer in denial, and it was agreed of record that all defenses might be given under this answer.

The court made a special finding of facts, and stated conclusions of law. They are substantially as follows:

"First. That, on the 18th day of February, A. D. 1888,

the defendant made a contract with one Louis M. Smalley to erect a dwelling house upon the south half of lot number twenty-eight, of the town of Elkhart, of the county of Elkhart, and State of Indiana, excepting eighty feet off the east end thereof, of which said real estate the said defendant, at the time of entering into said contract and continuously from thence until the 10th day of September, A. D. 1888, was the owner in fee-simple; that by the terms of said contract the said Louis M. Smalley was to furnish all the materials and perform all the labor in the construction of the said dwelling for a given sum, and that changes in the plans and specifications might be made by defendant, to be charged for by the said Smalley, and that the said contract was reduced to writing and executed by the defendant and the said Smalley.

"Second. That subsequent to the execution of the said contract, and during the month of March, A. D. 1888, the said Smalley commenced the work of constructing the dwelling house, as per his written contract, and finished the same on the 16th day of August, A. D. 1888.

"Third. That during the entire period of the construction of the said dwelling house, the plaintiffs, Stafford Maxon and Eber Darling, were partners trading under the firm name of Maxon & Darling, and the said firm was engaged in the lumber business.

"Fourth. That about the fourth day of April, A. D. 1888, the said contractor, Louis M. Smalley, commenced to purchase lumber and materials of plaintiffs, to be used in the construction of the said dwelling, directing the plaintiffs to charge the same to the defendant, and continued so to purchase such materials of plaintiffs and to have the same so charged, until the 10th day of August, A. D. 1888, during which period he purchased all the items charged in the plaintiff's complaint at the dates and prices therein stated, amounting in the aggregate to

$252.68, all of which was so used in said dwelling, and that plaintiffs did charge the items, as the same were purchased, to the said defendant.

"Fifth. That the defendant did not authorize the said Smalley to purchase the said bill of lumber and material on his account, and did not know that the same were being so purchased, until some time in the month of July, A. D. 1888, at which time he inquired of the plaintiffs, at their place of business, (in substance) whether Smalley was buying lumber of them for his house, and in reply was informed that he was; that the bill was charged direct to the defendant; the book account was at said time shown to him and footed up in his presence, and the amount stated to him; that he made no objection to the charge being made to him, but requested plaintiffs to make out an itemized statement of it and present it to him the next time he came in from his run as a U. S. postal clerk, and said that he would fix it up at that time, and that subsequently to the said conversation plaintiffs sold a part of the items enumerated in their complaint, and plaintiffs did not know anything about the contract between defendant and Smalley, until all the items in said account were sold and charged, as aforesaid.

"Sixth. That on the 10th day of September, A. D. 1888, and within sixty days of the date of the last items purchased in the said bill, the plaintiffs filed in the proper recorder's office in the county of Elkhart, and State of Indiana, the notice of mechanic's lien, as set forth in the complaint, and the same was duly recorded on said date in the miscellaneous record of the said county, in book 4, at page 354; that the said notice of lien contains and describes more land than was owned at said date by said defendant; the word eight, in the exception in said description, should have been eighty to have properly described his said land; that the plat in which said lot is situate is the plat first laid out for the town (now city) of Elkhart, but is not designated of record as the 'original plat,' and no other plat is so designated.

"Seventh. That the amount now due plaintiffs, including interest on the account so purchased by Smalley and so charged to defendant, is $311.43.

"Eighth. That a reasonable fee for plaintiff's attorneys in the prosecution of this suit is $155." * * *

And, as conclusions of law upon the facts, the court finds:

"First. That by his acts in the month of July, 1888, as set forth in No. 5, of the finding of the facts, the defendant ratified the acts of Smalley, and became bound for all the goods previously bought and for such goods as Smalley subsequently purchased in his name for the purposes of the completion of the defendant's said dwelling, and defendant is liable for the entire bill.

"Second. That the notice of lien is sufficiently definite to hold defendant's lot, as described in plaintiff's complaint."

The appellant excepted to the conclusions of law and moved for a judgment in his favor on the findings. This motion was overruled, and the court rendered judgment in favor of the appellees, and decreed a foreclosure of the lien. The appellant then filed a motion for a new trial; this motion was also overruled. Each of these decisions of the trial court is assigned as error in this court.

The office of a special finding or verdict is to determine the facts which give rise to legal conclusions embraced within the issues formed by the pleadings of the parties. Such facts are the source and cause of the law. They are the result or effect of the evidence, and are sometimes denominated the inferential or ultimate facts. The purpose of a judicial inquiry is to ascertain the facts upon which the law depends. Every ultimate fact is intimately related to many other facts. These attendant facts, not being of controlling legal importance, are denominated the evidentiary or subsidiary facts. The special findings, generally speaking, should be limited exclusively to the ultimate facts proved by the evidence. Ordinarily no evidence, no evidentiary facts, no conclusions of law, have any proper place in the special findings, and, if so found, must be disregarded in stating the legal conclusions.

The appellees' complaint alleges, that the appellant purchased materials of them for the construction of a dwelling house; that said materials were so used; that they gave notice of their intention to hold a lien thereon; that the value of said materials is a given amount, and that same is due and unpaid.

To entitle them to the relief prayed for, it was necessary that they should prove, and that the court should find, that there was a contract for the purchase of the material between them and the appellant, the value of the materials, and the amount due and unpaid. Such facts would entitle the appellees to a personal judgment. To entitle them to the enforcement of a lien, it was necessary to prove, and for the court to find, that the materials were furnished for, and used in, the construction of the house, and the giving of the notice of intention to hold a lien. If these facts are all found, they are sufficient to support the judgment rendered in favor of the appellees. But it is not expressly found therein that any contract of purchase was ever made between them. If it be conceded that under the agreement that all defenses might have been given under the answer of general denial, and that all affirmative matter in reply might be given without specially pleading the same, the inquiry arises as to the effect of subdivision No. 5 of the special findings as to establishing a contract.

He who ratifies and adopts a contract made in his name, although without his knowledge or authority, will be bound by it through all of its legitimate consequences the same as if he had authorized it in the first instance. The methods by which a contract may be ratified are as numerous and various as the methods by which a contract may be made without the intervention of an agent. There are certain well defined rules that govern ratification. The contract ratified must be one that the parties might have lawfully made in the first instance. The person who acts as agent must purport to be the agent of the principal, and the contract must be made upon the faith and credit of the principal. Ratification means adoption of that which was done for and in the name of another; hence, the contract, at its inception, must purport to be the contract of the principal. It is not sufficient to constitute ratification that the contract may have enured to the benefit of a person sought to be charged as principal. Some confusion has arisen as to the use of the word ratified, and as to whether ratification is a fact or a conclusion of law arising from the facts.

The terms "adopted" and "ratified" are properly applied only to contracts made by a party assuming to act for another. *Ellison* v. *Jackson, etc., Co.*, 12 Cal. 542, 19 Cent. L. J. 482; *Clough* v. *Clough*, 73 Me. 487.

These terms are frequently used in reference to the confirmation or renewal of contracts of infants and of persons of unsound mind, but not properly in its technical sense. Renewal is the proper designation of the conduct of a party under such circumstances. It is not a correct expression to say that a person adopts or ratifies his own act. That which is his own is already so, and needs no adoption. The terms ratified and adopt, of themselves, imply that some other person has acted other than the person who ratifies or adopts.

In its technical sense, ratification is itself a fact, and not a conclusion of law to be drawn from other facts or circumstances. *Carter* v. *Pomeroy*, 30 Ind. 438 (441).

The acts, words, and silence of the principal are sometimes spoken of as in themselves constituting a ratification, but this is not strictly accurate. They are rather the evidence of a ratification than the ratification itself. Mecham Agency, section 146.

Ratification, in its technical sense, may be pleaded in general terms, because it is a fact. *Voiles* v. *Beard*, 58 Ind. 510.

But when it is used in a sense akin to estoppel, it is not proper to plead it in general terms, but the acts done constituting it must be specially pleaded, and if it merely state legal conclusions, the pleading will be bad on demurrer. *Copenrath* v. *Kienby*, 83 Ind. 18; *Reinskopf* v. *Rogge*, 37 Ind. 207.

Ratification, as the term is applied to principal and agent, being a fact and not a legal conclusion, the special findings, in order to support the judgment, must find that a contract was entered into between the appellant and appellees, either directly or by a subsequent ratification. This the findings do not do. The facts stated in subdivision No. 5 are evidentiary and not ultimate facts. *Haggerty* v. *Juday*, 58 Ind. 154 (158).

Such facts are no more to be regarded in drawing the legal conclusions than the evidence itself. When the special findings and the conclusions of law are considered as an entirety, it is apparent that the court conceived the idea that ratification was not a question of fact, but a legal conclusion, and so placed it among the legal conclusions. Can this court transpose a fact improperly

cast among the conclusions of law and place it among
the finding of facts and then pronounce the proper judgment upon the facts? The rule is firmly settled that if
a conclusion of law be cast among the facts it must
be disregarded. It can not be used to help out the conclusions of law, as stated by the court. The reason for
a rule is equally as strong that a fact improperly cast
among the conclusions of law can not be considered as a
fact to supply any defect in the special findings. The
finding of a fact as a matter of law is not equivalent to
finding the fact as a fact. *Kealing* v. *Vansickle*, 74 Ind.
529 (536).

When matters of fact are stated as conclusions of law,
they are altogether out of place, and can exert no influence upon the case. *Smith, Admr.*, v. *Goodwin*, 86
Ind. 300 (303).

This is not an open question in this State. *Braden,
Admr.*, v. *Lemmon*, 127 Ind. 9 (14); *Jarvis* v. *Banta*, 83
Ind. 528.

There is good reason for the rule here announced, for
a fact is one thing and the law is another. If the court
improperly conceive a conclusion of law to be a matter
of fact, it is apparent that it proceeds upon an improper
basis, and likewise if it conceive a matter of fact to be a
conclusion of law. A court can not proceed intelligently
in the determination of the rights of parties litigant, unless it keep in mind the distinction between law and fact.
There is no finding of fact that the appellant ever purchased any material of the appellees. The findings are
not sufficient to support the judgment.

As said by BERKSHIRE, J., in *Kehr* v. *Hall*, 117 Ind.
405 (409): "Every fact must be found and stated in
the special finding necessary to the plaintiff's recovery,
or the judgment must be for the defendant."

Facts not found are presumed, as against the party who

has the burden of proof, not to exist. *Stix* v. *Sadler*, 109 Ind. 254.

We think the court erred in its conclusions of law. To prevent injustice, the judgment is reversed, at the costs of appellees, with instructions to grant a new trial to appellees if asked. *Buchanan* v. *Milligan*, 108 Ind. 433.

Ross, J., concurs in the result.

GAVIN, J., and DAVIS, J., dissent.

Filed Jan. 10, 1894.

No. 1,091.

*MAYBIN v. WEBSTER.

ASSIGNMENT OF ERRORS.—*Cause for New Trial.—How Assigned.*—A decision of the trial court, which properly constitutes a cause for new trial, can not be independently assigned as error on appeal, among which causes is a ruling on a motion to suppress a deposition.

EVIDENCE.—*Declarations.—Marriage, Breach of Contract.*—In an action for breach of marriage contract, a person who visited plaintiff when she was in a state of nervous prostration, is competent to testify to certain statements made to witness, which the witness, at plaintiff's request, communicated to defendant.

SAME.—*Motion to Strike Out.—Hearsay.—Cross-Examination.*—It is not error to overrule a motion to strike out evidence, on the ground that on cross-examination it was made to appear that the witness did not have a positive and distinct recollection as to some of the matters testified to by him on examination in chief, and that answers made by him in chief may have been based, in part, on hearsay.

MARRIAGE CONTRACT.—*Breach of.—Matters in Mitigation.—Set-Off.—Counterclaim.—Interrogatories to Jury.*—Matters in mitigation, in actions for breach of marriage contract, can not be considered as a set-off or counterclaim, and the jury, in answer to an interrogatory, need not state the amount allowed in mitigation, but should only state what matters were so allowed.

MISCONDUCT OF COUNSEL.—*Argument to Jury.—Exception, How Saved.*—If counsel, in argument to the jury, is guilty of misconduct in

* Spelled Mabin, in 129 Ind. 430.

making statements of a prejudicial character, not warranted by the evidence, and, on objection thereto being made, the court then and there instructs the jury to disregard such statements, the injured party, if he is not satisfied with such redress, should make his dissatisfaction known by calling the attention of the court to such action as, in his judgment, ought to be taken to remedy the wrong, and if such redress is refused, the party may except thereto and save the question for appellate tribunal.

Opinion on petition for rehearing by DAVIS, C. J.

From the Switzerland Circuit Court.

G. E. Downey and *J. K. Thompson*, for appellant.

G. M. Roberts, C. W. Stapp, F. M. Griffith, H. D. Mc-Mullen, H. R. McMullen and *W. R. Johnston*, for appellee.

DAVIS, J.—On the first trial of this case, in the Dearborn Circuit Court, appellee recovered judgment for six thousand dollars, which, on appeal to the Supreme Court, was reversed. *Mabin* v. *Webster*, 129 Ind. 430. The venue of the cause was then changed to the Switzerland Circuit Court, and resulted in judgment in favor of appellee for three thousand dollars.

The errors assigned by appellant in this court are: ·

"1st. Because said Switzerland Circuit Court erred in overruling the appellant's motion for a new trial of said cause.

"2d. Because said court erred in overruling the motion of the appellant to suppress parts of the deposition of Persis C. Chapin, taken on behalf of the appellee, read in evidence on the trial of said cause."

The ruling of the court on a motion to suppress a deposition is cause for a new trial. *Jeffersonville, etc., R. R. Co.* v. *Riley*, 39 Ind. 568.

It is well settled that rulings which properly constitute a cause for a new trial can not be independently assigned as error in this court. Elliott's App. Proced., sections 347, 351

The second error assigned in this case presents no question for our consideration.

The first question discussed by counsel for appellant relates to the admission of the testimony of Mrs. McConnel, a witness on behalf of appellee. This witness, over objection of appellant, testified that on one occasion she called to see appellee when she was suffering from nervous prostration, and that appellee then communicated to her certain statements which the witness, at her request, communicated to appellant. The questions asked were proper. The evidence sought to be elicited was pertinent. The answers of the witnesses may, in some respects, have been more comprehensive than the questions, but as the motion made by counsel for appellant to strike out parts of her testimony was sustained, appellant is in no position to complain.

The next question relates to the ruling of the court in refusing to strike out parts of the deposition of Persis Chapin. The fact that, on cross-examination, it was made to appear that the witness did not have a positive and distinct personal recollection as to some of the matters testified to by him in chief, and that the answers so made to questions propounded to him in chief may have been based, in part at least, on hearsay, did not constitute a sufficient reason for striking out his answers to such questions. The credibility of the witness, and the weight of his evidence as analyzed and dissected by the cross-examination, were proper questions for the consideration of the jury. There was no error in this ruling.

Complaint is also made of instructions given and refused, but the objections urged are general rather than specific. We have, however, carefully read all the instructions asked, given, modified, or refused, in the light of the argument of counsel in relation thereto. The in-

structions are numerous and lengthy, and we can not
undertake to set them out in this opinion. When considered together, as an entirety, the instructions given
fully and correctly state the law applicable to the case.
So far as we have been able to see, each of the instructions, standing alone, accurately states the law on the
question to which such instruction refers. As the instructions impress us, appellant has not in any respect
been prejudiced thereby. The attention of the jury was
explicitly directed to the matters which it was proper for
them to consider in mitigation of damages. There was
no error in either the giving or refusing of instructions.

A number of interrogatories which, on examination,
we find were in all respects proper in both substance
and form, were submitted to the jury by the court at the
request of the respective parties. The answers returned
thereto seem to have been responsive, full, and clear.
The appellant tendered one interrogatory in answer to
which the jury were asked to state the amount allowed
by them in mitigation of damages for the alleged breach
of contract, on account of the fact that he was afflicted
with epilepsy. The court struck out and refused to submit so much thereof as sought to have the jury fix the
amount they so considered in mitigation. The jury answered that such affliction was considered by them in
mitigation in determining the amount of the verdict.
This was all that was required on that branch of the case.
Matters in mitigation in this class of cases can not be
considered as a set-off or counterclaim.

The next question urged by counsel for appellant is
based on the alleged misconduct of one of the attorneys
for appellee in his argument to the jury, which is set out
in the bill of exceptions as follows:

"George M. Roberts, Esq., was addressing the jury on
behalf of the plaintiff, when said attorney, so acting,

made the following statement in argument to the jury, to wit: 'On rebuttal, we asked Mrs. Isdell to state whether her sister, Mary C. Webster, had a watch and bracelets in 1879, when she went to live with her. They objected to that; they were afraid to have her answer that question; they knew she would say her sister had the watch and bracelets in 1879, and that she did not get them afterwards.' To which the defendant then and there objected and excepted, and said counsel did not withdraw the statement, and thereupon, after objection made by counsel for the defendant, the court stated as follows, to wit: 'Gentlemen of the jury—The statement made by counsel in reference to what other counsel may have known, and what the witness may have sworn to, if permitted to testify, is not proper matter for you to consider, and is ordered stricken out by the court.' And still counsel for the plaintiff did not in any manner withdraw said statement. And the defendant then and there, at the proper time, and properly still objected and excepted to said statement of counsel, and the counsel proceeded with his argument of the cause.''

We have quoted in full all that appears in the bill of exceptions on this subject. When the alleged improper statement was made, counsel for appellant objected and excepted thereto, and thereupon the court clearly and unequivocally instructed the jury to not consider such statement. Counsel for appellant then renewed the objection and exception to the statement, but did not move the court to set aside the jury or take any other steps.

The rule applicable to the question here presented is, in our opinion, correctly stated by Judge COFFEY in *Grubb v. State*, 117 Ind. 277 (283): "Where counsel is guilty of misconduct, and the opposing party, at the time, objects, and the court, upon being asked to do so, neglects or refuses to take action in the matter, or to repair the injury to the satisfaction of the injured party, he can except and bring the question to this court. But, in such cases, if the court does all in its power to relieve the party injured from the consequences of such misconduct, there is no action of the court to which an exception can be taken, and consequently nothing to be reviewed in this court. In such cases, if the injured party thinks that the injury is of such a character that it can not be repaired by any action of the court, he should move to set aside the jury, or take such other steps as he may think will secure to him a fair and impartial trial. If he fails to do this, and permits the case to proceed to final determination, he must be deemed to have waived all questions arising out of such misconduct. *Coleman* v. *State*, 111 Ind. 563; *Henning* v. *State*, 106 Ind. 386. In this case, as the court did all that could be done, and, indeed, all it was asked by appellant to do, it must be considered by this court that all error on account of the misconduct of counsel for the State has been waived."

Without entering upon or deciding the question as to the character and effect of the statement which constitutes the alleged misconduct of counsel in this case, it will suffice to say that, in any event, on the authority cited, such statement can not be regarded as reversible error.

See, also, *Indianapolis Journal Newspaper Co.* v. *Pugh*, 6 Ind App. 510, 34 N. E. Rep. 991, and authorities there cited.

There is no error in the record, which would justify the reversal of the judgment of the court below.

Judgment affirmed.

Filed Nov. 2, 1893.

ON PETITION FOR A REHEARING.

DAVIS, C. J.—One of the grounds on which the petition for a rehearing is urged, is that the rule enunciated in *Grubbs* v. *State, supra,* and followed by us in the original opinion, in relation to the misconduct of counsel for appellee, in his argument to the jury, "is not well founded, either from a legal or common sense point of view."

We think counsel are in error. That decision, in our opinion, is not only good law, but is also sound common sense.

Counsel contend that "When a pernicious statement, such as the one under discussion, is lodged in the minds of jurors, and hammered in, as in this case, with all the force at the command of able counsel, it is as utterly impossible for a court to remove it by instructions as is the proverbial tale of the camel and the needle's eye, and for a court to instruct a jury to disregard such a statement, is to set a task beyond the powers of ordinary jurors."

Counsel underestimate the intelligence and impartiality of the average jury. The presumption is that the jury understood and obeyed the instruction of the court.

Reasoning on the line indicated, counsel for appellant insist that on account of such misconduct of the prevailing party, a new trial should have been granted. In other words, as we understand the argument of counsel, the only redress for such misconduct is to grant a new trial to the unsuccessful party.

As applied to this case, we are of the opinion that the better and wiser rule is stated in the opinion cited. Ordinarily, if counsel, in argument, is guilty of misconduct in making statements of a prejudicial character not warranted by the evidence, and, on objection thereto being made, the court then and there instructs and directs the jury to disregard such statements, if the injured party is not satisfied with such redress, he should make his dissatisfaction known by calling the attention of the court to such action as in his judgment ought to be taken to remedy the wrong.   Such misconduct on the part of counsel, in argument, should not be indulged, but the practical result of the rule for which counsel contend would be that in every case where counsel should be guilty of such misconduct a new trial could be demanded as a matter of right.   The cure, we fear, under such rule, would be more devastating than the disease.   Notwithstanding it is the duty of the trial court to see that counsel in argument keep within proper bounds, without objection or action of the parties, yet, if the court, through oversight or otherwise, fails, on his own motion, to discharge this duty, the party who is injured by such misconduct should not be allowed to remain silent until the verdict is returned, and then, if adverse to him, be awarded a new trial solely on the ground of such misconduct.

If we are right in this position, then it follows that when objection is made at the time to such improper argument, and the court, in response to such objection, instructs the jury to disregard the same, it is incumbent on the aggrieved party, if he desires different or greater satisfaction, to call attention of the court to the relief to which he thinks he is entitled, and if such redress is refused, he can then bring the question to the Appellate Court for review, but, in this case, it occurs to us that the court did all that it was necessary to do, under any view of the question, to redress the wrong of which complaint is made.   When the court instructed the jury to disregard the statement of counsel, no just cause, as it appears to us, existed for further complaint on the part of appellant.

It is earnestly insisted that the damages assessed are excessive. The basis of the argument in support of this proposition is that appellant is sixty-four years of age, and that he is an epileptic, that the disease is most aggravated, both in duration and intensity, making life most dreary and fruitless to him, and a source of the greatest solicitude and care to others, and is in such condition that marriage would probably aggravate the disease and shorten his life, and that appellee; who is fifty years of age, is not entitled to three thousand dollars for appellant's breach of the contract to marry her.

The evidence tends to prove that the parties had been engaged, by continuing agreements, renewed from time to time for eight years or more prior to the commencement of the suit, and that shortly before the complaint was filed appellant refused to consummate the marriage and repudiated the contract, and that appellant, as asserted by counsel for appellee, in their brief, and not controverted, was worth twenty-five thousand dollars.

When the facts and circumstances in this case are given the construction most favorable to appellant, the court can not say that the verdict of the jury is excessive. On the contrary, if appellee's theory of the case, as disclosed by her testimony, is correct, and, on this appeal, she is entitled to have it so considered, so far at least as this question is concerned, the amount of the recovery does not, in our judgment, evince, as contended by counsel, that there was the want of a just and full consideration by the jury of all things which they should have taken into account in making the assessment of damages.

The petition for rehearing is overruled.

Filed Jan. 31, 1894.

No. 1,075.

THE PITTSBURGH, CINCINNATI, CHICAGO AND ST. LOUIS
RAILWAY COMPANY *v.* JACOBS.

POOR PERSON.—*Right to Prosecute as.*—*Nonresident.*—The statute giving to certain persons the right to prosecute or defend as a poor person, applies to nonresidents as well as to residents, and in the event
such person is a nonresident, he can not be required to give bond
for costs, even though he might have brought his action in his own
State.

From the Clark Circuit Court.

S. Stansifer, for appellant.
J. H. Smith and *J. K. Marsh,* for appellee.

LOTZ, J.—The appellee brought this action to recover
damages for personal injuries sustained by her through
the alleged negligent conduct of the appellant.

In the court below, the appellant filed an affidavit
showing that the appellee was a nonresident of the State
of Indiana, and moved that she be required to give security for the costs of the action. This motion was sustained, and the appellee was ordered to file a cost bond
within a fixed time. The appellee then filed and presented to the court her affidavit showing that she was a
poor person and had not sufficient means to prosecute
her action, being wholly without money or property of
any kind whatever. On this showing, she moved that
she be permitted to prosecute her action as a poor person.

The appellant filed a counter-affidavit, from which it
appears that the appellee was a resident of the city of
Louisville, in the State of Kentucky, and that appellant's railroad extends to and into said city, and that its
principal office and officers are located there; that appel-

NOVEMBER TERM, 1893.   557

The Piitsburgh, Cincinnati, Chicago and St. Louis Ry. Co. v. Jacobs.

lee could sue in the courts of the State of Kentucky and obtain jurisdiction over the appellant therein.

The court sustained appellee's motion, and ordered that she be permitted to prosecute her suit as a poor person, without bond for costs, and appointed an attorney to assist her in said suit; and further ordered that the attorney serve without compensation from the county. This order and decision of the court is one of the errors assigned in this court.

The identical question here presented has not, to our knowledge, ever been decided in this State. The courts of this State are open equally to all residents of the State, with, perhaps, the bare exception of infants or persons under certain legal disabilities.

In the case of infants it is provided that before any process shall issue some responsible person shall consent in writing to appear as next friend, and such next friend shall be responsible for costs. Section 256, R. S. 1881.

The purpose of this statute, possibly, is to protect the estate of the person under disability rather than to secure the payment of the costs to the officers and person entitled to them.

Section 260, R. S. 1881, is as follows: "Any poor person, not having sufficient means to prosecute or defend an action, may apply to the court in which the action is intended to be brought, or is pending, for leave to prosecute or defend as a poor person. The court, if satisfied that such person has not sufficient means to prosecute or defend the action, shall admit the applicant to prosecute or defend as a poor person, and shall assign him an attorney to defend or prosecute the cause, and all other officers requisite for the prosecution or defense, who shall do their duty therein without taking any fee or reward therefor from such poor person."

It is apparent from the reading of this section, that the

courts are equally open to the rich and the poor. If a person be too poor to employ counsel to prepare and bring his action he may, nevertheless, appear in court and have counsel assigned him for that purpose, or having instituted his action or being made a defendant, he may have counsel assigned him to further prosecute or defend. Whatever is done for such a person under such circumstances is a clear gratuity, a charitable act.

By section 589, R. S. 1881, it is provided that "Plaintiffs who are not residents of this State, before commencing any action, shall file in the office of the clerk a written undertaking   *   *   *   for the payment of all costs."

If a nonresident plaintiff institute an action in the courts of this State, he is liable to have it dismissed for want of security for costs. Can such plaintiff avail himself of section 260, *supra*, and prosecute his action *in forma pauperis?* If so, then gratuity and charity may be extended to the unfortunate poor of other States, as well as our own. Is this the purpose of the statute? At common law the right to sue as a pauper did not exist in actions at law. But in equity, where the costs rested with the chancellor, it has been said that as a general rule "there is no sort or condition of persons who may not sue in a court of chancery; and this rule extends to the most distressed pauper, and that without being required to give security for costs." 8 Am. and Eng. Encycl. of Law, 545; 1 Daniel Ch. Pl., 37.

Under a statute of New York, similar to our own, in 10 Abb. N. Cas. 80, anonymous, it was said by Barrett, J.: "A nonresident should not be allowed to sue *in forma pauperis*. It could never have been the legislative intent to extend the privileges of the act to objects of charity from all quarters of the globe. The law even discriminates against nonresidents generally,

NOVEMBER TERM, 1893.   559

The Pittsburgh, Cincinnati, Chicago and St. Louis Ry. Co. v. Jacobs.

so far as to compel them to give security for costs. Then such statutes should be strictly construed against the appellant (2 Hill, 412)."

In *Christian* v. *Gouge*, 10 Abb. N. Cas. (N. Y.) 82, Sedgwick, J., said: "The letter and policy of the acts in relation to security to be given by nonresident plaintiffs, indicate that it is not unjust or impolitic to refuse leave to a nonresident to sue here, unless he give security for costs, even though in fact he is pecuniarily responsible. He must furnish some one who will respond for him in this State. If he can not, the State does not furnish him the means of pursuing a remedy here. It seems to me inconsistent with this policy, that an irresponsible non-resident should be allowed to sue without even a liability for costs."

In *Porter* v. *Jones*, 68 N. C. 320, the plaintiff was a resident of the State of Tennessee, and the statute of North Carolina enacts that any judge of the Superior Court may authorize *any person* to sue as a pauper when he shall comply with the terms of the act. It was held that a citizen of a sister State stands upon a very different footing from a citizen of a foreign government, and that the expression "any person" was broad enough to permit the plaintiff to sue as a poor person.

In *Wright, Admr.*, v. *McLarinan*, 92 Ind. 103, the plaintiff, while a minor, commenced an action by her next friend. The next friend was removed and she was then permitted to prosecute as a poor person. While the proceedings were pending, she attained full age, got married and became a nonresident of the State. On a motion to require her to give security for costs it was held that the fact that she had attained full age and became a nonresident did not invalidate the order permitting her to prosecute as a poor person.

The court said: "For aught that these things disclose she may have remained as needy as when the order was made.''

It should be borne in mind, however, in this last case that at the time the plaintiff instituted her suit she was under no obligation to give a cost bond. Her entry into the court was not attended with any conditions. Having once attained a rightful standing in court, she ought not lose it by reason of a failure to give security for costs resting upon a subsequent condition.

In *Hoey* v. *McCarthy*, 124 Ind. 464, this question is discussed to some extent, but as the Supreme Court refused to interfere with the discretion given to the trial court in ordering a nonresident plaintiff to give security for costs, nothing therein said can be considered as authority on the point here involved.

Fuller & Fuller Co. v. *Mehl*, 134 Ind. 60, 33 N. E. Rep. 773, was an action to have three chattel mortgages declared void. These mortgages were made by William Mehl, and one of them was executed to his children. The action was by the creditors of William, and the purpose was to subject the property covered by the mortgages to the payment of their debts. The children of William were made parties defendant. They were permitted ''to defend the action and to prosecute a cross-action for the foreclosure of their mortgage as poor persons and without cost bond, they being then nonresidents of the State of Indiana.''

In the course of the opinion the court, by HACKNEY, J., made use of this language: ''A strict construction of section 589, *supra*, as above, would, in a case like the one under consideration, defeat the object of section 260, *supra*, above quoted, in denying to poor persons whose rights must be enforced in the courts of this State the same opportunities for obtaining justice 'freely and without purchase; completely, and without denial; speedily, and without delay,' as are accorded to the rich. The Legislature did not deem it the part of wisdom to extend this salutary provision only to the poor of this State, but its language is so comprehensive as to include the poor whose rights are to be enforced in the courts of Indiana. The two statutes should be construed together: section 589, *supra*, as providing the rule, and section 260 as creating the exception. So construing the provisions, no error was committed by the court.''

It is undeniably true that there is a very marked difference between the attitude of a nonresident who comes voluntarily into the courts of this State and sets the machinery of justice in motion and that of a nonresident who is involuntarily brought into court, in the matter of giving security for costs.

In the latter case, the defendant may do whatever is necessary to preserve his rights, either by defending or prosecuting a cross-action to protect and secure his rights in the subject-matter of the controversy, and that, too, without being required to give a cost bond. If it were otherwise, an unfortunate nonresident might have his hands tied while being stripped of his rights.

Section 589, *supra*, does not apply to nonresidents who are sued in the courts of this State. It does not require a nonresident defendant to give security for costs, and there is no occasion to apply to the court for the privilege of defending or prosecuting a cross-action as a poor person in order to be excused from giving a cost bond.

The real point in decision in *Fuller & Fuller Co.* v. *Mehl*, *supra*, was whether or not a nonresident defendant, when sued in the courts of this State, may prosecute a cross-action without being required to give a cost bond. The court rightfully held that he could not be required to give security for costs. The court, however, in the language above quoted, seems to rest its decision on the fact that the defendants were excused from furnishing a cost bond because of being poor persons. If this be the proper construction of the language, then that case furnishes the rule for the decision here.

Appellant further contends that as it was made to appear by the counter-affidavit that the appellee could obtain jurisdiction over it in the courts of the State of which she was a resident, such fact should be taken into consideration in determining her right to prosecute as a poor person in the courts of this State.

Actions for the recovery of damages for personal injuries are transitory and may be brought in any jurisdiction in which the defendant resides. *Burns, Admr.*, v. *Grand Rapids, etc., R. R. Co.*, 113 Ind. 168 (172).

When the defendant is a resident of several States, we think it is the privilege of the plaintiff to determine in which jurisdiction she will prosecute her transitory action.

The court did not err in permitting the appellee to prosecute her action without giving security for costs.

The only other error assigned is that of overruling the demurrer to the second paragraph of complaint. We have examined this paragraph with care, and are satisfied that it was sufficient to withstand the demurrer.

Judgment affirmed, at costs of appellant.

Filed Jan. 23, 1894.

No. 1,053.

THE WESTERN UNION TELEGRAPH COMPANY *v.* BIERHAUS ET AL.

TELEGRAPH COMPANY.—*Action for the $100 Penalty.—When Will Not Lie.—Disclosure.—Statute Construed.*—An action to recover the $100 penalty imposed by the act of April 8, 1885 (section 5511, R. S. 1894), alleging an unlawful disclosure of a telegram, will not lie, the act of disclosure not being, by express terms nor by fair implication, within the meaning of the act providing for such penalty; and the statute, being a penal one, must be strictly construed.

SAME.—*Statute Construed.—Act of April 8, 1885.*—The act above referred to does not award liquidated damages for failing to perform a duty, but gives a penalty to a private individual, and was intended as a punishment for such wrongful acts only as were not covered by the criminal statutes.

SAME.—*Statute Construed.—Transmission and Delivery.—Disclosure.—Good Faith.*—The transmission of a telegram in good faith and with impartiality, as provided by statute, act 1885, means the forwarding of the message and delivery thereof accurately and without favor or preference, and does not include a non-disclosure of the telegram.

SAME.—*Statute Construed.—Messages.—Discrimination.*—The statute, section 5511, R. S. 1894, makes no discrimination between private dispatches and those of any other character, except messages of public and general interest, and those to and from officers of justice.

STATUTORY CONSTRUCTION.—*Criminal and Penal Statutes.—Double Punishment.*—Where one statute declares a given act to constitute a criminal offense, and prescribes a punishment therefor, a second enactment in the nature of a penal statute, should not be so construed as to bring the act constituting the crime within the purview thereof, unless by express terms it is so provided.

From the Daviess Circuit Court.

J. T. Beasley and *A. B. Williams,* for appellant.

W. R. Gardiner, C. G. Gardiner and *J. W. Ogdon,* for appellees.

REINHARD, J.—The appellees brought this action to recover from the appellant the penalty imposed by the act of April 8, 1885, the breach alleged being the disclosure of several telegraphic dispatches.

A separate demurrer addressed to each paragraph of complaint was overruled. There was a trial, and a finding and judgment in favor of appellees. But two questions are presented by the appeal, and they arise from the ruling upon the demurrer. They are these:

1. Can the statutory penalty of one hundred dollars be recovered on account of the willful disclosure of the contents of a telegraphic dispatch by the company through its agents or employes?

2. Can an action to recover such penalty be maintained in any county other than the one from which the dispatch was sent, and in which the contract was entered into?

The statute upon which this suit is sought to be maintained, as indicated by its title, was designed to enjoin certain duties upon telegraph and telephone companies, and to provide penalties for the violation of the same. Section 1 of the act provides, amongst other things, that the company shall, upon the usual terms, transmit any messages received for that purpose, "with impartiality and good faith, and in the order of time in which they are received, and shall in no manner discriminate in rates charged, or words or figures charged for, or manner or conditions of service between any of its patrons, but shall serve individuals, corporations and other telegraphic companies with impartiality."

Section 2 defines the duties of telephone companies.

Section 3 provides a penalty of one hundred dollars for each offense in violating any of the provisions of the foregoing sections, to be recovered by the party aggrieved in a civil action in any court of competent jurisdiction. R. S. 1894, sections 5511–5513.

This statute, by amendment, has taken the place of the act of May 6, 1853, which, upon the subject of our investigation, was similar, in its provisions, to the present statute. See R. S. 1881, section 4176.

It will be seen, at a glance, that there is no provision, in the enactment under consideration, prohibiting telegraph companies, in express terms, from divulging the contents of a telegraphic message. The question is, is such provision contained in the act by fair implication? or, in other words, can it be said to be fairly within the meaning of the act?

The question here presented has never been decided in our State, nor, so far as we have been able to discover, in the courts of any of our sister States. It is, therefore, with us at least, a question of first impression, but this will not lessen the duty of giving it a most careful consideration.

At first blush, the candid mind will naturally be impressed with the justness of an interpretation which would, without a glaring violation of legal principles, result in visiting a penalty upon any company that suffers its employes to divulge the contents of a message intended for none but the scrutiny of the addressee. It is true that we have a criminal statute making it an offense for any such employe to reveal the contents of any telegraphic dispatch, and providing a punishment for the same (R. S. 1894, section 2248), but public policy would, perhaps, dictate that the law should go a step further, and hold a rein over the companies themselves, so that every inducement would incline them not to retain in their service those who would thus betray a trust of so sacred a character. But it is not the office of a court, in construing a statute, to inject into it, by forced interpretation, matters which, according to the notions of the judge, should have been, but were not, placed there by the framers, however much such matters might conduce to the public interest, for if there is a want of proper legislation upon such subject, it is for the law-making power, and not for the courts, to supply the remedy.

There are certain well defined, and, in fact, elementary rules of interpretation to which the courts are bound to adhere in giving construction to a statute.

The act under consideration, as has been repeatedly decided, does not award liquidated damages for failing to perform a duty, but gives a penalty to a private individual, and being, therefore, highly penal in its character, must be strictly construed. Hence, if the act complained of is not clearly within the scope of prohibition contained in the statute, the latter must receive a construction such as will not involve penal consequences. *Western Union Tel. Co.* v. *Pendleton*, 95 Ind. 12; *Western Union Tel. Co.* v. *Mossler*, 95 Ind. 29; *Western Union Tel. Co.* v. *Harding*, 103 Ind. 505; *Western Union Tel. Co.* v. *Kinney*, 106 Ind. 468; *Western Union Tel. Co.* v. *Steele*, 108 Ind. 163; *Western Union Tel. Co.* v. *Wilson*, 108 Ind. 308; *Western Union Tel. Co.* v. *Brown*, 108 Ind. 538; *Western Union Tel. Co.* v. *Swain*, 109 Ind. 405; *Hadley* v. *Western Union Tel. Co.*, 115 Ind. 191.

The statute must be "at once strictly construed and pursued." Thompson Law of Electricity, section 450.

One of the first ends to be accomplished in finding the meaning of the statute is to ascertain its object and design.

As was said by ZOLLARS, J., in *Western Union Tel. Co.* v. *Wilson, supra:* "In construing statutes, the prime object is to ascertain and carry out the purpose of the Legislature in its enactment, and, while it is the duty of the court to yield to the words of the statute, still, in determining what meaning it was intended to have, it is proper to consider its spirit, the object it was intended to subserve, and the evils it was intended to remedy. Without doing violence to the language of the statute, the words used will be so construed as to bring the operation of the act within the intention of the Legislature."

Telegraph companies are *quasi* public corporations, and are, under the general duty they owe to the public, required to transmit and deliver any messages given to them for that purpose, on the payment or tender of the usual charges, with reasonable diligence and in the order of time in which such messages were delivered.

While these obligations rest upon such companies by virtue of their *quasi* public character, and; perhaps, as common law obligations, yet, in order to set this question at rest, many, if not all, the States of the Union have passed appropriate statutes requiring such companies, under penalties, to receive messages, and, on payment of the usual charges, to transmit them faithfully, without unreasonable delay, and in the order in which they are received, and without making unjust discriminations between patrons.   Thompson Law of Electricity, section 157, *et seq.*

Besides the statutes already referred to, the Legislature of this State also passed an act prohibiting, in express terms, the disclosure of telegraphic messages, and giving a remedy in damages to the party injured, to the extent of such injury, and making such company liable for failure or negligence in the performance of their duties generally.   R. S. 1894, section 5513.

It is not claimed by the learned counsel for appellees, that the civil and criminal statutes, other than the one under immediate consideration, do not furnish full and adequate remedies to the patrons of telegraph companies, in the transaction of their business, nor do we think such a position would be tenable.   The criminal statute fully punishes the wrongdoer, while the civil remedy gives ample redress for the consequences resulting from

unlawful disclosure. In addition to these, the penal statute
in hand makes the wrongful acts of the servants of these
corporations, such as partiality, discrimination, and bad
faith in the transmission of messages, a tort for which
the company is bound to respond in the penalty prescribed.

To our minds, it is clear that this penalty was intended to punish such wrongful acts only as were not
covered by the criminal statutes. Any other construction would impute to the law-making power an intention
to assess a double punishment for the same offense. The
law, as interpreted in this State, abhors the infliction of
double penalties. It is for this reason that the courts
will refuse to adjudge punitive damages when the criminal law provides a punishment against the wrongdoer.
It is true the criminal statute here does not operate directly against the corporation, but the act constituting
the malfeasance is nevertheless punished. Corporations
are but fictitious persons, and all their acts and omissions are only the real acts or omissions of their agents.
Some of the authorities go so far as to hold that punitive
damages are allowed against corporations, if at all, only
in extreme cases. 5 Am. and Eng. Encyc. of Law, 23.

Our own courts hold, however, that punitive damages
may be recovered against a corporation for the wrongful
acts of its servants, where such damages might be recovered against the servant. *Jeffersonville R. R. Co.* v.
Rogers, 28 Ind. 1; *Jeffersonville R. R. Co.* v. *Rogers*, 38
Ind. 116; *Citizens' St. R. R. Co.* v. *Willoeby*, 134 Ind.
563, 33 N. E. Rep. 627.

We do not undertake to declare that a penal law in the
nature of the one under construction would be invalid
if there already existed a criminal statute against the
same act, as that question is not before us. But we do
give it as our conviction that when one statute declares

a given act to constitute a criminal offense, and prescribes a punishment therefor, a second enactment in the nature of a penal or *qui tam* statute should not be so construed as to bring the act constituting the crime or offense within the purview thereof, unless by express terms it is so provided. Here, in our view, both the letter and spirit is against the interpretation contended for, and it is the duty of the court, to avoid the penalty by construction, rather than to create it. *Western Union Tel. Co.* v. *Axtell*, 69 Ind. 199; *Western Union Tel. Co.* v. *Mossler, supra; Western Union Tel. Co.* v. *Harding, supra.*

While, as has been stated, the Supreme Court has never passed upon the exact question here in dispute, some of its rulings in recent cases are indicative of what it considered as the acts denounced by this statute, and for which the penalty is awarded. Thus it was declared that failure or delay in the transmission of messages was the only thing provided against by the law of 1853, and that the act of 1885 added to these the element of discrimination in rates charged, or manner or condition of service. *Western Union Tel. Co.* v. *Brown, supra; Hadley* v. *Western Union Tel. Co., supra.*

It is true that in some of the cases it is said that the statute in question denounces three distinct acts, viz: Bad faith, partiality, and discrimination. *Western Union Tel. Co.* v. *Steele, supra; Western Union Tel. Co.* v. *Swain, supra.*

But these acts can have reference only to the duty of transmission, as they are inseparably connected with the same by the language of the law itself. To divulge the contents of a message has no necessary connection with its transmission. It may be transmitted ever so faithfully and impartially, and yet its import may be disclosed, either before or after the transmission, or during the progress thereof. Our opinion is that transmission in good faith and with impartiality means the forwarding of the message and the delivery thereof, accurately and without favor or preference.

There is another feature in this case not unworthy of consideration. The complaint avers that the messages transmitted were of a private business nature, and some weight is sought to be given this fact in the brief of appellees' counsel. But the statute makes no discrimination between private dispatches and those of any other character, except that messages of public and general interest, and those to and from officers of justice, have preference over private dispatches.

If the appellees can recover the penalty in this action, what is there to hinder the sender of any dispatch, whatever its nature, from recovering it? Or will it be claimed that "bad faith" can be ascribed only to the disclosure of private messages?

The statute giving a remedy in special damages (section 5513, R. S. 1894) expressly confines it to cases in which the disclosure is that of a private dispatch, but not so with the act of 1885. It makes no such discrimination. It requires as much "good faith" in the transmission of a public or nonsecret message as in a private one. Can it be true that the Legislature intended to impose this penalty on telegraph companies for every disclosure by its servants? If so, we shall never see the end of the litigation to spring from it. And yet, not a case is to be found on record where the penalty has been claimed for any divulgence.

Without further extending this opinion, we give it as our conclusion that the action will not lie.

We think the demurrer should have been sustained.

As this disposes of the entire case, it will not be necessary for us to pass upon the question of jurisdiction of the trial court.

Judgment reversed.

Filed Jan. 9, 1894.

———————

No. 1,099.

Levi *v.* Hare.

Recovery.—*Entitled to Some Relief, but not All Demanded.—Jurisdiction.*—Where a party is entitled, under the averments of his complaint, to some relief, but not to all demanded, that fact does not debar him from recovering what he is entitled to.

Appellate Court Practice.—*Prejudicial Error.*—Before an appeal can avail anything, the appellant must show affirmatively that some prejudicial error was committed.

From the Hamilton Circuit Court.

W. Garver, W. S. Christian and *I. W. Christian,* for appellant.

T. J. Kane and *R. K. Kane,* for appellee.

Reinhard, J.—The complaint in this action is in three paragraphs. The first paragraph seeks to foreclose a lien on the "get" of a certain sire for $200, under sections 2839–2843, R. S. 1894, and also to recover a personal judgment for the indebtedness growing out of the services of said sire. The second paragraph is designed to enforce a similar lien and recover a further personal judgment for the services of a different sire for the amount of $100. The third paragraph counts on an ordinary book account for $25, for feeding appellant's mares.

Separate demurrers were addressed to the first and second paragraphs of the complaint, each assigning for cause of demurrer the want of jurisdiction in the court, and the insufficiency of the paragraph to constitute a cause of action. The demurrers were overruled and exceptions reserved,. and this ruling is assigned as error. Further specifications of error are the overruling of the motion in arrest of judgment, and that the court below had no jurisdiction of the subject-matter of the action.

By these assignments, it is sought to present the question whether the circuit court has jurisdiction to enforce the lien provided for in the sections of the statute above cited. If the question were properly before us, we must concede that it would be one of some difficulty. The statute seems to limit the jurisdiction for the enforcement of this class of statutory liens to the courts of, justices of the peace of the township in which the property may be found. Whether the lienor may invoke the general equity powers of the circuit court in such cases, we do not deem it incumbent upon us, at this time, to determine.

Each paragraph of the complaint to which the demurrer was addressed, showed such facts as entitled the appellee to a personal judgment for the services of his stallions. The action was by the owner of the stallions against the owner of the mares, or, in other words, between the parties to the original contract. Had the suit been waged for the foreclosure of the lien only, a different question would be presented. The appellee was entitled, under the averments of the complaint, to some relief, and if he was not entitled to all the relief demanded, that fact would not debar him from recovering what he was entitled to. *McLead* v. *Applegate, Guar.*, 127 Ind. 349.

We think the court had jurisdiction to render a personal judgment.

The overruling of the motion for a new trial is the only remaining error assigned. The insufficiency of the evidence was assigned as a cause for a new trial, but the argument of appellant's counsel is addressed solely to that branch of the evidence tending to establish the lien. If the evidence was sufficient to entitle the appellee to recover a personal judgment, no error was committed in overruling the motion for a new trial. It is not claimed that the court erred in admitting testimony introduced upon the subject of the lien, nor is it shown that any motion was made to strike out such testimony. The appellant might also have saved the question by an objection to that portion of the judgment directing a foreclosure of the lien, or by a motion to modify the judgment so as to eliminate from it the part relating to the lien, and by an assignment of error upon the ruling thereon. In some such way it was incumbent upon the appellant to present the question to this court. *Bayless* v. *Glenn*, 72 Ind. 5.

Having failed to do this, any error that may have been committed by the trial court upon this point is waived. It is the duty of the appellant to show affirmatively that some prejudicial error was committed. This he has failed to do.

Judgment affirmed.

Filed Jan. 30, 1894.

No. 991.

THE BOARD OF COMMISSIONERS OF SHELBY COUNTY v. BLAIR, ADMINISTRATOR.

PLEADING.— *Necessary Allegations.— Conclusion.— Personal Injury.— Damages.—Bridge.— County.*—In an action against a county for injuries sustained while crossing a bridge, the allegation "that the bridge complained of was constructed at a point where the defendant had a right to, and it was its duty to, construct it," is a mere conclusion, and does not take the place of the necessary allegations of fact showing that the county had authority to build it.

SAME.—*Sufficient Allegation.—Bridge.—Personal Injury.—County.*—In such case, an allegation "that the bridge complained of was situate and located over and across a mill-race, through which a large quantity of water flowed rapidly," is sufficient to show that the bridge spanned a watercourse.

COUNTY.—*Bridges.—Duty to Keep in Repair.*—A county is only bound to repair such bridges as it is authorized to build; and it is not necessary that the county should have built the bridge in order to give rise to the duty to keep in repair, for a bridge may become a county bridge by adoption, no matter by whom it is built, and such duty extends to approaches and railings.

BRIDGE.— *When a County Bridge.—Highway.—Mill-Race.*—Where the excavation of a mill-race across a highway necessitates the construction of a bridge across the race in order to restore the highway to a passable condition, a bridge so constructed, it matters not by whom, becomes a part of the highway.

ASSIGNMENT OF ERRORS.— *When Will not Lie.—Presumption.*—Where the record does not show when instructions, which have been refused, were tendered to the court, error can not be predicated upon such action, for every presumption will be indulged in favor of the action of the trial court.

EVIDENCE.—*Repairs of a Bridge Subsequent to Accident.—Admissible for What Purpose.*—In an action for injuries received at a bridge alleged to be defective, and received by reason of such defect, evidence that since the happening of the injuries complained of, there has been a new bridge put in across the watercourse, in the place of the old one, is admissible to prove that the bridge was a part of the highway, but not for the purpose of proving that the defendant had been negligent.

From the Decatur Circuit Court.

6

The Board of Commissioners of Shelby Co. v. Blair, Administrator.

O. J. Glessner, *D. L. Wilson*, *B. K. Elliott* and *W. F. Elliott*, for appellant.

T. B. Adams and *I. Carter*, for appellee.

Ross, J.—The appellee, Alonzo Blair, as administrator of the estate of Laura Beynon, deceased, instituted this action against the appellant, in the Shelby Circuit Court, to recover damages for the death of said Laura Beynon, alleged to have been caused by the negligence of the appellant in improperly constructing and in failing to keep in repair a bridge across a mill race in Shelby county. The venue of the cause was changed to the Decatur Circuit Court.

The complaint is in two paragraphs, to each of which a demurrer was filed by appellant and overruled by the court. The correctness of these rulings are the first questions presented on this appeal.

The first paragraph, omitting the caption, is as follows:

"In the above entitled cause, the plaintiff complains of the defendant and says, that on, to wit, the 27th day of May, 1891, he was appointed, by the Shelby Circuit Court, administrator of the estate of Laura Beynon, deceased; that he qualified, gave bond, entered upon the discharge of his duties as such administrator, and is now the legally qualified and acting administrator of said estate; that said Laura Beynon died intestate in said county on, to wit, the 23d day of March, 1891, leaving surviving her three children, whose names and ages are, respectively, Lewis Beynon, aged 11 years; Maggie Beynon, aged 8 years, and Alvin Beynon, aged 1 year; and also her husband, William Beynon, and that said children and husband are her next of kin and sole heirs at law; that said decedent was, at her death, 30 years old. And the plaintiff further says, that the defendant negligently

and improperly constructed and caused to be constructed
a county bridge on, in, and across the public county highway in said county, leading from the city of Shelbyville,
in said county, to Boggstown, in the same county, and
that said bridge was not within the corporate limits of
of any town or city; that said bridge was negligently and
improperly constructed in that, to wit, said bridge was
not constructed of sufficient width to make it safe for
persons to pass over it in vehicles drawn by horses in
case said horses should shy or become frightened from
any cause; that said bridge was constructed without any
side rails or protections at the sides thereof to prevent
horses from running off said bridge at the sides of the
same, or to prevent their. backing off or running off
said bridge the vehicles to which they were attached,
while passing on and over said bridge; that the boards
in the floor of said bridge were loose and movable, and.
made much noise and motion when either ridden or
driven over, and were not of sufficient thickness to make
a good and sufficient roadway; that the'boards in said
floor were so laid as to make cracks and holes through
which horses, when crossing said bridge, could see running water beneath; that the defendant permitted said
bridge to remain as so constructed, up to and including
the time hereinafter named, at which it is alleged said
Laura Beynon was injured, with this exception, that the
defendant suffered and permitted said bridge and the
floor thereof to rot and fall in decay, and the cracks and
holes on the floor of the same to become greatly enlarged
and so remain for a long time, to wit, five years before
the time at which said Laura Beynon was so injured;
that said bridge was of the length of, to wit, thirty feet;
of the height of, to wit, fifteen feet from the ground below, and of the width of only ten feet, and was situated
and located over and across a mill race, through which

a large quantity of water flowed rapidly, making much noise; that the defendant has accepted and maintained said bridge so constructed, and had used it as a county bridge in, across, and forming a part of said highway over which the public did travel for more than fifteen years immediately preceding the time when said decedent was injured; that there is now, and has been, for twenty years last past, much travel over said highway, and, at the time said decedent was so injured, there was no way by which persons lawfully traveling on said highway could cross said mill race, except by going on and over said bridge; that at said time there was a county bridge constructed and maintained by the defendant across Brandywine creek, at a point a little southeast of the bridge across said race, and at a distance of, to wit, seventy-five feet from it, and said bridge across said Brandywine creek was and is a part of said public highway leading from Shelbyville, Indiana, to Boggstown, Indiana; that both of said bridges were constructed at points where the defendant had a right to, and it was its duty to, construct them; that the floor of said bridge, at the time of said injury, was ten feet above the floor of the bridge across said race; that the said highway extending from the bridge across said race to said Brandywine bridge, ran over an approach to said bridge, which approach was also the approach to said race bridge, was constructed by the defendant, was steep and sharply curved, so that in passing over said highway from said Brandywine bridge, to said race bridge, there was a tendency, by reason of the steep grade and sharp curve, for vehicles to which horses were attached to run on the horses, and to run them and the vehicle off said race bridge, at the left hand side, all of which would have been avoided had such approach and said bridge been properly constructed

and maintained; that such approach was constructed by
the defendant, was a part of said public county highway,
and had been such for more than five years immediately
preceding the time of said injury; that on the 27th day
of ———, 1888, said bridge and approach were in the
condition herein described, and the defendant then knew
and had known, for all of five years immediately preceding, that they were in such condition; that on said day
decedent was in a wagon with, to wit, twenty children
from the age of five to ten years, and was being carefully
driven over said public highway and down said grade
from said Brandywine bridge on her way home, and,
while being there driven, the horses attached to said
wagon became frightened by the wagon running on them
in going down said grade, and at the movement and
noise of the boards in the floor of the bridge across said
race, and at the sight and sound of the water underneath
said bridge, and at other things unknown to the plaintiff, and ran off the said bridge at the left hand side,
and ran the wagon off said bridge at said side, and
without any fault or negligence of said decedent, or of
any of her next of kin, or of any one who was in said
wagon with her, she was thrown out of said wagon and
from said bridge into the water below, and on to some
large, rough timbers with sharp corners which the defendant had placed and permitted to be placed and remain at the side of said bridge, and was seriously and
fatally injured in her abdomen, back, spine, and lower
parts of her body, both internally and externally, from
which injuries she languished and suffered until the 23d
day of March, 1891, when she died; that her death was
due to the injuries she received on said 27th day of July;
that she did not know it was dangerous for her so to
travel over said highway on said day; that the defendant invited her to travel over said highway on said day,

and that there was no other way by which she could pass to her said home; that said highway leading from said city of Shelbyville to said town of Boggstown was and had been a public highway for more than fifty years before said 27th day of July, and that on said day the public generally were using and traveling over said highway and down said approach and on and across said race bridge; that the death of said decedent was caused by the negligence and wrong of the defendant as herein set out, and not by the negligence or fault or wrong of any one else; that by said negligence and wrong the said children have lost their mother and a mother's support, care, and love, and said husband has lost the service, companionship, and support of a faithful and loving wife, who, at the time of her death, was thirty years old, and prior to her injuries had been strong, healthy, and free from disease and pain, and they have thereby been damaged in a great sum of $10,000.

"Wherefore the plaintiff asks judgment for $10,000, costs, and all other proper relief."

The second paragraph is, in substance, the same as the first, except that instead of alleging that the county constructed the bridge, it is alleged that the county accepted and adopted the bridge, and for more than fifteen years past had continued "to accept and maintain said bridge" as a part of a public highway.

Inasmuch as counties are involuntary corporations, being mere local subdivisions of the State, and created by the sovereign power of the State, they are not liable for the negligence of their servants or agents unless made so by statute. *Union Civil Township* v. *Berryman*, 3 Ind. App. 344; *Board, etc.*, v. *Boswell*, 4 Ind. App. 133; *Vigo Township* v. *Board, etc.*, 111 Ind. 170; *Abbett* v. *Board, etc.*, 114 Ind. 61; *Board, etc.*, v. *Chipp's Admr.*, 131 Ind. 56; *Smith* v. *Board, etc.*, 131 Ind. 116; *Morris*

v. *Board, etc.,* 131 Ind. 285; *Board, etc.,* v. *Daily,* 132 Ind. 73.

And, in the absence of an express statute imposing a duty to keep its bridges in repair, a county is not liable for failure to do so. Elliott on Roads and Streets, p. 42; *Board, etc.,* v. *Chipp's Admr., supra.*

But the Legislature may charge them with the duty of maintaining highways and bridges within their boundaries, thereby creating a liability for neglect in the performance of the duty thus enjoined, if injury results. When once a duty is imposed, its breach resulting in an injury fixes the liability.

It is well settled that a county is not liable for injuries received by a traveler on a highway by reason of the imperfect or improper construction of a bridge, or by reason of its having become out of repair, except such bridge is one which it had authority to build, or one which it was the duty of the county to maintain. Hence, in an action against a county to recover for injuries received on account of a defective bridge, the facts alleged in the complaint, in order to be sufficient to withstand a demurrer, must show a duty resting upon the county and a breach of such duty. *Board, etc.,* v. *Brod,* 3 Ind. App. 585; *Board, etc.,* v. *Deprez, Admr.,* 87 Ind. 509; *Spicer* v. *Board, etc.,* 126 Ind. 369.

It is alleged, in the complaint, that the bridge complained of was constructed at a point "where the defendant had a right to and it was its duty to construct it." This is a mere conclusion, and does not take the place of the necessary allegations of fact showing that the county had authority to build it. *Board, etc.,* v. *Brod, supra.*

Section 2892, R. S. 1881, provides that the board of county commissioners shall cause all bridges in the county to be kept in repair, while sections 2880 and 2885 authorize such board to erect bridges over streams and watercourses. And it has been held that these statutes impose upon counties the duty of keeping all bridges over streams and watercourses, upon highways, in repair, and for a neglect of such duty, resulting in injury, a liability exists. *Park* v. *Board, etc.*, 3 Ind. App. 536; *House* v. *Board, etc.*, 60 Ind. 580; *Pritchett* v. *Board, etc.*, 62 Ind. 210; *Patton* v. *Board, etc.*, 96 Ind. 131; *Vaught* v. *Board, etc.*, 101 Ind. 123.

And, in some cases, the construction placed upon section 2892, *supra*, is that the county must use reasonable care to keep in repair all bridges upon the public highways of the county, regardless of the size of the bridge or the character of the streams or ditches which they span. *Board, etc.*, v. *Sisson*, 2 Ind. App. 311; *House* v. *Board, etc.*, *supra*; *Board, etc.*, v. *Pritchett*, 85 Ind. 68; *Board, etc.*, v. *Brown*, 89 Ind. 48; *Board, etc.*, v. *Bacon*, 96 Ind. 31; *Vaught* v. *Board, etc.*, *supra*; *Board, etc.*, v. *Legg, Admr.*, 110 Ind. 479; *Board, etc.*, v. *Arnett*, 116 Ind. 438.

In the case of *Board, etc.*, v. *Legg, Admr.*, 93 Ind. 523, ELLIOTT, J., speaking for the court, says: "It is charged in the third paragraph of the complaint before us, that the appellant had for more than ten years prior to the time appellee's intestate was injured, maintained the bridge; that the bridge formed a part of a public highway in the county of Howard; and that it was the duty of the defendants to keep the bridges on the public highway in the county of Howard in repair. We think that these allegations show that the bridge was one over which the county had control, and which it was bound to maintain."

And, when the same case was before the Supreme Court a second time, 110 Ind. 479, the court, in discussing the correctness of the instructions given on the trial

582. APPELLATE COURT OF INDIANA,

The Board of Commissioners of Shelby Co. v. Blair, Administrator.

of the cause, says: "The substance of the instructions thus objected to was, that a traveler, using a public highway of the county in the ordinary manner, and without any knowledge of defects in a bridge forming a part thereof, has a right to presume that it is in a safe condition, and to drive over and across the same with his team, in the usual manner. * * * It is contended on behalf of appellant, that the bridge, by the breaking down of which Davis was killed, was a small one, over an artificial ditch, dug for the purpose of draining wet lands; that, being such, it was not a bridge over a 'watercourse,' and such as the county was bound to keep in repair.

"The county board has general supervision over the bridges of the county, and must exercise reasonable care in keeping all bridges upon the public highways of the county in a safe condition, regardless of the size of the bridge or the character of the streams or ditches which they may span."

Again, in the case of *Board, etc., v. State, ex rel.*, 113 Ind. 179, the court says: "When a bridge is a part of a public county highway, the county, or, what in law is the same thing in this State, the board of commissioners, is bound to exercise reasonable care in the maintenance of it, so that injury may not result to persons traveling upon the highway. * * * The board of commissioners owes a duty to the public to keep the bridges forming a part of the public highways of the county in a safe condition, so as to prevent injury to persons traveling upon such highways."

And in the case of *Board, etc., v. Washington Township*, 121 Ind. 379, which was an action brought by the county to compel the township to pay part of the expense of maintaining a bridge which was a part of a free gravel road, the court says: "The common-law rule is that the county officers are bound to adopt and maintain a public bridge forming a part of a road, or else have it declared a nuisance. Under this rule the bridge in question must be regarded as a county bridge, which it is the duty of the county to maintain."

In the case of *Board, etc.*, v. *Bailey*, 122 Ind. 46, it is said: "The Legislature having restricted the authority of county commissioners to the erection and repair of bridges over streams or watercourses, thereby clearly indicated a purpose to employ the term 'bridge' according to its common-law acceptation, or in its technical sense. In that sense it denotes a structure erected over a river, creek, pond, lake, or stream of water flowing in a channel, between banks more or less defined, although such channel may be occasionally dry, in order to facilitate public passage over the same."

And again, in the same case, the court says: "We do not mean to say that the power and duty of county commissioners in respect to the erection and repair of bridges is necessarily confined to structures over natural watercourses and flowing streams, but their duties relate to the erecting and keeping in repair of the bridges over permanent watercourses, either natural or artificial, or over lakes, ponds, or other more or less permanent and continuous bodies of water which obstruct the convenient use of a highway for public travel."

Prior to the passage of the free gravel road laws, counties were not responsible for defective highways, and no action could be maintained against a county for negligence respecting highways. *Board, etc.*, v. *Rickel*, 106 Ind. 501, and cases cited.

Not only is there confusion and uncertainty in the adjudicated cases as to just what kind of a bridge is to be understood as a county bridge, but some confusion apparently exists in our statutes concerning the respect-

ive duties of counties and townships relative to the building and maintaining of bridges, the same general authority to build and the duty of keeping in repair bridges,
having been conferred and imposed both upon the county
commissioners and the township officers, and yet it has
been held that section 2892, *supra*, which imposes upon
the county the duty of keeping all bridges therein in repair, in so far as the traveling public is concerned, has
not been changed or the duty lessened by any of the subsequent acts imposing the same duty upon township and
road officers. *Board, etc.*, v. *Sisson, supra; Board, etc.*,
v. *Emmerson*, 95 Ind. 579; *Patton* v. *Board, etc., supra;
Vaught* v. *Board, etc.; supra; Board, etc.*, v. *Arnett, supra;
Board, etc.*, v. *Washington Township, supra.*

It is alleged in both paragraphs of the complaint under consideration, that the bridge complained of is a part
of a public highway in said county. Is that allegation
sufficient to show that the bridge was one which it was
the duty of the county to keep in repair?

We think that when the courts have said that under
section 2892, *supra*, the board of commissioners is bound
to keep in repair all the bridges which form a part of the
public highways of the county, a broader construction
was placed upon it than the Legislature intended. All
of the sections of the statute, those conferring upon the
board the authority to build bridges, as well as the one
imposing upon it the duty of keeping them in repair,
should be considered and construed together. In that
view of the intention of the Legislature, and so construing the several statutes, we are forced to the conclusion
that the county is only bound to repair such bridges as
it is authorized to build. It is not necessary that the
county should have built the bridge in order that it be
its duty to keep it in repair, for a bridge may become a

county bridge by adoption, no matter by whom it is built. *State, ex rel.,* v. *Board, etc.,* 80 Ind. 478.

And the duty thus resting upon county boards of keeping county bridges in repair, extends to the necessary approaches, and also to railings, when the same are needed to make a bridge reasonably safe for travel by those who exercise ordinary care in traveling over them. *Board, etc.,* v. *Sisson, supra.*

It is also alleged in each paragraph of the complaint, that the bridge complained of "was situated and located over and across a mill race, through which a large quantity of water flowed rapidly."

This allegation is sufficient to show that the bridge spanned a watercourse, for a mill race through which a large quantity of water flows, is an artificial watercourse. And the other allegations, showing the bridge to be a part of the public highway, show that it was clearly a county bridge within the meaning of the statute, and that it was the duty of the board of commissioners to keep it in repair.

The court did not err in overruling the demurrer to each paragraph of the complaint.

The fourth error assigned is that the court erred in overruling appellant's motion for judgment on the answers of the jury to interrogatories. In answer to interrogatories submitted to them, the jury found that the bridge complained of was built in 1864, by one Samuel Murphy, in and as a part of an existing public highway, spanning a mill race at that time constructed by him across said highway for his own use; that there was no necessity for a bridge at that point, before the digging of the mill race, but that the digging of the mill race occasioned the necessity for a bridge at that point; that neither appellant nor the officers of the township in which the bridge is located ever repaired it, but that appellant assumed and exercised control over it.

Counsel for appellant say: "Under such a state of facts the appellant was not and could not become liable for failure to keep the bridge in repair. The jury found, that the highway was in existence long before the race was dug; that the race was dug by Samuel Murphy, the mill owner, and the bridge built by him across the race for his own benefit; that the cutting of the mill race by him created a necessity for the bridge; that the county neither constructed nor authorized the construction of said bridge, and that it never assumed to keep it in repair."

To sustain this contention counsel cite the case of *Dygert* v. *Schenck*, 23 Wend. 445, where the court, in passing upon the question of the right of an individual to dig a ditch across a public highway and his duty to build and maintain a bridge across the same, says: "The very necessity for its erection arises out of a nuisance, which was the work of the defendant himself."

While the principle there announced is probably applicable to that case, it is not authority in the case under consideration. As heretofore stated, the law is settled in this State that the board of commissioners is to keep in repair all the bridges in the county over watercourses, either natural or artificial, which are necessarily parts of the public highways. If the excavation of the race necessitated the construction of a bridge in order to restore the highway and a bridge was constructed, it became a part of the highway and it matters not who may have built it. If it is such a bridge as the county must keep in repair, a failure on the part of the county in the performance of such duty, to the injury of a traveler without fault on his part, makes it liable therefor.

We do not pretend to hold that a county can be held

liable for failing to keep in repair every bridge which it may have assumed charge and control of, simply because it attempted to assume the responsibility of keeping the same in repair. It is not within the power of a county, through its officers, to create such a liability, for the liability exists from a breach of a duty which can be imposed only by a positive statute.

. Following the many cases already cited, if the bridge complained of was a necessary part of the highway, whether it crossed a river, lake, pond, ditch, or mill race, it was the duty of the county to keep it in repair.

The appellant was not entitled to judgment on the answers to interrogatories.

What we have said in passing upon the sufficiency of the complaint and the right of appellant to a judgment on the answers to the interrogatories, disposes of most of the objections made to instructions given, and also as to those requested by the appellant which the court refused to give.

The objections to the second instruction given by the court are not well taken. It is true that if the court, in its instructions, attempts to designate what facts are necessary to be established to entitle a party to recover, all of the necessary facts must be stated. For, if the court directs the jury that a party is entitled to recover upon proof of a state of facts less than what the law applicable to the issues require, it is error. We do not consider that the court, by this instruction, attempted to limit the material facts essential to a right to recover to the fact that it was only necessary for the appellee to prove either that the appellant constructed the bridge, or that subsequent to its erection appellant accepted and adopted it as a county bridge and as a part of a highway. Other instructions given by the court clearly indicated to the jury that it was necessary to prove more.

Appellant requested the court to give a number of instructions, which were refused by the court, and this ruling of the court is urged on this appeal for a reversal of the judgment.

Section 533, R. S. 1881, provides: "When the evidence is concluded, and either party desires special instructions to be given to the jury, such instructions shall be reduced to writing, numbered and signed by the party or his attorney asking the same, and delivered to the court."

And it is well settled that such instructions must be presented to the court before the argument begins. *Terry* v. *Shively*, 93 Ind. 413; *Evansville, etc., R. R. Co.* v. *Crist*, 116 Ind. 446.

Every reasonable and natural presumption will be indulged by this court in favor of the correctness of the rulings of the trial court. *Graves* v. *Duckwall*, 103 Ind. 560.

Hence, a party who alleges error in the rulings of the trial court, in order to justify this court in reversing the judgment, must present a record which shows affirmatively that an error was committed. The record in this case does not show when the instructions asked were tendered to the court, and if we indulge the presumption that the court rightfully refused them, unless the record shows affirmatively that they were refused wrongfully, we may assume they were refused because not tendered at the proper time. Considering together all the instructions given by the court, we think they were correct and sufficient under the issues in this case.

On the trial of the cause, George Francis, a witness called on behalf of the appellee, was asked the following question, viz: "Now tell the jury whether or not, since Mrs. Beynon was hurt, there has been a new bridge put in across the race." To this question the appellant objected, the objection was overruled, exception saved, and the witness permitted to testify. This ruling of the court appellant insists was error.

Evidence of repairs made after the happening of an accident is not competent to show antecedent negligence. *Terre Haute, etc., R. R. Co.* v. *Clem*, 123 Ind. 15, and cases cited; *Board, etc.,* v. *Pearson*, 129 Ind. 456.

The evidence complained of, while incompetent for the purpose of showing the appellant to have been negligent, or that the bridge was out of repair at the time appellee was injured, was nevertheless competent for the purpose of showing that the appellant had accepted and adopted it as a part of the public highway. It was a controverted question in the case, and one which it was necessary for the appellee to prove, that the bridge was a part of the highway, and that the appellant had accepted and adopted it as such.

Evidence that they exercised control over it by looking after and repairing it was competent for the purpose of showing that it had adopted it and considered it a part of the highway. If it had been conceded that the bridge was a part of the highway, and was kept in repair by the appellant, we think it would have been improper to have admitted the evidence complained of, for it is clear, under such issues, that its admission was for the purpose of proving negligence on the part of the appellant in keeping the bridge in repair. If evidence offered is competent for the purpose of establishing any fact pertinent to and within the issues, it is not error to admit it.

Several other minor questions have been mentioned in appellant's brief, but we can not see that they were prejudicial to appellant's rights, and for that reason we do not extend this opinion and enumerate and pass upon them separately.

It is unnecessary to examine the cross-errors assigned.

Buscher *v.* The City of Lafayette.

We find no error in the record, for which the judgment should be reversed.

Judgment affirmed.

GAVIN, J., took no part in the decision of this case.

Filed Jan. 9, 1894.

———◆———

No. 818.

BUSCHER *v.* THE CITY OF LAFAYETTE.

JURISDICTION.—*Appeal.*—*Amount in Controversy, How Determined.*—*Appellate Court.*—Where, in an action for damages, the jury find for the plaintiff in a certain sum, such sum is the amount in controversy on appeal, and determines the jurisdiction. Had the jury found generally for the defendant, the amount demanded in the complaint would determine that question.

SPECIAL VERDICT.—*Overruling Motion to Strike Out Evidentiary Facts and Legal Conclusions.*—*Harmless Error.*—*Duty of Court to Disregard.* —If a special verdict contain evidentiary facts or conclusions of law, the court, in passing upon the verdict and in rendering judgment thereon, must disregard the evidentiary facts and legal conclusions; hence, the overruling of a motion to strike out improper findings in a special verdict is not such error as will warrant a reversal of the judgment.

MUNICIPAL CORPORATION.— *Defective Sidewalk.*— *Personal Injury.*— *Damages.*—*Liability for.*—If a city permit a sidewalk to become out of repair so that a pedestrian, without knowledge or the means of ascertaining its condition, be injured while using the same, without fault on his part, it is liable therefor.

SAME.—*Streets and Sidewalks, When Sufficiently Constructed.*—*Presumption.*— *Notice.*—Where a city builds and maintains streets and sidewalks, which are reasonably safe for use by persons exercising ordinary care, it has fulfilled its duty in that respect. And pedestrians may presume that the city has done its duty in constructing and maintaining the same. Actual notice on the part of the corpo. ration, of the defective condition of a street or sidewalk is not necessary where such unsafe condition has existed for such time that, with reasonable diligence, it might have been known.

SAME.—*Special Finding.*—*Recovery.*—*Sidewalk.*—*Personal Injury.*—In an action for a personal injury, against a city, alleged to have been received by reason of a defective sidewalk, the plaintiff can not recover where the jury specially find that the walk where the plaintiff was injured "was in a reasonably safe condition for use in the customary and proper way, by persons exercising ordinary care."

From the Tippecanoe Superior Court.

J. R. Coffroth, A. L. Kumler, T. F. Gaylord and *T. A. Stuart*, for appellant.

J. F. McHugh, A. D. Wallace and *S. P. Baird*, for appellee.

Ross, J.—The appellant brought this action against the appellee, to recover damages for injuries received by her, caused by an alleged defect in a sidewalk in the city of Lafayette.

The appellant, in her complaint, demanded damages in the sum of five thousand dollars, but upon trial of the cause, the jury returned a special verdict, in which her damages were assessed at one thousand dollars. Upon the special verdict of the jury, judgment was rendered in favor of the appellee.

The first question presented for our consideration calls in question the jurisdiction of this court. It is urged that this court has no jurisdiction of the cause, for the reason that the amount in controversy exceeds thirty-five hundred dollars, and we are required to determine which controls, the demand in the complaint or the damages assessed by the jury. Had the jury returned a general verdict for the appellee, the appellant's damages would have been undetermined, and the demand of the complaint would be the amount in controversy, but when the amount to be recovered has once been ascertained and fixed it must control. When the jury determined that the appellant had been damaged in the sum of one thousand dollars, the amount in controversy became fixed, and, on appeal, that is the amount in controversy, and determines the jurisdiction of this court.

The appellant assigns in this court, for a reversal of the judgment, the following reasons, viz:

1st. "Because the court erred in overruling appellant's motion to strike out parts of the special verdict returned by the jury on the trial of this cause."

2d. "Because the court erred in overruling appellant's motion for a *venire de novo* herein."

3d. "Because the court erred in overruling appellant's motion for judgment in her favor, upon the facts found by the jury in their special verdict herein."

4th. "Because the court erred in sustaining the motion made by appellee, for judgment in its favor, upon the facts found by the jury in their special verdict herein."

5th. "Because the court erred in overruling appellant's motion in arrest of judgment herein."

When a jury returns a special verdict containing evidentiary facts, conclusions, or legal inferences, the court, in passing upon such a verdict and in rendering judgment thereon, must disregard such evidentiary facts, conclusions, and legal inferences, hence the overruling of the motion to strike out improper findings in a special verdict is not such error as will warrant a reversal of the judgment. Being improper, they neither add to nor take from the facts properly found, and if the verdict is sufficient without them they neither strengthen nor weaken it.

A special verdict, in order to be sufficient to sustain a judgment in favor of the party upon whom rests the burden of the issue, must find all the facts necessary to sustain such issue. *Waymire* v. *Lank*, 121 Ind. 1; *Town of Freedom* v. *Norris*, 128 Ind. 377; *Brazil Block Coal Co.* v. *Hoodlet*, 129 Ind. 327.

The special verdict returned by the jury in this case

probably contains conclusions, as well as legal inferences, yet they do not vitiate it.   *Reeves* v. *Grottendick*,
131 Ind. 107, and cases cited.

The motion for a *venire de novo* was properly overruled, unless the verdict was ambiguous, indefinite, or
wanting in form.   This verdict is not open to any of
these objections.

The third and fourth errors assigned may be considered
together, as they both call in question the correctness of
the courts ruling on the facts found.

The material facts found in the verdict, which we think
necessary to a determination of this case are, in substance, as follows: That the appellee, on the 20th day
of September, 1888, and for a long time prior thereto,
was a municipal corporation, organized under the general laws of the State of Indiana; that about sixty days
prior to said day a brick gutter had been constructed in
the sidewalk, on Salem street, an improved and generally used street in said city of Lafayette, in front of
the property of one Schuman, the gutter having been
built of brick, about eight inches long, four inches wide,
two inches thick, so laid that the bottom of the gutter
was from three and one-half to four inches wide, extending across the entire sidewalk; that bricks were placed
on end on each side of the bricks so laid for the bottom
of the gutter, at an angle of from twenty-six degrees at the
lot line to nineteen degrees at the curb line, thus forming
sides for the gutter, which was four and one-fourth inches
deep at the lot line, and two and one-half inches deep at
the curb line, and measured sixteen and one-half inches
across the top at the inner or fence line, and nineteen
and one-half inches at the outer or curb line, the top of
the gutter being on a level with the general surface of
the walk; that the gutter was so constructed that it did

not afford a firm foothold to one stepping into it; that on the night of said 20th day of September the appellant, in company with others, was walking along said sidewalk talking, and she stepped into said gutter and was thereby thrown down, and her ankle severely sprained and partially dislocated; that she had no knowledge of the condition of the sidewalk, or that there was a gutter there, and that she did not see it; that the night "was a bright, moonlight night, but occasionally the moon was obscured by the clouds"; that the appellant, at the time she was injured, was walking along the sidewalk "in a manner and way that an ordinarily prudent person would have done under like circumstances, and she had no knowledge of the condition of the sidewalk, or that there was a gutter there, nor was her attention attracted thereto, nor did she see said gutter before stepping into the same, and that she, at the time of receiving said injury, was walking along said sidewalk with ordinary and reasonable care, and without fault"; "that said sidewalk at said point, by reason of the existence of said gutter, so constructed as aforesaid, was in a reasonably safe condition for use in the customary and proper way, by persons exercising ordinary care;" that appellant, by reason of such injuries, was confined to her bed for three weeks, during which time she suffered great pain, and still suffers therefrom; that her nervous system was greatly shocked and she is sore and lame by reason thereof, but that she will probably recover.

A city is bound to maintain its streets and sidewalks in a reasonably safe condition for the use of persons travelling thereon. *City of Lafayette* v. *Larson*, 73 Ind. 367; *City of Crawfordsville* v. *Smith*, 79 Ind. 308; *City of Washington* v. *Small*, 86 Ind. 462; *City of Michigan City* v. *Boeckling*, 122 Ind. 39; *City of Columbus* v. *Strassner*, 124 Ind. 482.

If a city permits a sidewalk to become out of repair, so that a pedestrian, without knowledge or the means of ascertaining its condition, be injured while using the same, without fault on his part, it is liable therefor. But while the city is bound to maintain its sidewalks in a reasonably safe condition for the use of reasonably prudent and careful persons, it is not required to see that its sidewalks are absolutely perfect and safe, neither does it insure persons traveling thereon from injury. When it builds and maintains streets and sidewalks which are reasonably safe for use by persons exercising ordinary care, it has fulfilled its duty, and, if injury befall such persons, the city is not liable. It is impossible to construct a sidewalk absolutely free from defects and slight irregularities, inequalities, and obstructions. The law never exacts an impossible thing.

In the case of *City of Indianapolis* v. *Cook*, 99 Ind. 10, the court says: "There are slight inequalities in sidewalks and other trifling defects and obstructions against which one may possibly strike his foot and fall, but if injury might be avoided by the use of such care and caution as every reasonably prudent person ought to exercise for his own safety, the city would not be liable."

Actual notice on the part of the officials of a corporation, of the defective condition of a street or sidewalk, is not always necessary, for notice may be inferred, when the facts disclose the unsafe condition of the street to have existed for such a length of time that the officers might, with reasonable diligence, have known it. *City of Indianapolis* v. *Scott*, 72 Ind. 196; *City of Indianapolis* v. *Murphy*, 91 Ind. 382; *City of Aurora* v. *Bitner*, 100 Ind. 396; *City of Madison* v. *Baker*, 103 Ind. 41.

And pedestrians may presume that the city has done

its duty and has built and maintained sidewalks which
are reasonably safe for use, but, at the same time, the
pedestrian, in using the sidewalk, must exercise such
care as an ordinarily prudent person ought to exercise
in its use.   Those using it must exercise such care in its
use as is commensurate with the apparent danger to be
encountered, and a less degree of care on their part is
negligence.   It is also well settled that persons going
along a highway are bound to take notice of visible defects, and if they proceed and are injured they assume
the risk to a degree commensurate with the care the law
exacts from an ordinarily prudent person under like circumstances.

The jury found that the walk where the appellee was
injured "was in a reasonably safe condition for use in
the customary and proper way, by persons exercising ordinary care."   Nothing more was required of the city,
hence its duty to the public had been performed.   A
traveler traveling thereon has no right to use it other
than in the customary and proper way in which persons
exercising ordinary care would use it.   There were no
facts found by the jury, from which the court could infer that the appellee was negligent.

In arriving at this conclusion, we have not overlooked
the finding that the gutter was so constructed as not to
afford a firm foothold to one stepping into it "and was
likely to cause one using said sidewalk at that point to
fall."   All the facts found must be considered together,
and if they are not sufficient to warrant the court in inferring negligence as a matter of law, the judgment rendered thereon in favor of the appellee is right.   The
burden was upon the appellant to establish facts sufficient to warrant an inference of negligence on the part
of appellee, and if the facts found point as strongly to-

ward its freedom from fault as toward its negligence, the appellant must fail.

There was no error in rendering judgment in favor of the appellee, upon the facts found.

Judgment affirmed.

Filed Jan. 30, 1894.

<hr/>

No. 1,004.

HEDGE v. TALBOTT, ADMINISTRATOR.

EVIDENCE.—*Decedent's Estate.—Attorney.—History of a Land Transaction.—Competency.—Note.*—In an action on a claim against a decedent's estate, involving a note bearing eight per cent. interest alleged to have evolved out of a land transaction between the claimant and the decedent, the attorney for the decedent was permitted to testify to the facts in relation to the land transaction between the decedent and claimant's husband, with the statement by the court to the jury that plaintiff was not bound by anything that was said or done in her absence, but that the circumstances connected with the transaction were proper to go to the jury with the other evidence in the case.

Held, that such testimony, as a history of the transaction, subject to the limitations stated by the court, was proper to go to the jury, in order to make the evidence offered in relation to the transaction more intelligible.

SAME.—*Nonexecution of Note.—Circumstance for Jury.—Alleged Maker Having Money to Loan at Date of Execution.—Decedent's Estate.*—In such case, where the defenses interposed were nonexecution of the note and want of consideration, evidence that the decedent had, when the debt in question was said to have been created in 1876, on hand or in bank, from $300 to $1,500, and that decedent made a loan of $300 at six per cent. interest, about the time of the alleged execution of the note, and that decedent continued to have such sums of money at her command during all the time prior to the execution of the note, was admissible as a circumstance which the jury might consider in determining whether such debt was so created and allowed to stand as an open account from 1876 to 1887, and whether the note was then executed as evidence thereof, at eight per cent., when she had money to loan at six per cent.

From the Montgomery Circuit Court.

A. D. Thomas and *W. F. Whittington*, for appellant.

A. B. Anderson and *B. Crane*, for appellee.

DAVIS, C. J.—This was an action upon a promissory note for four hundred dollars, bearing interest at eight per cent. from date, filed by appellant against the estate of Isabel Durham. The defense interposed to the note was nonexecution of the note and want of consideration. A trial by jury resulted in verdict and judgment for appellee.

The only error assigned is the overruling of appellant's motion for a new trial.

This is the second time the case has been in this court. *Talbott, Admr.,* v. *Hedge,* 5 Ind. App. 555.

The evidence tends to prove that about 1874 said Durham sold and conveyed to appellant's husband one hundred and twenty acres of land for four thousand, eight hundred dollars, of which eight hundred was paid in cash, and notes were executed for the residue; that at the expiration of one year, when the first note became due, the real estate was reconveyed by the purchaser to her in discharge of said notes; that in consideration of the eight hundred dollars paid by him on the purchase price he was allowed the use and possession of the real estate for two years.

The theory of appellant was that said Isabel agreed to pay appellant four hundred dollars to join in the reconveyance of the real estate, and that in consideration of said agreement the note in suit was executed eleven years thereafter. There was some evidence, perhaps, slight though it may be, tending to support that contention. On the contrary, the theory of appellee was that said decedent never signed the note, but that if she did it was without consideration.

Appellee introduced evidence tending to prove that after the reconveyance appellant claimed she was entitled to something on account of the land transaction, and that the attorney who had the business in charge for Mrs. Durham insisted that she was entitled to nothing. Over objection of appellant, said attorney was permitted to testify to the facts in relation to the land transaction between said decedent and appellant's husband. This evidence was admitted by the trial court, with the statement, then made to the jury by the court, that appellant was not bound by anything that was said or done in her absence, but that the circumstances connected with that transaction were proper to go to the jury with the other evidence in the case. Under the circumstances, the history of that transaction was proper to go to the jury, subject to the limitation stated by the court, in order to make the evidence offered by the respective parties, in relation to the nature of that transaction, intelligible.

On the trial James C. Knox and Eugene Ashby, witnesses for appellee, who were familiar with her business affairs, over the objections and exceptions of appellant, were allowed to testify that she had before, and at, or about, the time the note purports to have been executed, money on hand which she desired to loan, and that in a conversation with one of them she requested him to find a borrower for her. This evidence tended to show that from 1876 to 1887 she had, at all times, or nearly so, in bank from $300 to $1,500, and that she made a loan of $300, at six per cent. interest, to one of the witnesses near the time of the alleged execution of the note in suit. In this connection it should be borne in mind that there was evidence introduced on the part of appellee, tending

to prove that the signature to the note was not that of
Mrs. Durham.

The fact that she was in easy financial circumstances
during all of these years, that she had money on hand,
and that she desired to find a borrower for her money,
did not prove that she did not promise, in 1876, to pay
appellant four hundred dollars, or that she did not, in
pursuance of 'that promise, execute the note in suit in
1887. The jury were required to determine whether the
promise was made in 1876, and whether the debt was afterwards paid, or whether the note was executed in consideration thereof in 1887. There was no direct evidence on the question of payment.

In such cases, relating to transactions of a remote
period, where it is (as it was in this case) difficult to apply other than circumstantial evidence, when the question is whether or not money has been paid, proof that
the party sought to be charged with the debt was in such
circumstances that he or she could or could not pay, has
been received as tending to show that he or she did or
did not pay. *Vogt* v. *Butler*, 105 Mo. 479, 16 S. W.
Rep. 512; *Stolp* v. *Blair*, 68 Ill. 541; *Dowling* v. *Dowling*,
10 Irish Com. Law, 236.

The evidence that said Isabel Durham had, when
the debt in question was said to have been created in
1876, on hand or in bank the amount of money hereinbefore mentioned, and that she continued to have such
money at her command during all the years prior to the
alleged execution of the note was admissible as a circumstance which the jury might consider in determining
whether such debt was so created and allowed to stand
as an open account from 1876 to 1887, and whether the
note was then executed as the evidence thereof. *Selig-
man* v. *Rogers*, 21 S. W. Rep. 94.

It was a question, under all the circumstances, whether

appellant, according to the usual experience of mankind, would allow such debt to stand as an open account for eleven years, or whether said decedent would execute a note bearing eight per cent. interest when she had money to loan at six per cent.

For the reasons stated there was no error in our opinion in allowing the evidence to go to the jury. With their knowledge of, and experience in, the common business affairs of life, this evidence was proper to be considered in connection with the other facts and circumstances in the case in determining whether the debt was created in 1876, whether it remained unpaid until 1887, and whether the note in suit was executed by said Isabel Durham.

It is undisputed, that when Isabel Durham died she was seventy years of age; that she took a reconveyance of the real estate, because the husband of appellant, at the end of the first year, found he could not pay therefor, and in doing this she surrendered his notes for the unpaid purchase money, on a part of which ($700) there was personal security, and the residue was secured by mortgage; that for the eight hundred dollars which he had paid thereon she allowed him the use and possession of the land, worth $400 per year, for two years. If appellant was, in justice, entitled to anything farther from Mrs. Durham, such fact, to say the least of it, is not clearly or satisfactorily explained, but if she had recovered in the court below, perhaps this court would not have reversed the judgment on the evidence.

However this may be, neither of the parties in interest could testify at the trial. The mouth of one was then sealed in death and the mouth of the other was closed by statute. The history of the transaction which constituted the alleged consideration of the note, and the financial situation of the parties, during the years mentioned, were, under the circumstances of this particular case, so far as the same were entered into on the trial, relevant and pertinent subjects of inquiry, as tending in some degree, at least, to throw light on the matters in controversy.

It is sufficient to say in conclusion, that it appears to the court, from an examination of the record, that the merits of the cause have been fairly tried in the court below. Section 658, R. S. 1881.

Judgment affirmed.

Filed Jan. 30, 1894.

No. 1,049.

THE TOLEDO, ST. LOUIS AND KANSAS CITY RAILROAD COMPANY *v.* FLY.

RAILROAD.—*Duty to Fence and Maintain Cattle-Guards.*—*Killing of Animal.*—*Denial of Obligation to Fence, etc.*—*Burden of Proof.*—*Evidence.*—A railroad company is not required to fence its track or put in a cattle-guard at a point where a fence or cattle-guard would materially interfere with the operation of the road in the discharge of its duty to the public, or would endanger the safety of its employes in operating it. But the burden of showing that a railroad ought not to be fenced, or a cattle-guard put in at a given place, is upon the railroad company; and where there is nothing in the evidence to indicate that the operation of the railroad, with reference to its duty to the public, would be interfered with, a judgment for damages for the killing of an animal which entered upon the track at a point where it was not fenced and a cattle-guard not maintained, will not be disturbed on appeal.

From the Montgomery Circuit Court.

C. Brown, S. O. Bayless and *C. G. Guenther,* for appellant.

J. West, for appellee.

GAVIN, J.—Appellee sued for damages by reason of the

killing of his horse, which entered upon appellant's track at a point where it ought to have been, but was not, fenced.

The only error argued relates to the sufficiency of the evidence, and the only point made upon that is that it is conclusively shown that, at the place where the horse entered, the company was not bound to fence.

There is evidence tending to show that the horse entered upon the appellant's right of way on the north side of it, from a highway which crossed it and where there was no cattle guard and wing fences. The railroad runs east and west, the highway runs northwest and southeast, crossing the railroad at an angle. This crossing is about one-quarter of a mile east of appellant's depot, at the town of Wingate. On the north side of the railroad there is a fence extending from the crossing east about seven hundred and seventy feet to a cattle-guard with proper wing fences. On the south side of the railroad there is no fence from the crossing to this cattle-guard. From this cattle-guard a switch track runs about three hundred feet west, where it joins the main track, the east end of the switch being a dead end, south of this switch track is a tile mill, and south of it a saw mill. The triangular piece of ground occupied by the tile mill and saw mill is open and unfenced on the southwest where the highway runs along it. From the crossing east to the west end of the switch is about four hundred and seventy feet. On the west side of the highway crossing, and eighty feet from where the horse entered the right of way, there is a cattle-guard and wing fences. The switch was put in and used solely to load tile from the tile factory, except there were perhaps at one time some cars of lumber on the switch, for a house for the owner of the tile factory. How much tile was loaded there, whether one car load or one hundred a year, does not appear. Cars have been seen on the switch track, but how frequently is not shown.

One witness testified that he had seen some switching done there, but had never seen any brakeman couple or uncouple cars there, although it was necessary to do so in getting cars in and out of the switch, and was also necessary, in so doing, for a brakeman to pass over some portion of the track from the crossing to the switch, what portion would be passed over being dependent on circumstances. A train is ordinarily about eight hundred feet long.

It further appears from the evidence, that there was, seven or eight years ago, a switch fence along the south side of the railroad from this crossing east to where the cattle-guard now is, and cattle-guards at the crossing, both a switch and the tile factory being then in existence, the present switch, however, having been put in to replace the former one torn out.

The location of the crossing and switch is shown by the following diagram:

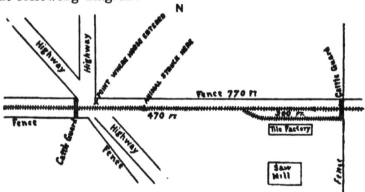

It is settled law that a railroad company is not required to fence its track at a point where a fence would materially interfere with the operation of the road in the discharge of its duty to the public, or endanger the safety of its employes in operating it, but the burden of showing that the road ought not to be fenced at the given place is upon the railroad company. *Toledo, etc., R. R. Co.* v. *Woody,* 5 Ind. App. 331; *Terre Haute, etc., R. R. Co.* v. *Schaefer,* 5 Ind. App. 86; *Pennsylvania Co.* v. *Lindley,* 2 Ind. App. 111; *Chicago, etc., R. R. Co.* v. *Modesitt,* 124 Ind. 212; *Pennsylvania Co.* v. *Mitchell,* 124 Ind. 473.

Counsel for the appellant insist that upon the evidence in this case we should adjudge, as a matter of law, that the road could not be fenced at the place in question.

Reliance is placed largely upon the case of *Indianapolis, etc., R. W. Co.* v. *Clay,* 4 Ind. App. 282, and cases cited therein. Without entering into a consideration of the propositions of law therein stated, which are relied upon by appellant, it is sufficient to say that the decision itself in that case is conclusively against appellant's position in this case.

There the business of the company at the point named and its necessities were proven much more fully than here, and still it was decided that the cattle-guard might have been maintained within two hundred feet of a switch.

In the case at bar there were four hundred and seventy feet of clear space between the crossing and the switch. If two hundred and seventy feet had been fenced off and protected, there would still have been more than enough left for the safe use of the switch, under this decision. *Toledo, etc., R. R. Co.* v. *Woody, supra,* is to the same effect, holding that the court could not say, as a matter of law, that the company could not safely erect cattle-guards and fences within two hundred feet of a switch.

There is, in the evidence, nothing to indicate that the operation of the road, with reference to its duty to the public, would be interfered with. The switch was for the use of the tile factory only. How many cars it needed does not appear, but if it needed and used many cars they could plainly be thrown into the switch without requiring the brakeman to travel over all of this four hundred and seventy feet.

The fact that the company maintained a cattle-guard on the west side of this crossing was strong evidence that it did not need for switching purposes a free space equal to the full length of the train, as argued by counsel.

Our conclusion is that there was no error.

Judgment affirmed.

Filed Jan. 9, 1894.

No. 927.

KELLEY *v.* KELLEY.

HARMLESS ERROR.—*Sustaining Demurrer to Paragraph of Answer.*—It is harmless error to sustain a demurrer to a paragraph of answer, even if good, where the facts provable under such paragraph were admissible under the general denial, which was also pleaded.

NEW TRIAL.—*Joint Motion.—Overruling as to One and Sustaining as to Another.*—A party can not be heard to complain of the overruling of a joint motion for a new trial, as to him, unless the motion is well taken as to all the parties who join in making it. In such case, the court may overrule as to one, and sustain it as to another.

SAME.—*Surprise as a Cause.*—Since a party who is surprised by the testimony of a witness may procure a continuance on account of such surprise, if, upon motion, he show proper grounds, a strong and clear case must be made before a reversal will be founded upon such cause as a ground for a new trial.

SAME.—*Newly Discovered Evidence.—When a Cause.—Diligence, When Sufficiently Shown.*—Newly discovered evidence is not a ground for a new trial, where no sufficient excuse is shown for the failure to have the testimony at the trial; nor is it sufficient for the party to state in his affidavit, that he could not, with reasonable diligence, have discovered such testimony, for it is incumbent upon him to set out, in his affidavit, the facts constituting diligence.

Kelley *v.* Kelley.

ASSAULT AND BATTERY.—*Instruction to Jury.—Conspiracy.—Evidence.*—
In an action for damages for an assault and battery, where there
was some evidence of a conspiracy leading up to the assault and
battery, it is not error for the court to instruct the jury as to what
constitutes a conspiracy, the jury being entitled to all the facts and
circumstances leading up to the assault and battery.

SAME.—*Instruction to Jury.—Assumption of Fact.*—In an action for
damages for assault and battery, where the court instructed the
jury that if it had been shown that plaintiff had occasionally been
meeting at her place of residence a person with whom she had had
improper relations, such fact would not justify an assault and battery upon her, such instruction was not erroneous on the ground
that it assumes the fact of assault and battery.

SAME.—*Damages, Elements of.—Special Proof.*—In an action for assault and battery, the jury has a right to consider all the elements
entering into the damages, without special proof as to amounts.

DAMAGES.—*Excessive, as a Cause for Reversal.*—A judgment will not
be reversed on the ground of excessive damages, unless the amount
is so large as to lead to the conclusion that it must have been the
result of prejudice, partiality, or corruption.

INSTRUCTIONS TO JURY.—*Party Must Ask for, or be Estopped to Complain of an Omission.*—A party desiring an instruction on a certain
point must ask for it, or he will not be heard to complain because
of the absence of such instruction.

From the Harrison Circuit Court.

J. V. Kelso and *C. D. Kelso*, for appellant.

J. K. Marrs, for appellee.

REINHARD, J.—One of the errors relied upon is the
sustaining of a demurrer to the appellant's second paragraph of answer. It is conceded that the facts pleaded
in this paragraph were admissible under the general denial, which was also pleaded. The error, if any, was
therefore harmless. Elliott's App. Proced., section 637,
and cases cited.

Another alleged error is the overruling of the joint
motion of appellant and his co-defendant for a new trial.
The appellant was sued jointly by the appellee with another for damages for an alleged assault and battery.
The defendants answered separately the general denial,

but the jury returned a joint verdict against the two for $3,200.

The defendants jointly moved for a new trial. The court sustained the motion as to the other defendant, but overruled it as to the appellant, on condition that appellee would remit $700 of the amount found in the verdict, which was done.

It is insisted by appellant's counsel, in argument, that the granting of a new trial to Marrs was a decision by the court that there was a failure of proof as to him, at least, and this being so a new trial should have been granted both, for the reason that when the evidence fails as to one of the parties against whom a verdict has been rendered, a joint motion for a new trial by all must be sustained.

In support of this contention counsel cite *Sperry* v. *Dickinson*, 82 Ind. 132, and *Graham* v. *Henderson*, 35 Ind. 195, and it must be conceded that these cases go far toward sustaining the position assumed.

We have reached the conclusion, however, after careful consideration, that the doctrine contended for is in conflict with the rule adhered to in many cases, since those above referred to were decided, viz., that a party can not be heard to complain of the overruling of a joint motion for a new trial as to him, unless the motion is well taken as to all the parties who join in making it; and, where the rights of the parties are separate and distinct, the party seeking a new trial should file a separate motion therefor. Elliott's App. Proced., section 839, and cases cited.

Our conclusion, therefore, is that there is no available error in the action of the court sustaining the motion for a new trial as to Marrs and overruling it as to the appellant.

It is further contended that the damages are excessive.

As we have seen, the verdict was for $3,200, of which $700 was remitted. The theory of the defense was that the appellant found the appellee, his wife, in bed with, and in the embraces of, another man, and that, therefore, even if he inflicted the injuries upon her of which she complains, the provocation was so great that it should naturally and properly palliate the offense so as to make it but little more than a nominal one. Moreover, it is insisted that no witness testified to the striking except the appellee herself, and that her appearance and conduct subsequent to the difficulty was such as to lead to the conclusion that no serious injury was sustained by her.

On the other hand, there was evidence tending to show that the man with whom the appellee was found in bed went there at the instance and request of the appellant, without the invitation and against the desires of the appellee, and for the purpose of enabling the appellant to secure evidence upon which to base an action for a divorce, and that the appellant inflicted serious injuries upon the appellee. If the theory of the appellee is the true one, and the jury by the verdict in effect found that it was, we can not say that $2,500 is in excess of what the appellee was entitled to recover.

A man who would thus deliberately debauch and bring shame and dishonor upon the wife he engaged to honor and protect deserves no commiseration at the hands of a court or jury.

It is true the gist of the action was not for the alleged misconduct of the appellant in bringing obloquy and disgrace upon his wife, but for an assault and battery, and yet, if the latter was established, we can not say that the jury had not the right to take into consideration the entire circumstances leading up to the point of the striking, and this would, of course, include the acts of the appellant in setting the trap into which he intended his wife to fall.

It is not our province to determine which of the theories was the correct one, but the jury having adopted the one relied upon by the appellee, and there being some evidence to support it, we would not feel justified in holding that the result reached was an erroneous one.

The rule that where the evidence is at all conflicting upon the material questions in issue this court will not undertake to weigh or determine it, is too well established to need the citation of authority in its support, and it is likewise settled beyond controversy, that unless the amount of the verdict is so large as to lead to the conclusion that it must have been the result of prejudice, partiality, or corruption, the judgment based upon it will not be disturbed on appeal. *Lake Erie, etc., R. W. Co.* v. *Acres,* 108 Ind. 548; *Farman* v. *Lauman,* 73 Ind. 568; *Louisville, etc., R. W. Co.* v. *Pedigo,* 108 Ind. 481.

A further ground for a new trial contained in the motion made in the court below was that the defendants were surprised by the testimony of the plaintiff. In this connection it is claimed that it was shown by affidavits filed in support of the motion that in a divorce proceeding between the appellant and appellee the latter testified that her husband did not strike, beat, or kick her, and in effect that appellant did not commit any assault and battery upon her whatever. While we find the affidavits substantially as claimed, it is also true that counter affidavits were filed by the appellee tending to show, not only that she was injured, but that she testified to such injuries upon the trial in the action for divorce.

Under the third subdivision of the section of the civil

Kelley *v.* Kelley.

code defining causes for a new trial, accident or surprise against which ordinary prudence could not have guarded is made a ground upon which a new trial may be granted. R. S. 1881, section 559.

But inasmuch as the party who claims to be surprised by the testimony of a witness might have procured a continuance on account of the surprise, if he had moved for it and shown proper grounds, a strong and clear case must be made before a reversal will be grounded upon such cause. *Louisville, etc., R. W. Co.* v. *Hendricks*, 128 Ind. 462; *Scheible* v. *Slagle*, 89 Ind. 323.

We do not think this is such a case. As we have seen, there was some evidence tending to show that the appellee did testify on the divorce trial that the appellant had struck and beaten her. Moreover, we do not think the appellant has brought himself within the rule that he must show that by proper diligence he could not have had the witnesses at the trial, as well as on a new trial. *Smith* v. *Harris*, 76 Ind. 104.

The appellant also insists that a new trial should have been granted him upon the ground of newly discovered evidence. The affidavits filed in support of the motion are the same as those relied upon to show surprise.

We do not think that the appellant shows himself entitled to a new trial for this cause. If the appellant, at the time of the trial, knew, as he says he did, that the appellee had testified to certain facts at the divorce trial, there is no reason shown why he was not prepared to establish this at the trial of this cause. She being a party to the action her former admissions would have been competent testimony for the appellant and his co-defendant at the trial, even though she did not herself go upon the stand as a witness. No sufficient excuse is shown for the appellant's failure to have the testimony at the trial. See *Allen* v. *Bond*, 112 Ind. 523.

The proposed testimony of persons who had seen the appellee the next morning after the difficulty and saw no marks of violence upon her or heard her make no complaint, does not add any strength to the appellant's position on the subject.

The mere fact that appellant did not, before the trial, know that these persons would testify to the facts which he now says he can prove by them, is not a showing of any diligence to discover the testimony. Nor is it sufficient for him to state in his affidavit, that he could not, with reasonable diligence, have discovered such testimony. It was incumbent upon him, in his affidavits, to set out the facts constituting the diligence used by him, so that the court might be enabled to decide whether due diligence was used, and if he made inquiries, the time, place, and circumstances should be stated. *Keisling* v. *Readle,* 1 Ind. App. 240; Elliott's App. Proced., section 857, and cases cited.

This was not done, and the appellant is in no position to complain.

Objection is made to some of the instructions given. Instructions numbered 4½, 5½, and 6½ are complained of. In these instructions the court undertook to define a conspiracy. It is urged that there is nothing in the evidence raising any question as to any conspiracy, and, if there was, it was only for the purpose of entering the appellee's house at the time the difficulty occurred.

There was evidence tending to show that Marrs, the appellant's co-defendant, was approached by the appellant and requested by him to accompany the appellant to appellee's house during the night of the difficulty, and that appellant said that "he had arranged it" with the party found in bed with the appellee. If there was a conspiracy by which such an arrangement was made, it was proper for the jury to consider it, both for the pur-

pose of connecting Marrs with the transaction and to
show the aggravating circumstances under which the
appellee was attacked. At all events, we can see no
harm in the mere definition of a conspiracy given the
jury by the court.

It is quite true, as contended, that a conspiracy to enter the appellee's premises under the circumstances
claimed would not necessarily tend to prove an assault
and battery. But if the assault and battery was otherwise established, we know of no good reason why the jury
might not consider all the facts and circumstances leading up to it.

In the fifth instruction the court told the jury that if
it had been shown that appellee had occasionally been
meeting at her place of residence the person found in
her bed with her and had had improper relations with
him, such fact would not justify an assault and battery
upon her. This instruction is assailed upon the ground
that it assumes that an assault and battery was committed. We do not so construe the instruction. The
court fully informed the jury, in other instructions, what
was necessary for the appellee to prove before she could
recover, and it can not be presumed that the jury was
misled by the instruction complained of.

Nor is there any force in the objection that the court
failed to tell the jury that the appellee's misconduct
might be considered by them in mitigation of the damages.

If the appellant desired an instruction upon this point,
or deemed it necessary to have a more explicit statement
of the rules of law upon the subject, he should have prepared an instruction such as he desired given, and requested the court to give it. Besides, in a subsequent
instruction, the court fully met the point by informing
the jury what they might consider in mitigation.

We do not think the court erred in giving the instructions referred to.

It is further urged that error was committed in an instruction to the effect that the jury, in estimating the damages, might consider the shame, humiliation, loss of honor, reputation, or social position, if any was shown. We think these things may be considered as among the natural results of an unlawful assault and battery. Where this is the case damages may be recovered on account of the results mentioned without specially pleading the same in the complaint. *Richter* v. *Meyers*, 5 Ind. App. 33; *Morgan* v. *Kendall*, 124 Ind. 454.

Nor does the fact that no evidence was introduced as to the extent of the damage for either of these injurious results render the instruction bad. The jury had the right to consider all the elements entering into the damages without special proof as to amounts, and estimate the latter by all the evidence given at the trial.

We think the instruction is fully sustained by the Supreme Court in *Wolf* v. *Trinkle*, 103 Ind. 355.

It is finally urged that the court erred in annexing a condition to its overruling of the motion for a new trial as to the appellant, viz., the condition that appellee remit $700 of the verdict. If there was error in this, it was not such as harmed the appellant. Had the court overruled the motion without the condition, the judgment would have been for $700 more than it is. But of this the appellant can not complain.

This disposes of all the questions presented, and we have not been able to discover any reversible error.

Judgment affirmed.

Filed Oct. 12, 1893; petition for a rehearing overruled Jan. 13, 1894.

No. 915.

HAMILTON ET AL., EXECUTORS, *v.* FEARY.

CONTRACT.—*Breach of.*—*Damages, When Remote and Consequential.*—*Recovery.*—A party injured by the breach of a contract or covenant is entitled to recover such damages only as proximately resulted from the breach and were within the contemplation of the parties when the contract was entered into. In such case, remote and consequential damages can not be recovered.

LANDLORD AND TENANT.—*Breach of Covenant to Repair.*—*Damages.*—*Personal Injury.*—*Recovery.*—Where a landlord leased premises, and covenanted with the tenant to repair and put in a safe condition an excavation thereon, which was in close proximity to a well from which the tenant had to obtain water for domestic purposes, and the landlord failed and refused to make such repairs, though often requested to do so, and the tenant, while at the well obtaining water, was precipitated into the excavation by the falling in of the earthen walls thereof, and was injured, the tenant can not recover damages for such injuries in an action for breach of covenant to repair, such damages being too remote and consequential, and not in contemplation of the parties to the covenant.

SAME.—*Breach of Covenant to Repair.*—*Remedy of Tenant.*—*Damages.*—*Recovery.*—*Personal Injury.*—In such case, on failure and refusal of the landlord to make the repairs, as he covenanted to do, the tenant had the right to make the necessary repairs himself and charge their cost to the landlord, and, under the principle that it is the tenant's duty to reduce the damages as much as reasonably lies in his power to do so, he could not be permitted to allow the defect in the premises to remain, being fully cognizant of the same, and then sue for the injuries resulting from the accident caused by the dangerous condition of the premises.

SAME.—*Tort.*—*Sufficiency of Complaint.*—*Failure to Show Negligence.*—*Personal Injury.*—In such case, the tenant can not recover in an action upon *tort*, where the complaint shows that the plaintiff knew of the existence of the excavation before she took possession of the premises, and, with such knowledge, continued to occupy the property during the period of the lease, after the landlord, upon demand, had failed and refused to make the repairs; that the landlord could not have given the tenant any further information of the defect than she admits she possessed; that the landlord practiced no fraud or deception upon the tenant in connection with the condition of the excavation; and that the cause of injury, if latent and not patent, was

no more patent to the landlord than to the tenant, therefore failing
to show the landlord guilty of negligence contributing to the injury.

From the Shelby Circuit Court.

T. B. Adams and *I. Carter* for appellant.

A. C. Harris, *K. M. Hord* and *E. K. Adams*, for appellee.

REINHARD, J.—This case was tried in the court below,
upon the second paragraph of the complaint, to which a
demurrer was overruled.

The appellee was the tenant of the appellant, in a
dwelling house owned by the latter.   The action was for
the recovery of damages for a personal injury sustained
by the appellee while in the occupancy of the premises.
The trial was by a jury, and there was a verdict in favor
of the appellee for $2,500, upon which, over appellant's
motion for a new trial, and other motions, judgment was
rendered.

The overruling of the demurrer is the first specification of error.

The substance of the paragraph of complaint to which
the demurrer was addressed, is as follows:

That on the 22d day of February, 1890, the appellee
leased, in writing, from the appellant the premises described; that by the terms of the lease appellee was to
pay, as rent therefor, the sum of $8.33 per month, in
advance; that the tenancy was to begin on said date and
to continue for six months thereafter; that she was to
keep the property in good condition, not sublet the same,
and to give possession thereof at the end of six months.
A copy of the lease was filed with this paragraph of complaint, as exhibit "A."

It is further alleged that appellee did not take possession under the lease on said day, and that after the execution of the lease, and before appellee took possession of the property, it was agreed between the parties that appellee should not, and would not, be required to pay the first month's rental until she had taken full possession.

It is then averred that there was, at that time, and for several months subsequent thereto, located upon said lot and in the rear of said house, a circular excavation, about five feet in depth and about seven feet in diameter, which appellant had caused to be made, intending thereby to make a cistern; that a portion of the said dwelling house was then badly in need of being papered, the walls being smoked and dingy in appearance; that after the signing of said lease, to wit, on the 24th day of February, 1890, and before any act had been done thereunder, and before possession had been taken by the appellee, and before there was any breach of the terms of said lease by either party, appellee having discovered for the first time the excavation aforesaid, and the condition of the walls aforesaid, refused to take possession of said premises under the said lease, or to pay any sum of money as rental for said premises under said lease, or to comply with any of the terms of said contract; that thereupon, and upon said day, appellee and appellant entered into a parol modification of said lease, as follows: That the said Hamilton, to induce appellee immediately to take possession of said premises as his tenant, and to pay him the said rental therefor, then and there agreed with appellee that if she would, on that day, take possession of said premises and continue as tenant therein for the said period of six months, at the rate and under the terms mentioned in said lease, and if she would, on that day, pay him the sum of $8.33 in cash, as the first month's rental, that he would immediately thereafter finish said excavation and make a good cistern, by making the same deeper and walling up the same, and would cover up and repair the said excavation so that the same would and could not endanger the lives or bodies of persons who should go upon said lot or in proximity to the place where the excavation existed; that appellant also agreed to paper said house and put the whole thereof in good condition for the use of the appellee, who desired the use of all of said property for a dwelling for herself and family; that thereupon, and before appellee had taken possession of said property, she paid the appellant the sum of $8.33, and immediately thereafter went into the possession of said premises under said lease and said modification thereof, and occupied the same under said lease, as modified, for and during the period aforesaid, for all of which she fully paid appellant at the rate aforesaid, and in all things fully performed her part of said agreement and the said modification thereof; that at the time of said renting, and during the period of said tenancy, the appellant had located and maintained, near the edge of said excavation, a well, in which was a pump, from which, under said lease, appellee obtained water for domestic purposes, said well being the only place on said lot from which water could be obtained; that appellant complied with his said agreement to paper the walls of the said house, but that, although often requested so to do, prior to the injuries herein set out, he neglected and refused to complete said cistern, and allowed the same to remain in the unfinished condition aforesaid during the whole of said period of six months; that heretofore, to wit, on the 26th day of July, 1890, and in the night time, and while appellee was prudently and carefully trying to get some needed water from said well by means of said pump, and while she was standing upon the ground near said excavation, and no nearer than was necessary in order to get said water, she being near to said pump and in the proper place to get water therefrom, the earth surrounding said excavation, and upon which she was standing, caved and fell into said excavation so suddenly and unexpectedly to her that, without any fault or negligence on her part, she was thereby precipitated and thrown violently and with great force into said excavation, and upon a piece of timber lying at the bottom thereof, resulting in serious bodily injury to her, as hereinafter set out; that said excavation was made, as set out, and without any walls or other barriers thereto, whereby said adjoining earth could be held in place, and that by reason of the same remaining in such condition during the period aforesaid, the earthen walls of said excavation had become, at the time of said injury, so undermined and in such dangerous condition as to result in the injury aforesaid, which condition was perceptible to appellant; that appellee had no knowledge, prior to said injury, that the earth surrounding said excavation was in said undermined and dangerous condition, and she believed, up to said time, that the same was firm and would support her weight thereon; that by reason of said fall appellee sustained the following injuries, to wit.

Then follow a description of the injuries and an averment that the same were not caused by the act, fault or negligence of the appellee, but were wholly the result of the said wrongful and negligent acts of appellant.

The complaint then proceeds to specify the damages and concludes with a prayer for $5,000 judgment.

A copy of the lease is set out, and, as indicated in the complaint, it contains no stipulation for the making of repairs on the part of the appellant. Assuming that the modified agreement was such as obligated the appellant to place the excavation in a condition of safety, does the appellee show herself entitled, by the averments of the complaint, to the remedy here pursued?

Appellee's counsel construe the action to be upon the contract to repair. As such, is the complaint sufficient? Without an express agreement to make repairs, it does not devolve upon the landlord to do so. This is conceded. Assuming that, in the present case, there is such an agreement, what redress is the tenant entitled to for a breach of the obligation?

Appellant's counsel contend that in such case the tenant may either abandon the premises, or make the repairs himself and recoup the expense therefor in an action by the landlord for rent.

On the other hand, the appellee's position is that the tenant need not pursue either of these remedies, but may sue in damages and recover for any injury proximately flowing from the breach of the covenant. Taylor Landlord and Tenant, section 330; *Buck* v. *Rodgers*, 39 Ind. 222; *McCoy* v. *Oldham*, 1 Ind. App. 372.

That this position is well taken, we shall not undertake to controvert.

It may be stated, as a general rule, that for a breach of contract in any case the injured party is entitled to recover such damages only as proximately resulted from the breach, and were within the contemplation of the parties when the contract was entered into. Damages which are remote and speculative can not be recovered. 5 Am. and Eng. Encyc. of Law, 13.

In this respect the rule is not different from what it would be if the contract to repair had been between the tenant and a mechanic or workman employed by her to do the work. The only damages recoverable in such case would be the difference between the price agreed upon and the actual cost of the work if the employer had hired another to do it, and possibly such other damages as were sustained by reason of the delay. This would be especially true if the employe had repudiated the con-

tract after reasonable notice to her, or had positively refused to perform it; for, upon such refusal, it would have
been the privilege of the employer to treat the contract
as rescinded, and she could have hired the work to be
done by another.

We shall not undertake to assert that if the employe
had repeatedly promised to do the work upon being requested to do so, and had thus led the employer to rely
upon his carrying out the promise, he might not be held
liable as for special and consequential damages, even for a
personal injury incurred under the circumstances of the
present case.   But even then there could be no recovery
unless the employer had done all that she reasonably
could do to reduce the damage as much as practicable.

Applying this rule to the case in hand, it may be
conceded that there are circumstances under which a
tenant may recover special and consequential damages for the breach of the landlord's covenant to repair.   Thus it was held in *Buck* v. *Rodgers, supra,* that
where the landlord had agreed to furnish his tenant a
sufficient quantity of rails to keep his fences in repair,
so as to protect the crops, and had failed to do so, and
the cattle had broken in and destroyed the crops, the
landlord was liable to the tenant for the damages occasioned by the injury to the crops.   But this and other
similar holdings are predicated upon the supposition that
the tenant or lessee had used such reasonable means as
were in his power to prevent or lessen the damages. The
Supreme Court has repeatedly declared and given effect
to this principle, and in a very recent case has expressly
decided that the case of *Buck* v. *Rodgers, supra,* was determined in full recognition of the same.   *Hendry* v.
Squier, 126 Ind. 19.

In the case just cited the lessor had agreed to place a
new roof upon the store house of which the lessee was

the occupant with a stock of goods. By the failure of
the lessor to comply with his covenant, the lessee's goods
were damaged by a leak in the roof, for which he sued
the lessor for damages. The complaint averred that the
tenant had repeatedly requested the landlord to make the
repair, but that the latter had failed and refused to do so.
It was held, that under these circumstances the tenant
could not recover the damages occasioned by the injury
to his goods; that upon the landlord's refusal he should
have made the repairs himself and charged them to the
landlord.

It is averred in the paragraph of complaint under consideration, that the appellant, "although often requested
so to do, prior to the injuries herein set out, neglected
and . *refused* to complete said cistern, and allowed the
same to remain in the unfinished condition aforesaid,
during the whole of said period of six months."

It was said, in the case of *Hendry* v. *Squier, supra :*
"As shown by the averments in the pleading, the condition of this roof was well known to the appellant long
before the time when the landlord was to repair it by
putting on a new roof. And it is further averred that
the appellant requested the repairs to be made, and the
appellees refused to make the repairs. This gave the
appellant the right to make the necessary repairs and
charge them to appellees. *Hopkins* v. *Ratliff*, 115 Ind.
213. Certainly, after such refusal appellant could not
voluntarily permit his goods to remain in the building and suffer injury, and recover the damage from the
appellees. Yet, under these circumstances, the appellant allows his goods to remain in this end of the building, and be damaged by the rainfall, when, for aught
that appears in the pleading, it would have been a small
expense to have repaired it, or that even a new roof upon

the building would have cost much less than the damages sustained to the goods.''

In this particular the case at bar does not differ materially from the case cited. In both cases the pleading showed that the landlord had, long before the injury, refused to make the repairs. Where this is the case it would seem to be fruitless for the tenant longer to rely upon the landlord's promise. He would have the right to make the necessary repairs himself and charge their cost to the landlord. Under the principle that it is his duty to reduce the damages as much as reasonably lies in his power to do so, he could not be permitted to allow the defect in the premises to remain, being himself fully cognizant of the same, and then sue for the accident resulting from the dangerous condition of the property.

The case under consideration can not be distinguished from the one cited by saying that in the latter case the tenant might have removed his goods to another part of the building. The court does not base its conclusion upon this fact. It holds that under such circumstances his remedy was to make the repairs and charge them to the landlord. This ruling does not conflict with the cases which decide that the tenant, instead of making such repairs himself, might recover in damages the diminution of the value of the rent during the time the premises remain out of repair. While in such cases the landlord is clearly guilty of a violation of his contract, the tenant can not remain inactive and allow special damages to accrue, and recover them from the landlord, when, at slight expense, he might have averted the injurious consequences complained of.

The principle adverted to applies not only to breaches of contracts, but to torts as well. ''In case of wrongful injury to person or property, the injured party is required to use reasonable exertion to lessen or moderate the resulting damage." 1 Suth. Dam., section 90, and cases cited in second edition.

As we have stated, the appellee treats this case as though the complaint declared upon a breach of contract and not upon tort. But it is our opinion that such damages are not the natural and ordinary result of a breach of the covenant, and were not in contemplation of the parties when the contract was entered into. Such damages are too remote and speculative, and could only be recovered as special and consequential damages, under circumstances hereinbefore adverted to.

We think if there is any liability under the facts set up in the complaint, it must be upon the theory of negligence, as upon tort. To determine whether or not there was actionable negligence, it must first be ascertained what if any duty the appellant owed the appellee and the manner in which the appellant failed to discharge such duty. The duties owing by a landlord to his tenant are various, but they are limited. The landlord does not insure the safety of the premises, nor does he impliedly warrant them to be inhabitable or fit for certain uses, and, as a general rule, the tenant, under the maxim *caveat emptor*, assumes all the risks incident to the occupancy, having complete control and dominion over the premises. To this general rule there are, however, several exceptions. Thus the landlord is liable where the premises contain some hidden defect or defects, or are infected with some noxious disease, rendering them dangerous or uninhabitable, and of which dangerous elements or defects the landlord had some knowledge or information, but which were not open to the view of the tenant and of which he was ignorant or uninformed. And so the landlord is answerable where he controls or retains possession of a portion of the premises, or a portion is used in common by two or more tenants, and an injury occurs through some negligence or fault of the landlord upon that portion over which he has the control or which is used in common. Still another instance of liability on the part of the owner is where he, though not bound to do so, undertakes to make repairs, and makes them in so negligent or unskillful a manner as to produce injury to the tenant. Also, where the landlord has covenanted to make repairs, and upon being notified has repeatedly promised and led the tenant to believe in good faith that he will make them. The liability of the lessor in these, and perhaps other instances, arises from the principle that he owes the lessee a duty, and if, by the lessor's failure or negligence to discharge such duty, and without any contributing fault of the lessee, the latter sustains injury, a right of action arises in favor of the lessee or tenant, for the damages sustained. Buswell Pers. Inj., section 82, *et seq.;* 1 Taylor L. and T. (8th ed.), section 175a; 1 Wood L. and T. (2d ed.), section 379; *Lucas* v. *Coulter*, 104 Ind. 81; *Deller* v. *Hofferberth*, 127 Ind. 414; *Purcell* v. *English*, 86 Ind. 34; *Toole* v. *Beckett*, 67 Me. 544; *Gregor* v. *Cady*, 82 Me. 131; *Kirby* v. *Boylston Market Ass'n*, 80 Mass. 249; *Bowe* v. *Hunking*, 135 Mass. 380; *Minor* v. *Sharon*, 112 Mass. 477; *Gill* v. *Middleton*, 105 Mass. 477; *Wellington* v. *Downer, etc., Oil Co.*, 104 Mass. 64; *Cowen* v. *Sunderland*, 145 Mass. 363; *Willy* v. *Mulledy*, 78 N. Y. 310; *Cesar* v. *Karutz*, 60 N. Y. 229; *McAlpin* v. *Powell*, 70 N. Y. 126, 26 Atl. Rep. 155; *Arnold* v. *Clark*, 45 N. Y. Sup. Ct. 252; *Flynn* v. *Hatton*, 43 How. Pr. 333; *Butler* v. *Cushing*, 46 Hun, 521; *Snyder* v. *Gorden*, 46 Hun, 538; *Kabus* v. *Frost*, 50 N. Y. S. C. 72; *Scott* v. *Simons*, 54 N. H. 426; *Little* v. *McAdaras*, 38 Mo. App. 187; *Reichenbacher* v. *Pahmeyer*, 8 Ill. App. 217; *Mendel* v. *Fink*, 8 Ill. App. 378; *Pollack* v. *Pioche*,

35 Cal. 416, 95 Am. Dec. 115, with notes; *Godley* v. *Hagerty*, 20 Pa. St. 387.

The appellee admits, in her complaint, that she knew of the existence of the excavation even before she took possession of the premises, and with such knowledge continued to occupy the property for the period of six months, though the appellant had, upon demand, failed and refused to make the repair which he had covenanted to make. The appellant could not have given the appellee any more information of the defect than she admits she possessed. To avoid this dilemma she undertakes to aver that the hidden portion of the defect consisted in the ruinous condition of the banks of the excavation, and not in the excavation itself, and she insists that it was the duty of the appellant to have disclosed these to her. She does not aver that the appellant had any peculiar knowledge of these other than she had herself; at least the facts pleaded 'show that she had ample time and opportunity for investigation, and there is no pretense that the appellant practiced any fraud or deception upon her in connection with the condition of the walls of the excavation. It must be clear, therefore, that if the cause of the injury was a latent and not a patent danger, it was no more patent to the owner than to the lessee, and it does not appear wherein he violated any duty in failing to apprise her of the same. If we should treat the complaint, therefore, upon the theory of a latent defect, we encounter the insurmountable obstacle that it fails to show the appellant guilty of any negligence; and hence, whether the appellee was guilty of contributory negligence or not, there is no right of action. See Buswell Pers. Inj., section 84; Taylor Landlord and Tenant, section 175a.

But if we take the other end of the dilemma, and say that the particular duty which the appellant owed the appellee here was not to disclose to her the existence of the latent defect of the banks of the excavation, but to fill up the latter and place the premises in safe condition, we then come back to the other obstacle, already mentioned in reviewing the complaint as upon contract, that the appellee has failed to reduce or moderate the damages, as she could have done by making the repairs herself and charging them to the appellant.

In addition to all this, it is very questionable, we apprehend, whether, under the pleading, she does not show herself guilty of contributory negligence. The well from which she got water was in close proximity to the alleged dangerous excavation. She had occupied the premises with the dangerous excavation from February to July. The banks were not walled up, and there was nothing to prevent the changing seasons from having their full effect upon the earth surrounding the cavity. The appellee was bound to make use not only of her senses, but also of her knowledge and reasoning faculties. She must have known that during all this time the earth constituting these embankments had become liable, under the varying influences of the atmosphere and the weather, to crumble and give way, and hence it is very difficult to perceive how she could have been free from contributory fault by venturing so near to the dangerous pitfall. And so, if we regard this complaint as counting upon tort for negligence, and there was fault in the appellant in failing to repair, or in failing to disclose the defect, there was likewise fault on the part of appellee in not avoiding the danger.

From what we have said, it must be apparent, we think, that we regard the complaint as totally insufficient to state a cause of action, either as upon contract, for consequential and special damages, or as upon tort, for the negligent failure of the appellant to perform his duty as landlord.

Our conclusion is that the demurrer should have been sustained.

In view of this conclusion, it will not be necessary to consider errors alleged to have occurred after the ruling upon the demurrer.

Judgment reversed.

Ross, J., was absent.

Filed Oct. 20, 1893; petition for a rehearing overruled Jan. 12, 1894.

--------◆--------

No. 937.

KERLIN v. THE NATIONAL ACCIDENT ASSOCIATION.

INSURANCE.—*Accident Insurance.*—*Premium, What Amounts to Payment of.*—*Tender of Full Amount of Premium.*—*Promise by Agent to Apply a Debt Owing by Him to Insured on Premium.*—*Presumption.*—Where, at the time of the execution of an application for accident insurance, the person seeking insurance exhibited, offered, and tendered to the company's soliciting and collecting agent, the full amount of the first annual premium for the policy, and the agent was owing the insured a sum less than the amount of the premium, and the agent told the insured to pay him, the agent, the excess of the premium over the amount owing by the agent to the insured, and he, the agent, would pay to the company the amount owing by the agent to the insured, and the insured, acting in entire good faith, paid the sum in excess of the debt owing by the agent to him, and relied, in good faith, upon the agent's statement, that he, the agent, would pay to the insurance company the remainder of the premium, this, in law, would be a sufficient payment of the premium by the insured; and the insured is not bound to see that the agent pays the money to the company, but he has the right to presume that it has been so paid, until he has notice to the contrary. .

SAME.—*Authority of Agent.*—*Waiver.*—In such case the agent, acting in the general scope of his authority, had the power to waive the payment of the premium in several different installments, and to accept payment in advance, his powers in such matters being equal to the powers of the officers of the company at the home office.

SAME.—*Authority of Agent.*—*Special Limitation.*—*Notice of.*—In such case, if the party acts in good faith with the agent, relying upon the statements made by such agent, within the scope of his apparent authority, the principal will be bound by such statements, and if there is any limitation on the power of the agent, within the scope of the particular business, it is the duty of the principal to bring the same to knowledge of the applicant.

SAME.—*Contract.*—*Construction.*—The same principles of law ordinarily govern the construction of insurance contracts that govern the construction of other contracts.

Opinion on petition for rehearing by DAVIS, C. J.

From the Marion Superior Court.

F. M. Finch and *J. A. Finch*, for appellant.

A. J. Beveridge, for appellee.

DAVIS, J.—Appellant instituted this action against appellee, upon a certificate of membership issued to her husband, Isaac N. Kerlin, for the principal sum of three thousand dollars, in the event of his violent death by accidental means, conditioned upon his performance of all the stipulations, agreements and conditions contained in said certificate of membership and his application therefor, which is made a part thereof.

The application, made on the 18th of August, 1889, contains the following:

"I agree to pay annually, not to exceed $30, the amount assessed therefor, in advance, without notice, so long as I apply to the home office for its continuance, to be paid as follows: The first monthly payment, of $7.50, to be made on the 20th day of September, 1889, and one payment of like amount due the same day of each of the next succeeding three months, to be apportioned to the expense and indemnity funds, as provided in the charter and regulations of said association, and in default of any payment being made by 12 o'clock noon, of the day when due, as above specified, said membership and insurance shall then and thereby become void, and can only be reinstated by tendering payment to the home office, and, if accepted, the reinstatement takes effect from and after the date of such payment, and no claim can be made for any injury occurring between the dates of such forfeiture and such reinstatement.''

On the same day the certificate was issued, containing, among others, the following provisions:

''This certificate shall not take effect unless payment is made or secured as agreed.   * * *   .

''In consideration of the facts and warranties in said application, and the agreement to fully perform all the provisions and conditions of this contract, all of which are conditions precedent.''

The appellee answered the complaint by general denial, and trial by jury resulted in verdict and judgment in favor of appellant for the full amount of the certificate. On appeal to general term, the judgment was reversed, and from the decision of the superior court at general term this appeal is prosecuted.

Several questions are presented, in support of which numerous authorities are cited, but these questions are so related and interwoven with one another that the determination of one or two propositions will be decisive of the entire controversy.

The evidence is, in some particulars, conflicting and contradictory, but there is evidence in the record tending to show that said Isaac N. Kerlin was carrying a certificate in the National Accident Association, which was about to expire, and that one Disher, who was an agent of the appellee, with authority to solicit applications and to collect premiums, but who was not authorized to contract insurance or to issue policies, called to see Kerlin in regard to the renewal of such certificate.

Said Kerlin was a baggageman, running on a railroad from Indianapolis to Chicago, and at the time the agent called on him he was in his car in the Union Station at Indianapolis, and the train was about ready to go. After the application had been written, but whether before or after it was signed, is not clear, and just before the train started, the agent asked Kerlin why he could not then pay all the premiums, as he had done before, to which Kerlin replied that he guessed he might, and said: "Just write up a new application," to which the agent replied that he had not the time, and that the application which he had written "would do just as well," and thereupon Kerlin replied "all right," and there tendered the agent thirty dollars—three ten-dollar bills—in payment of the entire premium for the year, and the agent in his testimony, says: "I told him *that I had ten dollars that he had loaned me a while back* that I would apply on it (the premium), and he could retain the ten dollars," and, therefore, the agent only took twenty dollars of the money so tendered, and gave to Kerlin a receipt for thirty dollars in payment of the premium in full, and agreed to pay the ten dollars to the company in discharge of his debt to Kerlin.

Disher, in October, paid $7.50 to the company, and the company, as the several installments became due, according to the terms of the application as written, each month gave to said Disher, as such agent, a statement or list of collections to be made by him from different members, including, among others, the name of Kerlin. Such statements were placed in the hands of Disher in September, October, November and December, and there is evidence tending to show that when the respective installments became due, according to the terms of the application, at the request of the agent, the time of payment of the several amounts by Kerlin was extended by the company.

The company was not aware of the payment of the entire premium by Kerlin to Disher, and neither did Kerlin have any notice or knowledge of the failure of Disher to pay the full amount to the company, or of the alleged extensions in his behalf.

For some of these months, the list placed in the hands of Disher for collection amounted to as much as $145. Such collections were placed in his hands about the first of the month; he made the collections during the month and "used the money (so collected for the company) right along," until he made his return and settlement, about the first of the next succeeding month. This also appears to have been his manner of doing business for and as the agent of the company, previous to the renewal of the policy in question.

On or about the 31st of December, 1889, Kerlin was killed in a railroad accident, and a few days thereafter Disher reported to the home office that during the month he had collected one installment of the Kerlin premium, which he then offered to pay to the company, but the company, because of the death of Kerlin, refused to accept the money, etc.

One of the contentions of counsel for appellant is that the jury was warranted in finding for appellant, on the theory that inasmuch as the appellee did not declare a forfeiture for failure to pay the several amounts on the premiums in installments at the time prescribed in the application, but, on the contrary, extended the time of payment so that in December the agent had in his hands for collection one installment at least of said premium, which, when he made his return about the first of January, he reported that he had collected, and then offered to pay, the appellee had, by reason of such facts, waived the alleged forfeiture, and that the insurance must be regarded as having been in full force at the time of the death of Kerlin.

The rule thus invoked is stated as follows: "Imposing or collecting an assessment by a mutual insurance company, after the company has knowledge of facts entitling it to consider the policy no longer binding upon it, without its assent, is, upon this principle, held to be a waiver of the right to claim the forfeiture which it might otherwise have insisted upon." *Murray* v. *Home Benefit Life Ass'n*, 90 Cal. 402, 25 Am. St. Rep. 133; *Phenix Ins. Co.* v. *Tomlinson*, 125 Ind. 84.

Without entering upon the discussion of this proposition, it will suffice to say that in the view we take of the case, on the record, as it comes before us, the question has no controlling weight, so far as the decision of the court on this appeal is concerned.

The trial court gave the jury the following instruction: "If, at the time of the execution of the application by Mr. Kerlin, he exhibited, offered, and tendered to the defendant's agent the full sum of thirty dollars in cash as premium for the policy in question, and the agent was owing Mr. Kerlin ten dollars, and told the latter to pay him only the sum of twenty dollars cash on such premium, and he, the agent, would pay to the company the other ten dollars, and Mr. Kerlin, acting in entire good faith, paid the twenty dollars in cash and relied, in good faith, upon the agent's statement that the latter would pay to the defendant the other ten dollars, this, in law, would be a sufficient payment of the premium by Mr. Kerlin."

It is substantially conceded by the learned counsel for the respective parties, in their able oral argument, and also in their cogent briefs, that the vital question in the case turns upon the proposition as to whether the law applicable to the facts in the case, which the evidence tends to establish, is correctly stated in the instruction quoted. In other words, if the trial court erred, under the circumstances, in giving this instruction, the decision of the superior court in general term should be affirmed; otherwise, such decision should be reversed, with instructions to affirm the judgment rendered at special term.

It is first insisted by counsel for the appellee, that said agent had no right, at the time the application was made, to waive the payment of the different installments of the premium at the respective times, in the several amounts stipulated in the application; that in the face of the terms of the application, the company was not bound by his agreement that the entire annual premium of thirty dollars might be paid in advance; that Kerlin had no right to rely on the statement of the agent that it was not necessary to change or rewrite the application to correspond with the facts. In short, that any and all such agreements or statements were merged into the written contract when the application was signed. In this connection it should be remembered that Disher was authorized to solicit the insurance and to collect the premium, and that he might agree with the applicant, before or at the time the application was made, that the premium should be paid all in cash or in the future in installments.

It is well settled, as said by this court in a recent case, that "Where an agent, acting within the general scope of his authority, undertakes to make out an application for insurance, and fails to state therein such facts and circumstances as the applicant directs, which, if stated therein, would affect the rights of the assured under the policy issued therein, such omission must be imputed to

the company, and not to the assured." *Phenix Ins. Co.*
v. *Lorenz*, 7 Ind. App. 266, 33 N. E. Rep. 444.

So, if, at the time the application is made or the insurance is contracted, circumstances or conditions exist
which are in conflict with the terms and conditions of
the application or policy, and the agent of the company
knew of their existence, "and agreed that as to them the
conditions" of the application should not be effective,
the insurer can not take advantage of their existence to
defeat a recovery after loss has occurred. *Phenix Ins.
Co.* v. *Lorenz, supra; Howe* v. *Provident Fund Society,*
7 Ind. App. 586.

In his excellent work on Insurance, Mr. May, in
speaking of the powers of what are known as soliciting
agents, says: "In short, the agent may do in this behalf what could be done at the home office, if the application were filled up there upon conference with the officers." Sections 120 and 123, May on Insurance.

In our opinion, under the authorities cited, Disher, as
the agent of the company, had the right, on the occasion
in question, to do all that could have been done, in relation to such matters, by the officers of the company at
the home office.

If it was conceded that Disher was, as contended by
appellee, a soliciting and collecting agent, he had the
authority to waive the payment of the premium in installments and to accept payment of the entire annual
premium in advance. His acts and his knowledge, in
respect to the matters in controversy, and within the
scope of his agency, on that occasion, are the acts and
knowledge of the company. When he assured Kerlin,
under the circumstances stated, that he could pay the
entire annual premium in advance, and that it was not
necessary to change the application, or write a new one
so as to make its terms, as to payment of the premium,

correspond with the facts, the company is bound by his statements and acts on that subject.

Coming to the principal questions presented, counsel for appellee states them as follows:

"First.—(a) Can an agent substitute his own indebtedness to the insured for the premium due the association?

"(b) Can the insured pay his premium due the association by cancelling the debt which he owes the agent?

"(c) Is the substitution of the agent's indebtedness to the insured, payment of the premium to the association?

"(d) Is the cancellation of a debt owed by an insurance agent to the person he insures, a payment of the premium, and does such an arrangement render the association liable?

"(e) Can a novation be effected without the consent of all parties?"

In support of his contention that an agent or an insurance company can not pay his debt to the insured by agreeing to pay the insured's premium to the company, and thereby bind the company without its consent or ratification, the learned counsel cites the following, among other, authorities: Ostrander on Insurance, p. 240; *Ferebee* v. *N. C. Mut. Home Ins. Co.*, 68 N. C. 11; *Texas Mut. Life Ins. Co.* v. *Davidge*, 51 Tex. 244; *Co-operative Life Assurance Co.* v. *McCormico*, 33 Miss. 233; *Hoffman* v. *Insurance Co.*, 92 U. S. 161; *Aultman & Co.* v. *Lee*, 43 Ia. 404; *Drain* v. *Doggett*, 41 Ia. 682; *Wheeler and Wilson Mfg. Co.* v. *Givan*, 65 Mo. 89; *Herring* v. *Hottendorf*, 74 N. C. 588; *Wiley* v. *Mahood*, 10 W. Va. 206; *Williams* v. *Johnston*, 92 N. C. 532; *McCormick* v. *Keith*, 8 Nev. 142.

It may be conceded that the foregoing authorities support the general proposition that the agent, in the absence of authority, either express or implied, can accept only money in discharge of the debt due his principal, and that he can not extinguish a debt to his principal by setting off against it his own debt; that he can not, in such cases, substitute his own indebtedness to the insured for the premium due from him to the association.

The question in this case is not, however, so narrow as stated by counsel for appellee, but the question which we are to determine is whether the actual tender of the full amount of the premium to the duly authorized agent of the company, under the circumstances referred to in the instruction, and the refusal of the agent to accept it, was sufficient to constitute payment of the premium, or, in other words, is the company, under the circumstances disclosed, bound or estopped by his waiver of the actual payment of the cash?

Counsel for appellee, however, while conceding that if the full amount of premium—$30—had been paid to the agent, the company would have been bound, although the agent might have used $10 of the money so received in paying his debt to Kerlin, says that "The fact that the insured has the actual cash in hand, and offers it to the agent, who is told by the agent to keep it in cancellation of the debt which the agent owes the insured, does not make it any more binding upon the association than if no tender had been actually made. It is not, in effect, payment. The agent must actually receive the cash or some equivalent which the association might convert into cash. Having done this, the agent is bound to pay the association, or the association can prosecute him for embezzlement."

Otherwise, it is urged, "A dishonest agent could make any arrangement he saw fit, swear to it, and bind the company."

In the first place, "the fair inference from the fact of appointment is, that the agent is a suitable person and conversant with his business. The applicant naturally and rightfully so looks upon him." May on Insurance, section 120.

Therefore, if an agent acting for an insurance company or association should possess the character described, the law would say, in the words of an old and terse expression, "for seeing somebody must be a loser by this deceit, it is more reason that he that employs and puts confidence in the deceiver, should be a loser than a stranger." *Hern* v. *Nichols*, 1 Salkeld, 289.

In the consideration of the question as to whether the general principles which underlie the authorities cited apply to the proposition which we have under investigation, we should keep in view the fact that the agent must be regarded and treated "as a suitable person,"with power to act within the scope of his apparent authority.

Kerlin, within these limits, had the right to rely upon the statements and acts of Disher, and if he was, in fact, misled by the agent, as the result of which either the beneficiary in the certificate or the company must suffer, it is more reasonable that the appellee should be loser than the appellant. Also, it should be borne in mind that "life insurance is a cash business," and that Kerlin, for the reasons stated in the authorities hereinbefore cited, could not, without the consent of the company, pay the premium due the company, through a novation of parties, by the terms of which the debt owing to him by Disher was discharged, and the agent substituted in his place as debtor to the company. Further, it should not be forgotten that there was evidence tending to show that the agent "had ten dollars" which he had previously borrowed of Kerlin, and that Kerlin actually tendered the agent, in cash, the full amount of the premium, of which the agent took only twenty dollars, and declined to accept ten dollars for the reason, as stated by him, in substance and effect, that the ten dollars which he had and the twenty dollars which he then accepted made the full amount of the premium for one year, and that he would pay the money to the company. Disher was the only witness who testified in relation to the transaction between him and Kerlin.

Appellee insists that the witness, on account of contradictory statements made out of court, his failure to pay over the money which he may have received, if any, and for other reasons, is discredited, and not worthy of belief. The question as to his credibility as a witness, and as to the weight which should be given his testimony on the trial, can not be reviewed by the court. These were matters proper for the consideration of the jury. Moreover, the appellee, through his long continuation in the service of the company, as solicitor and collector, may be said to have given him accredit to the public as a suitable and worthy agent for the transaction of the business in which he was engaged for the company, and, therefore, if it was within our province to do so, we would not be disposed, under the circumstances, to enter upon a review or analysis of the evidence as to his credibility as a witness.

Insurance companies act largely through agents who are appointed to facilitate and promote their business. Such agents must be presumed to be clothed with the power to transact the business which is intrusted to them, and the fair inference from their appointment is that they understand and are honest in the business in which they are engaged. If agents so appointed, with authority to solicit applications and to collect premiums, had not the authority to bind the company within the scope of their employment, the business of insurance companies would be confined to the limited sphere of negotiations with those only to whom the home office is accessible. When agents so appointed, especially after being long continued in such positions, are not suitable, worthy, and reliable, the fault, if any, rests on the insurance company, who is responsible therefor, and not on the public. With these preliminary observations, we will proceed to an examination of the authorities relied on by counsel for the respective parties.

In *Halleck* v. *Commercial Ins. Co.*, 26 N. J. 268, it appeared that in March, 1855, and before and after that time, George W. Breck was a local agent at Bath, New York, of a foreign insurance company, with authority to make surveys, receive proposals for insurance, and to receive premiums upon risks accepted by the company, but was not authorized to make insurance or issue policies. Halleck applied to such agent for insurance, and was told what the insurance would be, which the applicant then offered to pay, and Breck said he would consider it as paid, but would leave it with the plaintiff, who was a banker and with whom the agent kept an account, till the policy arrived, when he, Breck, would call and get the money. Afterwards, and before the policy was delivered, and before the premium was paid, the property burned. One of the provisions of the contract was that no insurance should be binding until the premium was paid. The company, so far as appears, had no notice of the arrangement with the agent. The company refused to pay the insurance, because, among other reasons, the premium had not been paid. The court held that the company was liable.

In the course of the opinion the court said: "The case shows that the plaintiff, when he made his application, offered Breck the premium, who said he would con-

sider it as paid, but would leave it with the plaintiff, ·
who was his banker, till the policy arrived, when he
would call and get it. Would it have made the payment
more real if the plaintiff had handed Breck the money,
and Breck had deposited it with his banker?''

In the case at bar, we pause to ask whether it would
have made the payment more real if Kerlin had handed
the additional ten dollars to Disher, and Disher had paid
it to Kerlin?

Continuing, the court said: ''The money was, in
legal effect, paid to Breck, and by him placed in deposit.
It was, in contemplation of law, an actual payment to
the company, as much so as if Breck had transmitted
the money, as well as the application, to the company.
But if not an actual payment, the defendants are estopped
from saying that it is not. They must be considered as
doing what Breck did, viz., saying to the plaintiff on the
2d of March, when he tendered them the money, we
will consider it as paid. *New York Central Ins. Co.* v.
National Protection Ins. Co., 20 Barb. 468.''

In this connection it is proper to remark that it is immaterial whether Disher was a general agent or whether
he was simply a soliciting and collecting agent. If only
the latter, he had, as we have seen, full authority to do
all that could have been done at the home office in regard to the matters here in difference. A general agent,
we apprehend, would not have had power to do more in
this respect. He seems to have been an agent clothed
with full power to solicit applications and to collect premiums in this territory. The questions which we are considering relate to the application and to the alleged payment of the premium then made. Within the scope of
the business intrusted to him he had, so far as the record

discloses, all the authority that a general agent could have exercised in the same matter.

In the case of *Chickering* v. *Globe Mut. Ins. Co.*, 116 Mass. 321, the agent was indebted to the insured and told him he would take care of the premium for him. The insured thereafter died before the premium was paid. The policy provided that the failure to pay the premium should work a forfeiture of the insurance.

The court, in discussing the matter, says: "It is not contended that the fact, that the premium had become due, was forgotten by the assured, or that the necessity of prompt and punctual payment was overlooked."

This sentence, under the evidence, will apply with equal force to the case in hand.

Continuing, the court in the above case, says: "It is clear ón the evidence that an arrangement of some sort was proposed and discussed for the purpose of meeting that necessity, and the jury might have found from the evidence that Chickering not only relied upon that arrangement, but had every assurance that it had been carried into effect."

So, we might add, the jury evidently found in this case.

In *Mississippi Valley Life Ins. Co.* v. *Neyland*, 9 Bush, (Ky.) 430, the court says: "The weight of modern authority is that a general agent of an insurance company, whose business it is to solicit applications for insurance and receive the first premiums, has the right to waive the condition requiring the payment in money, and to accept the promissory note of the applicant or of a third party in lieu thereof, or to undertake to make the payment to the company himself, and that when the cash payment is actually waived in either of these modes the contract binds the company, notwithstanding the recital in the policy that it is not to be binding until the cash portion of the first premium is actually paid in money. *Galt* v. *National Protective Ins. Co.*, 25 Barb. 189; *Boehen* v. *Williamsburg Ins. Co.*, 35 N. Y. 131; *Sheldon* v. *Connecticut Mutual Life Ins. Co.*, 25 Conn. 207.

"The powers of these general agents are *prima facie* co-extensive with the business intrusted to their care, and while acting within the scope of their duties and apparent authority parties dealing with them have the right to presume that they can waive any of the conditions of the contract that might be waived by the principal officers of the corporation."

We also quote from *Wooddy* v. *Old Dominion Ins. Co.*, 31 Grattan (Va.) 362, as follows: "Rowzie (the agent) says that when the twelve dollars and fifty cents, the amount of the premium, were tendered to him, he is clear in his recollection that he at the time owed the appellant that amount for rent past due. If he had then paid over that amount to appellant in discharge of the rent due, and the appellant had immediately handed it back to him for the premium, nobody will doubt that the premium would have been actually paid."

So in the case at bar, if Disher had paid to Kerlin the ten dollars he was owing him, and Kerlin had then handed the ten dollars back to Disher, the entire premium, if Disher is believed, would have been paid. See, also, *Lycoming Fire Ins. Co.* v. *Ward*, 90 Ill. 545.

In the opinion of the court in the case of *New York Life Ins. Co.* v. *McGowan*, 18 Kan. 300, we find the following: "As to the first objection, it is sufficient to say that the application was made to and accepted by an authorized agent of the company. The note was given and accepted as payment. An agent of an insurance company whose business it is to solicit applications for insurance, and receive the first premiums, has the right to waive the condition requiring the payment in money." To the same general effect are: *Southern Life Ins. Co.* v. *Booker,* 9 Heisk. (Tenn.), 606; *Sheldon* v. *Connecticut Mutual Life Ins. Co.,* 25 Conn. 207; *Home Ins. Co.* v. *Gilman,* 112 Ind. 7; *Jones* v. *Ætna Ins. Co.,* (U. S. C. C. Mass.) 8 Ins. L. J. 415; *Hartford Life, etc., Ins. Co.* v. *Hayden* (Ky.), 13 S. W. Rep. 585; *Gerbich* v. *Amazon Ins. Co.,* U. S. D. C., Ohio, 4 Ins. L. J. 240; May on Insurance (3d ed.), section 134, and other authorities there cited.

In *Root* v. *Ross,* 29 Vt. 488, the agent of the debtor took money to the attorney of the creditor for the purpose of paying the debt. A dispute arose as to the correct amount tendered and the money was handed to a bystander to count, said bystander being an officer who, at the time, held a writ of attachment against the creditor. The officer counted it, found the amount and then attached it as the property of the creditor. The attorney of the creditor refused to consider the transaction as payment. But it was held to constitute payment, even though it was shown that there was connivance between the agent of defendant and the party who attached the money.

Counsel for appellee, as we have before said, insist that to constitute payment in this case the money, thirty dollars, should actually have been delivered by Kerlin to Disher for the purpose of extinguishing the debt to the company, and that the agent must have received it for the same purpose. His farther contention may be best stated in his own words, which we quote from printed brief as follows:

"The question of waiver.

"It can not be said that Disher's agreement to pay the company, upon Kerlin's cancellation of the debt due him from Disher, was a waiver.

"In *Cronkhite* v. *Accident Ins. Co.,* 35 Fed. Rep. 26, payment of the premium was not made when due, and the general agent of the company extended the time. At the expiration of this time the insured, in company with the soliciting agent, tried to find the general agent and pay the premium. But they could not find him. The soliciting agent told the insured that he, the soliciting agent, would pay the company and look to the insured to reimburse him. But the soliciting agent did not pay the company. The insured, having been injured thereafter, brought suit on the policy, and Judge Brewer, now on the Supreme Bench of the United States, held that the insured could not recover because the arrangement between the insured and the soliciting agent of the company, whereby the latter agreed to pay the company instead of the former, who would thus become indebted to the latter, was not payment of the premium.

"In *Bane* v. *Travelers' Ins. Co.*, 85 Ky. 677, the insured was in the employ of a railway company, and, in consideration of his policy, assigned to the insurance company his claim on the railway company for wages still to be earned. Part of this was paid by the railway company. The insured quit work and the remainder of the claim remained unpaid by the railway company. The insured began work again for the railway company, and had ten dollars due him from the company at the time of injury, which the insurance company had not collected. Neither had the insurance company demanded such amount from the railway company, nor had it notified the insured of its nonpayment. The insured was injured and brought suit on his policy. The court held that although the company had accepted the assignment of the claim of the insured against the railway company, and although the railway company had money in its possession due the insured, nevertheless, such an arrangement was not payment, and the policy was forfeited.

"In *Belleville Mut. Ins. Co.* v. *Van Winkle,* 1 Beas.

(N. J.), 333, Van Winkle applied to the insurance company for insurance on his property. The company stated its terms and Van Winkle accepted them. Van Winkle had some money owing him by the company, and this much was applied on the premium. Van Winkle offered to make out his note for the remainder (a note being the usual method of paying the company), but the agent told him not to do so, as he did not know how much the balance would be, but that he would let Van Winkle know right away, and Van Winkle could then give the necessary note. Van Winkle asked the agent if he, Van Winkle, was insured, and the agent replied: 'Most certainly you are. I shall make out the policy and send you at once.' Before this could be done, or the note given, the property was destroyed. The court held that Van Winkle could not recover.

"In *Buffum* v. *Fayette Mut. Fire Ins. Co.*, 3 Allen (Mass.), 360, the laws of the company provided for payment of the premium before the company was bound. The insured obtained delays from the president and treasurer of the company until April. Upon the day when payment was due, according to such extension, insured called at the company's offices and asked further extension. The treasurer told him that he, the treasurer, would be responsible, and that the insured might pay him. The court held that under such an arrangement the company was not liable. On page 361, the court says: 'Nothing was actually received, nor did Chadwick [the treasurer] make himself liable to the company, so that they could have charged the sureties on his bond for the amount of the premium. * * * It is quite obvious that Chadwick did not, as agent of the company, agree that he would use their funds to pay this premium. But it was in his private capacity that he agreed to advance the money. And though he was treasurer, his private agreement would not bind the company. If he made a valid agreement in his private capacity, the remedy would be against him if he violated it; and no claim against the company could arise out of it.'

"In *Garlick* v. *Miss. Valley Ins. Co.*, 44 Ia. 553, the policy provided that the insurance should not be operative while any part of the premium or premium note remained unpaid after due. After one payment became due, the insurance company urged payment, part of which was made and accepted. Thereafter the loss occurred. The court held that the plaintiff could not recover, and that the acceptance of part of the premium after it was due was no waiver. The policy also provided that the insurance should be terminated upon the company's giving notice to the insured and refunding a ratable portion of the premium. This the company failed to do; held, nevertheless, that the company was not liable. The secretary of the company informed the insured that the company was liable, which statement put plaintiff at his ease, and he relied upon it. The court held that this was no waiver. On page 554, the court says: 'The premium note being past due and partly unpaid at the time of the loss, we must hold that the policy was suspended under the provisions of article 14, unless the provisions creating such suspension were waived by the defendant. * * After the maturity of the premium note, the plaintiff paid the defendant a part thereof. It is contended by the plaintiff * * that the receipt of such payment by the defendant must have had the effect to restore the policy to operation, because otherwise the defendant would receive plaintiff's money without rendering any return or consideration therefor. To this it may be replied that part payment of the note should have no greater effect than part payment of an original cash premium, where, by contract, full payment is made necessary to put the policy in operation.' ''

There is great force in the reasoning in these authorities. It will be observed that in many instances they are not in harmony with the authorities hereinbefore cited. In some respects the authorities can not be reconciled, but as applied to the facts in this case, we regard the differences, as a rule, as being more apparent than real. For instance, in none of the cases relied on, cited by counsel for appellee, was there an actual tender by the insured of the full amount of the premium, in money, to an agent or officer of the company authorized to receive it. In this case, the tender of the three ten-dollar bills must be regarded by this court as having been made for the purpose of paying the annual premium of thirty dollars in full. The agent to whom the tender was made, and who, as we have seen, was authorized to make the collection, declined to receive it. He stated, on the contrary, in substance, to the insured, I have in my hands ten dollars which you loaned me, therefore I shall only take twenty dollars of this money, which, with what I owe you, will make the thirty dollars, the full amount of the premium. We must assume, so far as the instruction in question is concerned, that Kerlin acted in entire good faith; that he made no effort to secure such an adjustment;' that he entered into no agreement which by inference, or otherwise, could be construed as a fraud on the rights of the company. Then the inquiry arises, what more could Kerlin have done? He certainly was not required to desert his post of duty and go to the home office to pay the ten dollars which the agent had refused to accept. He was assured by the agent, the representative of the company, that so far as he was concerned the premium was paid. It was not his duty to see whether twenty dollars or thirty dollars or any other amount was paid by the agent to the company.

In conclusion, as applied to the facts and circumstances of this case, concerning which, so far as relates to this question, there is absolutely no dispute or controversy (except as to certain alleged contradictory statements of the agent made out of court, and his want of credit as a witness for the reason urged, to which we have hereinbefore briefly referred), we are of the opinion, after patient and careful investigation and examination, that there was no error in giving the instruction hereinbefore set out, for which the judgment of the trial court should be reversed.

Other questions ancillary to the one we have decided are discussed, but if we are right in the conclusion above stated, there is nothing presented in the discussion of any such questions which would justify a different result than the one we have reached.

The decision at the general term is therefore reversed, with instructions to affirm the judgment rendered at the special term.

Ross, J., absent.

Filed Oct. 19, 1893.

On Petition for a Rehearing.

Davis, C. J.—The learned and eloquent counsel for appellee has filed an able, earnest, and interesting brief in support of his petition for a rehearing in this case, and, at the risk of being prolix, we will review the questions presented.

The certificate constitutes the contract on which the rights of the parties must be determined, except in so far as the parties or their authorized agents may have waived or modified the terms thereof. In this case, however, there is no claim that there was any waiver, change, or modification of the terms of the certificate, either before or after it was issued, except such as are necessarily incident to or grow out of what took place between Disher and Kerlin when the application was written and the premium was paid or waived before the certificate was issued.

The court has neither power nor inclination to change or overthrow the contract entered into between Kerlin and the company, nor to make a new one for the parties.

Counsel is in error, in our judgment, in assuming that the courts of the country are holding that there are no rights, in behalf of the company, in an insurance contract which any body is bound to respect. Counsel is also mistaken in the assertion that notwithstanding every provision of the contract is violated by the insured, the claimant under the policy is allowed to come into court and recover. Corporations have the same rights under the law as individuals. They are entitled to neither more nor less consideration. All, the rich and the poor, the strong and the weak, the high and the low, stand equal before the law. Accident and life insurance companies, it may be conceded, when properly managed and conducted, in harmony with the spirit of the better class of such organizations, are beneficent institutions. The same principles of law ordinarily govern the construction of insurance contracts that govern the construction of other contracts. The law applicable to agents of insurance companies stands upon the same footing as the law applicable to agents of other persons and corporations.

It is insisted that the court has not taken into consideration "the actual policy contract in this particular case."

That part of the contract to which reference is made is set out, and was considered in the original opinion. It

will be observed that the language, "the company shall
not be liable by virtue of the policy until the premium
therefor be actually paid," in the policy, in *Home Ins.
Co.* v. *Gilman, Exr.,* 112 Ind. 7 (12), is fully as strong
as the provisions on this subject in the certificate in this
case.

It is next urged that the court erred in holding that
under the contract the insured could make any arrangement with Disher waiving any requirement of the contract.

The controling questions in the decision of this case
are predicated on the proposition that Disher was the
authorized agent of the company to solicit insurance and
to collect premiums, with power to agree as to the time
when the same should be paid, whether in several installments, as written in the application by him, or in
one payment, in advance, as agreed to between the parties on that occasion, which the agent failed to reduce to
writing, and in agreeing on such terms as to the time of
payment, as were agreed upon in this case, and in writing the application, he was acting for and in behalf of
the company, and all he did at that time in relation to
the change of the time of the payment, and his statement
that it was not necessary in consequence of such change
as to when the payments should be made, to rewrite or
change the application to correspond therewith, were
binding on the company, and this underlying principle
must be kept in view in considering what has been and
will be said by the court in this and the original opinion.
Howe v. *Provident Fund Society, supra,* and other authorities cited in original opinion.

It should also be borne in mind that the arrangement
to which exception is taken was made before the policy
or certificate was issued and delivered.   *Crouse* v. *Hartford Fire Ins. Co.,* 79 Mich. 249; *Zell* v. *Herman Farm-*

ers' Mut. Ins. Co., 75 Wis. 521, and authorities cited *supra.*

Moreover, the general rule, as we understand it, is that ordinarily a party, acting in good faith, dealing with an agent, in such cases, may rely upon the statements made by such agent within the scope of his apparent authority, and that the principal will be bound by such statements, and if there is any restriction or limitation on their power, as such agents, within the scope of the particular business in which they are engaged, it is the duty of the company to bring the same to the knowledge of the applicant. Section 126, May on Insurance; *Howe* v. *Provident Fund Society, supra.*

What was said by Judge MITCHELL, in the Gilman case, is applicable here: "For all that appears, the assured was fully justified in presuming that the agent was authorized to make the arrangements disclosed."

We quote further from language cited by Judge MITCHELL with approval in that case: "If the agent be authorized to receive the premium, an agreement between the assured and the agent that the latter will be responsible to the company for the amount, and hold the assured as his personal debtor therefor, is a waiver of the stipulation in the policy that it shall not be binding until the premium is received by the company or its accredited agent."

It will be observed that we do not, in this opinion, go to the extent which the language quoted seems to sanction.

In this case the company sent its trusted representative, with authority to solicit the insurance and to collect the premiums, to Kerlin, who tendered to the agent thirty dollars, the full premium, in pursuance of the agreement, but the agent accepted twenty dollars only of the amount and refused to take ten dollars of the money because he had ten dollars which he had previously borrowed of Kerlin, and thereupon assured Kerlin that the full amount should be regarded as paid, and that he would pay the thirty dollars to the company.

The certificate was thereupon issued by the company and delivered to Kerlin, but the agent concealed the facts we have just mentioned from the company, and only paid to the company seven dollars and fifty cents of the amount received by him.

Now, it will be observed, we did not hold, in the original opinion, that Disher was a general agent, but what we did decide on this question was, that acting within the scope of his authority he did, under the circumstances of this case, have power to waive the payment of the premium in several different installments and to accept payment in advance, that is to say, he had the right to solicit the insurance and to agree with the applicant as to whether the annual premium should be paid in one or several installments. Neither did we hold, as counsel seem to think, that an agent may discharge his debt to the insured by agreeing to stand in his place with reference to his indebtedness to the company, without the latter's knowledge or consent. What we did decide, was that when an applicant for insurance offers and tenders, to an agent of the company who has authority to solicit the insurance and to collect the premiums, as hereinbefore stated, at the time the application is made in good faith, the full amount of the premium, in accordance with the terms of the agreement, and the agent accepts a part of the money so tendered, and refuses to take the residue on the ground that he has in his hands such amount, previously borrowed of the applicant, and agrees to regard the entire amount of the premium as paid by the applicant and to pay the money so had and received by him to the company, and the certificate is afterwards issued and delivered to the applicant, the applicant is not bound to see that the agent pays the money to the company, but he has the right to presume that it has been so paid, until he has notice to the contrary.

It should be borne in mind, in considering these questions, that Kerlin was not responsible for the failure of the agent to write the application as to the terms of payment of the premium, in accordance with the agreement in reference thereto, between him and the agent. See *Howe* v. *Provident Fund Society, supra,* and authorities there cited.

If we are correct in this position, the payment of the twenty dollars to Disher was binding on the company, and, if this is also true, it occurs to us that the logical conclusion is that the refusal of the agent to accept the ten dollars when tendered was a waiver of the payment of that part of the premium as a condition precedent to the taking effect of the policy or certificate.

In view of the subsequent delivery of the certificate to the insured, these facts, under the circumstances, should, in our opinion, be regarded as the equivalent of the payment of the entire premium when the application was made, in pursuance of the understanding between the agent and insured that the full premium should be so paid in advance, at least until the insured had notice that such payment or arrangement was not satisfactory to the company.

The original opinion was, we thought, sufficiently specific on these questions, and whether we have more clearly expressed our ideas in these additional remarks, the profession will determine.

Our reasoning and conclusions throughout are limited and applied to the facts and circumstances which constitute the foundation of this case, and, on careful review of the argument of counsel, we are not able to see how a different conclusion could be reached in this court.

On the question of the cancellation of the policy, a reference to the original opinion will show that what we said on that subject was in response to the argument of counsel for appellant, and, as we did not reach a conclusion thereon, it is not necessary to prolong this opinion in reference thereto.

The petition for a rehearing is overruled.

Filed Jan. 13, 1894.

No. 781.

SULT v. WARREN SCHOOL TOWNSHIP.

SPECIAL VERDICT.—*Failure to Find a Fact in Issue.—Burden of Proof.* —Where a special verdict is silent as to any fact in issue, such fact must be held as found against the party who was bound to prove it.

CONTRACT.—*Subscription.—Recovery of.—Substantial Compliance with Terms of Must be Shown.—Schoolhouse.—Township Trustee.*—Where citizens of a school township petition for the location of a school district and the erection of a schoolhouse therein, designating the size of the house, location, etc., and subscribing sums of money to aid in the construction thereof, to be paid when the walls are erected to the square, and the subscription is accepted by the trustee, before the amounts subscribed can be recovered the school township must show a substantial compliance with the terms of subscription.

From the Huntington Circuit Court.

M. L. Spencer, W. A. Branyan and *J. C. Branyan,* for appellant.

J. B. Kenner and *U. S. Lesh,* for appellee.

DAVIS, C. J.—It is alleged in the complaint, that appellant, with others, executed to appellee a subscription in writing, by the terms of which appellant agreed to pay appellee fifty dollars when a school district was located and a school house made of brick was erected therein to the completion of the walls. The subscription, a copy of which is filed with the complaint, is as follows:

"*To Thomas Bolinger, Trustee of Warren Township, Huntington County, State of Indiana:*

"We, the undersigned citizens of the town of Bippus, in said township, respectfully petition and ask you to locate at said town a public school, and erect a schoolhouse there, to be maintained at the public expense, as such, out of the tuition fund, which we believe should be fifty-four feet in length and forty-two feet in width, and two stories high, and divided into two rooms, made of brick, with suitable wooden finish, which we think should be at a cost of $3,000, and we will contribute to the said sum, for the construction thereof, the sum of money set opposite our names in the aid thereof, as soon as the walls thereof are erected to the square.

"Witness: LAFAYETTE SULT, $50.00.
                  ."(OTHERS.)"

It is further alleged in the complaint, that in pursuance of said petition and subscription the township trustee granted the request, accepted the donation, located and ordered the construction of the building, and completed the same all substantially, in accordance with said request and petition, and that such location and erection of said building was on the strength of the subscription aforesaid, and that without such subscription and money subscribed the said building would not have been erected, as there was not sufficient money in the treasury of said township to do the work, etc.

The sufficiency of the complaint has not been in any manner questioned.

The appellant filed an answer in one paragraph, in

which he expressly waived the answer of general denial, admitted the signing and delivery of the subscription, but pleaded specially that the same was not accepted by the appellee, and that no schoolhouse, as proposed in said offer, has ever been erected, and that appellee (the trustee) refused to comply with the offer and refused to build such house, but instead thereof announced to appellant and his co-subscribers that he did not rely upon their subscription, but would build a house to suit his own notion, from the public funds of the township, and did so build the same, that is to say thirty-eight feet long and twenty-eight feet wide and two stories high, instead of forty-two feet wide and fifty-four feet long, as proposed in the subscription, and that the same was built at a place remote from the town, all over the remonstrances of said subscribers, etc.

A demurrer was overruled to this answer, and a reply of general denial thereto was filed. On trial by a jury, there was a general verdict for appellant, which, on motion for new trial by appellee, was set aside. On the next trial, the jury returned a special verdict, in which they found, in substance, that the subscription paper above set out was signed by appellant and delivered to appellee (the trustee), and that the same was accepted by the trustee. The residue of the verdict is as follows:

"Afterwards and before any work was done or any material was furnished for the building of a schoolhouse in said district, and while he was still trustee of said school township, he declared to some of the subscribers, that he did not expect them to pay said subscription; that he was building said school house where he pleased and as he pleased, without any reliance upon said subscription, and that he did not want the same; and we find that the plaintiff abandoned said petition, * * and

VOL. 8—42

that in lieu thereof he erected near the town of Bippus, in said township, a school house twenty-eight feet wide and thirty-eight feet long, with a cloak room fourteen feet and eight inches wide by twenty feet long, said building being two stories high with only one room down stairs and one room up stairs for pupils to occupy, of which the lower room was for the school district and the upper room was for the township as a high school or graded school which the pupils of said district, in high school grade, could use in common with the pupils of the same grade of the other school districts of said township. We find that the seating capacity in the lower room of said house was for sixty-eight or seventy pupils, and that there were at least seventy-seven at the time enrolled for attendance in said room. We further find that said building was not constructed on the faith of said subscription, and that the subscription had been mutually abandoned by all parties thereto, before any work had been commenced or any material furnished, and that demand was made on defendant, after said building was up to the square and before suit.''

Then follows the formal conclusion.

There was no objection made by either party to the verdict. Neither party filed a motion for a *venire de novo* or a motion for a new trial. Each party moved for a judgment in his favor on the verdict. The court sustained appellee's motion, to which ruling appellant excepted. The evidence is not in the record.

The errors assigned by appellant are:

1. That the court erred in overruling appellant's motion for a judgment in his favor on the special verdict.

2. That the court erred in sustaining appellee's motion for judgment in its favor, and in rendering judgment thereon.

Appellee assigns as cross error the overruling of the demurrer to appellant's answer.

The answer denies the acceptance of the subscription, denies that it was relied or acted upon by appellee, and also denies a compliance with its terms, and it may be regarded as equivalent to a general denial.

The sufficiency of the answer, regarded merely as a general denial, is not, in fact, controverted by appellee in argument, although counsel say that they "do not waive the point;" and on this theory, if no other, there was, in our opinion, no error in overruling the demurrer thereto.

The principal—the controlling—question for our consideration is, was appellee entitled to recover judgment on the special verdict of the jury?

The rule is settled that if a special verdict is silent as to any fact in issue such fact must be held as found against the party who was bound to prove it. *Louisville, etc., R. W. Co.* v. *Buck*, 116 Ind. 566 (575); *Evansville, etc., R. R. Co.,* v. *Maddux*, 134 Ind. 571, 33 N. E. Rep. 345.

The burden was on appellee to establish, under the terms of the subscription and the allegations of the complaint, that the township had substantially complied with the conditions precedent, by locating at said town of Bippus and erecting to the square a schoolhouse of the kind and character designated. It was not necessary for appellee to prove a literal compliance in the performance of the conditions precedent, as to the location, size or character of the schoolhouse, but it was incumbent upon appellee to show a substantial compliance with such terms. The verdict does not, in express terms, find that the appellee has complied substantially in the performance of the conditions precedent, but it does appear that the subscription was not relied or acted upon, and that it was rescinded and abandoned by mutual agreement of the parties, before any work had been commenced or any material had been furnished, and that the trustee, in lieu of such compliance, built a house materially less in size and capacity near the town of Bippus. Circumstances might have been shown which would have authorized the court in saying that as to size and location there was a substantial compliance, but nothing of this kind appears in the verdict.

If the question of compliance was a mixed question of law and fact, still the finding does not include all the facts which would be involved in a performance of the condition precedent; and if so much of the finding as involves conclusions of law was rejected, there would not remain either a general finding or sufficient facts to show a substantial performance of the conditions of the subscription on the part of appellee. *Cook* v. *McNaughton*, 128 Ind. 410.

If all the statements or conclusions in regard to the agreement or intent of the parties, subsequent to the acceptance of the subscription, were eliminated and disregarded, the court could not say as a matter of law on the facts which would remain in the verdict, that appellee had substantially complied with the terms of the agreement in the performance of the condition precedent. It does not appear how near the school house erected was to the town. Neither are any facts or circumstances found which would warrant the conclusion that the size of the house erected was a substantial compliance either with the words or spirit of the contract, but it does appear insufficient in capacity to accommodate the pupils enrolled for attendance there.

In the view we take of the case, we are not required to consider the question as to the power of the trustee to abandon or rescind the contract after he accepted the subscription; but if it was conceded that the agreement was not in any respect rescinded, abandoned, or modified, it was necessary, as we have seen, before appellee could recover, to show at least a substantial compliance with the terms of the contract, on the part of the township.

The judgment of the court below is reversed, with instructions to grant appellee a new trial if moved for within ninety days, otherwise to render judgment in favor of appellant, on the verdict of the jury, all at costs of appellee.

Filed Jan. 24, 1894.

No. 1,210.

SMITH ET AL. *v.* THE STATE, EX REL. ELY.

DRAINAGE.—*Foreclosure of Lien.*—*Misdescription of Land.*—*When Description Sufficient to Put Parties Upon Inquiry.*—*Estoppel.*—Where, in an action to foreclose a drainage lien, the land was described as 443 acres, in reserve 53, township 29 north, range 10 east, whereas, in fact, only about 150 acres of such land lay in township 29, and reserve and range as stated, the remainder lying in township 28 north, reserve and range as above stated, such description was sufficient to put the defendants on inquiry, and they can not plead that they were misled thereby and induced to refrain from remonstrating, and confine the decree alone to the land lying in township 29.

From the Huntington Circuit Court.

J. B. Kenner and *U. S. Lesh,* for appellants.
T. E. Ellison, for appellee.

LOTZ, J.—In the year of 1883, William Branstrator and others filed their petition, in the Allen Superior Court, asking for the establishment of a ditch to drain their lands. The proceedings were commenced under the act of April the 8th, 1881 (sections 4273 to 4284, inclusive, R. S. 1881), and resulted in the construction of the ditch for the purposes sought.

The appellants' lands were assessed for the construction thereof. The report of the drainage commissioners described their lands in two separate tracts or parcels.

This action was brought to foreclose the lien on said lands. The complaint was in three paragraphs. The third paragraph, as an incident to the foreclosure, asked for the reformation of the description of one tract contained in said report.

The appellants answered the complaint by the general denial, and by a special answer, as follows:

"And for a second and further answer by all the defendants to the first and third paragraphs of the complaint, defendants say that they are the owners of the land described in the plaintiff's complaint, and they aver that after said petition was filed the court referred the matter to the commissioners, and said commissioners made their report, in which they placed an assessment of benefits for the construction of said work on the following described real estate, belonging to these defendants, to wit: 'All of reserve 53 except 200 acres off the northeast side thereof, in township 29 north, range 10 east.' That said commissioners made their report and filed the same in the Superior Court of Allen county, and that said report only purported to assess benefits against the lands of these defendants in township 29, and these defendants examined said assessment, saw such fact, and, while the number of acres were large, defendants knew that it was impossible to exactly tell how many acres of such reserve lay in township 29, and defendants were informed and believed that the amount of the assessment was largely in excess of the actual amounts of assessments, and defendants aver that they were led to believe, and did believe, that their lands only lying in township 29 were assessed, and they further believed this from the fact that the whole of said land was not benefited, to wit: 'All of the lands in said reserve 53, lying south of the line dividing Union and Jackson townships were not in any manner benefited.'

"They further aver that had said report of said commissioners reported benefits in the south part of said reserve 53, they would have remonstrated against said report; but believing and seeing by the report that it was not so assessed, they acquiesced in the report.

"Wherefore they aver that they were misled by such report, and deprived of their rights.

"Wherefore they pray that said decree confine the lien to the lands in township 29, in reserve 53, and none other, and for all further and proper relief."

To this answer a demurrer was filed and overruled, and a reply being filed, the issues joined were tried by the court, and resulted in a finding and judgment for appellee.

The only assignment of error discussed by counsel is, that of overruling the motion for a new trial.

On the trial of the cause, the appellants produced seven witnesses, whose testimony tended to show that the lands in Union township, being the south part of reserve 53, in township 28, were not benefited by the drain and could not be drained by it.   After this evidence had been given, the appellee moved to strike it all out.   This motion was sustained.   This ruling is one of the causes assigned for a new trial.

On a former appeal of this cause in the Supreme Court, *State, ex rel., v. Smith,* 124 Ind. 302, that court said: "Whether the appellee may controvert the validity of the assessment, upon the ground that she was misled by the description, or whether she may interpose other defenses, we do not decide.''

Appellants insist, if we understand their contention, that they were misled by the description as contained in the report of the drainage commissioners, and that one of the methods of showing this is to prove that the lands were not benefited by the drain.

Conceding, without deciding, this question, we do not see how the appellants were injured by the ruling of the court in striking out the evidence bearing upon the lands benefited; for the undisputed evidence in the case, as shown by the report of the commissioners, is that appellants' lands were assessed in two tracts, one as follows: ''All of reserve 53 except 200 acres off the northeast side thereof, township 29, range 10; 443 acres; $4,900.'' The second, ''East half of 200 acres off the northeast side of reserve 53, township 29, range 10; 100 acres; $1,100.''

The undisputed evidence further shows that reserve 53 lies part in township 29 and part in township 28. Of the 443 acres contained in the first above described tract, only about 150 acres lay in township 29, and the remainder lay in township 28.

The appellants, or their ancestors, were notified by the report, that under the first description, 443 acres were assessed benefits in reserve 53. They knew they had only 150 acres in township 29. This description was sufficient to put them upon their inquiry, and we do not see how they were misled and induced to refrain from remonstrating.

There is no available error in this ruling of the court. The other causes for a new trial relate to matters largely in the discretion of the court. We have examined each of them, and find no reversible error.

Judgment affirmed, at costs of appellants.

Filed Jan. 26, 1894.

No. 962.

FISHER v. FISHER, ADMINISTRATOR.

PROMISSORY NOTE.—*Consideration, Sufficiency of.*—*Burden of Proof.*— In an action on a promissory note, in which illegality of consideration is pleaded as a defense, the note imports sufficient consideration, and the burden is on the defendant to show that the consideration was illegal.

VERDICT.—*Sufficiency of Evidence to Sustain.*—That the evidence is sufficient to sustain the verdict, see opinion.

From the Huntington Circuit Court.

J. C. Branyan, L. P. Milligan, S. E. Cook, M. L. Spencer and *J. C. Branyan*, for appellant.

J. B. Kenner and *U. S. Lesh*, for appellee.

DAVIS, C. J.—This case is here for the third time. *Fisher* v. *Fisher*, 113 Ind. 474; *Fisher, Admr.*, v. *Fisher*, 131 Ind. 462.

The case was again tried, and the special finding of the facts by the court and conclusions of law thereon were against appellant, who appeals to this court and assigns as error the overruling of his motion for a new trial. The motion for a new trial contains two reasons:

1. That the finding and decision of the court is not sustained by sufficient evidence.

2. That the decision of the court is contrary to law.

The appellant contends that the note was given by him to cover his part of the loss sustained in dealings in margins in wheat on the Chicago board of trade in a gambling transaction, and that the note is, for that reason, without any consideration, and void.

If the transaction was a gaming one, illegal and void, and constituted the consideration for the note, appellee would not have a right to recover; for, if the transaction between the parties was illegal, they were *in pari delicto*, and will not be aided by the courts in profiting by their own wrong.

The court, however, in this case, after hearing all the evidence, has found "that said note was not executed for an illegal consideration, to wit, gambling in grain, but that the transaction out of which the same grew was a legitimate purchase of grain which was intended to be delivered, and warehouse receipts for the delivery of said grain were actually delivered, and the consideration of said note is and was for money advanced by Frank T. Fisher, deceased, to Tillman H. Fisher, and is a valid and legal one," and, therefore, the only question for us to determine is whether there is any evidence in the record tending to support the finding.

It should be remembered, in this connection, that this finding was not essential to a recovery on the part of appellee. In this State a promissory note imports a sufficient consideration, and the burden was on appellant to show that such consideration was illegal. *Fisher* v. *Fisher, supra.*

If the finding was silent on this question, the court would assume that appellant had failed to prove the alleged illegality of the consideration. *Louisville, etc., R. W. Co.* v. *Buck*, 116 Ind. 566.

We find, on examination of the record in this case, that there was some evidence, at least, tending to prove that said Tillman H. Fisher, appellant, and Frank T. Fisher, since deceased, were cousins; that about 1876 or 1877 they resided in Chicago, Illinois, and that appellant then approached said decedent, then in full life, with the statement that the wheat crop was short and that there was some prospect of a Turkish war, and, therefore, that there was a good opportunity to make money in purchase of wheat, and that thereupon they purchased of or through Ramsey Bros. & Co., regular and reputable members

NOVEMBER TERM, 1893.   667

Toledo, St. Louis and Kansas City Railroad Company v. Reeves.

of the Chicago board of trade, and buyers, sellers, and shippers of grain, twenty thousand bushels of wheat, which was in the warehouse, and which was delivered to Ramsey Bros. & Co., and was then delivered by said firm to them, in the shape of warehouse receipts, and that it was the intention of Ramsey Bros. & Co., who were a responsible and reliable firm, to deliver the wheat to them, and that they could have obtained the wheat if they had called for it, and that they carried the wheat on options or margins, with said firm, for ten or fifteen days, and that the wheat depreciated in value and they closed out at a loss of over nine hundred dollars, all of which was paid by said Frank T. Fisher to said Ramsey Bros. & Co., and that in a settlement of said transaction, between said Tillman and Frank, appellant executed his note to said decedent for his half of the loss. *Whitesides* v. *Hunt*, 97 Ind. 191.

This court can not disturb the judgment of the trial court on the evidence.

Judgment affirmed.

Filed Jan. 26, 1894.

No. 941.

TOLEDO, ST. LOUIS AND KANSAS CITY RAILROAD COMPANY v. REEVES.

DECEDENT'S ESTATE.—*Letters of Administration.*—*When and Where May be Granted.*—*Resident Dying Leaving no Assets in the State.*—Letters of administration may be granted under subdivision 1, section 2228, R. S. 1881, in the county where, at his death, the intestate was an inhabitant, leaving no assets in the State, and none coming into it afterward. One of the various reasons for administration, under such circumstances, may be to prosecute some claim of indeterminate value, as for the death of the intestate, as provided by section 284, R. S. 1881.

Toledo, St. Louis and Kansas City Railroad Company v. Reeves.

SAME.—*Administrator, Cause for Removal of.—Discretion, Abuse of.— Inventory.—Bond.*—The failure of an administrator to give bond or to file an inventory in the time required by statute, or, if no assets, a statement showing such fact, is good ground for removal; but as to such matters the circuit court has a wide discretion, and unless a clear abuse of discretion is shown, the action of the court will not be disturbed on appeal.

From the Montgomery Circuit Court.

S. O. Bayless and *C. G. Guenther*, for appellant.

G. W. Paul, M. D. White and *W. M. Reeves*, for appellee.

REINHARD, J.—The appellant filed, in the court below, a petition for the revocation of letters of administration, that had been issued to the appellee, and for his removal as such administrator. The ground relied upon in such petition is that the decedent had no estate in the county or State in which the letters were granted at the time of his death, although at such time he was an inhabitant of the county. It is shown that the purpose for which the letters were issued was to enable the appellee to prosecute an action for negligence against the appellant for causing the decedent's death.

It was stated in the petition that said appellee had never filed an inventory of his decedent's estate, although the statutory period for filing the same had expired. The appellee's application for letters, and the order of the court granting the same to him, were set out in the petition. The court sustained a demurrer to the appellant's petition, and the correctness of this ruling is the only question presented for our determination.

The proceedings for the appointment of an administrator, in this State, are purely statutory, and must be conducted in conformity to the statute governing the same. Henry Ind. Prob. Law, p. 4; *Croxton v. Renner*, 103 Ind. 223.

The statute under which administrators are appointed provides that letters may be granted in the county—

1. Where, at his death, the intestate was an inhabitant.

2. Where, not being an inhabitant of this State, he leaves assets.

3. Where, not being an inhabitant, and dying out of the State, he leaves assets.

4. Where, not being an inhabitant, he dies out of the State, not leaving assets in any county thereof, but assets of such intestate shall afterward come into it.

5. But where, not being an inhabitant, he shall die out of the State, leaving assets in several counties, etc. R. S. 1881, section 2228.

The section of the statute above set out was first enacted, in practically its present state, under the revision of 1843. R. S. 1843, section 92, subd. 1.

According to the showing in the petition, the power of the circuit court to grant letters in the present case does not fall within any of the provisions contained in any of the subdivisions of section 2228, *supra*, unless it be under the first subdivision, as in all the subsequent ones it was necessary that the intestate should have died the owner of some assets.

As preliminary to the determination of the question now in hand, it may be stated as the settled law of this State:

1. That the appellant has such an interest in the subject-matter of the proceeding to revoke the letters of the appellee as entitles it to institute and maintain the same in a proper case.

2. Where the decedent is not a resident of the State, and has no assets at the time of the application for letters, such letters may not properly issue, but if they are nevertheless issued, the act is *coram non judice* and void,

and the letters will be revoked in a proceeding such as this. *Jeffersonville R. R. Co.* v. *Swayne's Admr.*, 26 Ind. 477.

We proceed to determine whether the court has power to grant letters of administration in a county of this State where the intestate was, at the time of his death, a resident, leaving no assets in the State and none coming into it afterward. That the court has such power under the plain letter of the first subdivision of section 2228, *supra*, we think must be obvious. There is, in that subdivision, no condition annexed to the power of granting such letters other than the one that the intestate must have been an inhabitant. It is not required, in terms, that he should have had some assets or that assets belonging to him should have come into the State after his death. The clause under consideration stands alone, and is in no manner connected with or dependent upon the following subdivisions regarding the requirement that he must have had assets.

With the statute so clear and unambiguous, it would seem that there need be no difficulty in reaching the conclusion that the appellee's appointment was authorized. It is urged, however, that in cases where an intestate had no assets to administer, the Legislature could not have intended to confer on the circuit court the power of granting letters of administration, inasmuch as it would be useless and profitless to have an administrator where no assets are to be administered. But we are not able to say that the appointment of an administrator may not subserve a useful purpose, even where there are no tangible assets to administer. There are instances in which such appointment may become proper and necessary in order to prosecute some claim of indeterminate value, or to make satisfaction of record of a claim which had been paid but not satisfied, and perhaps for other purposes.

It is further contended that because section 2260, R. S. 1881, requires the filing of an inventory within sixty days after the appointment, and section 2242, the filing of a bond of not less than double the value of the personal estate to be administered, it must have been contemplated by the Legislature that in every case where an administrator is appointed there must be some personal property to be administered. We do not think this conclusion necessarily follows. The filing of the inventory is required, doubtless, to enable the court to determine the extent of the assets of the estate, and if none such exist when the inventory is to be filed, it should be so stated in the writing which is filed in lieu of the inventory. Some bond should also be filed, so as to hold the administrator to a responsibility in the performance of his duties. A failure to file these is good ground for removal, but, as to such matters, the circuit court has a wide discretion, as it likewise possesses in the matter of the appointment, and unless a clear abuse is shown, the action of such court will not be interfered with on appeal.

The statute under which appellant says, in its petition, that the appellee is proceeding to recover damages for causing the death of the intestate, provides that when the death of one is caused by the wrongful act or omission of another, the personal representative of the dead person may maintain an action for damages against the wrongdoer, if such deceased person, had he lived, might have maintained against such wrongdoer a similar action for an injury for the same act or omission. R. S. 1881, section 284.

The words "personal representative" here undoubtedly include an administrator, and we are of opinion that he may be appointed for the purpose of prosecuting such an action. His appointment, in such cases, is not to make assets for the estate of the deceased, for the section cited further provides that the damages must enure to the exclusive benefit of the widow and children, if any, or next of kin.

The administrator, in such cases, does not represent the creditors of the estate, being merely a trustee for those entitled to the damages for the purpose of collecting and disbursing the same. While it is true that the right of action is, strictly speaking, no part of the assets of the estate proper, yet the action may result in a fund belonging exclusively to the widow and children or next of kin of which the administrator becomes the trustee.

The right to maintain such an action did not exist at common law, as in cases of personal injury the cause of action expired with the death of the injured party. The statute under which the right of action is conferred was enacted by the revision of 1852. 2 R. S. 1852, p. 205, section 784.

At that time, the statute granting the power to appoint an administrator in the county where the deceased was an inhabitant at his death, without assets, was in force. It must have been the view of the law-making body that a remedy then existed in favor of all persons affected by the act, otherwise the right to maintain the action would have been extended to parties that might be injured and did not then possess such right. While legislative interpretation of a statute is not usually given great weight, it is not, especially in doubtful cases, without its influence upon the courts.

We are loth to believe that the Legislature intended to confer the right of action upon an administrator, when, at the same time, there was no power in the court to appoint one for the purpose of instituting such action. If the contention of appellant's counsel should prevail, no action could ever be maintained under section 284, *supra*,

Decker *et al. v.* Washburn.

if the deceased was without assets. The result of such a ruling would be that the families of those unfortunates whose death is brought about by the misconduct of others, and without fault of their own, and who die without property, would be absolutely without remedy, and the salutary provision of the statute could never be invoked with success, in behalf of their indigent families, while those who have property left them would alone be benefited by the enactment.

Our opinion is that the court had ample authority to grant letters of administration to the appellee, and that the court below committed no error in sustaining the demurrer to the appellant's petition.

Judgment affirmed.

Filed Nov. 3, 1893; petition for a rehearing overruled Jan. 26, 1894.

No. 1,061.

DECKER ET AL. *v.* WASHBURN.

EVIDENCE.—*Insufficiency of.*—*Highway.*—*Proceeding to Establish.*—*Damages.*—In a proceeding to establish a highway, the judgment in a former proceeding relating to the same subject-matter, which had been rendered more than six years prior to the commencement of the subsequent action, the damages in the former proceeding having never been paid, nor the highway, as established thereby, never having been opened or worked as such, the judgment in the former proceeding is not a proper basis for damages in the subsequent action, and that being the only evidence, there is clearly a failure of proof.

HIGHWAY.—*Proceeding to Establish.*—*Judgment Functus Officio.*—*Subsequent Proceeding De Novo.*—Where a highway has been established, but has not been opened or used within six years from the time of its establishment, the judgment establishing the highway becomes *functus officio,* or inoperative, and the only way in which the high-way may be again established is by a proceeding *de novo.*

From the Pulaski Circuit Court.

J. C. Nelson, Q. A. Myers, H. A. Steis and *M. M. Hathaway,* for appellant.

B. Borders, for appellee.

REINHARD, J.—In a highway proceeding, tried in the court below upon appeal from the board of commissioners, the appellee recovered a personal judgment for five hundred dollars, from which this appeal is prosecuted.

The insufficiency of the evidence to sustain the finding and judgment is relied upon to bring about a reversal. The only evidence presented to the trial court upon this question was a former judgment by the same court in a similar proceeding to open and establish the highway in question, in which proceeding the appellee had been awarded a judgment for five hundred dollars.

It is contended, by appellants' counsel, that this judgment was not a proper basis for the damages in the present action, and there being no other evidence, the court erred in overruling the motion for a new trial.

It is proper to state here that the question we are about to pass upon was presented, also, by way of demurrer to the answer setting up the former judgment, and by timely objection and exception to the introduction of the record of the former proceedings containing the original judgment.

The appellee's contention is that the former judgment of the Pulaski Circuit Court was an adjudication, not only upon the question of the public utility of the proposed highway, but also upon the subject of damages. It is agreed that the judgment just referred to had been rendered more than six years prior to the time of the commencement of the present proceedings, before the commissioners, and that the highway, as laid out and established in such former proceedings, had never been opened or worked as such, and that the former judgment for damages remains unpaid.

Section 5032, R. S. 1881, provides that "Every public highway already laid out or which may hereafter be laid out, and which shall not be opened and used within six years from the time of its being so laid out, shall cease to be a highway for any purpose whatever."

It is not claimed that any portion of this proposed highway was opened and used during the interval between the two judgments. The remaining portion of the section quoted does not, therefore, have any application to the question in hand.

We think the provisions of this statute are too plain to be misunderstood. The words "laid out" doubtless mean established, surveyed, declared a road. It seems to us that the statute applies to precisely such a case as we have here. A highway has been "laid out,"—that is to say, it has been established and declared to be a highway by the judgment of the court. But it has not been opened or used within six years from the time it was laid out. It has therefore ceased to be a highway altogether, and the former judgment of the court, by virtue of which it was laid out, at the expiration of six years from the date of its rendition, became *functus officio*. This includes, of course, the judgment for damages.

We are strengthened in this view, we think, by the fact that the order for the opening of the highway is enforceable only upon the payment of the damages assessed. If the damages are not paid, the road is not to be opened, and, conversely, if the road is not opened, there would be no consideration for the judgment of damages. When the six years' limitation had expired, the entire judgment ceased to be operative. That which was once declared to be a highway, upon certain conditions being complied with, has now ceased to be such, and the compliance with the conditions will not serve to restore to it its former character. The only manner in which it may be again declared as such is by a new proceeding, the same as if none before had ever been had.

We fully agree with the learned counsel for appellee, that the only way in which the citizens' land may be taken for a public highway is by the proceedings prescribed in the statute, R. S. 1881, section 5015, *et seq.*

We also agree with counsel that after such proceedings have culminated in a judgment there is no way provided by which a new proceeding may be instituted for again having the proposed road laid out or established. But we think this restriction is itself limited by the statute to the period of six years. If, within that time, the conditions upon which the judgment remains in operation thereafter are not complied with, the judgment dies, as it were, and the territory declared to be a public highway, but not opened or used as such, no longer retains its separate identity, but becomes again a portion of the mass of real property out of which it had been set apart for the use of the public. It seems to us that the statute was designed to meet just such cases as the one under consideration. In our view of the case, the learned trial court erred in treating the former judgment as still in force. There was no evidence to support the judgment for damages. The motion for a new trial should have been sustained.

Judgment reversed.

Filed Jan. 2, 1894.

No. 1,087.

JOHNSON *v.* WILLIAMS.

PRINCIPAL AND AGENT.—*Rendering Services at Request of Another.—Recovery.—Broker.—License.*—Where a person not engaged in a regular business of stock and exchange broker renders services at the instance and request of another, in the sale of bank stock, the former is entitled to recover of the latter the reasonable value of the services rendered, such services not being in violation of section 5269, *et seq.*, R. S. 1881.

From the Grant Circuit Court.

G. W. Harvey and *A. De Wolf*, for appellant.
W. H. Carroll and *G. G. Wharton*, for appellee.

Ross, J.—This action was brought by the appellee against the appellant to recover for services rendered appellant in the sale of some bank stock. The only question presented on this appeal is as to the correctness of the conclusions of law made by the court upon the facts found.

The facts found, with the conclusions of law thereon, are as follows:

1. "That the plaintiff, at the instance and request of the defendant, sold forty-five shares of bank stock belonging to the defendant, and that the services so rendered in selling said bank stock were reasonably worth one hundred and eighty dollars."

2. "That the plaintiff, at the time he sold said bank stock, was not licensed to carry on the business of stock and exchange broker, in buying or selling stock, bank notes, gold, silver, promissory notes, and bills of exchange."

3. "That at the time of making said sale of said bank stock the plaintiff was not engaged in a regular business of stock and exchange broker, in buying or selling stock,

bank notes, gold, silver, promissory notes, and bills of exchange.''

''And as conclusions of law upon the facts the court finds: 1st. That the plaintiff ought to recover of and from the defendant the sum of one hundred and eighty dollars.''

The contention of counsel for appellant is that the appellee was not entitled to recover, because he was acting as a broker, contrary to sections 5269, 5274 and 2090, R. S. 1881.

We think it unnecessary to pursue and determine all the questions so ably presented by counsel for appellant, for the reason that counsel's reasoning is predicated upon a state of facts contrary to what is shown by the record in this case. In determining the correctness of the conclusions of law drawn by the court, we can look simply to the facts found by the court within the issues.

Had the court found as a fact that the appellee was acting as a broker in making the sale of bank stock for appellant, we would probably be called upon to put a construction upon the sections of the statute, *supra*. However, the court found as a fact that the appellee ''was not engaged in a regular business of stock and exchange broker.'' Whether or not he was so engaged is a question of fact to be determined from the evidence, and the appellant does not question the correctness of the facts found. The court having found that he was not acting as a broker, the conclusions were right.

The court did not err in its conclusions of law.

Judgment affirmed.

Filed Jan. 10, 1894.

No. 1,058.

THE STATE NATIONAL BANK OF SPRINGFIELD, ILLINOIS, *v.* BENNETT.

EVIDENCE.—*Conditional Examination of Plaintiff by Defendant.—Use of in Several Cases.—Agreement as to.—Grounds of Objection.*—Where defendant took what is styled a "conditional examination of plaintiff," under an agreement in which it is stated that there are several cases involving similar questions, the agreement providing that any testimony that may be thus taken at the instance of the defendant may be used by the plaintiff, at his option, so far as the same may be relevant, in each and all of such cases, and according the same right to the defendant, but providing that neither party to the agreement waives any question as to the competency or relevancy of such testimony; in such case, the only grounds of objection to such testimony that will be heard are those as to its relevancy or incompetency.

SAME.—*Patent-Right Note.—Statutory Requirement.—Ignorance of.*—In an action on a note given for a patent-right, where the note did not disclose the fact that it was "given for a patent-right," as required by statute, there was no substantial error in refusing to permit plaintiff, an assignee and nonresident, to show that its officers had no knowledge of such statutory requirement, for the want of such knowledge could not be considered as tending to establish plaintiff's good faith.

SAME.—*Action by Assignee of Note for Patent-Right.—Notice.—Newspaper Articles Charging Payees with Fraud.*—In an action on a promissory note given for a patent-right, by the assignee thereof, the note not having been drawn in compliance with the law of this State, it was not error for the court to admit in evidence certain newspaper accounts of the arrest of one of the payees of the note, about two months before the assignment thereof, in which articles the payees were charged with swindling parties by selling a patent-right which had expired, the court instructing the jury that the articles were to be considered only as bearing upon the question of notice to plaintiff, the assignee, other evidence having been admitted tending to show that plaintiff's officers had read these articles before they purchased the note in suit.

APPELLATE COURT PRACTICE.—*Evidence.—What Objections Considered.*—The Appellate Court will consider only such grounds of objection in relation to evidence as were presented to the trial court.

INSTRUCTIONS TO JURY.—*Law Applicable to Issues, to Evidence.*—The rule that instructions should be applicable to the evidence does not preclude the court from stating to the jury the law applicable to the issues made by the parties.

SAME.—*Not Signed.—Refused.—No Question Saved.*—No question can be saved as to instructions asked by a party and refused, where the instructions are not signed by the party or his attorney.

PROMISSORY NOTE.—*Purchaser Fraudulently Refraining from Inquiry.— Good Faith.—Notice.*—Where the purchaser of a note fraudulently refrained from inquiry lest he should thereby discover the transaction out of which it originated, he can not assume the attitude of a holder in good faith without notice.

From the Hamilton Circuit Court.

G. Shirts and *I. A. Kilbourne*, for appellant.

J. A. Roberts, *M. Vestal*, *W. S. Christian* and *I. W. Christian*, for appellee.

GAVIN, J.—Appellant sued appellee upon a promissory note dated November 8th, 1890, due in one year, executed to Bernard & Hunter, payable at the Citizens' State Bank of Noblesville, Ind., the note having been assigned to appellant by indorsement thereon before maturity and for a valuable consideration.

For answer appellee set up:

1st. That the note was given for the right to sell a certain patent fence, and that the affidavit and copy of letters patent, required by section 6054, R. S. 1881, had not been filed in the proper clerk's office, nor had the words "given for a patent-right" been inserted therein, according to the terms of this statute.

2d. Want of consideration.

3d. That the consideration of the note was the right to use and sell a certain patent fence, and false representations, in that it was not patented as represented, which were relied upon by appellee.

In each paragraph it is averred that appellant had, at the time of the purchase of the note, full knowledge of the facts therein set forth.

The only questions here presented arise upon the motion for new trial.

What is styled the "conditional examination of plaintiff," being the evidence of its officers, was taken by appellee under an agreement, in which it is recited that there are several cases involving similar questions, and is also provided "that any testimony that may be thus taken at the instance of the defendant in this case may be used by the plaintiff, at its option, and also at the plaintiff's option, such testimony so far as the same may be relevant may be admitted in evidence in each and all of said cases.

The defendant in each of said cases has the right also, if they shall so desire, to introduce such testimony in said several cases. But neither party to this agreement waives any question as to the competency or relevancy of any such testimony."

By the terms of this agreement, the only objections which could be heard are those relating to the competency or relevancy of this testimony, and appellants are precluded from questioning it on the ground that it is taken as a "conditional examination" rather than as a deposition.

Under the circumstances of this case, there was no material error in refusing to permit appellant to show that its officers had no knowledge of the law of Indiana regarding patent-right notes. Such want of knowledge could not be considered as tending to establish the good faith of appellant.

The sixth, seventh, eighth, and ninth specifications relate to evidence admitted over appellant's objection. No ground of objection whatever was stated to the court. Consequently, no question is saved for our consideration. The general rule is that the Appellate Court will consider only such grounds of objections as are presented to the trial court. *Swaim* v. *Swaim*, 134 Ind. 596, 33 N. E. Rep. 792; *Noftsger* v. *Smith*, 6 Ind. App. 54, 32 N. E. Rep. 1024.

The court admitted in evidence certain newspaper accounts of the arrest of one of the payees of this note, at Muncie, Ind., about two months before the assignment of this note, in which the payees were charged with swindling parties by selling for $144 some right connected with a fence claimed to be patented but on which the patent had long ago expired. The jury were expressly instructed that the articles were to be considered only as bearing upon the question of notice to appellant. In view of the evidence tending to show that appellant's officers read these articles before they purchased the note in suit, and that they understood the Muncie transactions were but a part of the regular business of Bernard & Hunter, in the course of which this note had been taken, the evidence was competent for the purpose for which it was admitted.

The objection raised by the fifteenth cause for new trial is subject to the same infirmity found in the sixth, seventh, etc.

Instructions Nos. 2, 3, 5, 6, given by the court, are complained of. These instructions state the law as to the issue formed by the first paragraph of the answer. Objection is made to them for the reason that they are inapplicable to the evidence as claimed by appellant. The objection urged against them goes rather to the sufficiency of the evidence to sustain the answer, than to the correctness of the instructions, which state the law fairly and correctly as applicable to the issue made by the pleading.

If the written contract showed, as asserted by counsel, that no patent right, either real or claimed, entered into the consideration of the note, then there was a failure of proof as to this issue. But the rule that an instruction should be applicable to the evidence, as laid down in *Summerlot* v. *Hamilton*, 121 Ind. 87, can not be construed to mean that the court errs in stating to the jury correctly the law applicable to the issues made by the parties.

The instructions stated the law correctly as far as they went, and did not, in any degree, intimate to the jury that the written contract referred to sustained the answer.

If the appellant desired the court to place a construction upon this contract, he should have asked for it. Elliott's App. Proced., section 647; *Barnett* v. *State*, 100 Ind. 171.

Section 6055, R. S. 1881, applies in terms to any "patent-right or right claimed" to be a patent-right. We are unaware of any rule of law requiring such "claim" to be made in writing, nor can we see any good reason for such a requirement.

Counsel argue that whether appellant fraudulently refrained from inquiry was not the issue in this case, but simply whether or not it had notice of the vice in the consideration of the note.

Where the consideration of the note is illegal, or it is obtained from the maker by fraud, the burden is upon the holder to show that he purchased it in good faith, without notice, and in the usual course of business. *Giberson* v. *Jolley*, 120 Ind. 301; *Tescher* v. *Merea*, 118 Ind. 586; *First National Bank* v. *Ruhl*, 122 Ind. 279; *Schmueckle* v. *Waters*, 125 Ind. 265; *Farmers' Loan and Trust Co.* v. *Canada, etc., R. W. Co.*, 127 Ind. 250; *Bunting* v. *Mick*, 5 Ind. App. 289.

In *Schmueckle* v. *Waters, supra*, it is said by MITCHELL, Judge: "Where, however, the circumstances show that the purchaser of paper refrained from making inquiry lest he should thereby become acquainted with the trans-

action out of which the note originated, he can not occupy the attitude of a holder in good faith without notice.''

The rule thus laid down we regard as an extremely
equitable and salutary one. No man should be permitted
to willfully close his eyes and then excuse himself upon
the ground that he did not see. The instructions upon
the question of notice we regard as being fully as favorable to appellant as he was entitled to ask.

The instructions asked were not, so far as the record
discloses, signed by the appellant or its attorneys. The
contention of appellee must, therefore, be sustained, and
we are compelled to hold that no question thereon is
saved. *Board, etc.,* v. *Legg,* 110 Ind. 479; *State* v. *Sutton,* 99 Ind. 300; *Beatty* v. *Brummett,* 94 Ind. 76;
Darnell v. *Sallee,* 7 Ind. App. 581, 34 N. E. Rep. 1020.

We have, however, examined the instructions asked,
as set out in the record, and are of opinion that so far as
they state the law they are fully covered by the charges
given.

The evidence fully sustains the verdict.

We have found no material error in the cause, and the
judgment is, therefore, affirmed.

DAVIS, C. J., did not participate in this decision.

Filed Jan. 23, 1894.

No. 1,080.

THE EVANSVILLE AND TERRE HAUTE RAILROAD COMPANY *v.* CLASPELL.

DEMURRER TO EVIDENCE.—*Effect of.*—Where a party demurs to evidence, he admits the truthfulness of all the evidence favorable to his adversary, together with all the inferences which might be reasonably drawn therefrom by the jury, and the demurring party withdraws from the jury all evidence adduced by him, and, so far as there is any conflict in the evidence of the opposing party, that which is favorable to the demurring party must be disregarded.

From the Gibson Circuit Court.

J. E. Iglehart, E. Taylor and *J. H. Miller,* for appellant.

M. W. Field, for appellee.

GAVIN, J.—This appeal is from a judgment recovered by appellee for damages on account of the death of his minor son while in appellant's employ.

The sole question argued in this court arises upon the demurrer to the evidence, which was overruled by the court. Appellant's contention is that its demurrer should have been sustained by reason of the failure to prove the employment.

The principles which should govern the court in passing upon the demurrer to the evidence are well settled.

By demurring to the evidence, the appellant admitted the truth of all the evidence favorable to appellee, together with all the inferences which might be reasonably drawn therefrom by the jury; and further, by demurring, the appellant withdrew from the jury all evidence adduced by it, and so far as there was any conflict in the evidence of the appellee, that which was favorable to appellant must be disregarded. *Leavitt* v. *Terre Haute, etc., R. R. Co.,* 5 Ind. App. 513; *Hartman* v. *Cincin-*

nati, etc., R. R. Co., 4 Ind. App. 372; *Lake Shore, etc., R. W. Co.* v. *Foster*, 104 Ind. 293; *Palmer* v. *Chicago, etc., R. R. Co.*, 112 Ind. 250, and cases there cited.

, The evidence in this case shows, that appellant was running, ordinarily, two trains per day over a branch road of about forty miles in length; that appellee's son had been working on one of the trains for five or six days before his death, doing such work as a brakeman ordinarily does, helping load and unload freight, setting brakes and switches, etc.; that when the accident occurred he was engaged in carrying out a command of the conductor with reference to the train work; that before the accident appellant's superintendent sent to the conductor of the train on which the deceased was working, and the only regular conductor on this branch road, a message, saying: "As soon as we get a good brakeman· to fill Claspell's place, send him to Evansville, and I will put him on the local, and notify him to this effect."

The proposition to find a substitute for Claspell, who was employed on this branch road, had been under consideration for thirty days before this letter was written. The conductor of the train had employed a number of men at different times as brakemen on his train, and the company had recognized them as employes.

The conductor testifies: "One time he (deceased) kicked to me and said, 'I am going on twenty-two years, and I want to learn, and I want to get a job as brakeman,' and I told him I couldn't take him. He came around there every morning, and kept begging me; he said he had nothing to do. I said all right, if he would get on there and learn, and be careful, I would take him. He went out with me regular for six trips, I think."

These are some of the facts proved favorable to appellee's claim. From them, we are of opinion that the jury might fairly and reasonably infer that the company was seeking a substitute for Claspell; that the conductor employed the deceased with that in view, and that the employment was within the scope of his apparent authority, and the company was bound thereby. *Louisville, etc., R. W. Co.* v. *Willis*, 83 Ky. 57; *Wachter* v. *Phœnix Ass. Co.*, 132 Pa. St. 428; *Cincinnati, etc., R. R. Co.* v. *Carper*, 112 Ind. 27; *Commercial, etc., Ass. Co.* v. *State, ex rel.*, 113 Ind. 331; *Kerlin* v. *National, etc., Acc. Assn.*, 8 Ind. App. 628, 35 N. E. Rep. 39.

Judgment affirmed.

Ross, J., absent.

Filed Jan. 26, 1894.

———————◆———————

No. 854.

ANDIS v. LOWE, ADMINISTRATRIX.

DECEDENT'S ESTATE.—*Priority of Right of Administration.*—*Statute Construed.*—*Petition for Removal, etc.*—*Necessary Allegations.*—*Qualification to Administer.*—The statute giving sons the priority of right over daughters to administer on their deceased parent's estate, where there is no widow or widower of the deceased, is mandatory, and the court has no discretion in reference thereto, if application is made within twenty days. If, however, in such a case, letters have been issued to a daughter of the deceased, and a son of the deceased makes application for letters of administration, and asks that the former letters be revoked and that such daughter be removed as administratrix, he must clearly show in his petition, by alleged facts, that he possesses the necessary qualifications to entitle him to act as administrator, or the petition will be insufficient on demurrer.

From the Hancock Circuit Court.

E. Marsh, W. W. Cook, W. H. Martz and *B. F. Davis*, for appellant.

C. G. Offutt and *R. A. Black*, for appellee.

REINHARD, J.—This proceeding was instituted in the court below, by the appellant, against the appellee, for the removal of the appellee as administratrix of the estate of Isabella Andis, deceased, and for the appointment of the appellant in her stead.

The petition states, in substance, that on the 27th day of March, 1892, Isabella Andis died in Hancock county, Indiana, intestate, leaving an estate therein of $600 in value, and leaving surviving her no husband, but leaving surviving her as her only children and only heirs at law the petitioner and Samuel Andis, John R. Andis, Margaret E. Osborn, wife of Alexander Osborn, and Mary E. Lowe, wife of Uriah Lowe; that at the time of said decedent's death the appellee was and still is the wife of said Uriah Lowe; that each of said decedent's children above named was, at the time of her death, and still is, a resident of Hancock county, Ind.; that immediately upon the death and burial of said decedent, to wit: On the 29th day of March, 1892, and without the knowledge or consent of the petitioner, the appellee made application to the clerk of the Hancock Circuit Court for letters of administration upon the estate of said decedent, and, also, on said day filed the written consent of her said husband that she should be appointed as such administratrix, and that thereupon the clerk issued letters of administration upon said estate to the appellee, she executing her bond and otherwise qualifying as such, and that she has been acting as such administratrix ever since that time, to the exclusion of the petitioner and the brothers of the appellee and appellant, each of whom, as well as the petitioner, has the lawful right to be preferred as administrator of said estate, but that said appointment has not yet been confirmed by the court.

Wherefore, the petitioner asks that said appointment be not confirmed by the court, and that said Mary E.

Lowe be removed as such administratrix and her letters revoked, and that he, as well as his said brothers, be allowed to administer upon said estate, which applicant is willing and ready to do.

The petition was duly verified.

The appellee appeared and demurred to the petition; the demurrer was sustained and an exception saved, and judgment rendered on the demurrer. An appeal was taken to the Supreme Court, and, by that tribunal, the cause was transferred to this court, under the provisions of the act conferring jurisdiction on the Appellate Court in such cases. Acts 1893, p. 29, section 1, subd. 8 and 9.

It is agreed by the counsel on opposing sides, that the petitioner and the appellee and her brothers were all the "next of kin" of the decedent, in equal degree; but it is contended on behalf of the appellant, that as the appellee was a female the brothers had the prior right to the appointment.

It is provided by statute that at any time after the death of an intestate the proper clerk of court, having examined the person applying for letters, and such persons as may be deemed proper to be examined, under oath, touching the time and place of the death of the intestate, whether he left a will, and concerning the qualifications of such person, and there being no such will, shall grant letters of administration in the following order:

1. To the widow or widower.

2. To the next of kin.

3. To the largest creditor applying and residing in the State.

4. If no person thus entitled to administer shall apply within twenty days after the death of the intestate,

the clerk of the court shall appoint a competent inhabitant of the county, to whom the letters shall issue.   R.
S. 1881, section 2227.

In a subsequent section, it is enacted that if several
persons of the same degree of kindred are entitled to administration, letters may be granted to one or more of
them, but males shall be preferred to females, relatives
of the whole blood to those of the half blood, and unmarried to married women.   R. S. 1881, section 2229.

Other things being equal, it is doubtless the policy of
the law that where there is no widow or widower of the
decedent, and there are brothers and sisters, the former
shall have the prior right to administer upon the estate,
and, we may say in passing, this provision is mandatory,
and leaves the court without discretion, if the application be made within the twenty days.   Henry Prob.
Law, section 12; Croswell Exr. and Admr., section 170;
Jones v. *Bittinger*, 110 Ind. 476.

If letters are issued out of the order of the statute,
however, they are not void, but may be revoked on application, if the proper showing be made, when the court
will appoint the persons entitled thereto.   *Jones* v. *Bittinger, supra.*

But in order to bring the applicant for revocation and
appointment within the letter and spirit of the statute,
he must show in his petition the facts that give him the
right of priority.   In the present case, the petitioner discloses that he is a son and the appellee a daughter of the
decedent, and if he is otherwise qualified he would doubtless be entitled to administer in preference to the appellee, and the former appointment must be set aside or confirmation thereof withheld.   But has he shown himself
so qualified?

It will be noticed that the petition fails to allege that
the petitioner and his brothers are, or that either of them

is, of proper age and possesses the necessary qualifications that entitle him to act as such administrator. Under the rule that the averments of a pleading will be most strongly construed against the pleader, we must presume that the petitioner did not possess such qualifications.

It is true the petition avers that the petitioner as well as his brothers has each "the lawful right to be preferred as administrator of said estate," but this is not sufficient. The statement quoted is, at most, but a legal conclusion and not a fact. But it is facts and not conclusions that must be pleaded in order to make the pleading good. For aught that appears, the petitioner may be an infant or otherwise disqualified from taking upon himself the responsible position of administering upon the estate. He should have made a clear case upon paper, showing that he was fully qualified to receive the appointment. Having failed to do this, he can not complain of the ruling of the court in sustaining his demurrer.

Judgment affirmed.

Filed Sept. 29, 1893; petition for a rehearing overruled Jan. 30, 1894.

No. 914.

CUTSHAW ET AL. *v.* FARGO ET AL.

FAILURE OF PROOF.—*Action on Account by A. for Goods Sold and Delivered to B.—Proof of Sale by C. to B.—Recovery.—Evidence, Sufficiency of.—Partnership.—Corporation.*—Where several plaintiffs join in an action, as partners, for goods sold and delivered to the defendants, and the evidence develops the fact that defendants purchased the goods of A. & Co., and that A. & Co. is a corporation of which plaintiffs are the sole stockholders, the plaintiffs can not recover, the cause of action being one in favor of the corporation, for which the stockholders can not, as individuals, recover, the corporation being, in legal contemplation, separate and distinct from its members or stockholders.

SAME.—*Legal Capacity to Sue.—Waiver.—Real Parties in Interest.— Variance.—Amendment of Pleading.—Presumption.*—In such case, the defect is not that plaintiffs have not legal capacity to sue, and subject to the principle of waiver. The want of legal capacity to sue has reference to legal disability, such as infancy, idiocy, etc. Neither are the plaintiffs, the stockholders, the real parties in interest; nor is the variance between the complaint and the proof such as this court will presume to have been cured by amendment.

From the Washington Circuit Court.

H. Morris, J. A. Zaring and *M. B. Hottell*, for appellants.

D. M. Alspaugh and *J. C. Lawler*, for appellees.

GAVIN, C. J.—This was a suit upon an account, together with an attachment proceeding, brought by the appellees Charles H., Charles E., Samuel M., and Frank M. Fargo.

The complaint is as follows:

"The plaintiffs in the above entitled cause, doing business under the firm-name and style of 'C. H. Fargo & Co.,' complain of the defendants in said cause, who are partners, doing business in the firm name and style of 'Cutshaw Bros.,' and say that the said defendants are indebted to the said plaintiffs in the sum of nine hundred and seventy-one dollars and fourteen cents, for goods sold and delivered by said plaintiffs to said defendants, at their special instance and request, a bill of particulars of which is filed herewith, marked exhibit 'A,' and made a part of this complaint; that said sum is wholly due and unpaid. Wherefore the plaintiffs demand judgment," etc.

To this complaint a general denial was filed. There

was a trial and judgment for appellees, over a motion for new trial presented by appellants.

Numerous questions have been argued by counsel, but the determination of one will be decisive of this case, and that question arises upon the sufficiency of the evidence as presented under the motion for a new trial.

The evidence shows, without contradiction, that appellants purchased the goods described in the bill of particulars from C. H. Fargo & Co., and that "C. H. Fargo & Co. is a corporation, and not a partnership, although the appellees are the sole stockholders in such corporation.

Counsel for the appellees urge vigorously that the corporation is, in the eyes of the law, an individual, separate and distinct from its members or stockholders; that the right to contract and sue upon its contracts is inherent in the corporation, and that the stockholders can not, as individuals, recover upon causes of action belonging to the corporation; they further claim that the evidence in this case wholly fails to show any sale by appellees to appellants, or any contract by appellants with appellees.

With these views of counsel we are compelled to agree, although quite reluctantly, under the circumstances of this case.

It is of the very essence of a corporation that it should possess an existence and an individual personality distinct from that of its members.

As defined by Chief Justice MARSHALL: "A corporation is an artificial being, invisible, intangible and existing only in contemplation of law." "Among the most important (of its attributes) are immortality, and if the expression may be allowed individuality, properties by which a perpetual succession of many persons are considered as the same, and may act as an individual."

Dartmouth College v. *Woodward*, 4 Wheat. 517 (636).

"The great object of an incorporation is, to bestow the character and properties of individuality on a collective and changing body of men." *Providence Bank* v. *Billings*, 4 Pet. 514 (562).

"A corporation is recognized by the law as having an existence as an artificial person distinct from the members which compose it." 4 Am. and Eng. Encyc. of Law, 203.

The case then turns upon this proposition: Can one man sue for goods alleged to have been sold by him, and recover on proof of goods sold by another?

We can not agree to an affirmative answer to this proposition.

Appellees insist that appellants are estopped to question the existence of a partnership, because they dealt with appellees as a partnership. There is, however, no evidence of such a fact. On the contrary, the evidence is that appellants dealt not with plaintiffs but with some one else; that is, with the corporation.

It is also claimed that the objection is one to the capacity to sue, and has been waived. In this counsel are in error. Appellees have ample capacity to sue and maintain this action if the proof will support their complaint.

The objection that the plaintiff has not legal capacity to sue refers to some legal disability such as infancy or idiocy. *Pence* v. *Aughe, Guar.*, 101 Ind. 317.

The fact proved does not constitute matter in abatement, but goes to the merits. *Morningstar* v. *Cunningham*, 110 Ind. 328; *Pixley* v. *Van Nostern*, 100 Ind. 34.

Neither is there here a simple defect of parties, as in *Thomas* v. *Wood*, 61 Ind. 132, or *Bledsoe* v. *Irvin*, 35 Ind. 293, cited by appellees. On the contrary, an issue is raised by the general denial, on the main fact alleged in the complaint, to wit, that plaintiffs sold the appellants the goods described.

To sustain their complaint, plaintiffs were required to prove that they did sell them. Instead of this, they proved that they did not sell them, but some one else did.

A complaint, to be good upon demurrer for want of facts, must show a good cause of action in favor of the plaintiff, not in favor of some one else. If the complaint showed that the goods had been sold by the corporation, and not by the plaintiffs, it would certainly be bad upon demurrer.

"A complaint by A., which shows a cause of action in favor of B., does not state facts sufficient to constitute a cause of action in favor of A., and a demurrer for want of facts raises the question." *Bond* v. *Armstrong*, 88 Ind. 65; *Louisville, etc., R. R. Co.* v. *Lohges*, 6 Ind. App. 288, 33 N. E. Rep. 449; *Holman* v. *Langtree*, 40 Ind. 349; *Richardson* v. *Snider*, 72 Ind. 425.

The allegation that appellees sold the goods, being necessary to make the complaint good on demurrer, it was required to be shown by the proof. The plaintiffs being unable to establish even a *prima facie* obligation to themselves, the case is not brought within the rule of those cases wherein it is held that matter questioning the interest of the plaintiff must be set up specially. *Curtis* v. *Gooding*, 99 Ind. 45.

Finally, it is urged by appellees that the plaintiffs are the real parties in interest, and for that reason entitled to maintain this action, being all of the stockholders in said corporation.

As we have already shown, the corporation has an existence and personality which is separate and distinct from its members. Its rights and liabilities are to be

worked out through its corporate existence, and not
through its individual members.

If this suit were brought by the corporation, we do
not think it could be reasonably contended that the suit
could be defeated on the ground that it should be maintained by the individual members of the corporation as
the real parties in interest.

The stockholders are not, in legal contemplation, the
real parties in interest in the claim proved in this case.
As stockholders, they may finally be entitled to the proceeds of this suit, or they may not.   That will depend
upon the financial obligations of the corporation, to which
the fund thus derived is first applicable.   Whatever interest these stockholders may finally have in such proceeds will be not a direct interest in this particular cause
of action, but a general interest in all the assets of the
corporation, to be received in due time and proper manner from the corporation.

The principle is plainly laid down in Morawetz on
Corp., section 233, which is as follows: "It is of great
importance that the title to property be kept free from
complication or uncertainty.   The title to property vested
in a corporation should therefore not be affected by acts
of the shareholders, except when acting in such corporate name.   Although all the shares in a corporation belong to a single person, and there are no creditors, a
conveyance or transfer by the sole shareholder, in his
own name, of property vested in the corporate name,
would not affect the legal title.   The title would in legal
contemplation remain in the fictitious entity called the
corporation, irrespective of the equities which the transaction might give rise to."

In the well considered case of *Button* v. *Hoffman*, 61
Wis. 20, it is held that one who becomes the owner of
all the capital stock of a private corporation does not

thereby become the legal owner of its property, and can not maintain replevin therefor in his own name.

The case of *Hasselman* v. *Japanese, etc., Co.*, 2 Ind. App. 180, does not aid appellees. It simply holds that where the contract is really made with the corporation, even though by a name other than its corporate name, it may recover upon it.

We are constrained to hold that the motion for a new trial should have been sustained.

Judgment reversed.

Filed June 6, 1893.

On Petition for a Rehearing.

Gavin, J.—Appellees, in their petition, insist that the complaint in this cause should be deemed amended by substituting, as plaintiffs, the name of the corporation to whom the evidence showed the debt to be due. While our statutes are very liberal upon the subject of amendments which the Appellate Court will deem made, there must be some limit beyond which we can not properly go. To aid the appellees, we should be required to pass that limit, according to our own adjudicated cases.

The question is decided adverse to appellees' contention in *Snyder* v. *State, ex rel.*, 21 Ind. 77, where the court says, with reference to a similar claim: "But it is claimed, that if the action was wrongfully brought in this respect, it could have been amended below, and will be deemed amended here. But, in our opinion, such a radical amendment as a total change of one of the parties to the action, or which is in substance the same thing, a total change of the person suing as relator can not be deemed to be made here."

This ruling is followed in *Taggart* v. *State, ex rel.*, 49 Ind. 42, and in five similar cases in following pages of that report.

Kibby *et al.* *v.* Kibby, Administrator.

If such steps had been taken in the court below, after attention was called to the point in question, as that a proper judgment had been rendered in accordance with the proof, there would then be greater force in the argument of counsel. *Hubler* v. *Pullen,* 9 Ind. 273; *Pittsburgh, etc., R. W. Co.* v. *Martin,* 82 Ind. 476.

The petition for a rehearing is overruled.

Filed Jan. 24, 1894.

No. 741.

KIBBY ET AL. *v.* KIBBY, ADMINISTRATOR.

From the Grant Circuit Court.

J. C. Branyan, G. E. Meyers, J. S. Branyan and *F. W. Swezey,* for appellants.

D. H. Fouts, A. M. Waltz and *J. A. Kersey,* for appellee.

DAVIS, C. J.—The appellants filed, as a claim against the estate of their father, a note purporting to have been executed by him to them in June, 1891, for two thousand dollars. No answer was filed by appellee. The case stood for trial on such defense as might lawfully be given in evidence under the statute. A trial by jury resulted in verdict and judgment against appellants. In this court, the only error assigned is that the trial court erred in overruling appellants' motion for a new trial.

The reasons contained in the motion for a new trial are that the verdict is not supported by sufficient evidence, and is contrary to law.

We have carefully read the entire record, and the facts are that Jonah Kibby departed this life intestate, in January, 1892, leaving surviving him a widow, by whom he had no children, and five children, two sons and three daughters, by a former wife, also that his estate at that time consisted of one hundred and twenty acres of land, and personal property to the amount of twelve hundred dollars, and that for almost a year prior to his death he was terribly afflicted with an incurable cancer in and about the lips and mouth.

There is also evidence tending to show that appellants—the sons of Jonah Kibby—were kind to their father, and assisted in caring for him in his great affliction; that he suffered intensely, and a part of the time, at least, was not in his right mind, and that said appellant, John E. Kibby, had great influence over his father, and could easily talk or persuade him into doing anything he wished him to do.

No one testified to the execution of the note in suit—when, how or for what it was given does not appear,—but several witnesses testified

Kibby *et al. v.* Kibby, Administrator.

that, in their opinion, the signature to the note was in the handwriting of Jonah Kibby. The cross-examination discloses that the witnesses were not positive as to whether the signature was his, but this was their opinion from the limited knowledge they had of his handwriting.

The appellant Paul Kibby testified that he never heard of the existence of the note until after the death of his father.

We can only say that if the note was executed by said Jonah Kibby the only consideration therefor, so far as any inference can be drawn in relation thereto, from anything appearing in the record, grows out of the services rendered by appellants in assisting in caring for their father during his last illness.

Whether the note was executed, whether its execution was secured when said Jonah Kibby was not in his right mind, or through the undue influence of John E. Kibby, or whether there was any consideration for the note, were all questions for the jury to determine.

The fact, if true, that the jury would have been justified in the conclusion that the note was duly executed by Jonah Kibby for a good and valuable consideration is no reason why this court, because a contrary result was reached, should set aside the verdict. The jury were not bound to conclude, on the evidence introduced, that appellants had established every material point in issue, the burden of which was on them, by a preponderance of the evidence. Neither was the conclusion irresistible that appellee had not established, by such preponderance, one, at least, of the affirmative defenses on which the estate relied to defeat the action.

In addition to what has been said, we will say that it does not appear, except inferentially, that there was any intent on the part of appellants, or either of them, when the services were rendered, to charge anything therefor, neither is it shown in any manner that said decedent expected to pay them for such services.

Moreover, we fail to find any statement in the record that the note was introduced in evidence. We do find a statement that it was offered in evidence, and that the objection made to reading it in evidence was overruled; but if the note was then, or thereafter, introduced or read in evidence, the record is silent on that subject. There is no copy of the note in the record at the place where it was offered in evidence. We notice in one place in the bill of exceptions, between two pages in the testimony of the witness John Patterson, a slip of paper, at the top of which there appears, "Note exhibit A in evidence," following which there is a copy of the note in suit, but there is nothing either preceding or following to indicate that the note was read in evidence. If, however, this defect or omission in the record was overlooked, this court could not, under the circumstances shown by the record, and to some of which we have briefly called attention, disturb the verdict of the jury on the evidence.

The judgment is affirmed.

REINHARD, J., absent.

Filed Dec. 14, 1893.

INDEX.

ABATEMENT.
See CRIMINAL LAW, 6.

ABSTRACT.
See REAL ESTATE, 1.

ACCEPTANCE.
See SALE.

ACCIDENT INSURANCE.
See INSURANCE, 2.

ACCORD AND SATISFACTION.
See PLEADING, 23.

What Amounts to.—Delivery of Check for Less than Amount Due.—Debtor and Creditor.—Where a debtor sends a creditor a check in settlement of an account, the check being less than the amount due, an acceptance of the check by the creditor will not amount to an accord and satisfaction of the amount due, unless the creditor must have understood, from the words used by the debtor, in connection with the delivery of the check, that they were to accept it in full of their claim.   *Pottlitzer* v. *Wesson, 472*

ACCOUNT.
See INSTRUCTIONS TO JURY, 6.

ACTION.
See EVIDENCE, 11, 27; FAILURE OF PROOF, 1; HUSBAND AND WIFE, 1; PLEADING, 6, 28; POOR PERSON.

ADMINISTRATOR.
See DECEDENTS' ESTATES, 1, 6, 7.

ADMISSIONS.
See ASSIGNMENT OF ERRORS, 1.

When Sufficient to Shift Burden of Proof.—Open and Close.—Promissory Note.—Attorney's Fees.—Chattel Mortgage.—Decedent's Estate.—Where an administrator, in an action on a contested claim, for the purpose of obtaining the opening and close of the evidence and argument in the case, after the jury had been impanneled and before the claimant had introduced any evidence, admitted the execution of the notes (they being secured by chattel mortgage) forming the basis of the claim, and also admitted the reasonableness of attorney's fees as set forth in the claim, such admissions are not sufficient to entitle the estate to the open and close in the case, for the reason that the admissions do not shift the burden of proof so that the claimant might have complete recovery and relief on his claim, without the necessity of introducing evidence, the claimant being entitled to make proof of attorney's fees, above the amount stated in the claim, and, also, to make proof of the

(700)

chattel mortgage, the admissions not being broad enough to satisfy
the issues in these respects.

McCloskey, Admr., v. Davis, Admx., 190

ADVERSE POSSESSION.

See REAL ESTATE, 2.

AFFIDAVIT.

See RECORD, 1.

AMENDMENT OF PLEADING.

See FAILURE OF PROOF, 2; PRACTICE, 2.

ANIMALS.

See NEGLIGENCE; RAILROAD, 9.

ANSWER.

See DEMURRER, 2; PLEADING, 2, 18, 26; REPLEVIN, 1; VARIANCE.

APPEAL.

See APPELLATE COURT PRACTICE; ASSIGNMENT OF ERRORS; JUSTICE OF
THE PEACE, 2; JURISDICTION; NEW TRIAL, 1; PRACTICE, 1; STREETS
AND ALLEYS, 1.

1. *Appellate Court.—Jurisdiction.—Money Demand.—Originating Before a Mayor.—*An appeal can not be taken from a judgment of a
circuit court on a money demand not exceeding $50, exclusive of
interest and costs, where the action originated before a mayor of
a city. *Lake Erie, etc., R. R. Co. v. Yard, 199*

2. *Trial, What Amounts to. — Mayor. — Misdemeanor. — Plea of not
Guilty.—Finding of Guilty by Agreement.—*Where a person was arrested upon an affidavit filed before a mayor, and, upon arraignment, pleaded not guilty, but consented, by his attorney, that the
court, without the hearing of testimony, might find the defendant guilty as charged, and the court, in accordance with the agreement, found the defendant guilty, the defendant is entitled to an
appeal, there having been a trial in legal contemplation, whether
the court actually heard any evidence or not.

State v. Gardner, 440

APPELLATE COURT.

See APPEAL, 1; JUDICIAL NOTICE; JURISDICTION.

*Decision of.—Law of Case.—*A decision of the Appellate Court in a case
remains the law of the case throughout all its subsequent stages.

Board, etc., v. Cole, 485

APPELLATE COURT PRACTICE.

See EVIDENCE, 1, 4; PRACTICE, 1; RECORD, 2.

1. *Sufficiency of Evidence.—*The Appellate Court can not, on appeal,
weigh conflicting evidence to ascertain the real facts, but it must
take that view of the evidence most favorable to the appellee, and
affirm the judgment if there be evidence which fairly supports
the finding. *Mazelin v. Ronyer, 27*

2. *Reversal of Judgment.—Special Verdict.—New Trial.—Question of
Fact.—*The jury are the exclusive judges of all questions of fact;
and where the trial court has overruled a motion for a new
trial, one reason for which was that the verdict fails to find all
the facts proven by the evidence, the appellate tribunal will not
disturb that ruling unless it clearly and affirmatively appears from
uncontradicted evidence that the facts established thereby, if
stated in the special verdict, would have authorized a different
judgment. *Colton v. Lewis, 40*

of a conspiracy leading up to the assault and battery, it is not error for the court to instruct the jury as to what constitutes a conspiracy, the jury being entitled to all the facts and circumstances leading up to the assault and battery.

Kelley v. *Kelley, 606*

2. *Instruction to Jury.—Assumption of Fact.*—In an action for damages for assault and battery, where the court instructed the jury that if it had been shown that plaintiff had occasionally been meeting at her place of residence a person with whom she had had improper relations, such fact would not justify an assault and battery upon her, such instruction was not erroneous on the ground that it assumes the fact of assault and battery. *Ib.*

3. *Damages, Elements of.—Special Proof.*—In an action for assault and battery, the jury has a right to consider all the elements entering into the damages, without special proof as to amounts. *Ib.*

ASSESSMENT OF DAMAGES.

See PLEA IN ABATEMENT.

Presumption.—Plea in Abatement.—Whatever damages, present and prospective, that might properly have been assessed in a proceeding under a writ of assessment of damages, will be presumed to have been assessed, and such assessment, unless appealed from, is a final adjudication for such injuries, and the land-owner can not seek any other remedy against the same party or parties defendant, while such proceeding is pending.

Rehman v. *New Albany, etc., R. R. Co., 200*

ASSETS.

See PARTNERSHIP.

ASSIGNEE.

See EVIDENCE, 27.

ASSIGNMENT.

See EVIDENCE, 11; VENDOR AND VENDEE.

ASSIGNMENT OF ERRORS.

1. *Joint Assignment.—Admitting Sufficiency of One Ground of Error.— Effect.*—Where an appellant assigns as error that the answers of appellee do not state facts sufficient to constitute a defense to appellant's complaint, and, also, in another assignment, avers that the overruling of appellant's demurrer to the second, third, and fifth paragraphs of answer, and then concedes the sufficiency of the second paragraph of answer, no question is presented by such assignments.

Walter A. Wood Mowing and Reaping Machine Co. v. *Field, 107*

2. *Questioning Admissibility of Evidence.—Errors Jointly Assigned.— When Unavailable.*—When an assignment of error is that the court erred in the admission of certain testimony given by several witnesses upon divers subjects, the assignment is unavailable if any part of such evidence was properly admitted.

Louisville, etc., R. W. Co. v. *Renicker, 404*

3. *Assignment Must be Based Upon Proper Exception.—Misconduct of Counsel.*—Where error is predicated upon the misconduct of counsel, no question is presented, on appeal, unless the trial court was given an opportunity to correct the error. No valid exception can be saved unless based upon a ruling of the court.

Welsh, Exec., v. *Brown, 421*

4. *Assignment, Insufficiency of.—Evidence.*—Where an assignment of

error is that "the court erred in refusing to allow the plaintiff * * to testify as to matters that occurred prior to the death of Nathan Gray," the assignment is not well made, and is insufficient, where the record shows that plaintiff was permitted to testify to many such matters. *Cleland* v. *Applegate, 499*

5. *Omission of Name from Title.—Supplied in Body of Assignment.—Sufficiency.*—An omission to give the name of a party appellant in the title of an assignment of error may be supplied in the body of the assignment, and the assignment in that respect will be sufficient. *Ferguson* v. *Despo, 523*

6. *Cause for New Trial.—How Assigned.*—A decision of the trial court, which properly constitutes a cause for new trial, can not be independently assigned as error on appeal, among which causes is a ruling on a motion to suppress a deposition. *Maybin* v. *Webster, 547*

7. *When Will not Lie.—Presumption.*—Where the record does not show when instructions, which have been refused, were tendered to the court, error can not be predicated upon such action, for every presumption will be indulged in favor of the action of the trial court. *Board, etc.,* v. *Blair, Admr., 574*

ASSUMPTION OF FACT.

See ASSAULT AND BATTERY, 2; INSTRUCTIONS TO JURY, 12.

ATTORNEY.

See EVIDENCE, 22.

ATTORNEY AND CLIENT.

See ATTORNEY'S FEES.

When Such Relation Exists.—Contract.—Professional Services.—Attorney's Fees.—Decedents' Estates.—A. died testate, devising almost his entire estate to B. and C., in trust for D., E. and F., three nieces. C. did not qualify, but B. qualified to look after the interest of his wife, a *cestui quie trust.* G. was appointed administrator with the will annexed. A suit was instituted to set aside the will. G., as administrator, employed, among other attorneys, H. and I. to defend and sustain the will, for which services they were paid in full, the first trial resulting in a disagreement of the jury. Before the second trial of the case, G. resigned his trust, and H. was appointed administrator *de bonis non,* with the will annexed, and I. was appointed guardian of a minor child of D., deceased. In the second trial, B., H. and I., among others, were defendants in their respective trust capacities. H. and I. prepared the case for trial, interviewed witnesses brought to their office by B., and assisted at the trial, as attorneys, in the presence of B. H. and I. bring suit against B. for professional services rendered for him in the second trial of the cause.

Held, that the fact that H. and I. interviewed witnesses brought to their office by B., in preparation for trial, and assisted, as attorneys at the trial, in the presence of B., raises no presumption of employment by B.

Held, also, that the evidence is insufficient to sustain the verdict rendered in favor of plaintiffs. *Miles, Tr.,* v. *De Wolf, 153*

ATTORNEY'S FEES.

See ADMISSIONS; ATTORNEY AND CLIENT; PLEADING, 13.

When Recoverable.—Contract.—Attorney and Client.—A contract to pay attorney's fees is a contract of indemnity to secure the holder of the note against any liability which he may incur in the event he should be compelled to employ an attorney to enforce the collection of the debt, and the plaintiff is not entitled to judgment for attorney's fees, unless an attorney, of necessity, was employed to collect the debt. *Judson* v. *Ramaine, 390*

BILL OF EXCEPTIONS.

See RECORD, 1, 2.

*Who May Sign.—Expiration of Judge's Term of Office.—*A person who was judge and presided at the trial of a cause, has no power to sign a bill of exceptions and make the same a part of the record in such cause, after he has ceased to be judge. Such function should be performed by his successor.

Cincinnati, etc., R. W. Co. v. *Grames, 112*

BOND.

See DECEDENTS' ESTATES, 6; PLEADING, 6.

BRIDGES.

See COUNTY; EVIDENCE, 21; PLEADING, 29, 30.

*When a County Bridge.—Highway.—Mill-Race.—*Where the excavation of a mill-race across a highway necessitates the construction of a bridge across the race in order to restore the highway to a passable condition, a bridge so constructed, it matters not by whom, becomes a part of the highway. *Board, etc.,* v. *Blair, Admr., 574*

BROKER.

See PRINCIPAL AND AGENT, 5.

BURDEN OF PROOF.

See ADMISSIONS; PROMISSORY NOTE, 1; RAILROAD, 9; SPECIAL VERDICT, 6.

CARE.

See RAILROAD, 3.

CERTIFICATE OF STOCK.

See GARNISHMENT.

CERTIORARI.

See RECORD, 2.

CHATTEL MORTGAGE.

See ADMISSIONS.

CHECK.

See ACCORD AND SATISFACTION.

COLLATERAL ATTACK.

See JUDGMENT, 2; JUSTICE OF THE PEACE, 1.

COMMON CARRIER.

1. *Loss of Goods.—When Unnecessary to Aver Want of Contributory Negligence.—*In an action against a common carrier for goods destroyed while in its possession, it is unnecessary to aver that the loss was not occasioned by plaintiff's negligence, the carrier for hire being an insurer against loss or injury from whatever cause, except only the acts of God and the public enemy.

Evansville, etc., R. R. Co. v. *Keith, 57*

2. *Delivery, What Amounts to.—Complaint, Sufficiency of.—*In such

case, the complaint is sufficient as showing a delivery of the goods (baled hay) intended for immediate transportation, which alleges the placing of the goods, in a condition to be carried, at the usual place of loading the same. *Ib.*

3. *Freight Charges.—When Prepayment Waived.—Liability.*—While a common carrier is not bound to receive freight for transportation until the charges therefor have been paid, the right to prepayment may be waived, and the liability of the carrier attached in the absence of such payment. *Ib.*

4. *Freight Charges.—Tender, When Unnecessary to Aver.*—In such case, where the complaint shows that the goods were tendered to, and accepted by, the carrier, and were destroyed by fire before being shipped, it is not necessary to aver that the charges for transportation were tendered. *Ib.*

COMMON SCHOOLS.

See CONTRACT, 1.

COMPLAINT.

See APPELLATE COURT PRACTICE, 3; COMMON CARRIER, 1, 2, 4; DECE DENTS' ESTATES, 7; MINES AND MINING, 2, 3; MUNICIPAL CORPORATION, 1, 2; PLEADING, 4, 5, 6, 8, 9, 11, 12, 14, 15, 17, 21, 22, 24, 27, 28, 29, 30; STREETS AND ALLEYS, 2.

CONSIDERATION.

See PROMISSORY NOTE, 1.

CONSPIRACY.

See ASSAULT AND BATTERY, 1.

CONSTABLE.

See REPLEVIN, 3.

CONTRACT.

See ACCORD AND SATISFACTION; ATTORNEY'S FEES; ATTORNEY AND CLIENT; COVENANT; GUARDIAN AND WARD, 1; INSURANCE, 5; LIFE INSURANCE, 3, 5; MARRIAGE CONTRACT; PRINCIPAL AND AGENT, 3, 4; PLEADING, 18; REAL ESTATE, 1; SALE.

1. *Common Schools.—Employment of Teacher.—Verbal Contract Valid. —Township Trustee.*—A verbal contract of employment as a teacher in the public schools, entered into by a township trustee and the teacher, is valid and binding, there being no statute requiring it to be reduced to writing. *Jackson School Tp.*v. *Shera, 330*

2. *Made for Benefit of Third Person.—May Accept and Enforce, or Rescind.*—A person in whose favor a contract has been made, may accept the same and enforce it; as, where A. assumes the payment of a debt owing by B. to C., C. may accept and enforce the contract against A., or C. may rescind it before it is accepted. *Judson* v. *Romaine, 390*

3. *Breach of.—Damages, When Remote and Consequential.—Recovery.* —A party injured by the breach of a contract or covenant is entitled to recover such damages only as proximately resulted from the breach and were within the contemplation of the parties when the contract was entered into. In such case, remote and consequential damages can not be recovered.
Hamilton, Exec., v. *Feary, 615*

4. *Subscription.—Recovery of.—Substantial Compliance with Terms of Must be Shown.—Schoolhouse.—Township Trustee.*—Where citizens of a school township petition for the location of a school district

and the erection of a schoolhouse therein, designating the size of the house, location, etc., and subscribing sums of money to aid in the construction thereof, to be paid when the walls are erected to the square, and the subscription is accepted by the trustee, before the amounts subscribed can be recovered the school township must show a substantial compliance with the terms of subscription. *Sult* v. *Warren School Tp.*, *655*

CONTRIBUTORY NEGLIGENCE.

See COMMON CARRIER, 1; INSTRUCTIONS TO JURY, 3; MINES AND MINING, 2; PHYSICIAN AND PATIENT, 2; RAILROAD, 2.

1. *Railroad Crossing.—Exception to Rule Requiring Traveler to Stop and Listen.*—A person approaching a railroad crossing is required to look and listen, because it is the part of a prudent man to do so, for the reason that a due regard for his own safety requires it. If, however, the facts and circumstances under which he approaches it are such as to mislead him, and such as would naturally create in his mind a sense of security and belief that there is no danger, to such an extent that a man of prudence would ordinarily act upon it, then the reason and rule for the precaution fails, as where one railroad train follows another, at a high rate of speed, with but twelve seconds of time between them, the view of the track being materially obstructed.
Grand Rapids, etc., R. R. Co. v. *Cox*, *29*

2. *When a Question of Law.—Question of Fact.*—Where the facts are undisputed, and but one legitimate inference can be fairly drawn from them, the court may take the question of negligence from the jury; but if the undisputed facts are of such a character that different men might reasonably and fairly base upon them different conclusions, then the determination of the question is for the jury. *Ib.*

3. *Mixed Question of Law and Fact. — Province of Jury.* — As to whether a party is guilty of contributory negligence in attempting to lead his horses past an object in the highway, at which they had taken fright, and so attempting was injured, is a mixed question of law and fact, the determination of which properly rests with the jury. *Hindman* v. *Timme*, *416*

CONVEYANCE.

See ESTOPPEL, 3; EVIDENCE, 22.

CORPORATION.

See FAILURE OF PROOF, 1; GARNISHMENT; PLEADING, 4.

COUNTERCLAIM.

See MARRIAGE CONTRACT; PLEADING, 13, 19, 20.

COUNTY.

See EXECUTION, 2; PLEADING, 29, 30.

Bridges.—Duty to Keep in Repair.—A county is only bound to repair such bridges as it is authorized to build; and it is not necessary that the county should have built the bridge in order to give rise to the duty to keep in repair, for a bridge may become a county bridge by adoption, no matter by whom it is built, and such duty extends to approaches and railings.
Board, etc., v. *Blair, Admr.*, *574*

COVENANT.

See DECEDENTS' ESTATES, 3; LANDLORD AND TENANT, 1, 2.

CRIMINAL LAW.

alleging whether such act was with or without malice, or whether the firearm was loaded or empty, the *gravamen* of the indictment being the willful pointing of the firearm at another.

Graham v. *State, 497*

DAMAGES.

See ASSAULT AND BATTERY, 3; CONTRACT, 3; ESTOPPEL, 1; EVIDENCE, 6, 24; LANDLORD AND TENANT, 1, 2; MINES AND MINING, 1; MUNICIPAL CORPORATION, 2, 4; PLEADING 12, 13, 17, 22, 29; PRINCIPAL AND AGENT, 1; SPECIAL VERDICT, 4; TELEGRAPH COMPANY, 1, 2; VERDICT, 1.

Excessive, as a Cause for Reversal.—A judgment will not be reversed on the ground of excessive damages, unless the amount is so large as to lead to the conclusion that it must have been the result of prejudice, partiality, or corruption. *Kelley* v. *Kelley, 606*

DEBTOR AND CREDITOR.

See ACCORD AND SATISFACTION.

DECEDENTS' ESTATES.

See ADMISSIONS; ATTORNEY AND CLIENT; EVIDENCE, 22, 23; PLEADING, 28; PRINCIPAL AND AGENT, 2.

1. *Final Settlement.—What Does not Amount to.—Administrator De Bonis Non.*—Where an administrator filed what purports to be his final report, to which exceptions were filed by claimants, but the exceptions are subsequently withdrawn, with right to enforce and collect their claims in the future, and the order concludes as follows: "And the estate is continued as to matters embraced in the exceptions only for further administration as the court may authorize and direct, and said * * [A.] now tenders his resignation as such administrator, which is accepted, and said administrator finally discharged," the provisions of the order continuing the estate for certain purposes, and accepting the resignation of the administrator, are wholly inconsistent with the idea of final settlement, and an administrator *de bonis non* may be appointed under the provisions of section 2240, R. S. 1881.

Green v. *Brown, Admr., 110*

2. *Right of Widow to Take Both Under the Will and the Law.*—If a widow accept a bequest, she does not thereby forfeit her statutory allowance ($500), where there is nothing in the will inconsistent with the widow's right to take both the bequest and the statutory allowance. *Richards, Admr.,* v. *Hollis, 353*

3. *Liability of Devisees for Breach of Decedent's Covenant.—Final Settlement.*—The devisees of a decedent are liable in damages to the covenantee for a breach of the decedent's covenant, occurring after the decedent's death and after the final settlement of the decedent's estate. *Harman* v. *Dorman, 461*

4. *Claim.—Witness.—Competency.—Adverse Interest.—Principal and Surety.*—In an action on a claim against a decedent's estate, wherein the claimant alleged that he, as surety for the decedent, was compelled to pay the amount due on a certain note, the note, which was introduced in evidence, purporting to have been executed as the joint and several obligation of all the makers, *i. e.*, the decedent, the claimant and one A., A. is incompetent as a witness to testify as to the question of principal and suretyship in such transaction, A.'s interest in the controversy being adverse to that of the estate, and the mere fact that A., at the time of the trial, was insolvent, does not strip him of such interest.

Thornburg, Admr., v. *Allman, 531*

DECISION.
See Appellate Court.

DEFENSE.
See Insurance, 1; Railroad, 1.

DELIVERY.
See Common Carrier, 2; Life Insurance, 4; Pleading, 9; Special Finding, 2; Telegraph Company, 9.

DEMAND.
See Mechanic's Lien, 5.

DEMURRER.
See Harmless Error, 2, 3, 4; Pleading, 1, 8, 10, 26; Practice, 2; Replevin, 1.

DEMURRER TO EVIDENCE.

Effect of.—Where a party demurs to evidence, he admits the truthfulness of all the evidence favorable to his adversary, together with all the inferences which might be reasonably drawn therefrom by the jury, and the demurring party withdraws from the jury all evidence adduced by him, and, so far as there is any conflict in the evidence of the opposing party, that which is favorable to the demurring party must be disregarded.

Evansville, etc., R. R. Co. v. *Claspell, 685*

DESCRIPTION.

See DRAINAGE; MECHANIC'S LIEN, 1, 2.

DISCLOSURE.

See TELEGRAPH COMPANY, 9.

DISCRETION.

See DECEDENTS' ESTATES, 6; EVIDENCE, 12, 18.

DISCRIMINATION.

See TELEGRAPH COMPANY, 10.

DISCUSSION.

See APPELLATE COURT PRACTICE, 4.

DRAINAGE.

See JUDGMENT, 3.

Foreclosure of Lien.—*Misdescription of Land.*—*When Description Sufficient to Put Parties Upon Inquiry.*—*Estoppel.*—Where, in an action to foreclose a drainage lien, the land was described as 443 acres, in reserve 53, township 29 north, range 10 east, whereas, in fact, only about 150 acres of such land lay in township 29, and reserve and range as stated, the remainder lying in township 28 north, reserve and range as above stated, such description was sufficient to have put the defendants on their inquiry, and they can not plead that they were misled thereby and induced to refrain from remonstrating, and confine the decree alone to the land lying in township 29. *Smith* v. *State, ex rel., 661*

DUPLICITY.

See CRIMINAL LAW, 1.

DURESS.

See PLEADING, 21.

EARNEST MONEY.

See REAL ESTATE, 1.

ELECTION.

See DECEDENTS' ESTATES, 2.

EMPLOYER AND EMPLOYE.

See JUDGMENT, 4; MASTER AND SERVANT.

1. *Personal Injury.*—*Knowledge of Defects and Danger by Employe.*—*Assumption of Risks.*—*Judgment on Answers to Interrogatories, Non Obstante.*—In an action for damages for personal injuries received while in the employment of rolling car wheels, in which a general verdict was rendered for plaintiff, it was not error for the court, on motion, to render judgment for defendant on the answers to interrogatories, which established the fact that plaintiff had knowledge of the defective condition of the track on

which the wneeis were rolled, and of the danger attendant thereon, the want of such knowledge by plaintiff being essential to the sufficiency of the complaint. *Lynch* v. *Chicago, etc., R. R. Co., 516*

2. *Knowledge of Condition of Appliance.*—In such case, a finding that the employe knew the condition of the track, fastens upon him not only knowledge of some, but of all the defects existing in the track. *Ib.*

ESTOPPEL.

See ARBITRATION, 1; DRAINAGE; INSTRUCTIONS TO JURY, 14; PRINCIPAL AND AGENT, 3.

1. *Street Improvement.—Lien.—Damages.— Wrongful Appropriation of Land.*—In an action to enforce a lien for street improvement, an appeal having been taken from the improvement proceedings, and a judgment rendered on appeal declaring such proceedings null and void, the defendants are estopped to deny the city's right to the land appropriated for such street, and the resulting lien of the contractor, where, after such judgment annulling the improvement proceedings, the defendants accepted damages of the city for the appropriation of the land as above mentioned. And the rule is the same whether the land-owner accepts damages in proceedings under the writ of assessment or in a suit for damages. *Morris* v. *Watson, 1*

2. *Real Estate.— Vendor and Vendee.—Lien.—Representations of Third Party.—Purchase on Faith of.*—Where a party, previous to a conveyance, has informed the grantor or grantee of lands conveyed, that he has no lien on such lands, and the grantee purchased the lands, relying upon such representations, the party making such representations is estopped from asserting a lien thereon, which he may have had at the time of making such representations; and it is not necessary to show that he intended, by his statements, to defraud, for the fraud consists, not in making the statements, but in attempting to enforce his lien, to the injury of the party whom he induced to purchase the land upon his representations. *Lacy* v. *Eller, 286*

3. *Mortgage Deed.—Conveyance by Mortgagee.—Action by Mortgagor for Improvements Made at Request.*—Where A. conveyed land to B. as indemnity for a debt of security, by a deed absolute upon its face, though in fact only a mortgage, and B. conveys the land without the consent of A., by such conveyance B. will be held to have treated the deed as an absolute conveyance, and in an action by A. for improvements made on such land at the instance and request of B., B. will be estopped from asserting that the deed from A. to him was only a mortgage. *Tyler* v. *Johnson, 536*

EVIDENCE.

See ADMISSIONS; APPELLATE COURT PRACTICE, 1, 8; ARBITRATION, 2; ASSAULT AND BATTERY, 1; ASSIGNMENT OF ERRORS, 4; FAILURE OF PROOF, 1; GUARDIAN AND WARD, 2, 3; JUDGMENT, 5; NEW TRIAL, 4; PRINCIPAL AND AGENT, 2; RAILROAD, 9; REAL ESTATE, 2; REPLEVIN, 3; TELEGRAPH COMPANY, 6; VARIANCE; VERDICT, 3, 4, 5.

1. *Objection, When not Well Made.*—An objection to evidence that it is irrelevant and immaterial, is unavailable, unless the evidence shows on its face that it is incompetent. *Keesling* v. *Doyle, 43*

2. *Malicious Prosecution.—Record of a Previous Action.— When Admissible.*—In an action for malicious prosecution, the record of a previous action is admissible in evidence, when it tends to prove or disprove malice or want of probable cause. *Ib.*

3. *Joint Objection.—When Unavailable.*—Where offered evidence is

admissible against one of two or more parties, it is not error to overrule a joint objection thereto. *Ib.*

4. *Public Records.—Notice.*—Public records are notice to the world, and it is not necessary to prove that a person has examined a record in order to bind him with notice of its contents. *Ib.*

5. *Conversation.— Real Estate.— Rent.*—Where the right to the possession of certain land is in litigation, a conversation had during such time, by one of the parties, as to his intention to rent the land, is inadmissible. *Ib.*

6. *Railroad.—Sparks.—Damages.—Scope of Inquiry.*—In an action against a railroad company, for negligently permitting sparks from its engine to be communicated to plaintiff's goods, it may be shown that other engines of the defendant, passing over the road where the property was destroyed, threw sparks, and that other fires occurred along or near the right of way, about the time the loss occurred, as tending to show the negligent habit of the officers and agents of the company.
Evansville, etc., R. R. Co. v. *Keith, 57*

7. *Railroad.—Spark Arrester.—Expert Testimony.*—In such case, it is proper for an expert witness to give his observation with reference to a certain spark-arresting device, for the purpose of showing its efficiency for the purpose intended. And there was no error in refusing to permit such witness to be contradicted by showing that fires occurred along the line of such road while such device was in use. *Ib.*

8. *Objections, How Made.*—All objections to the introduction of evidence, to be available on appeal, must be specific.
McCloskey, Admr., v. *Davis, Admx., 190*

9. *Subsidiary or Corroborative Fact.*—When the principal fact is given in evidence without objection, it is not reversible error to give in evidence a subsidiary or corroborative fact.
Bank of Westfield v. *Inman, 239*

10. *Law of Foreign State Not Pleaded.— When May be Shown by Parol.* —Where a plaintiff seeks to establish his cause of action by showing the loss of a remedy in a foreign State, by defendant's negligence, the existence of the remedy under the laws of such foreign State may be shown, without pleading the law of such State.
Bierhause v. *Western Union Tel. Co., 246*

11. *Transcript of Record of an Action.— When Admissible in Subsequent Action.—Assignment.*—Where a written assignment of a note shows that an action on the note was pending at the time the assignment was executed, it is proper to admit in evidence, in a subsequent action thereon by the assignee, a certified transcript of the record of such action showing the result thereof.
Baldwin v. *Threlkeld, 312*

12. *Proof of Contents of Destroyed Letters.—Discretion.*—The court may, in its discretion, reject evidence offered by plaintiff to prove the contents of letters destroyed by him after he had instituted his action; the court having the right to deduce, from such act, the inference of fraudulent design. *Ib.*

13. *Original Evidence, When May be Given.—Discretion.*—It is within the discretion of the court to admit original evidence at any stage of the proceeding, and unless abuse of discretion is shown, there can be no cause for reversal. *Ib.*

14. *Admission Without Objection.—Appellate Court Practice.*—The admission of evidence, without objection, can not be complained of on appeal. *Doan, Exec.,* v. *Dow, 324*

had, when the debt in question was said to have been created in 1876, on hand or in bank, from $300 to $1,500, and that decedent made a loan of $300 at six per cent. interest, about the time of the alleged execution of the note, and that decedent continued to have such sums of money at her command during all the time prior to the execution of the note, was admissible as a circumstance which the jury might consider in determining whether such debt was so created and allowed to stand as an open account from 1876 to 1887, and whether the note was then executed as evidence thereof, at eight per cent., when she had money to loan at six per cent. *Ib.*

24. *Insufficiency of.—Highway.—Proceeding to Establish.—Damages.—* In a proceeding to establish a highway, the judgment in a former proceeding relating to the same subject-matter, which had been rendered more than six years prior to the commencement of the subsequent action, the damages in the former proceeding having never been paid, nor the highway, as established thereby, never having been opened or worked as such, the judgment in the former proceeding is not a proper basis for damages in the subsequent action, and that being the only evidence, there is clearly a failure of proof. *Decker* v. *Washburn, 673*

25. *Conditional Examination of Plaintiff by Defendant.—Use of in Several Cases.—Agreement as to.—Grounds of Objection.—*Where defendant took what is styled a "conditional examination of plaintiff," under an agreement in which it is stated that there are several cases involving similar questions, the agreement providing that any testimony that may be thus taken at the instance of the defendant may be used by the plaintiff, at his option, so far as the same may be relevant, in each and all of such cases, and according the same right to the defendant, but providing that neither party to the agreement waives any question as to the competency or relevancy of such testimony; in such case, the only grounds of objection to such testimony that will be heard are those as to its relevancy or incompetency.
State Nat'l Bank v. *Bennett, 679*

26. *Patent-Right Note.—Statutory Requirement.—Ignorance of.—*In an action on a note given for a patent-right, where the note did not disclose the fact that it was "given for a patent-right," as required by statute, there was no substantial error in refusing to permit plaintiff, an assignee and nonresident, to show that its officers had no knowledge of such statutory requirement, for the want of such knowledge could not be considered as tending to establish plaintiff's good faith. *Ib.*

27. *Action by Assignee of Note for Patent-Right.—Notice.—Newspaper Articles Charging Payees with Fraud.—*In an action on a promissory note given for a patent-right, by the assignee thereof, the note not having been drawn in compliance with the law of this State, it was not error for the court to admit in evidence certain newspaper accounts of the arrest of one of the payees of the note, about two months before the assignment thereof, in which articles the payees were charged with swindling parties by selling a patent-right which had expired, the court instructing the jury that the articles were to be considered only as bearing upon the question of notice to plaintiff. the assignee, other evidence having been admitted tending to show that plaintiff's officers had read these articles before they purchased the note in suit. *Ib.*

EXCEPTIONS.

See INSTRUCTIONS TO JURY, 13; PRACTICE, 2; WAIVER.

FREIGHT.

See COMMON CARRIER, 3, 4; RAILROAD, 7, 8.

GARNISHMENT.

Certificate of Stock of Foreign Corporation.—Nonresident Defendant.— Not Subject to.—Replevin.—Answer of Res Adjudicata, Sufficiency of.—Suit was brought in this State against a nonresident, notice being given such defendant by publication. Proceedings in attachment and garnishment were instituted, which resulted in the garnishment of a certificate of stock of a foreign corporation, belonging to defendant, and held in trust for him, the only appearance, answer, or defense to such garnishment proceeding being an answer by the garnishee defendant, admitting that he held the certificate of stock as the property of the defendant. The defendant in the principal action was defaulted, and judgment being rendered against him, the certificate of stock was ordered to be sold. The defendant instituted an action in replevin against above plaintiff for recovery of possession of the certificate of stock. The defendant answered, setting up the above facts as a plea of *res adjudicata* in defense to the action.

Held, that the answer was insufficient on demurrer, it appearing that the principal defendant (plaintiff here) in the garnishment proceedings was a nonresident, and that the certificate of stock was issued by a foreign corporation, and, hence, not subject to garnishment in this State. *Smith* v. *Downey, 179*

GIFT.

See HUSBAND AND WIFE, 4.

GRAVEL ROAD.

See VERDICT, 1.

GUARDIAN AND WARD.

See HUSBAND AND WIFE, 1, 2.

1. *Contract.—When the Terms of May be Partly Enforced and Partly Disregarded.*—Where a ward, within three years from the final settlement of his guardian, employed counsel to institute suit to set aside certain allowances and to recover certain sums from the guardian, and the guardian promised that if he would not bring suit against him, he would hold all of such sums for him, and manage them for him until he, the ward, should marry and settle down, and then he would pay him all of such sums with their accretions, and would make him his, the guardian's, heir, the contract to make the ward the guardian's heir and to pay the sums of money are distinct and separate matters, and the promise to pay the sums of money may be separated from the promise to make the ward an heir, and be enforced against the guardian or his estate, without working any injustice, the forbearance to sue being sufficient consideration for such promise.

Doan, Exec., v. *Dow, 324*

2. *Evidence.—Statements of Guardian to Judge.—To a Former Attorney.* —In an action by a ward against his guardian to set aside certain allowances made the guardian, the presiding judge was competent to testify concerning the statements made by the guardian to procure the allowance of his claims; and, to the same effect, the statements of a person who had formerly, but was not at the time of the transaction testified to, been the attorney of the guardian, are admissible in evidence. *Ib.*

3. *Evidence.—Declarations of Guardian.—Amount of Estate.*—In such case, declarations of the guardian as to the amount of the ward's

estate, or what he expected it to be, were admissible in evidence to show its amount, and also to show that heavy charges made just before the close of the trust, were an afterthought, and were not contemplated nor intended by him when the ward was living with him as a member of his family.   *Ib.*

HARMLESS ERROR.

See DEMURRER, 2; INTERROGATORIES TO JURY, 1; JURY; PLEADING, 8;
REPLEVIN, 1; SPECIAL VERDICT, 5.

1. *Error Cured by Instruction.—Recovery.—Pleading, Bill of Particulars.*—In an action on account, the party is restricted, on recovery, to the items designated in the bill of particulars, and where evidence of items not so included is given, which might have been embraced in the verdict, any error which otherwise might have occurred will be deemed cured by an instruction that "the defendant would not be entitled to a verdict against the plaintiff on any item not included in such bill of particulars."
Bank of Westfield v. *Inman, 239*

2. *Overruling Demurrer to Paragraph of Complaint.*—Any error in overruling a demurrer to a paragraph of complaint will be deemed harmless, where it clearly appears that the judgment is founded upon another paragraph of the complaint.
Baldwin v. *Hutchison, 454*

3. *Sustaining Demurrer to Good Paragraph of Answer.*—It is harmless error to sustain a demurrer to a good paragraph of answer if there is a paragraph remaining under which the same facts may be proven.   *Pottlitzer* v. *Wesson, 472*

4. *Sustaining Demurrer to Paragraph of Answer.*—It is harmless error to sustain a demurrer to a paragraph of answer, even if good, where the facts provable under such paragraph were admissible under the general denial, which was also pleaded.
Kelley v. *Kelley, 606*

HIGHWAY.

See BRIDGES; EVIDENCE, 24; NEGLIGENCE.

Proceeding to Establish.—Judgment Functus Officio.—Subsequent Proceeding De Novo.—Where a highway has been established, but has not been opened or used within six years from the time of its establishment, the judgment establishing the highway becomes *functus officio,* or inoperative, and the only way in which the highway may be again established is by a proceeding *de novo.*
Decker v. *Washburn, 673*

HUSBAND AND WIFE.

1. *Right of Wife of Insane Man to Support Out of His Estate.—Remedy.—Can not Bring Action Against.—Guardian and Ward.*—The wife and minor children of an insane man, whose estate is in the hands of a guardian, should be provided, out of the estate, with such things as are reasonably necessary for their comfort and welfare, and if the guardian fail to make suitable provisions for them, application therefor may be made to the court under whose authority the guardian is acting, and the court should direct the guardian to make proper provisions; but the wife has no right of action, under such circumstances, against her husband's estate, for such support.   *Hallett* v. *Hallett, 305*

2. *Right of Wife and Children of Insane Man to Crops Raised by Them on His Lands.—Seizure by Guardian.—Remedy.*—The wife and minor children of an insane man have a right to the use, for their support, of grain (wheat) raised by them on the lands of

the husband and father, previous to the appointment of a guardian for him. The guardian has no right to the custody of such grain, and, on a seizure of the same by him, no right of action lies against him therefor, as guardian; but if any exists, it would be against him as an individual. *Ib.*

3. *Wife's Separate Estate.—What Consists of.*—Not only is the property actually acquired by gift, devise, or descent, preserved to the married woman, but also the proceeds of such property, whether the natural increase or the money procured by its sale or other property purchased with that money.

Parrett, Admr., v. Palmer, Admr., 356

4. *Wife's Separate Estate.—Use of by Husband with Wife's Consent. —Trustee.—Gift.*—Where the husband, with the wife's consent, used money belonging to the wife, as part of her separate estate. in building a family residence, and there was nothing to indicate that the wife intended the money as a gift, it will be presumed that, as to such money, the husband is the trustee of the wife, and the husband or his estate is liable to the wife for such money. *Ib.*

5. *Personal Property.—Rights in, How Affected by Marriage.—Governed by Law of Husband's Domicil.*—The respective rights of the husband and wife in their personal property, acquired by them by their marriage, are determined by the law of the place of their marital domicil, and that, in the absence of any contrary intention, is the domicil of the husband at the time of the marriage. *Ib.*

IMPROVEMENT.

See ESTOPPEL, 3.

INDEFINITENESS.

See PLEADING, 16.

INDICTMENT. •

See CRIMINAL LAW, 1, 2, 3, 4, 8.

INSTRUCTIONS TO JURY.

See ASSAULT AND BATTERY, 1, 2; HARMLESS ERROR, 1; MALICIOUS PROSECUTION.

1. *Those Given not in Record.—No Question as to Those Refused.— Presumption.*—Where instructions given are not in the record, no available question is presented as to those asked and refused, as it will be presumed that those given covered all proper points included in those refused. *Grand Rapids, etc., R. R. Co. v. Cox, 29*

2. *Refusal to Give.—When not Error.—Given in Substance.*—It is not error to refuse to give an instruction which is as fully and completely covered in substance, by an instruction given.

Keesling v. Doyle, 43

3. *Contributory Negligence.—When not a Bar to Recovery.*—In an action where certain paragraphs of the complaint make a case wherein the defendant is liable regardless of any contributory negligence on part of plaintiff, it is not error to refuse an instruction making contributory negligence a bar to recovery.

Evansville, etc., R. R. Co. v. Keith, 57

4. *Erroneous Instruction.—Warranty.—Breach of.—Machine.*—Where a machine is warranted to do good work when properly managed, an instruction to the jury that if, on fair trial, the machine could not be made to "work profitably and successfully," it did not

comply with the warranty, and the buyer might refuse to pay for it, is erroneous.

Walter A. Wood Mowing and Reaping Machine Co. v. *Field, 107*

5. *Error in Giving and Refusal to Give.—Presumption of Harm.—Unsatisfactory Evidence.*—Where the evidence is so unsatisfactory on the vital points in the case as to render it extremely doubtful, in the mind of the court, whether the verdict was right, error in giving and refusal to give instructions will be presumed to have been harmful, and will work a reversal.

City of Lafayette v. *Ashby, 214*

6. *Items of Account.—Restricting Consideration of Jury.—Exclusiveness. —Erroneous.*—Where many matters are given in evidence, among which are several hundred items of account, conversations, notes, and bank checks, without objection, an instruction which singles out three items of account and says, "these are all the matters proper for you to consider in arriving at a conclusion as to whether the defendant * * was indebted to plaintiff at the date of the execution of the note in suit, and as to whether the plaintiff is now, in fact, indebted to the defendant," is erroneous, the phrase, "these are all the matters," etc., conveying the idea of exclusiveness, *i. e.*, the only matters. *Bank of Westfield* v. *Inman, 239*

7. *Correct Statement of Law, Irrelevant.—Refusal to Give.—Modification by Court.*—Where an instruction, as asked, correctly states an abstract proposition of law, but is not relevant to the issue, it is not prejudicial error to refuse the instruction asked, or to give the instruction as modified by the court.

Lake Erie, etc., R. R. Co. v. *Arnold, 297*

8. *Instruction Stating Ground of Recovery.—Omission of Essential Element.—Reversible Error.*—Where an instruction purports to set out all the material averments necessary to be proven in order to entitle the plaintiff to recover, it is fatal error to omit any such material averment. *Jackson School Tp.* v. *Shera, 330*

9. *Joint Assignment.—When Unavailable.*—An assignment of error, which questions the sufficiency of instructions jointly and not severally, can avail nothing, unless all the instructions thus assigned are erroneous. *Hindman* v. *Timme, 416*

10. *Incomplete Instruction.—Remedy.*—If an instruction is correct as far as it goes, the party who desires a more complete and fuller statement of the law must ask for it, and thus only can error be ordinarily predicated upon the action of the court. *Ib.*

11. *Not Signed by Party or Attorneys.—Refusal not Error.*—It is not error to refuse instructions which are not signed by a party or his attorneys. *Ib.*

12. *Assuming Fact to be True.*—It is not error to assume an issuable fact as true in an instruction, if the fact be uncontroverted. *Ib.*

13. *Exceptions to.—How Saved.—Filing.*—Where written instructions have been given to the jury, or refused, and the proper exceptions taken, which are dated and signed by the judge, the record must show that the instructions were filed as a part of the record of the cause, or there will be no question saved, relating thereto, on appeal. *Killion* v. *Hulen, 494*

14. *Party Must Ask for, or be Estopped to Complain of an Omission.*—A party desiring an instruction on a certain point must ask for it, or he will not be heard to complain because of the absence of such instruction. *Kelley* v. *Kelley, 606*

15. *Law Applicable to Issues, to Evidence.*—The rule that instructions should be applicable to the evidence does not preclude the court

from stating to the jury the law applicable to the issues made by the parties. *State Nat'l Bank* v. *Bennett, 679*

16. *Not Signed.—Refused.—No Question Saved.*—No question can be saved as to instructions asked by a party and refused, where the instructions are not signed by the party or his attorney. *Ib.*

INSURANCE.

See ACCIDENT INSURANCE; LIFE INSURANCE; PARTNERSHIP; PLEADING, 2, 17; RAILROAD, 1.

1. *Policy on Merchandise.—Provision for Inventory Each Year.—When Failure to make not Matter of Defense.*—Where an insurance policy issued upon a stock of merchandise provided, as a condition of insurance, that the insured would make an itemized inventory of merchandise * * each year, and correct records of all purchases and freight paid, and all sales made from the time one inventory is made until another shall have been taken, etc., and about two months after the issuance of the policy the property was destroyed by fire, no inventory having been made, the failure of the assured to make an inventory of the merchandise is no matter of defense by the company, the assured having yet ten months in which to make such inventory, under the terms of the policy. *Citizens' Ins. Co.* v. *Sprague, 275*

2. *Accident Insurance.—Premium, What Amounts to Payment of.—Tender of Full Amount of Premium.—Promise by Agent to Apply a Debt Owing by Him to Insured on Premium.—Presumption.*—Where, at the time of the execution of an application for accident insurance, the person seeking insurance exhibited, offered, and tendered to the company's soliciting and collecting agent, the full amount of the first annual premium for the policy, and the agent was owing the insured a sum less than the amount of the premium, and the agent told the insured to pay him, the agent, the excess of the premium over the amount owing by the agent to the insured, and he, the agent, would pay to the company the amount owing by the agent to the insured, and the insured, acting in entire good faith, paid the sum in excess of the debt owing by the agent to him, and relied, in good faith, upon the agent's statement, that he, the agent, would pay to the insurance company the remainder of the premium, this, in law, would be a sufficient payment of the premium by the insured; and the insured is not bound to see that the agent pays the money to the company, but he has the right to presume that it has been so paid, until he has notice to the contrary.

Kerlin v. *National Accident Ass'n, 628*

3. *Authority of Agent.—Waiver.*—In such case the agent, acting in the general scope of his authority, had the power to waive the payment of the premium in several different installments, and to accept payment in advance, his powers in such matters being equal to the powers of the officers of the company at the home office. *Ib.*

4. *Authority of Agent.—Special Limitation.—Notice of.*—In such case, if the party acts in good faith with the agent, relying upon the statements made by such agent, within the scope of his apparent authority, the principal will be bound by such statements, and if there is any limitation on the power of the agent, within the scope of the particular business, it is the duty of the principal to bring the same to the knowledge of the applicant. *Ib.*

5. *Contract.—Construction.*—The same principles of law ordinarily

govern the construction of insurance contracts that govern the
construction of other contracts.   *Ib.*

INTERROGATORIES TO JURY.

See EMPLOYER AND EMPLOYE, 1; JUDGMENT, 4; MARRIAGE; CONTRACT;
          PHYSICIAN AND PATIENT, 2.

1. *Refusal to Submit.— When Not Available Error.—*Where answers
   to interrogatories refused, taken in connection with the answers
   made to interrogatories submitted to the jury, could not have controlled the general verdict, there was no available error in refusing them.   *Grand Rapids, etc., R. R. Co.* v. *Cox, 29*

2. *When General Verdict Controlled By.—*It is only when the answers
   to interrogatories are absolutely irreconcilable with the general
   verdict that the general verdict will be controlled by them.   *Ib.*

INVENTORY.

See DECEDENTS' ESTATES, 6.

IRRELEVANCY.

See INSTRUCTIONS TO JURY, 7.

JEOPARDY.

See CRIMINAL LAW, 5, 6, 7.

JOINDER.

See CRIMINAL LAW, 3.

JUDGE.

See BILL OF EXCEPTIONS; JUDICIAL NOTICE.

JUDGMENT.

See EMPLOYER AND EMPLOYE, 1; EVIDENCE, 17; EXECUTION, 1; HIGH-
   WAY; PHYSICIAN AND PATIENT, 2; REPLEVIN, 3; REVERSAL OF
   JUDGMENT; WAIVER.

1. *Arrest of.— When Motion for Will Lie.— Verdict Against Part Only
   of Defendants.—Motion to Modify.— Venire de Novo.—*Where a
   verdict does not find against all the defendants in the action and
   the court is proceeding to render judgment against all, the defendants against whom there is no finding may move in arrest of judgment as to them, there being an intrinsic cause appearing on the
   face of the record which shows that some of the defendants were
   entitled to such relief because there was no verdict against them.
   Other, and perhaps more appropriate, remedies would be by motion for judgment in their favor, motion to modify, or for *venire
   de novo.*   *Westfield Gas and Milling Co.* v. *Abernathy, 73*

2. *Voidable.—Collateral Attack.—*In an action for work and labor
   performed, on a demand for $3, the jury returned a verdict as fol-
   lows: "We, the jury, find for the plaintiff," upon which the
   court rendered judgment for plaintiff for $3 and for costs of suit,
   taxed at $14.75.
   Held, that the judgment was merely voidable and not void, and could
   not be collaterally attacked.   *Fruits* v. *Elmore, 278*

3. *Railroad.—Drainage Lien.—Foreclosure of.— When Personal Judgment May be Rendered Against Railroad Company.—*A personal judgment may be rendered against a railroad company, in an action
   to foreclose a drainage lien against the railroad of the company,
   a sale of the road under the lien being forbidden upon the ground
   of public policy, and the court having the power to furnish a
   remedy for an existing right.
                   Louisville, etc., R. W. Co. v. *State, ex rel., 377*

4. *On Answers to Interrogatories.—Employer and Employe.—Co-Employe.—Personal Injury.*—In an action for personal injuries received by the negligence of a co-employe, the defendant was entitled to judgment on answers to interrogatories, which established the fact that such co-employe was competent to do the work in which he was engaged at the time of the injuries.

American Wire Nail Co. v. *Connelly, 398*

5. *Sufficiency of Evidence to Support.*—The judgment of the trial court will not be disturbed where the evidence is conflicting, or where there is some evidence which supports the finding upon which the judgment is founded. *Haase* v. *State, 488*

JUDICIAL NOTICE.

Judges.—Terms of Office.—The Appellate Court judicially knows who the judges of the courts of general jurisdiction of the State are, and when their terms of office expire.

Cincinnati, etc., R. W. Co. v. *Grames, 112*

JURISDICTION.

See APPEAL, 1; JUSTICE OF THE PEACE, 1, 2; RECOVERY, 2.

Appeal.—Amount in Controversy, How Determined.—Appellate Court.—Where, in an action for damages, the jury find for the plaintiff in a certain sum, such sum is the amount in controversy on appeal, and determines the jurisdiction. Had the jury found generally for the defendant, the amount demanded in the complaint would determine that question. *Buscher* v. *City of Lafayette, 590*

JURY.

See CONTRIBUTORY NEGLIGENCE, 3; INSTRUCTIONS TO JURY, 6.

Misconduct of.—Taking Note in Suit to Jury Room.—Plea of Non Est Factum.—Signature.—Harmless Error.—Practice.—When an action is brought on a promissory note, and a plea of *non est factum* is entered, and the jury are allowed, over defendant's objection, to take the note sued on to their room, but the record fails to show that they also took to their room the plea mentioned, to which defendant's signature was attached, and fails to show any comparison of the signature, there is no available error.

Smith v. *Thurston, 105*

JUSTICE OF THE PEACE.

1. *When Acting as Collecting Agent Does not Deprive Justice of Jurisdiction.—Collateral Attack.—Presumption.—Waiver.*—Where a justice of the peace sits in judgment on the trial of a case based on account, the accounts having been, previous to bringing suit, placed in the hands of the justice for collection, the previous action of the justice as a collection agent of the subject-matter of the suit did not disqualify the justice to the extent of depriving him of jurisdiction, and a judgment rendered by the justice under such circumstances is not void and subject to collateral attack, except the disqualification is made to appear on the face of the record, or unless it was not known when it occurred; and it will be presumed that the parties had knowledge of any such disqualification until the contrary is made to appear affirmatively. Such disqualification may be waived, and would be waived unless disclosed at the earliest opportunity. *Baldwin* v. *Runyan, 344*

2. *Appeal from, How Tried.—Jurisdiction on Appeal.—How Determined.*—Where a case is appealed to the circuit court, from a justice of the peace, the cause is tried *de novo*, and the circuit court only inquires into the jurisdiction of the justice for the purpose of deciding whether it has itself jurisdiction, and when it has so found, it tries and disposes of the case as an original action. *Ib.*

LANDLORD AND TENANT.

LAW AND FACT.

LAW OF CASE.

LEGAL CAPACITY TO SUE.

LETTERS OF ADMINISTRATION.

See DECEDENTS' ESTATES, 5.

LICENSEE.

See MUNICIPAL CORPORATION, 1; PRINCIPAL AND AGENT, 5.

LIEN.

See DRAINAGE; ESTOPPEL, 1, 2; JUDGMENT, 3; MECHANIC'S LIEN; STREETS AND ALLEYS, 2; VENDOR'S LIEN.

LIFE INSURANCE.

1. *Warranties, What Amounts to.—Cancellation of Policy.*—Warranties in insurance policies are not favored in law, and the court will construe as a warranty that only which the parties have plainly and unequivocally declared to be such. And where the terms of the policy prescribe the penalty for misrepresentations in the application to be a right of cancellation of the policy by the company, it can not be held, by reason of the indefinite provisions of the application, to have intended a much severer penalty.

Union Central Life Ins. Co. v. *Pauly, 85*

2. *Warranties.—Construction of Policy.*—Where it is uncertain whether statements in an application for insurance are to be taken as warranties or representations, the construction most favorable to the policy-holder will be adopted. *Ib.*

3. *Consummated Contract.—Failure of Payment of Premium and Delivery of Policy.*—While a consummated contract may exist without either payment of premium or delivery of policy, yet such cases are exceptional, and must be supported by very strong and satisfactory proof. And where all the evidence is consistent with the idea that there were simply negotiations looking toward an insurance, such a contract can not be established thereby. *Ib.*

4. *Constructive Delivery of Policy.—Waiver of Payment of Premium.—Agent Holding Policy in Trust.*—Where there is no indication of any purpose to contract other than by a policy to be made and delivered upon payment of at least half of the premium, the fact that the insurance agent wrote the person seeking insurance, saying, "Your policy has come; the first time you are in town come around and get your policy," does not show a constructive delivery of the policy, a waiver of payment, and a consummation of the contract, neither does it show that the agent simply held the policy in trust for the insured. *Ib.*

5. *Refusal of Agent to Consummate Contract.—Sickness and Death of Insured.*—Considering the facts that the negotiations for a policy occurred about September 28; that the insured was notified by postal card of the arrival of his policy; that two or three weeks thereafter a son of the insured called for the policy and tendered the amount of the premium, the insured being sick October 10th, and still sick November 21st and 28th, and still sick and unable to go and get his policy on the 6th of December, the date of tender of the premium, the agent was justified in refusing to consummate the contract, and, upon the death of the insured, was justified in returning the policy to his principal. *Ib.*

MALICE.

See MALICIOUS PROSECUTION.

MALICIOUS PROSECUTION.

See EVIDENCE, 2.

Probable Cause.—Malice.— Instruction to Jury.—The court, in an action for malicious prosecution, instructed the jury that in determining the question of malice and want of probable cause, they might take into consideration certain things, all being issuable facts and proper to be considered by the jury in determining whether the prosecution was malicious and without probable cause. In this there was no error.   *Keesling* v. *Doyle, 43*

MALPRACTICE.

See PHYSICIAN AND PATIENT, 1.

MARRIAGE CONTRACT.

See EVIDENCE, 19.

Breach of.—Matters in Mitigation.—Set-Off.—Counterclaim.—Interrogatories to Jury.—Matters in mitigation, in actions for breach of marriage contract, can not be considered as a set-off or counterclaim, and the jury, in answer to an interrogatory, need not state the amount allowed in mitigation, but should only state what matters were so allowed.   *Maybin* v. *Webster, 547*

MASTER AND SERVANT.

See EMPLOYER AND EMPLOYE.

Employing a Minor.—Rules Governing Master's Liability.—Coemploye, Incompetency of.—Injury by.—Railroad.—If one knowingly hire a minor and require him to perform dangerous service, in opposition to the parent's will, he will be liable to the parent, if injury befall such minor while engaged in such service. In such case it is not a question of negligence that gives rise to the liability, but the wrong consists in opposing the will of the parent. But where such employment is simply without the consent of the parent, not against his express will, the question of liability is governed by the general rules applicable to such relation, viz: Instructing servant if unexperienced, providing usually safe machinery, tools, and place to work, and competent and skillful fellow-servants; and in case of an injury resulting from the incompetency of a fellow-servant, damages can not be recovered where it is not affirmatively shown that the injured party had no knowledge of such incompetency.

Toledo, etc., R. R. Co. v. *Trimble, 333*

MAYOR.

See APPEAL, 1, 2.

MECHANIC'S LIEN.

See PLEADING, 28.

1. *Notice.—Sufficiency of Description.—Materialman.*—A notice of intention to hold a materialman's lien, which described the property as "lot 6, 7 or 8 in Pray and Hunt's addition to the city of Indianapolis, Indiana, on the west side of Quince street, and about three-fourths of a square south of Prospect street," etc., is a sufficient description, being sufficiently certain "to enable a party familiar with the locality to identify the premises intended to be described, with reasonable certainty."   *Dalton* v. *Hoffman, 101*

2. *Complaint, Sufficiency of.—Notice.—Variance.—Description.*—In such case, where the complaint based upon the notice avers that lot 6 was the one on which the building was erected, the complaint makes a *prima facie* case, and the question as to whether the description in the complaint is at variance with that in the notice should be submitted for trial.   *Ib.*

3. *What Constitutes.—Labor.—Board, Groceries, Money Furnished, etc.—Railroad.*—In an action, on a mechanic's, etc., lien for labor performed as a foreman in the construction of the masonry

for a bridge for a railroad company, the account contained items, besides that for the labor performed, for board, groceries, tobacco, and money furnished the other employes of the contractors.

Held, that the item for labor properly constitutes a lien, but that the other items for board, groceries, etc., not being materials entering into the construction of the work, constituted no lien.

Ferguson v. *Despo, 523*

4. *Railroad Laborer.—Lien, How Obtained.—Notice.—Statute Repealed.* —Where labor was performed for a railway company in 1889 and 1890, in constructing masonry for a bridge, the employe, whether of a contractor or subcontractor, may have a lien for such work upon filing notice of intention to hold a lien, and no other notice (as provided by the act of March 6, 1883, section 9) is necessary, such section, as to notice, having been expressly repealed by the act of March 9, 1889, section 6. *Ib.*

5. *Demand.*—In such case, where notice of intention to hold a lien was duly filed, a demand for the money due is not necessary before an action will lie. *Ib.*

MESSAGE.

See TELEGRAPH COMPANY, 1, 2, 3, 4, 5, 6, 7, 9, 10.

MINES AND MINING.

1. *Falling In of Mine.—Right of Action.—Failure to Furnish Timbers for Props, etc.—Statutory Requirement.—Negligence.—Personal Injury.—Damages.*—Where, during the operation of the statute of March 6, 1885, requiring the owners or operators of coal mines to supply the workmen therein with suitable timber for props and supports to secure the workings from falling in, an employe therein, by reason of a failure to furnish such timbers, was injured by the falling in of the mine, but an action for such injuries was not commenced until after the taking effect of the act of March 9, 1891, relating to the same subject, there was a right of action against the operator of the mine, whether conferred by the act of 1885 or not, such right of action for negligence being given by common law; and the question whether or not the act of 1885 was repealed by that of 1891 can make no difference, as the statute of 1885 only defined what should be regarded as negligence *per se* in that particular. *Hochstettler* v. *Mosier Coal and Mining Co., 442*

2. *Contributory Negligence.—When Sufficiently Negatived.—Complaint.* —In such case, the complaint alleged that "without any fault or negligence on his part the slate which composed the roof in said mine at the point where he was at work fell upon him, greatly injuring him," etc., also averring that at the time the roof fell in upon him, he "was using all due care," and "had no knowledge of the unsafe and dangerous condition of the roof." These several averments, when construed together, are equivalent to one that the injury was incurred without any fault or negligence on appellant's part. *Ib.*

3. *Complaint, Sufficiency of.—Assumption of Risk of Employment.— Failure of Operator to Discharge Statutory Duty.*—Nor does the fact that the complaint, in such case, avers that plaintiff requested defendant, three days before the injury occurred, to furnish the caps and props "so that he [plaintiff] might make said neck or room secure and safe," disclose such a state of facts as would cast upon plaintiff the assumption of the risk of the employment, after defendant's refusal to furnish the supports. *Ib.*

MINOR.

See Master and Servant.

MISCONDUCT OF COUNSEL.

See Assignment of Errors, 3; Pleading, 13.

Argument to Jury.—Exception, How Saved.—If counsel, in argument to the jury, is guilty of misconduct in making statements of a prejudicial character, not warranted by the evidence, and, on objection thereto being made, the court then and there instructs the jury to disregard such statements, the injured party, if he is not satisfied with such redress, should make his dissatisfaction known by calling the attention of the court to such action as, in his judgment, ought to be taken to remedy the wrong, and if such redress is refused, the party may except thereto and save the question for the appellate tribunal.   *Maybin v. Webster, 547*

MISCONDUCT OF JURY.

See Jury.

MISDEMEANOR.

See Appeal, 2.

MORTGAGE DEED.

See Estoppel, 3.

MOTION.

See Judgment, 1; Waiver.

MUNICIPAL CORPORATION.

See Streets and Alleys, 1.

1. *Personal Injury.—Defective Sidewalk.—Notice.—Liability for Act of Licensee.—Sufficiency of Complaint.—Theory of.*—In an action against a municipal corporation, for personal injuries sustained by tripping upon a guy wire which had been erected by an electric light company, licensed to use the street, extending from the top of a pole, across the street, and attached to a tree, the complaint is sufficient, on demurrer, which proceeds upon the theory that the defendant had notice, when the wire was stretched across the street, that it was fastened to a decayed and unsafe tree outside and beyond the street (such tree having been blown down, and such wire suspended but a few inches above the sidewalk about an hour before the accident complained of), and that, by the exercise of reasonable diligence, appellant might have known of the continuance (about nine months) of such unsafe attachment up to the time of the accident, and alleging want of contributory negligence.   *City of Lafayette v. Ashby, 214*

2. *Open Drain or Sewer.—Failure to Keep in Repair.—Damages.— Complaint, Sufficiency of.*—Where the gist of an action stated in the complaint is negligence of the municipality in failing to keep a drain or open ditch in repair, by carelessly and negligently allowing the same to fill up with sand and other obstructions, and by building across the drain approaches to adjoining alleys without placing drains under the approaches, by reason of which obstructions the water overflowed the drain, and flowed into plaintiff's cellar, keeping it damp and unhealthful, injuring the foundation of the house, and destroying large quantities of personal property mentioned, the complaint states a cause of action.
        City of Valparaiso v. Cartwright, 429

3. *Special Verdict.—Sufficiency of.*—In such case, where the facts

found by the special verdict were, substantially, those alleged
in the complaint, and, in addition, that the ditch was so defectively constructed as not to be adequate to carry off the water,
the special verdict is sufficient to support the theory of the complaint, and plaintiff is entitled to recover. *Ib.*

4. *Defective Sidewalk.—Personal Injury.—Damages.—Liability for.—*
If a city permit a sidewalk to become out of repair so that a
pedestrian, without knowledge or the means of ascertaining its
condition, be injured while using the same, without fault on his
part, it is liable therefor. *Buscher v. City of Lafayette, 590*

5. *Streets and Sidewalks, When Sufficiently Constructed.—Presumption.
—Notice.—*Where a city builds and maintains streets and sidewalks, which are reasonably safe for use by persons exercising
ordinary care, it has fulfilled its duty in that respect. And pedestrians may presume that the city has done its duty in constructing and maintaining the same. Actual notice on the part of the
corporation, of the defective condition of a street or sidewalk is
not necessary, where such unsafe condition has existed for such
time that, with reasonable diligence, it might have been known.
Ib.

6. *Special Finding.—Recovery.—Sidewalk.—Personal Injury.—*In an
action for a personal injury, against a city, alleged to have been
received by reason of a defective sidewalk, the plaintiff can not
recover where the jury specially find that the walk where the
plaintiff was injured "was in a reasonably safe condition for use
in the customary and proper way, by persons exercising ordinary
care." *Ib.*

NEGLIGENCE.

See CONTRIBUTORY NEGLIGENCE; LANDLORD AND TENANT, 3; MINES
AND MINING, 1; PHYSICIAN AND PATIENT, 1; PLEADING, 5, 15;
TELEGRAPH COMPANY, 1, 5.

*Leaving Sick and Disabled Cow in Highway.—Injury from Fright of
Horses.—*In an action for damages for personal injury by reason
of plaintiff's horses taking fright at defendant's dead cow in the
highway, defendant's negligence was sufficiently established when
shown that he left the sick and disabled cow in the highway, having good reason to believe that she would die and was liable to
frighten the horses of passers-by, whether he knew, previous to
the accident, that the cow had died. *Hindman v. Timme, 416*

NEW TRIAL.

See APPELLATE COURT PRACTICE, 2; ASSIGNMENT OF ERRORS, 6; REC-
ORD, 1; WAIVER.

1. *Causes for.—Cause Improperly Assigned Raises no Question on Appeal.—*Rulings on motions to strike out pleadings and on demurrers are not proper causes for a new trial, and raise no question
when assigned as such. *Leiter v. Jackson, 98*

2. *Joint Motion.—Overruling as to One and Sustaining as to Another.
—*A party can not be heard to complain of the overruling of a
joint motion for a new trial, as to him, unless the motion is well
taken as to all the parties who join in making it. In such case, the
court may overrule as to one, and sustain it as to another.
Kelley v. Kelley, 606

3. *Surprise as a Cause.—*Since a party who is surprised by the testimony of a witness may procure a continuance on account of
such surprise, if, upon motion, he show proper grounds, a strong
and clear case must be made before a reversal will be founded
upon such cause as a ground for a new trial. *Ib.*

4. *Newly Discovered Evidence.—When a Cause.—Diligence, When Sufficiently Shown.*—Newly discovered evidence is not a ground for a new trial, where no sufficient excuse is shown for the failure to have the testimony at the trial; nor is it sufficient for the party to state in his affidavit, that he could not, with reasonable diligence, have discovered such testimony, for it is incumbent upon him to set out, in his affidavit, the facts constituting diligence.
I b.

NONRESIDENT.

See GARNISHMENT; POOR PERSON.

NOTICE.

See ARBITRATION, 1, 2; EVIDENCE, 4, 27; INSURANCE, 4; MECHANIC'S LIEN, 1, 2, 4; MUNICIPAL CORPORATION, 1, 5; PLEADING, 11; PROMISSORY NOTE, 2; RAILROAD, 8.

OBSTRUCTION OF HIGHWAY.

See CRIMINAL LAW, 1, 2.

OPEN AND CLOSE.

See ADMISSIONS.

PARTIES.

See PLEADING, 7; PLEA IN ABATEMENT.

PARTNERSHIP.

See FAILURE OF PROOF, 1.

Surviving Partners.—Continuing · Partnership Business.—Trustee and Cestui Que Trust.— Insurance.— Receiver.—Assets.—When a member of a partnership dies, the surviving partners hold the property and money of the partnership in trust for the partnership creditors; and where the surviving partners continue the business of the partnership in another firm-name, and insure the property in such name, and pay the premiums thereon, any money realized on the insurance policy, as well as all other funds of the partnership, belong to the *cestui que* trust, and primarily to the creditors of the firm; and, in such case, a receiver having been appointed, he is entitled to the possession and control of all the firm assets, including insurance money obtained by the surviving partners on a policy procured by them, and including profits realized in the continuance of the partnership business.
Bollenbacher v. First Nat'l Bank, 12

PASSENGER.

See RAILROAD, 6.

PATENT-RIGHT.

See EVIDENCE, 26, 27.

PAYMENT.

See COMMON CARRIER, 3; INSURANCE, 2; PLEADING, 23.

PERSONAL PROPERTY.

See HUSBAND AND WIFE, 5; VENDOR AND VENDEE.

PHYSICIAN AND PATIENT.

1. *Malpractice.— When Patient May Recover, When Not.—Mixed Negligence.*—In an action against a surgeon for malpractice, no recovery can be had by the patient against the surgeon, in any case, where both the surgeon and patient are free from negligence, or where the surgeon and patient are both guilty of negligence, or

where the surgeon is free from fault and the patient is guilty of negligence. It is only where the surgeon is guilty of negligence, and the patient is without negligence on his part, contributing in any degree to such injuries, that the patient can recover damages of the surgeon. *Young* v. *Mason, 264*

2. *Contributory Negligence.—Judgment on Answers to Interrogatories, non Obstante.*—In such an action, when the answers to interrogatories show that the patient, by his negligent conduct in disregard of his surgeon's instructions, and in interfering with the surgeon in the discharge of his duties, contributed to the injuries complained of, the defendant is entitled to judgment on such answers, notwithstanding a general verdict for the plaintiff. *Ib.*

PLAT.

See Record, 2.

PLEADING.

See Amendment of Pleading; Answer; Appellate Court Practice, 3; Common Carrier, 2, 4; Complaint; Counterclaim; Decedents' Estates, 7; Garnishment; Harmless Error, 1; Landlord and Tenant, 3; Mines and Mining, 3; Municipal Corporation, 1, 2; Reply; Streets and Alleys, 2; Variance.

1. *Answer, Inconsistent and Repugnant.—Demurrer.*—Where a paragraph of answer to a complaint on a promissory note, was that the note was given in part payment of a wheat-harvesting machine which was sold upon a written warranty, alleging a breach of such warranty, and that the plaintiff did not become the owner or holder of the note in suit until after maturity, "or if it did become such owner, it was only for the purpose of collecting the same * * or with the agreement and understanding * * that * * [said assignor] would keep * * the plaintiff whole and harmless,"—the answer is so inconsistent and repugnant that it can withstand a demurrer. *Second Nat'l Bank* v. *Hart, 19*

2. *Action on Insurance Policy.—Answer.—Confession and Avoidance. —General Denial.*—To a complaint on an insurance policy, alleging loss of insured property by tornado, cyclone or hurricane, the defendant answered that the loss was caused by a very high wind forcing a boat of the Cincinnati and Memphis Packet Co. against the property. The answer is insufficient as a confession and avoidance, neither is it good as a denial, and no defense is stated to the action. The further allegation of an investigation by the assured and the insurer, and the bringing of an action for damages by the insured against the Cincinnati and Memphis Packet Co. did not show a release of the insurer from liability. *Queen Ins. Co.* v. *Hudnut Co., 22*

3. *General Allegations Controlled by Special.*—Special allegations in a pleading, inconsistent with the general allegation, control the general statement. *Ib.*

4. *Corporate Existence.— When Sufficiently Shown.*—Where an action is brought against a defendant implying a corporation, the complaint need not expressly allege that the defendant is a corporation. *Lake Erie, etc., R. R. Co.* v. *Griffin, 47*

5. *Railroad.—Allowing Fire to Escape from Right of Way.—Negligence, General Allegation of.*—In an action for damages against a railroad company, for allowing fire to escape from its right of way, etc., the complaint is sufficient where it charges negligence in general terms, without alleging the specific acts constituting the negligence; and the same is true as to the freedom of plaintiff from contributory negligence. *Ib.*

pleading is sufficient on the theory of injury and damage by reason of the sale to plaintiff of the forged and worthless note.

Baldwin v. *Threlkeld, 312*

13. *Counterclaim, Sufficiency of.—Action for Attorney's Fees.—Misconduct of Attorney.—Damages.—*In an action for attorney's fees, a counterclaim is sufficient, on demurrer, which alleged, in substance, that the plaintiff, as defendant's attorney in cases forming the basis of the fees, acted in disregard and contrary to defendant's instructions, in continuing the cases until the next term of court, thereby causing defendant, by such wrongful conduct, to pay —— dollars additional costs, to his damage.

O'Halloran v. *Marshall, 394*

14. *Complaint.— Sufficiency of, How Determined. — Theory of.—*The theory and sufficiency of a complaint must be determined from the facts alleged, and not simply from the statements or admissions of the parties. *American Wire Nail Co.* v. *Connelly, 398*

15. *Complaint.—Negligence.—General Allegations Sufficient.—*In an action based on tort, negligence may be alleged in general terms without setting forth the specific acts constituting the same.

Hindman v. *Timme, 416*

16. *Indefiniteness.—Remedy for.—*The usual remedy for indefiniteness in pleading is by motion to make more specific. *Ib.*

17. *Complaint, Sufficiency of.—Exhibit.—Insurance.—Damages.—Fraudulent Representations.—*Where a controversy arose between an insurance company and the beneficiary of a policy issued by it, and the controversy was settled by a compromise agreement, in which the company paid the beneficiary $600, the policy being for $3,-000, and subsequently the beneficiary brought suit to recover damages alleged to have been sustained through false representations in procuring the settlement and compromise; the *gravamen* of the complaint is the fraud alleged to have been perpetrated upon plaintiff, and a copy of the policy need not be filed with the complaint. *Wabash Valley Protective Union* v. *James, 449*

18. *Answer.—Sustaining Demurrer to.—By-Law.—Contract.—Tort.—*In such case, it was not error to sustain a demurrer to an answer in bar setting up a by-law of the company, for the reason that the action is not on the policy nor on contract, but in tort. *Ib.*

19. *Counterclaim.—Essential Averments.—Can not be Aided by Other Pleadings.—*A counterclaim, to be sufficient, must contain all the essential averments of a complaint, and must state a cause of action in favor of the defendant and against the plaintiff, growing out of the subject-matter alleged in the complaint, without aid by reference to other pleadings. *Ib.*

20. *Counterclaim, When Insufficient.—Release.— Warranty, Breach of.—*In an action for damages for fraudulent representations in the settlement of a disputed insurance policy, wherein it appears that the plaintiff is standing upon and retaining the consideration of the settlement, it was not error to sustain a demurrer to a counterclaim for damages, founded upon a breach of warranty, in the release executed to defendant by plaintiff, to defend the payment, in settlement, against all claimants whomsoever. *Ib.*

21. *Complaint, Sufficiency of.— To Recover Money Obtained by Duress.—Threatened Prosecution for Statements as Witness.—Privileged Communication.—*In an action to recover money obtained through duress and without consideration, the complaint was sufficient which alleged, in substance, that plaintiff, having been duly subpœnæd, testified as a witness in the trial of a cause to which de-

fendant was a party, and, in response to questions asked him, testified that the character of defendant's son, a witness, was bad for truth and veracity, and that plaintiff testified on cross-examination that he had heard one A. and wife say that said son had stolen a sheep, all of which answers were made in good faith, and without malice, believing them to be true; that the defendant, the next day, threatened to prosecute plaintiff for such testimony, unless plaintiff paid him a certain sum of money; that plaintiff was a person of weak mind, of little education and experience in business affairs, ignorant of the law and of his rights and liabilities as a witness, easily influenced and overcome by a person of strong mind, all of which was known to defendant, and that defendant was a shrewd business man of wide experience, and of force and determination; that plaintiff, believing that defendant would carry out his threats, and by being put in fear of defendant, and against plaintiff's will, and upon defendant's promise not to prosecute him on account of said testimony, plaintiff paid defendant the sum of $900, which he seeks to recover.

Baldwin v. *Hutchison, 454*

22. *Complaint.—Allegation of Damages.—Due and Unpaid.—*In an action for damages for breach of covenant, it is not necessary to allege, in the complaint, that the damages sought are due and unpaid. *Harmon v. Dorman, 461*

23. *Reply, Sufficiency of.—Accord and Satisfaction.—Part Payment.—* In an action for balance due on a car load of bananas, to which the defendant answered that plaintiff received $550.70 in settlement of the car of bananas in suit, a reply that such sum was not accepted in full satisfaction of the amount due, but that it was received in part payment only, of which fact plaintiff had due notice, is sufficient on demurrer. *Pottlitzer v. Wesson, 472*

24. *Variance Between Allegations of Complaint and Exhibit.—Effect of.* —Where there is a conflict between the allegations of a complaint and a written instrument which is the basis thereof, and filed as an exhibit therewith, the latter controls.

Arcana Gas Co. v. Moore, 482

25. *Reply.—General Averment.—Statute of Limitations.—*To an answer setting up the six years' statute of limitations, a reply, in general terms, that defendant has made payments on the claim within six years, is sufficient without pleading the particulars.

Board, etc., v. Cole, 485

26. *Answer.—When too Narrow.—Demurrer.—*An answer must fully cover the entire complaint, or so much thereof as it purports to answer, or it will be insufficient on demurrer.

Walter A. Wood Mowing and Reaping Machine Co. v. Niehause, 502

27. *Complaint, Sufficiency of.—To Set Aside Final Settlement.—Decedent's Estate.—Fraud.—*The final settlement of an estate may be set aside for mistake, fraud or illegality, as provided by section 2403, R. S. 1881. And a complaint comes within the provisions of the above section which states, in substance, that the defendants, seeking to cheat and defraud plaintiff out of his right in the property left him by his father and mother, both deceased, by falsely representing to the court that this plaintiff was dead, his whereabouts not being known since 1872, it now being 1887, by reason of which representations they caused plaintiff's estate to be administered upon, etc., in which a final settlement was made,. etc., all of which proceedings were unknown to plaintiff, and

whereas, in truth and in fact, the whereabouts of plaintiff was known to defendants all of such time. Wherefore, etc.

Jaap v. *Digman, 509*

28. *Complaint, Sufficiency of Facts.—No Cause of Action Against Part of Defendants.—Subcontractor.—Mechanic's Lien.—Personal Liability.*—A railroad company contracted with A. to construct certain piers and abutments for a bridge, and A. in turn sublet the work to B., and B. contracted with C. for labor and materials. Under such contract, C. performed labor and furnished certain materials, and in due time filed his notice of intention to hold a lien for the same. C. brought suit against A. and B. and the railroad company for the amount due, praying judgment against the several defendants, and for a foreclosure of his lien, etc. Under such circumstances has C. a cause of action against A.?

Held, that, as the facts do not disclose any state of facts which would make A. personally liable to C., there being no privity between them, nor any principle of subrogation whereby C. could succeed to the rights of A., the benefits of the labor performed and the materials furnished by C. having enured, alone, to B. and the railroad company, no cause of action existed against A.

Ferguson v. *Despo, 523*

29. *Necessary Allegations.— Conclusion.— Personal Injury.—Damages. —Bridge.— County.*—In an action against a county for injuries sustained while crossing a bridge, the allegation "that the bridge complained of was constructed at a point where the defendant had a right to, and it was its duty to, construct it," is a mere conclusion, and does not take the place of the necessary allegations of fact showing that the county had authority to build it.

Board, etc., v. *Blair, Admr., 574*

30. *Sufficient Allegation.—Bridge.—Personal Injury.—County.*—In such case, an allegation "that the bridge complained of was situate and located over and across a mill-race, through which a large quantity of water flowed rapidly," is sufficient to show that the bridge spanned a watercourse. *Ib.*

PLEA IN ABATEMENT.

See Assessment of Damages.

Assessment of Damages.—Instituting Another Suit Pending Writ of Assessment.—Making Additional Defendants.—Railroad.—During the pendancy of a proceeding under a writ of assessment of damages for land appropriated by a railroad company, and for consequential damages, the plaintiff can not, over a plea in abatement, setting forth the pendency of the writ for assessment of damages, prosecute another action involving the same subject-matter, and affecting the same party defendant; and the fact that in the subsequent action plaintiff makes another party a co-defendant, can avail nothing as against the plea in abatement of the common defendant to both actions, setting up the pendency of the former suit; and the plea in abatement of the co-defendant joined in the subsequent action, setting up the same facts, can not prevail against a demurrer.

Rehman v. *New Albany, etc., R. R. Co., 200*

POINTING FIREARM.

See Criminal Law, 8.

POOR PERSON.

*Right to Prosecute as.—Nonresident.—*The statute giving to certain persons the right to prosecute or defend as a poor person, applies to nonresidents as well as to residents, and in the event such person is a nonresident, he can not be required to give bond for costs, even though he might have brought his action in his own State. *Pittsburgh, etc., R. W. Co.* v. *Jacobs, 556*

POSSESSION.

See REPLEVIN, 2.

PRACTICE.

See APPELLATE COURT PRACTICE; JURY; STREETS AND ALLEYS, 1; VERDICT, 3.

1. *Question, How Saved for Appellate Court.—Appeal.—Appellate Court Practice.*—In order to present a question for decision to the Appellate Court, as to irregularities or abuse of discretion in the proceedings of the trial court, the foundation must be laid in an exception to the ruling of the trial court. *Judson* v. *Romaine, 390*

2. *Pleading, Sustaining Demurrer to.—Exception.—Leave to Amend.*—Where a demurrer is sustained to a pleading, and exception is taken to such ruling, and leave is granted to amend, the excepting party may stand on his pleading and exception, or he may abandon his exception, and amend his pleading.
O'Halloran v. *Marshall, 394*

3. *Order for Production of Books for Inspection.—When Proper.*—The propriety of making an order, by the court, requiring one party to produce and give another party inspection of certain of its books, depends upon the averments of the pleadings and issues joined. *Wabash Valley Protective Union* v. *James, 449*

PRESUMPTION.

See ASSESSMENT OF DAMAGES; ASSIGNMENT OF ERRORS, 7; FAILURE OF PROOF, 2; INSTRUCTIONS TO JURY, 5; INSURANCE, 2; JUSTICE OF THE PEACE, 1; MUNICIPAL CORPORATION, 5; RAILROAD, 4, 5; RECORD, 2; SPECIAL FINDING, 2.

PRINCIPAL AND AGENT.

See INSURANCE, 3, 4.

1. *Agent Acting in Disregard of His Principal's Instruction.—Liability of Agent.—Damages.—Measure of.*—Where A. left money in the hands of B., as his agent, with instructions to loan the same to C., when C. and his wife should execute a mortgage upon a certain eighty acres of land unincumbered, and B., in disregard of such instructions, loaned the money to C. with a preëxisting mortgage on the land, he is liable to A. therefor, if loss resulted therefrom, in a sum not exceeding the amount of the preëxisting mortgage. *Welsh, Exec.,* v. *Brown, 421*

2. *Evidence.—When a Witness May Testify to a Conversation with Decedent.—Decedent's Estate.*—In an action by a decedent's representative, against decedent's agent, for damages resulting from a disregard, by the agent, of instructions concerning the loaning of money, the party with whom the agent contracted is competent to testify to a conversation which he had with the decedent before the agent turned over the money left with him by the decedent to loan and accepted a mortgage, wherein the decedent directed witness to tell said agent to turn over the money and accept a second mortgage. *Ib.*

3. *Contract.—Ratification, How Pleaded.—Estoppel.—Law and Fact.*—Ratification, as the term is applied to principal and agent, is a fact, and not a legal conclusion, and, as such, may be pleaded in general terms; but when used in a sense akin to estoppel, it is

not proper to plead it in general terms, but the acts constituting the ratification must be specially pleaded.

Minnich v. *Darling, 539*

4. *Contract.—Ratification, Definition of.*—The contract ratified must be one that the parties might have lawfully made in the first instance, and the person who acts as agent must purport to be the agent of the principal, and the contract must be made upon the faith and credit of the principal, ratification being an adoption of that which was done for and in the name of another. *Ib.*

5. *Rendering Services at Request of Another.—Recovery.—Broker.—License.*—Where a person not engaged in a regular business of stock and exchange broker renders services at the instance and request of another, in the sale of bank stock, the former is entitled to recover of the latter the reasonable value of the services rendered, such services not being in violation of section 5269, *et seq.,* R. S. 1881. *Johnson* v. *Williams, 677*

PRINCIPAL AND SURETY.

See DECEDENTS' ESTATES, 4.

PRIVILEGED COMMUNICATION.

See PLEADING, 21.

PROBABLE CAUSE.

See MALICIOUS PROSECUTION.

PROMISSORY NOTE.

See ADMISSIONS; EVIDENCE, 22, 23, 26, 27; PLEADING, 9, 10, 12; VENDOR AND VENDEE.

1. *Consideration, Sufficiency of.—Burden of Proof.*—In an action on a promissory note, in which illegality of consideration is pleaded as a defense, the note imports sufficient consideration, and the burden is on the defendant to show that the consideration was illegal. *Fisher* v. *Fisher, Admr., 665*

2. *Purchaser Fraudulently Refraining from Inquiry.—Good Faith.—Notice.*—Where the purchaser of a note fraudulently refrained from inquiry lest he should thereby discover the transaction out of which it originated, he can not assume the attitude of a holder in good faith without notice. *State Nat'l Bank* v. *Bennett, 679*

QUESTION OF FACT.

See LAW AND FACT.

QUESTION OF LAW.

See LAW AND FACT.

RAILROAD.

See COMMON CARRIER; CONTRIBUTORY NEGLIGENCE; EVIDENCE, 6, 7; JUDGMENT, 3; PLEADING, 5, 11; PLEA IN ABATEMENT; MASTER AND SERVANT; MECHANIC'S LIEN, 3, 4.

1. *Fire Escaping from Right of Way.—Insurance Indemnity no Defense.*—Where, by the actionable negligence of a railroad company, fire escapes from its right of way to adjoining property, which is thereby consumed, the owner of such property can recover his entire loss from such company, without regard to the amount of insurance that may have been paid to him thereon.

Lake Erie, etc., R. R. Co. v. *Griffin, 47*

2. *Contributory Negligence.—Special Verdict.—When Plaintiff is Free*

from Negligence.—Railroad Crossing.—Personal Injury.—A. and B., as shown by special verdict, approached a railroad crossing with a wagon and team of horses, under the following circumstances and manner: A. driving and B. sitting in seat with A. On both sides of the street forming the crossing were buildings, which obstructed the view of persons approaching the railroad and materially interfered with their hearing approaching trains; also, box cars projecting into the street from each side, on a switch eight feet from main track, between main track and A. and B., obstructed the view of approaching trains. A. and B., who had made the crossing but a short time before, from the east, were returning. When about fifty feet from the tracks, they stopped their team and looked and listened for approaching trains, and could see and hear none. Then they started to make the crossing, driving in a walk, one listening and looking south for approaching trains and the other listening and looking north for the same. In such manner they approached the crossing, neither seeing nor hearing any, nor any signal of an approaching train, and could not have seen or heard the approach of the train, the company failing to give the statutory signals. While the horses were upon the main track, a train coming from the south and running at the rate of thirty miles an hour, ran against and upon the team and the wagon, injuring B., etc.

Held, that the facts found by the special verdict are sufficient to warrant the court in inferring that B. exercised care commensurate with the danger encountered, and was not guilty of contributory negligence. *Cincinnati, etc., R. W. Co.* v. *Grames, 112*

3. *Railroad Crossing.—Care Required of Traveler in Crossing.*—It is incumbent upon a traveler on a highway, riding in a wagon and about to cross a railroad track, who can not see or hear an approaching train on account of obstructions which are known to him, to use greater precaution to protect himself from injury than where the view is unobstructed, and the opportunity for using the senses of sight and hearing is unimpaired. Care commensurate with the known danger is required.　　　　*Ib.*

4. *Presumptions.—Lawful Conduct.—Statutory Signals.—Railroad Employes.—Traveler.*—While a traveler on a highway may presume that the employes of a railroad company will obey the law and give the required warning, so, also, those in charge of the train may assume that the traveler will take every precaution commensurate with the danger which he is about to encounter.　　*Ib.*

5. *Presumption of Contributory Negligence.— Recovery.*—Where a traveler is injured at a railroad crossing, the law raises the presumption that the fault was his own, and he must rebut this presumption before he can recover.　　　　　　　*Ib.*

6. *Passenger.—Demanding Extra Fare for Part of Passage Covered by Surrendered Ticket.—Rights of Passenger.—Expulsion.*—Where A. purchased a railroad ticket entitling him to passage from X. to Z., and boarded a train carrying passengers between such points, and surrendered his ticket to the conductor, which was accepted, and upon the arrival of the train at Y., an intermediate station between X. and Z., the conductor demanded fare of A. from Y. to Z., claiming that A.'s ticket entitled him to passage only from X. to Y., it was not the duty of A. to pay the extra fare demanded of him and afterwards settle the question in dispute, with the company or its agents, nor will his failure so to do be considered in mitigation of damages. The passenger was as much entitled to stand on his rights (having paid his fare) as the company was

to stand on theirs (believing the fare not to have been paid), and whether he should pay the extra fare and stay on the train, or refuse pay and suffer expulsion, was a matter solely in the discretion of A. *Lake Erie, etc., R. R. Co.* v. *Arnold, 297*

7. *Duty to Keep Premises Safe for All Persons Transacting Business With It.—Delivering and Receiving Freight.*—A railroad company, which is a common carrier of goods, and by its conduct invites or induces the public to use its premises, such as depots and other places set apart for receiving and discharging freight, is under special obligation to keep such premises safe for such use for all persons coming upon the premises to transact business with such company, and among those who are entitled to this protection are such persons as come there for the purpose of delivering or receiving freight. *Toledo, etc., R. R. Co.* v. *Hauck, 367*

8. *Freight, Delivering and Receiving.—Safe Premises, Duty of Company as to.—Notice.*—Where a box car had been left on a side track, to be loaded with freight, and the consignee of the car was storing her goods therein at the precise point where she was directed to use it for that purpose, there was an implied agreement that the company would protect her from all approaching trains, and that she should not be molested or endangered in her person or property by any act of the company or its servants; and, in such case, the mere fact that a freight train had arrived and passed the box car, on the main track, was no notice to her that such train would enter the side track and endanger her safety by being pushed violently against the car in which she was lawfully engaged in her work of putting away her goods; nor was it her duty, under such circumstances, to leave the car and watch the movements of the freight train. *Ib.*

9. *Duty to Fence and Maintain Cattle-Guards.—Killing of Animal.—Denial of Obligation to Fence, etc.—Burden of Proof.—Evidence.* —A railroad company is not required to fence its track or put in a cattle-guard at a point where a fence or cattle-guard would materially interfere with the operation of the road in the discharge of its duty to the public, or would endanger the safety of its employes in operating it. But the burden of showing that a railroad ought not to be fenced, or a cattle-guard put in at a given place, is upon the railroad company; and where there is nothing in the evidence to indicate that the operation of the railroad, with reference to its duty to the public, would be interfered with, a judgment for damages for the killing of an animal which entered upon the track at a point where it was not fenced and a cattle-guard not maintained, will not be disturbed on appeal. *Toledo, etc., R. R. Co.* v. *Fly, 602*

RATIFICATION.

See Principal and Agent, 3, 4.

REAL ESTATE.

See Evidence, 5; Estoppel, 1, 2, 3.

1. *Contract of Sale.— Construction of.— Title.— Abstract.—Earnest Money.—Forfeiture.*—Where a contract for the sale of real estate provides, among other things, that "said conveyance is to be made by warranty deed, with all liens and taxes discharged, but subject to all existing leases," and that "a full abstract is to be furnished by us, and said abstract and deed to be subject to reasonable examination and approval by," * * * the vendee, acknowledging the payment of $500, as earnest money, which the vendee should forfeit, if he failed to carry out the terms of the

agreement, provided the title proved good; under such contract the vendee was not bound to consummate the purchase on failure of the vendor to furnish an abstract showing title in him, and hence the earnest money was not forfeited on failure of the vendee to carry out the terms of the contract.

Constantine v. *East, 291*

2. *Evidence.—Proof of Title by Adverse Possession.—Erroneous.—*In such case, in an action to recover the earnest money, it was error to admit proof of title by adverse possession. *Ib.*

REAL PARTIES IN INTEREST.
See FAILURE OF PROOF, 2.

RECEIVER.
See PARTNERSHIP.

RECORD.
See APPELLATE COURT PRACTICE, 6; EVIDENCE, 2, 4, 11.

1. *Affidavits in Support of Motion for New Trial.—How Made Part of Record.—Bill of Exceptions.—Order of Court.—*Affidavits in support of a motion for a new trial can only be made a part of the record by bill of exceptions or order of the court; simply attaching the affidavits to the motion, and marking them as exhibits, is not sufficient. *Lake Erie, etc., R. R. Co.* v. *Arnold, 297*

2. *Plat, When May be Inserted After Bill is Signed by Judge.—Certiorari.—Presumption.—Appellate Court Practice.—*It is not necessary to incorporate a plat into a bill of exceptions before the judge has signed the same, but it is sufficient to refer to such evidence (the plat) by the words "here insert," and afterwards insert the plat in its proper place in the record, and such action will not be ground for *certiorari.* In the absence of any showing or statement to the contrary, the court will presume that the transcript of the record, on appeal, duly authenticated by the certificate of the clerk, is correct. *Toledo, etc., R. R. Co.* v. *Cupp, 388*

RECOVERY.
See CONTRACT, 3, 4; FAILURE OF PROOF, 1; HARMLESS ERROR, 1; INSTRUCTIONS TO JURY, 3, 8; LANDLORD AND TENANT, 1, 2; MUNICIPAL CORPORATION, 6; PRINCIPAL AND AGENT, 5; SPECIAL VERDICT, 2, 3, 4; VERDICT, 3.

1. *When Contrary to Law.—Theory.—*A party must recover *secundum allegata et probata,* or not at all. If the evidence fails to establish the material allegations of the complaint, a recovery by the plaintiff would be contrary to law. The plaintiff must recover, if at all, upon the theory of the complaint.

Louisville, etc., R. W. Co. v. *Renicker, 404*

2. *Entitled to Some Relief, but not All Demanded.—Jurisdiction.—*Where a party is entitled, under the averments of his complaint, to some relief, but not to all demanded, that fact does not debar him from recovering what he is entitled to. *Levi* v. *Hare, 571*

RELEASE.
See PLEADING, 20.

RELIEF.
See RECOVERY, 2.

RENT.
See EVIDENCE, 5

REPLEVIN.

See GARNISHMENT.

1. *Answer of Property in Third Person.—Sustaining Demurrer to.—Harmless Error.—General Denial.*—In an action of replevin, it is not available error to sustain a demurrer to a paragraph of answer which only amounts to an answer of property in a third person, such fact being provable under the general denial.

Fruits v. *Elmore, 278*

2. *Possession Must be Shown.*—Replevin can not be maintained unless the evidence shows the actual or constructive possession of the property in the defendant at the time when the suit was instituted. *Ib.*

2. *Evidence.—Judgment.—Execution.—Constable.*—In such case, the suit being against a constable, among others, who had levied an execution on the property in question, the judgment and writ of execution are admissible in evidence as tending to show the right of possession. *Ib.*

REPLY.

See PLEADING, 23, 25.

REPRESENTATION.

See ESTOPPEL, 2.

REPUGNANCY.

See PLEADING, 1.

RETURN.

See EXECUTION, 2.

REVERSAL OF JUDGMENT.

See APPELLATE COURT PRACTICE, 2.

SALE.

See REAL ESTATE, 1; VENDOR AND VENDEE.

Executory Contract.—Order for Goods.—What Amounts to Acceptance of Goods.—Vendor and Vendee.—The following order was made of Hoadley & Co., New Orleans, May 13, 1891: "Ship Pottlitzer Bros., Fort Wayne, and Pottlitzer Bros., Lafayette, car each of straight run bananas out of steamer 'Hewes,' at $1.50 per bunch," and May 14, Hoadley & Co. shipped a car of bananas to Pottlitzer Bros., at Lafayette, which arrived May 17, and vendees, on inspecting the bananas, wired vendors, May 18 and 19, that they would not accept the bananas as "straight run," to which the vendors replied at once, by telegram and by letter, that the bananas were "straight run," and that they must accept them as such, after which vendees took the bananas into their possession and sold them.

Held, that the conduct of the vendees constituted an acceptance of the bananas as per order. *Pottlitzer* v. *Wesson, 472*

SCHOOLHOUSE.

See CONTRACT, 4.

SCHOOL TEACHER.

See CONTRACT, 1.

SET-OFF.

See MARRIAGE CONTRACT.

SEWER.

See MUNICIPAL CORPORATION, **2.**

SHERIFF.

See EXECUTION, 2.

SHORTHAND REPORTER.

See STENOGRAPHER.

SIDEWALK.

See MUNICIPAL CORPORATION, 1, 4, 5, 6.

SPECIAL FINDING.

See LAW AND FACT; MUNICIPAL CORPORATION, 6.

1. *When Sufficient.*—A special finding will be sufficient which contains the ultimate facts necessary to support the conclusions of law, disregarding evidentiary facts and conclusions of law stated therein. *Baldwin v. Threlkeld, 312*

2. *When Delivery Need Not Be Shown.*—*Presumption.*—It is not necessary that a special finding, in an action for balance of purchase price of a personal chattel, should show a delivery. The sale being complete, it will be presumed that the vendee obtained possession. *Ib.*

SPECIAL VERDICT.

See APPELLATE COURT PRACTICE, 2; INTERROGATORIES TO JURY; MUNICIPAL CORPORATION, 3; RAILROAD, 2.

1. *Province of Jury, of Court.*—*Conclusion of Law.*—Where a special verdict is requested, it is the province of the jury to find only the ultimate facts established by the evidence, leaving the conclusions of law thereon to be stated by the court. *Cincinnati, etc., R. W. Co. v. Grames, 112*

2. *Failure to Find Essential Fact.*—*Not Aided by Intendment.*—*Recovery.*—Where a special verdict fails to find any fact essential to support the complaint, the plaintiff must fail. The special verdict can not be aided by intendment. *Shipps v. Atkinson, 505*

3. *Recovery.*—*Omission of Essential Fact.*—*Money Paid Out and Expended.*—In an action for money paid out and expended, on failure of the vendee to accept a phaeton ordered of plaintiff, the plaintiff can not recover, where the special verdict returned contains no finding as to the amount expended. *Ib.*

4. *Recovery.*—*Omission of Essential Fact.*—*Damages.*—*Vendor and Vendee.*—In such case, where the plaintiff retains the property and sues for damages (the difference between the contract and the market value at date fixed for delivery), the plaintiff can not recover, where the special verdict contains no finding as to such damages. *Ib.*

5. *Overruling Motion to Strike Out Evidentiary Facts and Legal Conclusions.*—*Harmless Error.*—*Duty of Court to Disregard.*—If a special verdict contain evidentiary facts or conclusions of law, the court, in passing upon the verdict and in rendering judgment thereon, must disregard the evidentiary facts and legal conclusions; hence, the overruling of a motion to strike out improper findings in a special verdict is not such error as will warrant a reversal of the judgment. *Buscher v. City of Lafayette, 590*

6. *Failure to Find a Fact in Issue.*—*Burden of Proof.*—Where a special verdict is silent as to any fact in issue, such fact must be held as found against the party who was bound to prove it. *Sult v. Warren School Tp., 655*

STATUTE CONSTRUED.

See CRIMINAL LAW, 8; DECEDENTS' ESTATES, 7; TELEGRAPH COMPANY, 7, 8, 9, 10.

STATUTE OF LIMITATIONS.

See PLEADING, 25.

STATUTORY CONSTRUCTION.

Criminal and Penal Statutes.—Double Punishment.—Where one statute declares a given act to constitute a criminal offense, and prescribes a punishment therefor, a second enactment in the nature of a penal statute, should not be so construed as to bring the act constituting the crime within the purview. thereof, unless by express terms it is so provided.

Western Union Tel. Co. v. *Bierhaus, 563*

STENOGRAPHER.

Duties of.—Transcript.—Time for.—It is not the duty of an official reporter to know that time, or what time, has been granted in which to file a bill of exceptions. It is simply her duty to furnish the transcript within the time given her by the party ordering the same, if such time is reasonable and sufficient.

Arcana Gas Co. v. *Moore, 482*

STREETS AND ALLEYS.

See ESTOPPEL, 1; MUNICIPAL CORPORATION, 5.

1. *Improvement Proceedings.—Appeal from.—Effect of Appeal Judgment.—Practice.—Municipal Corporation.*—Where an appeal is taken from proceedings to improve a street, the city is not compelled to stop the work while the appeal is pending; and, in such case, if, on appeal, the city prevails, the work may be finished under the original proceedings, but if the property-owner is successful, and the court decides that there is some irregularity in the proceedings, the city may correct the same or begin anew, according to the determination of the court on appeal. If, however, the court, on appeal, adjudges the entire proceedings void, and no appeal is taken from such judgment, and the city does not proceed anew under the statute, it amounts to an abandonment of the appropriation of the land, and the title to the property reverts to the owner. *Morris* v. *Watson, 1*

2. *Improvement Lien.—Complaint, Sufficiency of.—Statute Repealed.—Act of 1869.—Act of 1889.*—Where the theory of a complaint for the foreclosure of a lien alleged to have accrued by reason of certain street improvements, was that the contract was made and work performed under the act of 1869, relating thereto, the complaint was insufficient on demurrer, the contract having been made and work performed under the act of 1889, relating to the same subject and repealing the former act. *Coons* v. *Cluggish, 232*

SUBCONTRACTOR.

See PLEADING, 28.

SUBSCRIPTION.

See CONTRACT, 4.

TELEGRAPH COMPANY.

1. *Message.—Legal Transaction.—Negligence in Transmission and Delivery.—Special Damages.*—If a telegraphic message show that it relates to a commercial or legal transaction of value, it is sufficient to

apprise the company of its character, and, for failure to use due diligence, it must respond in all special, proximate damages.
Bierhaus v. Western Union Tel. Co., 246

2. *Message.—Legal Transaction.—Damages.*—Where a telegram has been negligently and unnecessarily delayed, either in transmission or delivery, and thereby the collection of a debt has been defeated or rendered improbable, a substantial injury has been sustained for which special damages may be recovered. *Ib.*

3. *Knowledge by Company of its Inability to Promptly Send Message.—Duty of.—Liability.*—Where a telegraph company receives a message for transmission, knowing at the time of its inability to transmit the message promptly, and does not so inform the sender, the company will be held responsible for any damages flowing from a delay in the transmission of the message. *Ib.*

4. *Telegram.—Free Delivery.—Limitation to Certain Hours.—Knowledge of by Sender.—Liability for Delay.*—Where a telegram is received for transmission and delivery, and the sender is informed of a rule at the office of destination that free delivery of telegrams will not be made beyond a certain hour in the day, until the succeeding day, the company will not be responsible for any damages resulting from a delay in delivery, in compliance with such rule and custom. *Ib.*

5. *Telegram.—Liability of Company for Mental Suffering Caused by Its Negligence.*—A recovery may be had for the mental anguish and suffering caused by negligence in transmission and delivery of a telegram, although no other pecuniary loss other than the cost of the message be shown.
Western Union Tel. Co. v. Cline, 364

6. *Gist of Action.—Secondary Evidence.—Telegram.—Duty of Jury.*—In an action against a telegraph company for failure to transmit and deliver a telegram with due diligence, the negligence in transmission and delivery, and not the message, is the foundation of the action; and when some evidence of the terms of the original message is given without objection, the original not being in evidence, it is the duty of the jury to weigh the evidence, such as it was, and the court can not remove this duty by instructing them to return a verdict for the defendant. *Ib.*

7. *Action for the $100 Penalty.—When Will Not Lie.—Disclosure.—Statute Construed.*—An action to recover the $100 penalty imposed by the act of April 8, 1885 (section 5511, R. S. 1894), alleging an unlawful disclosure of a telegram, will not lie, the act of disclosure not being, by express terms nor by fair implication, within the meaning of the act providing for such penalty. And the statute being a penal one, must be strictly construed.
Western Union Tel. Co. v. Bierhaus, 563

8. *Statute Construed.—Act of April 8, 1885.*—The act above referred to does not award liquidated damages for failing to perform a duty, but gives a penalty to a private individual, and was intended as a punishment for such wrongful acts only as were not covered by the criminal statutes. *Ib.*

9. *Statute Construed.—Transmission and Delivery.—Disclosure.—Good Faith.*—The transmission of a telegram in good faith and with impartiality, as provided by statute, act 1885, means the forwarding of the message and delivery thereof, accurately and without favor or preference, and does not include a non-disclosure of the telegram. *Ib.*

10. *Statute Construed.—Messages.—Discrimination.*—The statute, sec-

tion 5511, R. S. 1894, makes no discrimination between private dispatches and those of any other character, except messages of public and general interest, and those to and from officers of justice. *Ib.*

TENDER.

See COMMON CARRIER, 4; INSURANCE, 2.

Purpose of.—When a tender has been made for one purpose, it can not be diverted to another. *Shively* v. *Knoblock, 433*

THEORY.

See MUNICIPAL CORPORATION, 1; PLEADING, 12, 14; RECOVERY, 1.

TITLE.

See REAL ESTATE, 1.

TORT.

See LANDLORD AND TENANT, 3; PLEADING, 18; VERDICT, 1.

TOWNSHIP TRUSTEE.

See CONTRACT, 1, 4.

See STENOGRAPHER.

TRIAL.

See APPEAL, 2.

TRUST AND TRUSTEE.

See HUSBAND AND WIFE, 4; LIFE INSURANCE, 4; PARTNERSHIP.

Power of Court to Remove Trustee.—A court of chancery has power, even independent of any statutory provision, or of directions contained in the instrument, to remove a trustee for good cause. *Mazelin* v. *Ronyer, 27*

VARIANCE.

See CRIMINAL LAW, 5; FAILURE OF PROOF, 2; MECHANIC'S LIEN, 2; PLEADING, 24.

Immaterial.—Pleading and Proof.—Where an allegation in the complaint was that plaintiff was injured while "attempting to drive them [his horses] and pass" the object, and the proof was that plaintiff was injured while attempting to "lead" his horses past the object after failing to drive them by, there was at most an immaterial variance which would be deemed cured by sections 391 and 392, R. S. 1881. *Hindman* v. *Timme, 416*

VENDOR AND VENDEE.

See ESTOPPEL, 2; SALE; SPECIAL VERDICT, 4; VENDOR'S LIEN.

Sale.—Assignment of Forged and Worthless Note.—Action for Value of Articles Sold.—Personalty.—Where a vendor sold a horse of the value of $500, and accepted therefor the vendee's note for $50 and the assignment of another note which proved to be forged and worthless, the vendor had a right to disregard the assignment and sue for the value of the horse. *Baldwin* v. *Threlkeld, 312*

VENDOR'S LIEN.

Series of Installments.—Good Only as to the Whole.—Former Adjudication.—The right to have a vendor's lien declared applies not to any single installment of a series of payments to be made, but to the entire amount of the installments, and if there was no such lien for the first installment due, neither is there one for any sub-

Lightning Source UK Ltd.
Milton Keynes UK
UKHW031827280119
336340UK00011B/1010/P

9 781528 375436